| 114TH CONGRESS<br>*2d Session* | HOUSE OF REPRESENTATIVES | REPORT<br>114–848 |
| --- | --- | --- |

# FINAL REPORT

OF THE

## SELECT COMMITTEE ON THE EVENTS SURROUNDING THE 2012 TERRORIST ATTACK IN BENGHAZI

## HOUSE OF REPRESENTATIVES

DECEMBER 7, 2016.—Referred to the House Calendar and ordered to be printed

# FINAL REPORT OF THE SELECT COMMITTEE ON THE EVENTS SURROUNDING THE 2012 TERRORIST ATTACK IN BENGHAZI

This version does not include the additional and minority views from the original report #114-848.

# FINAL REPORT

OF THE

## SELECT COMMITTEE ON THE EVENTS SURROUNDING THE 2012 TERRORIST ATTACK IN BENGHAZI

## HOUSE OF REPRESENTATIVES

DECEMBER 7, 2016.—Referred to the House Calendar and ordered to be printed

U.S. GOVERNMENT PUBLISHING OFFICE

22–867                           WASHINGTON : 2016

---

This report is dedicated to the memory and service of Glen A. Doherty, Sean P. Smith, J. Christopher Stevens, and Tyrone S. Woods

## COMMITTEE STAFF

PHILIP G. KIKO, *Staff Director & General Counsel*
CHRISTOPHER A. DONESA, *Deputy Staff Director*
DANA CHIPMAN, *Chief Counsel*

SARAH ADAMS, *Senior Advisor*
SARA BARRINEAU, *Investigator*
BRIAN BEATTIE, *Professional Staff Member*
KIMBERLY BETZ, *Member Liaison & Counsel*
ROB BORDEN, *Senior Advisor*
LUKE BURKE, *Investigator/Detailee*

SHERIA CLARKE, *Counsel*
CARLTON DAVIS, *Counsel*
MARK GRIDER, *Deputy General Counsel*
SHARON JACKSON, *Deputy Chief Counsel*
CRAIG MISSAKIAN, *Deputy Chief Counsel*
J. MAC TOLAR, *Senior Counsel*

JAMAL D. WARE, *Communications Director*
AMANDA DUVALL, *Deputy Communications Director*
MATT WOLKING, *Press Secretary*

DOUGLAS ALEXANDER, *Printing Clerk*
ANNE BINSTED, *Finance and Personnel Administrator*
FRANK CHANG, *Legal Intern*
GEORGE GERBO, *Staff Assistant*
ELIZABETH GORMAN, *Professional Staff Member*
CLARK HEDRICK, *Legal Intern*

ABIGAIL HELVERING, *Staff Assistant*
PAT KNUDSEN, *Shared Employee*
PAIGE LUEKEN, *Executive Assistant*
BARBARA MCCAFFREY, *Documents Clerk*
ELIZABETH MCWHORTER, *Security Manager*
WILLIAM SACRIPANTI, *Staff Assistant*
ELIZABETH STAREK, *Staff Assistant*
SHARON UTZ, *Professional Staff Member*

### MINORITY STAFF

SUSANNE SACHSMAN GROOMS, *Staff Director & General Counsel*
HEATHER SAWYER, *Chief Counsel*
DAVE RAPALLO, *Senior Advisor to the Ranking Member*

KRISTA BOYD, *Senior Counsel*
PETER KENNY, *Senior Counsel*
RONAK DESAI, *Counsel*
SHANNON GREEN, *Counsel*
VALERIE SHEN, *Counsel*
JENNIFER WERNER, *Communications Director*
PAUL BELL, *Deputy Communications Director*
Linda Cohen, *Senior Professional Staff Member*

LAURA RAUCH, *Senior Professional Staff Member*
DANIEL REBNORD, *Professional Staff Member*
BRENT WOOLFORK, *Professional Staff Member*
ERIN O'BRIEN, *Investigator/Detailee*
KENDAL ROBINSON, *Investigator/Detailee*
MONÉ ROSS, *Staff Assistant*

### MAJORITY INTERNS

J. MICHAEL ABLER
JEFF BECK
COURTNEY BALLENGER
MICHELLE BOWLING

CLAY BRYAN
AMANDA GONZALEZ
FRANCESCA SAVOIA
IVY WILBORN

# LETTER OF TRANSMITTAL

---

HOUSE OF REPRESENTATIVES,
SELECT COMMITTEE ON THE
EVENTS SURROUNDING THE
2012 TERRORIST ATTACK
IN BENGHAZI,
*Washington, December 7, 2016.*

HON. KAREN L. HAAS,
*Clerk, House of Representatives,*
*Washington, DC.*

DEAR MS. HAAS:

Pursuant to H. Res. 567 of the 113th Congress and section 4(a) of H. Res. 5 of the 114th Congress, I hereby transmit the attached report, "Final Report of the Select Committee on the Events Surrounding the 2012 Terrorist Attack in Benghazi."

Sincerely,

TREY GOWDY,
*Chairman.*

| 114TH CONGRESS 2d Session | HOUSE OF REPRESENTATIVES | REPORT 114–848 |
|---|---|---|

FINAL REPORT OF THE SELECT COMMITTEE ON THE EVENTS SURROUNDING THE 2012 TERRORIST ATTACK IN BENGHAZI

---

DECEMBER 7, 2016.—Referred to the House Calendar and ordered to be printed

---

Mr. GOWDY, from the Select Committee on the Events Surrounding the 2012 Terrorist Attack in Benghazi, submitted the following

# REPORT

together with

## ADDITIONAL AND MINORITY VIEWS

On July 8, 2016, the Select Committee on the Events Surrounding the 2012 Terrorist Attack in Benghazi, approved and reported the following investigative report to the House, pursuant to H. Res. 567 (113th Congress).

## CONTENTS

# ILLUSTRATIONS

State Department facility in Benghazi, Libya

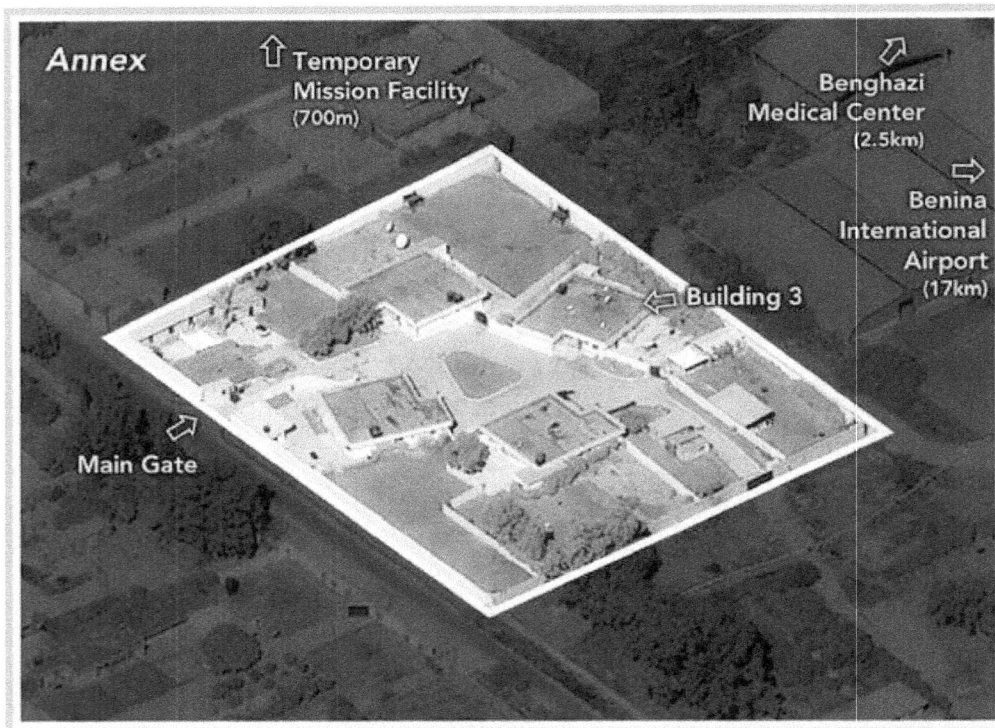

Central Intelligence Agency facility in Benghazi, Libya

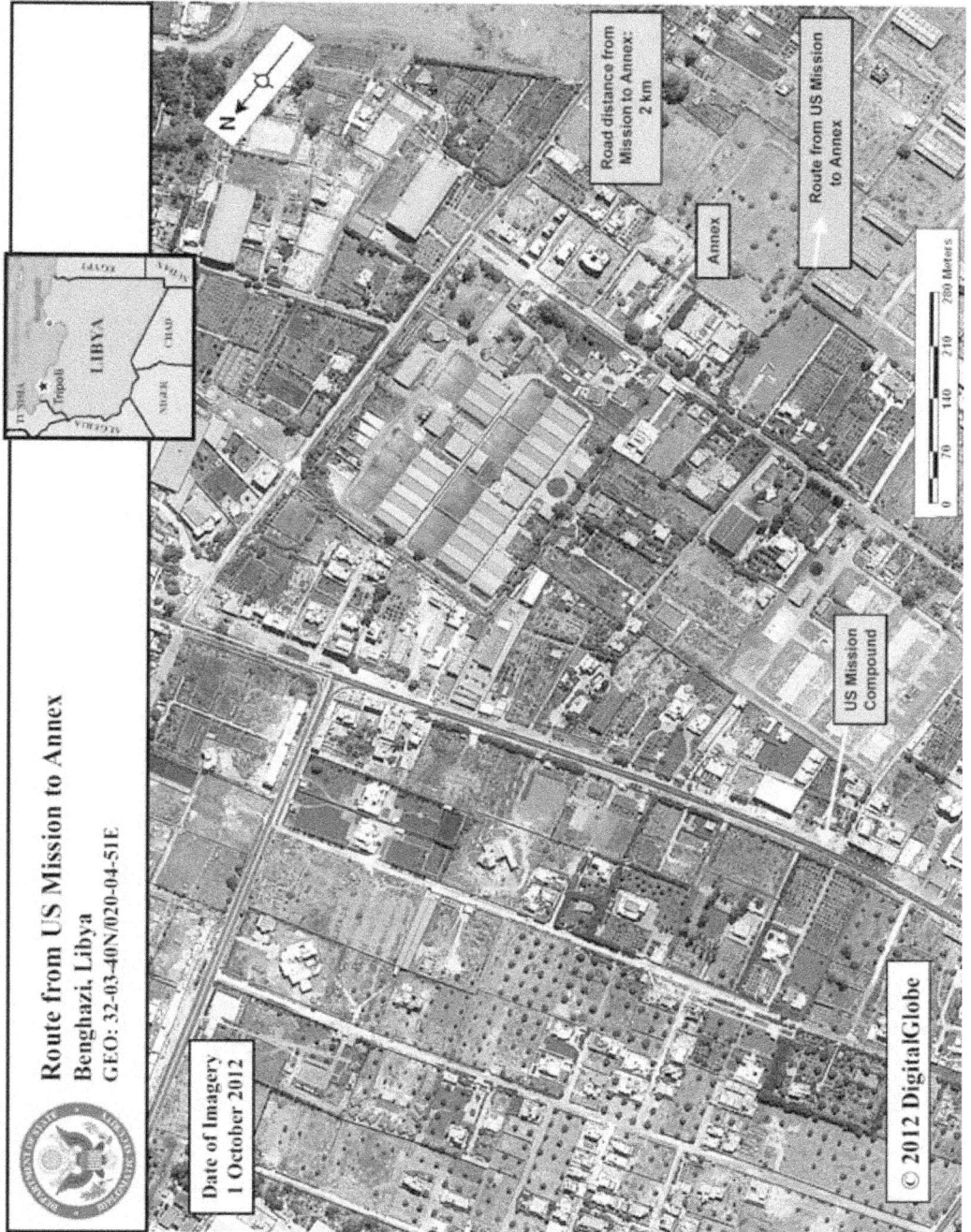

Route from US Mission to Annex
Benghazi, Libya
GEO: 32-03-40N/020-04-51E

Date of Imagery
1 October 2012

Road distance from
Mission to Annex:
2 km

Annex

Route from US Mission
to Annex

US Mission
Compound

© 2012 DigitalGlobe

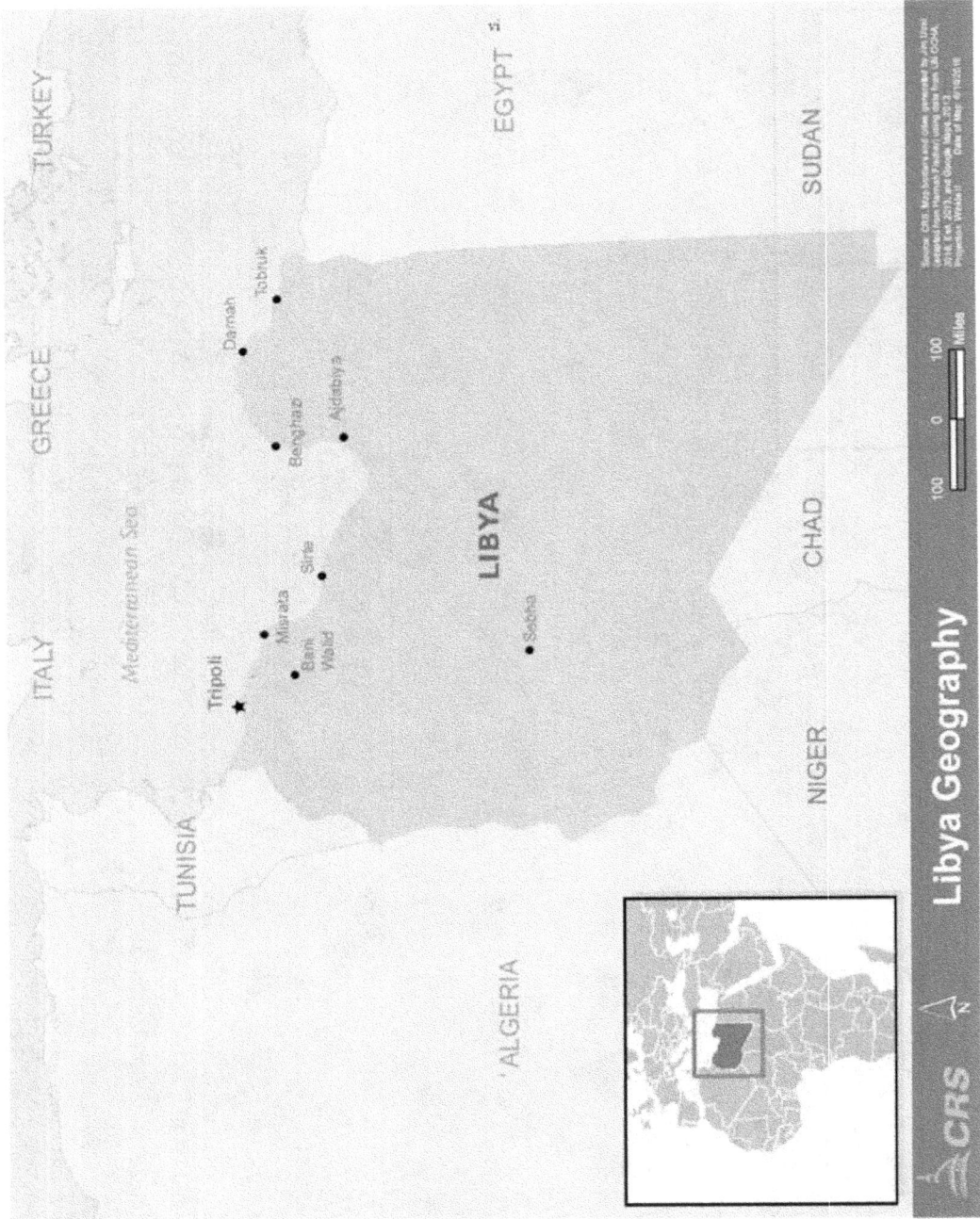

Libya Geography

7

Mediterranean Region

# PART I:

# Terrorist Attacks on U.S. Facilities in Benghazi

*"If you guys don't get here, we're all going to f---ing die."* [1]

> Diplomatic Security Agent in Benghazi during the attacks

*"I'm in Benghazi this week, lurking about with my eyes ever-peeled for RPG's hurtling towards my motorcade!"* [2]

> Ambassador Christopher Stevens, to the U.K. Ambassador on the morning of September 11, 2012

*"We're under attack."* [3]

> Ambassador Christopher Stevens, on the evening of September 11, 2012

---

[1] Testimony of GRS 4, Cent. Intel. Agency, Tr. at 33 (Mar. 1, 2016) [hereinafter GRS 4 Testimony] (on file with the Committee).

[2] Email from J. Christopher Stevens, U.S. Ambassador to Libya, to personal account of Dominic A.G. Asquith, U.K. Ambassador to Libya (Sept. 11, 2012, 5:40 AM) (on file with the Committee, C05390150).

[3] Testimony of Gregory Hicks, Deputy Chief of Mission, Libya, U.S. Dep't of State at 18 (Apr. 11, 2013) [hereinafter Hicks Apr. 2013 Testimony] (on file with the Committee).

# BACKGROUND: SEPTEMBER 2012 AND THE AMBASSADOR'S TRIP TO BENGHAZI

## Stevens' Decision to Travel to Benghazi

J. Christopher Stevens, a highly and widely respected diplomat, was sworn in as the United States Ambassador to Libya on May 14, 2012.[4] Thirteen months earlier in 2011, while Libya was still in the throes of a civil war, Stevens courageously arrived in Benghazi, Libya on a Greek cargo ship to serve as the United States' Special Representative to the Transitional National Council [TNC].[5]

Stevens remained Special Representative to the TNC for more than six months in 2011 and witnessed both the dictatorship of Muammar Qadhafi topple and the reopening of the U.S. Embassy in Tripoli, which had previously been evacuated at the beginning of the Libyan revolution in February of 2011.[6]

Stevens left Benghazi in November of 2011, to return to the United States, where he would be nominated and confirmed as Ambassador to Libya the following May.[7]

Stevens had a deep affection for the Libyan people in general and the people of Benghazi in particular. He also knew Libya as well as anyone in the U.S. Foreign Service. He would soon learn much had changed in Libya from the time he left as Special Representative in November of 2011 until the time he returned as Ambassador in May of 2012.

The Benghazi Mission compound where Stevens lived for several months in 2011 remained open while he was in the U.S. awaiting confirmation as Ambassador. The Benghazi Mission compound was protected by Diplomatic Security Agents and staffed by a Principal Officer who provided political reporting on the changes occurring in Benghazi as the country attempted to recover after the revolution.

In August of 2012, three months after Stevens returned to Libya as the newly confirmed Ambassador, the Principal Officer in Benghazi was nearing the end of his assignment. There would be a two-week gap between the Principal Officer's departure date and the arrival of the next Principal Officer.[8] No one was scheduled to fill this vacancy until September 15, 2012, so Ambassador Stevens chose to send Principal Officer 4, to cover the vacancy during the first week in September.[9] Stevens chose himself to cover the second week.[10] According to Gregory N. Hicks, who as the Deputy Chief of Mission was second in command at the time, Stevens "very much

---

[4] Public Schedule [for the Secretary of State] for May 14, 2012 found at www.State.gov/pa/prs/appt/2012/05/14/189814.htm.

[5] U.S. Representative to TNC Stevens provides an update on Libya, DIPNOTE, Aug. 3, 2011 found at https://blogs.state.gov/stories/2011/08/03/us-representative-t-n-c-stevens-provides-update-libya.

[6] A Guide to the U.S. History of Recognition, Diplomatic, and Consular Relations, by Country, Since 1776: [State Department/Office of the Historian] found at: https://history.state.gov/countries/libya.

[7] Biography of J. Christopher Stevens, Ambassador, Libya, found at: https://state.gov/r/pa/ec/biog/193075.htm.

[8] See Hicks Apr. 2013 Testimony at 9 ("[Principal Officer 3] left at the end of August, and the new Principal Officer was not arriving until—scheduled to arrive until September 15th or thereabouts.").

[9] See id. at 57 ("And so basically Chris announces at the meeting that [Principal Officer 4] is going to go to Benghazi to cover the first week in the gap, first week in September, and that he would cover the second week.").

[10] Id.

wanted to get back to Benghazi . . . he had not been able to go since his own arrival in Tripoli" in May of 2012.[11]

The timing of Stevens' visit to Benghazi was important for another reason as well. He was spearheading an effort to make Benghazi a permanent post, Hicks testified:

> One of the things he [Stevens] said to me was that, in his exit interview with Secretary Clinton, she expressed the hope that we could make the special mission in Benghazi a permanent constituent post. And Chris said that one of the first things he intended to do after his arrival was develop a proposal to move forward on that project.[12]

A trip to Benghazi would allow Stevens to personally assess the political and security situation and make a recommendation regarding whether the U.S. should have a permanent presence there. Discussions were already under way in Washington D.C. on how to fund a permanent post. Hicks stated:

> [W]e are only a month from the end of the fiscal year, so we have to get a [sic] or, we have to help Washington, the executive director's office of the Near East Bureau to put together a package to get it to [the Undersecretary for Management] Pat Kennedy for a decision by September 30th. Otherwise, we lose the money. Because we had surplus money available from Iraq—I can't remember, Iraq contingency fund I think—that had been notified by Pat Kennedy for transfer from Iraq—it wasn't going to get spent in Iraq, and so we were going to spend it in Libya and in Benghazi. But we had to get the justification forward to do that.[13]

While the end of the fiscal year funding deadline was looming, the Diplomatic Security Agent in charge at the Embassy in Tripoli was, nonetheless, concerned about Stevens' trip to Benghazi. Although his first planned trip to Benghazi in the beginning of August 2012 had to be canceled because of security,[14] Stevens was adamant, however, about going in September.[15] The Diplomatic Security Agent testified:

> Previous to this—to his decisions to going up there, there was—we would meet weekly to discuss the security situation in Libya. . . . [T]here was a specific meeting regarding what was happening in Benghazi. In that meeting, we reviewed incidents and probable causes, what's initiating it. And a lot of discussion was that it was the conflict or the incidents up there were, you know, local population against local population and that that they weren't specifically targeting Americans . . . up there. I expressed my

---

[11] *Id.* at 9.
[12] *Id.* at 7.
[13] *Id.* at 16–17.
[14] *See* Email from J. Christopher Stevens, U.S. Ambassador to Libya, to Principal Officer 3, Foreign Service Officer, U.S. Dep't of State, (Aug. 2, 2012, 2:45 PM) (on file with the Committee, C05390855).
[15] *See* Testimony of Diplomatic Security Agent 23, U.S. Dep't of State, Tr. at 69–70 (Oct. 10, 2013) [hereinafter Diplomatic Sec. Agent 23 Testimony] (on file with the Committee).

concerns about the incidents that did involve us. And the basic response was that they . . . were anomalies.

\*     \*     \*

It was the persons attending the meeting. I believe it was the Ambassador who actually said its anomalies; we can't account for anomalies. And other members of the group seemed to concur with that. And then this trip was planned because there was a gap in principal officer up there and the opening of the American corner. . . . I knew he was bound and determined to go.

I've been wracking my memory trying to remember the exact conversations I had with him on this. But I know he knew I didn't—the idea of him traveling there. But I knew he was determined to go. So doing everything I can to make it as safe as possible, given my resources and the environment—safety—compounds—both compounds, all the Americans there.[16]

Not only was the looming funding deadline an impetus for Stevens' trip, an upcoming trip by Hillary R. Clinton, Secretary of State, in the fall of 2012 was also a motivating factor for him to travel to Benghazi. The hope was to establish a permanent consulate in Benghazi for the Secretary to present to the Libyan government during her trip. Hicks discussed this with the Committee:

Q: Okay. We know that Ambassador Stevens went to Benghazi on September 10th. Was there anything about his trip to Benghazi in September of 2012 that was sort of a precursor for the Secretary's trip?

A: Well, you know, when we have a visit by a major political figure, like the Secretary of State, like the President, you know, we try to make that visit important publicly. And so we generally will create a list of what we call deliverables, items of importance to the bilateral relationship. So we hoped for the Secretary to announce the opening of a permanent consulate in Benghazi during her visit[.]

Q: Was there any reason that—was there anything related to making Benghazi a permanent post that was part of the purpose of Ambassador Stevens going to Benghazi in September?

A: Oh, absolutely. And so again, we had begun the process of developing a political rationale for having a permanent post in Benghazi. I sent in that rationale at the end of August to the executive director of the NEA [Near Eastern Affairs] bureau. We had begun a process of identifying locations and drawing plans for such a post.

---

[16] *Id.*

* * *

And we understood that the situation in eastern Libya was unstable and we wanted to—and Chris Stevens wanted to make sure that what we were doing was going—was the right course of action. And he personally, because he had the contacts in the region, because he had their trust. He was the only person that we felt could go to Benghazi and get a clear picture of the political situation there and the security situation there as well.[17]

The Secretary was planning to travel to Libya in October of 2012.[18]

## Benghazi: September 1-September 10, 2012

Security deficiencies plagued the Benghazi Mission compound in the lead-up to September 2012. With the departure of the Diplomatic Security Agent in charge at the end of August, only two Diplomatic Security Agents remained to secure the compound.[19] A Diplomatic Security Agent from Tripoli was routed to Benghazi to serve temporarily during the month of September putting three agents on the ground as of September 1, 2012.[20] None of the Diplomatic Security Agents in Benghazi had ever served at a high-threat post.[21]

In addition, the Mission compound's contracted quick reaction force, the February 17 Martyrs Brigade militia, which provided interior armed security at the Benghazi Mission compound, informed the Diplomatic Security Agents two days before the Ambassador was scheduled to arrive it would no longer provide off-compound security.[22] This meant the three Diplomatic Security Agents on the ground would have no security support for any transport or for any meetings held off of the compound during Stevens' visit. The Diplomatic Security Agents attributed the change in policy to an inter-militia power struggle.[23] The next day, however, the Principal Officer in Benghazi, joined a meeting with leading militia officials during which time they told him they could no longer guarantee the safety of the compound. The Principal Officer described the meeting:

> [T]here was a—it was a growing and nascent group of commanders who—militia commanders who were just becoming kind of players on the security scene. And some of the

---

[17] Testimony of Gregory N. Hicks, Deputy Chief of Mission at U.S. Embassy Tripoli, U.S. Dep't of State, Tr. at 50–51 (Apr. 14, 2016) [hereinafter Hicks Apr. 2016 Testimony] (on file with the Committee).

[18] Email from Huma Abedin, Deputy Chief of Staff for Operations, U.S. Dep't of State, to Philippe Reines, Deputy Ass't Sec'y for Public Affairs, U.S. Dep't of State (Sept. 12, 2012, 9:15 AM) (on file with the Committee, SCB0075710).

[19] See Email from Deputy Dir. for Maghreb Affairs, U.S. Dep't of State, to Diplomatic Sec. Agent 25, U.S. Dep't of State (Aug. 27, 2012 4:47 PM) (on file with the Committee, C05394203) ("Thanks for your call and clarification that DS has had no volunteers for Benghazi for the upcoming few months.").

[20] See Hicks Apr. 2013 Testimony at 56.

[21] See id. at 14 ("Principal Officer 4 is chosen to be Acting Principal Officer for the first week in September. And he goes to Benghazi and is there with three Diplomatic Sec. special agents, all of whom are brand new to the service and on temporary duty assignment.").

[22] See Diplomatic Sec. Agent 23 Testimony at 44–45.

[23] See Email from Diplomatic Sec. Agent 3, Diplomatic Sec. Service, U.S. Embassy Tripoli, Libya (Sept. 8, 2012 9:29 PM) (on file with the Committee, C05396013).

working assumptions were that they were doing this mainly for personal profit; others for religious and ideological reasons. It is trying to understand motivations of groups of people who may or may not become future leaders for the city of Benghazi or the country of Libya.

So these folks were identified as people who fit that billet, essentially, security official officials who may or may not have aspirations for larger roles in Benghazi.

\* \* \*

Libya Shield was a brand new organization at that time that was kind of emerging from the ranks of the [Supreme Security Council] and from other official organizations. They had numbers to them. What I characterize in here was what was the most fascinating part of the meeting to me. I was sitting with Wissam bin Hamid and Jumaa and I forget his name al Gha'abi. They were debating which militias they belonged to and who was in control of them and what their ideology was and what their ambitions were. And they weren't you know, they disagreed on many of those things.

And one member was—one of the commanders was a member of the other commander's brigade under that commander, and that commander was a member of that commander's brigade under that commander. So it was really difficult to determine who was in charge, and I think they right there in front of us were, you know, playing that out, which is a great opportunity to really get a sense of what's going on in the rest of the country.

\* \* \*

Q: [I]t looks like it's the second to last sentence or third to last sentence, it begins: They criticized the [U.S. Government] for supporting National Forces Alliance leader and prime minister candidate Mahmoud Jibril. Do you recall what their criticism of the U.S. Government was?

A: Yeah. So "supporting" is in quotations, right, and which is a false accusation against the United States. We don't support candidates in a foreign government's internal domestic election. But the general perception, because Mahmoud Jibril is an American citizen as well as a Libyan, is that the United States Government was backing him. He was a big political player, former prime minister and someone who was gaining it seemed to be at that time someone who may end up with another very high ranking position in the Libyan Government. That did not meet these particular militia commanders' idea of a beneficial Libyan structure for them, and so they were complaining about it.

Q: [Y]ou go on to write: If Jibril won, they said they would not continue to guarantee security in Benghazi, a critical function they asserted they were currently providing.

What was your understanding of what they meant when they said they would not continue to guarantee security in Benghazi?

A: Yeah, I did not take that as a threat against U.S. interests, the U.S. compound, U.S. persons, or anything else. I took that more as a general discussion of Benghazi, the security situation in Benghazi is generally deteriorating, if they at least their assertion that the general condition in Benghazi would deteriorate if they withdrew their security support.

Q: Did you understand what did they mean by withdrew their security support?

A: Well, I mean, that's one of the questions I was asking, right. What do you do? Who are you? Why are you Libya 1? Why are you Libya 2? What's your role? How do you fit into the security structure? And, as I said, you know, they didn't really have a very good picture of it themselves, so I couldn't come out with one.[24]

The meeting underscored that the militias in Benghazi controlled what little security environment existed there. Not having off-compound support from a militia would significantly threaten Stevens' safety.

### Stevens' Trip to Benghazi: September 10, 2012

Stevens arrived by a commercial airplane in Benghazi on the morning of September 10, 2012.[25] Traveling with him were two of the six Diplomatic Security Agents assigned to the Embassy in Tripoli. Four Diplomatic Security Agents remained behind at the Embassy along with four Department of Defense special operators who had previously served as part of the Site Security Team [SST].[26] In addition, the special operators had previously augmented security at the Benghazi Mission compound, but they were no longer able to do so.[27] Patrick F. Kennedy, the Under Secretary for Management, State Department, terminated the SST's responsibilities for the Embassy's security in August of 2012.[28] As a result, the SST was no longer able to travel with Stevens or augment security in Benghazi.[29]

---

[24] Testimony of Principal Officer 4, Foreign Service Officer, U.S. Dep't of State, Tr. at 64–68 (May 8, 2015) (on file with the Committee). *See also,* Email from J. Christopher Stevens, U.S. Ambassador to Libya, to Principal Officer 4, Foreign Service Officer, U.S. Dep't of State (Sept. 10, 2012 1:51 AM) (on file with the Committee, C05395344).

[25] Testimony of Diplomatic Sec. Agent 2, Tr. at 47 (Mar. 19, 2015) [hereinafter Diplomatic Sec. Agent 2].

[26] Testimony of Gregory N. Hicks, Deputy Chief of Mission at U.S. Embassy Tripoli, U.S. Dep't of State, Tr. at 12–14 (Apr. 11, 2013) [hereinafter Hicks Apr. 2013 Testimony] (on file with the Committee).

[27] Hicks Apr. 2016 Testimony at 17.

[28] *Id.* at 20, 33–35; *see also,* Email from Patrick Kennedy, Under Sec'y for Mgmt., U.S. Dep't of State, to Robert Neller, Lieutenant General, U.S. Dep't of Defense (July 15, 2012,) (on file with the Committee SCB0076533).

[29] *See* Hicks Apr. 2013 Testimony at 12–13.

The August 6th attack, or incident, if you will, AFRICOM decided to draw down the SST team from 16 members to 6. Chris concurred in that decision because he didn't really feel like he had, you know, much leverage other than that. And so [the Com-

Continued

In fact, during August 2012, the total number of State Department security agents assigned to the Embassy in Tripoli dropped from 34 individuals to six.[30] Losing 28 security agents reduced not only the security resources available to the Embassy, but also those available to the Benghazi Mission compound. With limited security agents in Tripoli, there were no surplus security agents to send to augment security in Benghazi—without leaving the Embassy in Tripoli at severe risk.

Hicks described the impact of the reduction in personnel on the overall security platform in Libya:

> [W]hen I arrived on July 31st . . . we had the 16 members of the SST and we had about 14 or so State security personnel, who were divided between either special agents or MSD, members of the mobile security detail teams.
>
> Through August, the MSD personnel are withdrawn until, by August 31st, . . . the security complement in Libya at the time was: In Tripoli is an RSO plus 5 assistant regional security officers protecting approximately 28 diplomatic personnel. And in Benghazi we have three DS special agents protecting two State Department personnel in our facilities.
>
> So the answer to your question . . . we had nine people to draw from when Chris decided you know, [Principal Officer 4] is chosen to be Acting Principal Officer for the first week in September. And he goes to Benghazi and is there with three Diplomatic Security special agents, all of whom are brand new to the service and on temporary duty assignment.
>
> So when Chris goes to Benghazi on the 10th of September, [Diplomatic Security Agent 23], the RSO, assigns two of our personnel in [Tripoli] to go with him. [N]ow we have, on the morning of September 11th, when [Principal Officer 4] flies back to Tripoli, we now have five Diplomatic security special agents protecting the Ambassador and Sean Smith. In Tripoli, we have four we have a Regional Security Officer and three Assistant Regional Security Officers to protect 28 diplomatic personnel.[31]

---

mander of the Site Security Team] and nine other members of the team left he may have discussed this in mid -August.

Full expectation was that when we, as the embassy, and working with the Defense Attaché, achieved the agreement of the Libyan Government to proceed with the counterterrorism mission under section 1208, and the training team was given diplomatic immunity, they would return and begin the training mission. So they left. So we have at the time, then, six members of the SST left, divided in two different locations, four and two. But they are still under AFRICOM authority.

General Ham issued a letter after the negotiation in Stuttgart over Eid al Fitr describing the relationship of the SST to the embassy going forward. I honestly cannot remember whether the contents of that letter are classified or not. I know it was transmitted to us over classified communications. But it was not Chief of Mission authority, I can tell you that. They were not told that they were under the authority of the Ambassador with respect to security, although they were told to cooperate I believe it told them to cooperate with the RSO for internal defense matters, if I remember correctly.

[30] *Id.* at 13–14.
[31] *Id.*

Publicity about Stevens' trip to Benghazi was reportedly limited. He previously told his staff and contacts on the ground "for security reasons we'll need to be careful about limiting moves off-compound and scheduling as many meetings as possible in the villa."[32] Stevens said he wanted to "avoid the RPG reception that the UK Amb[assador] got. . . ."[33]

Upon arriving in Benghazi on September 10, 2012, Stevens received a security briefing at the nearby Central Intelligence Agency [CIA] annex on the changing threat environment.[34] Due to the worsening security environment in Benghazi, the Diplomatic Security Agents at the compound requested support from the Annex's security team, the Global Response Staff [GRS], to supplement Stevens' movements off-compound in Benghazi.[35]

> Q: You talked during the last hour about the intelligence briefing that you provided to the Ambassador the night before the attack.
>
> What type of reaction did you get from the Ambassador from your briefing?
>
> A: He was interested. He took a lot of notes. It struck me a little bit that he was surprised at how fast the situation had deteriorated in eastern Libya.
>
> Q: And what did he do to give you that impression that he was surprised at how quickly——
>
> A: He was called in to go to his next appointment several times, and he refused to leave before we finished.
>
> Q: Okay, do you know who his next appointment was?
>
> A: Yes.
>
> Q: And what was that?
>
> A: Benghazi City Council, I believe.
>
> Q: Did the Ambassador ask any questions of you during the briefing?
>
> A: Yes, yeah, he asked a lot of questions.
>
> Q: And what were his questions along the lines of if you can recall?
>
> A: Specifically about the extremist groups that established presence in eastern Libya since the fall of the regime.
>
> Q: Okay, and do you recall at that time approximately how many extremist groups there were that had established a presence?
>
> A: Several.
>
> Q: Several?

---

[32] Email from J. Christopher Stevens, U.S. Ambassador to Libya, to a Locally Employed Staff, U.S. Dep't of State, and Principal Officer 4, U.S. Dep't of State (Sept. 8, 2012, 4:37 AM) (on file with the Committee, C05390147).

[33] Email from Principal Officer 3, U.S. Dep't of State, to J. Christopher Stevens, U.S. Ambassador to Libya (Aug. 1, 2012 10:49 AM) (on file with the Committee, C05390814).

[34] Diplomatic Sec. Agent 2 Testimony at 54.

[35] Id. at 59.

A: Yes.

Q: Well, from what you can remember, what are the names to the extent that you can remember?

A: Yes, AQIM; Al Qaeda; and Islamic Brethren; AQAP; Al Qaeda in the Arabian Peninsula; AQ Pakistan; EIJ, Egyptian Islamic Jihad. By that time, Ansar al-Sharia Derna had established a presence.[36]

Later in the evening of September 10th, Stevens—with Diplomatic Security Agents and GRS security—visited the Benghazi Local Council. Media was present upon his arrival.[37] One of the Diplomatic Security Agents testified:

Q: So, you knew prior to the council meeting that the press was going to show up?

A: Yes, and we tried to turn that off, but unfortunately, we couldn't. They showed up, but we sent them away.

Q: Okay. Were you surprised to learn that there would be press at the council meeting?

A: I was.[38]

Stevens' visit to Benghazi therefore became public to the extent it was not otherwise known.[39]

Stevens found the meeting with the Local Council fruitful, but noted Council members seemed to feel slighted that no sitting U.S. Ambassador had visited the city since the revolution ended.[40] This was a concern among the leaders in Benghazi at the time, as they feared the Libyan Government's control and power would remain in Tripoli as it had been during the Qadhafi regime, thus marginalizing not just Benghazi, but the whole of Eastern Libya. Stevens noted this concern in his personal diary:

They're an impressive & sincere group of professionals—proud of their service on committees, all working as volunteers. Their main problem is a lack of budget & authorities. Tripoli still runs the country & its bureaucrats are an uneven quality. There was a little sourness about why it has taken so long to get to Benghazi, and about Ambassadors who came to talk but don't do anything to follow up. But overall it was a positive meeting.[41]

### September 10 Phone Call on September 11 Preparedness

On September 10, 2012, the day Stevens arrived in Benghazi, American military forces were reminded to "do everything possible

---

[36] Officer A, Cent. Intel. Agency, Tr. at 116–118. (Mar 2, 2016) [hereinafter Officer A Testimony] (on file with the Committee).

[37] Diplomatic Sec. Agent 2 Testimony at 52.

[38] *Id.* at 52–53.

[39] *Id.*

[40] J. Christopher Stevens, U.S. Ambassador to Libya, Personal Diary, Unofficial Testimony prepared by Patrick F. Kennedy, *et al.* (Sept. 10, 2012) (on file with the Committee, STATE–SCB0048881).

[41] *Id.*

to protect the American people, both at home and abroad."[42] That day the President conducted a conference call with key national security principals to discuss the steps taken to protect U.S. persons and facilities abroad and force protection. Leon E. Panetta, Secretary of Defense, one of the conference call participants acknowledged they "were already tracking an inflammatory anti-Muslim video that was circulating on the Internet and inciting anger across the Middle East against the United States" and that they "braced for demonstrations in Cairo and elsewhere across the region."[43] Due to the Arab Spring, it was a time of heightened concern for that region in general. In particular, the discussion focused on several areas including Cairo, Tripoli, Tunis, Khartoum, and Sana'a, due to intelligence indicating potential demonstrations could erupt in those areas.[44]

Based on the September 10 conference call with national security principals and the President, the Defense Department placed its forces on "higher alert because of the potential for what could happen."[45] Yet, the intelligence and the call for a "heightened alert" did not cause any actual adjustment in its posture for assets that could respond to a crisis in North Africa.[46] Some assets were in the middle of training exercises, and others were in the middle of inspections. No fighter jets or tankers were placed on a "heightened alert" status.

## SEPTEMBER 11, 2012

### Morning in Benghazi: "Never Ending Security Threats"

The September 10 visit to Benghazi was Stevens' first since becoming Ambassador, and the city had changed since his departure in the fall of 2011.[47] A growing extremist movement had taken hold within the city limits and Stevens spent part of September 10th being briefed on what was happening from a security standpoint. One CIA officer described the declining security environment in Benghazi at the time:

> It was a really unique and difficult environment to operate in in eastern Libya. It was really a unique environment. It's a country that we have not had—I mean, as you know, it was a closed country and it was a police state, and it's not like it's a country that we had a ton of experience in how to operate in.

---

[42] Readout of the President's Meeting with Senior Administration Officials on Our Preparedness and Security Posture on the Eleventh Anniversary of September 11th, dated Sept. 10, 2012.

[43] Leon E. Panetta, *Worthy Fights: A Memoir of Leadership in War and Peace* 225 (2014).

[44] *Id.*

[45] *Id.*

[46] *Id. See also,* letter from Ashton B. Carter, Sec'y of Defense, to Trey Gowdy, Chairman, House Select Committee on Benghazi, Apr. 8, 2015 ("However, it is worth noting that none of the military forces listed above were placed on heightened alert ahead of the attacks on Benghazi on September 11, 2012.").

[47] J. Christopher Stevens, U.S. Ambassador to Libya, Personal Diary, Unofficial Transcript prepared by Patrick F. Kennedy, *et al.* (Sept. 10, 2012) (on file with the Committee, SCB0048881).

\*     \*     \*

New groups are forming. New groups are dissolving. Outside groups are interfering and starting to establish presence. So it was an extremely dynamic and fluid situation.

As I said, you know, we had the handicap of not having good SIGINT coverage within the country. And that goes back to the fact that Libya, in general, was a denied area for a long, long time for us, and it's an area that was very difficult to operate in.

Q: Now, **[redacted text]**. And I've noticed you've used the same word three times, "deteriorating." And one would think that a post-revolutionary country probably would be in not the greatest of positions to begin with.

A: Right.

Q: And what you're saying is it deteriorated even from that.

A: That's correct.

Q: And tell me why you have chosen to use that word and what you mean by "deteriorating"?

A: The level of armed conflict and fighting between the various groups increased. The level of assassinations, attacks on foreign entities increased. There were entire towns, specifically Derna and around it, that became very difficult to travel to; checkpoints that were manned by individuals dressed in Afghan garb, jihadi garb; a lot of evidence of foreign fighters coming in from outside the country.

Specifically in June of 2012, right before the elections, the Islamist militia had an overt show of force, where they had a military parade roll in from eastern Libya to downtown Benghazi. I mean, I guess it was a message to the Libyan electorate that we are here and we have a presence and we want to establish Islamic State inside Libya and we want sharia to be the law of the country. So there was, like, a lot of attempts to intimidate the populace in Libya by these extremist groups.[48]

Security concerns and the anniversary of September 11 kept Stevens on the Benghazi Mission compound for his day full of meetings.

According to his prepared agenda Stevens had meetings with the 17th February Brigade, the Arabian Gulf Oil Company, and the head of the al-Marfa Shipping and Maritime Services Company.[49]

Early on the morning of September 11th, one of the Diplomatic Security Agents in Benghazi was notified of an individual dressed in a uniform typically worn by the local police force conducting sur-

---

[48] Officer A Testimony at 147–49.

[49] Schedule for J. Christopher Stevens, Ambassador, Benghazi Libya: September 10–14 (on file with the Committee, C05396585).

veillance of the Mission.[50] The Diplomatic Security Agent in charge reported the incident to the head security officer in country at the Embassy in Tripoli and to staff at both the Benghazi Mission compound and the Annex, including Stevens.[51] The Diplomatic Security Agent described the incident:

> We received word from our local guards that this morning they observed a member of the police force assigned to the Mission at a construction site across the street from our main gate taking pictures of our compound. I briefed the Ambo and provided him drafts of letters notifying the [Libyan Ministry of Foreign Affairs] and police. Will let you know any further details.[52]

In Benghazi, the Supreme Security Council was the "most prominent" official police force, "assembled from former members of the various militias as an interim security measure."[53] It was "designed to be an interim security measure" following the revolution but had not coalesced into an established force and had little impact on the security incidents in Benghazi.[54]

Stevens' last meeting of the day was with the Turkish Consul General. He escorted the Turkish diplomat to the front gate of the compound that evening at 7:39 p.m. [1:39 p.m. in Washington D.C.].[55]

Stevens' last entry in his personal journal, dated September 11, 2012, read: "Never ending security threats . . . "[56]

## A Protest Begins at the U.S. Embassy in Cairo, Egypt on September 11

In the hours preceding the attacks in Benghazi, a protest of approximately 2,000 demonstrators assembled outside the U.S. Embassy in Cairo, Egypt.[57] Cairo is some 600 miles east of Benghazi. Plans for a demonstration in Cairo first began to coalesce in late August 2012 with the designated terrorist organization, Jamaa Islamiya, calling upon its supporters to protest the continued incarceration of its leader, Sheikh Omaar abdel Rahman, also known as the "Blind Sheik."[58] Rahman is serving a life prison sentence for his role in the 1993 World Trade Center bombing.[59] Additionally, in the days preceding the September 11 demonstration in Cairo, an

---

[50] Email from Diplomatic Sec. Agent 2 (Sept. 11, 2012, 5:00 PM) (on file with the Committee, C05271656).

[51] Id.; see also Diplomatic Sec. Agent 5 Testimony at 104–105; Diplomatic Sec. Agent 2 Testimony at 80.

[52] Email from a Diplomatic Sec. Agent (Sept. 11, 2012, 5:00 PM) (on file with the Committee, C05271656).

[53] U.S. Dep't of State, Cable, The Guns of August: security in eastern Libya (Aug. 8, 2012) (on file with the Committee, C055782149).

[54] Id.

[55] Comprehensive Timeline of Events—Benghazi (on file with the Committee, SCB0047843).

[56] J. Christopher Stevens, U.S. Ambassador to Libya, Personal Diary, Unofficial Transcript prepared by Patrick F. Kennedy, et al. (Sept. 10, 2012) (on file with the Committee, SCB0048881).

[57] Email to Susan E. Rice, U.S. Permanent Representative to the U.N. (Sept. 11, 2012, 7:55 PM) (on file with the Committee, C05390691) (re: FOR SER INFO: More on Cairo Embassy Attack).

[58] See Larry Bell, Muslim Brotherhood Fox Was Hired To Protect Our Benghazi Consulate Henhouse, FORBES (Dec. 2, 2012), http://www.forbes.com/sites/larrybell/2012/12/02/muslim-brotherhood-fox-was-hired-to-protect-our-benghazi-consulate-henhouse-interview.

[59] Id.

Arabic version of a trailer for a little known anti-Islamic film, produced in the United States, was posted on YouTube.[60] This trailer caught the attention of Muslims in Egypt and calls were made on television, in newspapers, and on social media, to protest the denigration of the Muslim faith as depicted in the movie trailer at the U.S. Embassy in Cairo on September 11, 2012.[61]

Multiple agencies of the U.S. government were aware of the impending demonstration in Egypt. The U.S. Embassy in Cairo notified the State Department, coordinated with Egyptian leaders, and ordered most of its personnel not to report to work that day.[62] The Department of Homeland Security issued an intelligence report on September 10, 2012 advising that the Cairo Embassy might be targeted as a means to call for the release of the Blind Sheik as well as in response to an anti-Islam film.[63]

Shortly after noon in Cairo [6 a.m. in Washington D.C.] on September 11, 2012, the U.S. Embassy in Cairo posted a tweet condemning those who would "hurt the religious feelings of Muslims."[64] A few hours later, demonstrators began gathering outside the perimeter wall of the Embassy in Cairo.[65] The crowd of demonstrators grew to nearly 2,000 people.[66] Armed with spray paint, a handful of demonstrators scaled the walls, tore down the American flag, ripped it to shreds, and replaced it with a black militant Islamic flag.[67] According to Kennedy, there were no weapons shown or used during the protest in Cairo.[68] Within hours, the

---

[60] The original trailer, in English, was posted in July 2012. *See* Phil Willon and Rebecca Keegan, *Timeline: "Innocence of Muslims" Unrest*, LA TIMES (Sept. 13, 2012), http:// articles.latimes.com/2012/sep/12/entertainment/la-et-mn-antiislam-film-sparks-violence-20120912.

[61] Nancy A. Youssef and Amina Ismail, *Anti-U.S. outrage over video began with Christian activist's phone call to a reporter*, MCCLATCHY NEWSPAPERS (Sept. 15, 2012), http://www. mcclatchydc.com/news/nation-world/world/article24737101.html; *see also*, Email from State Department Press Office, U.S. Dep't of State, to State Department Press Office, U.S. Dep't of State (Sept. 13, 2012 4:54 PM) (on file with the Committee, C05580045) (The film trailer "had actually been circulating at a relatively low level for some months out there in cyberspace and that it only caught fire in the region on the day or just before that day that we began to see these various protests.").

[62] *See id.* ("in the day or days prior to the protests that became violent at our Embassy in Cairo, the film had been shown on Egyptian television and was being quite heavily watched, and our social media tracking indicated that . . . we expected it to be localized to Egypt.").

[63] Catherine Herridge, *DHS report warned last week of call for 'burning the embassy down' in Cairo*, FOX NEWS, (Sept. 19, 2012), http://www.foxnews.com/politics/2012/09/19/dhs-report-warned-last-week-call-for-burning-embassy-down-in-cairo.print.html; *see also Intel agencies warned U.S. embassy in Egypt of possible violence over film*, AL ARABIYA NEWS (Sept. 18, 2012), http://www.alarabiya.net/articles/2012/09/18/238658.html.

[64] Email from Victoria J. Nuland, Spokesperson, U.S. Dep't of State, to Wendy Sherman, Under Sec'y for Political Affairs, U.S. Dep't of State, *et al.* (Sept. 12, 2012, 6:08 PM) (on file with the Committee, C05580024) (Subject: Today's Benghazi backgrounding points) ("The statement was issued from Embassy Cairo just after noon Cairo time on September 11, well before the incident at the Embassy."); see also Karen Yourish and David A. Fahrenthold, *Timeline on Libya and Egypt: Attacks and response*, WASH. POST, (Sept. 12, 2012), https:// www.washingtonpost.com/politics/decision2012/timeline-on-libya-and-egypt-attacks-and-response/ 2012/09/12/85288638-fd03-11e1-a31e-804fccb658f9_story.html?hpid=z1.

[65] Email to Susan E. Rice, U.S. Permanent Representative to the U.N. (Sept. 11, 2012, 7:55 PM) (on file with the Committee, C05390691) (re: FOR SER INFO: More on Cairo Embassy Attack).

[66] *Id.*

[67] *Id.*

[68] Email from Legislative Mgmt. Officer, U.S. Dep't of State, to H_Egypt, *et al.* (Sept. 12, 2012 7:55 PM) (on file with the Committee, C05562234) (Subject: Write up of U/S Kennedy Call with Hill re Libya) ("Attack in Cairo was a demonstration. There were no weapons shown or used. A few cans of spray paint.").

Egyptian police were able to "move the protesters off the compound peacefully."[69]

United States Africa Command [AFRICOM] was the U.S Combatant Command with responsibility for all of Africa, except Egypt. Despite Egypt not being in its area of responsibility, AFRICOM observed the Cairo protest throughout the day. Vice Admiral Charles J. Leidig, the Deputy Commander for Military Operations at AFRICOM, discussed AFRICOM's actions that day:

> [W]e had been observing the events on that day in Cairo and the protests, and we were concerned that those protests would cause other protests throughout the region, and particularly in North Africa. Even though Egypt is not in our area of responsibility, it surely has an affinity with the other countries that are in Northern Africa. So we were watching that carefully.
>
> So I actually recall staying at work until almost 1900 [7:00 p.m. in Libya] because we wanted to see if any riots or protests would break out, and they didn't.[70]

Despite the size of the crowd of demonstrators in Cairo and the length of the demonstration, the protest in Cairo prompted no change in force laydown for the forces that might respond to unrest in North Africa. In other words, neither the President's meeting with his Cabinet which included a discussion of the anti-Muslim film nor the anniversary of September 11, 2001, nor the demonstration in Cairo prompted any change in U.S. military posture or asset readiness in the region.

### The Anti-Muslim Film was a "Nonevent" in Libya

The protests in Cairo had little to no impact on the Benghazi Mission compound or throughout Libya. While the anti-Muslim film was one of the reasons protests were called for in Egypt, it was virtually unknown in Libya. Hicks testified regarding the reaction in Libya to the film:

> Q: Was it your understanding that the Cairo protest had been planned and called for?
>
> A: I believe I understood that at the time.
>
> Q: Okay. Had there been any similar protest in Libya that were planned and called for prior to that day?
>
> A: No there were not. And so we were interested in monitoring all our contacts, and monitoring social media, news outlets, to see if anything erupted in Libya that was comparable to what was happening in Cairo. And we wanted to do that, but we wanted to do that as safely as possible.

---

[69] Email to Susan E. Rice, U.S. Permanent Representative to the U.N. (Sept. 11, 2012, 7:55 PM) (on file with the Committee, C05390691) (re: FOR SER INFO: More on Cairo Embassy Attack) ("Egyptian police did finally move the protesters off the compound peacefully.").

[70] Testimony of Vice Admiral Charles J. Leidig, Deputy Commander for Military Operations, U.S. Africa Command, Tr. at 25–26 (Mar. 20, 2014) [hereinafter Leidig 2014 Testimony] (on file with the Committee).

\*     \*     \*

Q: Okay. We have heard reports that the demonstrations in Cairo were at least in part if not solely based on some sort of video or film trailer that was out that was demeaning to the Prophet Mohammed. Did you have that understanding at the time?

A: Of the Cairo——

Q: Yes.

A: —demonstrations?

Q: Yes.

A: I think maybe I did. I'm not sure.

Q: . Were you monitoring within Libya for any type of reaction to this film?

A: Yes.

Q: Okay. And how long had you been monitoring in Libya for any type of reaction to this film?

A: I think we had begun monitoring since about September 8th.

Q: Okay. And had you had any reaction or hits on your monitoring?

A: Very few, if any.

Q: So it appeared to be a nonevent in the country of Libya?

A: It was a nonevent in the country of Libya.

Q: Did you have any conversations with Ambassador Stevens regarding the demonstrations in Cairo and the actions that you were taking in response to that?

A: I had texted him and said, hey, are you watching TV? Embassy Cairo is under attack.

\*     \*     \*

Q: And did he respond?
A: He said, really? And I can't remember exactly what he said, but anyway it was, what's going on? And I said, the embassy's been breached, the flag's been taken down, the black flag has been raised in its place.

Q: Was that the sum total of your communication back and forth.

A: That was the sum total of our communication.[71]

One of the Diplomatic Security Agents in Benghazi told the Committee what happened after Stevens learned of the Cairo protests:

Q: Did you hear at any point during the day at some time about a protest in Cairo?

---

[71] Hicks Apr. 2016 Testimony at 64–68.

A: Yes. I can't remember exactly when, but I was made aware of the protests in Cairo, and the Ambassador had asked about it.

Q: And were you actually in a conversation with the Ambassador?

A: I was in a conversation with the Ambassador when he said, hey, something's going on in Cairo, and he asked me if I would be able to find out something about it for him.

Q: And were you able to?

A: I made some phone calls to the command center, in D.C. but there was no other information that I received other than that there was a protest, and they were actually in the process of evaluating the situation.[72]

As in Tripoli, the agents in Benghazi monitored social media for any planned or called-for demonstrations. On September 11, there was no indication in Benghazi that any protests over the film trailer were planned.[73] With the film being a virtual nonevent in Libya, the Diplomatic Security Agents saw no reason to change their security posture that day. One Diplomatic Security Agent recounted:

Q: And do you remember any conversations about whether or not, because of what the Ambassador had been hearing and asked you to follow-up on, or any other reasons, of potentially changing anything about the security setup for that evening?

A: No, no I—no, I can't think of any changes that we talked about making or made based on that.[74]

### Evening in Benghazi

On the evening of September 11, 2012, there were a total of seven U.S. personnel, including Stevens, on the ground at the compound at the time of the attack.[75] Sean P. Smith, who prior to working for the State Department served in the United States Air Force, was one of the U.S. personnel there. Smith was serving as the Information Management Officer. He had been in Benghazi on a temporary tour of duty from The Hague for 30 days. He arrived on September 1 and his role was to run the administrative component of the Mission. The other five U.S. personnel at the compound that evening included the two Diplomatic Security Agents who travelled with Stevens from Tripoli to Benghazi, and the three Diplomatic Security Agents assigned to Benghazi.

Stevens' last event of the day was a meeting with the Turkish Consul General, **[redacted text]**. The Consul General departed at 7:39 p.m. local time, and four British security team members de-

---

[72] Diplomatic Sec. Agent 2 Testimony at 82–83.

[73] Email from Agent 5, Diplomatic Sec. Agent, U.S. Dep't of State, to J. Christopher Stevens, U.S. Ambassador to Libya (Sept. 11, 2012 1:39 AM) (on file with the Committee, C05393199) (Subject: Daily Security Update).

[74] Diplomatic Sec. Agent 2 Testimony at 84–85.

[75] Diplomatic Sec. Agent 3 Testimony at 142.

parted at 8:27 p.m.[76] No other visitors were on the Mission compound that night. There was no evidence of any group assembled outside the Mission compound gate: large, small, peaceful or otherwise.

### THERE WAS NO PROTEST

All five Diplomatic Security Agents on the ground that night in Benghazi were consistent in their testimony—before the attack began, there was no protest.

One agent testified:

> Q: So the intelligence in and around Benghazi was that there was no planned protest?
>
> A: I did not hear of a planned protest, no.
>
> Q: No one communicated that to you.
>
> A: No, I did not hear that.[77]

Another agent testified:

> Q: Do you recall at any time during the day seeing any type of crowd form outside of the mission compound.
>
> A: Other than?
>
> Q: Other than normal activity that would have occurred in Benghazi, just people coming and going.
>
> A: So other than the attack and the attackers, no.
>
> Q: Okay. So there was no protest, to the best of your knowledge, the day of the attack.
>
> A: Not to my knowledge.[78]

Yet another agent testified:

> Q: From your perspective, had there been a protest?
>
> A: No. There was nothing out there up until, well, up until there was. I had been out of the gate at 8:30 that night. We had had personnel leaving the compound, and they drove away from our compound and didn't report anything, and I spoke with them subsequently, there was nothing out there.[79]

A fourth agent testified:

> Q: Prior to the attack occurred [sic], did you hear anything on the outside, such as chanting or any type of sounds [that] would be a protest?
>
> A: No, I never heard any sort of chanting or protest or anything.
>
> Q: Would it then be an accurate description to describe the attack as a sort of stealth attack?

---

[76] Video: DVR Footage of the Mission (Sept. 11, 2012, 1940 and 2027, respectively).
[77] Testimony of Diplomatic Sec. Agent 1, U.S. Dep't of State, Tr. at 50–51 (Mar. 6, 2015) [hereinafter Diplomatic Sec. Agent 1 Testimony] (on file with the Committee).
[78] Diplomatic Sec. Agent 2 Testimony at 123–124.
[79] Diplomatic Sec. Agent 3 Testimony at 31–32.

A: It was very sudden. As I had mentioned, conditions immediately before the only warning that I had that something was amiss was that—kind of that cry that I heard at assault on the main gate.

Q: So it was very sudden. And the first attackers that you saw enter, were they armed?

A: Yes.[80]

The fifth agent testified:

Q: If there had been something about a planned protest in Benghazi, would that be the type of information that you would have been interested in?

A: Yes.

Q: Do you recall any such information?

A: No.[81]

Hicks was asked "if there was . . . a protest [outside the facility], would that have been reported?"[82] In his view:

[A]bsolutely, I mean, we're talking about both security officers who know their trade, even though they are brand new, and one of the finest political officers in the history of the Foreign Service. You know, for there to have been a demonstration on Chris Stevens' front door and him not to have reported it is unbelievable. And secondly, if he had reported it, he would have been out the back door within minutes of any demonstration appearing anywhere near that facility. And there was a back gate to the facility, and, you know, it worked.[83]

## THE MISSION'S EMERGENCY ACTION PLAN

The Mission's emergency action plan relied on the Diplomatic Security Agents as well as the two contracted internal security support entities: The Blue Mountain Guard Force and the February 17 Martyrs Brigade. The Blue Mountain Guard Force consisted of unarmed guards whose primary role was static surveillance of the three entrance gates as well as the interior of the compound. These guards had access to an alarm should any danger present itself. According to one Diplomatic Security Agent:

The primary purpose of a local guard force is to man the perimeter and the gates in order to delay and deter potential security risks and to afford us additional notice . . . if there were to be a security risk. In addition, they were in charge of access control, so screening people as they

---

[80] Testimony of Diplomatic Sec. Agent 4, U.S. Dep't of State, Tr. at 144 (Mar. 16, 2015) [hereinafter Diplomatic Sec. Agent 4 Testimony] (on file with the Committee).

[81] Testimony of Diplomatic Sec. Agent 5, U.S. Dep't of State, Tr. at 105 (Apr. 1, 2015) [hereinafter Diplomatic Sec. Agent 5 Testimony] (on file with the Committee).

[82] Hicks Apr. 2013 Testimony at 81.

[83] Id. at 81–82.

were coming in the compound, screening vehicles as there were coming in the compound.[84]

The February 17 Martyrs Brigade consisted of a rotating set of three to four armed guards who lived on compound to operate as a quick reaction force to respond to any security incidents against the Mission. Their role was to augment security provided by the Diplomatic Security Agents. In addition, the February 17 Martyrs Brigade was supposed to send additional armed guards if an event occurred at the Mission compound. According to one Diplomatic Security Agent:

> Q: And [how] did their role and responsibility differ from the local guard force [Blue Mountain Group]?
>
> A: Well, they were armed primarily. But really what we counted on them to do was make a phone call to the 17th February Martyrs Brigade so that we could receive backup in case something happened.
>
> Q: Okay. So you were aware that they had a larger contingent of people that was to be available to——
>
> A: Right. Right.[85]

One Diplomatic Security Agent provided a description of the emergency action plan at the compound and how the local guards were expected to supplement this plan:

> The reaction plan, whether it was something small on the first or something larger ultimately on the 11th or 12th, and this is the plan that we actually followed, but the reaction plan is to shelter in place. That you would take the principal officers, you secure them in Villa C. The agent or whoever was in the [Tactical Operations Center] building would go operate the communications and reach out to the security elements that were supposed to react.
>
> The security elements that were supposed to react includes the local guard is supposed to just give us an alert, a heads up of what's going on. The three to four [February 17 Martyrs Brigade] members that live on the compound are supposed to take an active role in our internal defense; additionally, the 20 person [February 17 Martyrs Brigade] with heavy weapons and heavy vehicles 2 kilometers away that had responded in the past and were expected to respond to any event that necessitated them in the future. The security element encompassing other Americans was part of the react plan as well to support the [February 17 Martyrs Brigade] elements that were going to come as well.
>
> So we're talking almost 30 armed personnel where arrangements were made for them to respond to our location, and had done so in training and in actuality in past events. So whether the attack had happened—whether

---

[84] Diplomatic Sec. Agent 4 Testimony at 16.
[85] Diplomatic Sec. Agent 5 Testimony at 22.

something had happened on the first, and it didn't, although we had somebody armed armed personnel on the roof all night, a rotating presence, or something that did happen on the 11th or 12th, the expectations were for these elements to respond as they had done in the past.[86]

The unarmed Blue Mountain Guard Force was fully staffed the evening of September 11, 2012, with five guards. Two of those guards were assigned to the main entrance of the Benghazi Mission compound.[87] Three of the four armed February 17 Martyrs Brigade guards were at the compound at the time of the attack. One of the guards left early for a reported "family obligation" with no replacement. The three remaining guards were within the vicinity of the main gate just prior to the attack.[88]

### ALL IS QUIET AT THE FRONT GATE

The Diplomatic Security Agents at the compound did not observe any activity at the main gate during the hour leading up to the attack.[89] The only movement of note was the arrival of a local police vehicle at the main gate at approximately 9:02 p.m. [3:02 p.m. in Washington D.C.].[90] According to one of the Diplomatic Security Agents, the one security component consistently lacking at the compound on a regular basis "was the police support on the exterior of the compound."[91] On September 6, 2012, in the lead-up to Stevens' visit, the Mission requested the Libyan Ministry of Foreign Affairs provide one vehicle at each gate of the Mission "round the clock (24 hours/day) from Sept 10, 2012 to September 15, 2012" to supplement security during Stevens' visit.[92] As the morning began on September 11, no police vehicle was located at any of the compound gates.[93]

> Q: Who was—what was your understanding of who the SSC was?
>
> A: The Supreme Security Council. I knew that it was a pseudo militia/police force/military elements, of, again, different militia groups.
>
> Q: And do you know what the request had been for increased security?
>
> A: For at least two vehicles, I believe at each gate.

---

[86] See Diplomatic Sec. Agent 3 Testimony at 46–47 (for additional details on the reaction plans); see also Diplomatic Sec. Agent 4 Testimony at 20 and 82, and Diplomatic Sec. Agent 5 Testimony at 88 and 90.

[87] Letter from U.S. Dep't of State to Blue Mountain Group (Feb. 17, 2012) (on file with the Committee, C05395135) (Subject: Notice of Contract Award Contract No. SAQMMA–12–C–0092 Local Guard Services Benghazi, Libya).

[88] Diplomatic Sec. Agent 3 Testimony at 147.

[89] Diplomatic Sec. Agent 4 Testimony at 127; see also Diplomatic Sec. Agent 5 Testimony at 113–114; Diplomatic Sec. Agent 2 Testimony at 85; Diplomatic Sec. Agent 4 Testimony at 36 ("We did have visibility issues, especially at night with our CCTV system. For that reason one of the efforts that I tried to lead was having the ESO, Engineering Sec. Office, come out to install new CCTV cameras that we had received. Unfortunately, it wasn't to be. They were scheduled to arrive I believe the week after the attack.").

[90] DVR: Footage of the Mission. (Sept. 11, 2012).

[91] Diplomatic Sec. Agent 3 Testimony at 109.

[92] U.S. Dep't of State, Diplomatic Note #59 prepared for the Ministry of Foreign Affairs and International Cooperation, Dir. of Gen. Protocol Dep't Branch, Benghazi Office (Sept. 6, 2012) (on file with the Committee, C05389670).

[93] Diplomatic Sec. Agent 1 Testimony at 7.

Q: And how—had that request been granted?

A: They told me the request went in. I don't know specifics of whether it was granted. The first day [September 10] I do remember two vehicles outside, though.

Q: And did they express to you any concerns about the status of their request, that it hadn't been granted and that had caused concern for them?

A: That day, no, but the next day, there were—two vehicles weren't on—on stations, at the mission, so yeah, that was a concern.

Q: Okay. So that would have been on 9/11——

A: Yes.[94]

That evening, however, a vehicle arrived outside of the Mission compound's front gate at 9:02 p.m.

### WARNINGS AND INDICATORS PRIOR TO THE ATTACKS

Shortly before the attacks began, a **[redacted text]** extremist indicated **[redacted text]** on their way to attack the [Mission compound's front gate] in Benghazi.[95]

The Committee also found evidence that a former TNC security official also claimed he attempted to pass threat information directly to the CIA Benghazi Annex prior to the attack. A few days after the attacks, on September 15, 2012, the **[redacted text]**[96] **[redacted text]**[97] **[redacted text]**[98] **[redacted text]** the former TNC official tried to relay the information to the Director of the Libyan Intelligence Service and his assistant, who were both out of the country. **[Redacted text]**."[99]

**[Redacted text]**, however—but what the Committee has uncovered and verified—was the former TNC security official also claimed he attempted to pass this threat information directly to the CIA Benghazi Annex prior to the attack. This claim was acknowledged by both the Chief of Base in Benghazi and another CIA officer:[100]

Prior to the attacks, **[redacted text]**[101] **[redacted text]**[102] **[redacted text]**.[103]

**[Redacted text]**, the CIA was unable to confirm whether or not the former TNC security official's claim is true. A **[redacted text]**[104] **[redacted text]**[105]

The CIA also reviewed **[redacted text]**[106]

---

[94] *Id.*

[95] **[Redacted text]**.

[96] **[Redacted text]**.

[97] *Id.*

[98] *Id.*

[99] *Id.*

[100] Officer A Testimony at 100; *see also,* Testimony of Chief of Base, Cent. Intel. Agency, Tr. at 130 (July 16, 2015) [hereinafter Chief of Base Testimony] (on file with the Committee).

[101] Officer A Testimony at 57, 59–60.

[102] Officer A Testimony at 85.

[103] *See* Officer A Testimony at 86. *But see,* Chief of Base Testimony at 139 (**[redacted text]**.").

[104] Officer A Testimony at 63–64.

[105] *Id.* at 64.

[106] Attestation regarding **[redacted text]**.

A third person also claimed he tried to contact the U.S. government prior to the attack. A Libyan Special Advisor on Security "claimed he had tried to warn the U.S. government of the potential for an attack on the Consulate prior to the attack taking place."[107] This individual "left Libya immediately after the attack" and "was afraid of potential threats against him, based in part on his assumption that there were documents in the Consulate likely found by the attackers, that they might interpret as him sympathizing with the U.S. Government."[108]

## THE FIRST ATTACK ON THE BENGHAZI MISSION BEGINS

At 9:42 p.m., the Libyan police vehicle at the front gate of the Benghazi Mission compound rapidly departed at the same time attackers advanced toward the main entrance.[109] Prior to that, the Libyan police did not warn the Diplomatic Security Agents at the compound, the unarmed Blue Mountain Guards, or the armed February 17 Martyrs Brigade members of the surging attackers or of their own departure.[110]

As the police vehicle fled, dozens of armed men rushed the compound and an explosion occurred near the main gate.[111] It was the beginning of what would be not one, but several attacks on the Benghazi Mission compound.

The Diplomatic Security Agents recalled first hearing taunts and chants when the attackers rushed the compound and then a loud explosion. They knew they were in imminent danger. According to one Diplomatic Security Agent:

Q: And how did you find out about the attack?

A: I heard a loud explosion and chanting outside.

Q: When you say chanting, what would be——

A: Yelling, screaming.[112]

Attackers quickly breached the main gate pouring onto the compound.[113] One Diplomatic Security Agent described his reaction:

I see the men on the compound. I immediately picked up the PA system, and I say, attention on compound, attention on compound, this is not a drill. Repeat, this is not a drill.[114]

The Diplomatic Security Agent immediately activated the alarm in accordance with the Compound's Emergency Action Plan calling for shelter in place.[115] He stated: "The react plan is exactly what

---

[107] See Email to [Tripoli Station], Sept. 21, 2012 [REQUEST 1000790 to REQUEST 1000795].

[108] Id.

[109] Diplomatic Sec. Agent 3 at 140 ("I can say within 30 seconds to a minute, before the attack started the single police car that was out there was a truck and it departed the scene."); see also, DVR Footage of the Mission (Sept. 11, 2012, 9:42 PM).

[110] Id. at 141.

[111] See Diplomatic Sec. Agent 4 Testimony at 144. See also, Diplomatic Sec. Agent 2 at 85–86; DVR Footage of the Mission (Sept. 11, 2012, 2142.53).

[112] Diplomatic Sec. Agent 1 Testimony at 55.

[113] DVR Footage of the Mission (Sept. 11, 2012, 2143.50).

[114] Diplomatic Sec. Agent 3 Testimony at 137.

[115] Id.

happened: shelter in place, contact your support elements, and wait for their arrival." [116]

As the alarm was sounding, two unarmed Blue Mountain Guards fled through the main gate. [117] Immediately upon the initial breach of the main gate, the attackers were engaged briefly by gunfire by one or more February 17 Martyrs Brigade guards. According to one Diplomatic Security Agent, one of the guards was shot during this engagement:

> At least one of them got shot. One of the local guards at least one, if not two, of the local guards were shot, as well, in the process. It was as this group moved from building to building and we sheltered per our react plan. [118]

With minimal resistance at the main entrance, the attackers quickly pushed onto the compound and cornered the armed February 17 Martyrs Brigade guards inside their barracks and set fire to the barracks. [119] The guards incurred no fatalities that evening. Besides the initial exchange of gunfire at the main entrance, no additional gunfire was directed toward the attackers on the compound prior to the end of the first wave of attacks at the Benghazi Mission compound.

After the alarm was initiated, the Diplomatic Security Agent in the Tactical Operations Center [TOC] immediately called the GRS personnel at the Annex, located approximately one mile from the Benghazi Mission compound. [120]

The Diplomatic Security Agents were able to establish an open line of communication through a shared radio **[redacted text]** with the Annex during the attack allowing the two locations to have continuous communication. [121]

At the same time, another Diplomatic Security Agent relocated to the TOC and tried to call the 17th February guards on the Mission compound for help. [122] After this attempt failed, the Diplomatic Security Agent called the Annex compound and asked them to contact the headquarters of the February 17 Martyrs Brigade to request support. [123] The Diplomatic Security Agent also called the Libyan Ministry of Foreign Affairs for support. [124] The agents in the TOC then notified the lead security officer in Tripoli. [125] One Diplomatic Security Agent described their actions:

> So we are in the TOC office. The other agent and I began to make our calls. I notify the second American compound via radio. The other agent notifies the February 17 Martyrs Brigade members. And then I subsequently notify Tripoli, who subsequently notifies D.C.; it is either State ops or the command center. We basically have an open line

---

[116] *Id.* at 142.

[117] DVR Footage of the Mission (Sept. 11, 2012, 2142).

[118] Diplomatic Sec. Agent 3 Testimony at 147.

[119] *Id.*

[120] *Id.* at 141.

[121] *Id.*

[122] Diplomatic Sec. Agent 4 Testimony at 129.

[123] *Id.*

[124] *Id.* at 148; Diplomatic Sec. Agent 3 Testimony at 141.

[125] Diplomatic Sec. Agent 3 Testimony at 141; *see also,* Email to Principal Officer 4, U.S. Dep't of State (Sept. 14, 2012, 8:07 AM). (Subject: Re: Log of events on 9/11/12–9/12/12) (on file with the Committee, SCB00472640).

via radio with the other Americans at the second compound. And I keep Tripoli on speakerphone almost the whole time as we are working through and relaying what is going on.[126]

Meanwhile, Stevens, Smith, and one Diplomatic Security Agent retreated to the safe haven of Villa C, a dedicated area within the Villa that was reinforced with a metal barred-door.[127] The Diplomatic Security Agent who was with Stevens and Smith described what happened:

> I remember hearing the chants. I mean, they were fairly close already. I mean, yelling distance, which is pretty close especially in a city setting. So my impression is that I don't have much time. So I ran right to my room, you know, put my helmet on, put my vest on, grabbed my weapons, my additional weapons, and I turned to lock the gate, and basically, it was a jail cell door with three locks on it. I locked all three locks. And at about that time Ambassador Stevens and Sean Smith were coming out to their rooms. Sean Smith was already, you know, donning his helmet and vest. I guided them both into the safe haven, and set myself up in the safe haven with—I was holding my M4."[128]

Two other Diplomatic Security Agents attempted to "go back to Villa C to also provide protection for Stevens, but not to shoot at this large group."[129]

The agents in Villa B attempted to go to Villa C, but they were met with a very large hostile force of 7 to 10 attackers with "AKs and RPGs."[130] The two agents made the tactical decision not to shoot at this large group because, "if we would have taken one of them out at the time, it could have gone substantially worse."[131] The Agents believed the attackers would have been "out for blood" and it would have inflamed an already bad situation.[132]

Because of this concern, the agents chose to return to Villa B, which also served as the cantina or cafeteria for the Mission compound.[133] After seeking refuge, one of the agents in Villa B then contacted the TOC in Tripoli and the other agent contacted the State Department's Diplomatic Security Command Center [DSCC] in Washington D.C. at 9:49 p.m. Benghazi time [3:49 p.m. in Washington, DC].[134]

Unknown to the Diplomatic Security Agents on the Mission compound, the attackers were a mix of local extremist groups, including the Benghazi-based Ansar al-Sharia, al-Qaeda in the Lands of

---

[126] Diplomatic Sec. Agent 3 Testimony at 141; Diplomatic Sec. Agent 4 Testimony at 128–29.

[127] Diplomatic Sec. Agent 3 Testimony at 141; *see also* Diplomatic Sec. Agent 5 Testimony at 114.

[128] Diplomatic Sec. Agent 5 Testimony at 114.

[129] Diplomatic Sec. Agent 3 Testimony at 142.

[130] Diplomatic Sec. Agent 1 Testimony at 58.

[131] *Id.*

[132] Diplomatic Sec. Agent 3 Testimony at 142.

[133] *Id.* at 141–142.

[134] Diplomatic Sec. Agent 2 Testimony at 86; *see also,* Email from the Diplomatic Sec. Command Ctr. to the Special Assistants for the Secretary, *et al.* (page 1) (Subject: Benghazi—Attack on Compound—09112012) (Sept. 11, 2012, 6:34 PM) (on file with the Committee, C05578314).

the Islamic Maghreb, and the Muhammad Jamal Network out of Egypt. Members of al-Qaeda in the Arabian Peninsula, al-Qaeda in Iraq and Abu Ubaydah Ibn Jarah Battalion also participated.[135]

The Diplomatic Security Agent located in the safe haven with Stevens and Smith described the weapons he saw during a direct encounter with the attackers:

> I could hear outside explosions, yelling, chanting, scream-ing, gunfire, and I reported all of this on the radio just saying, this is what my senses are telling me. Then people started banging on the doors of the building, so I reported that. Hey, there is banging on the doors. They are trying to come in, you know, we need immediate assistance. And there wasn't any response on the radio. Shortly after that, to my recollection, the doors were blown open. And about 70 individuals, you know, rushed into the building, all of them carrying AK–47s, grenades, RPGs, you know, a mix-ture throughout everyone.[136]

The attackers were unable to gain access to the safe haven be-cause the access point had been fortified by the Diplomatic Security Agent inside. Instead the attackers started a diesel fire just outside the safe haven at approximately 10 p.m.[137] At that time, the agents in the TOC reported to the Diplomatic Security Command Center that Stevens and Smith were located in the safe room.[138] Meanwhile, notice of the attack was disseminated in Washington D.C. at 4:05 p.m. [10:05 p.m. in Benghazi] through an "Ops Alert" by the State Department Operations Center, which notified senior Department officials, the White House Situation Room, and others the Benghazi Mission compound was under attack.[139]

As news of the attack spread in Washington D.C., Villa C, the main diplomatic building, was quickly engrossed in flames and heavy smoke.[140] Within minutes, Diplomatic Security Agents re-

---

[135] The Committee found no evidence of involvement by the Iranian government, specifically the Iranian Revolutionary Guard-Quds Force (IRGC–QF) as has been reported. Email from the State Department Operations Center (Sept. 11, 2012, 6:06 PM) (on file with the Committee, C05272001). At the time, there were two Ansar al-Sharia (AAS) branches in Libya, the one in Benghazi that was involved in the attack, and one in Darnah that was led by former Guanta-namo detainee Abu Sufyian bin Qumo. There is no evidence that Qumo had any direct involve-ment in the attacks on the Mission or the Annex on 11 and 12 September 2012. *See Terrorist Attack in Benghazi: The Secretary of State's View,* hearing before H. Comm. on Foreign Affairs, 113th Cong. 35 (2013). The other Ansar al-Sharia, the Abu Ubaydah Ibn Jarah Battalion, was led at the time by Ahmed Abu Khattalah, the lone person charged in connection with the attack. NCTC: Libya: Terrorists and Extremists Reportedly Associates with the Benghazi Attacks (Sept 9, 2013); NCTC Current: Libya: Update on Benghazi Suspects (Sept. 11, 2013); CIA WIRe: Libya: Terrorists and Extremists Reportedly Associated with the Benghazi Attacks (Jan 28, 2013); CIA WIRe: Libya: Terrorists and Extremists Reportedly Associated with the Benghazi At-tacks (Feb 26, 2013); CIA WIRe: Libya: Terrorists and Extremists Reportedly Associated with the Benghazi Attacks (Aug. 12, 2013); CIA WIRe: Libya: Terrorists and Extremists Reportedly Associated with the Benghazi Attacks (Sept. 9, 2013); CIA WIRe Libya: Terrorists and Extrem-ists Reportedly Associated with the Benghazi Attacks, (Mar. 24, 2014); CIA WIRe: Libya: Terror-ists and Extremists Reportedly Associated with the Benghazi Attacks (July 24, 2014).

[136] Diplomatic Sec. Agent 5 Testimony at 115.

[137] DVR Footage of the Mission (Sept. 11, 2012, 2202.07 and 2202.25, respectively).

[138] U.S. Dep't of State, DSCC's Timeline for Benghazi and Tripoli Events [hereinafter DSCC Timeline] (on file with the Committee, C05391498) ("Ambassador Stevens, who is currently in Benghazi, and for [sic] COM personnel are in the compound safe room.").

[139] Email from the State Department Operations Center (Sept. 11, 2012, 4:05 PM) (on file with the Committee, C05272001).

[140] DVR Footage of the Mission (Sept. 11, 2012, 2201–2207); *see also,* Email to Principal Offi-cer 4, U.S. Dep't of State (Sept. 14, 2012, 8:07 AM). (Subject: Re: Log of events on 9/11/12–9/12/12) (on file with the Committee, SCB00472640).

ported to the lead security agent in Tripoli that contact with Stevens had been lost.[141] A Diplomatic Security Agent described what happened next inside the Villa:

> And then slowly, people started to kind of trickle out. And then the lights started to kind of dim. My initial response or my initial thought was, well, they just knocked out the generators. You know, we have regular city power, but we also have backup generators. So flickering would be a likely, you know, cause of this. But in reality, it was smoke. And it took me about, you know, 2 or 3 seconds after that to determine that it was smoke. As soon as I realized it was smoke, I turned to the Ambassador and Sean Smith and I said, we are moving to the bathroom.[142]

As Villa C filled with smoke, the two Diplomatic Security Agents in the TOC also realized it was on fire:[143]

> Q: At what point did you notice that there was also— buildings had been put on fire, and how did that come to your attention?
>
> A: Well, as—it seemed like a long time. Of course, I can't say exactly how much time elapsed between when we began our call for help and to when help finally arrived. I can't say certainly. But monitoring what was going on on the ground via the security cameras, I could see that Villa C—I could see flames starting to lick out of the windows and black smoke started to pour out of the windows, and that's when I became aware that they were in very big trouble over there.[144]

The Diplomatic Security Agent inside Villa C with Stevens and Smith attempted to lead them to the bathroom in the safe haven.[145] Once in the bathroom he realized Stevens and Smith had not followed him. Due to the thick toxic smoke, he was unable to see them and did not hear a response from them when he called out.[146] Because of the flames, the agent became weak and overcome with smoke and heat. He left the bathroom and crawled to his bedroom where he eventually escaped through a window. After catching his breath, over and over again he crawled back through the bedroom window of Villa C to search for Stevens and Smith.[147]

> The last time I went out, you know, I decided that if I went back into the building that I wasn't going to come back out. The smoke and the heat were way too powerful, and way too strong, and it was extremely confusing feeling my way in a smoke-filled building. And I didn't want to get lost, and so I decided to climb up the ladder to the roof.

---

[141] Email to Principal Officer 4, U.S. Dep't of State (Sept. 14, 2012, 8:07 AM). (Subject: Re: Log of events on 9/11/12–9/12/12) (on file with the Committee, SCB00472640).

[142] Diplomatic Sec. Agent 5 Testimony at 117.

[143] Diplomatic Sec. Agent 4 Testimony at 131–132.

[144] *Id.*

[145] Diplomatic Sec. Agent 5 Testimony at 117.

[146] *Id.* at 114; *see also,* Diplomatic Sec. Agent 3 Testimony at 147; Comprehensive Timeline of Events—Benghazi, produced by the U.S. Dep't of State (Last Edit Nov. 1, 2012) (on file with the Committee, SCB0047845); Hicks Apr. 2013 Testimony at 25–26.

[147] Diplomatic Sec. Agent 5 Testimony at 117–120.

I climbed up the ladder, and pulled up the ladder behind me and that's the moment that I knew the Ambassador Stevens and Sean Smith were probably dead.[148]

As the agent retreated to the rooftop of Villa C, he began taking gunfire.[149] At 10:14 p.m. [4:14 p.m. in Washington D.C.], he reported to the agent located in the TOC that Stevens and Smith were missing and unaccounted for.[150]

While some of the attackers were trying to break into Villa C's safe haven, other attackers broke through Villa B's main door.[151] The attackers were unable to gain access to the Diplomatic Security Agents and local guard seeking refuge in the back because they had successfully barricaded the doors.[152]

> Q: So you said that the attackers who tried to come into the room were unsuccessful?
>
> A: Yes, they tried to breach it one time.[153]

### THE MISSION CALLS THE ANNEX FOR SUPPORT

When the attack started at 9:42 p.m. [3:42 p.m. in Washington D.C.], the Diplomatic Security Agent in the TOC immediately called the Annex for backup.[154] The agent testified:

> Several requests were made. Unbeknownst to us at the time, the situation outside our compound was hostile. Apparently the militia that attacked us had set up heavy gun trucks on all four corners of the block we were on, had prohibited traffic from entering from any location, and it was difficult for the reaction forces to get to us.
>
> I can't tell you exactly when they arrived on compound. It is my assessment that it was approximately an hour and 5 minutes after. So if the attack started at 9:42, I don't think we see them on compound until 10:00, 10:45, 10:50, something along those lines.
>
> Now, it is my understanding that they fought their way in, and they ultimately split up into two groups, one of which literally fought their way in and climbed blocks and blocks of 10 to 12 foot high concrete walls, as well as the secondary group, who rallied with some February 17 Martyrs Brigade elements to come in through a different approach angle.
>
> So it was not as if they literally could have just walked across the street and walked in. The compound was overtaken, it was overrun. And it is my understanding it wasn't as simple as what it would have seemed on the surface.[155]

---

[148] Diplomatic Sec. Agent 5 Testimony at 121.

[149] *Id.* at 122; *see also,* Comprehensive Timeline of Events—Benghazi, produced by the U.S. Dep't of State (Last Edit Nov. 1, 2012) (on file with the Committee, SCB0047845).

[150] Diplomatic Sec. Agent 3 Testimony at 147.

[151] Diplomatic Sec. Agent 1 Testimony at 61–62.

[152] *Id.*

[153] *Id.*

[154] Diplomatic Sec. Agent 3 Testimony at 141.

[155] *Id.* at 143–44.

Once the request for assistance was made to the Annex, the security team there immediately began packing up and preparing to respond.

The GRS Team Lead described what happened after the Diplomatic Security Agent called and requested their help.

[A]pproximately 20 [minutes] to 10:00 [p.m.], I got a cell phone call on my phone from one of the ARSOs, State Department Regional Security Officers.

Give or take a few minutes or whatever it was, I'd get that phone call from [Diplomatic Security Agent 3], and he's obviously a bit worked up, and he says: Hey, we're under attack. And he tells me he's sitting in the TOC, their Tactical Operations Center, which is a separate building at the facility. And he says: I can see approximately 20 guys have come through the front gate, they are armed, and they are amassing on the soccer field, which is, you know, just in front of their—one of the living quarters buildings.

And I said: Okay. Gotcha. I said: Look, do me a favor, before you hang up or before I lose you on the cell phone network—we had previously given them one of our secure [re- dacted text] radios. I said: Pick up that radio in the TOC and just start giving me a play by play, just keep transmitting, and you know, once you get that radio, hang up the phone, and you know, we'll deal with it.

So once he hung up, I called—I made a radio call to all the guys, the GRS guys to return to the team room, and then, you know, within a few minutes guys start trickling in. Some guys kind of, you know—you know, it's in the evening, so some guys in shorts and T-shirt, other guys, you know, clearly just, you know, thrown pants, T-shirt or whatever on, you know, just asking: Hey, what's going on? Hey, I don't know. I don't have a lot of specifics other than I just got a call from [Diplomatic Security Agent 3]. He said the facility is under attack. So at that point, you know, I don't need to tell anybody what to do. As the guys trickle in, it's, you know, word of mouth, hey, start, you know, gathering gear, start getting your kit, you know, your helmet, night vision gear, ballistic armor, you know, weapons, all that good stuff.

And you know, shortly thereafter, the deputy chief of base walks in, and he says: Hey, what's going on. I heard you say call the guys to the team room. I said: Hey, Chief, not exactly sure, but the State facility, I just got a call and they're under attack.

And he asked me, he said: Well, did you tell chief of base yet?

I said: No, I'm just getting—he said: All right. Don't worry about it. I'll go tell him.

So we continue to kit up. The guys, you know, are doing their thing, start bringing our heavier weapons, equipment out to the car. We get the linguist, kind of get him—you know, get him some body armor, get him a helmet, and you know, kind of give him a quick brief. We kind of gravitate out to the vehicles.[156]

Once the Chief of Base was alerted, he met with the Team Lead and the Deputy Chief of Base to determine if they had received any additional information about what was happening at the Mission. The Chief of Base then began calling partner militia organizations for assistance.

So he starts working phones. I can hear him. You know, sometimes he's able to get through to people, and you know, I remember one conversation where he's given a quick data dump, and the guys says: All right. Hey, you know, call me back in 2 minutes.

So when he hangs up, he says: Hey, while—you know, I don't remember who he said it was, but while that person is making some phone calls, I'm going to call, you know, the other guy and just—you know, I said: Hey, look, Chief, what we want is technicals. So what we want is, you know, the trucks with bigger guns than what we have because I don't know what we're going into. So whether it be Dishka-type weapons or some type of heavy machine gun mounted on a truck, that's what I definitely want.[157]

While the Chief of Base was trying to generate assistance for the Annex team, the team members finished loading up their gear into two vehicles. The Team Lead was standing outside of the vehicles while the Chief of Base contacted their partner organizations. Meanwhile, the Annex team members became anxious to depart.

So while this is going on, one of my—like I said, the guys there are pretty much just kind of wrapping up, getting, you know, the ammo, and you know, first aid kits, all that stuff, and then they're basically standing by loading in front of the building. And one of the officers, my officers comes out, and he says: Hey, look, you know, we got to get going. We got to go. We got to go.

I said: Yeah, I know that, but I don't know what we're getting into, and the chief's trying to make some phone calls. I want to get some technicals to go with us because I don't know what we're—what we're going to get into.

\* \* \*

So he goes back into the car. Chief continues to, you know, work the phones. He makes contact with maybe another two or three guys, and then he circles back with that first person he made the phone call to, and the phone is shut off. And he tells me: Hey, it's not going through. It's shut off. I said: All right. Can you try the other guys back?

---

[156] Testimony of GRS-Team Lead, Cent. Intel. Agency, Tr. at 20–23 (Apr. 19, 2016) [hereinafter Team Lead Testimony] (on file with the Committee).
[157] Id. at 23–24.

So he proceeds to, you know, try to make follow up phone calls. You know, [one Team Member] pops out again, and he's like, hey, we got to go, we got to go, and at that point Chief is like, hey. Yeah, I know. I'm just trying—like, hang on. I'm trying to make some—we're trying to get the technicals. We're trying to, you know, get you guys some weapons.

\* \* \*

And then one of the other officers,[] came out. He's like, hey, you know, what do we got? I said: Look, Chief's trying to make phone calls. I really want to get some technicals.

\* \* \*

So at some point, you know, whatever, couple of minutes, it becomes kind of clear that there's nothing readily coming, or there's—like Chief isn't making positive coms with anybody who's saying, hey, I've got, you know, two, three, four, five technicals, they're going to meet you at whatever location. That's not happening. So I tell the chief, I say: Hey, Chief, look, we're going.

And to be honest with you, I don't recall Chief saying anything. Deputy chief, you know, kind of looks at me, and he's like, well, he's like, you know, [GRS-Team Lead], God speed, hopefully we'll see you guys back here shortly.

So at that point, we roll out. I can tell you between, you know, the time stamp on our CCTV, like I said roughly, I think my phone call came at like 21:43, depending on what timestamp you look at, we roll out at like 22:04, so 21, 23, 24 minutes, whatever.[158]

The Chief of Base described his actions after he learned about the attacks.

I was calling everybody I could think of. I think I called the police, LIS, other militia groups that—we were, you know, in an information-gathering mode, and trying to see who might be able to respond quickly to the Consulate, to the mission.

Q: How much success were you having in actually getting through to people at the police, at Libyan intel with other militias?

A: I didn't get through to Libyan intel, I don't think. They weren't actually very helpful to us in Benghazi at all.

Q: Okay.

A: But otherwise, I was getting through to the people.

Q: Okay. And what kind of response were you getting on the other end?

A: Well, there was a lot of disbelief and confusion, and trying to understand what was happening, what—basically, it

---

[158] *Id.* at 24–26.

was, as what you might, expect when something like that happens.[159]

Despite multiple attempts, the Chief of Base found his phone calls unfruitful. He was unable to generate any additional assistance from the partner organizations he called. He described his conversations with the organizations.

> A: Well, there was a lot of disbelief and confusion, and trying to understand what was happening, what—basically, it was, as you might, expect when something like that happens.
>
> Q: Did you hear anything that would give you any pause or reason for concern?
>
> A: Well, I was already concerned, to be honest with you. I mean, you know, we could hear the gunfire. There were even some tracer bullets flying overhead so we were, again, I was trying to get as much information as possible.[160]

The Chief of Base described what happened after the Annex team members finished loading their gear and were ready to depart.

> Q: So at some point, the GRS folks were kitted up, and what happened at that point that you can recall? Do you recall seeing them all kitted up?
>
> A: I was standing right in the area that they were getting their stuff. It took them, I would say, about 15 minutes to get ready. It was a very—to me, the time passed by very quickly.
>
> And people were going to CONEXes and getting ammunition and water, and getting batteries and MPGs and such. At one point, [the Team Lead] came to me, I would say maybe 15 minutes into it and said that he wanted to see if I could arrange a technical, or a gun truck, from 17th February. So I called back to 17th February and was working on getting that gun truck. So I was in contact with [the Team Lead].[161]

*   *   *

> Well, their response was, okay, but I don't have one, or it's going to be difficult. I have got to check. It was—it was not like immediately we are going to be able to—the person who I was talking to, who was one of their commanders whose name I don't remember.
>
> Q: And did you relay that back to [the Team Lead]?
>
> A: Yes.
>
> Q: What was his response?

---

[159] Testimony of the Chief of Base, Cent. Intel. Agency, Tr. at 24–25 (Nov. 19, 2015) [hereinafter Chief of Base Testimony] (on file with the Committee).
[160] *Id.* at 25.
[161] *Id.* at 29.

A: That's when they left to go on the rescue.[162]

The Chief of Base was adamant that he never told the Annex team members to "stand down."

> You said that you let them go. Did you give them an affirmative order for them to go?
>
> A: I think I was working with [the Team Lead] the whole time——
>
> Q: Okay.
>
> A: —in an effort to get them to get them gone, to have them go. So whether or not I gave an affirmative order, but I wanted them to go. They were cleared to go. And they went.
>
> Q: When you say they were cleared to go, is that you giving the clearance?
>
> A: Yes.
>
> Q: Did you have any discussions—do you recall having any discussions with the deputy chief of base about allowing the guys to go?
>
> A: I don't recall any. It was never—I never had any doubt about the GRS people going to the State Department compound. I had great concerns and great worry about it but I did not, I did not tell anybody to stand down.[163]

The Chief of Base acknowledged he may have told the team to wait while he was attempting to secure additional resources for them.

> I may have said wait because we were trying to get this technical truck that the team lead wanted. But it wasn't 10 minutes, or 5 minutes. It was a short period of time. And the only time I remember ever talking to [Annex team member] was when he came up, and I said I'm trying to get a technical truck for [the Team Lead]. There was nobody, myself or anybody else in Benghazi, that did anything to hold up the GRS deploying. The team lead was always cleared to go.[164]

He further added:

> People were coming and going the entire time. But I did not issue a stand-down order. And if there was a delay, there was a very short delay, basically the team lead we have to try to get this gun truck.
>
> \*　　\*　　\*
>
> I was doing everything, and to my knowledge, everybody on that base was doing everything. I think I carried an ammo can at one time to get those guys out the door.

---

162 *Id.* at 29.
163 *Id.* at 31–32.
164 *Id.* at 58–59.

So it's, you know, our GRS folks were very brave that night. But I, everything that I saw from during the kitting up of the team, to their departure till their return and heard in between, very much [the Team Lead] was in charge of it. Listening to the radio, he was in charge of it. So when [the Team Lead] was satisfied, I think, that we weren't going to get the support that we—that he wanted to get this gun truck to try to link it up—although I think they did link up at some point—that he left. He took the team and left.[165]

One GRS agent did not recall the Chief of Base telling the team to "stand down" but he did recall the Chief of Base telling them to "wait."[166]

Q: And what did you think when he told you to wait?

A: I believe at first I just said, okay, maybe he's talking to somebody that can help, and, you know, I respected the fact that he wanted us to wait and see if he can gather additional fire power to help. At some point, though, the wait was too long, and we decided, you know, we couldn't wait any longer and we left. We didn't know if that wait was going to be an indefinite wait and you're-not-going wait or a real wait or—but nothing was happening for several minutes.

And so we can hear the State Department's cries for help on the radio, and we just reached a point where we decided to leave on our own.[167]

The agent also acknowledged during the time the team was "kitting up" and after they loaded into the vehicles, the Chief of Base and the Team Lead attempted to obtain additional support from the Libyan partner organizations.

Q: When you said nothing happened—nothing was happening for several minutes, you're referring to what exactly? There were individuals on the phone?

A: Yes.

Q: So that was occurring, but for your purposes——

A: For our purposes, we were getting in and out of the vehicles, ready to go. We were just waiting for someone to say go. My understanding is they were trying to get us to link up with 17 Feb or have 17 Feb go there first, something to do with 17 Feb helping out. But there was never a clear, definitive, this is what's going on. Everything was chaotic. . . .[168]

Another Annex Team Member also recalled that the team was told to wait while the Chief of Base and the Team Lead were mak-

---

[165] *Id.* at 59–60.
[166] Testimony of GRS 3, Cent. Intel. Agency, Tr. at 52 (May 29, 2015) [hereinafter GRS 3 Testimony] (on file with the Committee).
[167] *Id.* at 50.
[168] *Id.* at 50–51.

ing phone calls. This member testified that once the team was ready to depart he approached the Chief of Base and the Team Lead, who were both making phone calls at the time. He explained what happened.

> A: Yep. Grab my machine gun, grab my night vision, grab my helmet and get back outside, and everybody else is doing their job. Cars are already staged. Looked at Ty. His car was up. He gave me a thumbs up. Had [GRS 3] and [GRS 1] in the car. And I went up to our chief of base and team leader, and they're standing in the courtyard, and I said, hey, we're ready to go.
>
> Q: Now the team leader at this point, you said you saw him on the way into the team room. He was not geared up. You saw him with his phone. You didn't see him on the phone?
>
> A: Not at first. When I came back out they were both on their phones.
>
> Q: Now, team leader and——
>
> A: And [the Chief of Base] were both on their phones. I looked at [the Chief of Base] and the team leader and said, hey, we're ready to go. [The Chief of Base] looked at the team leader, and he said tell these guys they need to wait. The team leader looks at me and says you guys need to wait. It's about 9:37. It's no more than 5 minutes if that.
>
> *     *     *
>
> So at this point in time, the chief told the team leader to wait.
>
> Q: Team leader told you to wait?
>
> A: Yes.
>
> Q: All right. What did you do next?
>
> A: Waited. Went back to the car and just radioed, hey, we got to wait guys. Just because the guys needed to know the information.
>
> *     *     *
>
> Q: All right. So you go back in the car. You're in the second car, in the SUV. You're with [GRS 5], and go to the radio and say we got to wait?
>
> A: And everybody is pretty cool about it. Nobody is getting upset.[169]

The team member was able to see what the Chief of Base and the Team Lead were doing when he returned to the vehicle:

> What I'm seeing, and I'm looking at [the Chief of Base and the Team Lead] off and on and they're just talking on their phones. And all I can see, as time goes on and we start

---

[169] Testimony of GRS 4, Cent. Intel. Agency, Tr. at 26–29 (Mar. 1, 2016) [hereinafter GRS 4 Testimony] (on file with the Committee).

getting calls, from [Diplomatic Security Agent 3] on the radio, saying, hey, the Consulate has been overrun. GRS, where the bleep are you? We do start getting a little bit more agitated.[170]

The team member continued:

Q: All right. So you said you heard [Diplomatic Security Agent 3] on the radio, and what did he say?

A: [Diplomatic Security Agent 3], and I can't recall his exact words. It's been 3 years, but I can recall the gist of it, and I can recall the emotions of it. It was, GRS, where are you? Consulate's been overrun. Where are you? Where are you? Get your asses over here. We need your help. Where are you? Another 10 minutes go by, and that's when I see [GRS 1] get out of his car. He goes to the driver's side. And I have my door closed, and I see him yelling at [the Chief of Base]. He's going like this. Now, I didn't hear it, but I asked him after what he said to him. He was just there. Him and [the Chief of Base] are jaw jacking.

He gets in the car. I said what's going on, dude? He said he's telling us to stand down. Now [GRS 1] told me that on the radio, but I said my vehicle was doors were closed, armored vehicle, but I remember seeing him go to the driver's side and just——

Q: So it was just you and [GRS 5] in your vehicle?

A: Yeah. And then I also reconfirmed that when I asked [GRS 1] later. He wasn't happy.

\* \* \*

We waited another 10 minutes, so it's been about 25 minutes.

Q: The first time you said you were ready to go in 5 minutes. Then you said there was 10 minutes. Then you waited another 10 minutes?

A: Close to 25 minutes.[171]

Although this team member's testimony regarding the amount of time that elapsed between the Mission's request for help and the team's departure was consistent with the testimony of other witnesses and the time indicated by the surveillance footage of the Annex, his testimony about when the attack began, and thus when the Mission called for help, differed. The witness, one of the co-authors of the book "13 Hours: The Inside Account of What Really Happened in Benghazi," testified that the attack began at 9:32 p.m., ten minutes earlier than other witnesses, documents and the surveillance footage indicates. He was asked why he believed the attack began at 9:32 p.m. and provided this explanation:

A: I remember hearing a call on the radio that all GRS needed to muster in the team room. I remember there was

---

[170] *Id.* at 30.
[171] *Id.* at 30–32.

not a sense of urgency in the voice. I remember looking at my watch. I remember it saying 9:32. And I have said that many times. I know it differs, but I know that's what it said.

Q: So let me stop you there. I know you said it many times. I've read that in the book. Everywhere else I've seen it's 9:42. How do you account for the difference?

A: Differences of what people want to hear, want to know. I was on the ground. I was looking. I was pissed off because somebody was bothering me at 9:32 at night because I wanted to go home.

Q: You were home.

A: I wanted to get the day over with. Nothing good comes when you get bothered at night, especially if you're in the military, and you're getting called by your leadership at 9:00 at night, nothing good comes of it. The difference, you'd have to ask the person that says it's 9:42. I don't know. I didn't see anybody else with me on that report there that night, though. We get a call 30 seconds later, roughly.

\* \* \*

Q: And I don't mean to pick apart your statement. So the book I believe—let me just quote you from the book. It says: At 9:02 p.m. an unexpected vehicle drove down the gravel road outside the compound. And a little bit later the SSC vehicle pulled away 40 minutes after it arrived. A little while later. Almost the moment the SSC pickup pulled away from the compound, shots and an explosion rang out?

A: Sure. And what Mitchell was doing with that is he was pulling stuff off the report. We had to get the book cleared.

Q: Okay.

A: So if you read it, too, he also says that [GRS 4] looked at his watch, and he has assured that it was 9:32 that he was called. So we're getting both what other people were saying. That's what we were trying to do, and [GRS 2] can help me out with the book here if I get too far into it. But we're trying to show that there are differences in what people saw. I know what I saw. I'm not going to say what other people saw, and what those other nine reports that went through, but I know what I saw on my watch.[172]

Another Annex Team member described his recollection of what happened between the time the Mission called for help and the Annex team departed. After the Team Lead told him the Mission was under attack, he got dressed, packed his gear, and loaded into a vehicle.

[I] Ran back in, told [Annex Team Member], we got all of our clothes on, ran out of the team room, got the big weap-

---

[172] *Id.* at 22–24.

ons . . . and we loaded up in the vehicles. It was probably about 5 minutes or so after we learned of the ongoing attack. And we're probably sitting there for a little while. We're sitting in the car, you know, just going over, double checking our weapons, double checking our gear, you know, kind of saying, hey, you know, what's going on, what's taking so long.

We're probably sitting there a good 15 minutes, and I get out of the car. I have the Chief of Base, the Deputy Chief of Base, and the team leader on the front porch. They're all three on the phone doing something.

And I just say: Hey, you know, we've got to get over there. We're losing the initiative. The Chief of Base looks at me, he says: Stand down, you need to wait. You need to come up with a plan.

And I say: No, it's too late to come up with a plan. We need to get over in the area, get eyes on, and then we can come up with a plan.

And that's kind of where I left it because they left it at that, and I got back in the car.[173]

The Annex Team Member's testimony was consistent with the other witnesses that while the team was "kitting up" and loading their gear into the vehicles, the Chief of Base and the Team Lead were making phone calls.

Q: So you were the only one out of the lead vehicle. And you got out of the vehicle and you said you saw the chief of base, the deputy chief of base, and the team lead. And where were they?

A: On the front porch of the building 3

\*　　\*　　\*

Q: And what were each of them doing?

A: They were on the phone.

Q: Okay. They were all on the phone?

A: Yes.

Q: Okay. And you said that—I'm just paraphrasing: We've got to get over there. We're losing the initiative. Did you say that? Does that sound right?

A: Yes.

Q: And did you say that to anybody in particular or all three of them?

A: Pretty much all three of them because I was looking directly at them.

Q: Okay. And what was the response that you got from all of them or any of them?

---

[173] GRS 1 Testimony at 73.

A: "Stand down. You need to wait." That was from the chief of base.

Q: Okay. Do you remember exactly what the chief—is that a paraphrase? Did he use those exact words? Do you remember?

A: He used those exact words.[174]

When asked why the team member had not disclosed the "stand down" order during previous testimony to Congress, he stated:

A: At the time, because a lot of it was that no—I mean, I didn't know why the stand down order was given. I mean, I guess [GRS team member] got told to wait, you know, that's what he says. I just know when we got told to stand down and when [the Team Lead] kind of gave the brief of kind of like why we're told to stand down, it was kind of understandable, you know.

But, yes, it shouldn't take you 23 minutes or 50 minutes to link up with the QRF, because even after we left there was still no link up. There was no communication between us and the 17 Feb. that I knew of. Because when we rolled in, we didn't know who we were going to be meeting.[175]

The team member believed that no matter what phrase the Chief of Base conveyed that night to direct the team, they would not have left unless they made the decision on their own to leave at the moment they did.

A: I mean, just like for the stand down. I don't think it came from anywhere else but [the Chief of Base]. . . .

So my biggest thing, I think, it was—I don't believe, you know, stand down. I think it was just like a heat-of-the-moment kind of thing. But to me, no matter what, when he said stand down, or wait, or don't go, whatever, he still—I believe if we didn't leave on our own, we would have never left.[176]

The Deputy Chief of Base also described what happened between the time the Annex was notified of the attack and the time the GRS Team departed.

I was sitting in my—I was sitting at my desk in the SCIF and I was working on—I was working on a cable I was writing regarding a meeting I had been to earlier in the day with the chief of base, and I remember looking at the clock that was in the lower corner of the computer screen noting that—for some reason it just stuck out—that it was 9:40 or 9:42. I remember looking at the time. And the GRS team leader, **[redacted text]**, came in, and grabbed me and pulled me out into the GRS room and said—said he had just received communication from [Agent 3] at the special mission that they had people inside the wire there.

---

[174] *Id.* at 78–79.
[175] *Id.* at 80.
[176] *Id.* at 130–31.

They had people inside the compound. And he said: We are going to go, we are going to go over there, you know, and get those guys, get them out of there. And I said: Okay, you know, got that, but we got to let the boss know about this and he needs to make the call before we do that. And he said, "yeah." So I went back in.

I got the Chief of Base, brought the Chief of Base out into the GRS team room where we were. The GRS team leader advised the chief of base what the situation was and said: We got to go get those guys. And the chief of base responded, "Absolutely." "Absolutely." Not, "I got to go call the chief of station." Not, "I got to go check with somebody in Washington." All he said was, "Absolutely." So I want to make that very clear because I know there's conflicting accounts about that discussion. There were three people in that discussion: myself, the GRS team leader, and the chief of base. And anybody writing any books or making movies, or whatever else, I can tell you none of those guys were in the room when that discussion occurred.[177]

The Deputy Chief of Base indicated the GRS team was loaded and ready to depart approximately 10 minutes after the Team Lead told them what was happening at the Mission.

So [the Team Lead] advised me that he had just gotten the call from [Diplomatic Security Agent 3] and then I—and then I told him, we got to, you know, we got to check with the chief of base on this. And I went and got him, and then we had that short discussion. And then, shortly thereafter, he advised the GRS team members to start gathering their equipment that they were going over there.

\* \* \*

And that took—that took about 10 minutes for them to get everything together.[178]

The Deputy Chief of Base raised a concern with the Chief of Base that they needed to attempt to confirm whether 17th February or any other friendly militia was at the base or would be arrive shortly in order to prevent that force from attacking the GRS team or vice versa. The Deputy Chief noted because one GRS team member was away from the base at the time, and the remaining were preparing to go to the Mission compound, the Annex effectively was without any defensive capability.

But what happened was, I said to the chief of base: Look it, you know, we got a real issue here with potential green-on-blue because we were still operating under the assumption that 17th February was going to show up.

And, in fact, a bunch of them about did, although it appears to be an uncoordinated response. They did, in fact, show up. So you got to remember that these guys that

[177] Testimony of Deputy Chief of Base, Cent. Intel. Agency, Tr. at 101–02 (June 4, 2015) [hereinafter Deputy Chief of Base Testimony] (on file with the Committee).
[178] *Id.* at 103.

went over there, the GRS guys, the six of them, **[redacted text]**. And I was really worried about that. If the city is blowing up, I got to make sure we get them back safely because what we were doing in making this decision, again, which the chief of base made instantly on the spot, without equivocation, was we were giving up all of our shooters to go over there and rescue the State Department people, as well as any QRF capability we would have had to rescue the case officer and the lone GRS guy **[redacted text]** if they got into an in extremis situation.

Now, on top of that, what the GRS guys took with them when they responded over there was every piece of heavy automatic weapons, and every really solid defensive weaponry capability that we had on the base. So while the chief of base agreed to do this right away, this was not a light—a decision taken lightly.

And, again, I feel like the narrative that I have seen in public does not account for this and does not account for the consideration that there was a green-on-blue situation that could have wiped all of those guys out. And then where would we have been? We wouldn't have had the ability to do anything to help the State Department people, and we wouldn't have had the ability to evacuate ourselves or defend ourselves if we came under attack.[179]

One GRS Agent explained it is not unusual for people to have a different recollection of what happened during the time the Diplomatic Security Agents called the Annex to request help.[180]

Q: Is it unusual in your perspective to have individuals with different accounts?

A: It's not—of course it's not unusual to have people have different accounts.[181]

The Annex Team departed at 10:05 p.m., twenty-three minutes after the Diplomatic Security Agent at the Mission called and asked for their help.[182]

After departing the Annex, the Annex Team faced a roadblock at the intersection of the main road leading to the Benghazi Mission compound. A militia was blocking the most direct route to the Mission compound. One GRS Team Member described what they encountered:

When we arrived, to the corner of the street that leads to the front gate, there was at least a couple vehicles there and some Libyans standing around outside. We slowly approached. We didn't know if they were friendly or hostile. They didn't appear to be a threat to us. They didn't raise their weapons at us, so we got out of the vehicles.

---

[179] *Id.* at 104–05.
[180] GRS 4 Testimony at 95.
[181] *Id.*
[182] DVR Footage of the CIA Annex (Sept. 11, 2012, 2005).

And at that time, the interpreter and [the Team Lead], I believe, started talking to somebody. We were receiving ineffective, sporadic fire. We returned fire and moved up the street. At that point, that's when our group split up.[183]

The Team Lead also described the roadblock:

Q: And describe what happened when you left the base?

A: So we roll out, and at this point there obviously was no communication via telephone that's got us anything. So my plan now is the route that we're going to take to get to the mission facility, I know there's two—three militia and/or proper Army compounds on the way. So my intentions are to basically stop into one of those facilities along the way, get the technicals that we were trying to get for support, and then roll to the mission facility.

So we come out to one of the main roads. One of the gates, back gates to one of the militia compounds, which is always sealed up and closed, is wide open, and there's militia guys moving all over the place.

I look up the street, and there is—I can see, you know, a bunch of other movement and what have you, personnel, militia guys, whatever, and we have to go north anyways, so I said: Hey, push on to, at that corner, there is what used to be a Libyan National Army base or compound right at the corner. I said: Hey, we're going to go to that compound because that's the direction we have to travel.

We get to that corner, and as I'm looking to pull in—and there's guys, you know, standing out in front. And as I'm looking there, and then I look at—essentially the path of the travel is across the main intersection and across the street, and generally speaking, where we would—the access road to the State facility is kind of up a couple of 100 yards or so on the right, and as I look up, there is—I can see a couple of technicals and a bunch of dismounted personnel with AKs or some type of rifle on them.

So I said: All right. You know what, guys, we're pushing to—through the intersection to that corner. Because there was already some type of force where we need to be, so I figured with the linguist there, roger that, we can try to utilize these guys to assist us.[184]

At the same time, the Diplomatic Security Agents at the compound were working to clear it. After they cleared Villa B, the Diplomatic Security Agents began searching Villa C, which was still on fire, for Stevens and Smith.[185] One Diplomatic Security Agent described the smoke in Villa C as so thick it prevented him "from see[ing] your hand in front of your face. There are no lights; the electricity [was] down."[186] Because the toxic smoke and heat were

[183] GRS 3 Testimony at 53–54.
[184] GRS Team Lead Testimony at 32–34.
[185] Diplomatic Sec. Agent 2 Testimony at 98.
[186] Diplomatic Sec. Agent 3 Testimony at 150.

so overwhelming, the Diplomatic Security Agents retrieved gas masks, which were ineffective:

> So I put the mask on. And we are being told repeatedly through this whole time by the other Americans that are there, "There is no good air in there. The device that you have does not provide air." I am aware of this. All you are going to do is go in there and become a victim, is what they are implying, which is accurate.[187]

As the agents are making their second round of attempts in and out of Villa C to locate Stevens, at 10:38 p.m. [4:38 p.m. in Washington D.C.], a local force, arrived at the Mission.[188] A few minutes later, the Annex Team arrived on the compound. After three of the Annex Team members cleared the main road and the main gate they entered the compound.[189] Two minutes later, the Annex Team Lead and the CIA linguist arrived through the main gate of the Mission.[190]

Over the course of the next 20 minutes, members of the Annex Team continued to clear portions of the compound while other Annex Team members joined the Diplomatic Security Agents in searching for Stevens and Smith.[191] One of the Diplomatic Security Agents described his attempts to find them:

> One of my biggest concerns is one of us in this recovery effort was going to go in there and become a victim ourselves, requiring our elements to stay on the X later, which is a bad situation. I would not want to put our guys at risk, any greater risk, by having to fish me out of that same situation where you are trying to pull somebody else out of.

> So I go in there a fourth time. I got the mask on. I go in as far as I have gone. I go directly in the safe haven, and I stay there longer than I should. I am stomping on the ground, I am feeling around, I am yelling for the Ambassador. I got nothing. The only and, again, the only guidance I had from the agent that was in there at the time was that he had him in the safe haven. I wasn't aware of any other location he may have been at that point.

> So I am in there, I don't know how long, a minute, [two], I don't know. I couldn't tell you how long exactly. But I start to feel the effects of oxygen deprivation. You start feeling it in the back of your head. Because I am just not getting air, because there is no good air in there. So I start thinking about, you know, putting our team in a worse position having to come retrieve me. I back out.

---

[187] *Id.* at 155.

[188] Comprehensive Timeline of Events—Benghazi, produced by the U.S. Dep't of State. (Last Edit Nov. 1, 2012) (on file with the committee, SCB0047843); *see also,* Video: DVR Footage of the Mission (Sept. 11, 2012, 2239–2240).

[189] Video: DVR Footage of the Mission (Sept. 11, 2012, 2245).

[190] Video: DVR Footage of the Mission (Sept. 11, 2012, 2247).

[191] Diplomatic Sec. Agent 3 Testimony at 155.

So, as I come out, I am grabbed by the team leader of the other Americans, who says, "You guys need to" . . . "get the fuck out of here." That is a quote.

And we pushed this off for the last 20 minutes, basically, where they repeatedly told us, you need to go, you need to go, and we have been adamant that we need to stay and recover or locate the Ambassador and Sean Smith. We have stayed up until this point.[192]

Diplomatic Security Agent 4 found Smith unresponsive inside Villa C.[193]

I go into the safe haven with the intention of recovering Smith and Stevens

Immediately upon entering the safe haven, it becomes very clear to me that it would be a very—that would be very difficult. The smoke is extremely thick and acrid. From what I understand now, that was a result of the accelerants used to start the fire. But open flame is not so much an issue; it's the volume and the toxic nature of the smoke that made it very difficult. Even immediately entering the room, I became very disoriented.

But using my internal map, my memory of the layout of the safe-haven area, I make my way along the wall searching and feeling my way. I make my way into the safe-haven closet, the safe room, where, according to our plan, everyone would've been staged. And I don't find anybody there. I go and make sure that—I go and work my way around the wall to the gate, the locked gate of the safe haven itself. And I'm able to confirm that the gate is still locked, it was locked by padlock from the inside. So I can make the assumption that nobody has entered the safe haven and nobody has left. So that limits the search area.

So I continue to search. I just kind of follow along the walls, calling out to the Ambassador and Smith and doing my best to feel around for them.

Q: So, at this point, you have zero visual visibility and you're feeling along the walls?

A: Uh-huh.

Q: And so did that mean that you were just necessarily a little limited in the surface area you could cover in terms of——

A: Right. Yeah. You're right; there was no visibility. So I was just trying to feel with my limbs, my hands and feet, and still maintain contract with the wall so that I wouldn't lose myself. But, nevertheless, I started to feel very disoriented myself. I started to be worried that, you know, I was really craving oxygen by that point, and I eventually found myself in the bathroom. I broke a window out to try

---

192 *Id.* at 155–156.
193 Diplomatic Sec. Agent 4 Testimony at 136.

and ventilate the space and to get some fresh air for myself. And I cleared my head a little bit.

I was able to get lower to the ground, and then I worked my way back out the way that I had come. And it was at that point in the hallway that I came across the body of Sean Smith. He was unresponsive. So I grabbed him and dragged him back down the hallway to the safe-haven window and then handed him off to the people waiting outside. It was when we had him outside in the clear air that—and we had a brief check of him, he had—he was unresponsive, not breathing, no pulse, and so felt that at that point he was already expired.[194]

At 11:01 p.m. [5:01 p.m. in Washington D.C.], Smith was reported as killed in action.[195] He was an only child, a husband and father of two. He was posthumously awarded the Thomas Jefferson Star for Foreign Service on May 3, 2013.

### Embassy Tripoli

At the U.S. Embassy in Tripoli, the Deputy Chief of Mission, the most senior member of the State Department team in Tripoli, and the Chief of Station, the most senior member of the CIA team in Libya, learned of the attack soon after it began.[196] At 9:45 p.m., three minutes after the attacks began, the senior Diplomatic Security Agent notified Hicks of the attack. After realizing he had a few missed calls on his cell phone, Hicks attempted to redial the number and reached Stevens:

I jumped up and reached into my phone at the same time I tried to connect with John which I did not do, he ran out immediately.

And I looked at my phone, and I saw two missed phone calls, one from a number I did not recognize, and the second from the Ambassador's telephone.

I punched the number that I did not recognize and called it back, to call it back, and I got Chris on the line. And he said, "Greg, we are under attack."[197]

The line went dead. Hicks was unable to reach Stevens again.

Individuals in the tactical operations center, the command center at the Embassy in Tripoli, quickly alerted other relevant Embassy staff when the attack was first reported.[198] Within minutes, the individuals in Tripoli took quick and decisive actions to execute two steps in response to the attacks that night. First, they submitted a request to divert an intelligence, surveillance, and reconnaissance asset— colloquially referred to as a "drone"—flying over another location in eastern Libya to Benghazi to provide tactical awareness of the situation on the ground. Second, the Chief of Station of the

---

[194] Id. at 136–137.

[195] Comprehensive Timeline of Events—Benghazi, produced by the U.S. Dep't of State. (Last Edit Nov. 1, 2012) (on file with the Committee, SCB0047843).

[196] Hicks Apr. 2013 Testimony at 18.

[197] Id.

[198] See Hicks Apr. 2016 Testimony at 72.

Annex in Tripoli prepared a rescue team, called "Team Tripoli," to respond forthwith to the attacks in Benghazi.

## Team Tripoli Response

In Tripoli, when word of the attacks reached the Embassy and the CIA Station, a team consisting of four Tripoli Station GRS members, one of whom was Glen Doherty, two Defense Department special operators, and a CIA linguist sprang into action. Using their initiative coupled with previously established contacts, in less than an hour, they managed to assemble a response team and acquire an aircraft for transport. The Chief of Station authorized this team, dubbed Team Tripoli, to respond to the attacks in Benghazi:

> [M]y specific direction to Team Tripoli was to provide quick reaction force to shore up base and to assist the [Benghazi Mission compound], the consulate there, and in so doing render any assistance to the Ambassador. So that was all kind of—they were a complementary set of objectives.
>
> One of the things, on a more tactical level, was the entire GRS contingent in Benghazi, save one officer, was forward deployed to the temporary mission facility. So they were, in my opinion, very vulnerable.
>
> At that time, I made the decision to deploy all except one of our GRS officers to Benghazi. That gave me certainly a sense of trepidation because that left us vulnerable to any sort of attack or follow on things. So that was part of my thought calculus doing that. I didn't hesitate, but I certainly thought about that and the ensuing consequences of leaving one GRS.[199]

While the mission of Team Tripoli was supported by the Department of State at Embassy Tripoli and supported by AFRICOM, it was a mission orchestrated solely by the CIA Chief of Station in Tripoli. As reported by one of the military members of Team Tripoli to the Committee:

> Q: Did AFRICOM headquarters or SOCAFRICA have any role in planning your deployment from Tripoli to Benghazi?
>
> A: No, sir.
>
> *　　*　　*
>
> Q: How about the Embassy itself there in Tripoli, were they directing the deployment from Tripoli to Benghazi?
>
> A: Not that I recall, sir.[200]

Fortuitously, earlier that day a CIA member of the team had brokered an initial agreement with the owner of an aircraft to charter

---

[199] Testimony of Chief of Station, Cent. Intel. Agency, Tr. at 112–13 (July 16, 2015) [hereinafter Chief of Station Testimony] (on file with the Committee).

[200] Testimony of Special Operator, U.S. Dep't of Defense, Tr. at 44–45 (Sept. 22, 2015) [hereinafter Special Operator Testimony] (on file with the Committee).

the aircraft as needed.[201] During the morning meeting, the CIA officer had queried the operator of the aircraft as to "How fast can you respond?" and the **[redacted text]** owner replied, "I am not sure; probably within 24 hours."[202] Because of this, Team Tripoli was able to quickly secure the aircraft for transport from Tripoli to Benghazi that night.

> A: Called back again that night and said, "We need you right now," and he was there. He showed up.
>
> Q: That was good timing, wasn't it?
>
> A: It was good timing, sir, convenient.[203]

                         *        *        *

> Q: And how long did it take from the time that call was made to the aircraft owner, what did he say about his ability to take off from Tripoli to Benghazi? How long a timeframe do you recall?
>
> A: I don't remember what time he said, but I know we had got there around 11:30 or midnight, but he was ready to go when we had gotten there. And they actually had expedited us through the airport. We didn't go through any— the actual airport procedures. We had weapons and ammo, obviously.

                         *        *        *

> Q: And was there no limitation on daylight only flight ops with this **[redacted text]**, as I understand was the limitation on the Libyan military C–130?
>
> A: I don't think they could fly at night, but he could because he was a privately owned company. The **[redacted text]** was privately owned.
>
> Q: But your understanding was, at least with respect to the Libya C–130——
>
> A: Daytime, sir.
>
> Q: That was limited to daytime ops?
>
> A: Yes, sir.[204]

At 12:30 a.m. [6:30 p.m. in Washington D.C.], the Team Tripoli departed the Tripoli Mitiga Airport with four GRS officers, including former U.S. Navy SEAL Glen A. Doherty, two military personnel, and a CIA officer acting as a linguist.[205]

---

[201] *Id.* at 37.

[202] *Id.*

[203] *Id.*

[204] *Id.* at 47–48.

[205] *See* U.S. Dep't of Defense, Timeline of the Department of Defense Actions on September 11–12, 2012 (May 1, 2013) (on file with the Committee) [hereinafter U.S. Dep't of Defense Timeline] ("A six-man security team from U.S. Embassy Tripoli, including two DoD personnel, departs for Benghazi"); *see also,* Special Operator Testimony at 41.

## The Defense Department is Alerted of the Attack

News of the attack traveled at varying speeds within the Defense Department. AFRICOM was the first combatant command to receive an alert about the attacks. By 4:32 p.m. in Washington D.C. [10:32 p.m. in Benghazi], news of the attack reached the Pentagon.

### AFRICOM ALERTED OF THE ATTACK

Members within the AFRICOM command structure learned of the attack just more than 30 minutes after it began. At AFRICOM headquarters in Stuttgart, Germany, Vice Admiral Charles J. Leidig Jr., the second in command for military operations, learned of the attack just over a half hour after it began.[206] He testified:

> The night of the attack, when I received the initial report at my quarters that night that there had been—I remember it exactly. I got a report at [10:15]. I tell people I saw the same Indiglo watch, and I was asleep in my bed. I went to bed, got up early, and it was my routine. So at [10:15], I rolled over and got a report that . . . the facility in Benghazi [had been overrun], but that the Ambassador was in a safe room and was safe. And that was the initial report I got at [10:15].[207]

Following notification, Admiral Leidig recalled his command center staff and returned to work.[208] Although the initial reports he received were that Stevens had been secured in a safe haven, he learned shortly upon returning to work that Stevens was missing:[209]

> When I got to the command center, the focus was on where is the Ambassador and trying to locate him. At that point I didn't know where the location that folks had went to. I didn't know who they were. I would later learn over the intervening hours that that was some folks from [the annex] who had come to move State Department personnel to the other facility. Again, it was several hours before I knew what the facility was, or the location, or where they were at. I just knew that they had moved to another location, and the reports we were getting from—most of our reporting at that point were coming from the defense attaché', our defense attaché' in Tripoli—was that they were safe, and they were fine, and that they were at this other facility. Our focus was trying to help gather information to see if we could locate where the Ambassador was.[210]

### PENTAGON ALERTED OF ATTACK

Almost an hour after the attacks started, at 4:32 p.m. in Washington D.C. [10:32 p.m. in Benghazi], nearly the same time the

---

[206] Leidig 2014 Testimony at 20.
[207] Id.
[208] Id. at 26.
[209] Id.
[210] Id. at 28.

Diplomatic Security Agents and the Annex security team members began clearing the Mission compound in Benghazi half a world away, word of the attack finally reached the Pentagon.[211] Although the Embassy in Tripoli and the Diplomatic Command Center at the State Department in Washington received word almost immediately that the Benghazi Mission compound was under attack, that notice did not make its way to the National Military Command Center, the operations center at the Pentagon, until 4:32 p.m. local time in Washington D.C.[212] Vice Admiral Kurt W. Tidd, the Director of Operations for the Joint Chiefs of Staff at the time of the attacks, testified his staff immediately alerted him about the attacks.[213] His staff simultaneously contacted AFRICOM to obtain additional information regarding the situation on the ground, while he notified members of the Secretary of Defense's staff.[214]

## ASSETS IDENTIFIED TO DEPLOY

As officials in Washington D.C. began to react to the attacks in Benghazi, it is important to describe and understand the assets available to respond, the state of those assets, and the military's policies and planning in force that applied to the assets' use and deployment.

## AFRICOM'S Posture and Force Laydown on September 11

In the days leading up to September 11, 2012, General Carter F. Ham, the Commander of the United States Africa Command [AFRICOM] conducted a "deep dive" into intelligence reports to guide their decision regarding whether any adjustment to the force posture needed to be made.[215] Leidig testified:

> [B]ased on General Ham's guidance, we actually did—we had been—the military always does planning for September 11th. We always know that there's a potential for, you know, some sort of terrorist activity on September 11th since its anniversary. General Ham had actually directed in the days running up to it that we do what we call a deep dive or a deep look at the intelligence to see if there was anything to indicated that there might be anything in our [area of responsibility]. We found nothing in any intelligence that would indicate that there was an attack or an incident being planned by terrorists in our [area of responsibility].[216]

Although AFRICOM's area of responsibility consists of the continent of Africa, with the exception of Egypt, its headquarters are based in Stuttgart, Germany. With the exception of a contingent stationed in Djibouti, a country on the Horn of Africa approximately 2,000 miles from Libya, AFRICOM did not have assigned

---

[211] U.S. Dep't of Defense Timeline.

[212] U.S. Dep't of Defense Timeline; *see* SCC Timeline (indicating the Diplomatic Security Command Center received notification of the attack at 3:49 PM EDT).

[213] Testimony of Vice Admiral Kurt Tidd, Assistant to the Chairman of the J. Chiefs of Staff, Dir. for Operations (J3), U.S. Dep't of Defense, Tr. at 8 (Apr. 4, 2016) [hereinafter Tidd Testimony] (on file with the Committee).

[214] *Id.* at 8–9.

[215] Leidig 2014 Testimony at 22.

[216] *Id.* at 22–23.

forces.[217] As a result, AFRICOM had to use United States European Command troops, aircraft, and bases in Europe including Ramstein, Germany; Sigonella and Aviano, Italy; and Rota, Spain to respond to events occurring on the African continent.[218]

## Planned Assets

### FAST PLATOONS

The assets AFRICOM would mostly likely call upon in response to a crisis situation were the Fleet Antiterrorism Security Team [FAST] platoons stationed in Rota, Spain. Those platoons were required to be ready to deploy within a certain time frame. FAST platoons, as of September 2012, were typically used to reinforce embassy security and operated from a fixed location within an embassy. FAST platoons did not deploy with their own vehicles, so they were dependent on other means for ground mobility. That reality made the FAST platoon less capable to rapidly respond as a quick-reaction force. Moreover, the FAST platoon's ability to move on a given timeline required the allocation of aircraft for deployment in a timely manner.

At the time, FAST platoons did not have dedicated airlift. This meant prior to being able to deploy, airlift would need to arrive from some other location, most likely Ramstein, Germany, to pick up the platoon for an onward deployment. The air base in Ramstein, Germany housed C–130s, large transport airframes that typically would be used to move the FAST platoons and associated equipment. In the days leading up to the attack, none of the C–130s in Ramstein were on any heightened alert. To effectuate movement, the Commander of United States Air Forces in Europe would need to take a series of steps to generate aircraft and prepare an air crew for deployment.[219]

### COMMANDER'S IN EXTREMIS FORCE

Another asset AFRICOM could call upon when circumstances warranted was the Commander's in Extremis Force [CIF] owned by European Command; it is one of the most capable quick response forces. General Ham described this force as "the force of first choice should there be an emergent situation."[220] It is a special operations response team that offers capabilities for emergency action in missions such as hostage rescue, noncombatant evacuation when the security situation is uncertain, or convoy security. The CIF can and does work with the U.S.-based Special Operations Force that also ultimately deployed the night of the attacks in Benghazi. Theoretically, since any deployment from the U.S. to the Middle East or North Africa will require significant time for the U.S.-based force to reach its destination, the CIF provides a more responsive capability when an emergency arises. It has dedicated aircraft for transportation. The CIF is tasked to be airborne in a set number

---

[217] Panetta Testimony at 13.
[218] *Id.* at 14–15.
[219] Testimony of General Philip G. Breedlove, Commander, U. S. European Command, Tr. at 21–22 (Apr. 7, 2016) [hereinafter Breedlove Testimony] (on file with the Committee).
[220] Testimony of General Carter F. Ham, Commander, U.S. Africa Command.Tr. at 28 (June 8, 2016) [hereinafter Ham 2016 Testimony] (on file with the Committee).

of hours once alerted, and the military's air traffic management system is supposed to provide two aircraft to ensure the CIF is airborne on the specified timeline. Unlike other assets deployed that night the CIF deploys with its own vehicles giving it the ability to drive from an airfield where deposited to a crisis site.

Typically stationed in Germany, in the days leading up to September 11 the CIF was actually deployed to Croatia to perform a joint exercise.[221] This training exercise had been planned for over a year.[222]

## U.S.-BASED SPECIAL OPERATIONS FORCE

One other asset that can be used in events similar to the attacks in Benghazi is a U.S.-based Special Operations Force [U.S. SOF]. That force offers capabilities that complement and expand upon the assets brought by the CIF.[223] Secretary of Defense Leon E. Panetta described the U.S. SOF as a "hostage rescue unit from our special operations team."[224] **[redacted text]**.[225] By design, the CIF would typically be able to reach an overseas target first, due to the distance required to deploy from the U.S.[226] If required, the CIF can assault a target immediately. If time permits, the preferred option is to hand the target over to the U.S. SOF, given its more robust capabilities.[227] Since the U.S. SOF deploys from the U.S., however, to respond to the attacks in Benghazi it must travel much farther than the CIF and other assets closer to Libya.

## Other Assets

### F–16S AT AVIANO AIR BASE

Aviano Air Base—situated in Aviano, Italy, approximately 50 miles north of Venice—is home to the 31st Fighter Wing of the United States Air Forces Europe. At the time of the attack, two squadrons each consisting of 21 F–16s were stationed at Aviano.[228] No tankers to provide air refueling for these F–16s were stationed at Aviano.[229] The assigned tankers were stationed in Mildenhall, England.[230]

On September 11, 2012, the air squadrons in Aviano were not on any heightened alert status, despite the call for a "heightened alert" during the President's call with Cabinet members—an alert sequence that would require the pilots and the aircraft to be ready in a short amount of time. Rather, they were in a training posture.[231] In fact, on that day, the 31st Fighter Wing was in the middle of a two-week inspection to ensure the Fighter Wing met Air

---

[221] Testimony of Army Major General Michael S. Repass, Commander, Special Operations Command Europe, Tr. at 18 (Apr. 15, 2016) [hereinafter Repass Testimony] (on file with the Committee).

[222] Id.

[223] Id.

[224] Leon E. Panetta, *Worthy Fights: A Memoir of Leadership in War and Peace* 225 (2014).

[225] Repass Testimony at 8.

[226] Id. at 8–9.

[227] Id. at 9.

[228] Testimony of Brigadier General Scott Zobrist, Commander, 31st Fighter Air Wing, U.S. Air Forces Europe, Tr. at 15 (Mar. 12, 2014) [hereinafter Zobrist Testimony] (on file with the Committee).

[229] Id. at 20.

[230] Id. at 21.

[231] Id. at 25.

Force requirements.[232] The aircraft were in a "true training configuration" which meant nothing was pre-loaded on the aircraft.[233] This also meant any live ordnances available at Aviano were not assembled, thus, prior to loading onto an F–16, the bomb had to be put together piece by piece.[234]

In addition to the fact that none of the F–16s was on any alert status but rather in a true training configuration on the anniversary of September 11, the distance between Aviano and Libya is approximately 1,000 miles or the equivalent of two-hour's flight time.[235] Because of that distance, an F–16 would have needed two air refuelings by the tankers that were stationed nearly 700 miles away in Mildenhall, England, at the time.[236]

These impediments to any fighter aircraft response from Aviano to North Africa were well known prior to September 11. Yet the alert posture of the aircraft at Aviano did not change in advance of that date, nor did the alert posture change after the protests in Cairo, Egypt.

General Ham testified he had not ordered any fighter aircraft at Aviano to be placed on alert in the days leading up to September 11 based on his assessment of the threat intelligence and the probability the type of attacks that would most likely occur would be small scale attacks.[237] Because of this, he believed if any attack were to occur, fighter aircraft would not be the right tool to respond.[238] Some other military officials agreed with General Ham's assessment that fighter aircraft would likely not be the right tool to respond to potential events in North Africa.

## REMOTELY PILOTED AIRCRAFT "DRONES"

At the time of the attacks, the Air Force operated four remotely-piloted aircraft—colloquially referred to as "drones"—from a base in southern Europe, approximately four hours from Benghazi. These drones were flown by a United States Air Force squadron located in the continental United States, and conducted missions over several countries including Libya.[239] None of the drones were armed, **[redacted text]**.[240] A pilot operating a drone on the night of the attack explained why:

Q: Was the aircraft armed?

A: No, the aircraft did not have Hellfires on it.

Q: Could it have been armed?

A: I guess "could" is a very subjective term in this case. So the aircraft had pylons which you could put Hellfires on, yes.

Q: If it was capable of being armed. Why wasn't it armed?

---

[232] *Id.* at 32.
[233] *Id.* at 36.
[234] *Id.* at 29–30.
[235] *Id.* at 56.
[236] *Id.*
[237] Ham Testimony at 28.
[238] *Id.*
[239] Testimony of Remotely Piloted Aircraft Pilot 1, U. S. Air Force, Tr. at 10–11 (May 25, 2016) [hereinafter Drone Pilot 1 Testimony] (on file with the Committee).
[240] **[Redacted text]**.

A: So as far as, like, the details of that decision, they're above my level as to why that wasn't armed. But from my understanding, the two reasons were—one is the political environment between Libya, Italy, America, and Europe was that we no longer needed missiles on our aircraft in Libya because it had stabilized from the Qadhafi regime, post-Qadhafi regime.

The second reason is, whenever we don't need missiles on the aircraft, we want to pull them off as soon as we can, because it provides an opportunity to put more gas on board, and with more gas on board, we can fly longer missions and we can provide more intelligence, surveillance, and reconnaissance to the Combined Air Operations Center.[241]

Armed drones had not been flown out of southern Europe since the fall of the Qadhafi regime. Another pilot who operated the drone that night added:

A: [W]e hadn't been armed in Libya since at some point after the Qadhafi stuff had happened. So at some point after that, it was—we knew we were no longer going to be armed in that theater.

Q: How did you know that?

A: I don't remember who mentioned it, but I remember hearing at some point that the—my understanding of it was that the [government hosting the drone base] did not want us flying an unmanned aircraft that was armed over their country, so therefore they restricted us from having armed unmanned aircraft.

Q: And did you ever hear anything like—was that through your chain of command or that was a fellow pilot?

A: My best guess would be that it was probably our operations supervisor who basically runs the mass brief at the beginning of each shift, you know, would have just mentioned one day: Hey, due to, you know, the [government hosting the drone base] not wanting us to have armed unmanned aircraft over their country, we're no longer going to be armed in Libya.[242]

One of the pilots added:

To the best of my knowledge, that is my understanding for what the trigger was for no longer arming the remote-piloted aircraft flying over Libya, was the takedown of Qadhafi.[243]

To utilize armed drones in a close air support environment, such as in Benghazi, a pilot would typically receive targeting instruc-

---

[241] Drone Pilot 1 Testimony at 24–25.
[242] Testimony of Remotely Piloted Aircraft Pilot 2, U.S. Air Force, Tr. at 15 (May 25, 2016) [hereinafter Drone Pilot 2 Testimony] (on file with the Committee).
[243] Id. at 27.

tions and clearance from a Joint Terminal Attack Controller [JTAC] on the ground.[244] One of the drone pilots explained:

> In a close air support environment, which is more akin to what [Benghazi] would be, that's where we would coordinate with a joint terminal attack controller, JTAC, on the ground, and he would give us what is called a nine-line in order to strike in that close air support environment. And that would be the clearance.
>
> And then the only other option would be to get a nine-line, which is equivalent to a strike clearance, from the actual Combined Air Operations Center via a chariot directed straight from the Combined Forces Air Component commander.[245]

Although there were no JTAC's on the ground in Benghazi that night, several of the GRS agents possessed the skillset from their prior military experience.[246] One agent testified:

> Q: And so how many of you had that, what [do] you call it again? What did you call it again?
>
> A: A nine line.
>
> Q: Nine line?
>
> A: Yes, sir. It's just calling for fire. Now they call them JTACs. When most of us were in the military it wasn't as specialized, but everyone on that team could have called in, called for fire.
>
> Q: Anybody——
>
> A: On our team, yes.
>
> Q: —could have called it?
>
> A: Yes, sir.
>
> Q: So how were you able to—I guess your capabilities—I'm talking about you personally, you were able to provide a nine line?
>
> A: Sure.
>
> Q: And how did you know how to do that?
>
> A: From the military. From prior training in the military.
>
> Q: Okay. Would you have had any way to communicate with the pilot if a pilot——
>
> A: We could have, yes.
>
> Q: All right. How could that have——
>
> A: Through radio.
>
> Q: Through radio. When you say we were all able to provide precision fire, are you talking about the GRS individuals?

---

[244] Id. at 25–26.
[245] Drone Pilot 1 Testimony at 23.
[246] GRS 5 Testimony at 43–45; see also, Drone Pilot 1 Testimony at 67 ("there were no JTACs in all of Libya.").

A: Only the GRS individuals, yes.

Q: Okay. Do you know if everybody was able to do that or——

A: Yes, I do.[247]

When asked whether former military personnel were capable of serving as a JTAC, one of the drone pilots acknowledged such a person could possess the skills necessary to direct a strike.[248] According to the witness from his perspective, the problem would be whether the military, without approval from the President, would have the authority to launch a missile toward a target at the direction of a skilled civilian.[249] However, as the pilot pointed out, authority to strike without a military JTAC on the ground could also have been provided by the Combined Forces Air Component Commander.[250]

The year before the attacks in Benghazi, the Defense Department had operated drones over Libya during Operation Odyssey Dawn, the U.S. led campaign against Qadhafi troops, and Operation Unified Protector, the NATO mission against Qadhafi troops. During both of those operations, the drones had been used to launch missiles toward targets in Libya.[251] During these operations, the drones were pre-loaded with missiles while stationed in southern Europe and always carried weapons during missions over Libya. At some point after the fall of Qadhafi, the drones operating over Libya no longer carried missiles.

After the fall of Qadhafi, the Defense Department continued to use drones and other ISR assets to gather intelligence information in Libya, especially regarding the growing number of Islamic extremist in country.

In August 2012, the Libyan government restricted the types of missions that could be flown in Libyan air space, primarily over Benghazi. General Ham explained:

Q: General, in the summer of 2012, August timeframe, ISR missions over Benghazi and Tripoli were suspended due to complaints from Libyans. I believe those ISR assets were Predators and they were under your command. Is that correct?

A: Yes.

Q: And what do you recall about the suspension or the complaints from the Libyans about those ISR assets operating in Libya?

A: There were complaints by the Libyan Government to the Embassy about overflights. **[Redacted text]**.

Q: Did those complaints impact your ability to operate those Predator assets at all during that time?

---

[247] GRS 5 Testimony at 43–45.
[248] Drone Pilot 1 Testimony at 65–66.
[249] *Id.* This appears to be a concise statement from his perspective of more complex legal and operational constraints.
[250] *Id.* at 30–31.
[251] Testimony of Remotely Piloted Aircraft Sensor Operator, U. S. Air Force, Tr. at 26 (June 9, 2016) [hereinafter Sensor Operator 1] (on file with the Committee).

A: I do not recall the complaints about the unmanned systems. I do recall complaints about the manned systems. And the manned systems, we would have to very carefully manage the time slots and when they could fly.

Q: Were those P–3s?

A: Yes.

General Ham described his assessment of the Libyans's request:

Sir, I think there were some honest Libyans who didn't like the noise. I mean, they're just kind of a constant buzz. They're low, and they're intrusive.

I think there were some Libyans who voiced concern to their government about a foreign power being intrusive.

And I believe there were Islamic terrorist organizations who were influencing members of the Libyan Government, because they knew what those aircraft were doing.[252]

### ASSETS AT SOUDA BAY, CRETE

While conducting oversight in Souda Bay, Members of the Committee received a briefing regarding special operations aircraft that were stationed at Souda Bay on the night of the attacks in Benghazi and could have been utilized in response to the attacks. The Committee sought confirmation of this information through interviews and requests for information from the Defense Department. The Defense Department has not denied the presence of these assets.

### MILITARY PERSONNEL IN LIBYA

The only Defense Department asset in Libya not considered that night were the military members of Team Tripoli. This was true because the Secretary was not even aware of their presence in Libya. At the time of his meeting with the President and for a period subsequent to that, the Secretary was not informed military personnel were making their way to Benghazi. In fact, he did not learn of this until the next day.[253] This means the only U.S. military asset to actually reach Benghazi during the attacks was an asset the Secretary did not know about, was not told about by his subordinates, and did not learn about until after the fact.

### FOREIGN EMERGENCY SUPPORT TEAM

The Foreign Emergency Support Team [FEST] is "the U.S. government's only interagency, on-call, short-notice team poised to respond to terrorist incidents worldwide."[254] Consisting of representatives from the Defense Department and other agencies, FEST deploys overseas at the request of the Chief of Mission or the State Department, and can augment both U.S. and host nation capabili-

---

[252] Ham 2016 Testimony at 168.
[253] Panetta Testimony at 45.
[254] Foreign Emergency Support Team (FEST) found at www.state.gov/j/ct/programs/fest/index.htm.

ties with specialized crisis response expertise.[255] Historically, it has deployed overseas in response to attacks on U.S. interests. For example, in 2000, after the USS Cole was attacked, a FEST team was deployed to Aden, Yemen.[256] Two years earlier, two FEST teams were deployed to Kenya and Tanzania. FEST has also been deployed in response to a hostage-taking crisis and abductions of Americans.[257] Typically, the State Department requests deployment of the FEST in conjunction with the Joint Staff. Once that decision is made, the FEST is capable of launching within four hours.[258]

Despite all of these capabilities, the Secretary recalls no discussion of a potential FEST deployment in response to the Benghazi attacks.[259] Mark I. Thompson, the person in charge of the FEST, contacted Kennedy about deploying the FEST on the night of the attacks. According to an email response sent to Thompson that evening, Kennedy "did not feel the dispatch of such a team to Libya is the appropriate response to the current situation."[260] Charlene R. Lamb, Deputy Assistant Secretary for Diplomatic Security, State Department also did not believe the FEST was an appropriate asset to be deployed that evening. Although in direct contrast to the State Department's own description and the historical record of prior deployments of the unit, Lamb described the FEST as "primarily focus[ing] on providing a strong communications package, policy experts, and investigative abilities."[261]

David H. Petraeus, Director, CIA, viewed the FEST as a "support element for the conduct of an operation to do a counter-terrorism or hostage rescue operation."[262] **[Redacted text]**.[263] Yet with Stevens considered missing for hours in Libya after the death of Smith, FEST expertise could have augmented the capabilities of the U.S. Embassy in Libya.

Tidd stated a FEST deployment was discussed briefly during the 7:30 meeting with the White House, but dismissed.[264] Kennedy and others at the State Department did not want to deploy the FEST in response to the attacks in Benghazi. Tidd indicated the State Department was concerned about putting individuals in country who were not "trigger pullers" and would potentially need rescuing.[265]

### The Practical and Policy Implications Associated with Deploying Assets

Throughout the course of the investigation, Defense Department witnesses provided insight into how various assets might have been

---

[255] See id.
[256] Foreign Emergency Support Team (FEST), http://2001-2009.state.gov/s/ct/about/c16664.htm.
[257] Id.
[258] Email from Mark I. Thompson (Sept. 11, 2012 9:58 PM) (on file with the Committee, C05562162) ("The team can launch within 4 hours of Deputies Committee decision.").
[259] Panetta Testimony at 182.
[260] Email to Mark I. Thompson (Sept. 11, 2012 10:43) (on file with the Committee, C05562162).
[261] Testimony of Charlene Lamb, Deputy Ass't Sec'y for Diplomatic Sec., U.S. Dep't of State, Tr. at 26 (Jan. 7, 2016) [hereinafter Lamb testimony] (on file with the Committee).
[262] Petraeus Testimony at 49
[263] Id.
[264] Tidd Testimony at 22.
[265] Id. at 23.

employed to respond to the events in Benghazi, and the constraints—whether imposed by policy or imposed by capability—of employing such assets.

### TIME AND DISTANCE

Given that the attacks occurred in Libya, military officials repeatedly emphasized any asset that would respond to the events would be necessarily constrained by the "tyranny of time and distance." The CIF commander described the difficulties of responding to events in Africa:

> So a lot of people that deploy to Africa or work on AFRICOM—work for AFRICOM—use the term "tyranny of distance" because it takes so long to move what could seemingly look like smaller distances. And there's not a robust network of airfields and staging points that there are, say, in a more developed area of the world, like Europe. So Europe is a much smaller area, and there's many developed airfields, fueling sites. Whereas, when you have Africa, it's, relatively speaking, much more undeveloped and exponentially times larger; so you are limited in your ability to move around with fuel, with time. And we call it the "tyranny of distance" because it's hard to get from point A to point B, and it takes a while.[266]

With respect to the response to Benghazi, the Secretary explained:

> I knew it was going to take some time [to move an asset into Libya], just because of the preparedness for the units and then the time and distance involved. You know, you've heard the term "tyranny of time and distance," and it's tough in this area.[267]

Tidd discussed the challenges faced to move forces as quickly as possible that night:

> Q: Admiral, one of the lingering questions that we have been trying to get a handle on is why it seemed to take so long to get the response forces off the ground. The FAST team was in Rota on a [specific] timeline. They were ready to move prior to that. They sat on the tarmac for about 6 hours before the planes got there.
>
> A: That is because we had no alert aircraft in Ramstein. So, literally, it was the middle of the night there. And I don't know all of the exact actions that they had to go to, but at Ramstein, they had to go and generate the airplanes, get the air crews, wake them up, brief them, tell them what we knew, and have the planes ready to go. We did not have an alert posture set for the aircraft.[268]

---

[266] Testimony of CIF Commander, Special Operations Command Europe, Tr. at 98 (Aug. 26, 2015) [hereinafter CIF Commander Testimony] (on file with the Committee).
[267] Panetta Testimony at 47.
[268] Tidd Testimony at 16.

\* \* \*

Everybody wanted them there instantaneously. And we were getting a lot of questions . . . Are they mov[ing] yet, are they moving yet? It was just taking a long time.[269]

Dr. James Miller, the Under Secretary of Defense for Policy at the time, provided a civilian's perspective on the logistical challenges faced by the Defense Department that night in response to the attacks:

The logistical issues were the tyranny of distance and time, first and foremost. So moving an asset from the [U.S.], the longest move, moving the FAST team, getting it prepared to deploy—the FAST teams, I should say, both from Rota—and then the EUCOM [CIF].

So there is, first, the distance to be traveled, the fact that it takes time. Second, they need time to spin up. And I later became deeply familiar with the various postures and so forth, but it is challenging to sustain a very short timeline for an extended period of time. And so each of the individual units we're talking about had a specific timeline for readiness. My impression was they were all working to shorten that timeline and to get prepared and to deploy even more rapidly than their timelines. But that I would consider a matter of logistics as well.[270]

Several witnesses also talked about the logistical obstacles to deploying F–16s in response to the attacks in Benghazi. Being able to deploy an aircraft and being able to actually utilize an aircraft in response to the events are separate questions. From the Defense Department's perspective, even if a F–16 was activated quickly and was able to fly to Benghazi before the final mortar attack, logistical constraints would still have impacted the capability to actually utilize the F–16s that night. Admiral James A. Winnefeld, the Vice Chairman of the Joint Chiefs of Staff, discussed those constraints:

But let's say you could just snap your fingers and there were F–16s suddenly over Benghazi immediately. It's the middle of the night; there's no joint tactical air controller on the ground. You don't even have any communications with the people on the ground. You don't even know where this is happening. If you're lucky and you've got a latitude and a longitude to point your systems at, you might be able to see the action going on on the ground, if there was action going on on the ground, but for most of the night there wasn't.[271]

Rear Admiral Richard B. Landolt, the Director of Operations for AFRICOM also explained the logistical and policy constraints of employing F–16s in response to the attack:

---

[269] Id.

[270] Testimony of Dr. James N. Miller, Under Sec'y of Defense for Policy, Tr. at 71–72 (May 10, 2016) [hereinafter Miller Testimony] (on file with the Committee).

[271] Testimony of Vice Admiral James A. Winnefeld, Vice Chairman, J. Chiefs of Staff, Tr. at 35–36 (Mar. 3, 2016) [hereinafter Winnefeld Testimony] (on file with the Committee).

A: You still have 3 to 4 hours of the flight time to get to, say, Benghazi. And then you need to spin up tanker aircraft because it can't do a round trip without them. And Admiral Leidig talked to General Franklin on that, so there was nothing on strip alert there in Aviano.

And tankers I believed were up in England, Mildenhall, I believe.

\*     \*     \*

Q: Were the F–16s—perhaps "dismissed" isn't the right word, but—pick a better word if you have one—but were they dismissed because of the [time it would take to activate] issue, or were they dismissed because there wasn't a viable mission for you to employ them?

A: I would almost say both reasons, because—yeah. So we spin it up, what are we going to do with it? I mean, you've got to put ordnance on it, you've got to refuel it, you've got to brief a mission. We don't know what the mission is. You know, this is an urban environment so—and we don't have people on the ground that can direct targeting. There were not tactical action controllers in Benghazi, as far as I know.[272]

Even if F–16s were generated in a timely manner and were able to arrive in Benghazi before the attacks ended, policy restrictions would have impacted their utility that night. As Winnefeld explained:

> No Air Force or Navy pilot will ever drop a bomb into an area where they are not certain who's there and what's going on unless there's communications with people on the ground and a JTAC or what we call a forward air controller airborne.

> So I mean, it was highly unlikely that we were going to be able to make a difference, even if we could get there in time with air power, so we chose not to do it.[273]

As mentioned previously, many of the GRS agents on the ground had the JTAC capabilities from prior military experience. Of course all of what is laid out above was well known beforehand. There was nothing new about the time and distance concerns in Africa or the positioning of U.S. assets that might be called upon to respond.

Not only did the Defense Department know any response to events in North Africa would be hampered by distance, the State Department also knew the military had such concerns because they were constantly reminded. Winnefeld testified he repeatedly warned the State Department of this issue:

> The tyranny of distance, in particularly North Africa, as I'm sure you've probably seen a picture of the U.S. imposed upon—you know, the entire continental U.S. fits neatly

---

[272] Testimony of Rear Admiral Richard B. Landolt, Dir. of Operations for U.S. Africa Command, Tr. at 38 (May 5, 2016) [hereinafter Landolt Testimony] (on file with the Committee).
[273] Winnefeld Testimony at 36.

into North Africa. It's a big place. We've constantly reminded State while I was the Vice Chairman and also, you know, National Security Council staff, gently, politely, that if you're counting on reactive forces from DOD to pull your fat out of the fire, basically, when there's an event going on, you're kidding yourselves. It's just too hard to get there. Usually, an event is over fairly quickly, and even in the best alert posture we can be in, it's going to be a couple of hours, two or three hours, before we can be someplace.

So what you should really be counting on is using these forces to either preemptively reinforce an area, like an embassy, or preemptively evacuate an area, like an embassy. Don't count on us to drop in in the middle of the night and stop a situation that's going on.

Now that won't prevent us from trying, certainly. If there's an event in a place that—you know, like a Benghazi and if we're postured in order to get there, we'll certainly try, we'll always try, but I've made it very clear to them—and they understand this—that they need to be very careful in their risk assessments. And it's a lot easier to reinforce and get out early than it is to save something that's under fire. And that has a lot to do not only with the tyranny of distance and how long it takes to get there, but you know, it's not easy to take a force and just drop it into the middle of an unknown area at night, and it's even harder when you're under fire. You know, V–22s don't like to fly when they're under fire, that sort of thing. So we've tried to make it very, very clear to [State], try, please, please, to do good risk assessment and evacuate or reinforce so that we don't have to rescue you in the middle of a firefight.[274]

### The President's Directive and The Secretary's Order

Just minutes after word of the attack reached the Secretary, he and General Martin E. Dempsey, Chairman of the Joint Chiefs of Staff, departed the Pentagon to attend a previously scheduled 5:00 p.m. meeting at the White House with President Obama and National Security Advisor Thomas E. Donilon.[275] The Secretary recalled two details about the attack on the U.S. facility in Benghazi: a building was on fire and Stevens was missing.[276] As the Secretary and Dempsey briefed the President on the evolving situation in Benghazi, Libya, the Secretary recalled the following guidance:

The President made clear that we ought to use all of the resources at our disposal to try to make sure we did everything possible to try to save lives there.[277]

Immediately following the meeting with the President, at roughly 6:00 p.m., the Secretary and Dempsey returned to the Pentagon

---

[274] Winnefeld Testimony at 74–75.
[275] Panetta Testimony at 22.
[276] *Id.* at 22–23
[277] *Id.* at 24.

and convened a meeting that included Ham, who was in Washington D.C. at the time, and relevant members of the Secretary's staff and the Joint Staff.[278]

During the meeting, three distinct capabilities were identified to deploy in response to the attacks in Benghazi: two FAST platoons, the CIF, and the U.S. SOF, capable of response to crises worldwide.[279] Again, the Secretary was not aware, and was not told, of any assets in Tripoli.

The Defense Department provided copies of maps identifying assets present in European Command, AFRICOM, and Central Command's areas of responsibility on September 11, September 12, and September 13 to the Committee. The assets identified on the maps were purportedly considered during this meeting, although the Joint Staff at the time did not keep a daily updated list of assets and their locations.[280] During its investigation, the Committee determined the maps failed to include assets that actually were deployed in response to Benghazi. For example, a C–17 medical airplane was deployed to Tripoli on September 12 to evacuate the wounded, deceased, and other American citizens. That asset was not identified on the maps provided by the Defense Department to the Committee. Given this discrepancy, the Committee requested it confirm whether there were any additional assets not identified on the maps or any assets withheld due to special access programs restrictions. It did not respond to the Committee's request. This failure to respond unnecessarily and unadvisedly leaves questions the Defense Department can easily answer, and it is in the public interest that it do so.

According to the Secretary, within an hour of his return to the Pentagon, he issued an order to deploy the identified assets.[281] The testimony of record is that the President's direction that night was clear: use all of the resources available to try to make sure we did everything possible to try to save lives there.[282] When asked whether he expected or needed the President to later extrapolate, clarify, or reissue that order, the Secretary said "no."[283] The Secretary insisted he understood the President's directive and no further communication with the President was necessary. Nor did any further communication with the President take place.

Similarly, the Secretary insists his own intentions and actions that night, in the aftermath of the President's orders, were also clear: deploy the identified assets immediately. The Secretary said his orders were active tense. "My orders were to deploy those forces, period. . . . [I]t was very clear: They are to deploy."[284] He did not order the preparation to deploy or the planning to deploy or the contemplation of deployment. His unequivocal testimony was that he ordered the identified assets to "deploy."[285]

By 7:00 p.m. in Washington [1:00 a.m. in Benghazi], nearly three hours after the attacks began, the Secretary issued what he be-

---

278 *Id.* at 22.
279 *Id.* at 24–25
280 *See* Winnefeld Testimony at 45.
281 Panetta Testimony at 25–26.
282 *Id.* at 23.
283 *Id.* at 49.
284 *Id.* at 26.
285 *Id.*

lieved, then and now, to be the only order needed to move the FAST platoons, the CIF, and the U.S. SOF.[286] Yet nearly two more hours elapsed before the Secretary's orders were relayed to those forces. Several more hours elapsed before any of those forces moved. During those crucial hours between the Secretary's order and the actual movement of forces, no one stood watch to steer the Defense Department's bureaucratic behemoth forward to ensure the Secretary's orders were carried out with the urgency demanded by the lives at stake in Benghazi. For much of the evening of September 11, principals in Washington D.C. considered Stevens to be missing and reliable information about his whereabouts was difficult to come by. For those on the ground and in the fight in Libya, the reality of a second American death was sinking in.

## THE SECOND ATTACK ON THE COMPOUND

### Evacuation to Annex

In Benghazi, the Diplomatic Security Agents determined Stevens would not have survived the fire in Villa C, and they were now engaged in a recovery mission.[287] According to Diplomatic Security Agent 4, "[W]e were unable to find Stevens. I was very—at that point, I think it was decided that this was probably a recovery mission. We were looking to recover his body."[288]

At 11:10 p.m. [5:10 p.m. in Washington], an explosive device detonated several meters inside the back gate, starting the second wave of attacks at the Benghazi Mission compound.[289] Around the same time, the drone arrived on station over the compound.[290] GRS officers returned fire after being fired on by the attackers, while the Diplomatic Security Agents loaded their vehicle and departed the compound under fire at 11:16 p.m. [5:16 p.m.].[291] Prior to leaving the compound, the Diplomatic Security Agents did not fire their weapons during the attacks. As one Diplomatic Security Agent explained:

> I feel now, and I felt then at the time, that I had the support. At that time there was no opportunity to shoot. There was a situation, it was a moment where it was myself and [another Diplomatic Security Agent], and we were very close quarters with an overwhelming force of armed combatants, and at that situation it would not have been the smart thing, it would not have been the tactical thing to fire your weapon at that time.[292]

The Diplomatic Security Agents loaded Sean Smith's body in their vehicle and departed the compound through the main gate. One Diplomatic Security Agent described what they saw as they exited the compound:

---

[286] *Id.* at 49.
[287] Diplomatic Sec. Agent 4 Testimony at 137–138.
[288] *Id.*
[289] Video: DVR Footage of the Mission (Sept. 11, 2012, 2310).
[290] *See* U.S. Dep't of Defense Timeline ("[At 11:10 PM EET t]he diverted surveillance aircraft arrives on station over the Benghazi facility.").
[291] Committee analysis of DVR Footage of the Mission (Sept. 11, 2012, 2210 to 2216).
[292] Diplomatic Sec. Agent 2 Testimony at 156.

As we were turning left to go outside the compound, we could see at the end of that access road a lot of cars and lights and people milling about. I ascertained that was probably a checkpoint or a blockade. And so we turned around and went the other way. It was at that point the attacking force kind of crossed paths with us, had then they opened fire on our vehicle, and we continued out.[293]

Another Diplomatic Security Agent provided further detail about the extensive attacks they encountered as they fled the Mission compound.[294]

The situation on the perimeter was getting substantially worse. As we loaded into the vehicle, the agent that had been taking in the most smoke that was in the safe haven with the Ambassador ultimately ends up being the one to drive. I still don't know why we allowed him to do that. He did a great job. That adrenaline kicked in.

As we pull out of the compound . . . we start taking fire. So, as we suspected, the individuals that attacked us, some of them had remained hidden in the fruit grove on the compound and were waiting for a situation to kill us.

So as soon as we got out of the way of the Libyans, they started shooting the side of our armored vehicle, on my side of the car actually. Ting ting, ting ting. I don't know, maybe 10 rounds is what hit us on our left side.

As we exit the compound, we turn right . . . There is a large crowd, 40, 50, 60 people. We can't tell if they are facing us, we can't tell if they are waiting for us, we don't know. We get, I don't know, 20 or 30 yards down this road; we see this crowd. We decide it is something we would rather not encounter. We turn around.

We go back close to the compound, and there is someone we presume to be a 17 February member waiting off to the side by the wall who is waving at us, "Don't go this way." That is enough for us to turn around. So we turn around again back toward the crowd, the large crowd that we don't know their intentions.

\* \* \*

Okay. So we are heading back in the direction we initially attempted to go. As we get about probably a third to two thirds to halfway down this road, we encounter an individual that is pulled off from a small group of people at a compound. . . . This individual is waving us into his compound as if to say, you know, this is somewhere safe, come in and we will protect you. We decide this is a terrible idea. We all advise for the driver to just keep going.

---

[293] Diplomatic Sec. Agent 4 Testimony at 138.
[294] Diplomatic Sec. Agent 3 Testimony at 158–162; *See also,* Comprehensive Timeline of Events—Benghazi, produced by the U.S. Dep't of State. (Last Edit Nov 01, 2012) (State-SCB0047846).

The second we pull alongside of this individual he raises an AK 47 and shoots at pointblank range, literally pointblank, inches. His gunfire impacts the entire right side of the vehicle. The ballistic glass and the armor proofing works, just like it is supposed to.

He shoots through all the way around the right side, up in the back window, breaks through the exterior glass, which is just factory glass, and impacts the ballistic resistant glass on the inside, which holds.

\* \* \*

So, at the same time this individual is shooting us with his AK 47, I don't think it is him but another member of his group throws two grenades under our vehicle. I specify that they were grenades because they went off immediately as opposed to being a fuse-lit explosive like the gelatin bombs we discussed earlier. Those would have taken a few seconds for the fuse to burn out. We didn't realize it at the time, but two of our tires had been blown out.

So, as we pass this gun, possibly a full magazine of AK–47 fire at pointblank range and two grenades under our vehicle, and we continue on. We didn't realize it at the time, but two of our tires had been blown out.

We approach the intersection with the next major road, where the large group was positioned, and, to our relief, they are not even paying attention to what is going on down the road. They have their backs to us.[295]

As the Diplomatic Security Agents drove away from the Mission compound toward the Annex, they noticed they were being followed.[296] The individuals following the agents detoured to a warehouse in the vicinity of the Annex near the parking area where attackers later staged the first attack on the Annex.[297] One Diplomatic Security Agent described what happened when the team arrived at the Annex:

Finally, we were able to turn, kind of get off the main road there where it was a lot quieter, and then we made our way to the Annex. Upon arrival at the Annex, you know, we pulled in, and immediately people came out and I parked the car, got out of the car, and you know, their eyeballs were about the size of saucers, just seeing the car, and seeing us. And immediately, they brought me into kind of a, you know, the kitchen area, which is where the med area was. And they just started pumping me, you know, with fluids, just chugging water, eating fruit, and

[295] Diplomatic Sec. Agent 3 Testimony at 158–163.
[296] *Id.*
[297] *Id. See also,* Diplomatic Sec. Agent 1 Testimony at 74–75; Diplomatic Sec. Agent 4 Testimony at 138; Diplomatic Sec. Agent 5 Testimony at 125.

my goal was just to get back up on my feet, get back out and keep fighting.[298]

The team of five Diplomatic Security Agents arrived with Smith's body at the Annex at 11:23 p.m. [5:23 p.m. in Washington].[299]

Back at the Benghazi Mission compound, the GRS team were no longer facing direct fire. The GRS departed through the compound's main gate and followed a different route to ensure no attackers were tailing them.[300] They arrived at the Annex approximately 20 minutes later and quickly took up fighting positions on the roofs of the Annex buildings.[301]

After the agents and the GRS departed the compound, attacks continued on the Mission compound with RPGs, small arms fire, and unknown explosions.[302] A mix of armed and unarmed individuals re-entered the compound through the back gate and subsequently looted the armored vehicles, removed paper and gear from the TOC, reset fires, and stole an armored Land Cruiser.[303]

## The First Attack on the Annex

As the situation continued to unfold in Benghazi, the Diplomatic Security Agents on the ground were periodically reporting back to the tactical operations center in Tripoli about the events on the ground. The Tripoli Chief of Station discussed requests for a medical evacuation:

> So the initial question that I asked for our GRS team lead: Do they need a Medevac, and what Medevac assistance do they need? At that time they didn't know, so that was one of our communications to AFRICOM was to put a warning order or we may be needing Medevac assistance.
>
> At that time also the location of—we had no indication—our main priority was the personnel at the—at the temporary mission facility and the whereabouts of the Ambassador.[304]

*   *   *

> A: I think there was a—and some of the decisions were an ongoing conversation that I had with our rep in Stuttgart was about do we need Medevac and where that Medevac would go. So initially in that, when we were still looking for the Ambassador and our team was at the airport, they just got—I didn't say we wanted a medical—a Medevac at that point because we didn't have any—I did have conversations with the GRS team lead in Benghazi: What is the status of your personnel? Do you need Medevac? And

---

[298] Diplomatic Sec. Agent 5 Testimony at 127.

[299] Video: DVR Footage of the CIA Annex (Sept. 11, 2012, 2338).

[300] Video: DVR Footage of the Mission (Sept. 11, 2012, 2219).

[301] GRS 2 Testimony at 53.

[302] Committee analysis of DVR Footage of the Mission (Sept. 11, 2012, 2219).

[303] Committee analysis of DVR Footage of the Mission (Sept. 11, 2012, 2219); *see also* Email to the DSCC Watch Team and the DSCC Mgmt. Team (Sept. 11, 2012, 7:59 PM) (on file with the Committee, C05409685). The Twitter account with handle @hadeelaish belonged to Hadeel al-Shalchi, a journalist for Reuters news.

[304] Chief of Station Testimony at 101.

that answer was no at that time, and the Ambassador was unlocated.

But what played into some of my calculus at that time was I didn't want to send a U.S. aircraft in Benghazi and maybe have the same dynamic of getting off the airport and not knowing what were going to be the parameters of that situation.

So that was—and the Defense Attaché was in that same conversation with elements in AFRICOM.[305]

Just before 12:30 a.m. [6:30 p.m. in Washington D.C.], individuals congregated and staged gun trucks at the far east intersection near the Annex. It was unclear to the agents at the Annex if these individuals were friend or foe. The GRS agents on the roof asked Annex management whether they were able to determine who was congregating outside of the Annex.[306] The next wave of attackers then used the east field as cover and concealment to advance toward the Annex wall.

[B]y that time, we had started to see people massing on that east side parking lot and starting to utilize that little house that had the family in it. They were coming through that front door. They would disappear where the front door was, and you could see them coming out the back door, and that's when we're trying to get our lights turned off, all the lights, get them off.

Q: So were there floodlights looking out or lighting the base?

A: Both. We were trying to get the ones looking in. We were trying to get those floodlights turned off. And the ones looking out, let them stay on. In the meantime, I'm calling on the radio going are we expecting friendlies from chief of base and our team leader. Are we expecting any friendlies? Are we expecting any friendlies? And I'm getting, I don't know, maybe, I don't know. In the meantime, they're coming towards us, and I'm asking **[redacted text]**, I said do you see any weapons? Because we're not going to shoot anybody unless we see a weapon. And you could tell they're moving tactically. They're moving sideways. They're playing hide and go seek. They don't realize we have night vision. Eventually, I'm not going to call that we got bad guys coming.[307]

The first assault on the Annex itself began at 12:34 a.m. [6:34 p.m in Washington D.C.], when attackers directed small arms fire at the Annex hitting the northeast portion of the property, where Annex Building 2 was located.[308] An IED was thrown over the wall near the Annex north recreation area in the vicinity of a GRS offi-

---

[305] *Id.* at 109.
[306] GRS 1 Testimony at 94.
[307] GRS 4 Testimony at 106–107.
[308] Video: DVR Footage of the CIA Annex (Sept. 11, 2012, 0034).

cer on the ground.[309] One GRS officer described the beginning of the first attack.

> But then you could hear, like there's a mass of cars that is forming. We're trying to figure out if it's 17 Feb. or if it was the police or who was it, you know. Of course, we got nothing back from the TL or the Chief of Base.

> But as I was walking the water back, something flew over the wall, exploded about 15 feet or so away from me. And at the same time, an RPG came up over the wall, and that's when the first assault on our compound happened.[310]

For the next 10 minutes, rounds of small arms fire, RPG fire and IED explosions impacted the Annex near the northeast corner.[311] Concurrently, starting at 12:41 a.m. [6:41 p.m. in Washington D.C.] the Annex took small arms fire and likely IED attacks from the east wall also aimed at Annex Building 2.[312] Over the next 10 minutes, there were attackers that were visible along the east wall and an explosive impacted against the east side of the Annex.[313]

After being repelled from the first assault, attackers were still visible in the east field at 12:59 a.m.; however, GRS refused to fire on their location at this time because their position was too close to a residence where a local family lived including children.[314]

### The Second Attack on the Annex

After being overwhelmed in the first attack, the attackers regrouped with a more aggressive second attack. At 1:10 a.m., this second attack was directed at the Annex, with a RPG striking Building 2.[315] The second attack included even heavier sustained fire and a larger number of attackers.

Over the next five minutes, there was sustained and heavy small arms fire from the east perimeter wall, small arms fire from the northeast corner, RPG strikes from the east field, and sustained fire.[316] The attackers retreated after taking heavy return fire from the Annex. One GRS agent described this attack:[317]

> Q: Okay. So the second attack, what happened?

> A: It was a lot more force, lasted probably twice as long as the first one. I got a little bit of shrapnel from something. I got a bunch of shrapnel from the light. That was pretty much it. We just repelled that one. And that was it until 5:15 when the mortars came in.[318]

---

[309] GRS 1 Testimony at 94. *See also,* Video: DVR Footage of the CIA Annex (Sept. 11, 2012, 0036).

[310] GRS 1 Testimony at 94.

[311] Committee analysis of DVR Footage of the CIA Annex (Sept. 11, 2012, from approximately 0034 to 0045).

[312] Video: DVR Footage of the CIA Annex (Sept. 11, 2012, 0036 and 0041, respectively).

[313] Committee analysis of DVR Footage of the CIA Annex (Sept. 11, 2012, from approximately 0040 to 0052).

[314] GRS 4 Testimony at 119–120.

[315] Video: DVR Footage of the CIA Annex (Sept. 11, 2012, 0110).

[316] Committee analysis of DVR Footage of the CIA Annex (Sept. 11, 2012, from approximately 0110 to 0115).

[317] Committee analysis of DVR Footage of the CIA Annex (Sept. 11, 2012, from approximately 0110 to 0200).

[318] GRS 1 Testimony at 97–98.

## Local Libyans Find Stevens

Shortly before the second attack on the Annex began, at approximately 1:00 a.m. [7:00 p.m. in Washington] local Libyans found the remains of Stevens in a bedroom in the main diplomatic building at the Benghazi Mission. One of the Libyans asked a member of the Libyan Army to help pull Stevens out of Villa C. A neighbor from a nearby compound who knew Stevens interceded and transported Stevens to the hospital.

The Libyan Army officer who helped pull out Stevens' remains kept the phone that had been with Stevens and began calling the numbers listed in the phone to report that an American was located at the hospital. These calls started around 2:03 a.m [8:03 p.m. in Washington D.C.].[319]

> I started receiving calls from somebody who claimed to have the Ambassador's—well, he didn't know that it was the Ambassador's phone, but he was calling from the Ambassador's phone, claiming that, you know, he had come in contact with some, what he suspected, Americans and found their phone, and he wanted to return the phone. So, at that point, I was also involved in trying to find out about the Ambassador's fate at this point and how this individual was in possession of his telephone.
>
> Q: All right. So you said you received a call from somebody who allegedly had the Ambassador——
>
> A: A Libyan, yes.
>
> Q: Okay. And how did that person reach out to you? How did they know to reach out to you?
>
> A: He used the Ambassador's phone and dialed a phone number that was stored on the phone. And that phone on the other end belonged to one of the Diplomatic Security——
>
> \*　　\*　　\*
>
> So how did that first conversation go with the individual on the other end of the line?
>
> A: I tried to get as much information from him as possible. Initially, he was coy, and he said several Americans, and I said, okay, well, put them on the phone. And he said, well, they're not around me right now. And that was kind of odd. And I asked him if they were injured or why can't you put them on the phone. And eventually he said that, yeah, they are in the hospital, and they cannot talk right now.[320]

The Chief of Station described learning about Stevens' location:

> Q: So at some point in the evening you learned the Ambassador is probably not being held hostage, is probably

---

[319] Officer A Testimony at 36–37.
[320] *Id.*

deceased. Do you remember about when that was and what—how you learned that?

A: I learned that—so I had two telephones for the two different Libyan cellular services. So I learned that from the Prime Minister's office representative who I was in contact with. He previously said: Oh, we believe the Ambassador is at a hospital, we believe he's unconscious, we believe—you know, can I speak with him? Oh, no. I'll try to get someone to speak with him. That was that line.

And then I got indications from the Libyan intelligence service, the President's office, and the charge or the DCM at about the same time. We got indications at the same time base was getting someone to go to identify a person because we had a base officer in telephonic communication with someone that had the Ambassador's phone.

Q: Yeah.

A: So during that whole time we were—knew the Ambassador's phone was located at that hospital. We had people telling us the Ambassador's at that hospital. We didn't know the status of the Ambassador, so—but all of those things happened within a relatively narrow timeframe.[321]

## Team Tripoli Arrives at Benghazi Airport

At 1:30 a.m. [7:30 p.m. in Washington D.C.], Glen Doherty and the other members of Team Tripoli landed at the Benghazi Benina International Airport.[322] Meanwhile at the Annex, there was a lull in the fighting.[323] One of the Team Tripoli members explained to the Committee the steps taken to obtain transportation from the Benghazi airport to the Annex:

Q: Was anyone present from the Libyan armed forces or local militia that you could liaison with upon arrival in Benghazi?

A: Not as soon as we landed sir.

Q: Okay. And you arrived at Benina airport?

A: We did.

Q: And what was the nature of activity going on at Benina at 02 in the morning?

A: It was completely dead. We were the only plane that had landed in quite some time, it looked like, and the guard actually came out in his pajamas and asked us what was going on.

Q: Okay. So there was no airport personnel. This was not a 24/7 airport?

---

321 Chief of Station Testimony at 122.
322 U.S. Dep't of Defense Timeline.
323 Special Operator Testimony at 52–53. *See also*, Video: DVR Footage of the CIA Annex (Sept. 11, 2012, 0158).

A: I don't think so, sir. It didn't appear to be. Only one individual came out to meet us once we had landed, and it was clear that he had been sleeping before that.[324]

When Team Tripoli arrived at the airport, "the Ambassador was still missing."[325] While trying to secure transport at the airport, Team Tripoli was receiving information Stevens was located at a hospital in Benghazi. One Team Tripoli member said, "One of the local militia had told us that he—they thought he was at the hospital. Reporting had indicated he was at the hospital."[326] The Chief of Station added details about their concern regarding the information they were receiving:

That whole atmosphere of getting drawn into that correspondence that our officer had with that individual who had the Ambassador's phone had a lot of the hallmarks of some type of entrapment. It wasn't straight up. It didn't—it wasn't: We have the Ambassador here, you want to come and get him. It was much more convoluted than that. So we were very leery of—that was just a very high security posture as we were going through.[327]

Based on their coordination and planning prior to leaving Tripoli, the Team expected to be met at the airport by elements of the Libyan Shield militia. When they arrived, however, no one was present at the airport.[328] One of the Team Tripoli special operators described what they encountered:

We didn't have a mode of transportation that was ours, so we were depending on those local militias. So it took us that long to find one that was capable of taking us into town. Again, initially we were trying to go to the hospital, which we were all being told, "No, we can't take you to the hospital. We can take you to the annex."

So that fight went on for a little while, with us thinking that he could possibly be at the hospital needing medical care. So we were pushing hard enough to go there that it prolonged our time at the airport. Then once we found out he was deceased, we had obviously gave that up, and they had no problem taking us to the annex.[329]

While at the airport, Team Tripoli was alerted that Stevens' **[redacted text]** personal tracking device—was pinging "within 25 meters of their current location on the airfield."[330]

Q: Okay. So I want to direct your attention to the first page of exhibit 1, the last bullet?

A: Okay.

---

[324] Special Operator Testimony at 52–53.
[325] *Id.* at 55.
[326] *Id.* at 55–56.
[327] Chief of Station Testimony at 125.
[328] Special Operator Testimony at 52.
[329] *Id.* at 58–59.
[330] Request 1–004067 IntBook 6–044.

Q: It reads: "Note: TF Green member informed **[redacted text]** that the AMBOs **[redacted text]**"—does that mean [personal tracking device]?

A: Correct.

Q: "It was pinging, and its location was within 25 meters of their current location on the airfield. Several militia members and vehicles were on the airfield and vehicles at the time." So just to be clear, how did you learn about that [personal tracking device] pinging?

A: My TL told me at the time because when that militia drove up, **[redacted text]** and I were unpacking gear, and we were situating. And I was checking my gear and that's when our TL came up and advised us what was going on in reference to the ping.

Q: So the TF Green individual would have informed the TL and he told you?

A: Could have been.

Q: What was your assessment at the time of the significance of that attack?

A: That someone was near the Ambassador, or at least recovered some of his gear or his phone or his [personal tracking device] system. Somehow they had his belongings.

Q: And they were standing very close to your team?

A: Correct.

\*     \*     \*

Q: So obviously, you talked about how one of your primary missions was to locate the Ambassador. And then you learned while you were at the airport that the Ambassador's [personal tracking device] is pinging within 25 meters of your current location. Did you or the other team members find that odd?

A: Yes.

Q: Can you elaborate on that?

A: It was unusual that somebody had some of the Ambassador's belongings.

Q: Okay.

A: Especially his [personal tracking device]. I don't know if it was his cell phone pinging, how they got the ping, or his personal [tracking device], but it was odd that they had some of his equipment.[331]

For the next three-plus hours after their arrival in Benghazi, Team Tripoli attempted to secure transportation from the airport to the hospital. Because Team Tripoli did not have full awareness of the local militias operating in Benghazi, nor relationships with

---

[331] Testimony of GRS Tripoli, Cent. Intel. Agency, Tr. at 32–35 (June 23, 2015) [hereinafter GRS Tripoli Testimony] (on file with the Committee).

local militias to contact for assistance, they relied on a Libya Shield official in Tripoli to vet the local militia elements that showed up at the airport offering assistance. Much of their time at the airport was spent identifying the "least of several bad options" as it related to choosing a militia for transport.[332] The Team's Tripoli contact recommended seeking transport with another branch of the Libya Shield, as the branch prearranged to transport them never arrived.[333] One Team Tripoli member stated:

> Q: Did you have any sense during the 2 and-a-half hours that you spent at Benina airport that you were being prevented from departing the airport? Could you have left at any time from 02 to 0430?
>
> A: We didn't have a mode of transportation that was ours, so we were depending on those local militias. So it took us that long to find one that was capable of taking us unto town. Again, initially we were trying to go to the hospital, which we were all being told, "No, we can't take you to the hospital. We can take you to the Annex." So that fight went on for a little while, with us thinking that he [the Ambassador] could possibly be at the hospital needing medical care. So we were pushing hard enough to go there that it prolonged our time at the airport. Then once we found out he was deceased, we had obviously gave that up, and they had no problem taking us to the Annex.[334]

The group that escorted Team Tripoli to the Annex was a branch of Libya Shield operating that night under **[redacted text]**.[335] According to a member of Team Tripoli, this was their "less bad" option for transport that night given the difficulty of trusting militias in a city where many have Islamist leanings and an anti-Western sentiment after the involvement of NATO in the Libya Revolution.[336]

> Q: And how were you going to proceed? What was the nature of your transport from Benina to the Annex?
>
> A: The Libya Shield commander had several gun trucks that we were using, as well as some Land Cruisers, to get us to the Annex.
>
> Q: And this again, Libya Shield 2, the less bad element of the militia?
>
> A: Less bad, yes.[337]

Team Tripoli left the airport at approximately 4:30 a.m.[338] A team member provided the Committee the following background information for their intended mission at the time, as it had transitioned from locating and potentially rescuing Stevens to an

---

[332] Special Operator Testimony at 56–57.
[333] *Id.* at 57.
[334] *Id.* at 62–63.
[335] *Id.* at 55.
[336] *Id.*
[337] *Id.*
[338] *Id.* at 51.

effort to start evacuating nonessential personnel from Benghazi back to Tripoli.

> Q: [W]hat did you understand about your mission as you were heading from Benina airport to the Annex? Was your mission then evacuation of nonessential personnel?

> A: It was nonessential personnel only prior to the mortar attack happening . . . we were going to take 14 personnel back with us to the airport, let the jet take off, take them back to Tripoli. We were going to come back to the Annex and help hold up with the GRS guys until further notice . . . the majority of those people [the GRS would have stayed there. Shooters, if you will.[339] . . . [W]e did not make the decisions for that [airplane] to come back. We didn't know how long we were going to have to stay at the Annex. We were under the understanding they wanted to stay. They did not want to leave. So we were just trying to get the nonessential personnel out to get further direction from Chief of Station back in Tripoli on what he wanted them to do . . . I believe it was the Chief of Base that wanted to keep some individuals there.[340]

## THE WHITE HOUSE CONVENES A MEETING

While Team Tripoli was urgently seeking transportation from the Benghazi airport to either the hospital or the Annex, Denis McDonough, the Deputy Assistant to the President for National Security Affairs convened a secure video teleconference meeting at 7:30 p.m. in Washington with the State Department and the Department of Defense.[341] The State Department attendees included: Cheryl D. Mills, Chief of Staff; Jacob J. Sullivan, Deputy Chief of Staff for Policy and Planning; Stephen D. Mull, Executive Secretary; Wendy R. Sherman, Under Secretary for Political Affairs; and Kennedy and the Secretary.[342]

The Defense Department was represented by Jeremy B. Bash, Chief of Staff to the Secretary of Defense, and Tidd.[343] The two representatives who normally would have participated in the meeting—the Vice Chairman of the Joint Chiefs of Staff and the Under Secretary of Defense for Policy—did not do so that night.

In the four hours since the initial attack on the Benghazi Mission compound, the Diplomatic Security Agents in Benghazi, with help from the team from the Annex, survived the initial onslaught, located the remains of their fallen colleague Smith, frantically searched for Stevens, escaped under heavy gunfire from the Mission compound to the Annex, avoided an ambush along the route, and arrived at the Annex only to withstand and repel additional attacks there.[344]

---

[339] *Id.* at 69–70.

[340] *Id.* at 70.

[341] *See* Email from Cheryl D. Mills to Beth E. Jones *et al.* (Sept. 11, 2012 7:03 PM) (on file with the Committee, SCB0066272) ("SVTC AT 7:30PM WITH WHITE HOUSE").

[342] *See id.*

[343] *See id.*

[344] Email to Victoria Nuland, *et al.* (Sept. 11, 2012 5:32 PM) (on file with the Committee, SCB0068365–67) (forwarding chain of emails regarding updates on the events in Libya).

Team Tripoli, after learning of the attack in Benghazi, quickly developed a plan to render assistance, secured private aircraft in Tripoli, packed gear, planned a mission, flew from Tripoli to Benghazi, and urgently negotiated with unknown militias seeking transportation to either the hospital or the Annex.

By stark contrast, in those same four hours, principals in Washington had merely managed to identify forces that could potentially deploy to Libya and convened a meeting to discuss those forces.

Despite the Secretary of Defense's clear directive and his intention that forces would move and move quickly, no forces had yet moved. Over 13 hours after the attack began, the first force—the farthest away—deployed. It would take nearly 18 hours for the FAST team to move, and over 20 hours from the beginning of the attack before the CIF moved.

### Forces are "Spinning Up As We Speak."

Moments before the White House meeting began, Bash emailed several people including Mills and Sullivan, notifying them of the assets the Secretary had ordered to respond to the attacks. He wrote:

> After Consulting with General Dempsey, General Ham and the Joint Staff, we have identified the forces that could move to Benghazi. They are spinning up as we speak. They include a SOF element that was in Croatia (which can fly to Suda [sic] Bay, Crete) and a Marine FAST team out of Roda [sic], Spain.
>
> Assuming Principals agree to deploy these elements, we will ask State to secure the approval from host nation. Please advise how you wish to convey that approval to us. Burns/Nides/Sherman to Miller/Winnefeld would be my recommended course.[345]

Even though the Secretary had already issued the order to deploy the identified forces and testified he fully expected his order was being carried out at the time, the plan was to "work through this issue" during the White House meeting.[346] As the Secretary reinforced: "I had the authority to deploy those forces. And I didn't have to ask anyone's permission to get those forces into place." [347] The Secretary further said his approach was "we need to move them and move them as fast as we can in order to respond. So I wanted no interference with those orders to get them deployed." [348] In fact, the Secretary added that during the meeting at the Pentagon, his orders were simultaneously being conveyed to those forces.[349] He noted: "[T]hese are elite units, and the purpose of

---

[345] Email from Jeremy Bash to Jacob J. Sullivan (Sept. 11, 2012 7:19 PM) (on file with the Committee, STATE–SCB0060705).

[346] Email from Jacob J. Sullivan to Jeremy Bash, *et al.* (Sept. 11, 2012 7:21 PM) (on file with the Committee, SCB0075439).

[347] Panetta Testimony at 32.

[348] *Id.* at 33.

[349] *Id.* at 34.

these units is to move when I give the order to move, and that's what I expected." [350]

Curiously, the two members of the Defense Department Bash identified in his "spinning up" email as the proper persons to "convey" "approval from the host nation"—Winnefeld and Miller—were not part of the White House meeting. In fact, Winnefeld was not even at the Pentagon. He had left to return to his residence to host a dinner party for foreign dignitaries and testified he received one update on the events during the dinner. After the dinner concluded around 10 p.m., he went to the secure communications facility in his home. An hour later, the mortar attacks began. Likewise, Miller was not at the Pentagon due to an unexpected family emergency. He asked Bash to participate in the White House meeting in his stead. [351]

### Purpose of Meeting

Despite the Secretary's expectation the assets he ordered to deploy would move as fast as possible in order to respond, the individuals who participated in the White House meeting, nevertheless, felt the need to "work through" the assets the Secretary had already ordered to deploy. [352] At the time of the White House meeting, the final decision about which assets to deploy had apparently not been made, according to them, despite the Secretary's recollection and testimony to the contrary. Tidd testified:

Q: And at the time of the meeting, what was the status of the assets that you all discussed? Were they preparing to deploy?

A: They were alerted. The final decision had not yet been made definitively, as I recall, but we came out of that meeting basically: send everything. [353]

Tidd described the purpose of the meeting convened by the White House as an opportunity to share information across agencies.

It was an information exchange to cross-level what does everybody know, is there any new information. The intelligence community was obviously providing information on other things that were going on, other locations that State was providing information on, other embassies where they had concerns. FBI. It was a general kind of a roundtable and round robin of everybody going around and passing out what information they had, what did they know. And then what were the asks. And then an opportunity for us to be able to say — when we got to the military, we talked about these are the type of forces that we can deploy, and

---

[350] *Id.* at 37.

[351] Miller Testimony at 63–64. Miller testified he attempted to participate in the meeting from his home, but was unable to connect to his call.

[352] Email from Jacob J. Sullivan to Jeremy Bash, *et al.* (Sept. 11, 2012 7:21 PM) (on file with the Committee, SCB0075439).

[353] Tidd Testimony at 23–24; *see also,* Email from Jacob J. Sullivan to Jeremy Bash, *et al.* (Sept. 11, 2012 7:21 PM) (on file with the Committee, SCB0075439) ("We should work through this issue in that venue.").

here's what we know, here's what we think, and here's what our recommendations are.[354]

Mills said essentially the same thing: "[T]he [White House meeting] was called because everyone was seeking both to exchange information and figure out how to coordinate resources to support our team."[355] Kennedy said this about the White House meeting:

The [meeting] was mainly, to the best of my recollection, simply a conforming of information, a sharing of information. Make sure everybody had the same understanding and everyone was doing whatever they could in their lane of responsibility to proceed.[356]

He elaborated:

Conforming, conforming means, in effect, reconciling. That I have heard this, you have heard that, what have you heard? Trying to make sure that we all, meaning across the entire U.S. Government, had the clearest coherent understanding of what was going on in the fog of war.[357]

Winnefeld typically would have participated in the meeting that night. However, after being notified of the attacks, he departed the Pentagon that night to attend a dinner engagement. Despite not participating in the discussion, Winnefeld explained why the White House meeting would be called:

[W]henever something like this happens, whether it's a hostage rescue, or you name it, particularly an emergent event, there's always a [meeting] like this, and there are a lot of really good points brought up by interagency partners about considerations and—in stream. They're very useful events, and we can very quickly resolve questions, like, does anybody have any objections if we sent forces into Tripoli? My supposition here is that that was a very quickly resolved; nobody has objections.[358]

From the Defense Department's perspective, it was an opportunity to notify the State Department and the White House of the assets it could deploy in response to the attacks as ordered by the Secretary and to seek concurrence.[359] Winnefeld explained:

[M]y sense is that the deputies sort of coordinated on what DOD intended to do. So the Secretary has decided he wanted to deploy the CIF and the [U.S. Based SOF] and the FAST platoons. That was exposed to the deputies in

---

[354] Tidd Testimony at 21–22.

[355] Mills Testimony at 47.

[356] Testimony of Patrick F. Kennedy, Under Sec'y for Mgmt., State Dep't, Tr. at 112 (Feb. 3, 2016) [hereinafter Kennedy Testimony] (on file with the Committee).

[357] *Id.* at 155.

[358] Winnefeld Testimony at 80–81.

[359] *See* Email from Jeremy Bash to Jacob J. Sullivan (Sept. 11, 2012 7:19 PM) (on file with the Committee, STATE–SCB0060705).

the deputies SVTC, and they all concurred with that. . . . [360]

Of course, Winnefeld did not participate in this particular White House meeting. Witnesses who actually were present and appeared before the Committee were surprisingly unable to recall details regarding the various issues and discussions during the White House meeting.

The Committee was, however, able to uncover several emails from participants summarizing the meeting. In striking contrast to the Secretary's testimony, one summary of the White House Meeting listed the theme of the meeting, not as deploying forces in an active tense, but as "getting forces ready to deploy" in a future tense.[361] Another summary described the deployment of assets in response to Benghazi as "likely" and "possibly" that evening.[362] According to these summaries, the conclusion from the meeting was that forces were not going to deploy "until order comes, to go to either Tripoli or Benghazi."[363]

But the Secretary was unequivocal the order had already come: President Obama, as the Commander in Chief, said do everything you can to help our people in Libya.[364] As the Secretary of Defense, he ordered assets to deploy—active tense with no further explanation, amplification, or instruction needed.

The two-hour "meeting"—in which neither the Commander in Chief nor the Secretary of Defense participated—was in fact much more detailed and involved than witnesses suggested and presents a new perspective on what was happening and being discussed in Washington D.C. even while an Ambassador was missing and a second U.S. facility was under attack half a world away.

## Discussions During the 7:30 White House Meeting

### DIPLOMATIC CLEARANCE

The issue of securing host nation approval, the last aspect of Bash's email, was discussed during the 7:30 White House meeting. According to a write-up of notes taken by Mull, the State Department emphasized any deployment of U.S. Forces into Libya needed approval from the Government of Libya.

> Overall theme: getting forces ready to deploy in case the crisis expands and a real threat materializes against Embassy Tripoli. DOD will send the details to U/S/Kennedy (i.e. plane numbers, troop numbers, airfield support needs, etc.) for us to make request to government of Libya (GOL).

---

[360] Winnefeld Testimony at 84. Winnefeld further explained that had there been a disagreement "the Secretary probably would have said: Look, get them moving anyway. And then he would be on the phone with the White House." *Id.* at 79–80.

[361] Email from State Dep't Operations Ctr. Watch Officer, to P StaffAssistants & D(N) StaffAssistants (Sept. 11, 2012 9:46 PM) (on file with the Committee, C05562037).

[362] Email to Harold Hongju Koh, *et al.* (Sept. 11, 2012 10:40 PM) (on file with the Committee, C05528017) ("There is likely to be a deployment very quickly, possibly this evening.").

[363] Email from State Dep't Operations Ctr. Watch Officer, to P StaffAssistants & D(N) StaffAssistants (Sept. 11, 2012 9:46 PM) (on file with the Committee, C05562037).

[364] Panetta Testimony at 23.

\*     \*     \*

Congressional angle: If any deployment is made, Congress will need to be notified under the War Powers Act . . . Libya must agree to any deployment.[365]

On the ground in Tripoli, the Defense Attaché had already begun working to obtain flight clearances from the Libyan government before the White House meeting even began.[366] Initially, he notified the Libyan government of a potential request for flight clearances as the night progressed.[367] Because he had given advance notice to the Libyan government that potential flight clearances would be needed, he fully expected the Libyan government to approve any formal request when it was made. He noted, however, that to submit a formal request, specific information about the tail numbers, expected arrival of the aircraft, the number of personnel, and types of weapons had to be conveyed to the Libyan government.[368] Not only did a formal request have to be made, a representative of the Libyan government had to be available to receive the paperwork for that request. There was no Libyan representative on duty overnight.[369] As to when formal approval was received, the Defense Attaché testified:

> Q: Can you recall when the actual—the relevant information that was needed, like tail numbers and things, when was that transmitted to the Government of Libya?
>
> A: I don't. But I would also come back to the fact that we had a green light from the Government of Libya to bring it in. It was just a question of when we were going to know the specific information that goes into a standard flight clearance request. So it had to have been, I would say, sometime midmorning to noon on the 12th. It could have been, I would say, sometime midmorning to noon on the 12th. It could have been a little bit after that.
>
> Q: And that's when you received the relevant information you need to pass on, or what happened?
>
> A: Probably both. In the course of the morning, leading up to the afternoon, we got the information we required, and then we were able to subsequently transmit it to the Libyans.[370]

## CIVILIAN CLOTHES

A request for the FAST Platoon to wear civilian attire appears to have generated from Kennedy during the White House meeting.[371] Kennedy, during his interview with the Committee, was unable to recall when the discussion regarding civilian attire was held

---

[365] Email from State Dep't Operations Ctr. Watch Officer, to P StaffAssistants & D(N) StaffAssistants (Sept. 11, 2012 9:46 PM) (on file with the Committee, C05562037).

[366] Testimony of Defense Attaché, U.S. Embassy Tripoli, U.S. Dep't of Defense, Tr. at 113–114 (Jan. 31, 2014) [hereinafter Defense Attaché 2014 Testimony] (on file with the Committee).

[367] Id.

[368] Id.

[369] Id. at 114.

[370] Defense Attaché Testimony at 159–160.

[371] See Email from Benjamin I. Fishman, Nat'l Sec. Council (Sept. 11, 2012 9:19 PM) (on file with the Committee, SCB000029–30).

that evening, but provided the following information about the substance of the discussion:

> [Y]ou wanted to make sure that the steps we were taking would enhance the security of our personnel, not potentially diminish the security of our personnel. Our personnel had been consolidated in Tripoli in one location, and all of them were there with the multiplied security forces of both the prime building and the Annex building. And I recall this discussion, generally speaking, and it was determined that the delay was not going to be significant and it was better to have the forces arrive in civilian clothes[.][372]

Tidd elaborated on the State Department's request for the FAST platoon to arrive in Libya in civilian clothing. He testified:

> Again, like I said, they wanted to minimize the signature that looked like a big military invasion, a big military arrival there. And the reason that I remember the discussion was I had to go back and find and make sure, as the FAST had moved out and was waiting for lift, and the question that I had to go back and ask AFRICOM was: in their rucksacks did they have civilian clothes that they could put on, or was this going to entail having to go back to their barracks and draw that equipment. They had what they needed, and so they didn't have to go anyplace.

> At the [White House] meeting, I couldn't speak for them. And I wanted to go back and verify that. Because what I wanted to know is: is it more important to get them there or to have the signature in civilian clothes? As it turned out, it didn't matter, because they had the civilian clothes with them already.[373]

Tidd did not agree that requiring the FAST platoon to wear civilian clothes was a step that would enhance security.[374] The Defense Department assessed the impact of the requirement as quite the opposite: it created an increased risk to the FAST platoon members as they traveled through Tripoli.[375]

Summaries of the White House meeting did not, in fact, highlight the potential security-enhancing benefit of the FAST platoon wearing civilian clothes. Instead, the benefit of having the FAST platoon wear civilian clothing was to cater to unexpressed Libyan government concerns about military appearances and to avoid "any impression of a U.S. invasion of Libya."[376] As Benjamin J. Rhodes,

---

[372] Kennedy Testimony at 173.

[373] Tidd Testimony at 28.

[374] *See* State Dep't Email (Sept. 11, 2012 10:40 PM) (on file with the Committee, C05528017) ("[T]here was discussion of the option of entering in plainclothes. . . .").

[375] *See id.* ("[The Joint Chiefs of Staff] explained . . . that the risks to the forces [] remaining in plainclothes increased as they transited from point of entry to the relevant location of action").

[376] Email from State Dep't Operations Ctr. Watch Officer, to P_StaffAssistants & D(N)_StaffAssistants (Sept. 11, 2012 9:46 PM) (on file with the Committee, C05562037) ("We made a request that any deployments should be in plain clothes to avoid any impression of a U.S. invasion of Libya."); *see also* State Dep't Email (Sept. 11, 2012 10:40 PM) (on file with the Committee, C05528017) ("Apparently Pat K expressed concern on the SVTC about Libyan reaction if uniformed US forces arrived in country in military aircraft"); Email from Benjamin I.

Deputy National Security Advisor for Strategic Communications, stated in an email to his colleague at the end of the meeting: "[T]he time for being overly sensitive to Libyan concerns about military appearances seems to be over."[377]

## The Plan from the Meeting

Although the Secretary told the Committee he fully expected his order to deploy was the only step needed to move forces in response to the attacks, records obtained by the Committee reflect a different understanding by others on the night of the attacks.

One email seems to indicate others may not have viewed the order as being as clear and immediate as the Secretary recalled. It read in relevant part:

> Per Amb. Mull, ROUGH notes from the 1930 [7:30 p.m.] EDT SVTC meeting:
>
> Overall theme: getting forces ready to deploy in case the crisis expands and a real threat materializes against Embassy Tripoli. DOD will send the details to U/S Kennedy (i.e. plane numbers, troop numbers, airfield support needs, etc.) for us to make requests to government of Libya (GOL).[378]
>
> There were 10 Action items from the White House meeting:

The first two action items in that email were redacted and not provided to the Committee. The next three items read as follows:

> 3) Fleet Antiterrorism Security Team (FAST): about **[redacted text]** Marines, they need six hours to prepare. They're currently at the Rota Air Base in Spain and will wait to deploy. Will not deploy until order comes to go to either Tripoli or Benghazi. We made a request that any deployments should be in plain clothes to avoid any impression of a U.S. invasion of Libya.
>
> 4) Congressional angle: If any deployment is made, Congress would need to be notified under the War Powers Act. Counselor Mills is working with L and H on this and it may come through Ops. Libya must agree to any deployment.
>
> 5) Efforts are continuing to locate Ambassador Stevens. A/S Beth Jones will work to reach out to the hospital to confirm the identity of the patient. . . .[379]

Phrases such as "getting forces ready to deploy" and forces "will not deploy until order comes to go to either Tripoli or Benghazi"

---

Fishman (Sept. 11, 2012 9:19 PM) (on file with the Committee, SCB000029–30) ("I don't know why Pat Kennedy is so concerned about what extra securit y [sic] folks are wearing. Does that come from Greg [Hicks]? The time for being overly sensitive to Libyan concerns about military appearances seems to be over.").

[377] Email from Benjamin I. Fishman (Sept. 11, 2012 9:19 PM) (on file with the Committee, SCB000029).

[378] Email from State Dep't Operations Ctr. Watch Officer, to P StaffAssistants & D(N) StaffAssistants (Sept. 11, 2012 9:46 PM) (on file with the Committee, C05562037).

[379] Id.

do not reflect an imminent deployment of the assets as ordered by the Secretary and as he testified before the Committee.

The declarative "Libya must agree to any deployment" is also inconsistent with what the Secretary testified to and similarly inconsistent with what the Secretary recalled President Obama telling him. At no point, according the Secretary of Defense, did a U.S. response to the attacks in Benghazi hinge on Libya agreeing with the actions ordered.[380]

Mull's summary of the White House meeting is, however, more consistent with Tidd's recollection of the meeting.[381]

Another email regarding the meeting with the White House reads in relevant part:

> All, I just got off a conference call with [State Department employee] who reported on a [White House meeting] this evening concerning the violence against USG facilities and personnel in Libya and Egypt, of which you likely have gotten separate notice. S[ecretary Clinton], Pat K[ennedy], and Beth Jones (possibly among others) attended for State. In short, there was a significant attack in Benghazi on the US consulate where the US Ambassador and 7 other USG employees were present[.]
>
> There is likely to be a deployment very quickly, possibly this evening, of forces to assist in Libya. Beth Jones is tasked with seeking consent of the GOL asap for entry into the country. Options under consideration for the deployment include: (1) a FAST team; (2) a [U.S.–Based SOF] . . . ; and (3) a Commander's Force. . . . DOD indicated they would circulate additional information on the options/decisions in the morning and we will need to be prepared to do a quick War Powers assessment and probably report by COB tomorrow.
>
> \*  \*  \*
>
> Apparently Pat K[ennedy] expressed concern on the [White House meeting] about Libyan reaction if uniformed US forces arrived in country in military aircraft; there was discussion of the option of entering in plainclothes, which JCS explained was possible but noted that the risks to the forces to remaining in plainclothes increased as they transited from point of entry to the relevant location of action.[382]

Another email framed the issue as follows:

> The U.S. military has begun notifying special units of likely deployment, with ultimate disposition pending State coordination with the Libyan government and final approval by the White House.
>
> State remains concerned that any U.S. military intervention be fully coordinated with the Libyan Government and

[380] Panetta Testimony at 67.
[381] Email from State Dep't Operations Ctr. Watch Officer, to P StaffAssistants & D(N) StaffAssistants (Sept. 11, 2012 9:46 PM) (on file with the Committee, C05562037).
[382] State Dep't Email (Sept. 11, 2012 10:40 PM) (on file with the Committee, C05528017).

convey Libyan concerns that [sic] about U.S. military presence, to include concerns that wheeled military vehicles should not be used and U.S. Military Forces should consider deploying in civilian attire.[383]

The plan described in this email was later conveyed to the Combatant Commands. While Bash's "spinning up" email indicated these forces were prepared to go to Benghazi vice Tripoli, it was clear by the end of the White House meeting that no forces were going to Benghazi.[384] It is worth noting that while this meeting was ongoing and even after it ended, Diplomatic Security Agents, the team from the Annex, and Team Tripoli were under attack at the Annex and Stevens was still missing.

These emails confirm the understanding among the individuals participating in the White House meeting that deployment to Benghazi was not imminent. As the Defense Department timeline shows, none of the orders given to the assets that night contained an order to deploy to Benghazi.[385] The FAST platoons were ordered to prepare to deploy, not to deploy.[386] The CIF and the U.S. based SOF were ordered to deploy only to an intermediate staging base, not to Benghazi or Tripoli.[387]

In fact, once the decision to activate the U.S. based SOF was made, the CIF was no longer an option to deploy to Libya as its mission then became to prepare for the arrival of the U.S. based Special Operations Force at the intermediate staging base.

Once the forces were ready to deploy, a subsequent execute order would then have to be given by the Secretary of Defense. This is inconsistent with the Secretary's belief that no further order was necessary from either the President or himself.

Admiral Tidd had this to say about deploying a FAST Team to Benghazi:

> We were looking at two FAST teams, but it very, very soon became evident that everybody was leaving Benghazi. And so I don't remember if it was just before the [White House meeting] or during the [meeting] or just right after. By the time we came out of the [meeting], it was pretty clear that nobody was going to be left in Benghazi. And so the decision—I think, at the [meeting], there was some discussion—but as I recall, we weren't going to send them to Benghazi, because everybody was going to be back in Tripoli by the time we could actually get them there.
>
>        *     *     *
>
> And I think even at this point we knew that everybody had moved—they had moved from the temporary diplomatic facility, they moved to the Annex, and they were moving or going to be moving, if they had not already

[383] Testimony of Jeremy Bash, Chief of Staff, U.S. Dep't of Defense, Tr. at 98–99 (Jan. 13, 2016) [hereinafter Bash Testimony] (on file with the Committee).

[384] Email from Jeremy Bash, Chief of Staff, U.S. Dep't of Defense, to Jacob Sullivan, Deputy Chief of Staff for Policy, U.S. Dep't of State (Sept. 11, 2012 1919) (on file with the Committee: STATE–SCB0060705).

[385] See generally, U.S. Dep't of Defense Timeline.

[386] Id.

[387] Id.

begun moving, from the Annex to the airport, and would be leaving at the airport as quickly as they could.

So it was pretty clear we weren't going to be able to get anything into Benghazi before the last people left. So, I don't think we ever went beyond the notion of moving the FAST into—the FAST platoon into Tripoli.[388]

While it may have been "pretty clear" to Tidd that "nobody was going to be left in Benghazi," it was not at all clear to those in Benghazi who were manning a rooftop exchanging gunfire with attackers.[389] Furthermore, the Diplomatic Security Agents and team from the Annex had to fight their way even from the Benghazi Mission compound to the Annex a short distance away while Team Tripoli had to negotiate with unknown militias for transportation from the Benghazi airport to the Annex. So, how the principals in Washington were certain U.S. personnel in Benghazi were going to be leaving Benghazi and how they were going to be leaving is itself unclear.

There is uncertainty attached to other statements made during the White House meeting too:

"State remains concerned that any U.S. military intervention be fully coordinated with the Libyan Government and convey Libyan concerns that [sic] about U.S. military presence, to include concerns that wheeled military vehicles should not be used and U.S. Military Forces should consider deploying in civilian attire."

"DOD indicated they would circulate additional information on the options/decisions in the morning and we will need to be prepared to do a quick War Powers assessment and probably report by COB tomorrow."

"Libya must agree to any deployment."

"Overall theme: getting forces ready to deploy in case the crisis expands and a real threat materializes against Embassy Tripoli."

This sentence is illuminating on a number of levels, including: "getting forces ready to deploy in case the crisis expands" begs the question of expanding how and where? At the time of the White House meeting, Sean Smith was dead, Ambassador Stevens was missing, and the remaining State Department personnel had to be rescued by the Team from the Annex while sustaining gunfire en route back to the Annex. Moreover the second clause in that sentence references a "real threat" materializing against "Embassy Tripoli." The real threat at the time was and remained in Benghazi.

Among the questions left even in the aftermath of investigating what happened before, during and after the attacks in Benghazi is how so many decision makers in Washington and elsewhere were unaware of the Annex in Benghazi and how the Washington decision-makers expected U.S. personnel remaining in Benghazi to

[388] Tidd Testimony at 25–27.
[389] Id. at 25–27.

evacuate or defend themselves for a prolonged period of time without assistance.

## The Orders: Prepare to Deploy and Deploy to an ISB

At 8:39 p.m., more than five hours after the attacks in Benghazi began and more than two hours after the Secretary gave his order to deploy, the Pentagon finally transmitted orders to the combatant commands regarding the FAST platoons, the CIF, and the U.S. Based Special Operations Force.[390] Specifically, the FAST platoons were ordered to "prepare to deploy."[391] The CIF and the U.S. Based Special Operations Force were ordered to deploy to an intermediate staging base.[392] No asset was ordered to deploy to Benghazi.[393]

Tidd provided authorization for each of those forces to move in an email transmitting the orders at 8:53 p.m. [2:53 a.m. in Benghazi]. The email reads in relevant part:

> discussions at Deputies, and followed up between [the Office of the Secretary of Defense] and the Chairman——
>
> [The Secretary of Defense] has directed deployment of the CIF to the [intermediate staging base] determined most suitable by AFRICOM . . .
>
> [The Secretary of Defense] has directed deployment of the [U.S. Based Special Operations Force] to the same [intermediate staging base] as the CIF.
>
> [The Secretary of Defense] has directed FAST to make all preps to deploy but hold departure until we are sure we have clearance to land in Tripoli. We'll work with State to nail that down, but intent is to get security force augmentation into [Tripoli/Tripoli] (not Benghazi, at least not initially) ASAP. Embassy making efforts to move all [American citizens] from [Annex] Compound Benghazi to Tripoli, possibly using same [commercial] Air that 5-pax team arrived on.
>
> \* \* \*
>
> Remember [the Secretary of Defense] holds final approval to deploy FAST, pending receipt of Tripoli country clearance. But the point is to get the Marines on the ground se-

---

[390] Email from Tidd (Sept. 11, 2012 8:53PM) (on file with the Committee, SCB001376). *See also,* Letter from Ashton B. Carter, Sec'y of Defense, to Trey Gowdy, Chairman, House Select Committee on Benghazi, Apr. 8, 2015, providing an explanation regarding the unclassified timeline:

> Has the U.S Department of Defense identified any information that would warrant any adjustments, correction or modification to the unclassified timeline it provide to Congress on November 9, 2012?

> One Point of clarification: the unclassified timeline has the SecDef Vocal Order (VOCO) for moving response forces at 0000–0200. This authorization was relayed and recorded at 0239 for FAST and CIF and at 0253 for [the U.S. SOF]. This is not to imply that timing of the VOCO as reflected in the unclassified timeline is inaccurate, but rather that receipt of this vocal order at [sic] was at 0239 and 0253, respectively.").

[391] *Id.*

[392] *Id.*

[393] *Id.*

curing the embassy in Tripoli as rapidly as we can move them.[394]

Tidd testified about his email:

> I'm looking at the timelines here, and I'm—I am thinking that—that [Deputy Director for Operations] had a conference call with the various watch centers of the commands that are listed here as a result of the decisions that came out of the [White House] meeting.
>
> And so the things that you see upfront—the [Secretary of Defense] [vocal order], the things to move, and then also forwarded request for information from AFRICOM and EUCOM for the following—I am guessing at this point now, but I think this might have been in response to—I gave him a verbal dump from the Deputies Committee meeting. He had this conference call. This is a report back with the information from the conference call. And then I turned around and replied on top of that with subsequent information that had been provided from phone calls that I had had at the same time.[395]

Winnefeld also provided his understanding of Tidd's email:

> All this is doing is reporting out what the Secretary has directed to do. And [Tidd] would not put this out unless the deputies had concurred with it. If the deputies had not concurred with the SecDef deciding to do these things, that would have been a big issue, but it wasn't. The deputies obviously concurred, so [Tidd] put it out: Hey, this is now official; Secretary says do this.[396]

It is unclear why concurrence from anyone attending the White House meeting was needed. The National Command Authority, the lawful source of military orders, consists of two people: the President and the Secretary of Defense.[397] Neither of them attended that meeting. Both the President and Secretary Panetta had already issued their orders. As the Secretary made clear:

> I had the authority to deploy those forces. And I ordered those forces to be deployed. And I didn't have to ask anybody's permission to get those forces in place.[398]

### PREPARE TO DEPLOY

The orders issued to the forces that night were different from the orders the Secretary gave earlier that evening. The Secretary had this to say about the orders he issued that night:

---

[394] Id.

[395] Tidd Testimony at 33.

[396] Winnefeld Testimony at 85. Winnefeld further explained that had there been a disagreement "the Secretary probably would have said: Look, get them moving anyway. And then he would be on the phone with the White house." Id. at 87.

[397] See Panetta Testimony at 32. Panetta elaborated, "My directions were clear; those forces were to be deployed, period. . . . So I wanted no interference with those orders to get them deployed." Id. at 33.

[398] Id.

Q: I just want to make sure this portion of the record is fair to you and that your testimony has the clarity that I think it has, but I'm going to give you an opportunity if I'm wrong.

You did not issue an order to prepare to deploy. You issued an order to deploy.

A: That's correct.

Q: So no one would have been waiting on you to issue a subsequent order?

A: That's correct.[399]

Leidig described the difference between a "prepare to deploy" order and an "execute" order:

They are two very distinct orders in the military. The first is prepare to deploy. And that's basically guidance from my boss, in this case, the Secretary of Defense and the Chairman, that you have permission to make every preparation necessary to execute this mission. But you do not have permission to actually to deploy them yet—you don't have permission to execute the mission.[400]

In contrast, Miller testified his understanding was an order to deploy has no operational distinction from an order to prepare to deploy:

The initial order was to deploy to forward basing in order to be able to then refuel if necessary, prepare to any additional degree necessary, which can largely be done in flight for these forces, to the extent that they weren't already as they got on the plane, and then to deploy into Libya.

[T]he order could have come in one of two ways, and it's a technical difference that in this instance and in any other instance has no operational impact, one form of the order says deploy to the intermediate staging base and prepare to deploy into Libya, and that additional authorization will be given prior to deployment into Libya; a second says deploy to the intermediate staging base and proceed to Libya unless given direction not to do so.

I don't know which of those—I don't recall which of those was in the order, but in any event, it's well understood that no time should elapse awaiting. In other words, if the form was to go to the ISB, go to the intermediate staging base and then get additional authority, it's incumbent on the commander to request that authority well in advance of when the force would be prepared to then deploy into Libya, and it's incumbent on the Secretary of Defense and the team supporting him to ensure that he makes a timely

---

[399] *Id.* at 49.
[400] Leidig 2014 Testimony at 64–65.

decision so that there's not additional time added to the timeline.[401]

Bash considered the orders that night a distinction without a difference because the intent of the Secretary was clear: the forces were to move.

> This was a real-time, very fluid, very dynamic set of meetings in which the Secretary, with his senior military, uniformed military advisers, the Chairman, the Vice, and the combatant commanders and others, were making real-time decisions

> So I just want to set that context, because I'm sure some people could look at this and say: Why were these words used or that discussion or this phrase used, "prepare to deploy" or "deploy"? My recollection was he was told of the situation, he was told about which units could respond, and he said: Go get them, do it, move.

> Q: So there would've been no further order necessary from him?

> A: Correct.

> Q: Wheels could have taken off and he would not have had to say another single, solitary word?

> A: Correct, and I believe that actually was the case.

> Q: All right. So he never amplified, clarified, withdrew, changed his instructions, which were deploy?

> A: He did not.[402]

Leidig, whom Ham described as his "most trusted advisor" and an "extraordinarily competent officer," testified because he was moving forces between two combatant commands' areas of responsibility he needed to receive a subsequent "execute" order to move the FAST Platoon into Libya.[403]

> Q: At what point did you receive an order to execute? At what point did you have the authority to launch assets into Libya?

> A: We were never given an execute order to move any forces until we got to move in the C–17 to evacuate folks out of Tripoli later that next morning. There was never an execute order to move any forces from Sigonella into Africa or from Rota into Africa until later. So, I mean, we did get an order eventually to move the FAST team into Tripoli to provide security, but during that evening hour, that incident, there were no execute orders to move forces into our AOR.

---

[401] Miller Testimony at 80–81.
[402] Bash Testimony at 26–27.
[403] *See* Ham Testimony at 51–52.

\* \* \*

Q: You said that you were never given an execute order until later. Who provides that execute order?

A: Execute order comes from the Secretary of Defense. So we were not given an—there was an order given to move forces to Sigonella. There was never an execute order given to move those forces into Libya.

Q: And when you received the execute order later on to deploy the forces into Libya, the FAST platoon into Tripoli, and then the C–17 to evacuate the medically injured, do you recall how that order was conveyed?

A: Do you mean, was it verbal, or was it in—usually in every case—I don't know specifically for those, but normally it's a VOCO, a vocal command, followed up by a written command. And so, in that case, it was probably both. It was probably a vocal command to get things moving, followed by a written command——

Q: And do you——

A: —but I don't know for sure.

Q: And do you recall the timeframe for when you received the vocal command to execute the movement of the FAST platoon into Tripoli and the——

A: No, I don't recall. It's on the timeline.

Q: Do you recall if it was before or after the mortar attacks occurred?

A: Oh, it was after.

Q: Okay. Thank you.

\* \* \*

Q: And just to be clear for the record, prior to receiving the vocal execute order, would you have——

A: Which vocal execute order?

Q: For either of the assets that were deployed into Libya, the FAST platoon or the C–17, did you have the authority to move those assets into Libya prior to receiving that VOCO?

A: No. I wouldn't move those without a—without an order from the Secretary or the Chairman. They're moving across COCOM boundaries.

Q: Okay. Thank you.[404]

Ham's recollection of the extent of the authority he had to move forces that night differed from Leidig and differed from the email

---

[404] Testimony of Vice Admiral Charles J. Leidig, Deputy Commander for Military Operations, US Africa Command, Tr. at 45–48 (Apr. 22, 2016) [hereinafter Leidig 2016 Testimony] (on file with the Committee). *But see,* Leidig 2016 Testimony at 48 (Q: There was some discussion about the term "prepare to deploy" and an "execute order," and I just wanted to ask you a couple questions about that. Would a lack of an execute order, or did a lack of an execute order on the night of the attacks ever slow down your forces? A: No.).

Tidd sent to the combatant commands relaying the Secretary's order.

Q: Can you explain what he means by the [Secretary of Defense] holding final approval to deploy FAST?

A: I think it means what it says. That is different than my recollection. Again, my belief is the Secretary had given authority to me to do that. So I think this is the J3 issuing instructions, but my recollection is different than what Vice Admiral Tidd has written here.

\* \* \*

Yeah. Right. The last sentence there I think is the important one.

\* \* \*

A: "But the point is to get the Marines on the ground securing the embassy in Tripoli as rapidly as we can move them."

Q: Well, I think one thing that we would like to try to kind of marry up is, even on the timeline, the orders that were given to some of the—specifically the FAST platoon was a prepare-to-deploy order. And there has been testimony that a prepare-to-deploy order is different from a deploy order. Perhaps you can provide us what the distinction is and how that played out on this night.

A: I can try to explain the distinction between the two. A prepare-to-deploy order simply is notifying a force that you must be prepared to deploy within a specified timeframe, so that you have to adjust your activities, whatever they may be, your personnel posture, your readiness, your training, the prestaging of equipment, depending on what the timeline is, so that you are prepared to deploy on the designated timeline. This is not an uncommon occurrence.

\* \* \*

And a deploy order simply says, "Go now," or whatever the specified timeframe is. So it's prepare to deploy, "I think I may need you, so I want you to be ready." A deploy order says, "I do need you. Deploy."

\* \* \*

So the three units that were of highest importance to me—the Commander's In-extremis Force, the Fleet Antiterrorism Security Team, and the [U.S.-Based SOF]—all already had prepared to—my understanding is all had prepared to deploy. They were already on various timelines to deploy. So that's what I believe their status was.

And my belief is that—and my recollection differs a bit from what Vice Admiral Tidd says—that when the Secretary made his decisions, my understanding of that was that the Secretary of Defense was transferring operational control to me for those forces for their deployment and employment.

Q: So if the Secretary of Defense's order was, in fact, "prepare to deploy" and not "deploy," was there an additional step needed to be—did the Secretary of Defense have to do anything additional to deploy those forces?

A: I don't know because I'm not familiar with the specifics. Typically, in a prepare-to-deploy order, there is a designated official who can order that unit to deploy. It doesn't always have to go back to the Secretary of Defense. It could be a combatant commander, it could be the Chairman of the Joint Chiefs, it could be a joint task force commander. But, in this particular case, I'm just not familiar with the specifics of the order.[405]

## DEPLOY TO AN ISB

The CIF, the force most capable of quickly responding to the attacks in Benghazi, was ordered instead to go to an intermediate staging base. Ham discussed this decision:

Q: Sir, given the fact that the CIF was on the continent, per se, did you ever consider employing the CIF for the hostage-rescue mission or the NEO by sending them directly to either Benghazi or to Tripoli?

A: I don't recall specifically, but I feel confident in saying that, as we weighed the options, the various courses of action of how the Commander's In-extremis Force might be employed, that there was some consideration to, you know, do they go somewhere other than the intermediate staging base. Should they go to Benghazi? Should they go to Tripoli?

My recollection is that the situation was certainly evolving. And, as previously discussed, my view was the situation, after an initial spike, the fighting had largely subsided, that Benghazi was probably not the right place for them to go. Get them to the staging base, where we now have many, many options.

One of the challenges, of course, is with a force like the Commander's In-extremis Force, once you operationally employ it someplace—so if you were to deploy into any place and they're on the ground, you now no longer have that force for other emergent contingencies. So we're very careful about making a decision as to where to go.

There are other complexities with inserting a force into Benghazi, to be sure, but, for me, it was, where's the best place for that force to be right now? And, in my view, I believe that—you know, certainly supported and with recommendations from the AFRICOM operations and intelligence staff—that the best place for them would be at the

---

[405] Ham Testimony at 133–136.

intermediate staging base so that they would be well-postured for subsequent missions.[406]

Tidd testified one reason the CIF and the U.S. SOF were ordered to an intermediate staging base and not to Libya directly was due to concerns expressed by the State Department regarding the number of military personnel that would arrive in country.[407] He testified:

Q: Sir, was it your decision, then, to send them back to an ISB first?

A: Yes . . . State was very, very concerned about what the footprint would look like in Tripoli. They didn't want it to look like we were invading.

That was the gist or that was the genesis of the discussion that occurred over whether or not when the FAST arrives at the airport in Tripoli—because they wanted to reinforce security at the embassy—but there was concern that it not have this image of a big, invading force.

And we knew that the FAST, when it arrived, did not have its own mobility. The embassy was going to have to provide trucks and vehicles to move them from the airport to the embassy. And there was just concern of parading a bunch of trucks or buses full of Marines in uniform, what kind of image that would present, recognizing it was going to be daylight when they arrived.[408]

## TEAM TRIPOLI NEGOTIATES TRANSPORTATION

Team Tripoli left the airport at approximately 4:30 a.m. A team member provided the committee the following background information for their intended mission at the time, as it had transitioned from locating and potentially rescuing Stevens to an effort to start evacuating nonessential personnel from Benghazi back to Tripoli.

Q: What did you understand about your mission as you were heading from Benina airport to the Annex? Was your mission then evacuation of nonessential personnel?

A: It was nonessential personnel only prior to the mortar attack happening . . . we were going to take 14 personnel back with us to the airport, let the jet take off, take them back to Tripoli. We were going to come back to the Annex and help hold up with the GRS guys until further notice . . . the majority of those people [the GRS] would have stayed there. Shooters, if you will. . . . We did not make the decisions for that [airplane] to come back. We didn't know how long we were going to have to stay at the Annex. We were under the understanding they wanted to stay. They did not want to leave. So we were just trying to get the nonessential personnel out to get further direction from Chief of Station back in Tripoli on what he want-

---

[406] Id. at 93–94.
[407] Tidd Testimony at 24.
[408] Id. at 22–23.

ed them to do . . . I believe it was the Chief of Base that wanted to keep some individuals there.[409]

## FINAL STAGES OF THE ATTACK

### Team Tripoli at the Annex

After Team Tripoli secured transportation, it arrived at the Annex just after 5:05 a.m. Former U.S. Navy SEAL Glen A. Doherty, one of the members of Team Tripoli, immediately joined Tyrone S. Woods, Diplomatic Security Agent 4, and other GRS agents on the rooftops of the Annex buildings. Within 10 minutes of the arrival of Team Tripoli, a new small arms attack began. One member of Team Tripoli described the small arms attack:

> Once we had gotten to the annex, we called probably three minutes out, and the GRS Team Lead was actually out there to meet us with the gate open. We didn't take any of the vehicles inside. We exited the vehicles and walked inside.

> We took the Libyan Shield commander inside with us so his guys would stay there, ultimately. Went directly to the main house where the TOC was. I think it was Building Three. Team leader started talking to chief of base, and I was talking to the [GRS Team Lead] on the security situation, wounded personnel, what did he need from us that he didn't have already, and how we could help the security posture.

> Shortly after us being there, we were all sitting outside while we were talking about this on the front patio of Building Three. We had some sporadic gunfire over the top of Building Three, and immediately following, the first mortar round hit. I believe it went long, hit out in the road where our convoy had been. The gate is obviously closed to the compound now. Next one hit short just behind Building Three on the wall towards the warehouse. The other three or four mortars hit directly on top of Building Three.[410]

One GRS agent described the mortar attack:

> It was about 5:30 in the morning—the sun was just coming up—because me and Tyrone had been talking about, you know, if they're going to attack us, it's going to happen here shortly because usually the time to attack is right before the sun comes up. About that time, [Doherty] came up on the roof after the guys from Tripoli had came in. I never met [Doherty]. He walks over to Tyrone and says hi to Tyrone. They had worked together on the teams. Tyrone introduced him to me, said that he was a sniper.

> I told him: Well, that's good. I hope we don't need you, but it will be great having another rifle up here.

---

[409] Special Operators Testimony at 65.
[410] *Id.* at 61.

He had turned to walk away, and it was about that time that there was an explosion against the back wall, and there was a mortar that hit the top of the back wall, which from our building was maybe 8 or 10 yards from the building.

[Agent 4] was in the corner where the ladder was at. Me and Tyrone were in the opposite corner facing out towards what we call Zombieland, and when that hit, small arms fire started coming from that direction, and Tyrone opened up with a machine gun. I started shooting with my assault rifle. I heard [Agent 4] yell out that he was hit.

I kind of glanced over. I saw his shadow sitting because the wall at the top of our building was about 3 feet tall, so there was a box that you had to step on to get up on to the ladder. So he was—I saw his image or the silhouette of him sitting on that box, and he was holding his head. What went through my mind is that he's breathing, so his heart is beating . . .

We're shooting. I kneel down to change magazines. As I come back up after changing magazines, the first mortar hits the top of the roof, hits almost directly into the wall, where the roof and the arc of the parapet or wall comes up, right into the corner of that. When that hit, it blew me back a little bit, knocked me back. I kind of caught myself. I saw Tyrone go down. . . . The mortar hit on my right.

As I come up, I bring my arm up to grab my gun, and from about here down, it was kind of hanging off at a 90 degree angle. I continued to try to grab my gun. Another mortar hit, and I kind of glanced over my right shoulder, and I saw [Doherty] go straight down. . . . As I tried to keep firing, my weapon is pretty much inoperable. I can't grab it with my hand. The third mortar hits and peppers me again with shrapnel. The best way I can describe it is it felt like I got stung by a thousand bees. At that point, I figured I might better get to cover because if another one comes, I'll be lucky if I survive that.

I kind of dove down to the wall, . . . and everything had went quiet. I kind of sat up and thought I was bleeding out because everything was wet around me. I realized that it was water because it was cold, and there was a water tank right there beside us that had gotten perforated. I don't know what the timeframe was.

I pulled out a tourniquet, and I was trying to get the tourniquet on. . . . At that point, I saw [GRS 1] come up over top of the roof, which I didn't know it then—I saw a shadow come up, and at that point, he had at first put two tourniquets on [Agent 4]; one on his leg, one on his arm. Then he come over to me, and he was sitting there. He told me to quit messing with my arm because I was trying to put it back in place. He grabbed my tourniquet, put it on, stood me up, and asked if I could walk myself over to the ladder so he could tend to Tyrone and [Doherty], and I said, yeah.

He had called for help on the radio, that we had wounded up there. By the time I got over to the ladder, there was three guys that had come up on the roof. I remember one later to find out it was one of the TF or the task force guys. He asked me if I could get off the roof.

I said, "Yeah, I'm going to have to" because I knew they had to tend to the guys up there. So I kind of put myself up on the parapet, hooked my good arm around the ladder, and kind of scooted myself over. I ended up climbing down the ladder.

I come around past the swimming pool to the front, and that's when I ran into [GRS Tripoli]. [GRS Tripoli] walked me in, laid me down in the building, building 3, and he went back—I think at that time, he went back out to help up top. Everybody inside was just kind of looking at me. I told them somebody needs to cut my clothes off because I know I'm bleeding from other spots. **[redacted text]** case officer I was with earlier that night, **[redacted text]**, asked me where the shears were. **[redacted text]** to cut my clothes off with. **[redacted text]** got those, come back, cut my clothes off. I wasn't bleeding profusely from anything else; I just had a bunch of little holes in me that were kind of oozing blood. And later they came down. I think [GRS Tripoli] came in and gave me an IV. They finally got [Diplomatic Security Agent 4] off, and that was pretty much the night there.[411]

As GRS agents on Building 3 fired back in response to the new attack, a well-aimed mortar attack commenced on the Annex mortally wounding Woods and Doherty and severely wounding another GRS agent and one Diplomatic Security Agent.[412]

In total, six 81-millimeter mortars assaulted the Annex.[413] Three mortars, including the first one, landed near the north perimeter wall. Three additional mortars landed on the roof of Building 3 within one minute at 5:18 a.m. Overall, the six mortar attacks were launched within 1 minute and 13 seconds.[414] A member of Team Tripoli testified:

Once the mortar round—the first mortar round hit outside the gate where the convoy was, we saw the vehicles driving away, the gun trucks that were out there driving away.[415]

Libya Shield sub-commander, **[redacted text]**, who was left behind during the mortar strike suggested, that attackers were well-aware that Team Tripoli was held up at the Benghazi airport while seeking transport and that the attackers may have planned an am-

---

[411] GRS 2 Testimony at 57.
[412] Video: DVR Footage of the CIA Annex (Sept. 11, 2012, 0517.40).
[413] Special Operator Testimony at 61.
[414] Committee analysis of DVR Footage of the CIA Annex (Sept. 11, 2012, from 0517 to 0519).
[415] Special Operator Testimony at 66.

bush that coincided with the arrival of the Team Tripoli members at the Annex:

> "It began to rain down on us. I really believe that this attack was planned. The accuracy with which the mortars hit us was too good for any regular revolutionaries."[416]

One witness told the Committee Libya Shield departed the Annex when the mortar strike began at the direction of an individual who was standing next to Abu Khattala during the attacks. He recounted what happened during the mortar attack:

> Q: When Team Tripoli arrived, were you outside? Were you inside?
>
> A: No, when they arrived, I was outside.
>
> Q: You were outside. Okay. And did you go inside at any point after they arrived?
>
> A: Yes. Luckily we went inside, because then the mortars landed.
>
> *     *     *
>
> Q: Did anybody from the Libyan Shield militia go inside as well?
>
> A: Yes.
>
> Q: All right. And can you explain the situation?
>
> A: When the Tripoli team arrived, they brought with them a commander of that force that escorted them from the airport to the Annex.
>
> Q: Okay. And he ended up going inside one of the villas?
>
> A: Yes.
>
> *     *     *
>
> I asked him to shut off his phone and stop talking on the phone after the mortar—especially specifically after the mortar landed.
>
> *     *     *
>
> He was talking to his force and wondering why they left him behind and informed them that we had just got hit with mortars, and he was trying to find out why they left him behind.[417]

The witness stated the Commander of the force was frantic and was "surprised that the attack took place when he thought that his force outside was securing the perimeter."[418] He testified about the Commander's actions:

> When he came inside, he was under the impression that the force that he brought with him, the commander that

---

[416] *Libya Rescue Squad Ran Into Fierce, Accurate Ambush*, Reuters (Sept. 12, 2012; 17:11), http://www.reuters.com/article/libya-ambassador-battle-idAFL5E8KCMYB20120912.

[417] Officer A Testimony at 118.

[418] *Id.*

he left behind and his forces will secure the area. But when he called them on the phone, he realized they had departed the area. And he asked them, why did you depart the area? And they said that the commander of the militia, Wissam bin Hamid, gave them orders to return to their base on the other side of town. And he asked them, why are you going back to the base and leaving me behind? And they told him that, oh, we are going to get more weapons and more additional forces.[419]

Wissam bin Hamid was standing with Abu Khattala during the attack[.][420]

One GRS member of Team Tripoli provided his assessment of the mortar attacks in an after-action interview conducted by the CIA. The GRS member was:

100% confident that the enemy was waiting for the QRF to arrive at the Annex so they could hit them upon arrival. Communication was given to local militias and police upon the arrival of the QRF team to Benghazi airport. Many Libyan militia members and police knew of the QRF team's arrival and movement to the annex.

He [was] confident it was a well-trained mortar team that hit the compound.[421]

A military member of Team Tripoli described his assessment of the mortar attacks that evening:

Q: And so what's your opinion on the skill of those who were actually employing the mortars that evening in the attack on the Benghazi Annex?

A: I would say personally that it was probably a skilled mortar team. It's not easy. And you, being a trained mortar man, know how hard that would be to shoot inside the city and get something on the target within two shots. That's difficult. I would say they were definitely a trained mortar team or had been trained to do something similar to that . . . I was kind of surprised. I had not heard of or seen anybody or talked to anyone that had been trained on mortars at all [during my time in Tripoli]. So it was unusual.[422]

The mortar attack was reported at 5:32 a.m. and a medical evacuation was requested.[423]

One CIA agent discussed his actions:

A: [M]inutes later is when we got attacked by the first few mortars.

Q: And you were in the SCIF when the mortar attack happened?

A: The initial, correct, yes, sir.

---

[419] *Id.*
[420] *Id.*
[421] CIA Document 1–004067 at 71.
[422] Special Operator Testimony at 82–83.
[423] DSCC Timeline.

Q: Well, actually I was trying to go to the bathroom; so I put my gear back on, and we were all stacked at the front door, myself, the team leader, the two DOD personnel, and there were several more volleys of impacts on the building, mortar fire. And I heard small arms going out from our team, and then small arms coming in on our building. And as soon as it subsided, I asked for [GRS Agent] because . . . he had [s]ome of my gear . . . and that's when he didn't answer up. And that's when one of the other GRS personnel said they were all down on the roof. So as soon as it subsided, we made our way to the roof.

Q: Okay, and then what actions did you take at that point?

A: I came around a few seconds after the main element . . . so I stepped back . . . and that's when I was met halfway down the ladder by the GRS operator [GRS 2]. And I put my light on him because I heard a funny noise, and it was obvious that he was severely injured. And that's when he came down on top of me. I noticed he was severely wounded, bleeding a lot and everything like that.

\* \* \*

Well, they actually put bathroom tile outside there, and so it was real slick. He ended up falling on top of me, and I ended up hyperextending my leg to the rear. So now I'm injured, so I drug him out because we started getting hit by small arms fire. So I dragged him around the corner. I started putting a tourniquet on his arm. He was bleeding from his left arm. He had a hole in his neck, and he had a hole in his chest.

So I put tourniquets on his arm and started patching up with the help of others from the shrapnel wounds. And it seemed like seconds later when I heard somebody say [GRS Tripoli] I have another one for you. That's when the second State Department guy, [Agent 4] . . . came down. And I pushed [GRS 2] up on to the couch, and that's when [Agent 4] was there.

\* \* \*

So I readjusted the tourniquet on his right leg, put another one on his right leg, and ended up putting a tourniquet on his left arm and packing his neck with combat gauze to help stop the bleeding. I ended up starting an IV on him. And then I went back to [GRS 2], put an IV in him. That's one of the State Department personnel—I don't know who it was—had morphine, and I made the call to give [Agent 4] morphine because he was in so much pain he started pawing at the tourniquets and the gauzes, some of the dressings I put on. And that seemed like seconds.

During this process is when **[redacted text]** asked me to . . . contact Tripoli and give them a SITREP. That's when I called Tripoli . . . [and] asked them for blood for [Agent

4] because I didn't think he was going to make it much longer.

\* \* \*

We had two severely injured, so I asked for blood, because I thought our plane, the one we rented, had taken off already. . . . And then, right after that, I went back in, made sure both patients were stable, and I worked on [Agent 4] more. I started another IV because he had sucked that one down so fast. And that's when I went outside, and the sun was actually up. I know it doesn't sound significant, but it was to me because I really felt with the sun up, it would give us time, room to breath, because hopefully it would drive away the attackers.

I was still handling care of the patients . . . And I was in the back of the truck with the wounded GRS guy because I had no—there was no more room to sit inside a vehicle, so we put a stretcher in the back of a small truck. I jumped in the back with him and held on to him, and we drove out the gate; and that's when we were met by several gun trucks and militia that were there to escort us. And we drove out, and it looked to be several militias or several different groups because it looked like they were trying to determine which way they were going to go to the airport.

So there was a few minutes delay there before we actually started to drive towards the airport. And that's when we made it back to the airport. And I loaded on a plane with the nonessential personnel, and the two wounded, and made it back to Tripoli where we landed in Tripoli because the hospital was close to the Tripoli airport.

\* \* \*

I gave [Agent 4] another morphine on the plane. I adjusted [GRS 2] bandage. And then when I was moving [Agent 4] off the plane—we were bring him off without the stretcher because the stretcher was so big and the plane was so small—he stopped breathing, so I had to give him CPR. Got him back breathing, and that's when the State Department nurse met me on the plane. . . .

And then we loaded them on to an ambulance, and at that point, the ambulance took them to Afia Hospital in Tripoli. And I went back in a Suburban with all the other State Department personnel and gear. And that was it. I received a call from the flight medic from Ramstein, the military airlift, and I went over the view of what I did and what I gave them as far as tourniquets, morphine, and IV bags, how much, and the times and stuff. And that was it in reference to my medical service.

Q: You said they asked if the patients were capable of going directly to Germany. Was that the request?

A: I believe, yeah. And I said, no, they need to go to the hospital now. This is when I just got [Agent 4] breathing again. But I made the suggestion, you know, I remember they said can they wait for the Ramstein bird. And I was like no, because I really think [the agent] was going to die any minute.

Q: We're coming close to the end of our hour. This is the last question. Setting modesty aside, do you believe that [the agent] or [GRS 2] would have survived to make it to Tripoli without your intervention?

A: No. [424]

## At the Time of the Mortar Attacks, No Asset was rn route to Libya

At 11:45 p.m. in Washington [5:45 a.m. in Benghazi], Denis R. McDonough sent an email to Sullivan, Sherman, Rhodes, Bash, Winnefeld, and other high level representatives of the Executive Branch with the subject line, "Quick level set before we head into tomorrow AM SVTC." [425] McDonough wrote:

The situation in Benghazi remains fluid. Amb. Chris Stevens remains unaccounted for; one State Department officer is confirmed dead (next of kin notification is complete); five State Department officers are accounted for and at another USG compound in Benghazi, which had been taking fire earlier in the evening (until at least 2030 EDT). . . . Five DOD personnel arrived in Benghazi about an hour ago from Tripoli to reinforce security there.

On our people in Libya, the Joint Staff is deploying three sets of teams into the region appropriate to the mission(s).

\* \* \*

And on getting the video(s) in question taken down, I reached [out] to YouTube to ask them to take down two videos: one that was not developed by Pastor Jones but which he is promoting, and another—of him burning the Prophet in effigy—that he did film. Sec. Panetta has also reached out to Pastor Jones to ask him to pull down his video, knowing that even if YouTube takes the video down, Pastor Jones can put it up somewhere else. . . .[426]

This McDonough email was sent more than six hours after President Obama and the Secretary first met to discuss the initial attack in Benghazi, more than six hours after the Commander in Chief said to do everything possible to help our people, more than five hours after the Secretary of Defense issued an order to deploy elements—active tense—and more than four hours after the Secretary's Chief of Staff sent an email saying elements were "spinning up." McDonough writes: "[T]he Joint Staff is deploying three

---

[424] Officer A Testimony at 37–46.
[425] Email from Denis R. McDonough to Wendy R. Sherman, *et al.* (Sept. 11, 2012 11:45 PM) (on file with the Committee, C05562167).
[426] *Id.*

sets of teams into the region appropriate to the mission(s)." [427] This "deploying" was supposed to occur hours earlier at the order of the Secretary.

Moreover, McDonough references "five DOD personnel arrived in Benghazi about an hour ago from Tripoli to reinforce security there." [428] This reference to DOD personnel is noteworthy because this "asset" or "element" was not even on the list of "assets" and "elements" provided to the Secretary of Defense. As discussed above, these individuals went to Benghazi from Tripoli at the direction of the Chief of Station in Libya, not at the order of anyone in Washington, D.C.

By this time, both McDonough and the Secretary of Defense had made calls to have the YouTube video removed from the internet. [429] Yet, none of the forces the Secretary ordered to deploy had actually moved.

Moments after McDonough sent this email, word of the mortar attacks on the Annex would make its way through the State Department, the White House, and the Defense Department.

At 1:40 a.m. in Washington, the assets the Secretary ordered to deploy more than six hours earlier had still not deployed, though Libya had finally given approval for assets to fly into Tripoli. [430] At that time, Winnefeld emailed McDonough and others relaying to them diplomatic clearance had been obtained from Libya allowing the FAST platoon to fly into Tripoli. [431] Of course, all State and CIA personnel had already evacuated the Annex in Benghazi, and the first aircraft evacuating the American personnel was preparing to depart for Tripoli within minutes. Winnefeld wrote:

> Two C–130s will move to Rota then Tripoli. One departs at 0600z, the other at 0700z. 3+40 transit time to Rota, 1 hour load time. Estimated arrival at Tripoli is 1300z. We now have country clearances for Spain and Libya. Working to expedite movement (for example, faster load time than one hour), but not sure we can go faster now that aircrews are on the ramp. [432]

Winnefeld's email meant this: Now that host nation approval had been obtained, the transport aircraft would depart Ramstein Air Base in Germany in 20 minutes to pick up the FAST team that was waiting in Rota, Spain.

### Evacuation to Benghazi Airport

After the lethal mortar strikes, the team at the Annex was determined to evacuate all personnel. A member of Team Tripoli testified:

---

[427] Email from Denis R. McDonough, Dep. Nat'l Sec. Advisor, Nat'l Sec. Council, to Wendy R. Sherman, Under Sec'y for Political Affairs, U.S. Dep't of State, et al. (Sept. 11, 2012 11:45 PM) (on file with the Committee, C05562167).
[428] Id.
[429] Id.
[430] Email from James A. Winnefeld, Jr., Vice Chairman, J. Chiefs of Staff, U.S. Dep't of Defense, to Benjamin J. Rhodes, Dep. Nat'l Sec. Advisor, White House, et al. (Sept. 12, 2012 1:40 AM) (on file with the Committee, C05562167).
[431] Id.
[432] Id.

We decided that the situation we had was untenable to stay at the compound. We didn't have enough shooters and there were too many wounded, and we were definitely going to lose our State Department wounded if we had stayed there much longer. So we were pushing to get out as fast as we could.[433]

A key issue remained in that, "There was no security vehicle, no gun trucks that would help us get to the airport. And we determined we could probably not make it with the vehicles we had inside the compound."[434] At 6:16 a.m., a 50-vehicle motorcade arrived at the Annex to provide transport support by the Libyan Military Intelligence. The motorcade included technical, pick-up trucks retrofitted with mounted machine gun-like weapons.[435]

The forces that arrived at the Annex shortly after the mortar attacks were able to transport all State Department and CIA personnel safely to the airport. The forces, known as Libyan Military Intelligence, arrived with 50 heavily-armed security vehicles.[436] Libyan Military Intelligence was not part of the Libyan government, nor affiliated with any of the militias the CIA or State Department had developed a relationship with during the prior 18 months since the Libyan revolution took place.[437] Instead, Libya Military Intelligence—whom the CIA did not even know existed until the night of the attacks—were comprised of former military officers under the Qadhafi regime who had gone into hiding in fear of being assassinated, and wanted to keep their presence in Benghazi as quiet as possible so as to not attract attention from the militias in control of Benghazi.[438] In other words, some of the very individuals the United States had helped remove from power during the Libyan revolution were the only Libyans that came to the assistance of the United States on the night of the Benghazi attacks.

The reason Libyan Military Intelligence was able to rescue the Americans from the CIA base after the mortar attacks—likely saving over two dozen lives—was due solely to the extraordinary efforts of Officer A, **[redacted text]** stationed in Benghazi. Officer A, **[redacted text]**, spent a lot of time on the night of the attacks trying to secure help. In the early morning hours of September 12, a commander in the February 17 militia told Officer A that February 17 would be unable to protect the Base and that they were leaving.[439] This commander referred Officer A to the National Police, who the commander said was taking over their duties. Officer A described the National Police as "next to helpless."[440] An officer in the National Police told Officer A "There's nothing I can do. . . . I cannot continue to secure the perimeter [of the Base]."[441]

---

[433] Special Operator Testimony at 68.
[434] Special Operator Testimony at 69.
[435] DVR Footage of the CIA Annex (Sept. 11, 2012, 0616); LMI insignia is printed on vehicles.
[436] TRIPOLI 27900, Sept. 19, 2012 [REQUEST 1–002982 to REQUEST 1–002991].
[437] Officer A Testimony at 71.
[438] Id. at 71–72.
[439] Id. at 19–20.
[440] Id. at 20.
[441] Id.

After some convincing by Officer A, the police officer referred Officer A to a colonel in Libyan Military Intelligence.[442] Officer A had never spoken to this individual before, nor was he even aware of Libyan Military Intelligence. Officer A first had a conversation with this individual around 4:30 am, and testified:

> And I immediately made contact with this commander. He asked how he could help, and I told him, again, our general location, and I said, you know, we need you to come and secure this area. He had an idea, at that point, of events happening in that part of the city, and he told me that he would need to put a big force together, he cannot just come with one of his—I mean, like, two or three vehicles, that he would need to put a large force together and for me to give him some time to put that force together.[443]

Immediately after the mortar attacks, Officer A called the colonel back and said, "[We] now really need you to come here."[444] Within minutes, the 50-truck force from Libyan Military Intelligence arrived and all American personnel safely evacuated to the airport.

The group that ultimately came to the rescue of and facilitated the evacuation of the Americans in Benghazi was not the Libyan Government the State Department had worked tirelessly to appease; nor was it the February 17 Martyrs Brigade, recommended by the Libyan Government and contractually obligated to provide security to the Mission Compound. Instead, the group that came to rescue the Americans that night, the Libyan Military Intelligence, was a group most U.S. Government personnel did not even know existed. This group, ironically, had close ties to the former Qadhafi regime—the very regime the United States had helped remove from power. It was also this group, not groups previously given credit by previous investigations, that came to the rescue of the Americans in those early morning hours —likely saving dozens of lives as a result.

It was the hard work and ingenuity of a single CIA case officer that located and developed this evacuation lead—a witness no other committee of Congress interviewed and a witness the CIA was reluctant to allow the Committee to interview.[445]

Despite the "assurance" some principals in Washington had that U.S. personnel in Benghazi were evacuating earlier, it was not until the rescuing convoy actually arrived to at the Annex that the evacuation of all U.S. personnel was fully understood by those on the ground in Benghazi.

Officer A described what happened after the Libyan Military Intelligence arrived: "We lined up the trucks in order of movement. And then everybody that was a non-shooter was in an up-armored vehicle, and all the shooters were in thin-skinned vehicles to be able to shoot out of their cars."[446] After loading into the available vehicles at the Annex, at 6:34 a.m. the majority of Annex personnel

---

[442] Id. at 23–24.
[443] Id. at 24.
[444] Id. at 27.
[445] Id. at 25–28.
[446] Special Operators Testimony at 71.

and all the Diplomatic Security Agents evacuated in the LMI motorcade.[447]

A few minutes later, two GRS and two CIA Staff officers evacuated the Annex alone in a Toyota pick-up truck after an attempted destruction of the CIA equipment.[448] One CIA personnel described the actions he took to destroy sensitive equipment:

> Q: So you said the last four folks there was yourself, [GRS 5], it was the chief of base, it was the GRS team lead. Did you see any type of interaction between the GRS team lead and the chief of base, any argument?
>
> A: No, and actually I felt bad because once the stuff detonated—whew.
>
> \* \* \*
>
> A: You know, I looked down and I was kneeling in a bunch of blood. I jumped in the truck, and the chief didn't say a word, you know, but I was pretty happy, you know, because the device went off and smoke was already billowing out of the office. The door was jammed open, and so I was pretty thrilled about that, you know, and then I jumped in and said, let's go, you know. And of course, the chief knew that [Woods] is dead, and anyway, it is—I felt bad about that. And then we took off and caught up with the rest of the convoy.[449]

## AMERICANS IN BENGHAZI EVACUATE

### Evacuation to Tripoli

The survivors and four Diplomatic Security Agents departed at 7:31 a.m. local and landed in Tripoli at 8:38 p.m. local.[450] The same private aircraft secured by Team Tripoli to come to the aid of those being attacked in Benghazi was the aircraft used to evacuate the first wave of Americans from Benghazi to Tripoli.

At 8:25 a.m. GRS and one Agent 3 received the body of Stevens from individuals delegated by the Libyan Ministry of Foreign Affairs.[451]

The second aircraft, a C–130 provided by the Libyan Air Force, departed with the remaining security officers and the remains of Stevens, Smith, Woods, and Doherty at 9:54 a.m. and arrived in Tripoli at 11:33 a.m.[452]

### Evacuation to Germany

At 2:15 p.m. on September 12, a C–17 departed Germany en route to Tripoli to evacuate the Americans.[453] This departure occurred over eight hours after the 6:05 a.m. AFRICOM order to de-

---

[447] DVR Footage of the CIA Annex (Sept. 11, 2012, 0634).

[448] Video: DVR Footage of the CIA Annex (Sept. 11, 2012, 0637).

[449] Testimony of **[redacted text]**, Cent. Intel. Agency, Tr. at 61–64 (Jun 19, 2015) [hereinafter **[redacted text]** Testimony] (on file with the Committee).

[450] *See,* U.S. Dep't of Defense Timeline.

[451] Diplomatic Sec. Agent 3 Testimony at 170–172.

[452] U.S. Dep't of Defense Timeline (estimating the times of arrival and departure).

[453] U.S. Dep't of Defense Timeline.

ploy the C–17 for use as part of the Medevac (medical evacuation).[454]

At 7:17 p.m. the C–17 departed Tripoli returning to Ramstein, Germany with the Benghazi-based U.S. personnel, non-essential U.S. Embassy State Department personnel and the remains of the fallen and arrived at 10:19p.m.[455]

### FOUR DIED. OTHER LIVES UNDOUBTEDLY SAVED

The initiative shown during the attacks by those on the ground in Benghazi and Tripoli not only embodied the service and sacrifice of those in military and the Foreign Service but undoubtedly saved the lives of other Americans.

The Diplomatic Security Agents followed their training and responded appropriately after the Mission compound was attacked. The Diplomatic Security Agents showed heroism in their efforts to protect Sean Smith and Chris Stevens and to enter a burning building in search of their missing colleagues.

Team Annex moved quickly and decisively to help fellow Americans at the Mission compound. Their actions during the night/early morning hours provided not only much needed intelligence about what was happening on the ground but also helped secure their State Department colleagues and saved the lives of fellow Americans.

Likewise, Team Tripoli, which included military personnel based at the Tripoli Annex, acted with purpose, precision and ingenuity that night. The Secretary and the Joint Staff did not know those personnel were in Tripoli, much less were they considered as one of the potential assets to respond to the events in Benghazi. In fact, they represent the only military "asset" to reach Benghazi during the attacks. They deployed themselves because fellow Americans needed them.

The creativity, valor and selfless sacrifice of the Diplomatic Security Agents, the team from the Benghazi Annex and Team Tripoli stand in some contrast to the discussions held during the White House meeting occurring at roughly the same time, half a world away, in the safe confines of the U.S.

## THE DEFENSE DEPARTMENT'S RESPONSE TO THE ATTACK WAS INSUFFICIENT

When the attacks in Benghazi began, the Defense Department was unprepared to respond. Despite there being a missing U.S. Ambassador, its response—from the start of the attack at 9:42 p.m. in Libya, to the amount of time it took for the forces to actually deploy late the next morning in Libya—at best illustrates a rusty bureaucratic process not in keeping with the gravity and urgency of the events happening on the ground.

The decisions made earlier in the year by senior State Department officials to maintain a presence in Benghazi without adequate security forces and an inadequately fortified Mission compound contributed to what amounted to a worst case scenario of circumstances that would test the military's preparedness and ability

---

[454] *Id.*
[455] *Id.*

to respond. Nevertheless, the Defense Department did not pass the test. Whether this failure is shouldered by it alone, or rests in part on decisions made by the State Department in Washington D.C. or with the White House who presided over a two hour meeting where half of the action items related to an anti-Muslim video wholly unconnected to the attacks, is one of the lingering questions about Benghazi.

To muster forces actually capable of responding to the second lethal attack in Benghazi, the Defense Department needed to overcome the "tyranny of distance." From the moment the first attack occurred, the clock began to tick, and with each passing hour, the need to immediately deploy forces became more crucial. Any forces deployed by AFRICOM faced two inherent challenges.

First, AFRICOM did not have a significant number of assigned forces. It had a standing arrangement with EUCOM to enable it to have access to EUCOM forces when a contingency arose. In essence, AFRICOM had to ask for help, creating another level of bureaucracy that ultimately played out in the orders to deploy forces.

Second, since any force AFRICOM would use in response to the attack were EUCOM assets, those forces would deploy from bases in Europe, not Northern Africa. In fact, elements of the forces that were ordered to deploy, although based in southern Europe, needed C–130s or other transport aircraft to fly from central Europe to their location to transport them on to Libya.

Of course, these challenges were known well in advance and came as no surprise. Whereas the facts and circumstances surrounding security related events in North Africa may change, the map and the time it takes to respond to the geographic challenges does not.

Whether any of this was taken into account when no change in force posture was ordered on September 10 following the meeting with the President or on September 11 as the situation in Cairo unfolded is unclear. What is clear is the Secretary of Defense testified he was clear on both what the President ordered and what he ordered subsequent to the initial attack. Yet, no asset was ever ordered to respond to Benghazi and the decisions made—and not made—coupled with a lack of urgency in Washington D.C. delayed the response even, in some instances, with an Ambassador missing.

## The Forces did not Meet Timelines

### ISSUES WITH FAST DEPLOYMENT

One of the FAST platoons ordered to deploy by the Secretary arrived in Tripoli at 8:56 p.m. local time [2:56 p.m. in Washington D.C.] the evening of September 12, nearly 24 hours after the attacks began.[456] As military witnesses have posited on many occasions, the mission of a FAST Platoon is not hostage rescue but to "put that layer of steel around a critical infrastructure of the United States to say to our enemy, 'Don't mess [with us].'"[457] Nevertheless, the timing of the FAST Platoon's arrival is problematic. When the Secretary identified a FAST Platoon as an asset to de-

[456] U.S. Dep't of Defense Timeline.
[457] Testimony of FAST Platoon Commander, U.S. Marines, Tr. at 35 (Sept. 2, 2015) [hereinafter FAST Commander Testimony] (on file with the Committee).

ploy and said "go," one U.S. facility in Libya had already been attacked, Sean Smith had been killed, Chris Stevens was missing, and the U.S. Embassy in Tripoli was facing threats of another attack. The fact that nearly 24 hours elapsed until those forces actually arrived in Tripoli to reinforce the security there belies the expectations of the American people that the U.S. Military can and will move expeditiously. The Secretary said this on the time it took for forces to arrive in Libya:

Q: Mr. Secretary, did you know it was going to take 23 hours to get the first assets in country?

A: No.

Q: So what did you expect it was going to take?

A: I knew it was going to take some time, just because of the preparedness for the units and then the time and distance involved. You know, you've heard the term "tyranny of time and distance," and it's tough in this area.

\* \* \*

But I didn't—and I assumed these units moved as quickly as possible and that, you know, we can get them in place as quickly as possible, recognizing that there is a time element that's involved. And, you know, I understand the time element involved here just because of the nature of moving the military.

I mean, as Secretary, I used to sit down with deployment orders all the time of units. And you go through a whole series of discussions about, you know, units that have to be deployed. And, normally, the timeframe to get these units deployed—it takes time. It takes time to put them on a plane. It takes time for them to locate, I understand that. But when you're dealing with the kind of elite units we're talking about here, my expectation is that they move as fast as they can.[458]

The Commander of the FAST Platoon testified he first became aware of the attack on the Mission compound in Benghazi through reports on Fox News.[459] At the time, the FAST Platoon was stationed in Rota, Spain.

So, that evening, I recall I was actually talking to my dad on Skype, watching the Armed Forces Network news channel, which rotates through news affiliates, and I think it was Fox News that night. And all of a sudden we see a consulate building on fire.

As soon as I hung up with him, I got on the phone with my commanding officer, and we had a short talk. . . . And he said something more or less in the lines of, "Make sure you do your laundry and you got enough soap."

---

[458] Panetta Testimony at 47–48.
[459] FAST Commander Testimony at 26.

A couple of hours later, he was calling me, telling me he was going to go down to the commander of CTF 68, who is the higher headquarters of FAST Company Europe, and that I needed to start getting my Marines together. This was around midnight [local time in Rota, Spain], so it would be on September 12.

Around midnight is when my platoon sergeant and I initiated the recall.

\* \* \*

Q: Let's back up a little bit. In terms of the Rota Naval Station, were there any air assets typically stationed at Rota?

A: No, sir. No. What we always planned upon is primarily aircraft coming from Ramstein, because that's where the preponderance of Air Force C–130s were[.] [460]

Almost three hours after the FAST Platoon Commander initiated the recall order, which required his Marines to return to base, he received official notification at 2:39 a.m. [8:39 p.m. in Washington D.C.] the platoon was activated and he was to prepared to deploy.

Q: When did you receive VOCO [vocal order] or a warning order that the FAST platoon was going to be mobilized?

A: Around 0230 is when we got the official notification. So that was our official [redacted]. We already had some lead-in to it, obviously.

\* \* \*

Q: —was it at 0239? Does that sound familiar?

A: Yes, sir.

\* \* \*

Q: What were your specific orders at that time?

A: Prepare my platoon to deploy to Libya. We didn't know where exactly we were going, but we knew through open media sources of what was going on on the deck.

At that time, we started to make contact with the embassy to gain S[ituational] A[wareness] of what was happening and what our potential mission would be. [461]

Three hours after he received official notification, at 5:45 a.m. local time [11:45 p.m. in Washington D.C.], the FAST Commander's platoon was prepped and ready to deploy.

Q: When was your platoon packed out and ready to get on a plane?

A: I believe it was around 0545. I know it was before 6.

Q: Obviously your company commander is aware of that.

---

[460] *Id.* at 27.
[461] *Id.* at 31–32.

A: Yes, sir.

Q: Did they notify anybody up the food chain that at 0545 you're ready to go?

A: Yes, sir.[462]

Yet, another six hours would elapse before C–130s arrived in Spain to transport the FAST Platoon to Libya. General Philip Breedlove, the Commander of the United States Air Forces in Europe, which is the component command which owned the C–130s used to transport the FAST Platoon, told the Committee he began generating C–130s on his own initiative after learning about the attacks in Benghazi.[463] Breedlove said repeatedly his C–130s were ready to deploy before he received official notification of deployment.[464]

The C–130s arrived six hours later, and the FAST Platoon loaded its gear within an hour.[465] Yet, another three hours would elapse before the FAST Platoon departed for Libya.[466] The FAST Platoon commander explained the cause of the delay:

A: After we were loaded, which was around [1:00 p.m. local time], so about an hour after the C–130s were there, we still did not lift off until [4:00 p.m. local time] was when the first aircraft took off.

* * *

Q: Why was there another delay to get off the ground?

A: So we were told multiple times to change what we were wearing, to change from cammies into civilian attire, civilian attire into cammies, cammies into civilian attire.

There was also some talk of whether or not we could carry our personal weapons. I was basically holding hard and fast to the point where we were carrying our personal weapons. Like, we've got a very violent thing going on the ground where we're going, so we're going to be carrying something that can protect ourselves.

But as far as what the Marines were wearing, that continually changed, and we had to make those changes inside of the aircraft.[467]

In fact, the FAST Platoon commander testified that during the course of three hours, he and his Marines changed in and out of their uniforms four times. Ham was not aware the FAST Platoon had been directed to change out of their uniforms until after the fact.[468] When asked whether he had any explanation for why it

---

[462] FAST Commander Testimony at 40.
[463] Breedlove Testimony at 21.
[464] Id.
[465] FAST Commander Testimony at 39–41.
[466] Id. at 41.
[467] Id. at 40–41.
[468] Ham Testimony at 90.

took so long for the FAST Platoon to arrive in Tripoli, he replied, "I do not."[469]

Although Dempsey told the U.S. Senate that once forces began moving, "nothing stopped us, nothing slowed us," it appears the U.S. Military's response that night was delayed—because it started too late.[470]

## Diplomatic Clearance

On the ground in Tripoli, the Defense Attaché had already begun working to obtain flight clearances from the Libyan government before the White House meeting began.[471] Initially, he notified the Libyan government of a potential request for flight clearances as the night progressed.[472] Because he had given advance notice to the Libyan government potential flight clearances would be needed, he fully expected the Libyan government to approve any formal request when it was made. He noted, however, that to submit a formal request, specific information about the tail numbers, expected arrival of the aircraft, the number of personnel, and types of weapons had to be conveyed to the Libyan government.[473] Not only did a formal request have to be made, a representative of the Libyan government had to be available to receive the paperwork for the request. There was no Libyan representative on duty overnight.[474] As to when formal approval was received, the Defense Attaché testified:

> Q: Can you recall when the actual—the relevant information that was needed, like tail numbers and things, when was that transmitted to the Government of Libya?
>
> A: I don't. But I would also come back to the fact that we had a green light from the Government of Libya to bring it in. It was just a question of when we were going to know the specific information that goes into a standard flight clearance request. So it had to have been, I would say, sometime midmorning to noon on the 12th. It could have been, I would say, sometime midmorning to noon on the 12th. It could have been a little bit after that.
>
> Q: And that's when you received the relevant information you need to pass on, or what happened?
>
> A: Probably both. In the course of the morning, leading up to the afternoon, we got the information we required, and then we were able to subsequently transmit it to the Libyans.[475]

An email from Winnefeld corroborates the Defense Attaché's recollection that the final relevant information needed to obtain host nation approval was received sometime mid-morning on Sep-

[469] Id. at 91.
[470] Department of Defense's Response to the Attack on U.S. Facilities in Benghazi, Libya, and the Findings of Its Internal Review Following the Attack, Hearing before the S. Comm. on Armed Services, 113th Cong. 66 (2013).
[471] Defense Attaché 2014 Testimony at 113–114.
[472] Id.
[473] Id.
[474] Id.
[475] Id. at 159–160.

tember 12. In Washington, at 1:40 a.m. [7:40 a.m. in Libya] on September 12, Winnefeld wrote, "Understand we now have dip clearance for the FAST platoon in Tripoli." [476] At least six hours had transpired between the time the Secretary ordered the deployment of forces and the Libyan Government approved deployment of those forces into Libya. Prior to this approval, no forces had begun moving.

Winnefeld did not believe the timing of host nation approval from the Government of Libya prevented forces from moving. [477] Rather, from his perspective, what most impacted the ability of the forces to move was the availability of airlifts coming from Ramstein, Germany. [478] Notably, Winnefeld stated one lesson learned that night was the need to "synch up" force deployment timelines with airlift availability timelines. [479] Nevertheless, the question still remains if the request for host nation approval from Libya was merely *pro forma* and did not delay deployment of forces, why did the forces not move until approval was obtained?

## PROBLEMS WITH CIF DEPLOYMENT

Twenty-two hours after the initial attack in Benghazi began, the CIF landed at the intermediate staging base in Sigonella, Italy. [480] On the night of the attacks, the CIF was located in Croatia participating in a training exercise. The CIF Commander provided the following information about his instructions that night:

A: The initial guidance was—I can't recall if someone said prepare to deploy or you will deploy. The notification we just operate under at all times, if you're notified, we are operating under the premise that we are going to deploy. But no one ever specifically said you would; or that, we would. And as the situation progressed from initial notification around 02, through the early morning hours and throughout the next day, there were various updates along that timeline

Q: And as the night progressed and the morning developed, at what point were you told you will deploy and this is the N Hour? At what point do you recall receiving an N Hour notification? Or did you receive one?

A: I can't recall the official N Hour notification that was set for official purposes. From my purview, when someone told me, that is when I started working off it at the tactical level so that we are prepared.

So, from my recollection, it was in the middle of the night, but I can't recall when the official N Hour was set. [481]

---

[476] Email from Admiral James Winnefeld, Jr., Vice Chairman of the J. Chiefs of Staff, U.S. Dep't of Defense, to Denis R. McDonough, Deputy Nat'l Sec. Advisor, White House, *et al.* (Sept. 12, 2012 1:19 AM) (on file with the Committee, C05562167).

[477] Winnefeld Testimony at 51.

[478] *Id.* at 90.

[479] *Id.* at 30.

[480] *See* U.S. Dep't of Defense Timeline ("[At 7:57 PM EET t]he EUCOM special operations force, and associated equipment, arrives at an intermediate staging base in southern Europe").

[481] CIF Commander Testimony at 58–59. Some forces that are required to move within a predetermined timeframe operate with a notification hour or "N-hour." The N-hour is the estab-

Continued

Notably, as he and his team were preparing after receiving their orders, the CIF Commander was receiving updates from his chain of command but never received any information about what was happening on the ground until he received word Ambassador Stevens had been killed.[482] Despite the updates he was receiving, he was never told State Department personnel had evacuated to the Annex or even that the Annex had been struck by mortars and two more Americans were killed.[483]

The CIF faced several obstacles that slowed its ability to deploy. First, before they could execute, they had to have a fork-lift brought in from Zadar, Croatia, which was approximately 180 miles away from their current location.[484] Once the forklift arrived, the CIF was able to load their pallets of gear and ammunition, then make the two-hour journey to Zagreb International Airport, where they would await their follow-on transportation.[485]

Despite these logistical obstacles, the CIF was packed and ready to go at approximately 7:00 a.m. local time [1:00 a.m. in Washington D.C.]. Yet, it was nearly another three hours until it was airborne. The CIF Commander described the delay:

> A: So in terms of the air, my recollection, I did not—I was waiting on the aircraft. I wasn't involved in the planning of the aircraft, is the best way to describe it. So I don't recall the N Hour sequence for the air movement. It was— for us, we packed up every quickly and then we were waiting at the airfield.
>
> And my comms—I packed up my comms and everything. So once we were sitting at the airfield about seven o'clock in the morning on September 12th, I had limited communications with what was going on. I was just waiting for the aircraft to show up.[486]

*   *   *

> A: But none of us knew—we weren't aware of the aircraft deploying time. On that set N Hour to move aircraft, I don't recall what that was.
>
> Q: Do you recall any efforts to try to coordinate back with SOECUER headquarters to say, "Hey, is there an N Hour Sequence in effect?
>
> Were you tracking an N Hour sequence of any type or was it more of a deliberate deployment sequence?
>
> A: I was tracking—for me, as a ground assault force, the second I heard what was going on, that was kind of what I was tracking. And we moved as quickly as we could. And once we found out that the crisis was not what it was originally articulated in terms of a U.S. Ambassador or any Am[erican] cit[izen] missing, and that he was killed

---

lished time that essentially starts the clock ticking for when the forces are required to be airborne.

[482] Id. at 63, 65.
[483] Id. at 65–66.
[484] General Repass Testimony at 54.
[485] Id. at 54–55
[486] CIF Commander Testimony at 76.

and nobody was—that crisis was no longer occurring as originally discussed, then it became deliberative.

So from my perspective, at that point the crisis was no longer ongoing and it was more of a deliberate process. So the N Hour sequence, I hate to use the term irrelevant, but I didn't know what my mission was going to be if there wasn't a crisis that we were prone to look at.[487]

In support of its training exercise, the CIF's two C–130 aircraft were located in Croatia.[488] Based on reports regarding the attack in Benghazi, and well before receiving an order to deploy, at approximately midnight local time [6:00 p.m. in Washington D.C.] the commander of the aircraft placed his pilots and air crews in "crew rest" in anticipation of a potential mission.[489] "Crew rest" is typically a 12-hour period in which the pilots and air crew rest prior to engaging in a mission. The 12-hour period can be waived to eight hours (or more in exigent circumstances). General Repass, the SOCEUR Commander, waived the crew rest to eight hours in order to facilitate the CIF's movement to the intermediate staging base at Sigonella, Italy.[490]

Once he received word of Stevens's death, the CIF Commander testified the mission transitioned from a crisis action planning event to a deliberate planning event.[491]

Q: Why did it transition from a crisis action planning event to a deliberate planning event? What was the nature of what his death generated in terms of your planning sequence?

A: From my recollection—and I wasn't in constant communications about all of that; I just remember hearing that he was killed, and there were no reports of any other missing American citizens or any life, limb, or eyesight threats to American personnel in the original crisis point. Once we heard of that, and then from that point we knew we were going to an ISB, for sure. So there is no longer an in extremis, as we call it, crisis, and personnel are safe, for a matter of speaking, it became a much more deliberate planning cycle.[492]

\*　　\*　　\*

I was waiting for orders, to be honest with you, from that point forward, outside of deploying. I knew I was going to deploy. Aside from that, the scope of that deployment in terms of a mission statement, was still unknown.[493]

Once the U.S. based Special Operations Force was activated, the CIF—the closest military asset capable of quickly deploying to Benghazi—transitioned to a supporting role to help facilitate what-

---

[487] *Id.* at 77–78.
[488] Repass Testimony at page 29.
[489] *Id.* at 49.
[490] *Id.* at 62.
[491] CIF Commander Testimony at 69.
[492] *Id.* at 69–70.
[493] *Id.* at 71.

ever mission was to be assigned to SOF forces.[494] As such, the CIF's primary responsibility was then to simply get to the intermediate staging base prior to the U.S. based Special Operations Force and assist them as required.[495] The CIF was essentially relegated to being an enabler of the U.S. based SOF, unless they were subsequently tasked otherwise.

Ham disagreed that the CIF's sole role became to prepare for the U.S.-based Special Operations Force. He testified:

> Q: Did you anticipate as you did your planning that the Commander's In-extremis Force was going to be relegated to being nothing more than enablers for the National Mission Force?
>
> A: In my view, that's an incorrect characterization of the Commander's In-extremis Force.
>
> \*　　\*　　\*
>
> Q: [W]hat would be a more accurate characterization?
>
> A: Mr. Chairman, in my view, the Commander's In-extremis Force, again, these are specially trained, equipped, prepared forces that can, as the name implies, conduct missions in extremis. **[Redacted text]**
>
> **[Redacted text]** but they can, in fact, accomplish that mission.
>
> And, Mr. Chairman, they do, in fact, have a mission to receive and prepare for arrival of the National Mission Force, but, in my view, their mission is much broader than just that.
>
> Q: I think the tension that we're trying—particularly those of us who have never served before—the tension we're trying to reconcile is, when General Repass testified—and he did a fantastic job, but one of the impressions we were all left with based on his testimony was, once the [U.S. SOF] was deployed, the CIF's role then became to go to the ISB and await the [U.S. SOF], which, in effect, took them out of the realm of other assets that could deploy otherwise. That is a fair characterization of his testimony.
>
> And I'm just wondering whether or not you agree that, once both of those assets are put in place—the [U.S. SOF], it's headed, it's got a longer travel time than the CIF—that the CIF's job was to go to the ISB and await the [U.S. SOF]?
>
> A: Mr. Chairman, I would say that that was one of their missions, certainly, to facilitate the arrival and the staging of the [U.S. SOF]. But, in my mind, that was an operational force that was available to me, a highly capable special operations force that was available.[496]

---

[494] Repass Testimony at page 60.
[495] *Id.* at 70.
[496] Ham Testimony at 91–92.

Even still, Ham believed the CIF's failure to meet its timeline was not justified and was inexcusable:

> Though I know now in hindsight that had the CIF made its timelines, they would not have been in position to affect the outcome as things eventually played out on the ground, the reality is, they should have made their timelines. And that's—there's no excuse for that. They should have made their timelines. They should have been postured for subsequent use. As it turns out, they would not have been needed, but we didn't know that at the time. So that, as I look back on this, the disappointment of the Commander's In-extremis Force not meeting its timeline is, to me, significant, and I believe the steps taken by the command and by the Department of Defense after that have addressed that situation.[497]

The Secretary had this to say about the CIF's deployment timeline:

> Q: Well that same unit then had to wait for aircraft till about if you look at the timeline here, 10:21 a.m.
>
> So that N-hour that was set at 11 o'clock east coast time on the night of the 11th, it was not until 11 hours later that EUCOM CIF was actually transported down to Sigonella from Croatia.
>
> Does that timeframe seem reasonable to you, given what you thought might be occurring in the region?
>
> A: I think it's a legitimate area to ask why did it take that long.[498]

### PROBLEMS WITH US SOF DEPLOYMENT

The U.S. SOF force is required to deploy within a specific number of hours after the order to deploy is given. As reflected in the Defense Department's timeline and after-action reviews, it actually took a significant amount of additional time to launch the U.S. SOF. Even given this delay, the U.S. SOF Force, which deployed from the United States, arrived at the staging base in southern Europe only an hour and a half after the CIF arrived.

By the time CIF and the U.S. SOF Force landed at Sigonella, the crisis in Benghazi had ended. In fact, the units arrived in Sigonella nearly 12 hours *after* all U.S. personnel had evacuated from Benghazi. The assets ultimately deployed by the Defense Department in response to the Benghazi attacks were not positioned to arrive prior to the final lethal attack on the Annex. The fact that this is true does not mitigate the question of why the world's most powerful military was not positioned to respond or why the urgency and ingenuity displayed by team members at the Annex and Team Tripoli was seemingly not shared by all decision makers in Washington.

---

[497] *Id.* at 108.
[498] Panetta Testimony at 176–177.

What was disturbing from the evidence the Committee found was that at the time of the final lethal attack at the Annex, no asset ordered deployed by the Secretary had even left the ground. Not a single asset had launched, save the military personnel from Tripoli who did so on their own accord and whose presence no one in Washington seemed aware of when discussing which assets to deploy. Nothing was on its way to Benghazi as a result of the Secretary's initial order to deploy.

More than 12 hours had passed since the first attack happened at the Mission compound, resulting in the death of Sean Smith (which was known) and Ambassador Stevens (which was not then known), yet in that time, the greatest military on earth was unable to launch one single asset toward the sound of the guns.

The CIF's response timeline and the U.S. SOF's timeline exposed flaws in a process designed to ensure that when a crisis erupts, the military's decision and deployment cycles will prove adequate to the challenge being confronted.

## The U.S. Government's Response Lacked a Sense of Urgency

Perhaps given the timing of the 7:30 p.m. meeting with the White House on September 11, shortly after all surviving State Department personnel had evacuated from the Mission compound to the Annex, there may have been a sense the worst of the attack was over. Indeed, Winnefeld stated when he was first briefed around 4:30 p.m. about the events in Benghazi, he recalled being told there had been an attack and the attack was over.[499] The job left to be done was no longer a hostage rescue situation but was, at best, recovering Stevens from a hospital and, at worst, recovering Stevens's remains.

This sense, in fact, was false and should have been viewed as limited, if not false, at the time. As the participants of the White House meeting would soon learn, events were continuing to unfold on the ground in Benghazi. Those leaving the Benghazi Mission compound were attacked and ambushed *en route* to the Annex and once the Diplomatic Security Agents and Team Annex arrived at the Annex the attacks continued. Moreover, preparing for what could theoretically happen in Tripoli, or other cities and facilities was understandable. However, the lack of urgency in responding to what was actually happening on the ground in Benghazi is difficult to reconcile.

Some may seek to argue a transferred focus onto Tripoli may explain why such topics as military attire, vehicles, and country clearances—topics that may seem irrelevant in a crisis situation—found their way into the discussions, and why other topics, such as deployment of the FEST, received short shrift. This belies the reality that—even as Bash indicated the assets were "spinning up" and the ensuing meeting took place—Ambassador Stevens was missing in Benghazi. There is no evidence news of his death had reached Washington D.C. Indeed, news of his death could not have reached Washington D.C. because it was not known at the time. So, pivoting toward a Tripoli security analysis and the possibilities of unrest and violence there is hard to reconcile with the reality of

---

[499] Winnefeld Testimony at 11.

what had happened in Benghazi, what was currently happening in Benghazi, and tragically what was soon to happen in Benghazi.

With the storming of the compound in Benghazi, the killing of Smith, and Stevens missing, discussing the nature of the vehicles to be used and the clothing to be worn by those seeking to provide aid seemed to place a disproportionate emphasis on how the Libyan government might respond. After all, the Libyan government was supposed to play an active role in preventing the attack in the first instance and certainly in responding afterward.

In addition, a fair review of read-outs and summaries of the White House meeting suggest the focus had already moved away from responding to Benghazi and toward responding to Tripoli and the broader region. Expressing concern about how forces might be received in Tripoli seems difficult to reconcile with an actively hostile security situation ongoing in Benghazi.

## The U.S. Government's Response Lacked Leadership

### THE DEFENSE DEPARTMENT THOUGHT STATE WAS EVACUATING THE AMERICANS IN BENGHAZI

The response to the attacks suffered from confusion and misinformation circulating between the agencies underscoring that no one effectively took charge of the U.S. Government's response the night and early morning of September 11–12. From the Defense Department's perspective, when the orders were issued, the plan on the ground was for the people in Benghazi, with the assistance from Team Tripoli, to make their way back to Tripoli. It would provide assets to augment the security in Tripoli where needed, and provide evacuation of the wounded and deceased. Several witnesses indicated that despite the Secretary's orders, the plan was not to insert any asset into Benghazi; their understanding was that assets needed to be sent to Tripoli to augment security at the Embassy, and that the State Department was working to move the State personnel from Benghazi to Tripoli.

Tidd confirmed this understanding of the response plan following the 7:30 meeting with the White House:

> By the time we came out of the [White House meeting], it was pretty clear that nobody was going to be left in Benghazi. And so the decision—I think at the [White House meeting] there was some discussion—but as I recall, we weren't going to send them to Benghazi, because everybody was going to be back in Tripoli by the time we could actually get them there.[500]

He further added:

> On the evening, at the time that all of this was transpiring, our mindset, our sense was that everything was going to Tripoli, that no one was left—or no one would be left in Benghazi. So that—that's—that was the mindset that we had.[501]

---

[500] Tidd Testimony at 26.
[501] *Id.* at 47.

Even the diplomatic security timeline of events reflected this was the plan as understood by individuals on the ground in Libya. At approximately 10:15 p.m. in Washington D.C., the Diplomatic Security Command Center received a call from the CIA Annex in Tripoli relaying the following information:

> The Response Team has been on the ground for approximately 60 minutes. They are waiting for to [sic] escort them to the [redacted] annex.

> \* \* \*

> Once the six-member Response Team arrives they will have non-essential employees and the remains of Sean P. Smith depart.[502]

Word of the plan to evacuate the individuals from Benghazi seemed to spread throughout the State Department. Susan E. Rice, U.S. Permanent Representative to the U.N., received an email update on the events of the evening which read: "Apparently the Department is considering an ordered departure of some personnel from both Tripoli and Benghazi."[503] One member of Team Tripoli also testified the plan, as he understood it, was to evacuate all non-essential personnel to Tripoli.[504]

Yet several other witnesses believed a very different plan was in place: No one was evacuating until Stevens was found.[505]

The Defense Department was working off of the premise everyone in Benghazi was being evacuated, others were clear that no one was leaving, and even State Department senior officials did not authorize the Diplomatic Security Agents to evacuate until Stevens was found. The Committee was also struck by the sheer number of government officials involved in the decision making the evening/early morning hours of September 11–12, who did not even know there was a separate U.S. facility in Benghazi referred to as the "Annex" or where the Annex was.

The first time it is clear all agencies understood the people in Benghazi were evacuating to Tripoli was after the final, lethal mortar attack at 11:15 p.m. in Washington D.C., [5:15 a.m. in Benghazi]—and over seven hours after the initial attack.[506]

The lack of clarity on evacuation versus location of the missing Ambassador was not the only example of conflicting and confusing directives during the attacks and aftermath in Benghazi.

The issue of military attire versus civilian clothes illustrated no one seemed to be taking charge and making final decisions. After the State Department request at the 7:30 p.m. White House meeting, the Defense Department began working the issue. Documents

[502] DSCC Timeline.

[503] Email from Senior Advisor to the U.S. Permanent Representative to the U.N., to Susan E. Rice, U.S. Permanent Representative to the U.N. (Sept. 11, 2012 10:37 PM) (on file with the Committee, SCB0051700).

[504] Special Operator Testimony at 69.

[505] See DSCC Timeline ("[At 11:13 PM EDT] response team has arrived at the [redacted] Annex. Station is telling him all DS staff told to evacuate. [Redacted] has 3 people willing to stay behind. Director Bultrowicz stated no, DS will not evacuate all members due to the outstanding issue of the Ambassador.").

[506] See Email from Cheryl D. Mills, Chief of Staff to the U.S. Sec'y of State, U.S. Dep't of State, to Denis R. McDonough, Deputy Nat'l Sec. Advisor, White House (Sept. 12, 2012 12:12 AM) (on file with the Committee, SCB0051706) ("we're pulling everyone out of Benghazi [starting shortly]").

from the Defense Department show, and the FAST Platoon Commander testified it was well into the next afternoon on September 12th before the final decision was made. He testified further the Marines changed in and out of uniform and civilian clothes several times because the orders kept changing.

### THE DEFENSE DEPARTMENT DID NOT ANTICIPATE ADDITIONAL ATTACKS IN BENGHAZI

Several Defense Department witnesses testified that following the attack at the Benghazi Mission compound, they did not anticipate any additional attacks. Landolt explained:

> But you also have to remember that the first firefight was around midnight. We didn't anticipate a second one at 5:00 in the morning.

> \* \* \*

> Q: In terms of, though, after the first attack, was there a sense that perhaps this thing had passed and the dust had settled and—-

> A: There was that sense.

> Q: Talk about that a little more. Was there a general agreement amongst yourself and General Ham and Admiral Leidig of that, well, we got through this thing with minimal damage? Or what was the process? What was the thought?

> A: Yeah, there was a sense that we needed more information, that it looked like the initial attack had ended. We had the one dead body on our hands, but we still had a missing Ambassador. And then the Embassy, through the DAT, was telling us that they were able to get a plane and they were going to fly people over. So I thought, okay, well, that will give us better situational awareness. So there was that lull where, Okay, let's wait and see what happens here.[507]

Although the Defense Department did not anticipate an additional attack, the people on the ground in Benghazi most assuredly did. One GRS agent on the ground testified:

> Q: Was there a sense from you that something was building to something larger later in the evening?

> A: Yes. And what we were worried about was an even larger force with gun-mounted weapons, which are much larger, overtaking the compound.

> Q: Okay. But in terms of individuals with small arms, that's something that you guys had sufficiently handled and were able to continue handling based on your defensive posture at the base?

> A: Right, but there was a limit to it. Like it's not something that we could have done for days. I mean, we were

---

[507] Landolt Testimony at 33–34.

able to do it for as long as we could, but it wasn't—there had to be something else.

Q: Okay. Was there ever a sense throughout the evening that the attacks were over and there was sort of a calmness——

A: Absolutely not.

Q: —around the base?

A: No. There were lulls, which are normal, but no, none of us, and when I say "us," the team, none of us thought it was over, no.[508]

### THE DEFENSE DEPARTMENT'S FOCUS SHIFTED FROM BENGHAZI TO THE REGION

The Defense Department's lack of comprehension of the events taking place in Benghazi, coupled with the emphasis on resolving potentially extraneous policy matters, hampered the administration's subsequent plan to respond to those events and dictated the urgency with which forces moved that night. As the CIF commander testified, their movements that night transitioned from crisis action to deliberate planning.[509] Winnefeld explained why:

> I think there are a number of factors in play. One, it wasn't a matter of not having enough urgency, I think it was more a matter of posture, coupled with the fact the focus was on regional challenges, not on something additional was going to happen in Benghazi later that night. And so when there was not the perception of an immediate threat right there . . . people are going to operate safely.[510]

> \* \* \*

> And remember, the reason we were moving the CIF, we were moving it to, what, Sigonella. . . . It was not because they were going to Benghazi.

> \* \* \*

> We were worried about the copycat attacks elsewhere in the region. And so I think they were more in a—it wasn't a lack of urgency, but it was—you know, they keep safety in mind. It was, okay, there could be a copycat attack; we need to reposture ourselves in theater. Let's do it, but let's not kill ourselves doing it.

> You know, in 20/20 hindsight, if anybody had known there was going to be a second attack and that potentially the CIF could end up going there, maybe they would have asked that question that you're asking. But again, their mindset was we're moving the CIF to Sigonella because something else could happen in the region.[511]

---

[508] GRS 5 Testimony at 65–66.
[509] CIF Commander Testimony at 69.
[510] Winnefeld Testimony at 39–40.
[511] *Id.* at 30–31.

THE DEFENSE DEPARTMENT'S RESPONSE LACKED URGENCY

Finally, the coordination for and deployment of the assets identified and ordered deployed by the Secretary lacked any real sense of urgency.

The Defense Department knew of the initial attack in Benghazi, which killed Sean P. Smith, less than an hour after the attack began.

Two hours after this initial attack began, the Secretary had met with the President and been given all of the authority he believed he needed to "use all of the resources at our disposal to try to make sure we did everything possible to try to save lives there."[512]

Three hours after the initial attack began, Bash emailed senior leaders at the State Department to inform them of the assets that could be deployed in response to the attack.

Five hours after the initial attack began, formal authorization to deploy the assets was issued.

Instead of setting the N hour at the time the Secretary of Defense gave his order before Bash's email, or even setting the N hour at the time orders were issued to the forces at 8:39 p.m., the Joint Staff coordinated with the U.S. SOF force to ask, "What would you like to set as N hour?"[513]

Given the urgency of the Secretary's intended deployment of these units and particularly in light of what was continuing to happen in Benghazi, this cannot be justified, particularly since it was already known the likelihood of further unrest in the region was significant.

N hour was ultimately set at 11:00 p.m.—more than seven hours after the attacks in Benghazi began, more than four hours after the Secretary gave the order to deploy the forces, and more than two hours after that order was finally relayed to the forces. Though, Petraeus quipped to the Committee, "N hour has nothing to do with this whatsoever, with great respect. That is completely irrelevant[,]" the setting of the N hour was symptomatic of a larger lack of urgency in responding to the situation on the ground.[514]

Almost six hours after first learning of the initial attack on U.S. facilities in Benghazi, no asset had been deployed to Benghazi or Tripoli. Moreover, no asset ordered by the Secretary was even moving toward Benghazi or Tripoli aside from military personnel in Tripoli who mustered the ingenuity, courage, and resolve to ferry themselves toward danger. At the White House, McDonough knew at 11:45 p.m. the situation in Benghazi remained "fluid," Stevens was still "unaccounted for," and one State Department officer had been killed. He included this in his 11:45 p.m. email on September 11.

Despite the fact that more than six hours had lapsed between the time the first attack was known and the time of this email, McDonough was still speaking of assets "deploying" rather than assets deployed. If there is evidence McDonough placed calls or sent

---

[512] Panetta Testimony at 23.

[513] Email from Vice Admiral Kurt Tidd, Dir. of Operations, J. Chiefs of Staff, U.S. Dep't of Defense, to Deputy Dir. of Operations, *et al.* (Sept. 11, 2012 8:53PM) (on file with the Committee, SCB001376).

[514] Testimony of General David A. Petraeus, Dir., Cent. Intel. Agency, Tr. at 16 (Mar. 19, 2016) [hereinafter Petraeus Testimony 2] (on file with the Committee).

emails inquiring about the status of the deployment, the White House has not shared that evidence with the Committee. Rather, what was learned is McDonough made mention of calling "YouTube" to request the taking down of two videos, and he references having had the Secretary call "Pastor Jones to ask him to pull down his video." Why McDonough had time to concern himself with "You Tube" videos while an Ambassador was missing and unaccounted for remains unclear. And why the Secretary of Defense was used to call "You Tube" and a "pastor" about a video—that had not and would not be linked to the attacks in Benghazi—rather than inquiring about the status of the asset deployment he ordered five hours earlier is also unclear.

What is clear is the United States Government sent personnel into a dangerous post-revolution environment in Benghazi, Libya. Those sent displayed heroism and valor. They also displayed a sense of urgency in discharging the mission assigned to them. Chris Stevens had the urgency to travel to Benghazi because decisions needed to be made before the end of the fiscal year. Chris Stevens felt the urgency to assign himself to cover a one-week gap in the Principal Officer position in Benghazi.

Those Americans assigned to work at a nearby Annex had the sense of urgency to fight their way onto the Benghazi Mission compound because a sister U.S. agency was under attack. Diplomatic Security Agents had the urgency to return time and time again into a burning building in search of Smith and Stevens. Diplomatic Security Agents and the team from the Annex no doubt felt the urgency when they fought their way from the compound to the Annex overcoming point-blank machine gun fire and grenade attacks.

Team Tripoli sensed the urgency of what was happening in Benghazi and negotiated for private aircraft to race toward the danger in defense of fellow Americans. Tyrone S. Woods and Glen A. Doherty felt the urgency of defending a second U.S. facility against a series of coordinated attacks before ultimately being killed by precision mortar attacks.

There was life and death urgency felt in Libya with split-second decisions being made: Do I fire on this crowd or not? Do we fire in the direction of a residence or not? Do we return to a smoke and fire engulfed building yet again in search of fallen colleagues? Do we go to the hospital to find Stevens or to the Annex? How do we fly from Tripoli to Benghazi?

If that same degree of urgency was felt among the decision makers in Washington it is not reflected in the time within which decisions were made nor in the topics being debated in and around the deployment.

The "tyranny of time and distance" may well explain why no U.S. military asset—save the bravery of the men serving in Tripoli—made it to Benghazi. It does not explain why no asset was even headed toward Benghazi. The "tyranny of time and distance" does not explain why Washington D.C. leaders were preoccupied with ancillary issues when they were responsible for sending our fellow Americans into harm's way in the first instance.

Half of the action items that emerged from the White House meeting convened in response to the killing of an American Foreign Service officer and an attack on an American diplomatic facility related to a video. Half. There is more of a record of phone calls from White House officials to "YouTube" and a virtually anonymous "pastor" than there were calls imploring the Defense Department to move with greater urgency. The preoccupation the administration felt with safeguarding the feelings of the Libyan government and dealing with an anti-Muslim video (which video prompted no change in force posture or readiness even after protests erupted in Cairo) is a foreshadowing of what would become an administration wide effort to conflate that same video with the attacks in Benghazi.

# PART II:

# Internal and Public Government Communications about the Terrorist Attacks in Benghazi

*"Two of our officers were killed in Benghazi by an Al Queda-like [sic] group."*

> The Secretary of State to her daughter, September 11, 2012[1]

*"We know that the attack in Libya had nothing to do with the film. It was a planned attack—not a protest."*

> Summary of a statement by the Secretary of State to the Egyptian Prime Minister, September 12, 2012[2]

*"To underscore that these protests are rooted in an Internet video, and not a broader failure of policy."*

> Benjamin J. Rhodes, defining one of the goals of Ambassador Susan E. Rice's appearances on the Sunday news programs following the Benghazi attacks, September 14, 2012[3]

*"I gave Hillary a hug and shook her hand, and she said we are going to have the filmmaker arrested who was responsible for the death of my son."*

> Diary entry of Charles Woods, father of Tyrone Woods, September 14, 2012[4]

---

[1] Email from Hillary R. Clinton ("H"), Sec'y of State, U.S. Dep't of State, to Chelsea Clinton ("Diane Reynolds") (Sept. 11, 2012, 11:12 PM) (on file with the Committee, C05795467).

[2] Email from U.S. Dep't of State, to S_CallNotes, (Sept. 12, 2012, 7:11 PM) (on file with the Committee, C05561911).

[3] Email from Benjamin J. Rhodes, Deputy Nat'l Sec. Advisor for Strategic Commc'cs, Nat'l Sec. Council, to Dagoberto Vega, Special Ass't to the President and Dir. of Broadcast Media, White House, *et al.* (Sept. 14, 2012, 8:09 PM) [hereinafter Rhodes Memo] (on file with the Committee, C05415285).

[4] Fox News Insider, *Father of Benghazi Victim Reveals Journal Entry Documenting Meeting With Hillary,* YOUTUBE (Jan. 13, 2016), http://www.youtube.com/watch?v=dMx0huMabos.

## The Security Environment

The attacks in Benghazi did not occur in a vacuum. They took place amidst a severely deteriorating security situation in eastern Libya—a permissive environment where extremist organizations were infiltrating the region, setting up camps, and carrying out attacks against Western targets.[5] In June 2012, State Department security officials were discussing "an active terrorist cell in Benghazi" that was "planning and implementing attack operations against western interests including the U.S. Mission in Benghazi[.]"[6] That same month another security official in Libya reported to Washington about the "increase in extremist activity" and described his "fear that we have passed a threshold where we will see more targeting, attacks, and incidents involving western targets."[7] The official cited a series of recent attacks and noted that a source had warned of a "group attack" on an American facility.[8] He specifically mentioned "[t]argeting [and] attacks by extremist groups particularly in the eastern portion of Libya," where Benghazi is located.[9]

In the months leading up to September 11, 2012, several major security incidents had taken place in Benghazi against Western targets, including:

- April 2, 2012: Attack on a United Kingdom [UK] armored vehicle;

- April 6, 2012: Improvised Explosive Device [IED] attack on the State Department facility in Benghazi;

- April 10, 2012: IED attack on the motorcade of the United Nations Envoy;

- April 27, 2012: IED attack on a courthouse in Benghazi;

- May 22, 2012: Rocket Propelled Grenade [RPG] attack on the International Committee for the Red Cross [ICRC] facility in Benghazi;

- June 6, 2012: IED attack on the State Department facility in Benghazi;

- June 11, 2012: RPG attack on the UK Ambassador's motorcade;

- June 12, 2012: RPG attack on the ICRC;

- July 29, 2012: IED found at Tibesti Hotel; and

- August 5, 2012: Attack on the ICRC facility.

The threat environment in Benghazi was so severe that on September 11, 2012, on the anniversary of September 11, one Diplomatic Security agent in Benghazi feared an attack that night and was not planning on going to sleep. He testified:

---

[5] This deteriorating security environment is discussed in detail in Section III of the report.

[6] Memorandum from James Bacigalupo, Regional Dir. of the Near East Asia Bureau of Diplomatic Sec., U.S. Dep't of State, to Charlene Lamb, Deputy Ass't Sec'y for Diplomatic Sec., U.S. Dep't of State (June 15, 2012) (on file with the Committee, C05578316).

[7] Email from Diplomatic Sec. Agent 24, U.S. Dep't of State, to Diplomatic Sec. Agent 25, U.S. Dep't of State (June 14, 2012) (on file with the Committee, C05388987).

[8] Id.

[9] Id.

You know, I wasn't going to go to sleep that night. I was probably going to stay up throughout the night just because, one, it's September 11, you know, and what was happening in Egypt. So if anything was to happen, it would happen late at night, early morning. So I wasn't going to go to bed. I believe [Agent 2] was along the same mindset, but we hadn't ratified whether, yes, this is what we are doing. It was just people are going to stay up. I had taken my weapon and ammunition and put it in my room. [Agent 2] had done the same thing. And I believe they had—[Agent 5] had his weapon with him as well in his room.[10]

Sean P. Smith, the Information Management Officer at the Benghazi Mission compound, also feared an attack, telling a community of online gamers shortly before the attack: "[A]ssuming we don't die tonight. We saw one of our 'police' that guard the compound taking pictures."[11]

It was against this backdrop that the September 11, 2012 attacks against U.S. facilities in Benghazi took place.

## THE PROTESTS IN CAIRO

In Cairo, Egypt earlier that day, approximately 2,000 protestors demonstrated outside the U.S. Embassy—a protest that began in the middle of the day.[12] A handful of protestors scaled the embassy wall, tore down the American flag, and sprayed graffiti inside the compound.[13] Some protestors were eventually removed by Egyptian police. No Americans were injured or killed in the event.

In Cairo, protests had been planned for days in advance on social media as a result of a video posted on YouTube about the prophet Muhammad.[14] On September 10, 2012, the CIA warned of social media chatter calling for a demonstration in front of the Embassy in Cairo,[15] and Americans at the Embassy were sent home early due to the impending protests.[16]

Although the attacks in Benghazi occurred later on the same day, they had little else in common with the Cairo protests. Significant differences included:

---

[10] Testimony of Diplomatic Security Agent 1 [Agent 1], Diplomatic Sec. Agent, U.S. Dep't of State, Tr. at 49–50 (Mar. 6, 2015) [hereinafter Agent 1 Testimony] (on file with the Committee).

[11] Matt Smith, *Ex-SEALs, Online Gaming Maven among Benghazi Dead*, CNN (Sept. 13, 2012, 8:53 PM), http://www.cnn.com/2012/09/13/us/benghazi-victims.

[12] *See, e.g.*, Email to Susan E. Rice, U.S. Ambassador to the U.N., *et al.*, (Sept. 11, 2012, 7:55 PM) (on file with the Committee, C05390691).

[13] *See, e.g., id.*

[14] Sara Lynch and Oren Dorell, *Deadly embassy attacks were days in the making*, USA Today, (Sept. 12, 2012, 8:36 PM), http://usatoday30.usatoday.com/news/world/story/2012/09/12/libyan-officials-us-ambassador-killed-in-attack/57752828/1.

[15] *See, e.g.*, email from Victoria J. Nuland, Spokesperson, U.S. Dep't of State, to Erin Pelton, Dir. of Commc'cs and Spokesperson, U.S. Mission to the U.N. (Sept. 15, 2012, 7:18 PM) (on file with the Committee, C05622933).

[16] *Egypt Protesters Scale U.S. Embassy Wall, Take Flag*, CBS/AP (Sept. 11, 2012, 5:16 PM), http://www.cbsnews.com/news/egypt-protesters-scale-us-embassy-wall-take-flag.

- In Cairo, plans for the protest appeared on social media well before the actual demonstration.[17] In Benghazi the attacks occurred without warnings on social media;[18]

- In Cairo, protestors did not brandish or use weapons.[19] In Benghazi, attackers were armed with assault weapons, rocket propelled grenades, and sophisticated mortars;[20]

- In Cairo, protestors spray painted walls and did other minor damage.[21] In Benghazi, the attackers burned down buildings and pounded U.S. facilities with mortars and machine gun fire;[22] and

- In Cairo, the protest was confined to a single location.[23] In Benghazi, the attacks spanned nearly eight hours over two different locations.[24]

Diplomatic Security personnel in Washington D.C. recognized differences as well. At 5:13 p.m. on September 11, 2012 James Bacigalupo, Regional Director for Diplomatic Security, Near Eastern Affairs Bureau, State Department, notified all regional security officers:

> Within the last few hours we have had one demonstration in which protestors infiltrated the perimeter of the compound in Cairo and an armed attack on our compound in Benghazi. Both are currently on-going and may be in response to the release of an anti-Islamic documentary and upcoming demonstration by Terry Jones this evening.[25]

The differences also were noted by senior State Department officials as well. Victoria J. Nuland, Spokesperson, State Department, sent an email at 6:09 p.m. that included Jacob J. Sullivan, Deputy Chief of Staff and Director of Policy Planning, State Department, and Patrick F. Kennedy, Under Secretary for Management, State Department, among others. Nuland wrote:

> [Please] put out as two separate statements to bullpen, asap. On record, me.

> We can confirm that our office in Benghazi, Libya has been attacked by a group of militants. We are working with the Libyans now to try to restore security.

> In Cairo, we can confirm that Egyptian police have now removed the demonstrators who had entered our Embassy grounds earlier.

---

[17] Sara Lynch and Oren Dorell, *Deadly embassy attacks were days in the making,* USA TODAY, Sept. 16, 2012.

[18] *See, e.g.,* Testimony of Tripoli Chief of Station, Cent. Intel. Ageny, Tr. at 42–45, July 16, 2015 [hereinafter Tripoli COS Testimony] (on file with the Committee).

[19] *See, e.g.,* Email to Susan E. Rice, U.S. Permanent Rep. to the U.N. (Sept. 11, 2012, 7:55 PM) [hereinafter 7:55 P.M. Rice Email] (on file with Committee, C053906910).

[20] *See, e.g.,* Benghazi Accountability Review Board at 4, U.S. Dep't of State [hereinafter Benghazi ARB].

[21] 7:55 P.M. Rice Email, *supra* note 19.

[22] Benghazi ARB, *supra* note 20, at 4.

[23] *See, e.g.,* 7:55 P.M. Rice Email, *supra* note 19.

[24] Benghazi ARB, *supra* note 20, at 4.

[25] Email from James Bacigalupo, Regional Dir. of the Near East Asia Bureau of Diplomatic Sec., U.S. Dep't of State, to DS–IP–NEA–RSO (Sept. 11, 2012, 5:13 PM) (on file with the Committee, SCB0048896).

For [press] guidance, if pressed whether we see a connection between these two.

We have no information regarding a connection between these incidents.[26]

## WHAT BENGHAZI REPORTED DURING THE ATTACKS

All five Diplomatic Security agents at the Benghazi Mission spoke with the Diplomatic Security Command Center while the attacks were ongoing. Agent 5, the Diplomatic Security agent who was with Smith and Ambassador to Libya J. Christopher Stevens during the attack, recounted his story:

Okay, so the evening started with [Agent 4], [Agent 2] and I sitting at a table near the pool at the end of the night. Ambassador Stevens had come by and said, I'm going to bed. Sean Smith said the same thing and went, you know, went inside the villa, and we were just sitting out kind of relaxing at the end of the night.

While we were talking, I started hearing some kind of chanting, I thought it was. So I told the others, you know, I told the other two, hang on. Just listen for a minute. And what we heard was chanting. And it was my impression that it was coming closer. You know, so immediately when I realized, you know, that this is a potential security incident, or a potential something, I said, you know, get your gear, right now. I ran into Villa C where the Ambassador and Sean Smith were and the other two ran in a different direction.

I remember hearing the chants. I mean, they were fairly close already. I mean, yelling distance, which is pretty close especially in a city setting. So my impression is that I don't have much time. So I ran right to my room, you know, put my helmet on, put my vest on, grabbed my weapons, my additional weapons, and I turned to lock the gate, and basically, it was a jail cell door with three locks on it. I locked all three locks.

And at about that time, Ambassador Stevens and Sean Smith were coming out of their rooms. Sean Smith was already, you know, donning his helmet and vest. I guided them both into the safe haven, and I set myself up in the safe haven with—I was holding my M4. I had a pistol, a radio, a shotgun, and when we were, you know, when we were in there, I radioed the other guy, hey, we are all in the safe haven.

I could hear outside explosions, yelling, chanting, screaming, gunfire, and I reported all of this on the radio just saying, this is what my senses are telling me. Then people started banging on the doors of the building, so I reported that. Hey, there is banging on the doors. They are trying

[26] Email from Victoria Nuland, Spokesperson, U.S. Dep't of State, to Elizabeth Dibble, Deputy Ass't Sec'y in the Bureau of Near Eastern Affairs, U.S. Dep't of State, et al. (Sept. 11, 2012, 6:09 PM) (on file with the Committee, C05578255).

to come in, you know, we need immediate assistance. And there wasn't any response on the radio. Shortly after that, to my recollection, the doors were blown open. And about 70 individuals, you know, rushed into the building, all of them carrying AK–47s, grenades, RPGs, you know, a mixture throughout everyone. Different—there were a couple of different assault rifles.

And with the number of individuals that came into the building versus me, I chose just to stay in the shadow that I was in. So I was partially in the safe haven, partially outside the safe haven. This area was, you know, there was a big shadow where I was sitting, and my view through the jail cell door was into the common area. So I could see where everybody was going, and they began breaking everything. I could just hear glass breaking. I could hear stuff being thrown around. I could hear furniture being moved.

If I may just back up a little bit. When we made it into the safe haven, I handed my cell phone to the Ambassador. I said, call everybody on my cell phone. Call everybody that you know that can help us. At one point, I handed Sean Smith the shotgun, but just like me and everybody else that was in the safe haven, we were scared. But as a security professional with my military training and my agent training, I'm trained to remain more calm than a non-security professional.

So I took the weapon back from him seeing that he was visibly shaken. And I just waited to see what was unfolding. I was on the radio the whole time updating, you know, whispering. Turned the volume way down, you know, hey guys, they are in the building. Shortly after that, two individuals came up to the jail cell door and took out their AK–47s, and they are beating on the jail cell door. They also had grenades on them. And I thought they were going to take the grenades off and pit them on the locks and blow the locks.

So I tuned to the Ambassador, and said, you know, if they take their grenades off the door and put them on the locks, I'm going to start shooting. And when I go down, pick up the gun, and keep fighting. Thankfully, they didn't put the grenades on the locks. And they just kind of turned away, and walked to a different, you know, part of the house that I couldn't really see.

And then slowly, people started to kind of trickle out. And then the lights started to kind of dim. My initial response or my initial thought was, well, they just knocked out the generators. You know, we have regular city power but we also have backup generators. So flickering would be a likely, you know, cause of this. But in reality, it was smoke. And it took me about, you know, two or three seconds after that to determine that it was smoke.

As soon as I realized it was smoke, I turned to the Ambassador and Sean Smith and said, we are moving to the bathroom. And at that time, grabbed the Ambassador, Sean Smith was right behind him and we started crawling towards the bathroom. It's about a three- to four—meter crawl. And it only took seconds for us to reach—to reach the hallway that the bathroom was in. But by that time—seconds later, the smoke had already filled the entire room and I began basically army crawling like on my belly, and breathing though my hands like this, the last, you know, centimeter of air that was left.

And as soon as it became that thick, no light was visible from the lights that were fully on. The sounds were, you know, crackling and breaking of things from heat. And so to lead them to the bathroom, I was saying, Come on guys, follow me. And I was slapping my hands on the floor, or you know, hitting stuff with my hands if I felt anything. Like come on, you guys, follow me. Come on. We are going to the bathroom.

So I make it to the bathroom and nobody follows me in. The whole time I was slapping and saying, come on, follow me. My intention of going to the bathroom is because if we made it to the bathroom, I know there is a window that we can open. So what we would do is go into the bathroom, close the door, wet towels on the floor and open the window. And we could last, you know probably much longer in the bathroom than anywhere else in the house.

But because nobody followed me in, I wasn't going to close the door. So thinking about how I can better the situation, I open the window. And I thought that that could you know, provide some, you know, the lights in the bathroom. I could provide some light, or I could provide, you know, someplace with air and they could see that. But by opening the window, I stood up to open the window, and I thought my face was on fire. And I opened the window anyway and it just became a chimney and all the smoke started, you know, pouring out of the window and being sucked in my direction.

Because at that point that—I started to pass out. I could feel myself becoming weak and just overcome with smoke and heat. So I got back on the floor, took off my M4, because crawling with a slung weapon is extremely difficult. It was getting hung up on things, and I didn't want to be stuck in that building because of my M4. So I threw it in the bathroom, just left it there and started crawling towards my bedroom. And when I decided to do that, I was very clear to anybody else who could hear me, I'm moving to my bedroom. Come on guys, I'm moving to my bedroom. The whole time I'm hitting the floor, slapping, yelling. Come on, guys. Come on, you can do it. Let's go. Let's go. We are moving to my bedroom.

So I crawled to my bedroom. And as soon as I passed the threshold to my bedroom, you know, I had seconds left of life, essentially. And so I quickly went over to my window and started to crank open the metal shutters, but I was cranking the wrong way. So I had to turn back and crank it the other way. Then I had to open up the glass window, and then I had to pull a pin and push out this big metal gate. And as soon as I did that, I collapsed on to my little patio area.

And around the patio area was, you know, maybe a 2½-foot tall cinderblock wall. And as soon as I went out there, I just started taking fire immediately. I remember hearing explosions, which I equate to grenades. I remember feeling the cement exploding and hitting me in the face. And I remember the sounds. So after catching my breath, I jumped back into the building and I searched for the Ambassador and Sean Smith. I went as far as my threshold, and reached out into the—into the area we had just come from to see if I could feel anybody. But the smoke and heat were so intense that, I mean, the smoke was coming in though my eyes, even though they were closed. It was coming in through my nose. And I stayed in there until I could—physically couldn't do it any more.

When I was in the Navy, they engrain in you, 110 percent. And most people don't think you can do 110 percent, but it's part of my character. I do 110 percent and I stayed in there until—until I physically could not and mentally could not stay in there any longer.

I went back out of the building, caught my breath on the patio again, immediately taking rounds, the same stuff, whizzing, you know, jumped back into the building, and I had intentions—you know, I was just thinking of any way that I could possibly signal them or let them know where I was besides yelling and slapping and hitting stuff.

And I remembered that I had a lamp in my room, and I went over to my lamp and I turned on my lamp, thinking that they could see it in the smoke. But it didn't turn on. And so I held it up to my eye to see if it was working, and I remember seeing a very faint glow when it was this close. I remember feeling the heat of the lamp, and I could just barely see the actual light from it.

That's how thick the smoke was. And I went back to my threshold, searched around, still yelling, still saying, "Come on guys," you know, to my bedroom. No response. Nothing. I went back out and caught my breath again, still taking rounds. And I went back in one or two more times to try and find them, and I couldn't. The last time I went out, you know, I decided that if I went back into the building that I wasn't going to come back out. The smoke and heat were way too powerful, and way too strong, and it was extremely confusing feeling my way in a smoke-filled building. And I didn't want to get lost, and so I decided to climb up the ladder up to the roof.

I climbed up the ladder, and pulled up the ladder behind me and that's the moment that I knew that Ambassador Stevens and Sean Smith were probably dead. Immediately, upon getting up to the roof, I started radioing for my colleagues, you know, telling them the situation, you know, telling them my situation, you know, I am exhausted. I am completely exhausted. I gave everything I had. And I'm still thinking of ways to help, still thinking of ways to get the guys out.

So I remember that we have a skylight in the top of the building, and so I, you know, we had a little stash of gear up on the roof. So I went over and I grabbed an M4 magazine and I climbed up on to this little platform which is near the window. But it's protected by these metal bars. And I couldn't break the window. But I remember yelling and hitting it as hard as I possibly could.

The bad guys saw me up there, started shooting at me again. I remember seeing tracer fire right over my head. I remember hearing the whizzing of the rounds going past me. And so I climbed, you know, back down off the ledge and just got on the radio. "Hey, guys, I'm on a frying pan. This thing is hot. The smoke is coming out of the building and going right on to the roof. If I pick my head up I'm getting shot at, and I can't—I can't do this forever."

Finally, over the radio, [Agent 4] says, "[Agent 5], we are coming to get you." You know, at that time a couple of seconds were gone, and he was like, "Hang on. Hang on. We are coming to get you" I don't know how long I was up on the roof, but for me it was a while.

Finally, the other guys came over in a fully-armored vehicle and parked right at the base of kind of my location and set up a small perimeter, called me down off the roof. I climbed down and they were all amazed to see me still alive. Just my condition was, you know, my face was black. My eyeballs were black. My nose was black. Everything I had was black. But as a security professional, I said, "Give me a gun." [Agent 2] gave me a 9-millimeter pistol which I was a little unhappy about, but I took it anyway and stood—stood a position on the outside.

And [Agent 4]—[Agent 4] and [Agent 1] tried to go inside the building and find them, but shortly after that, their report was way too hot, way too smokey. You know, we are going to get lost in there. Somebody is going to die if we keep this up.[27]

---

[27] Testimony of Diplomatic Security Agent 5 [Agent 5], Diplomatic Sec. Agent, U.S. Dep't of State, Tr. at 123 (Apr. 1, 2015) [hereinafter Agent 5 Testimony] (on file with the Committee).

Agent 3, Diplomatic Security agent in charge at the Benghazi Mission compound, testified he was in constant contact with the Diplomatic Security Command Center:

> I was in the best position to see the attacks happen, unfold. I was in the TOC [Tactical Operations Center] at the special mission compound. I manned the cameras. You guys have seen the video. Any time you see the camera moving, that's me. Subsequently, I was also in a position to review the cameras and be aware of all the situational awareness at the second compound, all of which I have shared. Much of the attack was passed in real-time through my phone to DS command center.[28]

Agent 3 also testified about what he saw:

> It was 9:42 at night, and I was wrapping up work and had some emails. My shift should have been done three or four hours earlier. I'm in the TOC office in the TOC building. I hear several, three to four, gunshots and an explosion that seemed substantially closer than what I heard earlier, which was the fireworks. The fireworks I kind of expected to happen every night at about 9:30 give or take. Initially I thought they were just a little bit late.
>
> So I get up. I go to the window, which is actually covered by two bookcases and has sandbags on the outside, so not to see anything, but actually to hear a little better I go to the window. I think I heard the shots or explosions first and then something more subsequent than that, either an additional explosion or additional gunfire, that sounded very close. I turn. I glance maybe a second, probably less, at the surveillance camera monitors and see a large group of personnel coming on. They're already on the compound, effectively in the middle of compound C. Right where this small roundabout is, there's a camera on a pole there. And I saw a large group. My original assessment was 16 to 20 armed men, a couple of them with banners[.][29]

Agent 3 testified this information was being relayed back to the Diplomatic Security Command Center [DSCC]:

> We are relaying what is going on via the cameras, where slowly the barrack buildings [Villa C], which is one of the villas on the compound on the map, is set on fire, and then slowly those forces migrate over to our side, where they pin us in, basically, in both of our locations, in Villa B and the TOC building, where they proceed to gain entry into Villa B and attempt to kick the door in to the TOC building for 10 to 15 minutes. . . . [t]he situation on the ground was rough out there. There was heavy weapons. Some guys have grenades that have already gone off. Everybody is armed with either a pistol or a long gun. Some-

---

[28] Testimony of Diplomatic Security Agent 3 [Agent 3], Diplomatic Sec. Agent, U.S. Dep't of State, Tr. at 77 (Oct. 8, 2013) [hereinafter Agent 3 Testimony] (on file with the Committee).
[29] *Id.* at 135–136.

body shows up at some point with, like, a bazooka. So it is tough.[30]

Diplomatic Security Agent 1 called the DSCC when attackers were attempting to break into the room where he and another agent had barricaded themselves. He testified:

Q: You mentioned earlier that you used your BlackBerry to call the DS Command Center. When did you first call the DS Command Center during this sequence of events?

A: So before they breached, when they made the first attempt, the first attempt they didn't breach into the room yet. But it was imminent that they were going to breach and they were going to come in. So at that point we bunkered in and started to proceed making calls. So [Agent 2] was calling Tripoli and I called the Command Center. I believe it was 18 minutes after the attack.[31]

Diplomatic Security Agent 2 also spoke with the DSCC during the attacks. He testified:

I stayed on the roof of that building for the majority of the night. I made several phone calls back and forth to the DS Command Center in D.C. relaying information. I also made phone calls to one of the Ambassador's contacts to try to get some atmospherics about what was going on in the rest of the city, should we need to do a ground evac.[32]

Agent 2 told the Committee he was providing "general situational awareness" to the DSCC so they could "make accurate decisions." He testified:

A: Yeah. He wanted to know the status of the accountability of the Americans who were on post, specifically the Ambassador, what information we had. There were also additional reports coming in that the Ambassador might have been at a hospital in a burn unit and we were trying to verify the validity of those claims. And then just general situational awareness for the Command Center in D.C.

Q: So your sense of kind of your—what you were doing there was kind of giving an ongoing as things were unfolding so that they would have the information to help assess how to continue responding?

A: Yes. My intent was to provide them the information that I had so they had timely information so they could make accurate decisions.[33]

---

[30] Id. at 145–146.
[31] Agent 1 Testimony at 62.
[32] Testimony of [Agent 2], Diplomatic Sec. Agent, U.S. Dep't of State, Tr. at 100 (Mar. 19, 2015) [hereinafter Agent 2 Testimony] (on file with the Committee).
[33] Id. at 102.

Diplomatic Security Agent 4 testified it was his job to "immediately" contact the DSCC in the event of an attack.[34] He testified about the beginning of the attack:

Q: Would it be then an accurate description to describe the attack as sort of a stealth attack?

A: It was very sudden. As I had mentioned, the only warning that I had that something was amiss was that—kind of that cry that I heard at the main gate. So it was very sudden.[35]

Agent 4 also testified of the attack:

A: No, I never told them that there was a protest.

Q: Was it your assessment that there was a protest?

A: No.

Q: Do you believe there was a protest?

A: I don't.[36]

At the Diplomatic Security Command Center, Charlene R. Lamb, Deputy Assistant Secretary for International Programs, State Department, was monitoring the situation in real time and was aware of the reports coming in from the agents under attack in Benghazi. She testified she was in "constant contact" with the agents on the ground and had an "almost full-time connection" to them:

A: I was in my office, and I received a phone call, I don't remember if it was directly from the command center or if it was from the desk officer, but I received a phone call that notified me that there was a problem.

Q: And that's what they said, it was a problem? Did they elaborate? Did they tell you anything more?

A: They said that they had the RSO on the phone and that the compound was under attack. And I didn't ask any more questions. I believe I notified Scott Bultrowicz, [Principal Deputy Assistant Secretary for Diplomatic Security, State Department] and we both went down to the command center.

\* \* \*

Q: And so once you learned of the attack, then what did you do?

A: I had a liaison officer that worked for me who had employees that worked in the Annex there, so I immediately called him on my way down to the command center and asked him to join me in the command center. And when we went in there, we initially tried to assess the situation the best we could, and then we started working on trying

---

[34] Testimony of Diplomatic Security Agent 4 [Agent 4], Diplomatic Sec. Agent, U.S. Dep't of State, Tr. at 85 (Mar. 16, 2015) [hereinafter Agent 4 Testimony] (on file with the Committee).
[35] Id. at 144.
[36] Id. at 155.

to identify security assets who could help them with the situation that was unfolding.

Q: And what assets would those have been?

A: Assets that were at the Annex facility. We made phone calls to Stuttgart, to AFRICOM [United States Africa Command] and EUCOM [United States Europe Command] to see if they had any assets in theater that were nearby that could possibly be drawn on for additional support.

Q: And did you discuss those assets and deployment with PDAS [Principal Desputy Assistant Secretary] Bultrowicz or Under Secretary Kennedy?

A: Yes. PDAS Scott Bultrowicz was in the room, he was on the phone with Pat Kennedy and Eric Boswell, and he was relaying information. As we were getting information in, he would relay it to them——

\* \* \*

Q: And was the DS command center your only source of information that night or were you in constant contact with the Annex as well via your liaison?

A: Yes. My liaison had constant contact with the Annex. We had almost full-time connection to the DS agents that were on the ground, and then we were—you know, towards the end, we were getting information off of Twitter and public media. So those were our primary sources of information.[37]

A senior watch officer at the DSCC described the events as "a full on attack against our compound."[38] The same individual also said there was "zip, nothing nada" when asked if there was any rioting in Benghazi reported prior to the attack.[39]

At 6:34 p.m. on September 11, 2012, the DSCC sent a "terrorism event information" to the Office of the Secretary.[40] The update noted that "host nation militia forces have responded to the U.S. Consulate in Benghazi" and "were engaged with the attackers."[41]

Lamb testified information received by the DSCC—directly from all of the agents on the ground—was relayed to Kennedy.[42] None of the Diplomatic Security agents on the ground reported anything about a protest in Benghazi. None of the Diplomatic Security agents on the ground reported anything about a video.

Kennedy testified that he passed on information from the DSCC directly to Secretary of State Hillary R. Clinton:

I stayed in my office, except for the SVTC [Secure Video Teleconference] the chairman referred to, monitoring my

---

[37] Testimony of Charlene Lamb, Deputy Ass't Sec'y for Diplomatic Sec., U.S. Dep't of State, Tr. at 14–16 (Jan. 7, 2016) [hereinafter Lamb Testimony] (on file with the Committee).

[38] Email from Diplomatic Sec. Agent 27, U.S. Dep't of State, to svcSMARTCrossLow (Sept. 12 2012, 10:20 AM) (on file with the Committee, C05389586).

[39] Email from Diplomatic Sec. Agent 27, U.S. Dep't of State (Sept. 18, 2012, 1:16 PM) (on file with the Committee, C05390678).

[40] Email from U.S. Dep't of State to S_SpecialAssistants (Sept. 11, 2012, 6:34 PM) (on file with the Committee, C05578699).

[41] Id.

[42] Lamb Testimony at 15.

telephone, monitoring my emails, and making telephone calls or coordinating activities as were required. . . . I went up several times to brief the Secretary on the latest information that I was receiving from Diplomatic Security, which was receiving it from the ground.[43]

## KNOWLEDGE BY SENIOR STATE DEPARTMENT OFFICIALS

At 4:06 p.m. in Washington D.C. on September 11, 2012, 24 minutes after the attacks began in Benghazi, the State Department Operations Center issued a widely disseminated email to Department officials, including the Office of the Secretary, indicating an attack was occurring. With the subject "U.S. Diplomatic Mission in Benghazi Under Attack," the email stated:

> The Regional Security Officer reports the diplomatic mission is under attack. Embassy Tripoli reports approximately 20 armed people fired shots; explosions have been heard as well. Ambassador Stevens, who is currently in Benghazi, and four COM [Chief of Mission] personnel are in the compound safe haven. The 17th of February militia is providing security support.[44]

Forty eight minutes later, a 4:54 p.m. update email stated:

> Embassy Tripoli reports the firing at the U.S. Diplomatic Mission in Benghazi has stopped and the compound has been cleared. A response team is on site attempting to locate COM personnel.[45]

A 6:07 p.m. update email with the subject "Ansar al-Sharia Claims Responsibility for Benghazi Attack" stated:

> Embassy Tripoli reports the group claimed responsibility on Facebook and Twitter and has called for attack on Embassy Tripoli.[46]

Gregory N. Hicks, Deputy Chief of Mission in Tripoli, was the United States' highest ranking official in Tripoli at the time of the attacks in Benghazi. Hicks testified that he talked with Ambassador Stevens moments after the attack started:

> A: I punched the number that I did not recognize and called it back, to call it back, and I got Chris on the line. And he said, "Greg, we are under attack." And I am walking outside, trying to get outside, because we have notoriously bad cell phone connectivity at our residence, and usually it's better outside. So I say, my response is,

---

[43] Testimony of Patrick F. Kennedy, Under Sec'y for Mgmt., U.S. Dep't of State, Tr. at 119 (Feb. 3, 2016) [hereinafter Kennedy Testimony] (on file with the Committee).

[44] Email from OpsAlert@state.gov to S_Special Assistants, et al. (Sept. 11, 2012, 4:05 PM) (on file with the Committee, C05272001).

[45] Email from OpsAlert@state.gov to S_SpecialAssistants, et al. (Sept. 11, 2012, 4:54 PM) (on file with the Committee, C05272001).

[46] Email from OpsAlert@state.gov to S_SpecialAssistants, et al. (Sept. 11, 2012, 6:07 PM) (on file with the Committee, C05272001).

"Okay," and I am about to say something else, and the line clicks.

I try to reach him back on the—I begin walking immediately to our tactical operations center, because I knew that everybody would be gathering there, and I could then also summon everybody that needed to be at the—to begin the process of responding. And I am trying to call back on those numbers to reconnect, and not getting—either not getting a signal or not getting a response.

Q: And did you ever make a connection with the Ambassador again?

A: No. I never did.

Q: That was the last you spoke to him?

A: That was the last I spoke to him.[47]

Hicks also testified that Stevens would have reported a protest had one occurred prior to the attack:

Absolutely, I mean, we're talking about both security officers who know their trade, even though they are brand new, and one of the finest political officers in the history of the Foreign Service. You know, for there to have been a demonstration on Chris Stevens' front door and him not to have reported it is unbelievable. And secondly, if he had reported it, he would have been out the back door within minutes of any demonstration appearing anywhere near that facility. And there was a back gate to the facility, and, you know, it worked.[48]

Throughout the course of the evening, Hicks was on the phone with Elizabeth Jones, Acting Assistant Secretary of State, Near Eastern Affairs, State Department,who was in Washington D.C. at the time, updating her about the events on the ground in Benghazi. Jones testified:

I sat down and called Greg Hicks and said, Tell me what is going on. I have this report from my special assistant, from the op[erations] center; what's going on? He said, I talked to Chris 20 minutes ago. Chris called me. He said, We're under attack.

I said, What do you mean we're under attack? He said there are people firing guns at us, firing weapons, firing at us. And I said, Where is Chris?

He said—he said that the RSO [Regional Security Officer] told him that they had taken—that Chris had said, We're going to the safe haven, and the regional security officer in Tripoli have reported, yes, the security officers in Benghazi had taken the ambassador to the safe haven.

---

[47] Testimony of Gregory N. Hicks, Deputy Chief of Mission at U.S. Embassy Tripoli, U.S. Dep't of State, Tr. at 18–19 (Apr. 11, 2013) [hereinafter Hicks Testimony] (on file with the Committee).

[48] Id. at 81–82.

I said, Okay. You talked to him 20 minutes ago. Call him again. He said, I've been trying. He doesn't answer the phone.

I asked, Who else was in the—in the building, where was Chris exactly, who else was in the building. He explained that Sean Smith was, that's the communicator, that there were three RSOs there and that they would—they were moving the two to the safe haven and that the others were trying to protect the building.

I immediately notified by email as many people as I could think of off the top of my head on the Seventh Floor [senior State Department leaders], that I had spoken to Greg, that this is what the situation was, that—that I would continue to stay in touch with him. In the meantime, I had a secure call from my CIA counterpart saying the same thing, We're hearing that Benghazi is under attack. I said, Is your annex under attack, which I knew to be a few minutes away.

He said, No. And I continued to be in touch with him, the—my CIA colleague and my staff. I decided to not work out of my office initially but work closer to where the secure phone is, which is on the other end of the suite and stayed in very close touch with Greg essentially all night long till the next morning.

The—what I did in the second phone call, I believe it was with Greg, I said, Okay. Who are you talking to in the Libyan government?

He said, I've talked to—I've forgotten, the chief of staff of various of the senior people.

I said, Talk to the President, talk to the Prime Minister, don't just stay with the chief of staff. Talk to the senior people yourself and ask them for help. Tell them they've got to get their people up there, not—get their people up there to go over to the compound to render assistance to get the—get the attackers out of there, and I kept asking, Have you heard from Chris? Have you heard from Chris?

No, we can't find him. No, he's not—no, he's not answering. That was the first. And I don't remember the timeline anymore. It seemed like forever, but it probably w[as]n't that long.[49]

Jones testified that she spoke with Hicks throughout the evening, almost every ten minutes:

Q: Okay. As the night wore on, was the phone just essentially left almost in permanent communication with Tripoli?

A: Yes.

---

[49] Testimony of Elizabeth Jones, Acting Ass't Sec'y, U.S. Dep't of State, Tr. at 39–40 (July 11, 2013) [hereinafter Jones Testimony] (on file with the Committee).

Q: I mean, do you have that capability that you have an open line that just essentially stays open, or is this—or calling every 5 or 10 minutes? I'm just curious how that works.

A: Yeah. No, that's a good question. I didn't have an open line.

We did two things. I stayed in my office with my front office team and with my staff assistants and with—Agent 1 was there. We, at the same time, started a task force in the Operations Center, so the Libya desk officers were up there helping manage some of the more routine issues, getting the evacuation going, working with EX [logistics] on those kinds of issues and sort of doing the—helping us with the nuts and bolts on implementing the things that we were deciding that we needed to do.

Because DS kept the open—Diplomatic Secretary kept an open line—actually, I don't know that it was an open line. They had communication directly with the RSO. I basically worked primarily with Greg Hicks on his cell phone because that worked better in terms of Embassy communications and I could reach him wherever he was—wherever he was in the compound when he was moving around. So I communicated by my office manager dialing him directly on his cell phone.

So it was not an open line, but it was—I don't know that we talked every 10 minutes, but it seemed like it was every 10 minutes. It was close to that.[50]

After some of Jones' discussions with Hicks, an assistant from the Office of the Secretary drafted emails about Jones' conversations with Hicks. These emails were disseminated to senior officials within the State Department, including Sullivan, Nuland, and William J. Burns, the Deputy Secretary of State.[51]

At 4:49 p.m., just over an hour after the attacks began, an assistant in the Office of the Secretary wrote:

Beth Jones just spoke with DCM Tripoli Greg Hicks, who advised a Libyan militia (we now know this is the 17th Feb brigade, as requested by Emb[assy] office) is responding to the attack on the diplomatic mission in Benghazi. The QRF [Quick Reaction Force] is in the compound, engaging the attackers, taking fire, and working its way through the compound to get to the villa, where Ambassador Stevens is in safe haven for extraction. The ARSO [Assistant Regional Security Officer] is also there in the compound. Greg spoke with Amb Stevens by phone 20 minutes before my call (which was about ten minutes ago). Greg will talk to the Prime Minister's Chief of Staff, and then speak with the Foreign Minister . . . Embassy is

---

[50] *Id.* at 79–80.
[51] *See, e.g.,* Email from U.S. Dep't of State to Victoria J. Nuland, Spokesperson, U.S. Dep't of State, *et al.* (Sept. 11, 2012, 5:32 PM) (on file with the Committee, C05391036).

sending medical assistance to Benghazi to be on stand-by. More updates to follow.[52]

At 5:13 p.m. a new email was sent to the group. It stated:

Just spoke again with Greg Hicks, who confirmed the party includes Ambassador Stevens plus three, not plus four. Hicks has been in contact twice with the Libyan President's office and twice with the Libyan PM's [Prime Minister's] office; their offices assured him they are fully engaged and consider themselves personal friends of Ambassador Stevens. Hicks has been coordinating with the [CIA] who has learned from the QRF about the status of the compound—currently they are clearing the compound and working to access the party. I also urged Libyan Ambassador to the U.S. Aujali to engage on this immediately at the highest level.[53]

An email at 5:32 p.m., the first in the chain sent to Cheryl Mills, Chief of Staff and Counselor, State Department, stated:

The fighting has stopped, DCM Greg Hicks just confirmed to me. He also confirmed one fatality: Sean Smith—a TDY'er from The Hague—has died. His body has been recovered. The five ARSO's are accounted for, but they're still trying to find the Ambassador. The Principal Officer's residence is still on fire with toxic smoke. I have spoken to A/S [Assistant Secretary] Gordon and Liz Dibble is contacting the Charge at The Hague, **[redacted text]**, to inform them.[54]

A 5:55 p.m. email to the same chain sent by an assistant in the Office of the Secretary stated:

I just spoke again to Greg Hicks, who himself spoke again to the offices of the Libyan President and Prime Minister, asking them to provide firefighting equipment to the Benghazi compound. He said the PD shop at Embassy Tripoli has found postings on Facebook indicating that the "Tripoli Council" plans to carry out an attack on Embassy Tripoli. He said he was promised increased police protection but it had not yet materialized.

Greg said his team reports that the extremist group Ansar Al Sharia has taken credit for the attack in Benghazi. He heard reports that the February 17 Brigade is currently engaged in a running battle with Ansar Al Sharia; he asked the offices of the President and PM to pursue Ansar al Sharia.

---

[52] Email from U.S. Dep't of State to William J. Burns, Deputy Sec'y of State, U.S. Dep't of State, *et al.* (Sept. 11, 2012, 4:49 PM) (on file with the Committee, C05391036).

[53] Email from U.S. Dep't of State to Jacob J. Sullivan, Deputy Chief of Staff and Dir. of Policy Planning, U.S. Dep't of State, *et al.* (Sept. 11, 2012, 5:13 PM) (on file with the Committee, C05391036).

[54] Email from U.S. Dep't of State to Cheryl D. Mills, Chief of Staff & Counselor to the U.S. Sec'y of State, U.S. Dep't of State, *et al.* (Sept. 11, 2012, 5:32 PM) (on file with the Committee, C05391036).

On working to locate Ambassador Stevens, the RSO team and militia are still on compound, which is 50 acres—Greg expressed the hope that Ambassador Stevens is in hiding somewhere on the compound. The PO's residence is still on fire.[55]

These emails consistently used the term "attack." None of these emails mentioned anything about a protest. None of these emails mentioned anything about a video.

Hicks also spoke directly with the Secretary while the attacks were still ongoing. He testified:

A: No. I really didn't get—you know, about 2:00 a.m. [8:00 p.m. in Washington D.C.], the Secretary called——

Q: Okay.

A: —along with—her senior staff was on the——

Q: Okay. Do you recall who was on that call?

A: It was Wendy Sherman, Cheryl Mills, Steve Mull, Beth Jones, Liz—I am not sure whether Liz Dibble was on the phone or not at that time. I know Beth Jones was. Jake Sullivan.

And so I briefed her on what was going on, talked about the situation. And at 2:00 a.m., of course, Chris [Stevens] is in the hospital, although the Libyan Government will not confirm that he's in the hospital. All they will tell us is he's in a safe place, or they will imply that he's with us at the [Annex] facility, which, of course, we have to feed back to them and say, no, we don't know where he is. It is a constant conversation, and I'm still talking to the same people.

The Vice Minister of the Interior chimes in sometime before midnight. And I'm pressing him to get their firefighters to the building to put the fire out, assuming that if they go to put the fire out, that they will send some security people with the firefighters to protect the firefighters. We tried everything that we could.

So we brief her on what's going on. She asks, How can we help? And I said, Well, we could use some reinforcements. And we have—we know we have wounded. And——

Q: What was the answer?

A: The answer was that the FAST team in Rota was being mobilized to come to Tripoli, and there would be a medevac flight coming down to pick up wounded.

And then we discussed also whether we were going to— they asked me if we were going to stay in the residential compound. And I said, no, we needed to consolidate our facilities here, because we basically sent everybody we have to protect us to Tripoli to rescue them.

---

[55] Email from U.S. Dep't of State to Victoria J. Nuland, Spokesperson, U.S. Dep't of State, *et al.* (Sept. 11, 2012, 5:55PM) (on file with the Committee, C05391036).

Q: To?

A: To Benghazi. Sorry. Benghazi. Apologies. And they said, good.

Q: And how long does that call last?

A: Ten minutes.[56]

None of the information coming directly from the agents on the ground in Benghazi during the attacks mentioned anything about a video or a protest. These first-hand accounts made their way to the Office of the Secretary through multiple channels quickly: through the Diplomatic Security Command Center; through the State Department Operations Center; through emails recounting Jones' phone calls with Hicks; through Kennedy, who briefed the Secretary directly; and through Hicks himself during a phone call with the Secretary.

## THE SECRETARY'S STATEMENT

The principal public statement from the U.S. government the night of the Benghazi attacks, September 11, 2012, came from the Secretary of State and was issued at 10:08 p.m. It stated in full:

### STATEMENT ON THE ATTACK IN BENGHAZI

I condemn in the strongest terms the attack on our mission in Benghazi today. As we work to secure our personnel and facilities, we have confirmed that one of our State Department officers was killed. We are heartbroken by this terrible loss. Our thoughts and prayers are with his family and those who have suffered in this attack.

This evening, I called Libyan President Magariaf to coordinate additional support to protect Americans in Libya. President Magariaf expressed his condemnation and condolences and pledged his government's full cooperation.

Some have sought to justify this vicious behavior as a response to inflammatory material posted on the Internet. The United States deplores any intentional effort to denigrate the religious beliefs of others. Our commitment to religious tolerance goes back to the very beginning of our nation. But let me be clear: There is never any justification for violent acts of this kind.

In light of the events of today, the United States government is working with partner countries around the world to protect our personnel, our missions, and American citizens worldwide.[57]

The decision for the Secretary to issue the statement appears to have been made earlier that evening during a 7:30 p.m. secure video teleconference [SVTC], a meeting hosted by the White House,

---

[56] Hicks Testimony at 32–34.
[57] Press Release, U.S. Dep't of State, Statement on the Attack in Benghazi (Sept. 11, 2012), http://www.state.gov/secretary/20092013clinton/rm/2012/09/197628.htm [hereinafter September 11 Statement].

that included senior officials from the State Department, Intelligence Community, and Defense Department to discuss the events unfolding in Benghazi.

Rough notes from the White House meeting describe ten specific action items. One of these action items stated:

> The Secretary will issue a statement tonight condemning the attacks and stating an official American was killed. . . . S may issue another statement to distance the United States from the Pastor Jones video.[58]

The Secretary did not, however, issue two statements that evening. She issued one. And that single statement condemned the attack, stated an American was killed, and distanced the United States from an internet video. In doing so, the statement—specifically the language "[s]ome have sought to justify this vicious behavior as a response to inflammatory material posted on the Internet"—appeared to connect, or at least conflate, the attacks in Benghazi with the video.[59] This connection between the attacks and the video continued for over a week, leading the public to believe that a video-inspired protest led to the attacks that killed Ambassador Chris Stevens and Sean Smith, Tyrone Woods, and Glen Doherty.

The 7:30 p.m. White House meeting was convened to discuss the Benghazi attacks and included the Secretary of State and other high level officials from the State Department, Defense Department, and White House. The meeting, however, contained a great deal of discussion regarding the video. Matt Olsen, Director, National Counterterrorism Center, was a participant in the meeting. He testified:

> Q: Was there any discussion of sort of the video and Benghazi being linked on the call?
>
> A: I don't remember specifically, you know, how we talked about it. I'm sure that we did, right, because we were—the fact is that it came—the discussion of taking the video down was part of our conversation in this call that was really focused on what was going on in Benghazi.[60]

Olsen also said:

> And in my own mind, at the time, I recall linking the two, you know, that this—we were thinking about what had happened in Cairo, we were thinking, okay, now this seems to be happening in Benghazi, and we're worried about other, obviously, other diplomatic posts in the Middle East and North Africa.
>
> On that particular issue, one thing that I recall in thinking, again, sort of preparing for coming here, sort of trying to recollect as much as possible, one of the issues that Denis [McDonough] asked me—and I think Nick Ras-

---

[58] Email from Watch Officer, U.S. Dep't of State, to P_StaffAssistants & D(N)_StaffAssistants (Sept. 11, 2012, 9:46 PM) (on file with the Committee, C05562037).

[59] September 11 Statement, *supra* note 57.

[60] Testimony of Matthew Olsen, Dir., Nat'l Counterterrorism Center, Tr. at 17–18 (Feb. 16, 2016) [hereinafter Olsen Testimony] (on file with the Committee).

mussen, my deputy, was there as well—was to see if we could work with—if we could contact Google to talk with them about enforcing their terms of service, which was the way that we often thought about offensive or problematic content.[61]

Five of the ten action items from the rough notes of the 7:30 p.m. meeting reference the video—including an item mentioning Leon E. Panetta, Secretary of Defense, and Martin E. Dempsey, Chairman of the Joint Chiefs of Staff, reaching out to "Pastor Jones" directly.[62] For nearly two years the White House had been issuing public statements in the wake of actions committed by "Pastor Jones,"[63] although no connection at the time linked "Pastor Jones" or the video to the Benghazi attacks.

Avril Haines, Deputy Counsel to the President for National Security Affairs, held a conference call after the 7:30 p.m. meeting. Rough notes from the call stated:

> There is likely to be a statement from S[ecretary Clinton] this evening addressing the violence and distancing the USG [United States government] from the videos that are believed to have instigated it (at least in part); while no one is sure of the cause, exactly, there is reportedly a new Terry Jones video threatening to burn Korans and a second film that includes a number of insulting statement about Mohamed.[64]

The fact the 7:30 p.m. White House meeting, which took place while Ambassador Stevens was considered missing and before Tyrone S. Woods and Glen A. Doherty were killed, was about the attacks in Benghazi but much of the conversation focused on the video is surprising given no direct link or solid evidence existed connecting the attacks in Benghazi and the video at the time the White House meeting took place. The State Department senior officials at the White House meeting had access to eyewitness accounts to the attack in real time. The Diplomatic Security Command Center was in direct contact with the Diplomatic Security Agents on the ground in Benghazi and sent out multiple updates about the situation, including a "Terrorism Event Notification."[65] The State Department Watch Center had also notified Sullivan and

---

[61] *Id.* at 18.

[62] Email from Watch Officer, U.S. Dep't of State, to P StaffAssistants and D(N) StaffAssistants (Sept. 11, 2012) (on file with the Committee, C05562037).

[63] *See, e.g.,* Krissah Thompson and Tara Bahrampour, *Obama renews call for religious tolerance after Koran-burning canceled,* WASH. POST, Sept. 10, 2012 ("Obama denied that his administration's forceful intervention—Defense Secretary Robert M. Gates made a personal appeal to the Gainesville pastor, the Rev. Terry Jones—had unnecessarily drawn attention to the pastor's plans."); and *Obama criticizes Quran burning, Afghan attacks,* NBC News, April 2, 2011, www.nbcnews.com/id/42396945/ns/world_news-south_and_central_asia/t/obama-criticizes-quran-burning-afghan-attacks/#.VloSrvkjrJaR ("At least 10 people have been killed and 83 injured in the southern Afghan city of Kandahar, officials said on Saturday, on a second day of violent protests over the actions of extremist Christian preacher Terry Jones . . . 'No religion tolerates the slaughter and beheading of innocent people, and there is no justification for such a dishonorable and deplorable act,' Obama said.").

[64] Email from Attorney, U.S. Dep't of State, to Harold Koh, Legal Advisor, U.S. Dep't of State, *et al.* (Sept. 11, 2012, 10:40 PM) (on file with the Committee, C05528017).

[65] Email from DS Command Center to DSCC_C DS Seniors, DSCC_E TIA/PII, DSCC_E TIA/ITA, and DS–IP (Sept. 12, 2012, 5:05 AM) (on file with the Committee, C05389586).

Mills that it was setting up a direct telephone line to Benghazi.[66] There was no mention of the video from the agents on the ground. Hicks—one of the last people to talk to Stevens before he died—said there was virtually no discussion about the video in Libya leading up to the attacks.

That did not, however, deter participants at theWhite House meeting—led by Denis McDonough, Deputy National Security Advisor to the President—from extensively discussing the video.

As a result of the White House meeting, the Secretary of State issued a statement about the attacks later that evening. Rather than relaying known facts from those experiencing the attacks firsthand, however, the Secretary's statement created a narrative tying the events in Benghazi to the video, despite a dearth of actual evidence. This was done by mentioning the video and the attacks in the same sentence: "Some have sought to justify this vicious behavior as a response to inflammatory material posted on the Internet."[67]

Sullivan testified about the decision to include that sentence in the statement:

> Q: Do you recall whose idea it was to include that sentence?
>
> A: I believe that it was my idea to include that sentence. It was either mine or Toria's [State Department spokesperson] or a combination of the two of us, but I thought it was important to include that sentence.
>
> Q: And why is that?
>
> A: Well there are two aspects to this. One was we didn't know the motivation of the actual attackers of Benghazi, so I didn't want to say they did it because of the video, and so I chose the words very carefully to say that some have sought to justify it on that basis.
>
> But I thought it was really important for us to be able to express our views on the video and to say there is never any justification for violent acts of this kind, as well as to say we deplore efforts to denigrate the religious beliefs of others because I was deeply concerned that we could potentially face attacks on our embassies elsewhere. And, unfortunately, that's exactly what happened.[68]

Sullivan did not say why it would not have been equally or even more important to denounce the video when it began circulating in the Middle East days earlier, or after the protests in Cairo where the link to the video was clear. Sullivan testified:

> I thought very hard about exactly how to formulate this. I didn't want to say the attackers did this because of the video. That's why I chose to use the phrase "justify," be-

[66] Email from U.S. Dep't of State to Jacob J. Sullivan, Deputy Chief of Staff and Dir. of Policy Planning, U.S. Dep't of State, et al. (Sept. 11, 2012, 4:38 PM) (on file with the Committee, C05561866).

[67] Id.

[68] Testimony of Jacob J. Sullivan, Deputy Chief of Staff and Dir. of Policy Planning, U.S. Dep't of State, Tr. at 220 (Jan. 12, 2016) [hereinafter Sullivan Testimony] (on file with the Committee).

cause I just wanted to talk more generally about people who might justify the attack on the basis of the video. Who would those people be? They would be the kind of people that would go try to gin up protests elsewhere, whether in Benghazi again or in Tripoli or anywhere else around the region.

And my first concern in getting this out was to do everything we could do to try to prevent further violence from happening. And I really thought it was important for the Secretary to get on the record on this issue. And in the days that followed, I thought it was important for her to continue getting on the record on this issue, especially as we dealt with these assaults on our embassies across the region.

So I thought hard about this paragraph. I thought hard about making sure we formulated it in a way that was accurate to say that just some had sought to justify it. Obviously, we have all seen a lot of public reporting linking things as well. So this, to me, was an important paragraph to include in this statement.[69]

Sullivan apparently did not engage in nearly as much thought about the video when it first appeared online, or even when the U.S. Embassy was breached by protestors in Cairo earlier on September 11, 2012. Where there was a known connection to the video, Sullivan was silent. Where the video was not connected by even a scintilla of reliable evidence at the time, Sullivan thought it important enough to include.

Dan Schwerin, Speechwriter, Department of State, helped draft the statement that went out that evening. Schwerin told the Committee the statement was intended to speak to a global audience. He testified:

Q: You talked about speaking to a global audience. What did you mean by that?

A: I mean any time the Secretary of State speaks, the world is listening. We had—it was a period of unrest across the Middle East, North Africa, and beyond; specifically, in the Muslim world, which was a source of concern; and how to lower that temperature and speak to that situation was an important issue.

Q: Was that focused on the video?

A: The video was the source of that unrest across the world in that period. And so, you know, lowering the temperature of that situation was one of our goals.[70]

While protests around the Middle East flared up in the following days, at the time of the Benghazi attacks the protest in Cairo represented the only instance of unrest.

---

[69] *Id.* at 221.
[70] Testimony of Daniel B. Schwerin, Staff Assistant and Speechwriter, U.S. Dep't of State, Tr. at 21 (Oct. 9, 2015) [hereinafter Schwerin Testimony] (on file with the Committee).

Megan Rooney, Speechwriter, Department of State, also worked on the statement and told the Committee that it was a "common-sense conclusion" that the video somehow sparked what happened in Benghazi, because it had done so in Cairo. She testified:

Q: Right. As you sit here today, do you recall anything generally about the conversation specific to the video that night?

A: No. Only that we thought it belonged in the statement.

Q: Do you recall why you thought it belonged in the statement?

\* \* \*

A: . . . I believed that it played a role in sparking the events of that night. And that any sort of conversation about what had happened, and what has to happen now would have to be taken into account in some way.

Q: Okay, just so I understand, it was your view that night that the video should be referred to in the statement because in your mind, the video had played some role in the attack in Benghazi?

A: Yeah, in sparking them or triggering them or motivating some of the people that night. Yeah, yes.

Q: And so you were kind of going back to your point about one of the goals for this speech was to explain to the American people what had happened. For that reason you wanted to refer to the video. Is that fair?

A: Yeah. I would say that's fair.

Q: And as best you can, could you just tell us what you based that conclusion on, or that opinion that the video somehow sparked what occurred in Benghazi?

A: Well, at the time it seems like the commonsense conclusion. You know, there was this incident happening in the same—not far from Benghazi, just a few countries to the—well, shoot, one country to the east. God, I'm failing on the geography—a nearby country, Cairo, Egypt, on the same day there was this protest that seemed—that was similarly targeting an American facility that similarly had our facility breached in this alarming way. And that seemed to be very clearly connected to this video since, again, I believe that not long before that protest broke out, the video had been broadcast on Egyptian news. So, you know, I was learning about what was happening in Egypt, and oh, look, the same day, something is happening at an American facility not far from there. . . .[71]

The gist is: a statement connecting the video with the Benghazi attacks was included by a speechwriter because the "thought"—half a world away—was that "commonsense" dictated it. But that same

[71] Testimony of Megan E. Rooney, Policy Advisor and Speechwriter, U.S. Dep't of State, Tr. at 48–51 (Oct. 9, 2015) [hereinafter Rooney Testimony] (on file with the Committee).

commonsense would not dictate listening to and following the real time information being provided by eyewitnesses who survived the initial attack and were preparing for subsequent attacks.

Benjamin J. Rhodes, Deputy National Security Advisor to the President for Strategic Communications, spoke with Sullivan about the statement before it was released. Rhodes testified the sentence "Some have sought to justify this vicious behavior as a response to inflammatory material posted on the Internet" was not about Benghazi but served to respond "to the general events taking place in the region as a whole."[72] He also said:

> A: Again, our concern—one of our concerns was that we saw efforts to utilize the video to incite protests, including the type of violent protests that we saw in Cairo. And so I recall that we wanted to have messaging in the statement that sought to reduce tensions associated with the video.
>
> Q: So was this sentence not meant to convey anything regarding Benghazi and Libya?
>
> A: No, I don't believe so.
>
> Q: You don't think—this sentence was not about Libya in any way, shape, or form?
>
> A: Again, I believe that it was intended to address the broader context in the region.
>
> Q: So that's what has me wondering. Then was there vicious behavior in other places that day?
>
> A: Yes. Certainly in Cairo.
>
> Q: But no—I mean, Pat Kennedy described Cairo as spray paint and rocks. Obviously, Benghazi was much different. So you're saying that vicious behavior applies to Cairo but doesn't apply to Benghazi?
>
> A: Again, I think it applies generally to the fact that we had indications that there were individuals who might seek to use this video to justify violence?
>
> Q: I'm asking about the two terms: vicious behavior. You said this sentence doesn't apply to Libya in a general sense or Benghazi in a specific sense, but does apply to other events in the region; namely, Cairo. Is that accurate?
>
> A: Again, this is taking place in the context where we have a protest that turned violent at our Embassy in Cairo, and we have the attacks in Benghazi. The situation is fluid. There are indications that we are getting from the State Department that there are other actors who are seeking to incite people related to this video. And so one of the objectives in our messaging was to have a statement that, again, sought to minimize our association with this video.

---

[72] Testimony of Benjamin J. Rhodes, Deputy Nat'l Sec. Advisor for Strategic Commc'cs, Nat'l Sec. Council, Tr. at 50–51 (Feb. 2, 2016) [hereinafter Rhodes Testimony] (on file with the Committee).

Q: And I understand you conveyed that is one of your objectives, but I'm specifically, again, just for the record, asking that sentence you said does not apply, is not meant in any way to convey anything about Libya, it's about Cairo and the rest of the region.

A: Again, it's not intended to assign responsibility for what happened in Benghazi. It's meant to describe the context of what happened, what's happening in the region.

Q: You mentioned context a couple of times here. When I look at context, I look at this document. The heading is "Statement on the Attack in Benghazi." Paragraph one: I condemn in the strongest way the attack on our mission in Benghazi. We are securing personnel and facilities. One of our officers was killed in Benghazi. Next paragraph: I have talked to the Libyan President. So everything in this document is about Libya and Benghazi except you're saying this sentence doesn't apply to Libya and Benghazi.

A: Again, as I look at this statement, my recollection is one of the objectives was to convey that we were doing everything we could to secure our diplomats in facilities around the world. If you look, for example, at the last sentence of the statement, it's intended to be about that general principle that we will work with partner countries around the world to protect our personnel, our missions, and our American citizens.[73]

Moreover, at Rhodes' direction, the Secretary's statement was the only statement issued on behalf of the United States government that night.[74] This put additional emphasis on its contents. Rhodes told the Committee:

A: You know, I recall telling my staff that that would be our comment for the night. So the people who work for me in the NSC press office, you know, everybody was being asked to respond to inquiries, and I remember determining that, you know, we would just have that one statement be our comment for the night.

Q: What was the thinking behind that, have that one statement coming from the State Department be the sole statement from the U.S. Government?

A: Again, my recollection is that this was an attack that had targeted our Ambassador, that it was appropriate for the Secretary of State to be speaking for the U.S. Government given that this had happened to people who worked in her department, and again, that made them the appropriate agency to issue a comment.[75]

---

[73] *Id.* at 61–64.
[74] *See* Email from Benjamin Rhodes, Deputy Nat'l Sec. Advisor for Strategic Commc'cs, Nat'l Sec. Council, to Steven Warren, Spokesman, U.S. Dep't of Defense, *et al.* (Sept. 11, 2012, 9:53 PM) (on file with the Committee, C05562046) ("[L]et the State Department' statement be our [USG] comment for the night.").
[75] Rhodes Testimony at 15.

The Secretary's private comments, however, were different than her public comments. In a phone call with Libyan President Mohammed el-Magariaf at approximately 6:00 p.m. in Washington D.C., the Secretary did not mention the video nor did she connect the video with the attacks. A summary of the phone call is below:

Secretary Clinton: Mr. President.

Libyan General National Congress President Magarif: Your Excellency.

S: I appreciate you taking my call at this late hour.

M: No problem. It's my duty.

S: As you know, our diplomatic mission in Benghazi was attacked earlier this evening. We need your immediate help, as one of our diplomats was killed and our Ambassador, who you know, is missing. We have asked for the Libyan government to provide additional security to the compound immediately as there is a gun battle ongoing, which I understand Ansar al Sharia is claiming responsibility for. We also need to provide additional capacity for firefighting as there are reports that the principle officers residence has been bombed or set on fire. We believe that it is important for your government, as well as ours, to condemn this attack in the strongest possible terms and promise these criminals will be brought to justice. I also need you to help us secure our mission in Tripoli. We have serious threats on social media sites, like Facebook, and it is important that your government take all possible measures, in an urgent manner, to secure our facilities. We need you to have people who you are confident in, who will follow your direction, and that your government trusts to secure our compounds.

M: Please accept my condolences for the death of the American at the compound and our sincere apologies for what has happened. We promise to find the criminals and bring them to justice. We will do our utmost to protect American buildings and every American citizen in Libya. We were just in the midst of an emergency meeting with the Prime Minister and all of his deputies to address this situation.

S: If there is anything that you need or that I can do please do not hesitate to call me at any time, day or night.

M: Thank you.

S: Thank you.

M: Good Night.[76]

In her call with the Libyan President, the Secretary mentioned a number of key facts not included in her public statement: that Stevens was still missing at the time;[77] that the extremist organi-

---

[76] Email from U.S. Dep't of State to S_CallNotes (Sept. 11, 2012, 11:34 PM) (on file with the Committee, C05561906).

[77] Id. ("[O]ur Ambassador, who you know, is missing.").

zation Ansar al Sharia had taken credit for the attacks;[78] that the compound may have been bombed and set on fire;[79] and that the administration intended to bring the perpetrators to justice.[80] Significantly, she also did not mention the video she referred to in her public statement.

The Secretary also sent a private email to her daughter that evening about an hour after her public statement. The email said:

> Two of our officers were killed in Benghazi by an Al Queda-like [sic] group: The Ambassador, whom I hand-picked and a young communications officer on temporary duty w a wife and two very young children. Very hard day and I fear more of the same tomorrow.[81]

In that email, the Secretary states two individuals had been killed "by an Al Queda-like [sic] group."[82] This key fact had been omitted from the Secretary's public statement. In sharing this fact with her daughter, the Secretary acknowledged the attack—with a link to al-Qaeda—was in fact terrorism. In omitting this fact from her public statement, however, the Secretary sent a very different message to the public—a message that suggested a protest over the video.

It was not until ten days later the Secretary told the American people the events in Benghazi were terrorist attacks.[83]

## THE DAY AFTER THE ATTACKS

The day after the attacks was a day of mourning for the families of the four Americans who lost their lives—Ambassador J. Christopher Stevens, Sean P. Smith, Tyrone S. Woods, and Glen A. Doherty. It was also a time of mourning and reflection for America. However, the day after the attacks also saw a marked difference in information shared by the administration with the American people compared with information shared by the administration privately.

### Public Statements Conflated the Video and the Attacks

The following day brought additional press inquiries and additional statements. After the Secretary's statement on the evening of September 11, two more Americans, Tyrone Woods and Glen Doherty, died in Benghazi as a result of the mortar attacks on the Annex.[84]

---

[78] *Id.* ("I understand Ansar al Sharia is claiming responsibility[.]").

[79] *Id.* ("[T]he principle officers residence has been bombed or set on fire.").

[80] *Id.* ("[I]t is important for your government, as well as ours, to condemn this attack in the strongest possible terms and promise these criminals will be brought to justice.").

[81] Email from Hillary R. Clinton ("H"), Sec'y of State, U.S. Dep't of State, to Chelsea Clinton ("Diane Reynolds") (Sept. 11, 2012, 11:12 PM) (on file with the Committee, C05795467).

[82] *Id.*

[83] Glenn Kessler, *From video to terrorist attack: a definitive timeline of administration statements on the Libya attack*, WASH. POST (Sept. 27, 2012), https://www.washingtonpost.com/blogs/fact-checker/post/from-video-to-terrorist-attack-a-definitive-timeline-of-administration-statements-on-the-libya-attack/2012/09/26/86105782-0826-11e2-afff-d6c7f20a83bf_blog.html.

[84] Scott Neuman, *U.S. Ambassador To Libya, Three Other Americans Killed in Benghazi Attack*, NPR (Sept. 12, 2012, 7:45 AM), http://www.npr.org/sections/thetwo-way/2012/09/12/160992840/u-s-ambassador-to-libya-three-other-americans-killed-in-benghazi-attack.

The administration needed to act quickly to ensure each agency was on the same page about how to message the attacks. At 8:14 a.m. the morning after the attacks, Bernadette Meehan, Deputy Spokesperson, National Security Council, sent an email to nearly two dozen people from the White House, Defense Department, State Department, and intelligence community stating:

> Both the President and Secretary Clinton released statements this morning. Both are pasted below. Please refer to those for any comments for the time being. **To ensure we are all in sync on messaging for the rest of the day, Ben Rhodes will host a conference call for USG communicators on this chain at 9:15 ET today. . . .**[85]

Rhodes responded, stating simply "If possible, let's do this at 9 to get a little ahead of potential statements by S[ecretary Clinton] and POTUS [the President] later this morning.[86]

The message emanating from the White House the morning after the attacks—similar to the message delivered by the U.S. government the night before through the Secretary's statement—was that the video and the attack on U.S. facilities in Benghazi would be mentioned in the same breath.[87] This therefore served the purpose of continuing to connect the two issues. As a result, this created confusion among the American public and the press as to whether or not these two events were directly related.

In the President's statement announcing the deaths of four Americans, he referred to "efforts to denigrate the religious beliefs of others"—i.e. the video—and the "senseless violence that took the lives of these public servants"—i.e. the Benghazi attacks—in the same sentence.[88] The statement, titled "Statement by the President on the Attack in Benghazi" read:

> I strongly condemn the outrageous attack on our diplomatic facility in Benghazi, which took the lives of four Americans, including Ambassador Chris Stevens. Right now, the American people have the families of those we lost in our thoughts and prayers. They exemplified America's commitment to freedom, justice, and partnership with nations and people around the globe, and stand in stark contrast to those who callously took their lives.
>
> I have directed my Administration to provide all necessary resources to support the security of our personnel in Libya, and to increase security at our diplomatic posts around the globe. While the United States rejects efforts to denigrate the religious beliefs of others, we must all unequivocally

---

[85] Email from Bernadette M. Meehan, Deputy Spokesperson, Nat'l Sec. Council, to Benjamin J. Rhodes, Deputy Nat'l Sec. Advisor for Strategic Commc'cs, Nat'l Sec. Council, et al. (Sept. 12, 2012, 8:14 AM) (emphasis original) (on file with the Committee, SCB000897).

[86] Email from Mr. Rhodes to Ms. Meehan, et al. (Sept. 12, 2012, 8:31 AM) (on file with the Committee, SCB000897).

[87] See Press Release, The White House Office of the Press Secretary, Statement by the President on the Attack in Benghazi (Sept. 12, 2012), https://www.whitehouse.gov/the-press-office/2012/09/12/statement-president-attack-benghazi ("While the United States rejects efforts to denigrate the religious beliefs of others, we must all unequivocally oppose the kind of senseless violence that took the lives of these public servants.").

[88] Press Release, The White House Office of the Press Secretary, Remarks by the President on the Deaths of U.S. Embassy Staff in Libya (Sept. 12, 2012), https://www.whitehouse.gov/the-press-office/2012/09/12/remarks-president-deaths-us-embassy-staff-libya.

oppose the kind of senseless violence that took the lives of these public servants.[89]

Later that morning the President addressed the Nation in a televised address from the Rose Garden about the attacks. The President said in part:

> Yesterday, four of these extraordinary Americans were killed in an attack on our diplomatic post in Benghazi. Among those killed was our Ambassador, Chris Stevens, as well as Foreign Service Officer Sean Smith. We are still notifying the families of the others who were killed. And today, the American people stand united in holding the families of the four Americans in our thoughts and in our prayers.
>
> The United States condemns in the strongest terms this outrageous and shocking attack. We're working with the government of Libya to secure our diplomats. I've also directed my administration to increase our security at diplomatic posts around the world. And make no mistake, we will work with the Libyan government to bring to justice the killers who attacked our people.
>
> Since our founding, the United States has been a nation that respects all faiths. We reject all efforts to denigrate the religious beliefs of others. But there is absolutely no justification to this type of senseless violence. None. The world must stand together to unequivocally reject these brutal acts.[90]

In the speech about the attacks, drafted by Rhodes and similar to the President's statement about the attacks earlier in the morning, the President refers to "efforts to denigrate the religious beliefs of others"[91]—i.e. the video. These comments, in a public address, gave a strong and continually reinforced impression to the public: the video was somehow linked to the attacks.

The Secretary also made remarks about the attacks on the morning of September 12, 2012. She said in part:

> We are working to determine the precise motivations and methods of those who carried out this assault. Some have sought to justify this vicious behavior, along with the protest that took place at our Embassy in Cairo yesterday, as a response to inflammatory material posted on the internet. America's commitment to religious tolerance goes back to the very beginning of our nation. But let me be clear—there is no justification for this, none. Violence like this is no way to honor religion or faith. And as long as there are

---

[89] Id.

[90] Press Release, The White House Office of the Press Secretary, Statement by the President on the Attack in Benghazi (Sept. 12, 2012), https://www.whitehouse.gov/the-press-office/2012/09/12/statement-president-attack-benghazi.

[91] Id.

those who would take innocent life in the name of God, the world will never know a true and lasting peace.[92]

Rooney, who helped draft the speech, told the Committee it was geared towards the American people:

> We knew basically a few things that we wanted to accomplish. If indeed some people had died, we knew that we wanted to give her some material that she could say about them, so she could say gracious things about them, which we knew she would have wanted to do. We knew that we would want to give her some sort of a—something that she could say that would summarize what had happened, anticipating that, you know, if Americans were waking up and turning on their TV in the morning and their Secretary of State was standing there, that they would—one of the questions on their mind would be what, what happened. We wanted to be able to give her some language that would at least begin to answer that.[93]

The fact the speech served in part to answer a question on the minds of many Americans—"what happened"—is interesting because Rooney never talked with anybody in the Bureau of Near Eastern Affairs (NEA) while she was drafting the speech. The individuals in NEA had been on the phone all night with State Department personnel in Benghazi receiving real-time updates about what was transpiring.[94] Rooney testified:

> Q: Did you speak to anybody in the NEA bureau about what had happened in the attacks?
>
> A: I don't recall speaking to anyone in the NEA bureau.
>
> Q: Is that something you would have done? I mean, you talked earlier about the process. If you're writing a speech about China, you go to——
>
> A: Right.
>
> Q: —the China experts and ask them. I mean, did that happen that night with regard to Libya?
>
> A: No, I don't think so. I don't recall any conversation with anyone from—no.[95]

Instead, the only actual description in the statement of what had occurred in Benghazi was a late addition to the speech from Sullivan. Schwerin, who also worked on the speech, explained:

> A: He said, you know, we have to keep making edits. He didn't tell me the substance of the conversations he had had, just that there were more edits to make.
>
> Q: Okay. What kind of edits?

---

[92] *Secretary Clinton Delivers Remarks on the Deaths of U.S. Personnel in Benghazi, Libya*, DIPNOTE (Sept. 12, 2012), https://blogs.state.gov/stories/2012/09/12/secretary-clinton-delivers-remarks-deaths-us-personnel-benghazi-libya.
[93] Rooney Testimony at 35–36.
[94] Jones Testimony at 79–80.
[95] Rooney Testimony at 39.

A: I can't, you know, all these years later, tell you which sentences we changed, but the only thing that I remember is, I think the formulation "heavily-armed militants" we added that morning in his office. But I could not beyond that give you chapter and verse about what we changed.[96]

The public statements by the President and Secretary of State did not call the events in Benghazi a terrorist attack.

The President also conducted an interview with Steve Kroft of *60 Minutes* that same morning. Kroft began the interview by asking the President about the attack and the President's reluctance to call the attack a terrorist attack in his earlier Rose Garden remarks. Again, the President did not call what had transpired in Benghazi a terrorist attack:

Q: Mr. President, this morning you went out of your way to avoid the use of the word "terrorism" in connection with the Libya attack.

A: Right.

Q: Do you believe that this was a terrorist attack?

A: Well, it's too early to know exactly how this came about, what group was involved, but obviously it was an attack on Americans. And we are going to be working with the Libyan government to make sure that we bring these folks to justice, one way or the other.

Q: This has been described as a mob action, but there are reports that they were very heavily armed with grenades. That doesn't sound like your normal demonstration.

A: As I said, we're still investigating exactly what happened. I don't want to jump the gun on this. But you're right that this is not a situation that was exactly the same as what happened in Egypt, and my suspicion is, is that there are folks involved in this who were looking to target Americans from the start.[97]

Later in the interview, the President raised the issue of the video while referring to the Benghazi attacks, implying the film was an "excuse for violence against Americans" and conflating the two issues.[98] The President said:

And I do have to say that, more broadly, we believe in the First Amendment. It is one of the hallmarks of our Constitution that I'm sworn to uphold. And so we are always going to uphold the rights for individuals to speak their mind. On the other hand, this film is not representative of who we are and our values, and I think it's important for

---

[96] Schwerin Testimony at 36.

[97] *See* Email from Bernadette M. Meehan, Spokesperson, Nat'l Sec. Council, to Victoria J. Nuland, Spokesperson, Dep't of State, & Patrick H. Ventrell, Spokesperson, U.S. Dep't of State (Sept. 13, 2012, 9:17 AM) (on file with the Committee, C05527907) (Attaching transcript of the Interview of the President by Steve Kroft, 60 Minutes).

[98] *Id.*

us to communicate that. That's never an excuse for violence against Americans[.][99]

## Private Statements Tell a Different Story

While administration officials may have been in sync with their public messaging regarding the Benghazi attacks on September 12, the messages shared privately told a completely different story.

Minutes before the President delivered his speech in the Rose Garden, Sullivan wrote in an email to Rhodes and others:

> There was not really much violence in Egypt. And we are not saying that the violence in Libya erupted "over inflammatory videos."[100]

Sullivan's private acknowledgement differs notably from the consistent public remarks connecting the video and the attacks in both the President's and the Secretary's statements that day.

On September 12, 2012, the President made separate phone calls to Libya President Mohamad Magariaf and Egyptian President Mohamed Morsi. In his phone call with the Egyptian President, the President "said that he rejects efforts to denigrate Islam, but underscored there is never any justification for violence against innocents and acts that endanger American personnel and facilities."[101] This is a reference to the video, which was the cause of the protest against the U.S. Embassy in Cairo.

In his phone call with the Libyan President, the President said the two countries "must work together to do whatever is necessary to identify the perpetrators of this attack and bring them to justice."[102] Notably, however, President Obama did not make a reference to the video.

The Secretary also had a phone call with an Egyptian leader, Prime Minister Hisham Kandil, on the afternoon of September 12. According to the call notes, the Secretary told the Prime Minister the following:

> We know that the attack in Libya had nothing to do with the film. It was a planned attack—not a protest. . . . Your [sic] not kidding. Based on the information we saw today we believe the group that claimed responsibility for this was affiliated with al-Qaeda.[103]

Not only did the Secretary tell the Prime Minister "the attack in Libya had nothing to do with the film," she strengthened the statement by prefacing it with "we know."[104] Such a definitive declaration made privately to another world leader stands in stark con-

---

[99] Id.

[100] Email from Jacob J. Sullivan, Deputy Chief of Staff and Dir. of Policy Planning, U.S. Dep't of State, to Senior Dir. for Commc'cs and Public Diplomacy, Afghanistan and Pakistan, U.S. Dep't of State, et al. (Sept. 12, 2012, 10:30 AM) (on file with the Committee, C05578214).

[101] Press Release, The White House Office of the Press Secretary, Readout of the President's Call with Egyptian President Morsi (Sept. 13, 2012), https://www.whitehouse.gov/the-press-office/2012/09/13/readout-president-s-call-egyptian-president-morsi.

[102] Press Release, The White House Office of the Press Secretary, Readout of the President's Call with Libyan President Magariaf (Sept. 13, 2012), https://www.whitehouse.gov/the-press-office/2012/09/13/readout-president-s-call-libyan-president-magariaf.

[103] Email from U.S. Dep't of State to S_CallNotes (Sept. 12, 2012, 7:11 PM) (on file with the Committee, C05561911).

[104] Id.

trast to her speech earlier in the day to the American people where she mentioned the attack—"this vicious behavior"—in the same breath as the video—"inflammatory material posted on the internet." [105]

Kennedy was also emphatic in privately conveying that no protests had occurred prior to the attack. In a separate, private briefing to congressional staff Kennedy was specifically asked whether this was "an attack under the cover of a protest." [106] Kennedy, who oversaw the Bureau of Diplomatic Security and had ready access to real-time information from the Diplomatic Security agents on the ground in Benghazi, replied "[n]o this was a direct breaching attack." [107]

Kennedy's assertions also aligned with the intelligence product, the Executive Update, produced by the CIA analysts earlier that day and shared with senior administration officials. That piece stated "the presence of armed assailants from the outset suggests this was an intentional assault and not the escalation of a peaceful protest." [108] This piece—which was part of the President's Daily Brief and likely discussed with the President's Chief of Staff on September 13, 2012—is discussed at length in Appendix H.

Whether or not a protest occurred prior to the attack was a significant fact at the time because the absence of a protest would clearly distinguish what happened in Benghazi from what transpired in Cairo. If it therefore became clear no protests occurred in Benghazi over the video, then the administration would therefore no longer be able to connect the two events in statements about Benghazi.

Privately, Kennedy did not hesitate to explain no protests had occurred prior to the attack.[109] Publicly, however, it took the administration more than two weeks to do so.[110]

## SEPTEMBER 13 INTELLIGENCE ASSESSMENT

On September 11 and September 12, public comments by administration officials had relied mainly on press reports and eyewitness accounts. On September 13 the Central Intelligence Agency [CIA] published its first intelligence assessment exclusively regarding the Benghazi attacks. This assessment, known as a WIRe [World Intelligence Review] was the key intelligence piece produced by CIA an-

---

[105] Though some may claim that "vicious behavior" also occurred in Cairo, in the Secretary's September 12 speech she specifically separates the "vicious behavior" from what transpired in Cairo by saying "this vicious behavior, along with the protest that took place at our Embassy in Cairo yesterday . . ." *Secretary Clinton Delivers Remarks on the Deaths of U.S. Personnel in Benghazi, Libya,* DIPNOTE (Sept. 12, 2012), https://blogs.state.gov/stories/2012/09/12/secretary-clinton-delivers-remarks-deaths-us-personnel-benghazi-libya.

[106] Email from Legislative Management Officer for Near Eastern Affairs, U.S. Dep't of State, to H_Egypt, *et al.* (Sept. 12, 2012, 7:55 PM) (on file with the Committee, C05580110).

[107] Email from Legislative Management Officer, U.S. Dep't of State, to H_Egypt, *et al.* (Sept 12, 2012, 7:55 PM) (on file with the Committee, C05562234).

[108] Middle East and North Africa Situation Report, Sept. 12, 2012, 0700 EDT (on file with CIA, REQUEST 17–0345 to REQUEST 0346).

[109] *See* Email to H_Egypt, *et al.* (Sept 12, 2012, 7:55 PM) (on file with the Committee, C05562234) (answering question about whether the attack was under the cover of a protest, Kennedy responded "[n]o this was a direct breaching attack.").

[110] Press Release, Office of the Dir. of Nat'l Intel., Statement by the Director of Public Affairs for ODNI, Shawn Turner, on the intelligence related to the terrorist attack on the U.S. Consulate in Benghazi, Libya (Sept. 28, 2012), https://www.dni.gov/index.php/newsroom/press-releases/96-press-releases-2012/731-statement-by-the-odni-s-director-of-public-affairs-on-intelligence-related-to-the-terrorist-attack-on-the-u-s-consulate-in-benghazi.

alysts immediately following the Benghazi attacks. It was titled "Libya: Government Poorly Positioned To Address Attacks." [111] As both Michael J Morell, Deputy Director, Central Intelligence Agency, and the Director of the Office of Terrorism Analysis (OTA)—an office of **[redacted text]** analysts focused on terrorism issues—acknowledge, this was the first time the analysts had coordinated a piece about the Benghazi attacks among the entire intelligence community.

The OTA Director described the purposes of this piece to the Committee:

> This is something that by this point we would have been writing on a regular basis trying to sort out. . . . [T]o have done a WIRe would've been really the first time where we said we're going to stand back, we're going to really make sure this was fully IC coordinated. We're going to work through this and say this is a more formal look. So I don't believe it was tasked so much as it was time for us to really take a full look at where we were.[112]

Additionally, this particular piece was also included as part of the President's Daily Brief [PDB].

Morell explained:

> Q: So the PDB staff would have edited this particular WIRe?
>
> A: Yes, because it was a PDB.
>
> Q: This particular WIRe was a PDB?
>
> A: Yes.[113]

As a PDB, this piece received wide distribution throughout the intelligence community. As Morell notes in his book, this piece "would be published and shown to senior policy-makers and to Congress on the morning of September 13." [114]

This September 13 piece was the pivotal piece coming from the intelligence community for several reasons. One, it was the first time the analysts had taken a step back to assess what had actually occurred in Benghazi; two, this piece was widely distributed across the U.S. government;[115] and three, Morell viewed this piece as the "assessment" of the analysts when he edited the talking points for the House Permanent Select Committee on Intelligence two days later.[116]

Despite the September 13 piece being heavily vetted, going through the PDB process, and being widely distributed, the piece was rife with errors as the analysts themselves would later acknowledge. There were improper footnotes, poor and confusing

---

[111] Cent. Intel. Agency, Libya: Government Poorly Positioned to Address Attacks, World Intelligence Review, Sept. 13, 2012 [hereinafter September 13 WIRe] (on file with CIA, REQUEST 17–0067 to REQUEST 17–0070).

[112] Testimony of Dir. of the Office of Terrorism Analysis, Cent. Intel. Agency, Tr. at 105 (Nov. 13, 2015) (on file with the Committee).

[113] Testimony of Michael Morell, Deputy Dir., Cent. Intel. Agency, Tr. at 39–41 (Sept. 28, 2015) [hereinafter Morell Testimony] (on file with the Committee).

[114] MICHAEL MORELL, THE GREAT WAR OF OUR TIME: THE CIA'S FIGHT AGAINST TERRORISM—FROM AL QA'IDA TO ISIS 217 (2015).

[115] Id.

[116] Morell Testimony at 135.

phrasing, and most importantly, headlines that were not supported by any text. The result was a very poorly written piece containing inaccurate information that was relied on by those analyzing, discussing, and messaging the Benghazi attacks.

The focus of the September 13 piece was twofold: the ability of the Libyan government to respond to the attacks, and the fact extremists had participated in the attacks. A timeline of the attacks and the sequence of events leading up to the attacks were not discussed in the piece. Whether or not a protest occurred prior to the attacks was not a focal point of the piece, nor was it an issue the analysts found to be particularly germane. As the manager of the analysts who wrote the piece testified:

> A: We weren't particularly concerned, worried about, or thinking about protests when we wrote this.
>
> Q: That was the next question I was going to ask you. Yeah.
>
> A: I want to make that very, very clear. Because in CTC [Counterterrorism Center] when something like this happens, we look at who do we think did it and are they about to do it again and is there anything we can do to stop it.
>
> So we did not think the question of protests was particularly germane to answering that question. In fact, it was fully probably a week. And we had several conversations among ourselves and even with more senior people in the DI [Directorate of Analysis] about, why in the hell would everybody care about protests?
>
> We just—we weren't tracking on it because it wasn't germane to what we were trying to do, which it doesn't really excuse our sloppy work, particularly in that paragraph here. I mean the ticks are the ticks. They are based on reporting. But our assessment was just imprecisely written. We weren't careful enough about it.[117]

The fact the piece was not focused on protests—nor did the analysts find the issue of protests germane—is ironic given this piece has received so much attention by Morell and others as supporting evidence that the analysts did in fact believe a protest had occurred.[118] That is because this is the only intelligence assessment written by the CIA that can support the analytic line that a protest had occurred prior to the attacks.[119]

Further, it was put in the intelligence piece by accident—a mistake that was not caught during what was supposed to be a rigorous and airtight editing process.

In his book, Morell says "[t]he September 13 piece—the first piece to go beyond a simple factual update—said four things. First,

---

[117] Testimony of **[redacted text]** Team Chief, Office of Terrorism Analysis, Cent. Intel. Agency, Tr. at 52–53 (Feb. 10, 2016) [hereinafter **[redacted text]** Team Chief Testimony] (on file with the Committee).

[118] Morell Testimony at 50.

[119] The CIA notes that a September 15 WIRe "includes reporting that 'members of an AAS-affiliated group stated that they took advantage of a planned demonstration . . .'" However, citing a report is different than crafting an assessment. A report is just that, a report—citing information from somebody else. An assessment, however, is the collective thoughts of analysts after synthesizing multiple pieces of intelligence to reach an analytic conclusion.

that the assault on the [Benghazi Mission compound] had been a spontaneous event that evolved from a protest outside the [Benghazi Mission compound]."[120] Except Morell is wrong. The piece did not say this at all. In fact, the exact language of the piece reads: "We assess the attacks on Tuesday against the US Consulate in Benghazi began spontaneously following the protests at the US Embassy in Cairo and evolved into a direct assault against the Consulate and a separate US facility in the city."[121] In his book, Morell alters the plain language of this piece, "began spontaneously following protests at the US Embassy in *Cairo,*" with the wording in his book, "a spontaneous event that evolved from a protest outside the *[Benghazi Mission compound]*."[122]

On the first page of the September 13 piece, titled "Libya: Government Poorly Positioned To Address Attacks," there is a single mention of "the early stages of the protest" buried in one of the bullet points.[123] The Director of the Office of Terrorism Analysis acknowledged the supporting evidence for this statement was incorrect. She testified:

> Q: "I'm sorry. In the early stages of the protest"—so a direct reference to a protest——
>
> A: Yes.
>
> Q: "Benghazi's top Ministry of Interior official personally ordered the withdrawal of Libyan Security Forces protecting the consulate saying he believed the action would avoid violence, according to the press reporting."
>
> A: Correct.
>
> Q: And we talked about that earlier.
>
> A: Yes.
>
> Q: Just really quickly, flip back to footnote 16, can you read the date on footnote 16? What's the date of that?
>
> A: That is 2012/09/04, so that would obviously be wrong.[124]

The article cited to support the mention of a protest in this instance was titled "Libyan Parliament Speaker, Interior Minister Discuss Country's Security" and was from Doha Libya TV in Arabic from September 4, 2012.[125] In other words, the analysts used an article from September 4, 2012—a full week before the lethal attacks—to support the premise that a protest had occurred just prior to the attack on September 11. A simple source check by the reader—or during any of the multiple levels of allegedly "rigorous" editing—would have caught the blatantly obvious error of relying on a news article from September 4 to support an event that occurred on September 11.

---

[120] MORELL, *supra* note 114, at 218.

[121] *Id.* at 218.

[122] *Id.* (emphasis added).

[123] Cent. Intel. Agency, Libya: Government Poorly Positioned to Address Attacks, World Intelligence Review, Sept. 13, 2012 [hereinafter September 13 WIRe] (on file with CIA, REQUEST 17–0067 to REQUEST 17–0070).

[124] OTA Dir. Testimony at 128.

[125] September 13 WIRe, *supra* note 123.

Yet it was not this mention of a protest in the piece that caught Morell's attention. Rather, it was a headline on the following page titled "Extremists Capitalized on Benghazi Protests." This page was a text box, which the OTA Director described as:

> So a text box is material that we believe is related to the storyline, to the analytic—to the arc of the story but is something that we kind of separate out, because sometimes it doesn't flow from the analytic argument but it's information we think is important to include. So think of it as an adjunct to the piece.[126]

While the title of this text box was "Extremists Capitalized on Benghazi Protests," nothing in the actual text box supports that title.[127] The summary paragraph in the text box, through which the rest of the text box would flow, read:

> We assess the attacks on Tuesday against the US Consulate in Benghazi began spontaneously following the protests at the US Embassy in Cairo and evolved into a direct assault against the Consulate and a separate US facility in the city. Extremists with ties to al-Qa-ida were involved in the attacks, according to signals intelligence.[128]

There is no mention—or even hint—of any protest in Benghazi in that paragraph or in any other text in the text box. Rather, the only mention of a protest relates to what had transpired in Cairo.[129]

After a discussion of this document during their interviews with the Committee, both Morell and the OTA Director acknowledged this fact. Morell testified:

> Q: I'm trying to tie it all back to the headline——
>
> A: Yep.
>
> Q: —"Extremists Capitalized on Benghazi Protests," I'm having a hard time understanding how that headline is supported by the evidence.
>
> A: Right.
>
> Q: So far, nothing in the actual text of the WIRe supports that, and so now we're looking at each footnote, footnote 29—source note 29, we've looked at the New York Times article, the body of the article doesn't support that, just the headline, and now we're looking at source note 30, "according to [redacted text]." You know, where in here does it support that but for collateral, is my question to you.
>
> A: And so—look, I don't know the answer to your question, right, why they wrote it the way they did.[130]

The OTA Director testified:

---

[126] OTA Dir. Testimony at 109.
[127] September 13 WIRe, *supra* note 123, at 2.
[128] *Id.*
[129] *Id.*
[130] Morell Testimony at 49.

Q: Okay. Let's look at the first bullet point. . . . That's a lengthy sentence.

A: Not good trade craft. We try and make them shorter.

Q: Is there anything in that sentence or that bullet point that denotes that there was a protest in Benghazi that you can see?

A: "After hearing how protesters breached the"—so, no, not in Benghazi.

Q: Not in Benghazi, okay.

Let's look at the next tick. . . .

Is there anything in that tick that mentions a protest in Benghazi?

A: No.

Q: All right. Let's look at the third tick. . . . Is there anything in that tick that mentions a protest in Benghazi?

A: No.

Q: And then I'm just going to read the last paragraph here. . . .

Is there anything in that paragraph that mentions the protest in Benghazi?

A: No.[131]

The OTA Director also told the Committee the text box in the September 13 intelligence piece was not supposed to be about whether or not protests had occurred in Benghazi prior to the attack.[132] Instead, it was supposed to focus on the involvement of extremists in the attacks. That was the point the analysts were trying to drive—extremists, not protests. This was true of the headline of the text box, too. The key word in that headline, according to the OTA Director, was "extremists," not "protests." She testified:

Q: So the headline for this text box, "Extremists Capitalized on Benghazi Protests," do you see any supporting evidence in the five paragraphs I've just read that support that headline?

A: So the headline—and I admit that in retrospect, if I could go back and change this headline, I would. Because the headline, it was more meant to be about the, we know extremists were involved and less about whether or not there were protests.

So if you look at this idea that the first, the topic sentence that talks—so, sorry, the second sentence, where the bullets are then following immediately after, about extremists with the ties to Al Qaeda were involved. We then go on in the first bullet to talk about we know that there was, you know **[redacted text]**. That bullet was to not only talk about AQIM but to also talk a little bit about motivation.

---

[131] OTA Dir. Testimony at 110–12.
[132] Id. at 112–13.

The second bullet that talks about, you know, again, extremists, as we were calling at that point, Ansar al-Sharia in Benghazi claimed responsibility, and also talked about the timing that this was spontaneous, **[redacted text]**. So, again, this idea of preplanning, timing, and those involved.

And the third bullet was, I think, meant to illustrate that this was a series that the extremists were involved at various points that was an opportunistic attack sequence, as we talk about. They took advantage of opportunities to attack U.S. facilities at various points throughout the night.

So are those things directly supporting in the way we would like the title of this? No. Was it meant—and as I said, so if I could take back that title, I would.

Q: Sure. "Extremists" is the key word in the title?

A: Yes, not the protests.[133]

She later called the title of the text box the "unfortunate title,"[134] and, as the head of the Office of Terrorism Analysis, ultimately took responsibility for it.[135]

While there may have been no text in the text box to support the title, as it turns out, the title was intended to be something different. According to the manager of the analysts who wrote the piece, the title of the text box was supposed to be "Extremists Capitalized on Cairo Protests."[136] That small but vital difference—from Cairo to Benghazi—had major implications in how people in the administration were able to message the attacks, and was used as support in the days and weeks after this piece was published for the claim that protests had occurred prior to the Benghazi attacks.

Even worse, this mistake was not caught until more than a week later, when the analysts were updating their assessment. The manager of the analysts who wrote the piece testified:

Q: The title here: "Extremists Capitalized on Benghazi Protests." So we talked to [the OTA Director] about this. She called it an unfortunate title?

A: It was a—we made a mistake.

Q: Okay. So when you say "we made a mistake," I mean, where—how would that have been——

A: So, God, how do I begin?

\* \* \*

A: . . . So "Extremists Capitalized on Benghazi Protests." Benghazi was supposed to be Cairo. So——

Q: Okay.

A: But let me explain that. So—and, frankly, it's a mistake that we didn't even notice until we published the

---

[133] *Id.* at 112–13.
[134] *Id.* at 135.
[135] *Id.* at 112–113.
[136] **[Redacted text]** Team Chief Testimony at 49, 136.

WIRe on the 24th, where I was talking to a senior person as he was reviewing it, and he was looking back and asking, I thought: Oh, my God, we were talking about Cairo.[137]

She also testified:

Q: So I guess this is why I'm a little confused is you say in the title Benghazi should have been Cairo?

A: The title probably should have read something like extremists motivated to attack in Benghazi because of protests in Cairo.[138]

In the end, Morell conceded the obvious—this piece could have been written better. He testified:

Right. And if you want to get a bottom line from me, from me, I don't think this was as well done as it could have been for a lot of reasons. I have reasons beyond yours as to why I don't think this is as well done as it could be, and you're pointing out some additional ones. So I don't think it is as well done as it could have been.[139]

In addition to this piece being poorly written—conveniently, in a way relied on by senior administration officials with respect to a key point—it also contained sourcing inaccuracies. One of these was described above. The lack of attention paid to sourcing has implications on future pieces shared with the President and other senior executive branch officials.[140] From papers in high school, theses in college, law review articles to scientific research, assertions made are expected to be properly documented with sources to support them. Yet when it comes to CIA analysts and pieces they write for the President, for some reason these footnotes do not receive the scrutiny they deserve. Morell explains:

A: So context number two, right, is that analysts don't spend a lot of time making sure that these footnotes match. Okay. They just don't. They just don't.

Q: Is that a problem?

A: It certainly is when you have a situation like this.

Q: I'm a lawyer. I mean, if you're writing a Law Review article, those things are going to be footnoted to death.

A: Is it a problem? Yes. Is it a problem? Yes. So those are the few pieces of context, right, is they believed is what they believed, right? They had a set of—they believed they had a set of information, a set of data points that took them there. Third, I think you've got to be a little bit careful going through this sentence by sentence and source by source, because analysts aren't as careful as they need to be.

---

[137] *Id.* at 48–49.
[138] *Id.* at 54.
[139] Morell Testimony at 56.
[140] *Id.*

Q: Why aren't they as careful as they need to be? If you're producing a piece for the [President], shouldn't every sentence have a valid source note?

A: Yes, absolutely. You're absolutely right. I couldn't agree with you more.[141]

The OTA Director also acknowledged there is not enough emphasis on making sure the footnotes, known inside the CIA as source attributions, are accurate—especially for pieces that become PDBs. She testified:

A: The editing process would have differed for a PDB in that it would have also gone through an additional layer of review or several additional layers of review. So a WIRe ceases, the review ceases pretty much after the office director, as I said, except for some technical edits.

A PDB, our process is more—there are additional levels that include a review within the organization we call PASS. There's also then the DA [Directorate of Analysis] front office would have reviewed a PDB, and then it would also have gone to ODNI [Office of the Director of National Intelligence].

\* \* \*

Q: Okay. So there are more senior analysts that would review a PDB?

A: Yes.

Q: Does it undergo a certain extra level of rigor for attributing sources and making sure everything lines up properly?

A: Attributing sources, not necessarily.[142]

Despite these myriad errors—the inaccurate title, the faulty sourcing, the lack of evidence in the text to support a headline—Morell and others have used this piece, and the title of the text box specifically, as the "assessment" of the analysts to buttress their statements that protests in Benghazi had occurred prior to the attacks.[143] In fact, the title "Extremists Capitalized on Benghazi Protests" alone does count as an "assessment" by the analysts. As the manager of the analysts testified:

A: And our assessment—again, it's embarrassing, it's poorly done—was that they had—really the title as it stood was what our assessment was, but we didn't explain it well—that they capitalized on these protests in Benghazi.

Q: Okay. So your title is what the assessment was, but that's not supported—and this is my analysis—not supported, Benghazi protests, by anything underneath——

A: That's true.

---

[141] Id. at 52–53.
[142] OTA Dir. Testimony at 106–08.
[143] See e.g. Morell Testimony at 50.

Q: —in the ticks. Okay. So is that actually an assessment, extremists capitalized on Benghazi protests, or is the assessment sort of the body under here, the paragraph, the three ticks, and then the final paragraph?

A: Well, it's all assessment. It's just sloppily done.

Q: Okay. So extremists capitalized on Benghazi protests, even though there's no supporting evidence for that statement in this box——

A: Yeah. Like I said, we weren't thinking about the protests or we would have been, frankly, far more careful about how we couched them.[144]

In other words, the title of the text box itself was an assessment by the analysts. That title was inaccurate. That title was an accident and was supposed to be something else entirely, but nobody caught it. The analysts were not even focused on the issue of protests. Yet it was that title the administration could point to—and ultimately relied upon—to say the analysts had assessed that protests had occurred prior to the Benghazi attacks. That title is the only analytic piece fully vetted by the intelligence community prior to Morell's editing of the talking points and the appearance on the Sunday talk shows by Susan E. Rice, U.S. Permanent Representative to the United Nations, where she said protests had occurred in Benghazi.

Nevertheless, despite the incorrect title and numerous other faults with the September 13 piece, there is still no assessment by the analysts that tied what transpired in Benghazi to the internet video. Even among the legion of mistakes made, the piece did not authoritatively connect Benghazi with protests or an internet video.

## THE CONFLATION CONTINUES

While the inaccurate and poorly written CIA analysis on September 13 gave an opening for administration officials to claim protests had occurred prior to the Benghazi attack, the public connection and conflation by administration officials between Benghazi and the video continued. This occurred despite any assessment by the CIA analysts of the video playing a role in the Benghazi attacks.

During her remarks at the opening plenary of the U.S.-Morocco strategic dialogue on September 13, 2012, the Secretary of State said there is "no justification, none at all, for responding to this video with violence. We condemn the violence that has resulted in the strongest terms."[145] These comments were similar to prior public comments she had made regarding the video.

A draft of the Secretary's comments, however, shows an attempt to draw a stronger link between Benghazi and the video—something unsupportable by the intelligence at the time, and not part of the CIA's assessment—than she stated publicly. A draft of the

---

[144] **[Redacted text]** Team Chief Testimony at 55.

[145] Hillary R. Clinton, Sec'y of State, U.S. Dep't of State, Remarks at the Opening Plenary of the U.S.-Morocco Strategic Dialogue (Sept.13, 2012), http://www.state.gov/secretary/20092013clinton/rm/2012/09/197711.htm.

Secretary's speech states: "But as I said yesterday, there is no justification—none—for responding to an Internet video with murder. We condemn the violence that has resulted in the strongest terms."[146]

This subtle change from the draft to her speech—from "murder" to "violence"—is important. While some violence had occurred at other United States diplomatic facilities across the Arab World such as Cairo, murder had only occurred at one: Benghazi.[147] By changing that one word, from "murder" to "violence," the Secretary did not draw an irrebuttable, direct link between the video and Benghazi—a link she had told the Egyptian Prime Minister she knew did not exist[148]—but instead continued to indirectly connect and conflate the two events to the American public, thus allowing her to claim she did not make a direct public connection between the video and the Benghazi attacks.

That same day, Thomas R. Nides, Deputy Secretary of State for Management and Resources, had a meeting with the new Egyptian Ambassador to the U.S. According to a summary of that meeting, "Nides said he understood the difference between the targeted attack in Libya and the way the protest escalated in Egypt."[149] While this message was shared privately by the Deputy Secretary of State to the Egyptian Ambassador two days after the attacks, it was not until two weeks later that the administration finally shared this message publicly with the American people.[150]

At a press briefing later in the day on September 13, Nuland openly talked about the video while discussing the Benghazi attacks.[151] At the briefing, she was asked whether any of the information she provided during the background briefing the day before had changed; said she did not have anything significantly different than what she had said privately on background.[152] Yet when asked about the Benghazi attack, she answered the question, then pivoted to talking about the video:

> Q: Toria, can you tell us whether there's been any progress towards determining whether the Benghazi attack was purely spontaneous or was premeditated by militants, and also whether there's been any further determination about the extent to which the Cairo, Benghazi, and now Yemen attacks were related in some way other than just theme?

---

[146] Email from Jacob J. Sullivan, Deputy Chief of Staff and Dir. of Policy Planning, U.S. Dep't of State, to Daniel B. Schwerin, Speechwriter, U.S. Dep't of State, *et al.* (Sept. 13, 2012, 9:22 AM) (on file with the Committee, SCB00100122).

[147] Benghazi was the only U.S. facility during this time period where terrorists killed an American government official.

[148] *See* Email from U.S. Dep't of State to S_CallNotes (Sept. 12, 2012, 7:11 PM) (on file with the Committee, C05561911) (attaching notes from phone call with Egyptian Prime Minister).

[149] Email from Operations Center, U.S. Dep't of State to Prem G. Kumar, Dir. for Israeli and Palestinian Affairs, White House (Sept. 13, 2012, 12:29 PM) (on file with the Committee, C05562242).

[150] Press Release, Office of the Dir. of National Intel., Statement by the Director of Public Affairs for ODNI, Shawn Turner, on the intelligence related to the terrorist attack on the U.S. Consulate in Benghazi, Libya (Sept. 28, 2012), https://www.dni.gov/index.php/newsroom/press-releases/96-press-releases-2012/731-statement-by-the-odni-s-director-of-public-affairs-on-intelligence-related-to-the-terrorist-attack-on-the-u-s-consulate-in-benghazi.

[151] Daily Press Briefing by Spokesperson Victoria Nuland, Bureau of Public Affairs, U.S. Dep't of State (Sept. 13, 2012), http://www.state.gov/r/pa/prs/dpb/2012/09/197729.htm.

[152] *Id.*

A: Well, as we said yesterday when we were on background, we are very cautious about drawing any conclusions with regard to who the perpetrators were, what their motivations were, whether it was premeditated, whether they had any external contacts, whether there was any link, until we have a chance to investigate along with the Libyans. So I know that's going to be frustrating for you, but we really want to make sure that we do this right and we don't jump to conclusions.

That said, obviously, there are plenty of people around the region citing this disgusting video as something that has been motivating. As the Secretary said this morning, while we as Americans, of course, respect free speech, respect free expression, there is never an excuse for it to become violent.[153]

While the question addresses Cairo, Benghazi, and Yemen, Nuland does not differentiate among the three events and instead notes "there are plenty of people around the region citing this disgusting video as something that has been motivating."[154] Nuland's failure to separate what transpired in Benghazi from what transpired in Cairo on the same day and Yemen one day later resulted in an administration official connecting again, publicly, Benghazi with the other two events—and thus Benghazi with the video.

Two days after the attacks ended, September 14, Jay Carney, Press Secretary, White House, held a press briefing at the White House. Reporters pressed on whether the administration believed the events in Benghazi were a reaction to the video:

A: Jake, let's be clear, these protests were in reaction to a video that had spread to the region——

Q: At Benghazi? What happened at Benghazi——

A: We certainly don't know. We don't know otherwise. We have no information to suggest that it was a preplanned attack. The unrest we've seen around the region has been in reaction to a video that Muslims, many Muslims find offensive. And while the violence is reprehensible and unjustified, it is not a reaction to the 9/11 anniversary that we know of, or to U.S. policy.

Q: But the group around the Benghazi post was well armed. It was a well-coordinated attack. Do you think it was a spontaneous protest against a movie?

A: Look, this is obviously under investigation, and I don't have——

Q: But your operating assumption is that that was in response to the video, in Benghazi? I just want to clear that up. That's the framework? That's the operating assumption?

A: Look, it's not an assumption——

---

[153] Id.
[154] Id.

Q: Because there are administration officials who don't—who dispute that, who say that it looks like this was something other than a protest.

A: I think there has been news reports on this, Jake, even in the press, which some of it has been speculative. What I'm telling you is this is under investigation. The unrest around the region has been in response to this video. We do not, at this moment, have information to suggest or to tell you that would indicate that any of this unrest was preplanned.[155]

In his response to a question about what happened at Benghazi, Carney switches gears to talking about the general unrest in the region as a whole—which was a result of the video. Carney does not distinguish the events in Benghazi from the events around the rest of the region thus connecting and conflating the two issues and again giving the impression that what happened in Benghazi happened as a result of the video. Carney is also asked twice whether or not a protest had occurred in Benghazi. Similar to his comments about the video, Carney talks about unrest in the region as a whole, conflating protests and Benghazi, and failing to distinguish Benghazi from what had transpired elsewhere in the region.

Despite these public comments by senior administration officials, those on the ground in Libya knew otherwise. That same morning a public information officer from the Embassy in Tripoli sent an email to colleagues in Tripoli and at the State Department headquarters in Washington D.C. regarding "messaging on the attacks in Libya."[156] The email said:

Colleagues, I . . . want to share with all of you, our view at Embassy Tripoli that we must be cautious in our local messaging with regard to the inflammatory film trailer, adapting it to Libyan conditions. Our monitoring of the Libyan media and conversations with Libyans suggests that the film is not as explosive of an issue here as it appears to be in other countries in the region. The overwhelming majority of the FB [Facebook] comments and tweets we're [sic] received from Libyans since the Ambassador's death have expressed deep sympathy, sorrow, and regret. They have expressed anger at the attackers, and emphasized that this attack does not represent Libyans or Islam. Relatively few have even mentioned the inflammatory video. So if we post messaging about the video specifically, we may draw unwanted attention to it. And it is becoming increasingly clear that the series of events in Benghazi was much more terrorist attack than a protest which escalated into violence. It is our opinion that in our messaging, we want to distinguish, not conflate, the events in other countries with this well-planned attack by mili-

---

[155] Press Briefing by Press Secretary Jay Carney, Office of the Press Secretary, The White House (Sept. 14, 2012), https://www.whitehouse.gov/the-press-office/2012/09/14/press-briefing-press-secretary-jay-carney-9142012.

[156] Email from Public Affairs Officer, U.S. Embassy Tripoli, to Spokesperson, U.S. Dep't of State, et al. (Sept 14, 2012, 6:43 AM) (on file with the Committee, C05396788).

tant extremists. I have discussed this with Charge Hicks and shares PAS's view.[157]

The purpose of this email was to discuss messaging to the Libyan people—similar to the part of the Secretary's September 11 statement where her aides noted she wanted to speak to the region to "lower the temperature."[158] What is significant about this email, however, is that in discussing messaging to the Libyans, the video is not emphasized at all—in fact the messaging on the ground in Libya sought to distinguish what happened from other countries.[159] This again contrasts with the statements of senior administration officials, speaking to the American people, who consistently connect the video and Benghazi.

## THE TALKING POINTS

The talking points provided by the CIA to the House Permanent Select Committee on Intelligence [HPSCI] on September 15, 2012 were flawed. The individual who made the most substantial changes to those talking points was Michael Morell.[160] While much has been written about these talking points and the flawed process undertaken to create them, this section focuses on what specific information Morell had at his disposal when he made the changes to the talking points, how this information affected his editing of the talking points, and subsequent portrayal of the talking points by others.

### Information from Tripoli

While the September 13 WIRe represented an "assessment" that CIA analysts believed a protest had occurred prior to the Benghazi attack, CIA case officers and security personnel in Libya knew that was not the case. For the first two days after the attacks, the Chief of Station in Tripoli had been debriefing eyewitnesses to find out what happened and worked with his CIA counterparts—who had been in Benghazi—to contact their sources and collect as much information as possible about the attacks.[161] The Chief of Station knew no protests or demonstrations occurred prior to the attack. None of the eyewitnesses he spoke with mentioned anything about protests.[162] The Chief of Station testified he first learned that Washington D.C. created a narrative that protests had occurred around September 13 or 14:

> Q: I guess the first question would be, when did you first become aware that there was a belief back in Washington that the Benghazi attack was carried out without a significant degree of preplanning, and that the attack had somehow evolved from a demonstration at the consulate, or per-

[157] Id.

[158] Schwerin Testimony at 17.

[159] Email from Public Affairs Officer, U.S. Embassy Tripoli, to Spokesperson, U.S. Dep't of State, et al. (Sept 14, 2012, 6:43 AM) (on file with the Committee, C05396788).

[160] White House e-mails on 2012 attacks in Benghazi, Libya, Washington Post, http://apps.washingtonpost.com/g/page/politics/white-house-e-mails-on-2012-attacks-in-benghazi-libya/157.

[161] Testimony of Tripoli Chief of Station, Cent. Intel. Agency, Tr. at 129–31, 189 (July, 16, 2015) [hereinafter Chief of Station Testimony] (on file with the Committee).

[162] Id. at 122–123.

haps used a demonstration as cover? About three things there, but when did you first become aware of those misconceptions?

A: I want to say it was when—probably the 13th or 14th we were asked to coordinate on that first intelligence report that came out.

Q: Sure.

A: We provided our edits or our contributions to that. They weren't incorporated or included.[163]

This was just the first time—in what would become a pattern—of analysts and others at CIA headquarters relying on accounts from the press and other sources over that of America's highest ranking intelligence officer in Libya.[164]

The earliest evidence the Committee has seen where the Chief of Station told CIA headquarters a protest did not occur in Benghazi came early in the morning on Friday September 14, 2012.[165] A Worldwide Unrest Update sent to Morell's assistants and chief of staff said:

Tripoli: COS [Chief of Station] passed the following update being formulated by NE [Near East] now.

1. Fighters were trained, not an undisciplined militia. State compound was an assult/probe [sic] vice flash mob. This is based on the observations of CIA officers who were in the fight assessing the fighting method of the attackers.

2. Multiple militias and fluid political dynamics in Benghazi. Central government not able to project influence/power.

3. Mortar attack was precise on base location. Per JSOC [Joint Special Operations Command] operation on the gorund [sic] one short, one long, two direct hits. Their assessment this was a well-trained group—not militia rabble. JSOC officer is training the Libyan Special Forces and noted that they are not as capable of preci-

---

[163] *Id.* at 178.

[164] The CIA told the Committee this part of the report "suggests the intelligence community had no information on which to base our initial assessment that a protest preceded the attacks on the State compound. To the contrary, a significant body of information available immediately following the attacks indicated that there was a protest." This "significant body of information," however, was almost exclusively press reporting, and with one exception, this information was not cited in either the September 13 or September 15 WIRe pieces.

On September 16, 2012, at the direction of Michael Morell, the CIA analysts finally tackled the issue of protests head-on. They wrote: "We have contradictory reporting about whether non-violent demonstrations occurred prior to the attack on the US Consulate. The Station's assessment that there were no peaceful protests on the day of the attack is in contrast to other reports that peaceful protests preceded the violent assault." As supporting evidence for this paragraph the analysts used *only* public news articles from the Washington Post, Los Angeles Times, and National Public Radio—all of which were at least three days old—in addition to articles by Al Jazirah and the Guardian of London. They did not cite any intelligence reports, instead relying on the Internet.

[165] Email from [EA to DDCIA] to DIR–EAs, (Sept. 14, 2012, 8:27 AM) (on file with the CIA, REQUEST 1–001673 to 1–001674).

sion mortar fire as was witness [sic] on 12 September.[166]

Morell explained the purpose of these Worldwide Unrest Updates:

> When the unrest began across the Muslim world as a result of the video, there was unrest, there were protests, the administration was deeply concerned about the prospect—possibility prospect of violence against U.S. facilities and U.S. persons. We were having daily deputies meetings to discuss the safety of Americans and the safety of U.S. facilities overseas, two a day deputies meetings, one in the morning and one at night.
>
> One of the things the director and I did—and I don't know which one of us in particular did—one of us asked [**redacted text**] where there was unrest as a result of the video to do a daily update, right? This is the daily update from Tripoli for that day in response to that request.[167]

In other words, the daily updates were done for Morell, sent to his Executive Assistants, and written for his consumption. Despite this, Morell assumed the analysts received these updates as well. He testified:

> Q: Did this actually go to the analysts?
>
> A: I assume so. I assume so.
>
> Q: Okay. Why would you assume it went to the analyst if it was created for you?
>
> A: Because I believe all the updates—the updates were shared. I mean, that's something we can check, okay, something we can check.
>
> Q: So you believe that this worldwide unrest update was shared with you?
>
> A: Absolutely. And something you can ask [the OTA Director].[168]

The Committee asked the OTA Director, if she received this document. She was not aware they did. She testified:

> At the time, I was not aware. I have since become aware. I believe this was part of the daily email that was being done at the behest of DD/CIA.[169]

The manager of the analysts who conducted the analysis also does not remember seeing this email. She testified:

> Q: Is this something that would have made it to your desk or your analysts' desks?
>
> A: Not this email. . . .

---

166 *Id.*
167 Morell Testimony at 111.
168 *Id.* at 114–15.
169 OTA Dir. Testimony at 130.

Q: Okay. Under Tripoli it says "COS [Chief of Station] passed the following update being formulated by NE now." And then there are seven, I guess, individual updates. Those seven updates in this format, is that something that would have been passed to your team?

A: No, I've never seen this.

Q: Okay. I'm just trying to understand——

A: Well, let me say, I don't remember seeing it. And I don't know that my team would have passed it. I do know [Chief of Station] was unhappy with our call on protests because——[170]

When asked about this specific Worldwide Unrest Update from the Chief of Station, Morell responded:

A: So, look, the point is—the point is—the point is there is a flood of information coming in, right, and it's not my job as the deputy director of CIA to assess all this stuff. Right?

Q: Right.

A: It's the job of the analyst. So I'm looking at it from the perspective of, geez, is there anything here that's going to lead me to raise questions with the analyst?

Q: Okay. And was there anything in this particular email, the worldwide unrest update that caused you to raise questions with the analyst?

A: So this is not the—this is not from the 14th. So, no.[171]

As noted earlier, the email was sent at 8:27 a.m. on September 14, 2012. It is unclear why Morell did not acknowledge this fact.

That afternoon, the Chief of Station also wrote an email directly to one of the analysts in the Office of Terrorism Analysis.[172] That email, in response to a request to coordinate on talking points for a phone call for David Petraeus, Director, Central Intelligence Agency, on the Libya attack, said:

We are verifying some of the events that took place in fornt [sic] of the State department facility with some of the embassy personnel. The RSO [Regional Security Officer] noted that he was not aware of a protest in front of the consulate (the DOS [Department of State] facility where the Ambo and the ARSO's were staying. (could it have been the AAmerican [sic] corner?) We will be talking to the lead **[redacted text]** who was in Benghazi to obtain additional background. I also do not agree with the assessment that the attack was opportunistic [sic] in origin. The GRS Agents and xx operators on the scene noted that the fighters were moving and shooting in a fashion that indicated training—and set them apart for the militias fighters typi-

---

[170] **[Redacted text]** Team Chief Testimony at 61–62.
[171] Morell Testimony at 117–18.
[172] Email from Tripoli Chief of Station, Cent. Intel. Agency, to [Office of Terrorism Analysis Analyst] (Sept. 14, 2012, 4:05 PM) (on file with the CIA, REQUEST 15–0005).

cally found in Benghazi. Perhaps most compelling point was the comment by the **[redacted text]** who noted the percise [sic] and timing of mortar fire—one short, one long two direct hits. He noted that the Libyan special forces are unable to use mortars so effectively and that U.S. forces mortar company would be hard pressed to repeat the same performace [sic] as he witnessed in Benghazi.

I am basing my assessment mostly on the data from the guys on the ground (not all source) and dealing with Libyan contacts. Thanks for letting [sic] have an opportunity to co[o]rd[inate].[173]

The Chief of Station noted he was relying on information from "guys on the ground" and "Libyan contacts." [174]

Even though this email was written to an analyst, the analysts sent it up the chain. The manager of the analysts testified:

> Q: Okay. So this email is from chief of station to her. Do you recall whether or not she forwarded this to you or disseminated this——
>
> A: Oh yeah. She forwarded it. Everything from the [Chief of Station] I saw.
>
> Q: So when you received this email, is this something you would have pushed up the chain?
>
> A: Oh, yeah. Chief of Station, you know, disagreeing with something is no small thing. I mean, the chiefs of station are not required for coordination. But we absolutely, and especially NCTC [National Counterterrorism Center], take into account what they have to say.
>
> Q: All right. So you sounded confident that you pushed this up the chain. I guess my question——
>
> A: I don't remember doing it, but, I mean, I would have.
>
> Q: Okay. And you would have sent that to?
>
> A: [OTA Director].
>
> Q: [OTA Director]. Okay.
>
> A: And my boss, my——
>
> Q: Okay. And you don't know whether or not [the OTA Director] would have sent it on further?
>
> A: I'm sure [the OTA Director] would have sent it on further. But I don't—well, I say that. I can't be sure what any other person does. But [the OTA Director] has excellent judgment and a whole ton of bureaucratic savvy. So——[175]

The Chief of Station believes the email made its way up to Morell. He testified:

> Q: Do you know how high up the contents of your email outlining your inform[ation] made it? Beyond the person at

---

[173] *Id.*
[174] *Id.*
[175] **[Redacted text]** Team Chief Testimony at 68–69.

CT that was coordinating it, do you have any idea? Did it make it to Mr. Morell, for example?

A: I believe it made it to Mr. Morell.

Q: Okay.

A: Because this is one of the responses. The reason why I say that——

Q: Yeah.

A: —it went—this was a response. He was aware of our view that either—so I have all—I don't have any reason to doubt it didn't make it to him.

Q: Yeah.

A: And his questions to us were consistent that he got this specific information or something like it.[176]

Morell, however, testified he does not remember receiving this email. He told the committee:

Q: Okay. You don't believe this is something that you have ever seen?

A: Not that I remember.[177]

## Drafting the Talking Points

Petraeus testified the House Permanent Select Committee on Intelligence [HPSCI] did not ask for unclassified talking points when he met with them on September 14, 2012, but rather he offered to provide them to the Committee. Petraeus testified:

A: Yeah. The Ranking Member asked: What can we say about this publicly? And so I said: Okay, we'll come up with something for you. And, frankly, the thinking was we could do something very quickly, give it to him, he could have it that afternoon, and he could know what he could and could not say.

Q: So your expectations were this was something that would be done internally at the CIA and knocked out quickly and sent over in the afternoon?

A: Yeah, yeah. And, obviously, that would be inappropriate in the end because it would need to be sent through the intelligence community, so it had to be an IC. And then, of course, since it's now going to be used publicly, then the respective public affairs offices of various organizations get involved. And then since it has overall government implications, then you end up having to get State and FBI. There's security concerns and a variety of other issues that start to get factored in. So it became quite an involved process in the end.

Q: But what was your understanding of how the process would evolve when the tasking was first issued by HPSCI?

[176] Chief of Station Testimony at 208–09.
[177] Morell Testimony at 119.

A: I'm not sure I had a very clear—yeah, staff come up with some talking points.[178]

The OTA Director accompanied Petraeus to the HPSCI meeting, and upon returning to her office, drafted an initial set of talking points. She testified:

> So as I said, the coffee was that morning. I immediately came back. And knowing the sense of urgency that the Members had, I took that as my, you know, top task was to get them talking points because they had all said they were going to be going out and speaking to the media and to constituents and they wanted to know what they could say.
>
> So I put together the talking points. And I wanted them to be reflective of what the Members, of course, had just heard. Thinking back on this now, I think part of this is I definitely had in my mind that the Members had heard a fuller explanation from the director, but that this was my attempt to try and say of what they had heard what could they say in an unclassified setting.
>
> So I drafted these talking points immediately after that. And then at 11:15, so it was pretty quickly, then circulated them to make sure that everyone agreed with both the content and that they were unclassified.[179]

The first draft of the talking points contained six bullet points. Nowhere in any of these six bullet points is a mention of demonstrations or protests in Benghazi. The OTA Director acknowledged that these six bullet points were factually accurate—both at the time they were crafted and today.[180] The first bullet point was pulled almost verbatim from the September 13 WIRe, published the day before.[181]

The bullet points were:

- We believe based on currently available information that the attacks in Benghazi were spontaneously inspired by the protests at the US Embassy in Cairo and evolved into a direct assault against the US Consulate and subsequently its annex. This assessment may change as additional information is collected and analyzed and currently available information continues to be evaluated.

- The crowd almost certainly was a mix of individuals from across many sectors of Libyan society. That being said, we do know that Islamic extremists with ties to al-Qa'ida participated in the attack.

---

[178] Testimony of David Petraeus, Dir., Cent. Intel. Agency, Tr. at 50–51 (Mar. 19, 2016) (on file with the Committee).

[179] OTA Dir. Testimony at 194–95.

[180] OTA Dir. Testimony at 197.

[181] September 13 WIRe, *supra* note 123. The September 13 WIRe said "We assess the attacks on Tuesday against the US Consulate in Benghazi began spontaneously following the protests at the US Embassy in Cairo and evolved into a direct assault against the Consulate and a separate US facility in the city." The first bullet point stated "We believe based on currently available information that the attacks in Benghazi were spontaneously inspired by the protests at the US Embassy in Cairo and evolved into a direct assault against the US Consulate and subsequently its annex."

- Initial press reporting linked the attack to Ansar al-Sharia. The group has since released a statement that the its [sic] leadership did not order the attacks, but did not deny that some of its members were involved. Ansar al-Sharia's facebook page aims to spread sharia in Libya and emphasizes the need for jihad to counter what it views as false interpretations of Islam, according to an open source study.

- The wide availability of weapons and experienced fighters in Libya almost certainly contributed to the lethality of the attacks.

- Since April, there have been at least five other attacks against foreign interests in Benghazi by unidentified assailants, including the June attack against the British Ambassador's convoy. We cannot rule out that individuals had previously surveilled the US facilities, also contributing to the efficacy of the attacks.

- We are working with Libyan authorities and intelligence partners in an effort to help bring to justice those responsible for the deaths of US citizens.[182]

The OTA Director sent these six talking points out for coordination with other offices within the CIA at 11:15 a.m.[183] A member of the National Clandestine Service—the operators who work on the ground, as opposed to the analysts who sit at headquarters—asked: "Second tick says we *know* extremists with ties to AQ *participated* in the attack, which implies complicity in the deaths of the American officers. Do we know this?"[184] The OTA Director responds and says "Good point that it could be interpreted this way— perhaps better stated that we know they participated in the *protests*. We do not know who was responsible for the deaths."[185]

Given that no protests had occurred in Benghazi prior to the attack, this change had the effect of transforming the second bullet point from being accurate to being inaccurate. The OTA Director testified:

> Q: Sure. So I guess the way I read it is, you're trying to appease legal, which is always a challenge, by saying that—you wanted to back off the fact you know they participated in the attack because you don't want to interfere and potentially jeopardize the investigation, showing complicity to the attacks. So you altered it to we know they participated in protests at the time you believe they were protests.
>
> A: Correct.

---

[182] *Talking Points Timeline*, ABC NEWS, http://abcnews.go.com/images/Politics/Benghazi%20Talking%20Points%20Timeline.pdf (last visited May 17, 2016).

[183] *See* Email from [National Clandestine Service Officer] to [Near East Division, *et al.*] (Sept. 14, 2012, 2:52 PM) (on file with the CIA, REQUEST17–0443 to REQUEST 17–0449) (sending talking points to multiple offices within the CIA).

[184] Email from [National Clandestine Service Officer] to [Near East Division, *et al.*] (Sept. 14, 2012, 2:52 PM) (on file with the CIA, REQUEST 17–0443 to REQUEST 17–0449) (emphasis original).

[185] Email from Dir., Office of Terrorism Analysis, Cent. Intel. Agency, to [National Clandestine Service Officer] (Sept. 14, 2012, 3:19 PM) (on file with the CIA, REQUEST 17–0443 to REQUEST 17–0449) (emphasis added).

Q: But you didn't know for a fact that they [Islamic extremists with ties to al-Qa'ida] participated in the protests. You just knew that they were there.

A: Right.

Q: So the change went from being accurate to being inaccurate?

A: Correct.

Q: Okay and is that something you did solely on your own?

A: Yes.[186]

In a subsequent email, the word "protests" was changed to "violent demonstrations" in that same bullet point.[187] Those changes made it all the way through to the final version of the talking points, surviving the extensive deletions made near the end of this process by Morell.[188]

Shortly after this change was made, a meeting took place to discuss the talking points. The CIA's "Lessons Learned" after action review described this meeting:

> At some point between 4–5 p.m., a group of officers from OCA [Office of Congressional Affairs] and OPA [Office of Public Affairs] met in OPA spaces to discuss the talking points. Those officers included C [Chief]/OCA, COS [Chief of Staff]/OCA, D [Director]/OPA, the Chief of OPA's Media Relations Branch and two OPA spokespersons. Their efforts, over a period of approximately 30 minutes, culminated in a revised version of the talking points that was sent to CIA/COS and the DDCIA's [Deputy Director, Central Intelligence Agency] office by OPA at 4:42 p.m.

> Participants in this group editing session agree that they did not have a complete picture of intelligence regarding the events in Benghazi to guide them. Group members were working under tremendous time pressure. All agree that they were focused on several important considerations, including ensuring that the talking points contained no information that could compromise sources and methods, and that nothing was said that could compromise the then-nascent FBI investigation by prematurely attributing responsibility for the attacks on any one person or group.

> The group had access to an e-mail from NCS [National Clandestine Service] noting that the original talking points statement that "we do know that Islamic extremists participated in the attack" implied complicity in the deaths of American officers. The original drafter of the talking points agreed that we did not know who was responsible

---

186 OTA Dir. Testimony at 205–06.

187 See Email from [National Clandestine Service Officer] to [Near East Division, *et al.*] (Sept. 14, 2012, 2:52 PM) (on file with the CIA, REQUEST 17–0443 to REQUEST 17–0449).

188 See *Talking Points Timeline*, ABC NEWS, http://abcnews.go.com/images/Politics/Benghazi%20Talking%20Points%20Timeline.pdf (last visited May 17, 2016).

for the deaths and suggested that the language be changed to say "we know that they participated in the protests." While the editing group did not make this change, "attacks" in the second bullet was changed to "violent demonstration," effectively accomplishing the same purpose.

In addition, the word "attacks" in the first bullet of the talking points was changed to "demonstrations." The group also deleted reference in the second bullet to al-Qa'ida. The reasons underlying both changes are not clear, and participants in the editing session have incomplete recollections regarding the decision. Some have suggested that they believed the sentence was somewhat awkward and illogical as written, making reference to "attacks" "evolving into an assault," with "attacks" and "assault" seeming to be synonyms. In addition to these changes, the group added two sentences about CIA product discussing threats, a statement noting that the investigation was ongoing, and several non-substantive word changes.[189]

The meeting did not include the OTA Director, the drafter of the original talking points, or any substantive experts on Benghazi. The OTA Director testified:

Q: So how did we go from "attacks" in bullet point one at 3:33 to "demonstrations" in bullet point one at 4:42?

A: At some point in this process this entered into—it became opaque to me. At some point in this process, as I——

Q: I'm sorry. Were you comfortable with it occur[ing] that way given the fact that you were tasked with——

A: I didn't know it was occurring. So when I say it was opaque to me, I did not know this was happening.

At some point in this process, as I know you have seen from all this, there is a group from OPA, our Office of Public Affairs, our Office of Congressional Affairs, and others, took the talking points and made changes to them. And I was not consulted on those changes. So I cannot tell you how some of these changes took place. I was not involved. I was not consulted beforehand.[190]

That change in the first bullet point—from "attacks" to "demonstrations"—also survived Morell's extensive edits and was in the final version of the talking points.[191]

Around this same time, Morell first learned about the existence of the talking points. He testified:

So there was a weekly meeting on Syria, followed by our three-times-a-week meeting on counterterrorism. In between those two meetings, the director's chief of staff

[189] Letter from Michael Morell, Deputy Dir., Cent. Intel. Agency, to Sen. Richard M. Burr, S. Select Comm. on Intel., *Lessons Learned From Formulation of Unclassified Talking Points re the Events in Benghazi, 11–12 September 2012* [hereinafter Lessons Learned] (Aug. 6, 2013) (on file with the Committee), at 4–5.

[190] OTA Dir. Testimony at 209–10.

[191] *See Talking Points Timeline,* ABC NEWS, http://abcnews.go.com/images/Politics/Benghazi%20Talking%20Points%20Timeline.pdf (last visited May 17, 2016).

walked up to me in the director's conference room and said, here, you need to see these. You need to be aware of this, you need to get involved in this. I said, what's this? And he explained the origin of the talking points and he explained kind of where they were in the process. I skimmed the talking points, and I immediately reacted to the warning language [language indicating that five prior attacks had ococurred in Benghazi against foreign interests]. . . .

So I say to my EA [Executive Assistant], where is this in the process? And he said, it's being coordinated. I say, okay, I will deal with it in the morning.[192]

Morell testified he did not edit the talking points that evening, nor did he speak with anybody about them.[193] Instead, Morell edited them by himself the next morning, Saturday, September 15. He testified:

So I come in the next morning and my—and the next morning, by the way, is a deputies meeting at eight. Family day at CIA—once a year you allow families to come on the compound, walk around, visit offices, et cetera, et cetera—is at nine.

And first thing my EA tells me is that Denis McDonough, then the deputy National Security Advisor, wants to talk about—wants to talk about the talking points in the deputies meeting, and I say, okay. I have a conversation with General Petraeus about the talking points, and [Petraeus' Chief of Staff] was there, and I believe he would—if he were here, he would agree with what I'm about ready to tell you, that I told Director Petraeus that the talking points were stuck, that the State Department was objecting to the warning language, and I told him that I agreed that the warning language should be taken out, and the Director didn't say a word to me. He didn't tell me that he was going to put it in, he didn't say, keep—keep the warning language in there, I think it's really important. He didn't say anything.

We do our family day stuff, which includes literally hundreds of people coming through my office and shaking hands with me, and the whole time I'm thinking these talking points are sitting on my desk, actually my EA's desk.

So when the family thing is done, I go and edit the talking points and I literally edit them in 5, 10 minutes and I fly through them. And as you know, I made a bunch of changes, and the most significant of which is taking out the warning language. So that's kind of the—that's kind of the story there.[194]

---

[192] Morell Testimony at 124–25.
[193] *Id.* at 128–29.
[194] *Id.* at 126–28.

## New Information on September 15

When Morell edited the talking points on the morning of September 15, new information was fresh in his mind regarding the Benghazi attacks. That morning saw additional information written about Benghazi. A *New York Times* article was published that morning written by Peter Baker. It read in part:

> According to a guard at the compound, the attack began at about 9:30 p.m., without advance warning or any peaceful protest. "I started hearing, 'God is great! God is great!'" one guard said. "I thought to myself, maybe it is a passing funeral." (All the guards spoke on the condition of anonymity for their safety)
>
> "Attack, attack," the guard said as he heard an American calling over his walkie-talkie as the chants came closer. Suddenly, there came a barrage of gunfire, explosions, and rocket-propelled grenades.[195]

The Chief of Station found this article compelling. He testified:

> Q: They told them attack or they told them fire, so I mean—I don't know if you knew that at the time, but I mean, in reading this, it seems like some of the folks being interviewed here only know things that someone who was there would know. Did you read this——
>
> A: Oh yeah, I found this compelling.[196]

Morell, however, did not. He testified:

> Q: Are you familiar with Peter Baker at all?
>
> A: Yes, I believe I have met him.
>
> \*     \*     \*
>
> Q: Okay. All right. Your assessment of the New York Times as a media organization?
>
> A: My assessment of The New York Times is that, like any media organization, it gets a lot of things wrong. And my assessment of The New York Times is that its reporting and editorials are fairly biased, in my view.[197]

Morell then said:

> Q: So the same paragraph we were talking about on page two, here is the New York Times citing one guard from the consulate. I mean, how would you assess that in terms of credibility from what the guard said reported in The New York Times article?
>
> A: How would I assess it?
>
> Q: How would you assess it?

---

[195] Peter Baker, *et al., Diplomats' Bodies Return to U.S., and Libyan Guards Recount Deadly Riot*, N.Y. TIMES (Sept. 15, 2012), http://www.nytimes.com/2012/09/15/world/middleeast/ambassadors-body-back-in-us-libya-guards-recount-riot.html?_r=0.

[196] Chief of Station Testimony at 218.

[197] Morell Testimony at 106.

A: Michael Morell?

Q: Yes.

A: I wouldn't give it great credibility.

Q: Okay.

A: Right? I mean, it's a data point. It's a data point. It's one guard. You don't know who it is. You don't know the conditions under which he was talking. I mean, it's a data point. I wouldn't discount it totally, but I wouldn't say this is absolute fact.[198]

The CIA analysts published another WIRe that morning, September 15, with a new assessment.[199] This piece, co-written with the National Counterterrorism Center, had two main focuses: the extremists who participated in the Benghazi attacks, and Libyan authorities placing a high priority on tracking down the perpetrators of the attack.[200] Similar to the September 13 WIRe two days earlier, the notion of a protest and the discussion of a video were not central—or even minor—focuses of the piece.

The first paragraph of the September 15 WIRe contains the sentence "The level of planning and exact sequence of events leading to the attack remain intelligence gaps."[201] This indicates the analysts did not know definitively what had transpired prior to the attacks—perhaps whether or not protests in Benghazi had occurred, or the motivation or level of planning for the attacks—and signaled to the reader that information still needed to be gleaned about these events.

Morell also reviewed an email from the Chief of Station on the morning of September 15. That email stated in part:

> INTEL: Station notes the following information from the past 24hrs, which strengthen Station's assessment that the attacks were not/not spontaneous and not/not an escalation of protests. Press reports noted that at the time of the attack, circa 2130 local, guards posted at the U.S. Consulate in Benghazi and Libyans residing in the vicinity reported the absence of protests at the consulate and specific that the attack began without warning. A CIA officer on the scene noted that at approximately 2200 [10:00 p.m.], there was no sign of a protest at the Consulate. Libya General National Congress (GNC) President Magaryaf stated in an interview that the attacks were planned in advance by experienced individuals, most likely al-Qa'ida (AQ) and not former regime elements (FRE).[202]

Morell testified about receiving this email:

---

[198] *Id.* at 109.

[199] Cent. Intel. Agency, Libya: Variety of Extremists Participated in Benghazi Attacks, World Intelligence Review, Sept. 15, 2012 (on file with CIA, REQUEST 17–0262 to REQUEST 17–0265).

[200] *Id.*

[201] *Id.*

[202] Email from Tripoli Chief of Station, Cent. Intel. Agency, to [Morell Assistant] (Sept. 15, 2012) (on file with the CIA, REQUEST 15–0011 to REQUEST 15–0022).

I go through it, I read this, right, and the line in there about, we don't think this was a protest, right, jumps out at me. Why did it jump out at me? Because the analysts believed there was a protest. So here I have my analysts saying there was a protest, and I've got my Chief of Station, a guy I've got a lot of confidence in, right, telling me there was no protest.

The other thing that jumped out at me were that the reasons he gave . . . why he thinks there was no protest, the first is that there were press reports saying no protest, but what goes through my mind, right, is, look, I know that there's press reports that say there were protests. Okay? . . .

And then the next reason he gives is that a CIA officer on the scene noted that at approximately 2200, there was no sign of a protest at the consulate. And what goes through my mind then is, well, you know what, that's—2200 is 20 minutes after the attack started, right? Maybe everybody dispersed by then. What I react to now is that they didn't get there at 2200. They got to the corner, they got to the corner of the street that the TMF [Benghazi Mission compound] was on at about 10 minutes after 10:00. They didn't even—they didn't get to the TM—to the front of the TMF itself until 2240, an hour after the attack started. So not compelling at all, right?[203]

Morell also compared the language in this email from the Chief of Station to the language in the email the Chief of Station sent the day before.

Q: So [the September 15 email] is stronger than the assessment given by the Chief of Station a day earlier?

A: I certainly remember it that way.[204]

Morell likely reviewed another piece of intelligence the morning of September 15 titled "Observations from the 11–12 September, 2012 Attacks Against the U.S. Consulate and a Separate Facility in Benghazi, Libya."[205] Morell received this piece of intelligence in an email at 8:50 a.m. and testified that he "almost certainly would not have not read an email from the chief of staff [of the CIA]."[206] This email also noted there were "no signs of a protest" at 10:00 p.m. in Benghazi—less than 20 minutes after the attacks began—according to a CIA officer at the scene.[207]

It was with this information fresh in his mind—the two September 15 emails and the September 15 WIRe—along with the September 13 WIRe and the September 14 email from the Chief of Station, that Morell edited the talking points. At the time he edited the talking points, he had seen at least two reports from the Chief

[203] Morell Testimony at 146–47.
[204] *Id.* at 150.
[205] Email from Chief of Staff to Dir., Cent. Intel. Agency, to Michael Morell, Deputy Dir., Cent. Intel. Agency (Sept. 15, 2012) [hereinafter Dir. COS Email] (on file with the CIA, (REQUEST 1–002167).
[206] Morell Testimony at 144.
[207] Dir. COS Email, *supra* note 205.

of Station—and possibly more—indicating, in increasingly forceful language, that no protests had taken place. The analysts had not seen these emails. Morell therefore was the only person who had both the analytic assessments about Benghazi in addition to multiple emails from the Chief of Station—somebody Morell had worked closely with during the Arab Spring and recognized as an "outstanding intelligence officer." [208]

It was incumbent on Morell to take all of this information at his disposal into account when he edited the talking points. Morell, a former intelligence analyst who rose through the ranks analyzing disparate information and formulating assessments, disagreed. He testified:

> A: It's not my job, it's not my job to be the analyst, right? It's not my job to take all this information and come to an analytic conclusion. That's the job of the analysts. So when I—look, and had I done that, had I played analyst, right, and started editing the talking points and started changing them to reflect what the COS said, the analysts would have protested, because they—at that moment, they still believed that there had been a protest. So for me to take it out because the COS said there wasn't one would have gotten a reaction from the analysts. They would have seen me as politicizing analysis, all right?
>
> Q: How would that have politicized the analysis, the fact that you're——
>
> A: They would have seen it that way.
>
> Q: But you're taking judgments from somebody that you had worked with very closely, somebody that you had deemed an exemplary intelligence officer.
>
> A: Look, managers at CIA don't do analysis. When they are perceived to be doing the analysis, the analysts go nuts, right? Bob Gates was accused of that, other senior officials at CIA have been accused of that. Analysts go nuts when they think that managers are doing the analysis themselves, particularly when they disagree with the analysis. So the last thing I was going to do was change the analysts' analysis, right? [209]

Morell was not, however, creating an analytic assessment. Morell was editing talking points that would be used for public consumption. The process—and the product—is an inherently different one from internal CIA processes for formulating assessments. The analysts were not involved in the talking points process—only managers were.[210] The analysts did not have the same emails Morell did from the Chief of Station—only Morell had those.

Talking points—something the CIA rarely produces—are different from analytic assessments, which the CIA produces every day. Petraeus acknowledged this when he testified:

---

[208] Morell Testimony at 14.

[209] *Id.* at 152–53.

[210] *See, e.g.,* email from Dir., Office of Terrorism Analysis, Cent. Intel. Agency, to [NE Division] (Sept. 14, 2012) (on file with the CIA, REQUEST 17–0443 to 17–0444).

I mean, that was where finally once it—this was not—certainly no longer a CIA document. It wasn't even an intelligence community document, although that rightly should have been, and that's why it went to the IC referral process, but then, of course, you know, it's going to be interagency and not everyone has got a hand in this.[211]

The talking points were understood to be viewed as representative of an authoritative analytical assessment. As shown, however, this was not the case—no analysts worked on these talking points, as they were created and edited only by senior CIA managers and other senior officials in the administration. The distinction was never manifested on the document or otherwise made known to those relying on, or making representations based on, the talking points.

No process was in place to create the talking points, and no analysis was required to create them. The only expectation was to produce accurate information to Congress for them to share with the American people. That being the case, Morell—the only person with the complete universe of information at his disposal—could have edited the talking points to reflect the most up-to-date information—or at the very least to caveat the talking points with a reflection that different views existed. Morell did neither of these things.

Panetta—whom Morell worked for when Panetta was Director of the CIA—understands this concept well. He told the Committee:

> The last lesson I would tell you is don't use talking points that don't include language that makes very clear that the matter is under investigation and that these results are only preliminary. As former chief of staff, I've seen talking points, and I can understand how trouble can result as a result of that. I used to review those before anybody got a hold of them to make sure that they reflected what we wanted to inform the American people about, because the last thing you want to do is to mislead the American people.[212]

## THE SUNDAY TALK SHOWS

Perhaps as much as any other subject surrounding Benghazi, the appearance by Ambassador Rice on five Sunday morning talk shows following the attacks has been the most politically charged. After all, it was the fallout from her appearances that ultimately caused her to withdraw her name as a candidate—perhaps the leading candidate—to be the next Secretary of State.[213] Yet little is known about why she was selected by the administration to represent the United States government on the shows, what she did to prepare for those talk shows, what materials she reviewed, who

---

[211] Testimony of David Petraeus, Dir., Cent. Intel. Agency, Tr. at 62 (Jan. 6, 2016) (on file with the Committee).

[212] Testimony of Leon Panetta, Sec'y of Defense, U.S. Dep't of Defense, Tr. at 107 (Jan. 8, 2016) (on file with the Committee).

[213] Karen DeYoung & Anne Gearan, *Susan Rice withdraws as candidate for secretary of state*, WASH. POST (Dec. 13, 2012), https://www.washingtonpost.com/world/national-security/susan-rice-withdraws-as-candidate-for-secretary-of-state/2012/12/13/17ad344e-4567-11e2-8e70-e1993528222d_story.html.

she spoke with to learn information about the attacks, and most significantly why she said what she said.

It was not until two days before the shows, on Friday, September 14, when Rice learned she would be appearing on behalf of the administration.[214] She was the administration's third choice to appear on the shows—the first being the Secretary of State and the second being Tom Donilon, National Security Advisor to the President.[215] Rhodes was the White House official responsible for reaching out to Rice and asking her to appear. He testified:

A: I recall reaching out to Secretary Clinton first.

\* \* \*

Q: Did you get an affirmative "no" or did you just not hear back?

A: I don't remember hearing back.

Q: Did you call again and redouble your ask or did you move on to your second draft choice?

A: I believe I moved on because I knew that she, again, does not regularly appear on Sunday shows. So I don't remember thinking that it was likely that she would want to appear.

Q: And who else would you have asked after Secretary Clinton?

A: I remember asking Tom Donilon, the National Security Advisor.

Q: And what was his response?

A: He did not want to appear. And he too very rarely appeared on the Sunday shows.

Q: All right. Who was number three?

A: I believe it was Susan Rice, is my recollection.[216]

Although Rhodes testified the Secretary "does not regularly appear on Sunday shows," she had in fact appeared on multiple shows on two separate occasions within a seven month period to discuss Libya. On March 27, 2011—barely a week after the United States supported the UN in imposing a no fly zone over Libya and authorizing all means necessary to protect civilians—the Secretary appeared on *Meet the Press, Face the Nation,* and *This Week,* to talk about the U.S. intervention in Libya, which was being promoted as a civilian protection and humanitarian mission.[217] Seven months later—in the immediate wake of Qadhafi's death—she ap-

---

[214] Testimony of Susan E. Rice, former U.S. Ambassador to the U.N., Tr. at 30 (Feb. 2, 2016) [hereinafter Rice Testimony] (on file with the Committee).

[215] *See* Rhodes Testimony at 65–66 (stating Sec'y Clinton and Tom Donilon were first and second choices to appear).

[216] Rhodes Testimony at 65–66.

[217] *Meet the Press transcript for March 27, 2011,* NBC News (Mar. 27, 2011), http://www.nbcnews.com/id/42275424/ns/meet_the_press-transcripts/t/meet-press-transcript-march/#.VzoK0_krJaQ; *Face the Nation March 27, 2011 Transcript,* CBS News (Mar. 27, 2011), http://www.cbsnews.com/htdocs/pdf/FTN_032711.pdf;*'This Week' Transcript: Hillary Clinton, Robert Gates and Donald Rumsfeld,* ABC News (Mar. 27, 2011), http://abcnews.go.com/ThisWeek/week-transcript-hillary-clinton-robert-gates-donald-rumsfeld/story?id=13232096.

peared on *Meet the Press, This Week, State of the Union,* and *FoxNews Sunday* to talk about Qadhafi's death and the path forward in Libya.[218]

Mills testified the decision not to appear on the Sunday shows was the Secretary's:

> Q: Since the Secretary didn't appear, who made the decision that she wasn't going to appear?
>
> A: Well, she would always decide what she would do, if she was going to go on a show or not go on a show.
>
> Q: Okay. Were there recommendations that she took from you and others, such as Philippe Reines, Jake Sullivan, others?
>
> A: No. Candidly, the Secretary was so focused on what had happened to our team and what was happening in the region that I don't know that there was a moment's thought about it. She didn't often go on the shows. And she was, understandably, very concerned about how we support our teams and the losses that we had incurred.[219]

When Rhodes learned the Secretary would not represent the administration on the talk shows, he then asked Donilon to appear.[220] He also declined.[221] Rice—Rhodes' third choice for the task—accepted.[222] In doing so, the administration selected someone to talk to the American people about the Benghazi attacks who was neither involved in the security of any U.S. facilities in Benghazi nor involved in any way with the operational response to the attacks. In fact, the administration selected an individual who did not even know there was a CIA presence in Benghazi, let alone the fact that two Americans had died there.[223] She testified:

> Q: Did you learn between September 11 and September 16 that were was a CIA presence in Benghazi?
>
> A: I think—no. I think I learned subsequently.
>
> *     *     *
>
> Q: So nobody told you between the dates of September 11 and September 16 that two of the four Americans who were killed who were providing security actually worked for the CIA and not the State Department?
>
> A: Not that I recall.

---

[218] *Meet the Press transcript for October 23, 2011,* NBC (Oct. 23, 2011), http://www. nbcnews.com/id/45000791/ns/meet_the_press-transcripts/t/meet-press-transcript-october/#.V1cU1 9UrJaQ., *Clinton Warns Iran: U.S. Committed to Iraq,* ABC's *This Week* (Oct. 23, 2011), http:// abcnews.go.com/ThisWeek/video/interview-hillary-clinton-14796369; *State of the Union with Candy Crowley,* CNN (Oct. 23, 2011), http://transcripts.cnn.com/TRANSCRIPTS/1110/23/ sotu.01.html., and *Clinton Talks Iraq, Libya; Sen. Graham Challenges GOP Candidates; Bachmann Focused on Iowa,* FOX News Sunday (Oct. 23, 2011), http://www.foxnews.com/on-air/fox-news-sunday-chris-wallace/2011/10/23/clinton-talks-iraq-libya-sen-graham-challenges-gop-candidates-bachmann-focused-iowa#p//v/1234077958001.

[219] Testimony of Cheryl D. Mills, Chief of Staff to the U.S. Sec'y of State, U.S. Dep't of State, Tr. at 123 (Sept. 3, 2015) [hereinafter Mills Testimony] (on file with the Committee).

[220] Rhodes Testimony at 66.

[221] *Id.*

[222] *Id.*

[223] Rice Testimony at 107–08.

Q: All right.

Q: And you learned that subsequently?

A: To the best of my recollection, I learned it subsequently.[224]

In selecting Rice to appear on the Sunday talk shows, Rhodes chose an individual with limited knowledge of, and presumably limited participation in, the administration's reponse to the Benghazi attacks. Instead, while the attacks were happening, Rice was receiving—apparently in response to an email chain about the attack on the Benghazi Mission compound—a detailed update from staff about the number of retweets her Twitter account had generated.[225]

### How Rice Prepped for the Shows

On Friday, September 14, 2012, the Secretary's calendar included a meeting with Rice.[226] Both Rice and Mills testified they believed that meeting took place, even though neither had a specific recollection of it.[227] That Friday meeting was a standing meeting between the Secretary and Rice that would take place when Rice was in Washington.

Despite having no specific recollection of the meeting, Rice is confident she did not discuss the Sunday shows with the Secretary at the meeting.[228] This is because Rice first learned of her possible appearance on the Sunday shows in the early afternoon of September 14, after the scheduled meeting. She testified:

> I received a phone call as I was in my car on my way to Andrews for the ceremony receiving our fallen colleagues. And in that phone call from Ben [Rhodes], I was asked whether it would be possible, if Secretary Clinton were unable to appear on the shows, if I could appear on the shows. It was a contingency question at the time. And I said that, you know, I had other plans for the weekend and that it would not be my preference but if they needed me and there was not an alternative that I would be willing to do it.[229]

Both the Secretary and Rice attended the return of remains ceremony at Andrews Air Force Base that afternoon, and later that day, Friday September 14, Rhodes called Rice back to inform her she needed to do the Sunday shows.[230]

Ambassador Rice did not begin preparing for the shows until the following day, Saturday September 15. Her staff, led by Erin

---

[224] *Id.*

[225] *See* Email to Susan E. Rice, U.S. Permanent Rep. to the U.N. (Sept. 11, 2012, 7:43 P.M.) (on file with the Committee, C05561948) ("Today, you tweeted 7 times on the anniversary of the September 11 attacks, generating more than 600 retweets. By this measure, your twitter account had a big day—your second or third biggest since the start of the summer—and your volunteering pics got a few nice responses . . .").

[226] Email from Special Ass't to the Sec'y of State, U.S. Dep't of State, to Hillary R. Clinton ("H"), Sec'y of State, U.S. Dep't of State (Sept. 14, 2012, 7:29 AM) (on file with the Committee, SCB0045306–SCB0045307).

[227] Rice Testimony at 28; Mills Testimony at 138.

[228] Rice Testimony at 28.

[229] Rice Testimony at 26.

[230] *Id.*

Pelton, Communications Director and Spokesperson, prepared a book of briefing materials for Rice.[231] Rice testified she began reviewing these briefing materials on Saturday:

Q: So let's go forward to—did you do anything after speaking to Mr. Rhodes on Friday night to begin preparing?

A: No.

Q: What did you do the next morning to begin preparing?

A: I reviewed briefing materials.

Q: What briefing materials? Would that just be the same daily briefing materials that you received in the ordinary course, or was this different material?

A: It was both. I received my daily intelligence briefing on Saturday morning, and I also began reviewing a briefing book that had been prepared by my staff for—in preparation for the Sunday shows.[232]

These briefing materials contained little to no information about the Benghazi attacks. Pelton testified that in gathering briefing materials for the Sunday shows she explicitly did not focus on Benghazi, anticipating materials pertaining to Benghazi would come at a later time. She said:

Q: In your list of areas where you were attempting to collect the latest information, you left Benghazi out. Was that intentional, or were you just giving me some examples?

A: I don't recall preparing information about Benghazi. What I do recall is understanding that we would have access to talking points that would be provided by the intelligence community that were unclassified and consistent with our latest understanding of what had transpired in Benghazi.[233]

Pelton also testified she believed she would be receiving talking points regarding Benghazi that would not require her to seek out briefing materials about Benghazi on her own:

Well, I recall that in the process of preparing Ambassador Rice between Friday and Saturday, September 14th and 15th, that I was not focused on Benghazi because I was going to receive talking points that were appropriate for public use by the intelligence community. I don't remember how I came to know that I was going to get those materials.[234]

While Pelton did not include any information specific to Benghazi in the briefing book, Rice recalled other material that was in the briefing book. She testified:

---

[231] Testimony of Erin Pelton, Dir. of Commc'cs and Spokesperson, U.S. Mission to the U.N., Tr. at 44 (Feb. 11, 2016) [hereinafter Pelton Testimony] (on file with the Committee).
[232] Rice Testimony at 31.
[233] Pelton Testimony at 45.
[234] *Id.*

Q: As best you can, do you recall what was in that briefing book that your staff provided?

A: I recall it included statements that other senior administration officials had made, including the President and the Secretary. I recall it including background Q&A and top-line themes covering the wide range of issues that we anticipated would come up on the shows: the protests that occurred all around the world that week; obviously, also what happened in Benghazi.

And, also, because it was one week before the opening of the U.N. General Assembly in New York and Iran was expected to be a prominent issue, and Prime Minister Netanyahu's visit also a prominent issue, I recall preparing for that discussion as well.[235]

The "background Q&A" and "top line themes" came from Rhodes.[236] Pelton testified about how this information came about:

A: I don't recall all the specifics of our conversation [with Ben Rhodes]. However, I do recall at one point asking him to provide, for lack of a better term, a memo regarding the objectives of the Sunday show appearances.

Q: How did he respond to you?

A: He said he would write it.

Q: And did he eventually deliver that to you?

A: Yes.[237]

Rhodes delivered this memo at 8:09 p.m. on the evening of September 14 in an email with the subject "RE: PREP CALL with Susan: Saturday at 4:00 pm ET."[238] The memo contained four bullet points under "Goals," six bullet points under "Top-lines," and contained five questions and suggested answers regarding the Arab Spring, protests, and Benghazi, and an additional four questions and suggested answers regarding Israel and Iran.[239]

The four bullet points under the "Goals" section of the memo were the following:

To convey that the United States is doing everything that we can to protect our people and facilities abroad;

To underscore that these protests are rooted in an Internet video, and not a broader failure of policy;

To show that we will be resolute in bringing people who harm Americans to justice, and standing steadfast through these protests;

To reinforce the President and Administration's strength and steadiness in dealing with difficult challenges.[240]

---

[235] Rice Testimony at 33.
[236] Rhodes Memo, *supra* note 3.
[237] Pelton Testimony at 42.
[238] Rhodes Memo, *supra* note 3.
[239] *See id.*
[240] *Id.*

The second point was one of the most explicit directions from a senior administration official about the intent of the adminstration's communications strategy. The Chairman had the following exchange with Rhodes about these bullet points during Rhodes' testimony to the Committee:

Q: How about number two? They are not numbered, but let's just go second bullet, okay? "To underscore that these protests are rooted in an Internet video, and not a broader failure of policy." What policy were you worried about being considered a failure?

A: My recollection over the course of that week is that we were getting questions about whether this represented a failure of our policy in the Middle East and in response to the Arab Spring.

Q: And you wanted to underscore the point that it wasn't any of that, it was just a video.

A: We were anticipating getting those questions, and we wanted to convey that, again, the protests were rooted in this video.

Q: Were there other options other than just those two, a wholesale failure of the administration's policy or an Internet video? Was there something else? Those are your only two options?

A: Again, my recollection is that this reflects the way in which we were getting questions over the course of the week is it's a failure of policy. And we were at the same time seeking to deal with the ongoing fallout from the video. So those were the factors in play.

Q: I'm with you on wanting to explain to folks that it wasn't a failure of policy. You essentially gave yourself two choices: an Internet video or a broader failure of policy. And my question is, were those your only two options?

A: Again, that's what I recall being the subject of discussion over the course of that week in terms of the questions we were being asked.

Q: Well, with respect to Benghazi, it certainly would have—it's possible that it was not just those two options, right?

A: I'm not sure I understand the question.

Q: With respect to what happened in Benghazi, you're not limiting us to just those two options, right, a failure of policy or an Internet video?

A: Again, I believe in this specific bullet I'm referring to the ongoing protests that are taking place across the Middle East which were very much still going forward on that Friday.

Q: Right. But you agree—you knew Benghazi was going to come up when Ambassador Rice was going on the five Sunday talk shows?

A: Yes.

Q: We haven't had an ambassador killed since when?

A: It had been a long time. I don't remember specifically.

Q: So you knew that that was coming up?

A: I knew that was going to be one of the topics.

Q: Right. And your third bullet, which isn't numbered, but it's number three, "To show that we will be resolute in bringing people who harm Americans to justice." Can you think of a country where Americans were harmed other than Libya that she might have been asked about?

A: That would principally, I believe, refer to Libya.

Q: Okay. So you concede that the third item does apply to Libya. Let's go back to the second one. How about the second one? Are we to have drawn a contrast between the second bullet and the third bullet, or are they all inter-related?

A: Again, my recollection is she is going on to talk about several different issues: the attacks in Benghazi, the ongoing protests that were taking place across the Middle East, and issues related to Iran and Israel. And so these points refer to different elements of the topic.

Q: Well, at the time, what did you think was the impetus for the attack in Benghazi?

A: I did not have a judgment of my own at the time. I was going to rely on the information provided by the intelligence community.

Q: Did the intelligence community mention an Internet video to you?

A: The intelligence community at this point had suggested that it was an event that was motivated in part by the protests in Cairo.

Q: That was a great answer to a question I didn't ask. Did they mention the video?

A: No, what I'm saying is, my recollection is they at that point had said that insofar as there was any connection it was more to the events in Cairo being a motivating factor for individuals.

Q: Right. So you are preparing the Ambassador to go on five Sunday talk shows to talk about what you know is going to involve Benghazi and you don't want her to be stuck with the option of a failure of your policy. So you give the option of the Internet video. And my question is, who in the intelligence community told you that the attacks in Benghazi were linked to the video?

A: Again, I prepared these points on a Friday in which there were violent protests across the Middle East because of the video, a violent breach of our facility in Tunis, a violent breach of our facility at Khartoum, violence against an

American restaurant in Lebanon, at the very least. So I very much was focused on the fact that there were ongoing protests, and one of the subjects that she was going to be asked about were those protests. So insofar as I'm referring to protests in the video, I'm referring to the many protests that were continuing to take place over the course of that week in response to the video.

Q: So is it your testimony that the second bullet and the third bullet are totally unrelated?

A: They're referring to different elements of what she's going to have to talk about on the Sunday shows.

Q: So bullet number two was not about Libya or Benghazi at all.

A: It was not intended to assign responsibility for Benghazi.

Q: But yet you jump in the very next bullet to those who harm Americans. Can you see how someone reading that memo might be vexed?

A: Well, again, these are several statements of principle up top that I think speak to, again, all—in different parts of the issues that she is going to have to address. And then you can see in the actual contents how we intended to respond to those individual questions and instances.[241]

The fact Rhodes concedes the third bullet point references Libya is important. The bullet point immediately prior references the video, allowing for easy connection and conflation of the video and the Benghazi attacks.[242] This occurred in public statements by the administration prior to Rhodes' memo, and, having seen this memo, Rice appeared to again connect the video and Benghazi the next day when she appeared on the talk shows.

While this connection between the two events may have favored a particular narrative, even Rhodes admitted that he was not aware of any intelligence that existed to directly link the video to the attacks. He testified:

A: And, again, my recollection of any connection to the video was indirect through the fact that the protests in Cairo may have been a motivating factor for the events in Benghazi.

Q: Okay. So just to be clear, so there was no direct connection made between the video and the attacks in Benghazi from the intelligence community that you're aware of at that time?

A: That's my recollection. I recall that there were public reports of protests that were—that would have been included in, you know, the information we were receiving.

Q: But you certainly weren't relying on those public reports, were you?

---

[241] Rhodes Testimony at 75–80.
[242] Rhodes Memo, *supra* note 3.

A: We were relying on the intelligence community's assessment, and the intelligence community's assessment was that these were events that were motivated in part by the protests in Cairo.[243]

At 4:00 p.m. on Saturday September 15, 2012, a conference call was convened with Rice to discuss her appearance on the Sunday shows the following morning.[244] Rice participated in this conference call from Columbus, Ohio, where she was spending the day.[245] Rexon Ryu, Deputy to the U.S. Permanent Representative to the United Nations, State Department, testified there were no State Department people on the call:

Q: Okay. Do you recall—so you said Ben Rhodes. Were there any individuals, other than the USUN individual, were there any other people from the State Department that participated in that call?

A: There were no State Department people.

Q: Do you recall if there were additional individuals from the White House that participated?

A: Yes, there were.[246]

Rice testified David Plouffe, Senior Advisor to the President, was on the call.[247] Plouffe had previously served as the campaign manager for the President's 2008 presidential campaign.[248] While Rhodes testified Plouffe would "normally" appear on the Sunday show prep calls,[249] Rice testified she did not recall him being on prior calls and did not understand why he was on the call in this instance.[250]

No witness interviewed by the Committee was able to specifically identify State Department individuals on the call aside from Rice's staff.[251] In addition, nobody from the Federal Bureau of Investigation [FBI], Department of Defense, or Central Intelligence Agency participated in the call, which apparently consisted of just a small circle of Rice's advisors and communications staffers from the White House.

At the time of her appearance on the talk shows, it had been announced the FBI would take the lead on the investigation into finding out what had occurred.[252] The Department of Defense, along with White House operators, had been involved in sending troops towards Libya while the attacks were ongoing, and analysts from the Central Intelligence Agency had taken the lead on post-attack analysis of intelligence. The State Department had its compound in Benghazi attacked and, as such, it was the principal source of in-

---

[243] Rhodes Testimony at 106–07.
[244] Rhodes Memo, *supra* note 3.
[245] Rice Testimony at 38.
[246] Testimony of Rexon Y. Ryu, Deputy to the U.S. Ambassador to the U.N., Tr. at 83 (Aug. 25, 2015) (on file with the Committee) [hereinafter Ryu Testimony].
[247] Rice Testimony at 39.
[248] WASH. SPEAKERS BUREAU, https://www.washingtonspeakers.com/speakers/biography.cfm?SpeakerID=6495.
[249] Rhodes Testimony at 111.
[250] Rice Testimony at 40.
[251] *See, e.g.* Ryu Testimony at 73–74.
[252] *U.S. launching apparent terrorist hunt in Libya,* CBS NEWS (Oct. 18, 2012), http://www.cbsnews.com/news/us-launching-apparent-terrorist-hunt-in-libya.

formation from eyewitnesses to the attack. The fact that no individuals from either the Defense Department or White House operators participated in the Saturday prep call therefore limited the information pertaining to Benghazi provided to Rice. Moreover, it does not appear Rice sought out any information about the attacks or worked to ensure that she had a full understanding of the events outside of the talking points she was provided.

In addition, multiple witnesses testified Benghazi was barely mentioned on the prep call. This inattention is consistent with the lack of information pertaining to Benghazi in the briefing materials. Instead, Rhodes commented on the call that the CIA was preparing unclassified talking points pertaining to Benghazi, with the understanding that the talking points would be shared with Rice when they were completed.[253] Rice testified:

> A: I don't recall us talking about the CIA talking points. I recall being reminded that they were forthcoming and that we would be relying on them because they had been prepared for Members of Congress and they were our best distillation of what we knew at the time.
>
> Q: Okay. Who told you that?
>
> A: I'm not certain, but I believe it was Ben. And so we didn't talk about Benghazi, in fact, on the phone call, as I remember. We just said that those were the points.
>
> Q: Let's go into that a little bit more. If I understood you correctly, you said during this prep call for the Sunday talk shows you did not talk about the attacks in Benghazi at all. Is that correct?
>
> A: In any depth. I don't have any recollection of talking about them in any depth.[254]

Rice also testified it was her understanding these talking points would be vetted and cleared by the CIA—in other words, manifesting the subtext the talking points represented an authoritative product.

> A: As I said, to the best of my recollection, it was Mr. Rhodes on the phone.
>
> Q: And to the best of your recollection, what did he—how did he characterize the CIA talking points?
>
> A: As being carefully vetted and cleared, drafted by the CIA, and provided—produced for the purpose of being provided to Members of Congress and, thus, what we would also utilize.
>
> Q: So, as far as you were concerned or as far as you understood, the CIA talking points represented the best information about the attacks in Benghazi at the time.
>
> A: Yes. That's how I—that's what I understood them to be, and that's, in fact, what I knew them to be, because they

---

[253] Rice Testimony at 39–40; Rhodes Testimony at 76–78.
[254] Rice Testimony at 42.

mirrored very precisely the intelligence that I had also received.[255]

No CIA witness the Committee interviewed had any knowledge the HPSCI talking points were going to be shared with Rice to be used on the Sunday talk shows.

As discussed above, Rice, the individual selected by the White House to represent the administration on the Sunday talk shows following the deaths of Ambassador Chris Stevens—the first U.S. Ambassador to be killed in the field since 1979—Sean Smith, Glen Doherty, and Tyrone Woods, was not a central figure in the creation or management of the Benghazi compound, or in the government's response to the attacks. She was unaware at the time the CIA had a presence there and essentially relied on just three bullet points of material—that none of the authors of the bullet points knew would be provided to her—to discuss the Benghazi attacks on the Sunday talk shows.

Rice took umbrage when she was confronted with the suggestion that her role was to simply parrot the talking points provided to her, testifying:

> A: Sir, as I said earlier, I did not have any knowledge of how these talking points were edited.
>
> *   *   *
>
> Q: I understand. So you were just the spokesman. You had been given something, and they told you: Go on out there and do your duty and repeat what you were provided.
>
> A: No sir. I was also a member of the President's Cabinet and the National Security Council. I was a recipient of the most refined intelligence products. And I satisfied myself that what I had been asked to say in the unclassified points were consistent with what I had received in intelligence channels. Otherwise, I wouldn't have said it.[256]

While Rice is mostly correct in noting the unclassified talking points were consistent with what she had received through intelligence channels, there was one major difference, as discussed above. What Rice received through intelligence channels said "The currently available information suggests that the *attacks* in Benghazi were spontaneously inspired by protests at the US Embassy in Cairo and evolved into a direct assault against the U.S. diplomatic post in Benghazi and subsequently its annex."[257] Yet the unclassified talking points said "The currently available information suggests that the *demonstrations* in Benghazi were spontaneously inspired by protests at the U.S. Embassy in Cairo and evolved into a direct assault against the U.S. diplomatic post in Benghazi and subsequently its annex."[258] That change—from "at-

---

[255] Rice Testimony at 45–46.
[256] Rice Testimony at 157.
[257] September 13 WIRe, *supra* note 123 (emphasis added).
[258] *Talking Points Timeline,* ABC NEWS, http://abcnews.go.com/images/Politics/Benghazi%20Talking%20Points%20Timeline.pdf (emphasis added).

tacks" to "demonstrations"—significantly altered the meaning of the entire sentence.

In her interview before the Committee, Rice maintained the claim that the talking points were similar to the analysis. In fact she had reviewed the two documents side by side "very recently."[259] She testified:

Q: And do you know how closely those products mirrored that bullet point?

A: Virtually identical but not verbatim.

Q: Okay. And do you know, if it was not verbatim, what the differences were between what you read——

A: I can't tell you precisely, but if you—I do recall looking at them side-by-side and being comfortable that they were—well, at the time, I didn't look at them side-by-side, but I knew from having seen intelligence as early as that previous morning, Saturday morning, that this was very consistent with our latest information.

Q: And you have since looked at them side-by-side?

A: Yes.

Q: And you're still comfortable that what was in the intelligence is virtually identical to what's in that bullet point?

A: Yes.

Q: And do you recall how recently you looked at them side-by-side?

A: Very recently.

\* \* \*

Q: Sure. My question is you said that you looked at them recently side-by-side, correct?

A: Yes.

Q: And you were comfortable that what was in the finished intelligence is reflected here in this bullet point.

A: Yes.

Q: Okay. And did you recognize any differences between, looking at them side-by-side, what you saw in the intelligence versus what's in the bullet point?

A: Okay. So let me be precise. What's in this bullet point closely mirrored a similar paragraph in the finished intelligence product that I received at the same time. I'm not saying this is the sum total of what I saw.

Q: Sure. And you say it closely resembled or closely mirrored. My question is, what are the differences between what you reviewed and what's in here?

A: I don't recall any substantive differences.

Q: And you looked at this recently?

---

259 Rice Testimony at 50.

A: Yes.[260]

Despite the precision by Rice and the fact she had compared the documents side by side very recently, "attacks" and "demonstrations" are fundamentally different words with fundamentally different meanings. The specific language Rice received through intelligence channels relating to the attacks here was accurate, and what she read from the talking points based on demonstrations was not. The fact she testified she did not recall any substantive differences does not mean no substantive differences existed.

## What Rice Said on the Shows

Despite Rice's limited knowledge about the Benghazi attacks when she appeared on the Sunday talk shows, some of her comments were conclusory, some were based neither in evidence nor fact, and some went well beyond what even the flawed talking points indicated. Two months after she appeared on the talk shows, she stated publicly:

> When discussing the attacks against our facilities in Benghazi, I relied solely and squarely on the information provided to me by the intelligence community. I made clear that the information was preliminary and that our investigations would give us the definitive answers. Everyone, particularly the intelligence community, has worked in good faith to provide the best assessment based on the information available. You know the FBI and the State Department's Accountability Review Board are conducting investigations as we speak, and they will look into all aspects of this heinous terrorist attack to provide what will become the definitive accounting of what occurred.[261]

A close examination of what Rice actually did say on each of the Sunday morning shows, however, along with the Committee's interview with her, demonstrates she in fact went well beyond "solely and squarely" relying on the information provided to her by the intelligence community.[262] In addition, several aspects of her Benghazi remarks—conflating the video with the attack, the status of the FBI investigation, the number of attackers, and the amount of security present at the State Department compound, to name a few—drifted even farther from the information provided to her by the intelligence community. An analysis of some of Rice's comments is below.

### FACE THE NATION

*Face the Nation* was unlike the other four shows in that Libyan President Mohamed el-Magariaf appeared on the show immediately prior to Rice. During his interview with Bob Schieffer, *Face the Nation* host, el-Magariaf, who hailed from Benghazi, attended univer-

---

[260] *Id.* at 49–51.

[261] Krishnadev Calamur, *Susan Rice Says Benghazi Claims Were Based On Information From Intelligence,* NPR (Nov. 21, 2012), http://www.npr.org/sections/thetwo-way/2012/11/21/165686269/susan-rice-says-benghazi-claims-were-based-on-information-from-intelligence.

[262] *Id.* ("When discussing the attacks against our facilities in Benghazi, I relied solely and squarely on the information provided to me by the intelligence community.").

sity there, and had deep ties to the city, said there was "no doubt" the attacks were preplanned. El-Magariaf said of the attack:

Q: Was this a long-planned attack, as far as you know? Or what—what do you know about that?

A: The way these perpetrators acted and moved, I think we—and they're choosing the specific date for this so-called demonstration, I think we have no—this leaves us with no doubt that this was preplanned, determined—predetermined.

Q: And you believe that this was the work of al-Qaeda and you believe that it was led by foreigners. Is that—is that what you are telling us?

A: It was planned—definitely, it was planned by foreigners, by people who—who entered the country a few months ago, and they were planning this criminal act since their—since their arrival.

Schieffer also asked President el-Magariaf about the FBI traveling to Benghazi to investigate the attacks:

Q: Will it be safe for the FBI investigators from the United States to come in, are you advising them to stay away for a while?

A: Maybe it is better for them to stay for a—for a little while? For a little while, but until we—we—we—we do what we—we have to do ourselves. But, again, we'll be in need for—for their presence to help in further investigation. And, I mean any hasty action will—I think is not welcomed.

Rice appeared immediately after President el-Magariaf on the show. She testified to the Committee she heard el-Magariaf say the attacks were preplanned, and even though his comments did not align with the talking points she was given, she was unconcerned. She testified:

Q: My question was, how did you react to that?

A: I was surprised.

Q: And what did you do? Were you concerned that he may have known something that you did not know?

A: I didn't know what he knew. I knew what we knew and what the intelligence community's current best assessment was. And so it was my responsibility to faithfully relay that and not make something up on the fly based on what he said.[263]

When asked about President el-Magariaf's comments by Schieffer, though, Rice actually disagreed with him. She responded:

Q: But you do not agree with him that this was something that had been plotted out several months ago?

---

[263] Rice Testimony at 147.

A: We do not—we do not have information at present that leads us to conclude that this was premeditated or preplanned.

Q: Do you agree or disagree with him that al-Qaeda had some part in this?

A: Well, we'll have to find that out. I mean I think it's clear that there were extremist elements that joined in and escalated the violence. Whether they were al-Qaeda affiliates, whether they were Libyan-based extremists or al-Qaeda itself I think is one of the things we'll have to determine.[264]

Notwithstanding intelligence Rice had seen indicating that al-Qaeda extremists were involved in the attacks [265]—and that the first draft of the HPSCI talking points also noted this fact [266]—the fallout of Rice's disagreement with President el-Magariaf was large. According to Hicks, the top American official in Libya at the time, Rice's comments prevented the FBI from going to Benghazi for a number of weeks. He testified:

Q: Do you think those statements had an effect going forward? What difference did those statements make?

A: I think that they affected cooperation with the Libyans. I mean, I have heard from a friend who had dinner with President Magariaf in New York City that he was still angry at Ambassador Rice well after the incident.

You know, the Libyan Government doesn't have a deep bench. President, Prime Minister, Deputy Prime Minister, Minister. After that, nah, not much there. Some ministries, yeah, you can go—it goes three deep, it goes down three layers. Most ministries it's just the Minister. So if the President of the country isn't behind something, it's going to be pretty hard to make it happen.

And I firmly believe that the reason it took us so long to get the FBI to Benghazi is because of those Sunday talk shows. And, you know, frankly, we never, ever had official approval from the Libyan Government to send the FBI to Benghazi. We stitched together a series of lower-level agreements to support from relevant groups, and we sat around in the meeting and we said, well, guys, this is as good as it gets in Libya. And we looked at the legat [legal attaché] and said, call it in, this is your shot. Call it in to D.C. and see if they're ready—if they're willing to send a team. And that's how—that's how the FBI got to Benghazi.[267]

---

[264] "Face the Nation" transcripts, September 16, 2012: Libyan Pres. Magariaf, Amb. Rice and Sen. McCain, CBS News (Sept. 16, 2012), http://www.cbsnews.com/news/face-the-nation-transcripts-september-16-2012-libyan-pres-magariaf-amb-rice-and-sen-mccain.

[265] September 13 WIRe, supra note 123; Rice Testimony at 42.

[266] Talking Points Timeline, ABC News, http://abcnews.go.com/images/Politics/Benghazi%20Talking%20Points%20Timeline.pdf (last visited May 17, 2016).

[267] Hicks Testimony at 232.

In her interview with Bob Schieffer, Rice also discussed the FBI investigation. She said:

> Q: Madam Ambassador, he says this is something that has been in the planning stages for months. I understand you have been saying that you think it was spontaneous? Are we not on the same page here?
>
> A: Bob, let me tell you what we understand to be the assessment at present. First of all, very importantly, as you discussed with the President, there is an investigation that the United States government will launch led by the FBI, that has begun and——
>
> Q: (overlapping) But they are not there.
>
> A: They are not on the ground yet, but they have already begun looking at all sorts of evidence of—of various sorts already available to them and to us. And they will get on the ground and continue the investigation. So we'll want to see the results of that investigation to draw any definitive conclusions. But based on the best information we have to date, what our assessment is as of the present is in fact what began spontaneously in Benghazi as a reaction to what had transpired some hours earlier in Cairo where, of course, as you know, there was a violent protest outside of our embassy——

In her comments Rice states the FBI has "already begun looking at all sorts of evidence."[268] Yet nobody from the FBI or Justice Department was on the preparation call with her the day before the shows, and she did not know what evidence the FBI had already "begun" reviewing, despite her claim that the FBI was doing so. In addition, she did not rely on the HPSCI talking points here when discussing the FBI investigation, as the talking points indicated only "the investigation is ongoing;"[269] earlier she claimed she had solely relied on those points when talking about Benghazi.[270] The Chairman had the following exchange with her about this topic:

> Q: If you go back when the issue was first broached. "Well, Bob, let me tell you what we understand to be the assessment at present. First of all, very importantly, as you discussed with the president, there is an investigation that the United States government will launch, led by the FBI that has begun." Then your next comment is, "They are not on the ground yet but they have already begun looking at all sorts of evidence." What were they looking at that you knew about?
>
> A: I didn't know specifically what evidence, but I knew that the investigation had begun and that they would do

[268] "Face the Nation" transcripts, September 16, 2012: Libyan Pres. Magariaf, Amb. Rice and Sen. McCain, CBS NEWS (Sept. 16, 2012), http://www.cbsnews.com/news/face-the-nation-transcripts-september-16-2012-libyan-pres-magariaf-amb-rice-and-sen-mccain.
[269] Talking Points Timeline, ABC NEWS, http://abcnews.go.com/images/Politics/Benghazi%20Talking%20Points%20Timeline.pdf (last visited May 17, 2016).
[270] See, e.g., Krishnadev Calamur, Susan Rice Says Benghazi Claims Were Based On Information From Intelligence, NPR (Nov. 21, 2012), http://www.npr.org/sections/thetwo-way/2012/11/21/165686269/susan-rice-says-benghazi-claims-were-based-on-information-from-intelligence.

as they customarily do, try to gather as much evidence as possible.

Q: They do customarily try to do that; you are correct. But your statement was, "They have already begun looking at all sorts of evidence." Who told you that?

A: I don't recall exactly who told me that.

Q: Do you know when you would have been told that?

A: I don't know exactly when but sometime between September 11th and September 16th.

Q: And there was no one from law enforcement on the 4 p.m. call?

A: No, not to my knowledge.

Q: Do you recall talking to anyone with the Bureau [FBI] before you went on the Sunday morning talk shows?

A: No.

Q: Well, this is what I'm trying to reconcile. If you didn't talk to anyone with the FBI, who would have told you that they had all sorts of evidence?

A: I didn't say they had—"they have begun looking at all sorts of evidence." I was aware, as a senior U.S. policymaker, that we had announced there was an FBI investigation already underway and that that investigation would involve gathering and looking at all sorts of evidence.

Q: All right. But you go on to say "already available to them and to us." What evidence was already available to you?

A: To me personally, none.

Q: Then why would you have said "available to them and to us"?

A: I meant to the administration.

Q: Do you know what was available to the administration?

A: Not precisely at this point.

Q: Not at this point or not at the point that you——

A: At the time.

Q: You did not know at the time what evidence was available to the administration.

A: That's correct.

Q: Then why would you say "already available to them and to us"?

A: Because I knew that we had already begun the process of gathering information, both from an intelligence side as well as from the law enforcement side.

Q: All right. I'm with you on the intelligence side, but this—but I can't find an interview that you conducted where you did not use "the FBI." And what I'm trying to understand is what was the source of your information from the FBI.

A: I didn't have any specific information from the FBI. I was aware of and what I was trying to convey is that the FBI was in the process of beginning its investigation.

Q: So if you were to say they already had begun looking at all sorts of evidence of various sorts already available to them and to us, in fact, you were not available—you were not aware of what evidence they had.

A: I knew they were looking at intelligence among other sources of evidence.[271]

Rice used the imprimatur of the FBI as a highly respected law enforcement agency and then conflated the fact they had begun an investigation with her statement the Bureau was "already looking at all sorts of evidence." In reality, Rice had no idea what the FBI was doing and where the investigation stood. The FBI would ultimately secure possession of the surveillance video from cameras on the Benghazi compound over a week later, but that video was not yet available to the Bureau—or the U.S. government—and once it became available, it impeached many aspects of the administration's initial assessment about the attacks.

Other evidence available to the Bureau at the time of Rice's Sunday morning talk show appearances would have included eyewitness accounts from both State Department and CIA witnesses who survived the attacks. The administration either did not avail itself of these eyewitness accounts or completely ignored what these witnesses had to say. These accounts would contradict most of the administration's initial public statements about both the existence of a protest and a link between the attacks in Benghazi and an internet video.

Rice invoked the name of a premiere law enforcement agency, indicated all sorts of evidence was available to them and then proceeded to recite talking points that would later be utterly impeached by the information that was gathered by the Bureau. Currently, the FBI's investigative position is reflected in both the charging instrument in *U.S. v. Ahmed Abu Khattalah* as well as various pre-trial motions. Instead of validating Rice's comments, the FBI's current assessment of what happened in Benghazi is closer to being the opposite of what Rice described on national television.

When discussing the spontaneity of the attack, Rice also used definitive language about what had transpired. Such definitive language was not consistent with the HPSCI talking points. She had the following exchange with the Chairman about that comment:

Q: "Our best current assessment, based on the information that we have at present, is that, in fact, what this began as, it was a spontaneous"—what did you mean by "in fact"?

---

[271] Rice Testimony at 96–98.

A: What I meant was that what we understood to be the case at the time was as I described. It was spontaneous, not premeditated, et cetera.

Q: But why would you use the—why would you use the phrase "in fact"? Ranking Member Schiff took great pains to talk about all the qualifying language that you used. "In fact" strikes me as being more definitive than qualifying language.

A: Given all the qualifiers that I put in here, I was not trying to convey that what I was saying was the last and final word on this.

Q: Okay. What does the word "premeditated" mean to you?

A: It means that whoever was involved had planned in advance to do what they did.

Q: How much planning would need to have taken place for it to qualify as premeditated or preplanned?

A: I don't have a clear answer to that.

Q: Well, you specifically said it was not preplanned and not premeditated. So I'm trying to get an understanding of how short a period of time something would need to be planned to not be preplanned or premeditated. What time period?

A: I don't have a definitive answer to that question. What I was trying to do, sir, is to convey, consistent with the talking points that this was, to the best of our understanding, a spontaneous reaction. And, to me, the antithesis of "spontaneous" is "preplanned or premeditated." I was trying to say the same thing in a slightly different way.[272]

It is unclear why Rice used such definitive language when the talking points she reviewed and relied on did not use similarly strong language.

### THIS WEEK WITH GEORGE STEPHANOPOULOS

It was during her appearance on *This Week* when Rice made the clearest link between the video and the Benghazi attacks. She said:

Q: It just seems that the U.S. government is powerless as this—as this maelstrom erupts.

A: It's actually the opposite. First of all, let's be clear about what transpired here. What happened this week in Cairo, in Benghazi, in many other parts of the region . . .

Q: Tunisia, Khartoum . . .

A: . . .was a result—a direct result of a heinous and offensive video that was widely disseminated, that the U.S. government had nothing to do with, which we have made

---

[272] *Id.* at 101–102.

clear is reprehensible and disgusting. We have also been very clear in saying that there is no excuse for violence, there is—that we have condemned it in the strongest possible terms.

But let's look at what's happened. It's quite the opposite of being impotent. We have worked with the governments in Egypt. President Obama picked up the phone and talked to President Morsi in Egypt. And as soon as he did that, the security provided to our personnel in our embassies dramatically increased.[273]

In her comments, Rice stated "what happened this week in Cairo, in Benghazi, in many other parts of the region . . . was a result—a direct result—of a heinous and video that was widely disseminated."[274] Nowhere in the HPSCI talking points—which Rice said she relied on "solely and squarely"—is there a mention of a direct link to the video. In fact, there is no mention of a link to a video at all, and the Committee is not aware of any mention of a direct link to the video in any intelligence Rice reviewed prior to her appearance on *This Week*. In mentioning a direct link to the video, Rice strayed far beyond her talking points and provided incorrect information.

Rice told the Committee she was not trying to use the talking points here, and may have misspoke. She testified:

Q: Okay. We will go through those transcripts. But to the extent you were linking Benghazi and suggesting that there were protests there, your statement—and tell me if you disagree with this—your statement that what occurred in Benghazi was a result, and then for emphasis you say "a direct result," of the heinous and offensive video." I mean, do you believe that you went a little bit beyond what was in the talking points in making that statement?

A: I wasn't even trying to utilize the talking points here. I was talking about what had happened around the world. That's what I meant to be focused on.

Q: So when you included Benghazi, did you—was that—did you misspeak?

A: Quite possibly.

Q: Because you would agree that, at the time you made this statement on Mr. Tapper's show, the information you had did not—did not state that there was a direct connection between the video and what occurred in Benghazi.

A: That's right. And that's why I was, I think, more precise in the other transcripts.[275]

[273] *'This Week' Transcript: U.S. Ambassador to the United Nations Susan Rice*, ABC News (Sept. 16, 2012), http://abcnews.go.com/Politics/week-transcript-us-ambassador-united-nations-susan-rice/story?id=17240933.
[274] *Id.*
[275] Rice Testimony at 115–16.

Rice later testified that she was "very careful" to link the video to what happened in Cairo. Despite her comments on *This Week,* Rice told the Committee:

> What I can say is that I—we have been through this, but I was very careful to link the video to what happened in Cairo and to other posts around the world. I did not say that the attack on Benghazi was directly caused by the video.[276]

Morell, a career CIA analyst who rose through the ranks to become Deputy Director and Acting Director, disagrees with Rice's analysis of her own comments. Morell said that a "good bit of what she said was consistent with the CIA points, but she also said that the video had led to the protests in Benghazi. Why she said this I do not know. It is a question that only she can answer."[277]

Rice also stated on *This Week* that there was a "substantial" security presence at the United States "consulate" in Benghazi. She said:

> Q: Why was there such a security breakdown? Why was there not better security at the compound in Benghazi? Why were there not U.S. Marines at the embassy in Tripoli?
>
> A: Well, first of all, we had a substantial security presence with our personnel . . .
>
> Q: Not substantial enough, though, right?
>
> A: . . . with our personnel and the consulate in Benghazi. Tragically, two of the four Americans who were killed were there providing security. That was their function. And indeed, there were many other colleagues who were doing the same with them.
>
> It obviously didn't prove sufficient to the—the nature of the attack and sufficient in that—in that moment. And that's why, obviously, we have reinforced our remaining presence in Tripoli and why the president has very—been very clear that in Libya and throughout the region we are going to call on the governments, first of all, to assume their responsibilities to protect our facilities and our personnel, and we're reinforcing our facilities and our—our embassies where possible...

The State Department facility in Benghazi was not a consulate. The talking points provided to Rice about Benghazi did not mention anything about a consulate. In fact, the term "consulate" was specifically edited out of the talking points for accuracy before they were provided to Rice. A consulate is formally notified to the host government—something the Benghazi diplomatic post was not—and provides certain services to citizens.

As a former Assistant Secretary of State, Rice knew there was a difference between a consulate and diplomatic post. She testified

---

[276] *Id.* at 166.
[277] MORELL, *supra* note 114, at 228–29.

to the Committee that she may have misspoke on this point and, with a statement of fact, acknowledged the difference:

> Q: So, following along, top of page 4, you say, "With our personnel and the consulate in Benghazi." Was there a consulate in Benghazi?
>
> A: It was a diplomatic post.
>
> Q: Why did you say "consulate" if there was no consulate in Benghazi?
>
> A: I may have misspoke.
>
> Q: Okay. Is there a difference between a consulate and a diplomatic post?
>
> A: Yes, in fact, there is.[278]

In addition, the mention of a consulate may imply to some a stronger fortification than a diplomatic post, perhaps indicating an additional amount of security. While a "substantial security presence" is the point Rice was attempting to convey—and as the Accountability Review Board made clear—the security presence at the State Department facility in Benghazi was nowhere near substantial.[279]

Morell wrote in his book the "harder statement" for Rice to explain is why she "said that there was a 'substantial security presence' in Benghazi, as that point was not in either CIA or the White House talking points."[280] Rice explained to the Committee about what she meant when she said there was a substantial security presence:

> Q: What did you mean, you said, "We had a substantial security presence with our personnel"?
>
> A: I meant what I just said.
>
> Q: What does a substantial security presence mean to you?
>
> A: It means significant, more than one, more than two, more than three.
>
> Q: Did you have any indication of how many security personnel were actually with the State Department in Benghazi?
>
> A: Did I have any indication?
>
> Q: Did you have any indication at the time you made the comments how many State Department personnel, security personnel, were in Benghazi?
>
> A: I knew we had a Diplomatic Security presence.
>
> Q: Okay.
>
> A: I knew we had contractors.
>
> Q: Okay.

---

[278] Rice Testimony at 106.
[279] Benghazi ARB, *supra* note 20, at 31–33.
[280] MORELL, *supra* note 114, at 229.

A: I knew that two of the people who had been killed were there in a security capacity.

Q: Okay. But in terms of "substantial security presence," to you that means more than one individual?

A: It means—it can—certainly means more than one. But it doesn't mean—I wasn't trying to say it means 10, it means 20, it means 50. It was substantial.

Q: Is "substantial security presence" more than one? Is that—in all situations, does a substantial security presence mean more than one, or are you referring specifically to Benghazi in this case?

A: I was referring to Benghazi.

Q: Okay.

A: But I was also making the point, as you'll see subsequently, that it obviously didn't prove sufficient to the attack.

Q: Okay. So I just want to make sure I'm clear. "Substantial security presence," in your mind, can mean two individuals.

A: I didn't say that.

Q: You said more than one.

A: I said more than one, more than two—we can keep going. I didn't mean to imply.[281]

Rice was mistaken again in stating there were State Department security contractors in Benghazi. The security contractors who died in the Benghazi attacks worked for the CIA—and their job was to protect the CIA facility in Benghazi, not the State Department facility. Rice, whether intentionally or negligently, presented misleading information about the size of the security presence at the State Department facility in Benghazi.

### FOX NEWS SUNDAY

Rice also characterized the level of security in Benghazi on *Fox News Sunday*—something that was not in her talking points. She said:

Q: All right. And the last question, terror cells in Benghazi had carried out five attacks since April, including one at the same consulate, a bombing at the same consulate in June. Should U.S. security have been tighter at that consulate given the history of terror activity in Benghazi?

A: Well, we obviously did have a strong security presence. And, unfortunately, two of the four Americans who died in Benghazi were there to provide security. But it wasn't sufficient in the circumstances to prevent the overrun of the

---

281 Rice Testimony at 103–05.

consulate. This is among the things that will be looked at as the investigation unfolds and it's also why——

Q: Is there any feeling that it should have been stronger beforehand?

A: It's also why we increased our presence, our security presence in Tripoli in the aftermath of this, as well as in other parts of the world. I can't judge that, Chris. I'm—we have to see what the assessment reveals. But, obviously, there was a significant security presence defending our consulate and our other facility in Benghazi and that did not prove sufficient to the moment.[282]

When asked about the use of the word "strong" versus "substantial," as she said on *This Week,* Rice responded:

Q: Okay. Just a couple more questions about your interview with Mr. Wallace. Your next response: "Well, we obviously did have a strong security presence." What did you mean when you said "strong security presence"?

A: I think we had this exchange over another adjective I used.

Q: That was "substantial." I'm asking you about "strong."

A: The same answer applies.

Q: Same answer? Okay. So more than one?

A: That wasn't my prior answer.[283]

In her appearance on *Fox News Sunday&cedil;* Rice noted "two of the four Americans who died in Benghazi were there to provide security. But it wasn't sufficient in the circumstances to prevent the overrun of the consulate."[284] This statement implies the two security officers who died were tasked with protecting the State Department facility. They were not; their job was solely to protect the CIA facility and CIA personnel. In reality the two she referenced—Glen Doherty and Tyrone Woods—were killed because the inadequate security at the State Department facility in Benghazi was not sufficient to repel the initial attack thus necessitating aid from CIA contractors at the Annex in Benghazi and from Tripoli.

In the case of Glen Doherty, not only was he not in Benghazi to provide security for the Benghazi Mission compound, he was not in Benghazi at all—at least initially. He left Tripoli to respond to the attacks in Benghazi precisely because State Department security proved inadequate. And neither Doherty nor Tyrone Woods were killed in the "overrun of the consulate." As noted above, there was

---

[282] *Amb. Susan Rice, Rep. Mike Rogers discuss violence against Americans in the Middle East,* FOX NEWS SUNDAY (Sept. 16, 2012), http://www.foxnews.com/on-air/fox-news-sunday-chris-wallace/2012/09/16/amb-susan-rice-rep-mike-rogers-discuss-violence-against-americans-middle-east#p//v/1843960658001.

[283] Rice Testimony at 125.

[284] *Amb. Susan Rice, Rep. Mike Rogers discuss violence against Americans in the Middle East,* FOX NEWS SUNDAY (Sept. 16, 2012), http://www.foxnews.com/on-air/fox-news-sunday-chris-wallace/2012/09/16/amb-susan-rice-rep-mike-rogers-discuss-violence-against-americans-middle-east#p//v/1843960658001.

no "consulate" in Benghazi and the Benghazi Mission compound was "overrun" hours before Doherty and Woods were killed.

Rice's appearance on *Fox News Sunday* is also where she was imprecise—again—in discussing the FBI investigation. Specifically, she said:

> Q: Let's talk about the attack on the U.S. consulate in Benghazi this week that killed four Americans, including Ambassador Chris Stevens. The top Libyan official says that the attack on Tuesday was, quote, his words "preplanned." Al Qaeda says the operation was revenge for our killing a top Al Qaeda leader. What do we know?
>
> A: Well, first of all, Chris, we are obviously investigating this very closely. The FBI has a lead in this investigation. The information, the best information and the best assessment we have today is that in fact this was not a preplanned, premeditated attack. That what happened initially was that it was a spontaneous reaction to what had just transpired in Cairo as a consequence of the video. People gathered outside the embassy and then it grew very violent and those with extremist ties joined the fray and came with heavy weapons, which unfortunately are quite common in post-revolutionary Libya and that then spun out of control.[285]

Significantly, Rice noted the "FBI has a lead in this investigation."[286] This critical distinction may have incorrectly implied to some the FBI was making significant progress in the nascent investigation. The Chairman had the following exchange with Rice about this topic:

> Q: On one of the occasions, you said—this is to Chris Wallace—"The FBI has a lead in this investigation." How would you have learned that if you had not talked to the FBI?
>
> A: Because I was aware, as a senior policymaker, that the FBI has a lead role in conducting investigations in this circumstance and others like it.
>
> Q: But there's a tremendous difference between the FBI has "the lead" and the FBI has "a lead." "A lead" is a law enforcement term that we have a suspect, we have a lead.
>
> A: No, no, no. Excuse me. That was not what I was trying to say. I was saying they had the lead, as in the leadership role, not a lead on a suspect in the investigation.
>
> Q: All right. So at least with respect to that transcript, you intended the article "the" instead of the article "a" to modify the lead. You were not suggesting that they had a lead but that they were taking the lead in the investigation.
>
> A: That's what I meant.

---

[285] *Id.*
[286] *Id.*

Q: Okay. All right.[287]

In her interview with the Committee, Rice said that in the future, perhaps a "no comment" regarding an FBI investigation would be more appropriate. She had the following exchange with the Chairman:

Q: I guess this is what I am getting at, just from a broader perspective. We all hear, whether it's Attorney General Holder, Attorney General Lynch, really anybody in the criminal justice realm just doesn't comment on ongoing investigations. They don't make comments and use qualifying predicates. They just say: Look, I don't know. And I am not going to answer your question until the investigation is complete. Why not respond that way when you were asked on the Sunday morning talk shows?

A: Sir, I wasn't trying to qualify or characterize the investigation. I was trying to indicate that there was an investigation, that it was going to be thorough, and that it would reveal the best information as to what had transpired.

Q: I am not challenging that. I am just saying instead of saying, "Our best assessment at this time is that it was not premeditated, not preplanned, that it was spontaneous," one out of five references to the video, why not just say, "The investigation has just begun; we don't know; and I am not going to guess"?

A: Because our intelligence community, in response to a request from HPSCI, had provided talking points along the lines that we have discussed multiple times now. And those talking points, which you and your colleagues would have gone out with, were more detailed than simply saying, "I don't know."

Q: Right. But you and I both know in hindsight that the talking points, at least to some degree, were wrong. So I guess the lesson moving forward is maybe we should just say, "It's an ongoing investigation, and I am not going to comment on it."

A: Maybe we should.[288]

Rice also said the following on *Fox News Sunday:*

But we don't see at this point signs this was a coordinated plan, premeditated attack. Obviously, we will wait for the results of the investigation and we don't want to jump to conclusions before then. But I do think it's important for the American people to know our best current assessment.[289]

---

[287] Rice Testimony at 95.
[288] *Id.* at 146–147.
[289] *Amb. Susan Rice, Rep. Mike Rogers discuss violence against Americans in the Middle East,* FOX NEWS SUNDAY (Sept. 16, 2012), http://www.foxnews.com/on-air/fox-news-sunday-chris-

Continued

Rice testified to the Committee about these comments:

> Q: But when you said, "We don't see at this point signs," did you mean to say that there were no signs, or did you mean to say that there was no conclusion that it was a coordinated, premeditated attack?

> A: I didn't purport to draw any final conclusions at any point during these interviews. I was very careful to underscore that I was providing the current best information and that information could change.[290]

Rather than noting that no final conclusions had been drawn by the intelligence community about premeditation, however, Rice instead chose to state there were "no signs" at all of any premeditation.[291] In this regard she not only went beyond the talking points she was provided, but she was also incorrect.

In fact, multiple signs existed at the time she appeared on *Fox News Sunday* that the attack may have been premeditated. **[redacted text]**[292] Another piece of intelligence from September 13 indicated that an attack was imminent—mere minutes away—and known by multiple parties.[293] Rice could have made her point by simply saying "our current assessment is that the attack was neither coordinated nor premeditated." Instead, she chose to go a step further and, inaccurately, state "we don't at this point see signs this was a coordinated plan."[294]

### MEET THE PRESS

Rice's comments on *Meet the Press* are perhaps the most egregious diversion from the talking points provided to her about Benghazi. She said:

> Well, let us—let me tell you the—the best information we have at present. First of all, there's an FBI investigation which is ongoing. And we look to that investigation to give us the definitive word as to what transpired. But putting together the best information that we have available to us today, our current assessment is that what happened in Benghazi was in fact initially a spontaneous reaction to what had just transpired hours before in Cairo, almost a copycat of—of the demonstrations against our facility in Cairo, which were prompted, of course, by the video. What we think then transpired in Benghazi is that opportunistic extremist elements came to the consulate as this was unfolding. They came with heavy weapons which unfortu-

---

wallace/2012/09/16/amb-susan-rice-rep-mike-rogers-discuss-violence-against-americans-middle-east#p//v/1843960658001.

[290] Rice Testimony at 125.

[291] *See Amb. Susan Rice, Rep. Mike Rogers discuss violence against Americans in the Middle East,* FOX NEWS SUNDAY (Sept. 16, 2012), http://www.foxnews.com/on-air/fox-news-sunday-chris-wallace/2012/09/16/amb-susan-rice-rep-mike-rogers-discuss-violence-against-americans-middle-east#p//v/1843960658001.

[292] **[Redacted text]**.

[293] **[Redacted text]**.

[294] *Amb. Susan Rice, Rep. Mike Rogers discuss violence against Americans in the Middle East,* FOX NEWS SUNDAY (Sept. 16, 2012), http://www.foxnews.com/on-air/fox-news-sunday-chris-wallace/2012/09/16/amb-susan-rice-rep-mike-rogers-discuss-violence-against-americans-middle-east#p//v/1843960658001.

nately are readily available in post-revolutionary Libya. And it escalated into a much more violent episode. Obviously, that's—that's our best judgment now. We'll await the results of the investigation. And the president has been very clear—we'll work with the Libyan authorities to bring those responsible to justice.[295]

At the time of her appearance, Rice should have known what transpired in Benghazi was not a "copycat" of what had transpired in Cairo. On September 11, the day of the Cairo demonstrations and Benghazi attacks, she received frequent email updates about both events.[296] Additionally, Rice received daily intelligence briefings from the CIA, and she received a briefing each day from September 12 to September 15. Out of scores and scores of intelligence products pertaining to Benghazi provided to the Committee, not a single one said what transpired in Benghazi was "almost a copycat of" what transpired in Cairo.[297]

Rice acknowledges that nowhere in the talking points was information indicating the Benghazi attack was a copycat of the Cairo protest. She testified:

> Q: Now, you would agree with me that nowhere in the CIA talking points does it describe what occurred in Benghazi and what occurred in Cairo as almost a copycat of each other? You would agree with me on that?
>
> A: I would agree with you on that.
>
> Q: So would you also agree with me that describing what occurred in Benghazi as almost a copycat of Cairo was really overstating what was known at the time and certainly overstating what was in the talking points?
>
> A: I don't know that it was overstating or even misstating. But I would agree that the word "copycat" does not appear in the talking points.[298]

In a later portion of her *Meet the Press* appearance, Rice connected the video with the Benghazi attacks, as she had with other appearances on the talk shows. She said:

> Q: The president and the secretary of state have talked about a mob mentality. That's my words, not their words, but they talked about the—the tyranny of mobs operating

[295] *Meet the Press September 16: Benjamin Netanyahu, Susan Rice, Keith Ellison, Peter King, Bob Woodward, Jeffrey Goldberg, Andrea Mitchell,* NBC News (Sept. 16, 2012), http://www.nbcnews.com/id/49051097/ns/meet_the_press-transcripts/t/september-benjamin-netanyahu-susan-rice-keith-ellison-peter-king-bob-woodward-jeffrey-goldberg-andrea-mitchell/#.Vzozl_krJaQ.

[296] *See, e.g.,* Email from U.S. Dep't of State, to Susan E. Rice, U.S. Ambassador to the U.N., *et al.* (Sept. 11, 2012, 7:55 PM) (on file with the Committee, C05390691); Email from Senior Advisor to the U.S. Permanent Representative to the U.N., U.S. Mission to the U.N., to Susan E. Rice, U.S. Ambassador to the U.N., *et al.* (Sept. 11, 2012, 6:41 PM) (on file with the Committee, C05561948); *and* Email from Senior Advisor to the U.S. Permanent Representative to the U.N., U.S. Mission to the U.N., to Susan E. Rice, U.S. Ambassador to the U.N., *et al.* (Sept. 11, 2012, 11:53 PM) (on file with the Committee, SCB0051721).

[297] *Meet the Press September 16: Benjamin Netanyahu, Susan Rice, Keith Ellison, Peter King, Bob Woodward, Jeffrey Goldberg, Andrea Mitchell,* NBC News (Sept. 16, 2012), http://www.nbcnews.com/id/49051097/ns/meet_the_press-transcripts/t/september-benjamin-netanyahu-susan-rice-keith-ellison-peter-king-bob-woodward-jeffrey-goldberg-andrea-mitchell/#.Vzozl_krJaQ.

[298] Rice Testimony at 129–130.

in this part of the world. Here's the reality, if you look at foreign aid—U.S. direct foreign aid to the two countries involved here, in Libya and Egypt, this is what you'd see: two hundred million since 2011 to Libya, over a billion a year to Egypt and yet Americans are seeing these kinds of protests and attacks on our own diplomats. Would—what do you say to members of congress who are now weighing whether to suspend our aid to these countries if this is the response that America gets?

A: Well, first of all, David, let's put this in perspective. As I said, this is a response to a—a very offensive video. It's not the first time that American facilities have come under attack in the Middle East, going back to 1982 in—in Beirut, going back to the Khobar Towers in—in Saudi Arabia, or even the attack on our embassy in 2008 in Yemen.

Q: Or Iran in 1979.

A: This has—this has happened in the past, but there—and so I don't think that—that we should misunderstand what this is. The reason we provide aid in Egypt and in Libya is because it serves American interests because the relationships . . .[299]

In this part of the conversation, David Gregory, *Meet the Press* moderator, and Rice are discussing foreign aid to both Egypt and Libya. Gregory mentions both countries twice in the lead-in to his question. Rice responds and says to "put this in perspective . . . this is a response to a—a very offensive video. It's not the first time American facilities have come under attack in the Middle East . . ."[300] She does not distinguish what happened in Libya to what happened in Egypt in her response, and ties the video to both incidents. After a brief interjection by Gregory, Rice mentions providing aid to both Libya and Egypt.[301] Nowhere in Rice's comments is Libya distinguished from Egypt, indicating she did not intend for her comment about the video to apply to just Egypt, but rather both countries.

### STATE OF THE UNION

On *State of the Union*, Rice spoke of the number of attackers at the Benghazi Mission compound. Nowhere in the talking points—on which she said she solely and squarely relied—is there any mention of the number of protesters. Rice said:

Q: But this was sort of a reset, was it not? It was supposed to be a reset of U.S.-Muslim relations?

A: And indeed, in fact, there had been substantial improvements. I have been to Libya and walked the streets of Benghazi myself. And despite what we saw in that hor-

---

[299] *Meet the Press September 16: Benjamin Netanyahu, Susan Rice, Keith Ellison, Peter King, Bob Woodward, Jeffrey Goldberg, Andrea Mitchell*, NBC NEWS (Sept. 16, 2012), http://www.nbcnews.com/id/49051097/ns/meet_the_press-transcripts/t/september-benjamin-netanyahu-susan-rice-keith-ellison-peter-king-bob-woodward-jeffrey-goldberg-andrea-mitchell/#.Vzozl_krJaQ.

[300] *Id.*

[301] *See Id.*

rific incident where some mob was hijacked ultimately by a handful of extremists, the United States is extremely popular in Libya and the outpouring of sympathy and support for Ambassador Stevens and his colleagues from the government, from people is evidence of that . . .[302]

In her interview with the Committee, Rice acknowledged this information was not in the talking points and was unsure where she got the information about the number of attackers. She testified:

Q: Now, you respond, "And indeed, in fact, there had been substantial improvements. I have been to Libya and walked the streets of Benghazi myself. And despite what we saw in that horrific incident where some mob was hijacked ultimately by a handful of extremists, the United States is extremely popular in Libya and the outpouring of sympathy and support for Ambassador Stevens and his colleagues from the government, from people is evidence of that."

Where did you get the fact that there was a handful of extremists that had hijacked what occurred in Benghazi? I mean, our understanding, even at the time, the information was that there were 20 attackers. That went—that number went to 50-plus, and then it went to over 100. Where did you get the number "a handful," which, in my mind anyway, is about five?

A: I don't recall exactly where I got that from.

Q: It's not in the talking points, certainly.

A: Talking points say that "the demonstrations in Benghazi were spontaneously inspired by the protests at the U.S. Embassy in Cairo and evolved into a direct assault against the diplomatic post in Benghazi and subsequently its annex. There are indications that extremists participated in the violent demonstrations."

Q: That's correct. But nowhere in what you just read does the CIA or the intelligence community attribute a number to the number of extremists that took place in—took part in the attacks, correct?

A: Not in these talking points.

Q: Okay. Do you believe that you received that information from another source?

A: I don't recall.

Q: But you do believe somebody told you that?

A: I don't recall exactly how I acquired that information.[303]

Conveying a "handful" of individuals hijacked a mob had significant implications. By claiming only a handful of individuals, rather

---

[302] *State of the Union with Candy Crowley Interview with Susan Rice*, CNN (Sept. 16, 2012), http://transcripts.cnn.com/TRANSCRIPTS/1209/16/sotu.01.html.

[303] Rice Testimony at 121–22.

than a larger amount, were involved in the attack, Rice may have conveyed to the audience a sense that only a very small number of people were angry enough to attack the U.S. facility. Had Rice said more than a "handful" of people attacked the compound—which video evidence shows to be the case—she may have conveyed more widespread problems in Libya, potentially raising the very policy questions Rhodes strove so specifically to avoid in his September 14 briefing memo.[304]

While Rice was on message in the following clause of the sentence—"the United States is extremely popular in Libya," indicating a successful Libya policy—unfortunately, the United States evacuated its embassy in Tripoli in July 2014 and today does not have an official diplomatic presence in Libya.

## REACTIONS TO THE SUNDAY SHOWS

The reaction to Rice's comments on the Sunday talk shows was as divided as it was quick. Many felt Rice presented information not based in fact, while others believed she simply stuck assiduously to the talking points she had been given.

### "Off The Reservation on Five Networks!"

Even though the Secretary did not appear on the Sunday talk shows, she monitored what Rice said on those shows. As the transcript for each show became available late Sunday morning into early Sunday afternoon, Sullivan sent a copy of the transcript to the Secretary with an accompanying note. The first transcript he sent her was from *This Week*. Sullivan wrote:

> Here is Susan on this week. She wasn't asked about whether we had any intel. But she did make clear our view that this started spontaneously and then evolved. The only troubling sentence relates to the investigation, specifically: "And we'll see when the investigation unfolds whether what was—what transpired in Benghazi might have unfolded differently in different circumstances." But she got pushed there.
>
> Waiting on other transcripts.[305]

This note from Sullivan is interesting for two reasons. First, he writes that Rice makes clear their "view that this started spontaneously and then evolved."[306] Second, Sullivan expresses concern regarding Rice's comment on the investigation, where she said "[a]nd we'll see when the investigation unfolds whether what was—what transpired in Benghazi might have unfolded differently in different circumstances."[307]

The fact that Benghazi may have transpired differently—and not spontaneously as a result of Cairo, as intelligence indicated to be the case—contained serious policy implications. If Benghazi started

---

[304] *See* Rhodes Memo, *supra* note 3 ("[T]hese protests are rooted in an Internet video, and not a broader failure of policy.").

[305] Email from Jacob J. Sullivan, Deputy Chief of Staff and Dir. of Policy Planning, U.S. Dep't of State, to Hillary R. Clinton, Sec'y of State, U.S. Dep't of State (Sept. 16, 2012, 12:22 PM) (on file with the Committee, SCB0045373).

[306] *Id.*

[307] *Id.*

spontaneously and then evolved—as Sullivan seemed to indicate he and the Secretary believed—that would indicate a similarity with other areas in the Middle East, where protests had transpired as a result of the offensive video. If, on the other hand, Benghazi transpired differently—as a premeditated terrorist attack, for instance—such a scenario would call into question whether the United States was defeating terrorism, and would raise doubts about the government's policy towards Libya specifically, and perhaps the Middle East generally. The fact Rice raised this as a possibility appeared to be unsettling to Sullivan.

Sullivan later passed on the transcript to *State of the Union* with an accompanying note saying "Nothing to this one."[308] Sullivan also forwarded the transcript for *Meet the Press,* with an accompanying note simply saying "[g]ood."[309] Just three minutes later, the Secretary responded and said "[p]ls remind Panetta NOT to mention Tunisia—in fact no specifics preferable."[310] This may have been in response to the *Meet the Press* transcript, where moderator Gregory mentioned the evacuation of all but emergency personnel from diplomatic missions in Tunisia and Sudan, and that the Secretary of Defense has deployed forces to several areas to protect U.S. personnel.

Almost immediately after Rice's appearance on the shows, Pelton highlighted conflicting statements between Rice and Libya President el-Magariaf. At 9:41a.m. on Sunday, September 16, 2012 she wrote to Rhodes and others on the White House communications team:

> They open w Libyan President who says no doubt attack preplanned/predetermined. Says planned by foreigners. Says maybe better for FBI to stay away a little while though they need their help w investigation. She said in all other shows that no evidence this was premeditated, as we discussed. Just fyi.[311]

Pelton testified as to why she sent this email:

Q: Do you recall having drafted this email?

A: Yes.

Q: And what was the—why did you write this email?

A: I wrote this email to alert Ben that what the Libyan President had said on CBS was inconsistent with what Ambassador Rice had said on the other shows that we had already taped.

Q: Did that inconsistency concern you?

---

[308] Email from Jacob J. Sullivan, Deputy Chief of Staff and Dir. of Policy Planning, U.S. Dep't of State, to Hillary R. Clinton, Sec'y of State, U.S. Dep't of State (Sept. 16, 2012, 2:38 PM) (on file with the Committee, SCB0045387).

[309] Email from Jacob J. Sullivan, Deputy Chief of Staff and Dir. of Policy Planning, U.S. Dep't of State, to Hillary R. Clinton, Sec'y of State, U.S. Dep't of State (Sept. 16, 2012, 2:36 PM) (on file with the Committee, SCB0045390).

[310] Email from Sec'y Clinton to Mr. Sullivan (Sept. 16, 2012, 2:39 PM) (on file with the Committee, SCB0045390).

[311] Email from Erin Pelton, Dir. of Commc'cs and Spokesperson, U.S. Mission to the U.N., to Dagoberto Vega, Special Ass't to the President and Dir. of Broadcast Media, White House, and Benjamin J. Rhodes, Deputy Nat'l Sec. Advisor for Strategic Commc'cs, Nat'l Sec. Council (Sept. 16, 2012, 9:41 AM) (on file with the Committee, C05622905).

A: No.

Q: Why not?

A: Because what Ambassador Rice said reflected the best information that we had at the time.[312]

This email reflects the shortcomings of Rice's preparation for the Sunday shows, which was reflected in some of her comments. As described above, on her Saturday prep call were people from her office and the White House messaging team. No subject matter experts about Benghazi were on the call nor was anybody from the intelligence community. Pelton wrote "no evidence this was premeditated, as we discussed"[313]—likely indicating a discussion of this topic on the phone call the day before. This is a significant difference from simply saying "the current assessment does not indicate that this was premeditated." In fact, as noted above, **[redacted text]** intelligence existed at that point indicating the attack may have in fact been premeditated.[314]

Rice's comments on the Sunday talk shows were met with shock and disbelief by those closest to the facts of the situation. Subject matter experts with direct knowledge of the attacks expressed immediate concern about what Rice had said on the shows—and potential fallout as a result. Hicks—possibly the last person to talk with Stevens, and the highest ranking U.S. official in Libya on Sunday September 16, 2012—said he was not asked for any information in advance of Rice's appearance on the show. He testified:

Q: You became the charge on——

A: September 12th, 3 a.m.

Q: And you are the senior U.S. official, senior diplomat in country starting September 12th. And you've testified you had constant contact with Washington. So, are you—as I understand what you are saying, before the Sunday show—series of appearances on the Sunday shows, you were not part of the preparation and planning?

A: That's correct. I was not.

Q: You didn't get a chance to review talking points?

A: No, I did not.[315]

Hicks also testified about Rice's appearance on *Face the Nation:*

So Magariaf, at great personal risk to himself, goes to Benghazi to initiate an investigation and lend his own personal gravitas. Remember he's from the Benghazi area himself. So he goes to lend his own personal gravitas and reputation to an investigation of what happens. And he gets on—and he is on these programs speaking from Benghazi, and he says this was an attack by Islamic extremists, possibly with terrorist links. He describes what

312 Pelton Testimony at 114–15.

313 Email from Ms. Pelton to Mr. Vega and Mr. Rhodes (Sept. 16, 2012, 9:41 AM) (on file with the Committee, C05622905).

314 **[Redacted text]**.

315 Hicks Testimony at 281.

happens. He tells the truth of what happened. And so, you know, Ambassador Rice says what she says, contradicting what the President of Libya says from Benghazi.

There's a cardinal rule of diplomacy that we learn in our orientation class, and that rule is never inadvertently insult your interlocutor. The net impact of what has transpired is the spokesperson of the most powerful country in the world has basically said that the President of Libya is either a liar or doesn't know what he's talking about.

The impact of that is immeasurable. Magariaf has just lost face in front of not only his own people, but the world. And, you know, my jaw hit the floor as I watched this. I've never been—I have been a professional diplomat for 22 years. I have never been as embarrassed in my life, in my career as on that day. There have been other times when I've been embarrassed, but that's the most embarrassing moment of my career.[316]

Other subject matter experts within the State Department also recognized problems with what Rice said on the talk shows. State Department employees in Washington D.C. who had spoken with those on the ground in Libya after the attack were universal in their condemnation of Rice's statements. The Senior Libya Desk Officer, Bureau of Near Eastern Affairs, State Department, wrote: "I think Rice was off the reservation on this one."[317]

The Deputy Director, Office of Press and Public Diplomacy, Bureau of Near Eastern Affairs, State Department, responded: "Off the reservation on five networks!"[318]

The Senior Advisor for Strategic Communications, Bureau of Near East Affairs, State Department, wrote: "Yup. Luckily there's enough in her language to fudge exactly what she said/meant."[319]

He also wrote: "WH [White House] very worried about the politics. This was all their doing."[320]

While Snipe may not have known exactly what "worried" the White House, he had extensive experience at the State Department, and had been in contact with the Embassy in Tripoli. Contrary to what Rice said on the talk shows, he did not believe any protests or demonstrations had occurred prior to the attacks. He testified:

Q: And then you made a statement that, you know, based on your training and experience, essentially you had never seen anyone bring an RPG to a protest.

A: I mean——

[316] *Id.* at 83–84.
[317] Email from Senior Libya Desk Officer, Bureau of Near Eastern Affairs, U.S. Dep't of State, to Senior Advisor and Spokesperson, Bureau of Near Eastern Affairs, U.S. Dep't of State, Deputy Dir. for the Office of Press and Public Diplomacy, Bureau of Near Eastern Affairs, U.S. Dep't of State & Deputy Dir. for Maghreb Affairs, U.S. Dep't of State (Sept. 17, 2012, 2:16 PM) (on file with the Committee, C05580618).
[318] Email from **[redacted text]** to **[redacted text]**, **[redacted text]** & **[redacted text]** (Sept. 17, 2012, 2:18 PM) (on file with the Committee, C05580618).
[319] Email from **[redacted text]** to **[redacted text]**, **[redacted text]** & **[redacted text]** (Sept. 17, 2012, 2:17 PM) (on file with the Committee, C05580618).
[320] Email from **[redacted text]** to **[redacted text]**, **[redacted text]** & **[redacted text]** (Sept. 17, 2012, 2:19 PM) (on file with the Committee, C05580618).

Q: Or that would be unusual.

A: I think what I said was "bringing an RPG to a spontaneous protest." I mean, I've been to Yemen before, and, I
mean, knives, AK–47s, RPGs. I mean, that place is armed
to the teeth, and I think people bring an RPG to the toilet
sometimes. But when I said that, I was suggesting that, if
you were spontaneously protesting, an RPG might necessarily not be the first thing you grab next to your car
keys.[321]

The Deputy Director, Office of Maghreb Affairs, State Department, was surprised of the connection made to the video. She testified:

Q: Do you recall having any discussions with NEA about
the substance of what was said on the talk shows and
whether there was an agreement or disagreement with
what was conveyed?

A: Yes, ma'am. I recall that I was a little bit surprised.
The description of what was said—and, again, I didn't
watch the program myself—it just sounded more definitive
of what potentially had happened. But, again, I didn't
watch the show myself, and I didn't read the full transcript. I was too busy that day to do that.

Q: When you say you're a bit surprised, what were you
surprised regarding?

A: I was surprised in the way that they were described in
the press clips, that there was an indication that there was
some connection to the anti-Muslim video of concern that
had been circulating online, that there was some connection to that. In the press clips that I read, I remember seeing, like—okay.

Q: And I think, before, you just said that that was a pretty definitive statement.

A: In the way that I saw it excerpted in the press clips,
it seemed like the connection had been made to the video
more definitively.[322]

Diplomatic Security Agent 30, Diplomatic Security Command
Center, State Department, was in the Diplomatic Security Command Center while the attacks transpired and aware of real-time
information coming straight from Benghazi during the attack was
asked if there was any rioting in Benghazi reported prior to the attack. His response was: "Zip, nothing nada." [323]

---

[321] Testimony of Deputy Dir. for the Office of Press and Public Diplomacy, Bureau of Near
Eastern Affairs, U.S. Dep't of State, Tr. at 96–97 (Oct. 9, 2015) (on file with the Committee).
[322] Testimony of Deputy Dir. for Maghreb Affairs, U.S. Dep't of State, Tr. 33–34 (Dec. 17,
2015) (on file with the Committee).
[323] Email from Diplomatic Sec. Agent 30 (Sept. 18, 2012, 1:16 PM) (on file with the Committee, C05390678).

## Circling the Wagons

While many lower- and mid-level State Department employees in contact with the Embassy in Tripoli believed Rice went too far on the talk shows, senior officials at the State Department and White House did not appear to share that sentiment. Instead, these senior officials appeared concerned more about supporting Rice's statements and ensuring any future statements on the attacks were disciplined than ensuring they were reflective of what had actually transpired.

The day after Rice's appearance, The Deputy Director, Office of Maghreb Affairs, sent an email summarizing a meeting with McDonough. She wrote:

> DNSA McDonough apparently told the SVTS [Secure Video Teleconference] group today that everyone was required to "shut their pieholes" about the Benghazi attack in light of the FBI investigation, due to start tomorrow."[324]

McDonough's comments about the FBI investigation starting the following day stand in stark contrast with Rice's statements the day before that the FBI had already begun collecting "all sorts of evidence" in their investigation and had "a lead." In addition, McDonough's remark about not commenting in light of the FBI investigation directly address the issue that Sullivan raised with the Secretary the day before—the troubling sentence by Rice that the FBI investigation could uncover "Benghazi might have unfolded differently in different circumstances" from other protests across the Middle East.[325]

That same day, during her daily press briefing, Nuland was asked by reporters to comment on the Benghazi attacks even though there was an FBI investigation. Nuland attempted to address the dichotomy between her refusal to talk about Benghazi and Rice's willingness to do so on the Sunday shows. Nuland said:

> Q: Toria, in Friday's briefing, Friday evening, you essentially stated that all questions concerning any aspect of the Benghazi attack—the circumstances surrounding it, the outcome of it, et cetera—would henceforth be directed by you to the FBI since it's their investigation.
>
> And yet, on five Sunday shows yesterday, Ambassador Rice, who works for the same agency as you, was giving the latest U.S. assessment of how this event unfolded, specifically by saying we don't believe it was premeditated or preplanned, and by saying that those with heavy arms and so forth showed up, in essence, as she put it, to hijack an ongoing demonstration.
>
> So my first question for you is: Given that Ambassador Rice is out there talking publicly about it and not referring

---

[324] Email from Deputy Dir. for Maghreb Affairs, U.S. Dep't of State, to James N. Miller, Under Sec'y of Defense for Policy, U.S. Dep't of Defense (Sept. 17, 2012, 6:52 PM) (on file with the Committee, C05580200).

[325] Email from Mr. Sullivan to Sec'y Clinton (Sept. 16, 2012, 12:22 PM) (on file with the Committee, SCB0045373).

Bob Schieffer and Chris Wallace and the rest to the FBI, may we consider that we can again begin asking you questions at this podium about the circumstances of the attack? If it's fair for the Ambassador to discuss it, it should be fair in this room, correct?

A: Well, let me start by reminding you that Ambassador Rice outranks me, as does my own boss, so she is often at liberty to say more than I am. And I guess that's going to continue to be the case.

What I will say, though, is that Ambassador Rice, in her comments on every network over the weekend, was very clear, very precise, about what our initial assessment of what happened is. And this was not just her assessment. It was also an assessment that you've heard in comments coming from the intelligence community, in comments coming from the White House. I don't have anything to give you beyond that.

She also made clear, as I had on Friday, that there is an ongoing FBI investigation. So frankly, I'm not sure that it's useful to go beyond that. I'm not capable of going beyond that, and we'll have to just see what the FBI investigation brings us.

Q: You would acknowledge, however, that the account of the events, the preliminary account of the events that Ambassador Rice offered, diverges starkly from the account offered by the Libyan President, correct?

A: Well, we've heard a number of different things from Libya. I would simply say that what—the comments that Ambassador Rice made accurately reflect our government's initial assessment.[326]

Nuland also addressed a question as to whether or not protests had occurred outside the Benghazi compound. Her on-the-record response, in the wake of Rice's talk show appearances, was markedly different from what she told reporters in an off-the-record briefing back on September 12. Nuland said:

Q: And one last question, if I might, because Ambassador Rice spoke to this. She suggested that there had been an ongoing demonstration outside the Consulate or in the proximity of the Consulate in Benghazi that was, in essence, hijacked by more militant elements who came armed to the affair. I just want to nail this down with you. You are—you stand by this notion that there was, in fact, an ongoing demonstration?

A: I'd simply say that I don't have any information beyond what Ambassador Rice shared with you and that her as-

[326] Daily Press Briefing by Spokesperson Victoria Nuland, Bureau of Public Affairs, U.S. Dep't of State (Sept. 17, 2012), http://www.state.gov/r/pa/prs/dpb/2012/09/197821.htm [hereinafter Nuland Sept. 17 Briefing].

sessment does reflect our initial assessment as a government.[327]

Nuland, similar to the President in his *60 Minutes* interview five days prior, also refused to directly label what had occurred as a terrorist act. She said:

> Q: Simply on the basis of what Ambassador Rice has publicly disclosed, does the United States Government regard what happened in Benghazi as an act of terror?
>
> A: Again, I'm not going to put labels on this until we have a complete investigation, okay?
>
> Q: You don't—so you don't regard it as an act of terrorism?
>
> A: I don't think we know enough. I don't think we know enough. And we're going to continue to assess. She gave our preliminary assessment. We're going to have a full investigation now, and then we'll be in a better position to put labels on things, okay? [328]

Even the CIA appeared to take part in the effort to bolster Rice's statements. Five days after the attack, a September 17, 2012 email exchange between officials at the White House, State Department, Office of the Director of National Intelligence [ODNI], and the CIA took place to craft a written response to questions posed by Fox News reporter Catherine Herridge about Rice's statements the day before. The first draft of the response, which appears to have come from the CIA's Office of Public Affairs, makes a number of misstatements—chiefly one in the first paragraph:

> Off the record, I reviewed the timeline of what is known now, of course realizing that there will be interviews of witnesses, people on the ground etc. . . . to get the down to the minute details. Like you, we have the attack kicking off reportedly after 9:30 PM with small crowds gathering during that 9:00–10:00 PM hour. It's pretty clear, as we discussed, that there had been smaller protests during the day, nothing along the scale of what we saw in Cairo or later on in the week, but protests nonetheless.[329]

It is unclear what information, if any, the CIA public affairs officer relied on to claim "it's pretty clear . . . that there had been smaller protests during the day"[330]—no CIA intelligence product provided to the Committee contained any such information.

Seven days after the attacks, on September 18, 2012, Meehan sent an email to Patrick Ventrell, Director, Office of Press Relations, State Department and Nuland about message discipline. Her email said:

> Focus today on reiterating that our initial assessment stands, and was based on information available. Keeping

---

[327] *Id.*

[328] *Id.*

[329] Email from Media Spokesperson, Cent. Intel. Agency, to Tommy Vietor, Nat'l Sec. Spokesperson, Nat'l Sec. Council (Sept. 17, 2012, 4:01 PM) (on file with the Committee, C05562137).

[330] *Id.*

hard line about now waiting for the investigation to run its course; we will of course provide info as it comes to light. No discrepancy between what Rice said and what State and WH said early on regarding preplanned attack.[331]

Nuland appears to have followed that guidance. In her daily press briefing later that day, Nuland said:

> Q: Any more information on the investigation, on the timeline? There continues to be some question about whether the protests had all but dissipated before the attack in Benghazi began, or whether or not the protest was robust and ongoing and this attack at least used it for cover. And there also continue to be, frankly, some apparent differences between the characterization here that it was a coordinated attack and Ambassador Rice's assertion that it basically kind of grew out of the protest.

> A: Well, on your last point, I spoke to this extensively yesterday, making clear that Ambassador Rice was speaking on behalf of the government with regard to our initial assessments. I don't have any more details beyond those that we've already shared, and I don't expect to because I think all of the information is going to go to the FBI for their investigation, and when they're completed, then we'll have more information.

> Q: The idea that it grew—that the protest may have been used as cover, can you say whether or not the protest had basically dissipated when the attacks began?

> A: I personally have no more information than what I've given you, and I don't think that we as a government will be talking about these details until the FBI has completed its investigation so that we don't prejudice it.[332]

Carney also held a press briefing on September 18. During that briefing, he was asked about the conflict between Libyan officials and the administration as to what transpired in Benghazi—a conflict on full display on *Face the Nation* when Rice contradicted the Libyan President. Carney, like Rice on the talk shows, also connected the protests and violence across the region with the Benghazi attacks, linking the video to both events. He said:

> Q: I wanted to go back to the conflict between—the conflicting reports I guess between the administration and Libyan officials over what happened. On Friday, you seemed to cite that the videos were definitely part of it, but I get the sense that you're backing away from that a little bit today. Is there something that you've learned since?

---

[331] Email from Bernadette M. Meehan, Spokesperson, Nat'l Sec. Council, to Victoria J. Nuland, Spokesperson, U.S. Dep't of State & Patrick H. Ventrell, Spokesperson, U.S. Dep't of State (Sept. 18, 2012, 11:03 AM) (on file with the Committee, C05561843).

[332] Daily Press Briefing by Spokesperson Victoria Nuland, Bureau of Public Affairs, U.S. Dep't of State (Sept. 18, 2012), http://www.state.gov/r/pa/prs/dpb/2012/09/197912.htm#LIBYA.

A: No, no. I think what I am making clear and what Ambassador Rice made clear on Sunday is that reaction to the video was the precipitating factor in protests in violence across the region. And what I'm also saying is that we have—we made that assessment based on the evidence that we have, and that includes all the evidence that we have at this time.

I am not, unlike some others, going to prejudge the outcome of an investigation and categorically assert one way or the other what the motivations are or what happened exactly until that investigation is complete. And there are a lot of suppositions based on the number of weapons and other things about what really happened in Benghazi and I'd rather wait, and the President would rather wait, for that investigation to be completed.

Q: So you're not ruling out that——

A: Of course not. I'm not ruling out—if more information comes to light, that will obviously be a part of the investigation and we'll make it available when appropriate. But at this time, as Ambassador Rice said and as I said, our understanding and our belief based on the information we have is it was the video that caused the unrest in Cairo, and the video and the unrest in Cairo that helped—that precipitated some of the unrest in Benghazi and elsewhere. What other factors were involved is a matter of investigation.[333]

Eight days after the attacks, on September 19, 2012, the Special Assistant to the Spokesperson, State Department, sent Nuland an email, possibly in response to a press inquiry, regarding Rice's statements regarding security personnel on the Sunday shows. He wrote:

> This is the only piece I can find that could possibly be construed as the two security officials being there w/responsibility to protect the mission compound vice the annex. From the FOX News Sunday interview . . .[334]

Also on September 19, 2012, Sullivan drafted an "ALDAC"—a worldwide cable to all U.S. embassies—approved by the Secretary in which guidance was given on "outreach and messaging" about the widespread violence in the Middle East.[335] The cable continued to connect the attacks with the video:

> Since September 11, 2012, there have been widespread protests and violence against U.S. and some other diplomatic posts across the Muslim world. The proximate cause of the violence was the release by individuals in the United States of the video trailer for a film that many

[333] Press Briefing by Press Secretary Jay Carney, The White House (Sept. 18, 2012), https://www.whitehouse.gov/the-press-office/2012/09/18/press-briefing-press-secretary-jay-carney-9182012.

[334] Email from Special Ass't to the Spokesperson, U.S. Dep't of State, to Victoria J. Nuland, Spokesperson, U.S. Dep't of State (Sept. 19, 2012, 5:20 PM) (on file with the Committee, SCB0052773).

[335] Email from Special Ass't to the Deputy Chief of Staff and Dir. of Policy Planning, U.S. Dep't of State, to SWO-Cables (Sept. 19, 2012, 7:13 PM) (on file with the Committee, SCB0052812–SCB0052813).

Muslims find offensive. Diplomatic compounds have been breached in several countries including Libya, Egypt, Tunisia, and Yemen. In Benghazi, Libya four

U.S. personnel were killed in the violence[.] [336]

Even as late as September 20, 2012, Nuland was still supporting the claims made by Rice on the talk shows. When reporter Jennifer Rubin asked Nuland to comment on a CBS news report that "there was NO protest outside Libya embassy," Nuland responded, "Off: this does not square with our info." [337]

In the week following her appearances on the Sunday talk shows, Rice remained publicly silent about her comments. Privately, however, she was "constantly interested" in new information about the attacks. She testified:

> Q: Did you have any conversations with anybody, either on the night of September 16th or at any day thereafter up to the point where you learned there were no protests in Benghazi, on the issue of whether or not President Magarief was correct or whether or not you were correct in saying that the attack was spontaneous?

> A: I don't recall specific conversations, but I recall being constantly interested in understanding our evolving best assessment, with a mind to caring about its inconsistency with what I was—with what I said on the 16th.[338]

The absence of protests prior to the Benghazi attacks, however, remained a troubling issue for the administration. It was only a matter of time before this fact became widely known and disseminated publicly. Despite the best efforts by administration spokespersons to publicly support Rice's comments, however, the truth ultimately emerged to show much of what she said on the talk shows was incorrect.

## THE SHIFT

A week after the Benghazi attacks, administration officials began telling the public yet a different story. It started with Matthew G. Olsen, the Director of the National Counterterrorism Center.

### Matt Olsen's Testimony on September 19

On September 19, 2012, testifying before the Senate Homeland Security and Governmental Affairs Committee, Olsen firmly stated that what happened in Benghazi was in fact a terrorist attack. Olsen also testified that individuals affiliated with al-Qaeda or al-Qaeda's affiliates may have been involved in the attack. Olsen said:

> Q: So, let me begin by asking you whether you would say that Ambassador Stevens and the three other Americans died as a result of a terrorist attack.

---

[336] *Id.*
[337] Email from Victoria J. Nuland, Spokesperson, U.S. Dep't of State, to Jennifer Rubin ("J Rubin") (Sept. 20, 2012, 9:59 AM) (on file with the Committee, C05412001).
[338] Rice Testimony at 149.

A: Certainly on that particular question, I would say yes, they were killed in the course of a terrorist attack on our embassy.

Q: Right. And do we have reason to believe at this point that that terrorist attack was preplanned for September 11th or did the terrorists who were obviously planning it because it certainly seemed to be a coordinated terrorist attack just seize the moment of the demonstrations or protests against the film to carry out a terrorist attack?

A: A more complicated question, and one, Mr. Chairman, that we are spending a great deal of time looking at even as we speak. And it's a—it's a—obviously, an investigation here is ongoing and facts are being developed continually. The best information we have now, the facts that we have now indicate that this was an opportunistic attack on our embassy. The attack began and evolved and escalated over several hours at our embassy—our diplomatic post in Benghazi. It evolved and escalated over several hours.

It appears that individuals who were certainly well-armed seized on the opportunity presented as the events unfolded that evening and into the—into the morning hours of September 12th. We do know that a number of militants in the area, as I mentioned, are well-armed and maintain those arms. What we don't have at this point is specific intelligence that there was a significant advanced planning or coordination for this attack.

Again, we're still developing facts and still looking for any indications of substantial advanced planning; we just haven't seen that at this point. So, I think that's the most I would say at this point. I do want to emphasize that there is a classified briefing for all of Congress that will take place tomorrow.

Q: We'll be there. Let me come back to what you said— that there was evidence or intelligence that, as you indicated broadly a moment ago, that in eastern Libya, in the Benghazi area, there were a number of militant or violent extremist groups. Do we have any idea at this point who was responsible among those groups for the attack on the consulate?

A: This is the most important question that we're considering.

Q: Right.

A: We are focused on who was responsible for this attack. At this point, I would say is that a number of different elements appear to have been involved in the attack, including individuals connected to militant groups that are prevalent in eastern Libya, particularly in the Benghazi area, as well. We are looking at indications that individuals involved in the attack may have had connections to al-Qaeda or al-Qaeda's affiliates; in particular, al-Qaeda in the Islamic Maghreb.

Q: Right. So that question has not been determined yet—whether it was a militant—or a Libyan group or a group associated with al-Qaeda influence from abroad.

A: That's right. And I would—I would add that what—the picture that is emerging is one where a number of different individuals were involved, so it's not necessarily an either/or proposition.

Q: OK. OK, good, well——

A: Again, as you know, the FBI is leading the investigation and that's ongoing.[339]

Olsen's testimony that what had transpired in Benghazi was a terrorist attack and that there may be links to al-Qaeda was the first time an administration official had stated either of those facts publicly. He said the attacks were "opportunistic" and did not mention anything about a video. Olsen responded to Chairman Joseph I. Lieberman's questions directly, concisely, confidently, and factually. He did not couch his language, speculate, or go beyond the facts he knew. Additionally, what he said was accurate. Such fact-centered testimony stands in stark contrast to Rice's appearances on the talk shows.

Olsen told the Committee he wanted to talk about the connection to al-Qaeda at the Senate hearing; a possible al-Qaeda connection was a large factor in the post-attack analysis occurring within the intelligence community—a fact the IC had known for nearly a week.[340] Olsen testified:

But my thought at the time was this is not overly sensitive, and it is the kind of information that I was concerned, if we didn't—if I didn't say this in response to a question about who was responsible for this attack, it would be an omission that would be glaring in the—you know, as, on, Congress Members, themselves, were aware of this, right? Some of them serving on HPSCI or SSCI may well have seen the reporting. So it seemed to me the right thing to do to avoid being, you know, viewed as not being as forthcoming as I could be, even if it went beyond what had been publicly stated.

So that was my thinking at the time, why I thought that that was an important point to make and why I actually focused on it in advance of the hearings, so that folks would know that I was going to say it.[341]

Olsen knew at the time the administration had yet to publicly tie al-Qaeda to the Benghazi attacks. As such, he directed his head of legislative affairs to alert other Executive Branch agencies that he would likely make the connection at the hearing.[342] Meehan

---

[339] *Homeland Threats and Agency Responses: Hearing before the S. Committee on Homeland Security and Government Affairs,* 112th Cong. (2012) (statement of Matthew Olsen, Dir., Nat'l Counterterrorism Center).

[340] Olsen Testimony at 55–57 (discussing how long and from what sources intelligence community knew of al-Qaeda connection).

[341] *Id.* at 57–58.

[342] *Id.* at 53–54.

emailed Nuland about this possibility on the morning of the hearing. In an email with the subject "Change of Language per the call"—perhaps an indication of coordination between how the White House and State Department were going to respond to press inquiries that day about Benghazi—Meehan wrote:

> I am rushing to Jay's prep, and will circle up with the broader group after. But wanted to flag that Matt Olsen from NCTC will be on the Hill this morning . . . Wanted to flag that IF ASKED, Matt will use the line:
>
> There are indications some of the extremists involved in the attack may be linked to al-Qa'ida or its affiliates, but this assessment may change as additional information is collected and analyzed. In eastern Libya there are numerous armed groups, some of whom have al-Qa'ida sympathies.
>
> Flagging because it is an unclass session, so if he makes that statement, word will likely leak, and it is the first time someone from the USG will be saying that there might be a link to al-Qaeda. Ben and I discussed, and agreed that we refer questions to people involved in the investigation, note the investigation is still underway and no definitive conclusions yet, and if pressed, can point out there is no discrepancy with our original assessment because we always said our original assessment was based on info available at the time and that the investigation would provide further detail.
>
> Hopefully won't come up, but wanted to flag just in case.[343]

In her email, Meehan mentions a conversation with Rhodes and notes that "if pressed, can point out there is no discrepancy with our original assessment because we always said our original assessment was based on info available at the time and that the investigation would provide further detail."[344] What Meehan does not say is that the link to al-Qaeda was actually cited in the intelligence community's original assessment.[345] That was not new information, as Olsen acknowledged.[346]

Additionally, Meehan's email—reflecting other public statements by administration officials up to that point—noted she and Rhodes "agreed that we refer questions to people involved in the investigation." Olsen told the Committee the investigation did not in fact prohibit him from talking about what had been learned up to that point. He testified:

> Q: Was there anything about the FBI investigation that prohibited you from either, A, saying it was a terrorist attack, or, B, drawing a link to AQIM?

---

[343] Email from Bernadette M. Meehan, Spokesperson, U.S. Dep't of State, to Victoria J. Nuland, Spokesperson, U.S. Dep't of State, & Patrick H. Ventrell, Spokesperson, U.S. Dep't of State (Sept. 19, 2012, 10:22 AM) (on file with the Committee, C05561987).
[344] Id.
[345] September 13 WIRe, supra note 123.
[346] Olsen Testimony at 25.

A: No, nothing that I—no, I don't—certainly not the question of whether it was a terrorist attack or the way I phrased the answer to the question on who was responsible—on the connections to—you know, potential connections to terrorist groups.

Q: So if nothing about the ongoing investigation prohibited you from saying that, then why would others refer to the ongoing investigation when asked those very same questions?

A: —You know, I, obviously, don't know exactly why others. I do think there's a range of reasonable, you know, approaches to this question. In other words, I don't think there is one right approach.[347]

Olsen also testified his background as a prosecutor helps him create a fact-centered approach to sharing information. He said:

Q: Sure. As a prosecutor, the facts are very important to you. A fact is a fact, and you're going to share what that fact may be—is that fair to say?—as opposed to being concerned about public relations, in lack of a better phrase, or the impression people might get?

A: That's basically right, and that's sort of—that is the approach of being a prosecutor in terms of reliance on facts. I'm not—I shouldn't, you know, lead you to believe that I'm completely oblivious to——

Q: Of course

A: —the public impression that you can leave and the importance that that has too.[348]

Even though Olsen wanted to state publicly that al-Qaeda sympathizers may have been involved in the attack, he did not plan on saying definitively that it was a terrorist attack. While Olsen knew from the outset it was a terrorist attack—"all of those factors, you know, made it so that it was, to me, there was not really a question of whether it was a terrorist attack"[349]—he testified he had not given it a great deal of thought, but when asked directly by Lieberman, the logical response was to acknowledge that it was a terrorist attack.[350]

Olsen recognized almost immediately after the hearing he may have made news with what he had said with respect to the events being a terrorist attack. He told the Committee he wrote an email to the White House alerting them of what he had said. Olsen testified:

Q: So what were the repercussions of you saying it was a terrorist attack?

A: So one of the things I did afterwards was I wrote an email to both John Brennan and Denis McDonough—you know, Denis was the Deputy National Security Advisor

[347] Id. at 60.
[348] Id. at 61–62
[349] Id. at 100.
[350] Id. at 50–51.

and John was—John Brennan was the counterterrorism advisor—and explained to them—you know, I said something like, "I made some news today with my testimony. Here is why I testified that this was a terrorist attack," was my thought process. And they wrote back to me, saying, "You did the right thing," essentially, in emails that day. You know, "Understand you made the right points," or something like that.

But again, look, I was aware, again, in a way I hadn't really been before that what I was testifying to was potentially newsworthy, and, in fact, it was. So that's why I thought both let my press person think about what we need to do, ask him to think about what we may need to do, and then also, myself, reach out to John Brennan and Denis McDonough.[351]

Private reaction from senior officials at the State Department regarding Olsen's testimony, however, appeared less supportive. Nuland wrote to Sullivan, Mills, and Kennedy:

Fysa, and for Jake's drafting exercise; NCTC also called it a terrorist attack today: I had demurred on that as had Jay, pending investigation.[352]

Sullivan called the White House to inform them he was unaware Olsen was going to testify it was a terrorist attack. Meehan testified:

Q: Do you recall generally having any conversations with [Jake Sullivan] that week? Or in the immediate aftermath of the attack, that general period of September 2012?

A: I do recall having one phone conversation with him. I don't know whether it's in the scope of the 4 to 5 days that we're discussing.

Q: Okay. What was discussed in that conversation?

A: He raised that he had been unaware before Matt Olsen testified on the Hill, that Matt Olsen was going to make a link publicly to Al Qaeda in reference to the Benghazi attack.

Q: Why did he raise that issue with you?

A: I can't say why I was the individual that he called. I don't know.[353]

Even the Secretary expressed surprise at Olsen's testimony. Olsen testified:

---

[351] Id. at 71–72.

[352] Email from Victoria J. Nuland, Spokesperson, U.S. Dep't of State, to Jacob J. Sullivan, Deputy Chief of Staff and Dir. of Policy Planning, U.S. Dep't of State, Cheryl D. Mills, Chief of Staff to the U.S. Sec'y of State, U.S. Dep't of State, & Patrick F. Kennedy, Under Sec'y for Management, U.S. Dep't of State (Sept. 19, 2012, 2:45 PM) (on file with the Committee, C05561975).

[353] Testimony of Bernadette M. Meehan, Spokesperson, Nat'l Sec. Council, Tr. at 28–29 (Dec. 16, 2015) (on file with the Committee).

Q: Yeah. Did anybody express to you that they were disappointed in what you said, they were perplexed by what you said, that what you said may have thrown a message off kilter?

    \*  \*  \*

A: . . . But, you know, to your question I did hear at one point—and I don't remember exactly when—from Director Clapper that he'd heard from Secretary Clinton, you know, of some surprise about me saying that it was a terrorist attack. And he basically said—you know, I remember thinking he basically said, you know, "We're saying what we see," something like that.

But I remember hearing from him. He told me directly— I think we were either in a car or getting ready to get in his car to come downtown—that he'd gotten a call or had heard from Secretary Clinton about surprise that one of his guys was talking about this being a terrorist attack.[354]

The day after Olsen's testimony, September 20, 2012, the President participated in a town hall with Univision at the University of Miami. The President had the following exchange:

Q: We have reports that the White House said today that the attacks in Libya were a terrorist attack. Do you have information indicating that it was Iran, or al-Qaeda was behind organizing the protests?

A: Well, we're still doing an investigation, and there are going to be different circumstances in different countries. And so I don't want to speak to something until we have all the information. What we do know is that the natural protests that arose because of the outrage over the video were used as an excuse by extremists to see if they can also directly harm U.S. interests——

Q: Al-Qaeda?

A: Well, we don't know yet. And so we're going to continue to investigate this. We've insisted on, and have received so far full cooperation from countries like Egypt and Libya and Tunisia in not only protecting our diplomatic posts, but also to make sure that we discover who, in fact, is trying to take advantage of this. . . .[355]

The President said the government wanted to "discover who, in fact, is trying to take advantage of this." It is unclear if "this" is a reference to the video, protests, or something else. However, no assessment from the CIA ever stated anybody was "trying to take advantage" of the video, or even that there was a direct link between the video and the Benghazi attacks.

The President also stated, in response to a question that mentioned only Libya, the "natural protests that arose because of the

[354] Olsen Testimony at 82–83.
[355] Remarks by the President at Univision Town Hall with Jorge Ramos and Maria Elena Salinas, Miami, FL, Sept. 20, 2012.

outrage over the video were used as an excuse by extremists to see if they can also directly harm U.S. interests—." This statement was made two days after the U.S. government obtained access to the video footage from the Benghazi Mission compound, which did not show a protest outside the Benghazi Mission compound prior to the beginning of the attacks.

When asked if al-Qaeda was involved, the President responded "we don't know yet." The day before, however, Olsen testified under oath before Congress the government was "looking at indiciations that individuals involved in the attack may have had connections to al-Qaeda or al-Qaeda's affiliates; in particular, al-Qaeda in the Islamic Maghreb."

Two days after Olsen's testimony, on September 21, 2012, the Secretary said for the first time publicly that what happened in Benghazi was a "terrorist attack." [356]

Four days later, on September 25, 2012, the President said, during remarks to the United Nations General Assembly: "There are no words that excuse the killing of innocents. There's no video that justifies an attack on an embassy." [357]

It was not until the following day—a full week after Olsen made his comments and fifteen days after the attacks began—Carney finally acknowledged the President's position was that a terrorist attack occurred. Carney said:

> Q: Can I ask one more—are criticizing the President for not classifying what happened in Benghazi as a terrorist attack, going as far as you did or the NCTC director. Can you respond to that and explain why that is?

> A: The President spoke eloquently I believe about the attack that took the lives of four Americans at the United Nations General Assembly, and I think made very clear that it is wholly unacceptable to respond to a video, no matter how offensive, with violence, and it is wholly unacceptable, regardless of the reason, to attack embassies or diplomatic facilities and to kill diplomatic personnel.

> The President—our position is, as reflected by the NCTC director, that it was a terrorist attack. It is, I think by definition, a terrorist attack when there is a prolonged assault on an embassy with weapons.

> The broader questions here about who participated, what led to the attack on the facility in Benghazi—all those questions are under investigation at two levels, by the FBI and by the Accountability Review Board established by Secretary Clinton to look at issues of security in Benghazi and security at other diplomatic facilities.

---

[356] Hillary R. Clinton, Sec'y of State, U.S. Dep't of State, Remarks with Pakistani Foreign Minister Hina Rabbani Khar before Their Meeting (Sept.25, 2012), http://www.state.gov/secretary/20092013clinton/rm/2012/09/198060.htm.

[357] Press Release, The White House Office of the Press Secretary, Remarks by the President to the UN General Assembly (Sept. 13, 2012), https://www.whitehouse.gov/the-press-office/2012/09/25/remarks-president-un-general-assembly.

So, let's be clear, it was a terrorist attack and it was an inexcusable attack.[358]

## September 24 Intelligence Assessment

Two days before Carney finally acknowledged publicly that Benghazi was a terrorist attack, on September 24, 2012, the CIA published its new "assessment" about the Benghazi attacks, formally changing their old assessment which had been in place since September 13. In the September 24 piece, which was produced jointly with the National Counterterrorism Center, the analysts wrote "We now assess, based on new reporting, that the assault was deliberate and organized. Our most credible information indicates that there was not a protest ongoing at the time of the attack as first reported."[359]

The supporting intelligence used in this piece to support the new assessment was threefold. The first piece of intelligence was from September 19, 2012 and noted that attackers used fixed firing positions, capture or kill teams, and blockades to impede the escape of US personnel," **[redacted text]**[360]

The second piece of intelligence **[redacted text]** suggesting "the attack was put together at least several hours ahead of time."[361] Although this piece of intelligence was available as early as September 15—one day before Rice went on the Sunday talk shows and nine days before the analysts published their updated assessment—an internal CIA after action review noted that this piece of intelligence was "not viewed as credible enough" at the time to outweigh other reporting, such as news reports.[362]

The third piece of intelligence **[redacted text]** noted simply that the attackers "also employed effective mortar fire against the Embassy annex later in the night after US return fire repulsed their initial ground assault."[363] This piece of intelligence was formally available to analysts as early as September 14, and informally available to them as early as September 12.

Additionally, perhaps the most credible—and definitive—piece of intelligence indicating no protest had occurred prior to the Benghazi attacks was the video footage from the closed circuit televisions at the Special Mission Compound in Benghazi. The CIA had access to analysis of this footage by the Libyan Intelligence Service as early as September 18, 2012, and those in the CIA who saw the video on that date concluded immediately no protest occurred prior to the attacks. This intelligence was not cited in the update assessment.

The manager of the analysts testified the analysts began working on the piece before September 18. Given that fact—and that the information cited in the updated assessment as rationale for chang-

[358] Press Gaggle by Press Secretary Jay Carney Aboard Air Force One en route Ohio, Office of the Press Secretary, The White House (Sept. 26, 2012), https://www.whitehouse.gov/the-press-office/2012/09/26/press-gaggle-press-secretary-jay-carney-aboard-air-force-one-en-route-oh.

[359] Cent. Intel. Agency, Libya: Updated Assessment of Benghazi Attacks, World Intelligence Review, Sept. 24, 2012 (on file with CIA, IntBook29–076 to IntBook29–079).

[360] Id.

[361] Id.

[362] Intelligence Note, Memorandum for Acting Dir., Cent. Intel. Agency, Jan. 4, 2013 [hereinafter Analytic Line Review] (on file with CIA, REQUEST 17–0049 to REQUEST 17–0063).

[363] **[Redacted text]**.

ing the assessment was available on September 14, September 15, and September 19—why did it take the CIA until September 24 to publish the piece?

The answer appears to be the piece was held up in interagency coordination. The analysts did not want an interagency partner to file a formal dissent. The manager of the analysts testified:

> And, frankly, the WIRe that ran on the 24th actually got held up for 2 days in Coordination, trying to convince people in the IC [Intelligence Community], who hadn't seen this video yet because it wasn't back in country, that there were no protests.[364]

Other interagency partners—specifically the State Department—did not trust the Libyan government's assessment of the video, even though CIA officials in Tripoli had seen the actual video footage and concurred with the assessment.[365] This distrust held up interagency coordination of the piece for several days. It was not until September 24 when the actual video footage arrived at CIA headquarters, allowing for dissemination to other interagency partners.[366]

## September 28 ODNI Statement

On September 28, 2012, Shawn Turner, Director of Public Affairs, Office of the Director of National Intelligence, released a statement on the intelligence related to the Benghazi terrorist attacks. That statement read in full:

> In the aftermath of the terrorist attack on U.S. personnel and facilities in Benghazi, Libya, the Intelligence Community launched a comprehensive effort to determine the circumstances surrounding the assault and to identify the perpetrators. We also reviewed all available intelligence to determine if there might be follow-on attacks against our people or facilities in Libya or elsewhere in the world.

> As the Intelligence Community collects and analyzes more information related to the attack, our understanding of the event continues to evolve. In the immediate aftermath, there was information that led us to assess that the attack began spontaneously following protests earlier that day at our embassy in Cairo. We provided that initial assessment to Executive Branch officials and members of Congress, who used that information to discuss the attack publicly and provide updates as they became available. Throughout our investigation we continued to emphasize that information gathered was preliminary and evolving.

> As we learned more about the attack, we revised our initial assessment to reflect new information indicating that it was a deliberate and organized terrorist attack carried out by extremists. It remains unclear if any group or person exercised overall command and control of the attack,

---

[364] **[Redacted text]** Team Chief Testimony at 75–77, 92–95.
[365] *Id.* at 75–77.
[366] **[Redacted text]**.

and if extremist group leaders directed their members to participate. However, we do assess that some of those involved were linked to groups affiliated with, or sympathetic to al-Qa'ida. We continue to make progress, but there remain many unanswered questions. As more information becomes available our analysis will continue to evolve and we will obtain a more complete understanding of the circumstances surrounding the terrorist attack.

We continue to support the ongoing FBI investigation and the State Department review of the Benghazi terrorist attack, providing the full capabilities and resources of the Intelligence Community to those efforts. We also will continue to meet our responsibility to keep Congress fully and currently informed. For its part, the Intelligence Community will continue to follow the information about the tragic events in Benghazi wherever it leads. The President demands and expects that we will do this, as do Congress and the American people. As the Intelligence Community, we owe nothing less than our best efforts in this regard, especially to the families of the four courageous Americans who lost their lives at Benghazi in service of their country.[367]

Even though the issue of protests was heavily debated in the public at the time, the statement does not specifically address whether or not a protest occurred prior to the attacks—doing so would have undercut Rice's statements on the talk shows twelve days before. In addition, the issue of protests was not an "analytical focal point"[368] for the intelligence community and was more of a "subsidiary issue" to them.[369]

Rather, the statement only mentions it was a "deliberate and organized terrorist attack"[370]—still leaving open the possibility protests may have occurred. The statement did not mention anything about the internet video, let alone any connection between the video and Benghazi attacks. The statement, issued by the intelligence community and not the White House or State Department, did not connect the two events.[371]

As public statements tend to be, this statement was carefully worded. It notes only the initial intelligence community assessment that it "began spontaneously following protests earlier that day at our embassy in Cairo."[372] This wording can be directly tied to language in the September 13 WIRe.[373] The statement does not say,

---

[367] Press Release, Office of the Dir. of National Intel., Statement by the Director of Public Affairs for ODNI, Shawn Turner, on the intelligence related to the terrorist attack on the U.S. Consulate in Benghazi, Libya (Sept. 28, 2012), https://www.dni.gov/index.php/newsroom/press-releases/96-press-releases-2012/731-statement-by-the-odni-s-director-of-public-affairs-on-intelligence-related-to-the-terrorist-attack-on-the-u-s-consulate-in-benghazi.

[368] Olsen Testimony at 119.

[369] Olsen Testimony at 67.

[370] Press Release, Office of the Dir. of National Intel., Statement by the Director of Public Affairs for ODNI, Shawn Turner, on the intelligence related to the terrorist attack on the U.S. Consulate in Benghazi, Libya (Sept. 28, 2012), https://www.dni.gov/index.php/newsroom/press-releases/96-press-releases-2012/731-statement-by-the-odni-s-director-of-public-affairs-on-intelligence-related-to-the-terrorist-attack-on-the-u-s-consulate-in-benghazi.

[371] *See id.*

[372] *Id.*

[373] September 13 WIRe, *supra* note 123.

however, the intelligence community ever assessed that protests or demonstrations had occurred prior to the Benghazi attacks—something repeatedly mentioned by Rice on the talk shows. That is because, aside from the errant title in the September 13 WIRe, the intelligence community never formally coordinated such an assessment in writing.

The statement also says "[a]s we learned more about the attack, we revised our initial assessment to reflect new information indicating that it was a deliberate and organized terrorist attack carried out by extremists. . . . we do assess that some of those involved were linked to groups affiliated with, or sympathetic to al-Qa'ida."[374]

Given that the intelligence leading to the new assessment was more than a week old, and in some cases even older, why, then, did ODNI wait until September 28, 2012 to issue this statement? The answer lies in emails between senior administration officials.

The genesis for ODNI's statement occurred the day before as a result of a press report. The article, published on September 27, 2012 said the following:

> URGENT: U.S. intelligence officials knew from Day One that the assault on the U.S. Consulate in Libya was a terrorist attack and suspect Al Qaeda-tied elements were involved, sources told Fox News—though it took the administration a week to acknowledge it.
>
> The account conflicts with claims on the Sunday after the attack by U.S. Ambassador to the United Nations Susan Rice that the administration believed the strike was a "spontaneous" event triggered by protests in Egypt over an anti-Islam film.
>
> Sources said the administration internally labeled the attack terrorism from the first day to enable a certain type of policy response and that officials were looking for one specific suspect.
>
> In addition, sources confirm that FBI agents have not yet arrived in Benghazi in the aftermath of the attack.[375]

Upon seeing the article that morning, McDonough forwarded it to Robert Cardillo, Deputy Director, Office of the Director of National Intelligence, Morell, and John Brennan, Counterterrorism Advisor to the President. McDonough wrote:

Hey, guys,

This is the third report making this assertion. Is this correct?

Thanks,

---

[374] Press Release, Office of the Dir. of National Intel., Statement by the Director of Public Affairs for ODNI, Shawn Turner, on the intelligence related to the terrorist attack on the U.S. Consulate in Benghazi, Libya (Sept. 28, 2012), https://www.dni.gov/index.php/newsroom/press-releases/96-press-releases-2012/731-statement-by-the-odni-s-director-of-public-affairs-on-intelligence-related-to-the-terrorist-attack-on-the-u-s-consulate-in-benghazi.

[375] Email from Peter Velz, Media Monitor, White House, to DL–WHO-Press, et al. (Sept. 27, 2012, 10:15 AM) (on file with the Committee, C05415305).

Denis [376]

Cardillo responded, including Olsen and Nick Rasmussen, Deputy Director, National Counterterrorism Center. Cardillo wrote:

> I am fairly sure the answer is 'no.' And I've asked Matt and Nick to lay out on a timeline the evolution of our IC assessments from 12 September on. They're on cc so I'll ask when that can be ready. Robert.[377]

It is unclear which assertion McDonough and Cardillo were referring to, although Olsen told the Committee he believed from the beginning the assault on the U.S. facilities in Benghazi was a terrorist attack,[378] and Morell testified that "[i]n the minds of the [CIA] analysts from the get-go, this was a terrorist attack, and I think that is reflected in what they wrote."[379]

Olsen responded to the email, writing:

> All-
>
> As Robert suggests, I think the best way to approach this is to review and memorialize exactly what we were saying from the onset of the attack going forward. We've got a chronological catalog of all finished intelligence on the attack. And we'll put together today a time line summary that sets forth all key points and analytic judgments as they developed from 9/11 through the present. Nick and I will get started on the time line right away.
>
> —Matt [380]

That evening, Cardillo responded. He sent his response to the group, but also included Turner and Rexon Ryu. Cardillo wrote:

> NCTC has already made great progress in documenting the chronology of what we knew and what we published. My reading of that draft is that we can easily debunk Fox and refute the hits on Susan's statements on Sunday, 16 Sep. As I read the laydown, her comments were consistent with our intel assessment at that time. . . .[381]

McDonough responded to the email, and included Rhodes in the email chain. In his response, McDonough included another article from ABC News. The title of the ABC News article was "Some Administration Officials Were Concerned About Initial White House Push Blaming Benghazi Attack on Mob, Video" and read, in part:

> Even before Defense Secretary Leon Panetta contradicted the initial story about the attack on the U.S. consulate in Benghazi, Libya, today, Obama administration officials

---

[376] Email from Mr.McDonough, to Mr. Cardillo and Mr. Morell (Sept. 27, 2012, 10:57 AM) (on file with the Committee, C05415305).

[377] Email from Mr. Cardillo to Mr. McDonough, *et al.* (Sept. 27, 2012, 11:23 AM) (on file with the Committee, C05415305).

[378] Olsen Testimony at 100.

[379] Morell Testimony at 74.

[380] Email from Mr. Olsen to Mr. Cardillo, *et al.* (Sept. 27, 2012, 12:12 PM) (on file with the Committee, C05415305).

[381] Email from Mr. Cardillo to Mr. Olsen, Mr. McDonough, & Mr. Morell (Sept. 27, 2012, 7:47 PM) (on file with the Committee, C05415305).

told ABC News they were concerned after the White House began pushing the line that the attack was spontaneous and not the work of terrorists. . . . Panetta today said that the attack that killed four Americans on the anniversary of 9/11 was not only carried out by terrorists—it was pre-meditated. . . .

The White House first suggested the attack was spontaneous—the result of an anti-Muslim video that incited mobs throughout the region. . . .

But sources told ABC News that intelligence officials on the ground immediately suspected the attack was not tied to the movie at all. . . .

As of Thursday afternoon, officials from the Obama administration were not even 100 percent certain that the protest of the anti-Muslim film in Benghazi occurred outside the U.S. diplomatic post.[382]

McDonough wrote of this article, "The piece immediately below led ABC World News Tonight today. It is really galling."[383]
Rhodes responded three minutes later. He wrote:

I believe that we need something tomorrow. There is a narrative that is being aggressively pushed that the White House and Susan Rice deliberately misrepresented facts, which is being confirmed by anonymous intelligence sources and administration officials. In the absence of an affirmative statement that this has been an evolving set of facts guided by our increasing understanding of what took place, that narrative will only harden further. Already, it is a bell that is going to be very difficult to unring.[384]

In essence, Rhodes wanted to put out a statement not for the reason of informing the public about the updated intelligence assessment relating to the attacks, but to refute allegations Rice and the White House "deliberately misrepresented facts."[385]
Rhodes emailed the group again less than twenty minutes later, stating:

Again, I believe we have a very credible case that all we have done is follow the facts and inform people of those facts, while prioritizing the need for investigations to run their course. However, that case is being lost amidst the leaks of information (correct and incorrect) and uninformed assertions coming from a variety of places.[386]

Two things about Rhodes' response are noteworthy. One, he acknowledges some of the leaks are "correct," although he does not

---

[382] Email from Mr. McDonough to Mr. Cardillo, Mr. Olsen, Mr. Rhodes, and Mr. Morell (Sept. 27, 2012, 7:49 PM) (on file with the Committee, C05415305).
[383] Id.
[384] Email from Mr. Rhodes to Mr. McDonough, Mr. Olsen, Mr. Cardillo, and Mr. Morell (Sept. 27, 2012, 7:52 PM) (on file with the Committee, C05415305).
[385] Email from Mr. Rhodes to Mr. McDonough, Mr. Cardillo, Mr. Olsen, and Mr. Morell (Sept. 27, 2012, 7:56 PM) (on file with the Committee, C05415305).
[386] Email from Mr. Rhodes to Mr. Cardillo, Mr. McDonough, Mr. Olsen, and Mr. Morell (Sept. 27, 2012, 8:15 PM) (on file with the Committee, C05415305).

identify which ones; and two, he writes "I believe we have a very credible case that all we have done is follow the facts." [387] "Credible case" is hardly a definitive, full-throated defense of the administration's handling of the public explanation for the attacks in Benghazi.

The following morning Olsen emailed the group that he had provided a draft statement to Turner for eventual release. Rhodes responded, writing:

> Thank you for working this, as the most important thing is having a public baseline—informed by the facts—that we can all point to. We are well synched up with Shawn Turner as well.[388]

Rhodes testified to the Committee about his recollection of this statement:

> Well, my recollection is that there was an interest in providing a statement that clarified our understanding and the evolution of our understanding of the events in Benghazi that that statement was to be prepared by the intelligence community. I work with them in my coordinating role as they were preparing that statement.[389]

Rhodes' email that they are "synched up" with Turner,[390] and his testimony that he was in his "coordinating role" as the statement was prepared,[391] serves as a reminder the White House played a central role in the drafting of this statement—a statement that, by Rhodes' own admission, served not to inform the public but rather to push back against a narrative that the White House and Rice deliberately misrepresented facts. The statement itself, however, according to Olsen, was "speaking on behalf of the intelligence community at that point and not really beyond that." [392] The White House's involvement in the creation of the statement—through McDonough, Brennan, and Rhodes—continues to raise questions as to who ultimately controlled the message regarding Benghazi coming out of not just the intelligence community but the executive branch as a whole.

## THE LANDSCAPE

The political import of the attacks on the presidential campaign of 2012 is not a subject of the committee's investigation. Nevertheless, the House of Representatives did direct the Committee to investigate and study "internal and public executive branch communications about the attacks." [393] It would be naïve to assume this or any administration's public statements about a significant foreign policy event would be made without full awareness of the po-

---

[387] Id.

[388] Email from Mr. Rhodes to Mr. Cardillo, Mr. Olsen, Mr. McDonough, Mr. Morell (Sept. 28, 2012, 10:43 AM) (on file with the Committee, C05415305).

[389] Rhodes Testimony at 137.

[390] Email from Mr. Rhodes to Mr. Cardillo, Mr. Olsen, Mr. McDonough, Mr. Morell (Sept. 28, 2012, 10:43 AM) (on file with the Committee, C05415305).

[391] Rhodes Testimony at 137.

[392] Olsen Testimony at 117.

[393] H. Res. 567 113th Congress Section 3(a)(3).

litical effect of those statements. It is necessary to place the attacks and the administration's statements about them in context.

The Benghazi terrorist attacks occurred not only on the anniversary of the Sept 11, 2001 terrorist attacks but also in the middle of the 2012 presidential campaign. The first presidential debate was 22 days away and the election was 56 days away. The killing of a U.S. Ambassador in the line of duty—which had not occurred in 33 years—and three other Americans would inevitably become an issue in the campaign and even be discussed at the presidential debate on October 16, 2012.[394]

Prior to the attacks, the President and the Secretary of State took credit for the Administration's record in the war on terror, the perceived success of the intervention in Libya, and the toppling of its dictator, Muammar Qadhafi.[395] Nearly four years had passed without a significant incident at home or abroad, and killing Osama bin Laden represented an historic victory.[396] The President pointed to these successes in his campaign, including in a speech five days prior to the attacks:

> In a world of new threats and new challenges, you can choose leadership that has been tested and proven. Four years ago, I promised to end the war in Iraq: We did. I promised to refocus on the terrorists who actually attacked us on 9/11. We have. We've blunted the Taliban's momentum in Afghanistan, and in 2014, our longest war will be over. A new tower rises above the New York skyline, al-Qaeda is on the path to defeat, and Osama bin Laden is dead.[397]

The Benghazi attacks could certainly affect public perception of the administration's record in the war on terror and the narrative of success in Libya. Almost immediately, the press began asking questions about whether Benghazi represented a failure of the President's policies. In a press conference the day after the attacks, a reporter asked Carney directly: "Jay, is the U.S. doing something wrong policy-wise in Libya that brings this [the attack] on? Or is the policy fine, it's just this particular event?"[398] One publication summed up the situation by saying, "with the American Presidential election only two months away, the murder of four Americans serving their government overseas could be a game changer so far as Mr. Obama's re-election prospects are concerned."[399]

The attacks remained an issue throughout the campaign including at the second presidential debate where former Massachusetts Governor Mitt Romney used the attacks to question the administration's Middle East policy generally:

---

[394] *October 16, 2012 Debate Transcript,* COMM'N ON PRESIDENTIAL DEBATES (Oct. 16, 2012), http://www.debates.org/index.php?page=october-16-2012-the-second-obama-romney-presidential-debate.

[395] *See, e.g.,* Tom Cohen, *Obama makes war policy an election strength,* CNN (Oct. 24, 2011), http://www.cnn.com/2011/10/24/politics/obama-foreign-policy.

[396] *Id.*

[397] President Barack Obama, Speech at 2012 Democratic National Convention (Sept. 6, 2012).

[398] Press Gaggle by Press Secretary Jay Carney en route Las Vegas, NV, Office of the Press Secretary, The White House (Sept. 12, 2012), https://www.whitehouse.gov/the-press-office/2012/09/12/press-gaggle-press-secretary-jay-carney-en-route-las-vegas-nv-9122012.

[399] Con Coughlin, *The Murder of the US Ambassador to Libya is a Wake-up Call for Obama,* The Daily Telegraph (Sept. 12, 2012), http://blogs.telegraph.co.uk/news/concoughlin/100180611/murder-of-us-ambassador-is-a-wake-up-call-for-obama.

And this [the Benghazi attacks] calls into question the president's whole policy in the Middle East. Look what's happening in Syria, in Egypt, now in Libya. Consider the distance between ourselves and—and Israel, the president said that—that he was going to put daylight between us and Israel.

We have Iran four years closer to a nuclear bomb. Syria— Syria's not just a tragedy of 30,000 civilians being killed by a military, but also a strategic—strategically significant player for America.

The president's policies throughout the Middle East began with an apology tour and—and—and pursue a strategy of leading from behind, and this strategy is unraveling before our very eyes.[400]

Shortly after this statement, the candidates and the moderator debated whether the President called the Benghazi attacks a terrorist attack from day one.[401] The President's Rose Garden remarks were not his only public comments about the attacks on September 12. The President also taped a *60 Minutes* interview the same day, which aired on September 23.[402] During the interview the President said it was "too early to tell" when asked about his Rose Garden remarks and whether the attacks were terrorism.[403] The question and the President's answer were not included in the broadcast version because the interview was edited.[404]

Three days after the second debate, CBS posted additional portions of the *60 Minutes* transcript from the interview with the President on September 12, 2012.[405] The portion of the President refusing to call it a terrorist attack was still absent. It was not until November 6, 2012, two days before the election, when CBS finally posted publicly for the first time the entire transcript of the President's interview on September 12, 2012.[406]

The President of CBS News at the time, David Rhodes, is the brother of Ben Rhodes, who helped prepare the President for the second debate.[407] While Ben Rhodes denied to the Committee he talked with anybody at CBS prior to the September 23, 2012, airing of the President's interview, he did not know whether others in the White House did. Rhodes also did not testify as to whether

---

[400] *October 16, 2012 Debate Transcript,* Commission on Presidential Debates (Oct. 16, 2012), http://www.debates.org/index.php?page=october-16-2012-the-second-obama-romney-presidential-debate

[401] *October 16, 2012 Debate Transcript,* COMM'N ON PRESIDENTIAL DEBATES (Oct. 16, 2012), http://www.debates.org/index.php?page=october-16-2012-the-second-obama-romney-presidential-debate; Press Release, The White House Office of the Press Secretary, Remarks by the President on the Deaths of U.S. Embassy Staff in Libya (Sept. 12, 2012), https://www.whitehouse.gov/the-press-office/2012/09/12/remarks-president-deaths-us-embassy-staff-libya.

[402] Dylan Byers & MacKenzie Weinger, *CBS under fire for withhold Obama's Benghazi remarks,* POLITICO (Nov. 5, 2012), http://www.politico.com/blogs/media/2012/11/cbs-under-fire-for-withholding-obamas-benghazi-remarks-148513.

[403] *Id.*

[404] *Id.*

[405] *Id.*

[406] *Id.*

[407] Helene Cooper, *Obama's Prep Session Goal: Don't Repeat Mistakes of Last Debate,* N.Y. TIMES (Oct. 14, 2012), http://www.nytimes.com/2012/10/15/us/politics/a-serious-debate-prep-session-for-obama.html?_r=0.

or not he spoke with anybody at CBS after September 23, 2012, regarding the posting of the transcript to CBS' website. He testified:

> Q: And you may recall there was some bit of controversy over the interview that was actually aired by CBS because it did not include a portion of the President's remarks. Do you remember that?
>
> A: I have a recollection that there was some controversy about that, yes.
>
> Q: Did you or anybody else on your staff have any conversations with CBS about that 60 Minutes interview?
>
> A: I did not excuse me, what's the in what time period are you talking about?
>
> Q: Prior to it airing?
>
> A: I did not have any conversations with CBS after the interview taped prior to it aired.
>
> Q: Did anybody on your staff?
>
> A: Generally, when we have interviews like that with the President, the contacts with the network are handled by the White House press in the communications office, not the NSC.
>
> Q: Do you know if any of those communications actually occurred?
>
> A: I don't know.[408]

On October 1, 2012, the Secretary of State forwarded a *Salon* article titled "GOP's October Surprise?" which alleged Romney planned to attack the President as weak on terrorism.[409] Sidney Blumenthal emailed the article to the Secretary and took credit for it getting it "done and published." [410] The Secretary forwarded the email to Sullivan with the instruction, "Be sure Ben knows they need to be ready for this line of attack." Sullivan responded: "Will do." [411]

The White House told the Committee they would not allow the Committee to ask about this email during the Committee's interview with Rhodes, citing executive privilege and noting that preparing for a debate was a "core executive function." [412]

## MIXING INTELLIGENCE WITH POLITICS

In the months after the Benghazi attacks, politics continued to play a role in assigning blame for what had occurred and who said what. In addition to the usual politics of Republicans and Democrats lobbing accusations at one another, however, a different,

---

[408] Rhodes Testimony at 118–19.

[409] Craig Unger, *GOP's October surprise?*, SALON (Oct. 1, 2012), http://www.salon.com/2012/10/01/gops_october_surprise.

[410] *See* Email from Sidney Blumenthal to Hillary R. Clinton ("H"), Sec'y of State, U.S. Dep't of State (Oct. 1, 2012, 9:30 AM) (on file with the Committee, SCB0045545) ("Got done and published.").

[411] Email from Jacob J. Sullivan, Deputy Chief of Staff and Dir. of Policy Planning, U.S. Dep't of State, to Hillary R. Clinton ("H"), Sec'y of State, U.S. Dep't of State (Oct. 1, 2012, 3:37 PM) (on file with the Committee, SCB0045545).

[412] Phone Call between Office of White House Counsel and Committee Staff (Jan. 30, 2016).

quieter, type of politics was taking place regarding Benghazi: internal politics. At the center of it all was Morell.

## The Setup

On November 27, 2012, amid speculation the President would nominate her to become the next Secretary of State, Rice traveled to Capitol Hill to meet with three Senators to discuss her September 16 appearances on the Sunday talk shows.[413] Accompanying Rice to that meeting was Morell, who was at the time Acting Director of the CIA. Morell described why he attended the meeting:

> Q: Can you just generally describe what the purpose of that meeting was?
>
> A: Yes. So I got a phone call from Denis McDonough, who was then the deputy national security advisor. He told me that—of course I knew from the media that Susan was under attack for what she had said on the Sunday shows. He told me that Susan wanted to go to the Hill and have conversations with her critics. He told me that the President wanted me to go along with her. He made very clear to me that my job in going along with her was to talk about the classified analysis, to talk about the talking points, and importantly, to show, to actually show the Senators the consistency between the talking points and the classified analysis. That's what he told me my job was. And I said yes and I went.[414]

Morell agreed to the President's request and attended the meeting with Rice. In his book, however, Morell wrote: "In retrospect, attending the meeting was a mistake. The meeting was inherently political, and by attending, I inserted myself into a political issue . . . That is not where an intelligence officer should be."[415] Morell told the Committee:

> Q: Did you think your presence there was requested to insulate or protect Susan Rice in any way?
>
> A: I think my—I think my presence there was to show that what she said, right, about Benghazi was consistent, right, at least the protest, spontaneity part, right, was consistent with what the analysts really believed.
>
> Q: I guess what I'm trying to get at it, do you think in any way—I mean you're a career analyst, you're known or so I've heard you're known around the community as a very straight shooting, as a straight shooter, you call it like you see it. So the fact that you were accompanying her—did you know if the Secretary of State at that point had announced that she was going to step down? Do you know if Susan Rice at that point——

---

[413] Ed O'Keefe, *Susan Rice, CIA director meet with GOP critics on Libya*, WASH. POST (Nov. 27, 2012), https://www.washingtonpost.com/blogs/2chambers/wp/2012/11/27/susan-rice-cia-director-meet-with-gop-critics-on-libya.

[414] Morell Testimony at 202–203.

[415] MORELL, *supra* note 114, at 235.

A: Yes, I believe so, right? I believe that was the whole point—in fact, that is what Denis said, right, her possible nomination to be Secretary of State was at risk, absolutely.

Q: —So it was a very inherently political meeting——

A: Yes, it was.

Q: —that you were inserting yourself or that you had been asked to—it was a very inherently political meeting that you had been asked to attend.

A: Yes. But, again, I didn't realize it at the time. I really didn't. I didn't know I was walking myself into this political setting.[416]

In addition to explaining to the Senators how Rice's comments on the Sunday shows aligned with the intelligence at the time, Morell's attendance at the meeting served another purpose—it kept him at the forefront of the controversy surrounding the Benghazi talking points. While Rice was the administration's representative on the Sunday talk shows, Morell was the individual who edited the CIA talking points Rice says she relied on.[417] Having public criticism targeted towards Morell, a career intelligence official, instead of Rice, a political appointee in a politically charged environment, could be beneficial for a potential Secretary of State nominee.

## The Execution

In late 2012, Morell directed two internal CIA reviews take place regarding the talking points. One review, called the Analytic Line Review, went through each piece of CIA analysis after the Benghazi attacks to determine how strong the supporting evidence was for each of the analytic assessments.[418] The second review was about "Lessons Learned" from the internal process of creating the talking points for HPSCI.[419] Morell wanted to send these two internal reviews to Congress.[420]

Morell sent only the Analytic Line Review to Congress, which was completed in January 2013. The White House would not allow him to send the other document—containing drafts of the talking points and the process through which they were drafted—to Congress, "citing executive privilege."[421]

On March 19, 2013, Robert S. Litt, General Counsel, Office of the Director of National Intelligence, testified before HPSCI.[422] At the hearing, Litt provided the HPSCI Members two packages of documents: one was a small package that contained each draft version of the talking points, showing which changes had been made from

---

[416] Morell Testimony at 205–206.

[417] *See, e.g., HPSCI White Paper Talking Points for Use with the Media* at 63 (Sept. 14, 2012), https://assets.documentcloud.org/documents/701145/white-house-e-mails-on-benghazi-talking-points.pdf.

[418] Analytic Line Review, *supra* note 362.

[419] Lessons Learned, *supra* note 189.

[420] Morell Testimony at 208.

[421] *Id.*

[422] *Briefing—The Hon. Robert S. Litt (Benghazi Documents), Hearing Before the H. Permanent Select Comm. on Intelligence,* 113th Cong. (2013).

draft to draft; the other was a large package of roughly 100 pages that contained interagency emails regarding the drafting of the talking points. These documents were shared with the HPSCI Members, yet Litt claimed they were so sensitive that he took them back at the end of the briefing;[423] Members therefore would be unable to keep the documents or make any copies.

Two months later, on May 15, 2013, however, everything changed. The White House decided to release 100 pages of emails related to the talking points.[424] These were the same emails Litt had provided to HPSCI two months prior yet took back at the end of the hearing. In conjunction with the release, the White House asked Morell to brief the press on the evolution of the talking points. Just as he had when he accompanied Rice to the November 2012 meeting, Morell complied.[425]

Morell talked to the Committee about the White House's decision to release these emails:

> Q: And so the fact that you were forbidden from sharing an assessment with Congress over the possibility of executive privilege and then all of a sudden the documents were released publicly, did that seem to you to be a pretty large turnaround?
>
> A: So, you know, I don't remember, I simply don't remember why, you know, why the shift, right, why all of a sudden the administration decided to release these publicly. I don't remember being part of those discussions. I don't recall being part of those discussions. So I don't know why they decided all of a sudden to do it.
>
> Q: Do you think it might have been politically beneficial for them to all of a sudden release those documents?
>
> A: I think—I think—I'm speculating, now, okay, so speculating—I think that the criticism kept going up and up. The different theories about what was going on kept on expanding right, and the White House wanted to put that to rest by putting it all out there. That's my guess.
>
> Q: Did they put it all out there when they released those talking points?
>
> A: Not in my view.
>
> Q: Can you elaborate on that?
>
> A: Sure. So 2014, mid-2014, I open the newspaper and I see Ben Rhodes' talking points from the 15th of September, right, designed to prep Susan Rice for her Sunday shows. And I say to myself, I have not seen these things before. When I saw them in the media in mid-2014 it was the first time I ever saw them.[426]

---

[423] *Id.* at 4.

[424] Jake Tapper, *et al.*, *White House releases Benghazi e-mails*, CNN (May 16, 2013), http://www.cnn.com/2013/05/15/politics/benghazi-emails.

[425] MORELL, *supra* note 114, at 207.

[426] *Id.* at 208–09.

The decision by the White House to release the talking points pertaining to HPSCI and not the talking points drafted by Rhodes had one major effect: it kept the spotlight on Morell—who became front and center of this release by briefing the press at the request of the White House—the CIA, and their role in shaping the talking points. It also kept the spotlight away from others. Morell acknowledged this in his testimony:

> Q: And you said you feel that they should have been released with the package of the CIA talking points. What are the implications that they were not released with the talking points, the package, and they're coming out a year later? What does that mean?

> A: I don't know, right, I don't know, the counterfactual is hard to think through. I believe—I'm speculating now, okay—I believe there would have been less attention on CIA and more attention on the White House.[427]

Around the same time, Morell lobbied the White House to release video footage of the attack from the State Department compound in Benghazi. Morell, aware of the public debate over whether or not protests had occurred prior to attack, wanted the footage released to provide transparency to the American people so they could judge for themselves what had transpired and quell the political firestorm. After all, it was after a description of this video footage was shared with the CIA that CIA personnel began to definitively conclude no protest had occurred.[428]

In addition to Morell, James Clapper, Director, Office of the Director of National Intelligence, also wanted the surveillance tapes to be made public. The White House refused, however, and to this day, the tapes remain classified. Morell told the Committee:

> Q: So you had seen the videos of the TMF, you had seen NCTC analysis of the videos. Did you want those videos to be released as well?

> A: I did, I did.

> Q: And was there anybody who agreed with you that those videos should be declassified and released?

> A: Yes, the DNI agreed with me.

> Q: The DNI. When you say DNI, you're talking about DNI Clapper?

> A: Yes.

> Q: Were those videos released?

> A: No.

> Q: Why did you want those videos released?

> A: Because look, my view, not only strongly today because of all of this, but even at the time, my view is when

---

427 *Id.* at 217.
428 Email from [Tripoli **[redacted text]**] to [Near East Division] (Sept. 18, 2012, 1:14 PM) ("I know that we all agree as time has passed the pieces are starting to unravel particularly where there was protests earlier that day—I think we can officially say now that there were none.") (on file with CIA, REQUEST 1–002940 to REQUEST 1–002943).

there's—when there are questions about—when there are questions about what was done on a particular issue, particularly when there's questions of impropriety, the best thing to do is to get everything out, the best thing to do is to get all the information you can out. Let the American people see it all and let the American people decide.

You know, I thought the video—the NCTC analysis told the story of what actually happened that night and I thought the American people deserved to see it.

Q: And who prevented the video from being publicly released?

A: The White House—the White House never responded to the DNI and my repeated suggestions that it be released.

Q: So you were acting director of the CIA at the time?

A: Uh-huh.

Q: And Mr. Clapper was the director for national intelligence. And you two repeatedly pushed the White House to release this video?

A: Yes.

Q: And they did not.

A: Correct.

Q: And instead they released the package, so to speak, they released the package——

A: I don't remember the timing of our suggestion, right? But, yes, you're absolutely right.

Q: So they released the package and at the time they released the package they did not release [the Ben Rhodes talking points], which is——

A: The video.

Q: They did not release the video.

A: And they did not release [the Ben Rhodes talking points].[429]

### The Fallout

On April 17, 2014, the Rhodes talking points—which, in addition to the talking points provided to HPSCI and edited by Morell, were used by Rice to prepare for the Sunday talk shows—were released to Congress.[430] Later that month, the talking points became publicized for the first time.[431]

Around the time of the November 27, 2012 meeting between Rice and the three Senators, Lieberman said of Ambassador Rice:

---

[429] Morell Testimony at 210–11.

[430] Letter from Thomas B. Gibbons, Acting Ass't Sec'y of Legislative Affairs, U.S. Dep't of State, to Rep. Darrell Issa, Chairman, House Committee on Oversight and Gov. Reform, U.S. House of Representatives (May 20, 2013) (on file with the Committee).

[431] Press Release, Judicial Watch, Benghazi Documents Point to White House on Misleading Talking Points (Apr. 29, 2014), http://www.judicialwatch.org/press-room/press-releases/judicial-watch-benghazi-documents-point-white-house-misleading-talking-points.

I asked if she was briefed by the White House, the campaign, or the political operation, and she said she had seen no message points from the White House."[432]

As discussed above, Rice testified she only relied on the talking points provided to HPSCI when discussing Benghazi on the talk shows.[433] Rhodes, however, conceded the third bullet point in his talking points—"to show the U.S. would be resolute in bringing to justice people who harm Americans, and standing steadfast through these protests"—applied only to Libya.[434]

Morell said he first learned about Rhodes' talking points when he opened the newspaper. Morell, an intelligence officer for over three decades, also believed the talking points related to Benghazi. He told the Committee:

> Q: Okay. So let me take that first statement. You thought that these were related to Benghazi. I'm just reading through it here on the first page, I don't see Benghazi listed. Why do you think that they were related to Benghazi?
>
> A: Two reasons. One is Benghazi was what was on everyone's mind at the time. Benghazi had just happened, right, the previous Tuesday. This was the following Sunday, right, it was the kind of top-of-the-list issue. And two, the—there is a tick in here—let me find it—so the third tick under "goals," third tick under "goals" says: "To show that we will be resolute in bringing people to harm Americans to justice." That only happened in one place.
>
> Q: And that was in Benghazi?
>
> A: Yes.[435]

After learning of the existence of these talking points, Morell became bothered that Rhodes, a member of the National Security Council staff, had drafted what Morell viewed as a political document. Morell believes there should be a bright line between national security and politics, and he views the talking points drafted by Rhodes crossed that line. Morell testified:

> Q: Aside from the release of these talking points and the release of the package, is there anything in, at least under the goals and the top-lines, is there anything about this document that makes you uncomfortable as a CIA officer and career analyst?
>
> A: Yeah. So, as you know, I'm on the record on this, so the second goal, the second goal bothers me in two ways. The first way it bothers me is that it has a feeling of being political. It has a feeling of being political, right? Blame it on this, not on that, right? Just that concept of blame it on

[432] Ed O'Keefe, *Susan Rice, CIA director meet with GOP critics on Libya*, WASH. POST (Nov. 27, 2012), https://www.washingtonpost.com/blogs/2chambers/wp/2012/11/27/susan-rice-cia-director-meet-with-gop-critics-on-libya.

[433] Krishnadev Calamur, *Susan Rice Says Benghazi Claims Were Based On Information From Intelligence*, NPR (Nov. 21, 2012), http://www.npr.org/sections/thetwo-way/2012/11/21/165686269/susan-rice-says-benghazi-claims-were-based-on-information-from-intelligence.

[434] Rhodes Testimony at 78.

[435] Morell Testimony at 216–217.

this and blame it on that, not don't blame it on that, has a feeling of being political to me.

Q: Ben Rhodes worked at the White House?

A: Yes.

Q: So what's the problem if he writes something that——

A: Because Ben is on the National Security Council staff, right, and I believe, right, and there might be different views out there, but I believe, as a 33-year national security professional, that there should be a very, very sharp line between national security and politics. And I know that's not always the case, but that's what I believe, right? And I believe that that line was crossed here. That is a personal opinion, right?

The second thing, right, the second thing I don't like about that is the line, "not a broader failure of policy." The President himself is on the record as saying that he has deep regrets about Libya. We all have deep regrets about Libya. And I talked earlier about the regrets that I have about what the intelligence community should have written prior to the intervention. There are policymakers have regrets about what we did and didn't do in Libya, right, and the loss of stability there.

And so, you know, I don't think "and not a broader failure of policy" is correct as it relates to Benghazi, as it relates to Libya. You can have a debate about the rest of the region, but as it relates to Libya and Benghazi I don't think that's right.[436]

When asked about his central role in all of these events—the meeting with Rice at the White House's request, briefing the press at the White House's request after the release of the drafts of the HPSCI talking points, and being in the dark for nearly two years about the Rhodes talking points—Morell testified:

Q: So we talked earlier about the meeting you had with Senators McCain, Graham, Ayotte. We talked about how the—at Denis McDonough's request, perhaps the President's request, we talked about how you briefed media members when the package was released. You have been beaten up for a year and you briefed media members at the request of the White House, is what I believe you said. Did you feel in any way used by the White House when you discovered that these talking points also existed and you were completely kept in the dark until the public found out about them?

A: Look, I wish I would have known about them, okay, I wish I would have known about them.[437]

---

[436] *Id.* at 218–19.
[437] *Id.* at 222–23.

## THE FBI INVESTIGATION

Throughout the days and weeks after the attacks in Benghazi, administration officials used the pending FBI investigation as both a sword and a shield. When convenient, officials such as Rice and Carney made reference to the FBI.[438] When inconvenient, administration officials cited the ongoing FBI investigation as the reason they could not discuss certain matters.[439] On at least one occasion, an administration official cited the FBI investigation as evidence of a fact even though the FBI investigation had hardly begun.

It is worth nothing Ahmed Abu Khatallah was arrested in June 2014.[440] To date, he has still not been brought to trial. It was 23 months after his arrest that the Justice Department announced the Department would not seek the death penalty for Khatallah.[441] The Justice Department has, however, made certain legal filings wherein the government's theory of the case—hence its understanding of provable facts—is on public display.[442] The FBI investigation that administration officials claimed would definitively answer questions that emerged in the days and weeks after the attacks is still "ongoing"—two years after a single suspect was arrested and nearly four years after Ambassador Chris Stevens, Sean Smith, Tyrone Woods, and Glen Doherty were killed.

---

[438] *See, e.g., "Face the Nation" transcripts, September 16, 2012: Libyan Pres. Magariaf, Amb. Rice and Sen. McCain*, CBS NEWS (Sept. 16, 2012), http://www.cbsnews.com/news/face-the-nation-transcripts-september-16-2012-libyan-pres-magariaf-amb-rice-and-sen-mccain (". . . there is an investigation that the United States government will launch led by the FBI, that has begun and . . . they have already begun looking at all sorts of evidence of—of various sorts already available to them and to us."), and Press Briefing by Press Secretary Jay Carney, Office of the Press Secretary, The White House (Sept. 18, 2012), https://www.whitehouse.gov/the-press-office/2012/09/18/press-briefing-secretary-jay-carney-9182012 ("There is an ongoing investigation. The FBI is investigating. And that investigation will follow the facts wherever they lead.").

[439] *See, e.g.,* Nuland Sept. 17 Briefing, *supra* note 326.

[440] Karen DeYoung, *et al., U.S. captured Benghazi suspect in secret raid*, WASH. POST (June 17, 2014).

[441] Spencer Hsu, *U.S. will not seek death penalty for accused ringleader in Benghazi attacks*, WASH. POST (May 10, 2016).

[442] Gov't's Motion for Pretrial Detention at 5–9, U.S. v. Khatallah (E.D. Va July 1, 2014).

# PART III:

# Events Leading to the Benghazi Attacks

*"Probably failing to plan for the day after what I think was the right thing to do in intervening in Libya."* [1]

> The President, on what constituted the biggest mistake of his Presidency, April 10, 2016

*"When Qaddafi is himself removed, you should of course make a public statement before the cameras wherever you are . . . You must establish yourself in the historical record . . . The most important phrase is 'successful strategy.'"* [2]

> Sidney Blumenthal to the Secretary of State, August 22, 2011

*"We came, we saw, he died."* [3]

> The Secretary of State after the death of Muammar Qadhafi, October 20, 2011

*"The American people and the U.S. Congress will be understandably irritated if a revolution that the United States supported ends up spewing hatred or advocating violence against the United States."* [4]

> Jake Sullivan, August 29, 2011 Note for the Secretary, U.S. Interests in post-Qadhafi Libya

---

[1] *President Obama: Libya aftermath 'worst mistake' of presidency,* BBC NEWS (Apr. 11, 2016), http://www.bbc.com/news/world-us-canada-36013703.

[2] Email from Sidney Blumenthal ("Sid") to Hillary R. Clinton ("H") (Aug. 22, 2011, 11:25 AM) (on file with the Committee, SCB0051597).

[3] Corbett Daly, Clinton on Qaddafi: "We came, we saw, he died," CBS NEWS (Oct. 20, 2011), http://www.cbsnews.com/news/clinton-on-qaddafi-we-came-we-saw-he-died.

[4] *See* Email from Policy Planning staff, U.S. Dep't of State, to Jake Sullivan, Dir. of Policy Planning, U.S. Dep't of State (Aug. 29 2011, 5:01 PM) (on file with the Committee, SCB0060926–30) (attaching Note for the Secretary re: U.S. Interests in post-Qadhafi Libya).

## Introduction

John Christopher Stevens arrived in Benghazi, Libya on April 5, 2011, in the midst of a civil war. Stevens traveled to Benghazi from Malta by Greek cargo ship with $60,000 in currency and an eight-member Diplomatic Security protective detail. Also in the group was a junior reporting officer tasked with conducting political reporting, and two members of the Disaster Assistance Response Team from the United States Agency for International Development. Stevens' only instruction was to begin establishing contact with Libyan opposition forces seeking to overthrow the government of the Colonel Muammar Qadhafi. There was no military support for Stevens' arrival because of President Barack H. Obama's "no boots on the ground" policy, no protocol and no precedent to guide his activities, and no physical facility to house him and his team. Stevens' operation had an undefined diplomatic status and duration, and no authorized set of contacts to work with. He was asked to do a difficult job in a dangerous environment, and he courageously accepted the call.

Although the civil war ended in August 2011 with the fall of Tripoli, Libya was not officially liberated until October 23, 2011, after the death of Qadhafi.[5] Even then the security environment remained hazardous. In December 2011, the State Department's own threat rating system considered Libya a grave risk to American diplomats.[6] The situation deteriorated from there. In Benghazi alone, more than 60 major security incidents took place between January 1, 2012 and September 10, 2012. More than half of those security incidents occurred after April 6, 2012, the date of the first IED attack on the Benghazi Mission compound.[7]

As conditions worsened, the Benghazi Mission labored under an unusual, if not unprecedented, set of circumstances and conditions:

- From the beginning, senior Obama Administration officials were divided about what degree of commitment to make in Libya. A principal objective was to limit military engagement: the administration's "no boots on the ground" policy prevailed throughout the Benghazi Mission's existence in Libya. Apart from "no boots on the ground," U.S. policy remained indefinite and undefined throughout Stevens' tenure in Benghazi.

- After the Qadhafi regime fell, the administration sought to maintain a "light footprint" in the country, determined to avoid an extended state-building engagement.

- Because the Benghazi Mission existed in a state of diplomatic uncertainty—never having a clearly defined status—it was not required to meet security standards applicable to permanent U.S. embassies.

---

[5] Press Statement, Hillary R. Clinton, Sec'y of State, U.S. Dep't of State, Liberation of Libya (Oct. 23, 2011), http://www.state.gov/secretary/20092013clinton/rm/2011/10/175999.htm.

[6] See Email from Diplomatic Sec. Agent 24 to Diplomatic Sec. Agent 10 (Dec. 15, 2011, 9:03 AM) (on file with the Committee, C05388931) (discussing "US Mission Benghazi threat levels"); see also U.S. GOV'T ACCOUNTABILITY OFF., GAO–14–655, DIPLOMATIC SECURITY: OVERSEAS FACILITIES MAY FACE GREATER RISKS DUE TO GAPS IN SECURITY-RELATED ACTIVITIES, STANDARDS, AND POLICIES (2014), available at http://www.gao.gov/products.

[7] See Security Incidents in Benghazi, Libya from June 1, 2011 to Aug. 20, 2012 (on file with the Committee); see also Benghazi Spot Report, EAC and Significant Event Timeline (DS/IP/RD) (on file with the Committee, C05394332).

- Benghazi had no clear lines of authority to either Tripoli or Washington D.C. This delayed responses to Mission requests for physical security measures and personnel.

- Senior officials in Washington D.C. did not heed intelligence detailing the rise of extremists groups in Benghazi and eastern Libya prior to September 11, 2012.

In an April 10, 2016 interview, the President called "failing to prepare for the aftermath of the ousting of . . . Muammar Gaddafi . . . the worst mistake of his presidency."[8] Expressing regret over "failing to plan for the day after," the President called Libya a "mess."[9] This section describes the events, decisions, and non-decisions that led to the terrorist attacks which killed Chris Stevens, Sean Smith, Tyrone Woods and Glen Doherty.

## STEPS TOWARD U.S. INTERVENTION IN LIBYA

### February–March 2011: Early Debates and Decisions

The United States' intervention in Libya took root during the Arab Spring, a series of anti-government protests and revolutions in the Middle East and North Africa occurring in late 2010 and early 2011.[10] The protests, inspired by Tunisians, followed in Egypt and reached Yemen in late January of 2011.[11] Tunisian President Zine El Abidine Ben Ali was removed on January 14, 2011, following a month of protests.[12] In February 2011, Egyptian President Hosni Mubarak resigned.[13] Four days later, on February 15, 2011, Libyans staged their first demonstration in Benghazi.[14] It evolved into an armed conflict two days later, as loyalists of Qadhafi attempted to quell the protests.[15] A civil war then erupted. As Joan A. Polaschik, then Deputy Chief of Mission at the U.S. Embassy in Tripoli, described: "On Friday, in Tripoli, things started to get a little tense, sporadic gunfire. Then Saturday night, sustained gunfire, so we started having emergency action committee meetings that Sunday at the Embassy to talk about what our response should be."[16]

The President publicly addressed the conditions in Libya on February 23, 2011, stating: "Secretary Clinton and I just concluded a meeting that focused on the ongoing situation in Libya. Over the last few days, my national security team has been working around the clock to monitor the situation there and to coordinate with our

---

[8] *President Obama: Libya aftermath 'worst mistake' of presidency,* BBC NEWS (Apr. 11, 2016), http://www.bbc.com/news/world-us-canada-36013703.

[9] *Id.*

[10] Testimony of Benjamin I. Fishman, Director for North Africa and Jordan, National Sec. Staff, Tr. at 15–16 (Jan. 12, 2016) [hereinafter Fishman Testimony] (on file with the Committee).

[11] *Id.* at 14; *see generally, The Arab Spring: A Year of Revolution,* NPR (Dec. 18, 2011, 9:24 AM), http://www.npr.org/2011/12/17/143897126/the-arab-spring-a-year-of-revolution.

[12] *Id.*

[13] *Id.*

[14] *Id.*

[15] *See* Testimony of Joan A. Polaschik, U.S. Deputy Chief of Mission in Libya, U.S. Dep't of State, Tr. at 18 (Aug. 12, 2015) [hereinafter Polaschik Testimony] (on file with the Committee) ("Well, the uprising really started on February 17 in Benghazi. I believe it was a Thursday.").

[16] *Id.* at 18.

international partners about a way forward."[17] He called the violence "outrageous" and "unacceptable," asserted the protection of American citizens was his highest priority, and added: "I have also asked my administration to prepare the full range of options that we have to respond to this crisis."[18]

The U.S. suspended operations at the Embassy in Tripoli, Libya on February 25, 2011.[19] The suspension of operations and evacuation were important for reasons beyond the safety of the embassy personnel. Polaschik testified:

> I was very clear with the people on those policy planning discussions that I felt very strongly that the administration could not change its policy toward Qadhafi until we got all of the U.S. employees out safely because we did not have appropriate security at our Embassy in Tripoli. It met none of our State Department security standards.[20]

The same day, the President issued an Executive Order freezing the property in the United States of Qadhafi, his family members, and senior officials of the Libyan Government.[21]

On February 26, 2011, the international community responded with United Nations Security Council Resolution 1970, deploring "gross and systematic violations of human rights" and demanding an end to the violence.[22] The resolution also imposed an arms embargo and travel restrictions, froze the assets of Qadhafi and his inner circle, and referred the matter to the Prosecutor for the International Criminal Court.[23]

Secretary of State Hillary R. Clinton made calls to foreign leaders to garner support for the resolution.[24] She took an active role in mobilizing forces against the Qadhafi regime. Her staff described the efforts as "instrumental in securing the authorization, building the coalition, and tightening the noose around Qadhafi and his regime."[25]

---

[17] Jesse Lee, *President Obama Speaks on the Turmoil in Libya: "This Violence Must Stop,"* WHITE HOUSE BLOG (Feb. 23, 2011), https://www.whitehouse.gov/blog/2011/02/23/president-obama-speaks-turmoil-libya-violence-must-stop (providing full transcript of the President's remarks).

[18] *Id.*

[19] Patrick F. Kennedy, Under Sec'y of State for Mgmt., U.S. Dep't of State & Janet A. Sanderson, Deputy Ass't Sec'y of State, Bureau of Near Eastern Affairs, U.S. Dep't of State, *The Suspension of United States Embassy Operations in Libya,* U.S. DEP'T OF STATE (Feb. 25, 2011), http://www.state.gov/m/rls/remarks/2011/157173.htm. Jake Sullivan indicated in an August 21, 2011 email to Cheryl Mills and Victoria Nuland "February 26—HRC directs efforts to evacuate all U.S. embassy personnel from Tripoli and orders the closing of the embassy," but this date appears to be contradicted by the Department's public statement the previous day. *See* Email from Jacob J. Sullivan, Dir. of Policy Planning, U.S. Dep't of State, to Cheryl D. Mills, Chief of Staff and Counselor to the U.S. Sec'y of State, U.S. Dep't of State, and Victoria J. Nuland, Spokesperson, U.S. Dep't of State (Aug. 21, 2011, 07:39 PM) [hereinafter Tick Tock on Libya Email] (on file with the Committee, SCB0045101).

[20] Polaschik Testimony at 19. The U.S. Government did not sever diplomatic ties with Libya. Patrick F. Kennedy, Under Sec'y of State for Mgmt., U.S. Dep't of State & Janet A. Sanderson, Deputy Ass't Sec'y of State, Bureau of Near Eastern Affairs, *The Suspension of United States Embassy Operations in Libya,* DEP'T OF STATE (Feb. 25, 2011), http://www.state.gov/m/rls/remarks/2011/157173.htm. Rather, Ambassador Cretz and his staff worked from Washington, D.C. on Libyan matters. Polaschik Testimony at 20–21.

[21] Exec. Order No. 13566, 76 Fed. Reg. 11315 (Feb. 25, 2011).

[22] S.C. Res. 1970, ¶ 1 (Feb. 26, 2011), http://www.un.org/en/ga/search/view_doc.asp?symbol=S/RES/1970 (2011).

[23] *Id.*

[24] Tick Tock on Libya Email, *supra* note 19.

[25] *Id.*

## Unofficial Commentary and Advice

During this period, the Secretary received extensive and regular communications from Sidney S. Blumenthal. Blumenthal frequently offered commentary about developments in Libya (as well as more general commentary about other matters)—passing on self-styled "intelligence reports" prepared by Tyler S. Drumheller, a former official at the Central Intelligence Agency[26]—and recommending various courses of U.S. action. Although Blumenthal had been rejected by the White House for employment at the Department of State, and admittedly had no knowledge about Libya,[27] Secretary Clinton responded to his emails and in some cases forwarded them to her top policy aides and career foreign service officers in the Department for their reaction and comment. The Secretary described Blumenthal's emails as "unsolicited."[28]

On February 21, 2011, two days prior to the President's first public remarks on the matter,[29] Blumenthal suggested the U.S. "might consider advancing [a no-fly zone] tomorrow."[30] The Secretary forwarded the email to her Deputy Chief of Staff and Director of Policy Planning, Jacob J. Sullivan, and asked: "What do you think of this idea?"[31] Sullivan replied: "[H]onestly, we actually don't know what is happening from the air right now. As we gain more facts, we can consider."[32] In response, the Secretary reflected on what Admiral Michael G. Mullen, Chairman of the Joint Chiefs of Staff, noted publicly more than a week later, asking Sullivan: "I've heard contradictory reports as to whether or not there are planes flying and firing on crowds. What is the evidence that they are?"[33] The Secretary responded to Blumenthal: "We are looking at that for Security Council, which remains reluctant to 'interfere' in the internal affairs of a country. Stay tuned!"[34] When the U.N. resolution was ultimately introduced two weeks later, the U.S. strongly advocated for passage of the no-fly zone.[35]

On February 25, 2011, Blumenthal suggested other means of pressuring the Libyan leadership:

---

[26] Testimony of Sidney S. Blumenthal, Tr. at 67–68 (June 16, 2015) [hereinafter Blumenthal Testimony] (on file with the Committee).

[27] Id. at 99.

[28] Daniel Drezner, "The Unbearable Lightness of Hillary Clinton's Management Style," the Washington Post (May 20, 2015), www.washingtonpost.com/posteverything/wp/2015/05/20/the-unbearable-lightness -of-hillary-clintons-management-style.

[29] Jesse Lee, President Obama Speaks on the Turmoil in Libya: "This Violence Must Stop," WHITE HOUSE BLOG (Feb. 23, 2011), https://www.whitehouse.gov/blog/2011/02/23/president-obama-speaks-turmoil-libya-violence-must-stop (providing full transcript of the President's remarks).

[30] Email from Sidney S. Blumenthal ("sbwhoeop") to Hillary R. Clinton ("H"), Sec'y of State, U.S. Dep't of State (Feb. 21, 2011, 10:32 PM) (on file with the Committee, SCB0078044).

[31] Email from Hillary R. Clinton ("H"), Sec'y of State, U.S. Dep't of State, to Jacob J. Sullivan, Dir. of Policy Planning, U.S. Dep't of State (Feb. 21, 2011, 10:42 PM) (on file with the Committee, SCB0078044).

[32] Email from Jacob J. Sullivan, Dir. of Policy Planning, U.S. Dep't of State, to Hillary R. Clinton ("H"), Sec'y, U.S. Dep't of State (Feb. 22, 2011, 4:59 AM) (on file with the Committee, SCB0078044).

[33] Email from Hillary R. Clinton ("H"), Sec'y of State, U.S. Dep't of State, to Jacob J. Sullivan, Dir. of Policy Planning, U.S. Dep't of State (Feb. 22, 2011, 6:34 AM) (on file with the Committee, SCB0078044).

[34] Email from Hillary R. Clinton ("H"), Sec'y of State, U.S. Dep't of State, to Sidney Blumenthal (Feb. 22, 2011, 6:09 AM) (on file with the Committee, SCB0078042).

[35] See Email from Jacob J. Sullivan, Dir. of Policy Planning, U.S. Dep't of State, to "jake.sullivan[REDACTED]" (Mar. 16, 2011, 9:29AM) (on file with the Committee, SCB0075861) ("We are going to be actively engaged in New York today in discussions about the best course of action for the international community to take, including through the UN Security Council.").

Depending on the state of play within the U.N. Security Council, it might be useful to think about generating a statement from the UNSC that any officer or government official in the chain of command in Libya who is involved in deploying or using WMD would be subject to war crimes and crimes against humanity prosecution.[36]

The Secretary forwarded the suggestion to Sullivan, asking: "What about including this in UNSCR?"[37] The following day, Blumenthal sent the Secretary another unofficial "intelligence" report that began with a note: "This report is in part a response to your questions. There will be further information coming in the next day."[38] The Secretary forwarded the information to Sullivan with the request not to "share until we can talk."[39]

In a later email, Blumenthal suggested: "Someone should contact Mahmod Jipreel [Mahmoud Jibril]. He is balanced, level-headed and understands the situation well."[40] The Secretary forwarded the note to Sullivan, indicating she thought "we" were reaching out to the individuals Blumenthal had suggested.[41] Even though Jibril was on the list Blumenthal sent earlier, Sullivan responded: "I don't know about this Jipreel fellow."[42] It was the "hastily scheduled" and "behind closed doors" meeting between the Secretary and Jibril in Paris just one week later[43] that helped prompt the Secretary to become a leading advocate for Libyan intervention.[44]

## "Libya Options"

On March 8, 2011, Sullivan sent an email titled "Libya Options" to senior State Department officials.[45] In the email, he described the Department's "preferred end-state in Libya, at the most basic level."[46] The email spelled out five "successively more intrusive" strategic frameworks outlining various options against Qadhafi:

1. Provide material support to the Libyan opposition but take no direct offensive action;

[36] Email from Sidney S. Blumenthal ("sbwhoeop") to Hillary R. Clinton ("H"), Sec'y of State, U.S. Dep't of State (Feb. 25, 2011, 7:16 PM) (on file with the Committee, SCB0078066).

[37] Email from Hillary R. Clinton ("H"), Sec'y of State, U.S. Dep't of State, to Jacob J. Sullivan, Dir. of Policy Planning, U.S. Dep't of State (Feb. 26, 2011, 11:34 AM) (on file with the Committee, SCB0078066).

[38] Email from Sidney S. Blumenthal ("sbwhoeop") to Hillary R. Clinton ("H"), Sec'y of State, U.S. Dep't of State (Feb. 26, 2011, 10:58) (on file with the Committee, SCB0078104).

[39] Email from Hillary R. Clinton ("H"), Sec'y of State, U.S. Dep't of State, to Jacob J. Sullivan, Dir. of Policy Planning (Mar. 2, 2011, 7:18 AM) (on file with the Committee, SCB0078121).

[40] Email from Sidney S. Blumenthal ("sbwhoeop") to Hillary R. Clinton ("H"), Sec'y of State, U.S. Dep't of State (Mar. 7, 2011, 10:29 PM) (on file with the Committee, SCB0078150–0078153).

[41] Email from Hillary R. Clinton ("H"), Sec'y of State, U.S. Dep't of State, to Jacob J. Sullivan, Dir. of Policy Planning, U.S. Dep't of State (Mar. 7, 2011, 7:17 AM) (on file with the Committee, SCB0087150–0078153).

[42] Email from Jacob J. Sullivan, Dir. of Policy Planning, U.S. Dep't of State, to Hillary R. Clinton ("H"), Sec'y, U.S. Dep't of State (Mar. 7, 2011, 7:22 AM) (on file with the Committee, SCB0077210).

[43] Steven Lee Myers, *Clinton Meets in Paris With Libyan Rebel Leader*, N.Y. TIMES (Mar. 14, 2011), http://www.nytimes.com/2011/03/15/world/africa/15clinton.html.

[44] Joby Warrick, *Hillary's war: How conviction replaced skepticism in Libya intervention*, WASH. POST (Oct. 30, 2011), https://www.washingtonpost.com/world/national-security/hillarys-war-how-conviction-replaced-skepticism-in-libya-intervention/2011/10/28/gIQAhGS7WM_story.html.

[45] Email from Jacob J. Sullivan, Dir. of Policy Planning, U.S. Dep't of State, to James B. Steinberg, Deputy Sec'y of State, U.S. Dep't of State, et al. (Mar. 8, 2011, 8:13 PM) [hereinafter Libya Options Email](on file with the Committee, C05886430).

[46] *Id.*

2. Provide material support to the Libyan opposition and take only that direct action which is nonlethal and designed to shape the theater rather than take the fight to Qadhafi;

3. All options consistent with broad regional support and a clear legal basis;

4. Offensive aerial options but no ground troops; and

5. Whatever necessary to remove Qadhafi.[47]

In addition, Sullivan identified a number of immediate goals to be accomplished through intervention, something he noted was sent over to the National Security Staff. The immediate goal listed first was "to avoid a failed state, particularly one in which al-Qaeda and other extremists might take safe haven."[48] Another immediate goal was "[w]e seek the prevention of an exodus of Libyans."[49]

The State Department and other top officials expressed concern about the options, especially establishing a no-fly zone without military intervention.[50] For example, the Secretary of Defense, Robert M. Gates, the National Security Advisor, Thomas E. Donilon, and others "opposed military action, contending the United States had no clear national interests at stake and that operations could last far longer and cost more lives than anyone anticipated."[51] A senior State Department official warned he did not "think that we've ever established a NFZ [no fly zone] anywhere where we didn't ultimately have to go in militarily and stay for a long time (Iraq, Bosnia, implicitly Afghanistan, Kosovo)."[52] The official suggested a better option would be to stand by, "not get pulled into more Middle East wars," and gain a "better sense of what post use-of-force end state looks like."[53]

The President convened a meeting with his National Security Council to discuss the situation. Ultimately, he sided with the Secretary of State, who favored some level of intervention.[54]

Senior officials still cited complications. State Department policymakers did not see the question as simply one of how to "pressure

---

[47] *Id.* A sixth option presented "focusing not on actions against Qadhafi but on a negotiated solution" was to "Leverage a stalemate into some kind of negotiated solution, or at least a process." *Id.*

[48] *Id.*

[49] *Id.*

[50] *See id.* (sent from Philip H. Gordon on Mar. 9, 2011, 9:37 AM) (Philip Gordon stating "would also point out I don't think we've ever established a NFZ anywhere where we didn't go have to go in militarily and stay for a long time (Iraq, Bosnia, implicitly Afghanistan, Kosovo).").

[51] Kevin Sullivan, *A Tough Call on Libya That Still Haunts*, WASH. POST (Feb. 3, 2016), http://www.washingtonpost.com/sf/national/2016/02/03/a-tough-call-on-libya-that-still-haunts.

[52] Libya Options Emails, *supra* note 45 (Sent from Philip H. Gordon on Mar. 9, 2011, 9:37 AM) (Philip Gordon stating "would also point out I don't think we've ever established a NFZ anywhere where we didn't go have to go in militarily and stay for a long time (Iraq, Bosnia, implicitly Afghanistan, Kosovo).").

[53] *Id.*

[54] *See* Email from Jacob J. Sullivan, Dir. of Policy Planning, U.S. Dep't of State, to "jake.sullivan[REDACTED]" (Mar. 16, 2011, 9:29AM) (on file with the Committee, SCB0075861) ("Last night, the President led a meeting with his national security team on the situation in Libya and the way forward."); *see also* Kevin Sullivan, *A Tough Call on Libya That Still Haunts*, WASH. POST (Feb. 3, 2016), http://www.washingtonpost.com/sf/national/2016/02/03/a-tough-call-on-libya-that-still-haunts.

and isolate Qadhafi."[55] Philip H. Gordon, Assistant Secretary of State for European and Eurasian Affairs, framed the situation as follows:

> As I noted, it seems to me fundamental [sic] initial decision for us is which is greater strategic priority: a) avoiding getting pulled into Libyan conflict and owning it; or b) bringing about quick end of Qaddafy regime. So far we have rightly sought to achieve both of these objectives at the same time but with each passing day, as regime gets upper hand, it is forcing us to choose between them. As Jim [Deputy Secretary of State James B. Steinberg] pointed out it is always possible that developments on the ground force you later on to abandon such a first principle (as in Kosovo when two months of ineffective air strikes led us to reconsider the determination not to use ground forces) but knowing the objective in advance would help guide the operational decisions in the meantime. If it's a) we need to be ultra-cautious about steps designed to make it look like we are doing something but will not prove decisive (NFZ); and if it's b) we need to understand the risks and costs of establishing that as a redline.[56]

Sullivan concurred, saying: "[W]e have not already embraced objective (b)" and further responded: "I agree with you about the fundamental initial decision, although I don't think it's as simple as (a) or (b). It will inevitably be a calibration between the two. I agree with Jim that we can get drawn in *some* but not *all the way*, as long as we have a strong theory of the case to rest on."[57]

## Implementing U.S. Policy

A week later, on March 17, 2011, the United Nations Security Council adopted Security Council Resolution 1973, demanding an immediate ceasefire and authorizing member states to "take all necessary measures . . . to protect civilians and civilian populated areas under threat of attack," specifically including a no fly zone.[58] On March 18, 2011, the President announced: "If Qaddafi does not comply with the resolution, the international community will impose consequences, and the resolution will be enforced through military action."[59] He emphasized: "I also want to be clear about what we will not be doing. The United States is not going to deploy ground troops into Libya. And we are not going to use force to go beyond a well-defined goal—specifically, the protection of civilians in Libya."[60] The President added: "Our focus has been clear: pro-

---

[55] Email from Special Ass't to Sec'y of State, U.S. Dep't of State, to Jacob J. Sullivan, Dir. of Policy Planning, U.S. Dep't of State (Mar. 28, 2011, 8:13 PM) [hereinafter Libya Q & A for S London Trip 32811] (on file with the Committee, SCB0075863–0075871).

[56] Libya Options Emails, *supra* note 45 (Sent from Philip H. Gordon on Mar. 9, 2011, 9:37 AM).

[57] *Id.* (Sent from Jacob J. Sullivan on Mar. 9, 2011, 10:33 AM) (emphasis in original).

[58] S.C. Res. 1973, ¶ 4 (Mar. 17, 2011), http://www.un.org/press/en/2011/sc10200.doc.htm#Resolution.

[59] Press Release, The White House Office of the Press Secretary, The White House, Remarks by the President on the Situation in Libya (Mar. 18, 2011), https://www.whitehouse.gov/the-press-office/2011/03/18/remarks-president-situation-libya.

[60] *Id.*

tecting innocent civilians within Libya, and holding the Qadhafi regime accountable." [61]

To implement this policy, the President announced he had "directed Secretary Gates and our military to coordinate their planning, and tomorrow Secretary Clinton will travel to Paris for a meeting with our European allies and Arab partners about the enforcement of Resolution 1973." [62] The next day, March 19, 2011, "U.S. military forces commenced operations to assist an international effort authorized by the United Nations (U.N.) Security Council . . . to prevent a humanitarian catastrophe and address the threat posed to international peace and security by the crisis in Libya." [63]

Two days later, on March 21, 2011, the President formally notified the Speaker of the House of Representatives and the President Pro Tempore of the Senate of these operations. [64] In his letter, the President stated the nature and purpose of these operations as follows:

> As part of the multilateral response authorized under U.N. Security Council resolution 1973, U.S. military forces, under the command of Commander, U.S. Africa Command, began a series of strikes against air defense systems and military airfields for the purposes of preparing a no-fly zone. These strikes will be limited in their nature, duration and scope. Their purpose is to support an international coalition as it takes all necessary measures to enforce the terms of U.N. Security Council Resolution 1973. These limited U.S. actions will set the stage for further action by other coalition partners.
>
> United Nations Security Council Resolution 1973 authorized Member States, under Chapter VII of the U.N. Charter, to take all necessary measures to protect civilians and civilian populated areas under threat of attack in Libya, including the establishment and enforcement of a "no-fly zone" in the airspace of Libya. United States military efforts are discrete and focused on employing unique U.S. military capabilities to set the conditions for our European allies and Arab partners to carry out the measures authorized by the U.N. Security Council Resolution. . . .

---

[61] *Id.* President Obama further detailed what specific steps he believed Qadhafi needed to meet to comply with the resolution:

> The resolution that passed lays out very clear conditions that must be met. The United States, the United Kingdom, France, and Arab states agree that a cease-fire must be implemented immediately. That means all attacks against civilians must stop. Qaddafi must stop his troops from advancing on Benghazi, pull them back from Ajdabiya, Misrata, and Zawiya, and establish water, electricity and gas supplies to all areas. Humanitarian assistance must be allowed to reach the people of Libya. Let me be clear, these terms are not negotiable.

[62] *Id.* Secretary Clinton's staff later noted that, surrounding these events, Secretary Clinton "participates in a series of high-level video and teleconferences. . . . She is a leading voice for strong UNSC action and a NATO civilian protection mission." Tick Tock on Libya Email, *supra* note 19.

[63] Letter from the President to the Speaker of the House of Representatives and the President Pro Tempore of the Senate Regarding the Commencement of Operations in Libya (Mar. 21, 2011), https://www.whitehouse.gov/the-press-office/2011/03/21/letter-president-regarding-commencement-operations-libya.

[64] *Id.*

The United States has not deployed ground forces into Libya. United States forces are conducting a limited and well-defined mission in support of international efforts to protect civilians and prevent a humanitarian disaster. Accordingly, U.S. forces have targeted the Qadhafi regime's air defense systems, command and control structures, and other capabilities of Qadhafi's armed forces used to attack civilians and civilian populated areas. We will seek a rapid, but responsible, transition of operations to coalition, regional, or international organizations that are postured to continue activities as may be necessary to realize the objectives of U.N. Security Council Resolutions 1970 and 1973.[65]

While the President described the goal of the intervention in Libya as "well-defined" in his March 18, 2011 public remarks, the formal notification of the ensuing military operation to Congress left uncertainty and ambiguity in the eyes of some U.S. decisionmakers. Speaker John A. Boehner responded to the President by letter two days later on March 23, 2011, writing:

It is my hope that you will provide the American people and Congress a clear and robust assessment of the scope, objective, and purpose of our mission in Libya and how it will be achieved. Here are some of the questions I believe must be answered:

A United Nations Security Council resolution does not substitute for a U.S. political and military strategy. You have stated that Libyan leader Muammar Qadhafi must go, consistent with U.S. policy goals. But the U.N. resolution the U.S. helped develop and signed onto makes clear that regime change is not part of this mission. In light of this contradiction, is it an acceptable outcome for Qadhafi to remain in power after the military effort concludes in Libya? If not, how will he be removed from power? Why would the U.S. commit American resources to enforcing a U.N. resolution that is inconsistent with our stated policy goals and national interests? . . .

You have said that the support of the international community was critical to your decision to strike Libya. But, like many Americans, it appears many of our coalition partners are themselves unclear on the policy goals of this mission. If the coalition dissolves or partners continue to disengage, will the American military take on an increased role? Will we disengage?

Since the stated U.S. policy goal is removing Qadhafi from power, do you have an engagement strategy for the opposition forces? If the strife in Libya becomes a protracted conflict, what are your Administration's objectives for engaging with opposition forces, and what standards must a new regime meet to be recognized by our government? . . .

---

[65] *Id.*

Because of the conflicting messages from the Administration and our coalition partners, there is a lack of clarity over the objectives of this mission, what our national security interests are, and how it fits into our overarching policy for the Middle East. The American people deserve answers to these questions. And all of these concerns point to a fundamental question: what is your benchmark for success in Libya? [66]

## Selecting Chris Stevens

Notwithstanding the State Department's decision to suspend operations at its Embassy in Tripoli and its efforts underway through the United Nations to impose a no fly zone,[67] discussions were immediately under way between the White House and the Secretary and her advisors to return to Libya—specifically to Benghazi.[68] These discussions included sending a "diplomatic representative" to serve as a liaison with the Transitional National Council [TNC], an opposition group headquartered in Benghazi hoping to emerge as the new Libyan government.[69] Jeffrey D. Feltman, Assistant Secretary for Near Eastern Affairs, State Department, told the Committee "the TNC had asked in the meetings with Hillary Clinton for representation to be able to work directly on a continuing basis with the U.S. Government, which is why a decision was made to send a representative to Benghazi." [70]

The Secretary selected J. Christopher Stevens, a widely and highly respected career Foreign Service officer, to serve as the representative to the TNC.[71] Stevens previously served as Deputy

---

[66] Letter from John A. Boehner, Speaker of the House of Representatives, to Barack H. Obama, U.S. President (Mar. 23, 2011),
http://www.speaker.gov/UploadedFiles/POTUSLetter_032311.pdf. (also asking three specific questions relating to the military operation and its cost).

[67] Patrick F. Kennedy, Under Sec'y of State for Mgmt., U.S. Dep't of State & Janet A. Sanderson, Deputy Ass't Sec'y of State, Bureau of Near Eastern Affairs, U.S. Dep't of State, The Suspension of United States Embassy Operations in Libya, DEP'T OF STATE (Feb. 25, 2011), http://www.state.gov/m/rls/remarks/2011/157173.htm. Jake Sullivan indicated in an August 21, 2011 email to Cheryl Mills and Victoria Nuland "February 26—HRC directs efforts to evacuate all U.S. embassy personnel from Tripoli and orders the closing of the embassy." This date appears to be contradicted by the Department's public statement the previous day. See Email from Jake Sullivan, Dir. Policy Planning, U.S. Dep't of State to Cheryl D. Mills, Chief of Staff to U.S. Sec'y of State, U.S. Dep't of State and Victoria Nuland, Spokesperson, U.S. State Dep't (Aug. 21, 2011, 07:39 PM) (on file with the Committee, SCB0051146). See Email from Phillip H. Gordon to James B. Steinberg, et al. (Mar. 23, 2011, 6:55 PM) (on file with the Committee, SCB0045016) ("We are putting together S conference call with Juppe, Davutoglu and Hague tomorrow. Here is the outcome I think the call should seek to meet everybody's redlines.

**[Redacted text.**

[68] See Email from Donald Steinberg, U.S. Agency on Int'l Development, to Patrick F. Kennedy, Under Sec'y of State for Mgmt., U.S. Dep't of State (Mar. 30, 2011, 10:12 AM) (on file with the Committee, SCB0095926) ("As you know, we're under instructions from NSS and State to get our DART staff into Benghazi so we can begin our humanitarian assessments of needs and infrastructure.").

[69] See Email from Jacob J. Sullivan, Dir. of Policy Planning, U.S. Dep't of State, to Hillary R. Clinton ("H"), Sec'y of State, U.S. Dep't of State (Mar. 13, 2011, 10:55 AM) (on file with the Committee, SCB0045011) ("They urged us to find some kind of language that would suggest moving in that direction, and I noted our decisions to suspend the operations of the Libyan Embassy, have S meet with Mahmoud Jabril of the Council and send a diplomatic representative to Benghazi.").

[70] Testimony of Jeffrey D. Feltman, Ass't Sec'y of State, Bureau of Near Eastern Affairs, U.S. Dep't of State, Tr. at 24–25 (Dec. 8, 2015) [hereinafter Feltman Testimony] (on file with the Committee).

[71] See Benghazi: The Attacks and the Lessons Learned Before the S. Comm. on the Foreign Relations, 113th Cong. 9 (2013) (statement of the Hon. Hillary R. Clinton, Sec'y of State); Terrorist

Continued

Chief of Mission, the Embassy's number two post, in Tripoli from 2007 through 2009.[72] The Secretary told the Committee: "[w]hen the revolution broke out in Libya, we named Chris as our envoy to the opposition."[73] "I was the one who asked Chris to go to Libya as our envoy."[74] The Secretary told the Committee that Stevens "was one of our Nation's most accomplished diplomats."[75] Stevens had been a member of the U.S. Foreign Service since 1991. He had previously served overseas as Deputy Principal Officer and Section Chief in Jerusalem; Political Officer in Damascus; Consular/Political Officer in Cairo; and Consular/Economic Officer in Riyadh. In Washington he had served as Director of the Office of Multilateral Nuclear and Security Affairs; a Pearson Fellow with the Senate Foreign Relations Committee and Senator Richard G. Lugar; Special Assistant to the Under Secretary for Political Affairs at the State Department; and Iran desk officer and staff assistant in the Bureau of Near Eastern Affairs.[76]

While attending the March 14, 2011 G8 foreign ministers meeting in Paris to discuss the Libyan crisis,[77] the Secretary arranged to have a separate meeting with Jibril, the leader of the Transitional National Council.[78] She asked that Stevens be rerouted to join her and Ambassador Gene A. Cretz, the U.S. Ambassador to Libya, for the meeting with Jibril.[79] As a result of the meeting with Jibril, the Secretary was convinced the United States should support the TNC in its efforts to become the new Libyan government.[80]

The decision to send a representative to the TNC was seen as both practical and symbolic. Ambassador Cretz explained the rationale for having a presence in Benghazi, telling the Committee "the center of the revolution was in Benghazi. It was the place that the opposition . . . had centered around as its, in effect 'capital.'"[81] He testified several other coalition partners established envoys in Benghazi and "so it was only natural" the U.S. have a presence there as well since the United States had a stake in the outcome of the Libyan revolution.[82]

---

*Attack in Benghazi: The Secretary of State's View Before the H. Comm. on the Foreign Affairs,* 113th Cong. 7–8 (2013) (statement of the Hon. Hillary R. Clinton, Sec'y of State).

[72] *J. Christopher Stevens Bio,* ECON. POLICY J. (Sept. 12, 2012), http://www.economicpolicyjournal.com/2012/09/j-christopher-stephens-bio.html (last visited June 7, 2016).

[73] Testimony of Hillary R. Clinton, Sec'y of State, U.S. Dep't of State, Tr. at 20 (Oct. 22, 2015) [hereinafter Clinton Testimony] (on file with the Committee).

[74] *Id.* 21.

[75] *Id.* 20.

[76] *J. Christopher Stevens Bio,* ECON. POLICY J. (Sept. 12, 2012), http://www.economicpolicyjournal.com/2012/09/j-christopher-stephens-bio.html (last visited June 7, 2016).

[77] The G8 is comprised of eight of the world's major industrialized countries.

[78] *See* Email from Jeffrey D. Feltman, Ass't Sec'y of State, Bureau of Near Eastern Affairs, U.S. Dep't of State, to J. Christopher Stevens, U.S. Rep. to Transitional National Council (Mar. 11, 2011, 9:20 PM) (on file with the Committee, SCB0076601) (discussing Sec'y Clinton's meeting with Mr. Jibril in Paris).

[79] *Id.; see also* Email from Jeffrey D. Feltman, Ass't Sec'y of State, Bureau of Near Eastern Affairs, U.S. Dep't of State, to Huma Abedin, Deputy Chief of Staff to U.S. Sec'y of State, U.S. Dep't of State (Mar. 13, 2011, 10:02) (on file with the Committee, SCB0076612) (communicating that Feltman had been asked to redirect Ambassador Stevens to Paris).

[80] *See* Email from Jacob Sullivan, Dir. of Policy Planning, U.S. Dep't of State, to himself on a personal email account (Mar. 16, 2011, 9:29 AM) (on file with the Committee, SCB0075861).

[81] Testimony of Gene A. Cretz, U.S. Ambassador to Libya, Tr. at 32 (Jul. 31, 2015) [hereinafter Cretz Testimony] (on file with the Committee).

[82] *Id.* at 32–33.

# Delay

The administration then made plans to send Stevens to Benghazi. Following the Secretary's March 14, 2011 meeting in Paris with Jibril, Stevens did not return to the United States but remained in Europe to plan his entry into Libya.[83] He traveled to Stuttgart, Germany to meet with General Carter F. Ham, commander of the United States Africa Command [AFRICOM], to discuss the trip into Libya, including any potential rescue operations.[84] Stevens discussed travelling to Benghazi on a "helicopter to a coalition naval vessel that can go close to shore," and then "zodiac transport from ship to shore" for "day trips only, returning to the naval vessel to RON [rest overnight]."[85]

In addition to Stevens' activities, the Secretary and her advisors were coordinating with United States Agency for International Development's [USAID] Disaster Assistance Response Team to travel into Benghazi to assess firsthand the extent of the humanitarian crisis.[86] On March 15, 2011, however, USAID "pulled the plug" because of security concerns.[87] That same day, Stevens' mission to Benghazi expanded:

> The latest . . . is now that 12–13 people are going into Libya near Benghazi. It's John C. Stevens (lead), a JO (no name) who is fluent in Arabic, 10 DS agents (protective detail) and they are working on getting a Management Officer to go to do the admin/accounting work. There are at least 2 DOD military elements going along (SOC Forward types i.e. Special Forces). . . . Given how this has grown from our earlier discussions, I think $60,000 is needed rather than the $25,000 we initially thought. They are talking about this trip being up to 30 days.[88]

While Stevens was still in Europe coordinating his entry, the National Security Council ordered him to deploy "as soon as possible."[89] For the next week, the State Department and AFRICOM

---

[83] Email from Jeffrey D. Feltman, Ass't Sec'y of State, Bureau of Near Eastern Affairs, U.S. Dep't of State, to J. Christopher StevensJ. Christopher Stevens, U.S. Rep. to Transitional National Council (Mar. 11, 2011, 9:20 PM) (on file with the Committee, SCB0076601) ("I know you have your travel accommodations set for Rome. But S staff would like you to join the Secretary and Gene Cretz for a mtg in Paris with Mahmoud Jabril."). Testimony of Diplomatic Sec. Agent, Diplomatic Sec. Serv., U.S. Dep't of State, Tr. at 13 (February 10, 2015)[hereinafter Diplomatic Sec. Agent 6 Testimony] (on file with the Committee) ("[W]hen I left Washington, I went to Rome. And in Rome, I was met by the Envoy, Chris Stevens.").

[84] Email from Patrick F. Kennedy, Under Sec'y of State for Mgmt., U.S. Dep't of State to Joan A. Polaschik, Deputy Chief of Mission in Libya, U.S. Dep't of State, et al. (Mar. 24, 2011, 9:55 AM) (on file with the Committee, SCB0095893–98) (discussing Stevens' plan).

[85] Email from Joan A. Polaschik, Deputy Chief of Mission in Libya, U.S. Dep't of State, to Lee Lohman, Ex. Dir., Bureau of Near Eastern Affairs, U.S. Dep't of State, and Post Mgmt. Officer, Bureau of Near Eastern Affairs, U.S. Dep't of State (Mar. 23, 2011, 5:14 PM) (on file with the Committee, SCB0091885).

[86] See Email from Jacob J. Sullivan, Dir. of Policy Planning, U.S. Dep't of State, to William J. Burns, Deputy Sec'y of State, U.S. Dep't of State (Mar. 6, 2011, 3:48 PM) (on file with the Committee, SCB0095837–0095838) (discussing coordination with USAID and the situation in region).

[87] See Email from Patrick F. Kennedy, Under Sec'y of State for Mgmt., U.S. Dep't of State, to Eric J. Boswell, Ass't Sec'y of State, Bureau of Diplomatic Sec., U.S. Dep't of State, et al. (Mar. 15, 2011, 1:59 PM) (on file with the Committee, SCB0095877–0095879).

[88] See Email from Patrick F. Kennedy, Under Sec'y of State for Mgmt., U.S. Dep't of State (Mar. 15, 2011, 8:02 PM) (on file with the Committee, SCB0098178–0098179).

[89] See Email from Joan A. Polaschik, Deputy Chief of Mission in Libya, U.S. Dep't of State, to Lee Lohman, Ex. Dir. Bureau of Near Eastern Affairs, U.S. Dep't of State, and Post Mgmt.

Continued

engaged in extensive planning to enter Benghazi using the military to augment the State Department Diplomatic Security Agents.[90]

Within a matter of days, Stevens' team expanded again.[91] Senior State Department officials made the decision to add two USAID workers, consistent with Secretary Clinton's goal that the U.S. be seen as "visibly engaged on the humanitarian side."[92]

After weeks of planning, the Administration's no boots on the ground policy kept military assistance from accompanying Stevens to Benghazi.[93] On March 30, 2011, Kennedy informed other senior State Department leaders: "After over a week of joint planning . . . Mullen has decided that the 'no boots on the ground in Libya' policy precludes DOD assisting us in getting Stevens into Libya."[94] Specifically, Admiral Mullen deemed the use of military assets—even in civilian dress—to be in violation of the President's directive, and therefore forbade their use to get Stevens into Benghazi and assist in his protection there.[95] With no military assets to assist, Stevens "found a way to get himself there on a Greek cargo ship, just like a 19th-century American envoy."[96] Accompanying Stevens on the ferry to Benghazi was a junior reporting officer, two members of USAID's Disaster Assistance Response Team, and eight Diplomatic Security Agents.[97]

## SETTING UP OPERATIONS IN BENGHAZI

When Stevens arrived in Benghazi, he was authorized to stay for up to 30 days, security permitting.[98] His job was to "begin gathering information and meeting those Libyans who were rising up against the murderous dictator Qadhafi."[99] This was all the instruction he was given. "There was no protocol for how to move forward," the Secretary said. "No past precedent to follow. No list of important figures to look out for. Chris had to work from scratch

---

Officer, Bureau of Near Eastern Affairs, U.S. Dep't of State (Mar. 23, 2011, 5:14 PM) (on file with the Committee, SCB0091885). *See also* Email from Special Ass't, Office of Deputy Sec'y, U.S Dep't of State, to Thomas R. Nides, Deputy Sec'y of State, U.S. Dep't of State (Mar. 24, 2011, 1:47 PM) (on file with the Committee, SCB0075262).

[90]*See* Email from Joan A. Polaschik, Deputy Chief of Mission in Libya, U.S. Dep't of State, to Ronald L. Schlicher, *et al.* (Mar. 24, 2011, 9:40 AM) (on file with the Committee, SCB0095893–94) ("Per Chris' emails, he would travel into Benghazi via zodiac or helicopter. All mil assets would be US, including comms and medic. Seals would participate in civilian dress—an initiative that could prove problematic with the TNC. Travel would be day trips. RON on the US naval vessel.").

[91]Email from Janet A. Sanderson, Deputy Ass't Sec'y of State, Bureau of Near Eastern Affairs, to Patrick F. Kennedy, Under Sec'y of State for Mgmt., U.S. Dep't of State (Mar. 26, 2011, 12:02 PM) (on file with the Committee, SCB0094603) ("Pat, AID Administrator talked to Bill Burns last night and requested Stevens Mission include one or two DART team reps.").

[92]Email from Jacob J. Sullivan, Dir. of Policy Planning, U.S. Dep't of State, to William J. Burns, Deputy Sec'y of State, U.S. Dep't of State (Mar. 6, 2011, 3:48 PM) (on file with the Committee, SCB0095837–0095838).

[93]Email from Patrick F. Kennedy, Under Sec'y of State for Mgmt., U.S. Dep't of State, to Jacob J. Sullivan, Dir. of Policy Planning, U.S. Dep't of State, and Joseph E. Macmanus, Exec. Ass't, Office of the Sec'y (Mar. 30, 2011, 12:50 PM) (on file with the Committee, SCB0071180).

[94]*Id.*

[95]*Id.*

[96]Clinton Testimony at 20–21.

[97]*See* Email to Patrick F. Kennedy, Under Sec'y of State for Mgmt., U.S. Dep't of State (Mar. 30, 2011, 7:38 PM) (on file with the Committee, SCB0095929) (attaching Benghazi Party OPLAN at SCB0095929–35).

[98]*Id.*

[99]Clinton Testimony at 20; *see also* Email from Special Ass't, Office of Deputy Sec'y, U.S. Dep't of State, to Thomas R. Nides, Deputy Sec'y of State, U.S. Dep't of State (Apr. 5, 2011, 5:38 PM) (on file with the Committee, SCB0061086) ("Chris explained his mission, making it clear that he would like to meet all members of the TNC and as many local council members as possible to understand the extent of the TNC's support.").

to identify the key players on the ground and carve out his own set of rules for working with the opposition." [100]

Stevens' early days and months in Benghazi were consumed by ongoing, concurrent concerns: contending with severe civil unrest; establishing a Mission compound; and meeting with officials from the Libyan insurgency and other nations. Stevens was expected to accomplish all of this with an uncertain diplomatic status.

## The Tibesti Hotel

The lead Diplomatic Security Agent who traveled with Stevens into Benghazi testified: "[W]e tried to put a plan together as best we could. We didn't even know where we were going to set up once we arrived. Once we arrived, we looked at a couple locations. But prior to going there, it was somewhat fluid because it was just the unknown." [101]

After spending the first night on board the Greek cargo ship, the Aegean Pearl, and evaluating different locations, Stevens decided to stay at the Tibesti Hotel. [102] While State Department security rules do not apply to hotels, [103] the Diplomatic Security Agents on the ground sought out locations with security advantages. The Tibesti Hotel had limited setback [104] and "rudimentary barriers to control access." [105] "[T]here was [also] an attempt to provide perimeter security, but it wasn't very robust." [106] The lead Diplomatic Security Agent described the decision-making process:

> We went to see where the British were at, and they were kind of at a guest conference type center. It wasn't really big, but it was moderate sized, maybe two or three stories, had a compound. It was down along the water, so we ruled that place out. [107]

He also testified:

> [W]e went to one other hotel where there were some other journalists were staying. I don't recall the name of it, but it was a little bit smaller. It was right up against the highway. So we decided and it was a little bit closer to where the U.K. facility was, but we decided that wasn't really a good place for us. And then we went to the Tibesti and

---

[100] Remarks, Hillary R. Clinton, Sec'y of State, U.S. Dep't of State, Prepared Remarks: Secretary Clinton Remarks at Swearing-In Ceremony for Chris Stevens, Ambassador to Libya (May 14, 2012), http://www.state.gov/secretary/20092013clinton/rm/2012/05/197696.htm.

[101] Diplomatic Sec. Agent 6 Testimony at 30–31.

[102] *Id.* at 31, 49.

[103] See Testimony of Gentry O. Smith, Deputy Ass't Sec'y, Bureau of Diplomatic Sec., Countermeasures, U.S. Dep't of State, Tr. at 14–15 (Feb. 25, 2016) [hereinafter Smith Testimony] (on file with the Committee) ("There would not be any security standards for a hotel, but security recommendations that are made during times that we're in a hotel, a solid core door, just basic things that you would expect from even being in the States, solid core door, viewfinder, very good locking equipment on the door; in situations such as being overseas, to look for hotels where there would be a security presence from either the host country or that the hotel provide its own security and what are the security procedures that are followed at that hotel for its guests.").

[104] Diplomatic Sec. Agent 6 Testimony at 32.

[105] Testimony of Diplomatic Sec. Agent, Diplomatic Sec. Serv., U.S. Dep't of State, Tr. at 36 (Feb. 26, 2015) [hereinafter Diplomatic Sec. Agent 7 Testimony] (on file with the Committee).

[106] *Id.*

[107] Diplomatic Sec. Agent 6 Testimony at 31.

looked at that. At the time, there were some advantages for us to be there.[108]

* * *

There were a lot of journalists there that would make it easier for—[sic] and others staying there that would make it easier for Mr. Stevens to communicate with these people without us having to make unnecessary movements all the time. And there was a little bit of security at that hotel, very minimal. There was a presence.[109]

He also testified:

There wasn't a formalized police—I mean, there was probably somebody that called himself a police chief. And then you had the military—somewhat of a military presence, you know—that really wasn't focused on anything to do with our security. They had, you know, they were trying to fight the war. Then you had February 17, a militia that assisted us a little bit.[110]

Notwithstanding the minimal security advantages over other hotels, Stevens and the Diplomatic Security Agents remained concerned about the security vulnerabilities of the Tibesti Hotel.

## CIVIL WAR AND UNREST

Five days after Stevens arrived in Benghazi, he and his group were nearly forced to leave. Qadhafi's forces had regrouped around the city of Ajdabiya, approximately 100 miles south of Benghazi.[111] Stevens and the lead Diplomatic Security Agent, were concerned about the security in Benghazi if Qadhafi took Ajdabiya.[112] When asked why they did not depart Benghazi, the Diplomatic Security Agent in charge of the Mission told the Committee: "[W]e reexamined the issues, and at that time, we weren't worried about what was happening in Benghazi. We were worried about the forces coming forward. So they must have stopped."[113] Concerns about Stevens and his team's security reached the Secretary.[114]

Nevertheless, the security situation in Benghazi remained precarious. On April 15, 2011, the Mission held an emergency action

---

[108] Id. at 32.

[109] Id. at 32–33.

[110] Id. at 33.

[111] See Email from Gene A. Cretz, U.S. Ambassador to Libya, to Jeffery D. Feltman, Ass't Sec'y of State, Bureau of Near Eastern Affairs, U.S. Dep't of State, et al. (Apr. 10, 2011, 6:06 AM) (on file with the Committee, SCB0095985) ("It appears that qadhafi forces are at the eastern and western gate of adjdabiyah and that there is a real possibility of the city falling."); see also Rob Crilly, Libya: rebels flee stronghold of Ajdabiya as Gaddafi closes net, TELEGRAPH (Mar. 15, 2011), http://www.telegraph.co.uk/news/worldnews/africaandindianocean/libya/8383872/Libya-rebels-flee-stronghold-of-Ajdabiya-as-Gaddafi-closes-net.html.

[112] See Email from Patrick Kennedy, Under Sec'y of State for Mgmt., U.S. Dep't of State, to James Steinberg, Deputy Sec'y of State, U.S. Dep't of State, et al. (Apr. 10, 2011) (on file with the Committee, SCB0095985).

[113] Diplomatic Sec. Agent 6 Testimony at 99; see also Email from Patrick F. Kennedy, Under Sec'y of State for Mgmt., U.S. Dep't of State, to Joan A. Polaschik, Deputy Chief of Mission in Libya, U.S. Dep't of State (Apr. 10, 2011, 2:06 PM) (on file with the Committee, SCB0095970) (showing email exchange at the time).

[114] Email from Huma Abedin, Deputy Chief of Staff to U.S. Sec'y of State, U.S. Dep't of State, to Hillary R. Clinton ("H"), Sec'y of State, U.S. Dep't of State (April 10, 2011, 10:14 AM) (on file with the Committee, SCB0045049)

committee [EAC] meeting "to address several security issues that occurred or reported during the past 12 hours. The meeting was called by Stevens and was attended by all members of the Benghazi Mission." [115] An emergency action committee meeting is called "when there is an emergency or security incident, the committee will convene and discuss the incident as well as steps forward either to mitigate the incident or resolve the incident." [116] Charlene Lamb, Deputy Assistant Secretary, Diplomatic Security, International Programs, described EACs to the Committee: "They're usually chaired by the deputy chief of Mission. Sometimes they're chaired and/or attended by the Ambassador. And then the core members, at a minimum, the core members of your post security envelope and intelligence if they are present." [117]

The April 15, 2011 EAC highlighted three discreet incidents including: (1) military grade explosives were found with the Tibesti Hotel as the identified target; (2) two explosives were detonated outside the El Fadeel Hotel—the hotel used by the U.N. and UK; and (3) a large fire and pillar of smoke was seen emanating near the Hotel Uzo—the hotel occupied by many international journalists. [118] The EAC determined it would work with the Transitional National Council to focus on security. [119]

Less than 10 days later, on April 24, 2011, Stevens again considered whether it was safe enough to stay at the hotel. He informed State Department senior officials the Tibesti Hotel might not be safe enough in the long run and alternative facilities might be needed for a longer term stay. [120]

The Diplomatic Security Agents on the ground protecting Stevens and his team members described a high-risk security environment. The Agents spoke of explosions occurring near and around the Tibesti Hotel. [121] They described constant gunfire, including "a small-caliber round [that] came through the dining room where [Stevens] and the Swedish Consul were having dinner" and "a round that went through the window of our command post room in the hotel." [122] One Diplomatic Security Agent testified the car bomb explosions "reminded me of what I experienced in Kabul or Iraq. . . ." [123] Unlike Kabul or Iraq, however, there was no U.S. military presence in Libya.

Security would remain tenuous through the summer. On June 10, 2011, a credible threat to the Tibesti Hotel forced Stevens and

---

[115] Email from Diplomatic Sec. Command Ctr. (Apr. 15, 2011, 5:54 PM) (on file with the Committee, C05396062).

[116] Testimony of Diplomatic Sec. Agent, Diplomatic Sec. Serv., U.S. Dep't of State, Tr. at 50 (Apr. 15, 2015) [hereinafter Diplomatic Sec. Agent 8 Testimony] (on file with the Committee).

[117] Testimony of Charlene Lamb, Deputy Ass't Sec'y, Bureau of Diplomatic Sec., Int'l Programs, U.S. Dep't of State, Tr. at 174 (Jan. 7, 2016) [hereinafter Lamb Testimony] (on file with the Committee).

[118] See Email to DSCC_C DS Seniors (Apr. 15, 2011, 5:54 PM) (on file with the Committee, C05396062).

[119] See Email to DSCC_C DS Seniors (Apr. 15, 2011, 5:54 PM) (on file with the Committee, C05396062).

[120] See Email from Huma Abedin, Deputy Chief of Staff to U.S. Sec'y of State, U.S. Dep't of State, to Hillary R. Clinton ("H"), Sec'y of State, U.S. Dep't of State (Apr. 24, 2011, 10:25 AM) (on file with the Committee, SCB0045054) (forwarding email communicating Benghazi security update, hotels being targeted, cell arrested, increased security being sought, and may need to move out of hotel to villa).

[121] Diplomatic Sec. Agent 6 Testimony at 39–42.

[122] Testimony of Diplomatic Sec. Agent, Diplomatic Sec. Serv., U.S. Dep't of State, Tr. at 42. (Feb. 12, 2012) [hereinafter Diplomatic Sec. Agent 9 Testimony] (on file with the Committee).

[123] Diplomatic Sec. Agent 7 Testimony at 49.

his team out of the hotel and to a more secure location.[124] In late July 2011, a leading opposition figure, General Abdul Fatah Younis—a former Qadhafi loyalist who defected earlier in 2011 to join the opposition—was assassinated in Benghazi.[125]

## BENGHAZI MISSION: SUMMER 2011

Despite the unrest and security concerns in April 2011, senior leaders at the State Department were discussing continuing Stevens' diplomatic operation beyond the initial 30 days and into the summer of 2011. On April 14, 2011, a report was filed with Thomas Nides, the Deputy Secretary of State for Management and Resources:

> NEA will be drafting a paper for Steinberg, which essentially will ask for an expanded scope of work for Stevens— which will allow him to stay in Libya for longer than (90 days or more). Once NEA has some policy guidance about what Stevens should be seeking to accomplish in Libya, it will devise a plan for a new footprint on the ground—this will require needed resources and could shift the mission from an envoy situation to a more permanent presence. We will need to watch this closely and I've flagged for P and D(S) staff that you and Pat should be included in these discussions.[126]

Feltman explained to the Committee:

> It was more fluid . . . but it was certainly the idea was to be there more than a day or a week. The idea was to be there for long enough that we would have the type of insights into TNC thinking that you can't get from a single meeting, that we would have the type of access to other decisionmakers in the TNC that you can't have when you only are meeting with one or two persons. We needed somebody who could better understand what was happening, what was motivating the leadership of the TNC, what were they thinking. So the idea was not that this would necessarily be years and years and years but certainly more than a few weeks.[127]

---

[124] See Email from Special Ass't, Office of Deputy Sec'y, U.S. Dep't of State, to Thomas R. Nides, Deputy Sec'y of State, U.S. Dep't of State (June 10, 2011, 6:58 PM) (on file with the Committee, SCB0074991) (discussing relocation from Tibesti Hotel); see also Email from Jacob J. Sullivan, Dir. of Policy Planning, U.S. Dep't of State, to Hillary R. Clinton ("H"), Sec'y of State, U.S. Dep't of State (June 10, 2011, 4:01 PM)(on file with the Committee, SCB0045085).

[125] See Email to Benghazi Update (July 31, 2011, 10:35 AM) (on file with the Committee, C05394875) (communicating reports of General Yunus' death).

[126] Email from Special Ass't, Office of Deputy Sec'y, U.S. Dep't of State, to Thomas R. Nides, Deputy Sec'y of State, U.S. Dep't of State (Apr. 14, 2011, 6:48 AM) (on file with the Committee, SCB0075032). P is the designation for the Bureau of Political Affairs. D(S) is the designation for the Deputy Secretary of State Steinberg.

[127] Feltman Testimony at 42:

> Q: Okay. And then when you either prior to your trip or during your trip in May of 2011, were there discussions about continuing the presence in Benghazi for an indefinite period of time, maybe not years but at least the foreseeable future?

> A: Yes, there were. And the discussions were, what's the appropriate when I was there, part of our discussions were, what's the appropriate platform for maintaining a presence for that period in Benghazi?

> Q: And by "platform," do you mean number of personnel?

By the end of April 2011, the diplomatic team had increased to 17 Americans consisting of "Stevens, one reporting/public diplomacy officer, one Information Management Officer who is also doing Management work, four USAID officers, and ten Diplomatic Security special Agents who comprise the protective detail for the mission."[128] By the end of June 2011, security threats had forced Stevens and his team to relocate. The space constraints in the new locations forced the number of personnel in Benghazi to drop to nine, including five Diplomatic Security Agents.[129] Staffing remained unchanged throughout the summer.[130] William V. Roebuck, the Director of the Office of Maghreb Affairs, told Stevens:

> Other principals like Deputy Secretary Nides are operating under (and accept) the assumption that the mission will bulk back up to 17 as housing stabilizes and the security conditions permit. . . . I have the strong sense in any case that there would be little appetite for capping the mission at 9 people, given the equities the interagency has in the previously higher staffing figure.[131]

Notwithstanding the security threats and decreased staff, Stevens and his team faced increasing demands. According to Polaschik, who served in Benghazi in May 2011:

> Certainly, when I was there, I was working from, you know, 8 in the morning till midnight. And there were two reporting officers there.
>
> Just in terms of sustainability and getting the work done, 8 in the morning until midnight is never a good recipe, and, also, when you're trying to make sure that people are at a heightened state of alert that's appropriate for a very fluid security environment.
>
> So it wasn't a decision to say, oh, we need a long term presence. It was a decision that we don't have the re-

---

A: Number of personnel, communications, location. You know, at the time we were in a hotel

Q: The Tibesti Hotel?

A: The Tibesti Hotel. And so the discussion had already started about what were the alternatives to being in a place like that.

Q: Okay. And had there been some review of compounds and villas at that time?

A: Yes, it had started, and it was very difficult because there were not that many places available or appropriate. *Id.* at 43.

*See also* Email from Special Ass't, Office of Deputy Sec'y, U.S. Dep't of State, to Thomas R. Nides, Deputy Sec'y of State, U.S. Dep't of State (May 5, 2011, 7:00 PM) (on file with the Committee, SCB0061070) (**"NEA sees Benghazi turning into an eventual EBO—and all that entails on resources, DS, OBO, and Interagency discussion."** (emphasis in original)).

[128] Memorandum from Jeffrey D. Feltman, Assistant Sec'y of State, Bureau of Near Eastern Affairs, U.S. Dep't of State, to Patrick F. Kennedy, Under Sec'y of State for Mgmt., U.S. Dep't of State (June 10, 2011) [hereinafter June 10, 2011 Action Memo for Under Secretary Kennedy] (on file with the Committee, C05578649).

[129] *See* Email from Special Ass't, Office of Deputy Sec'y, U.S Dep't of State, to Thomas R. Nides, Deputy Sec'y of State, U.S. Dep't of State (June 21, 2011, 8:12 PM) (on file with the Committee, SCB0061058) (discussing staffing concerns and issues).

[130] *See id.* (discussing staffing concerns and issues).

[131] Email from William V. Roebuck, Dir. Office of Maghreb Affairs, Bureau of Near Eastern Affairs, U.S. Dep't of State, to J. Christopher Stevens, U.S. Rep. to Transitional Nat'l Council (June 21, 2011, 12:08 PM) (on file with the Committee, C05409676).

sources in place to get the work done that needs to get done.[132]

## Move to Mission Compound

With Washington's interest in extending Stevens' stay, he and his team searched for a new location—a challenging process in the middle of a civil war. The Post Management Officer for Libya, Bureau of Near Eastern Affairs, State Department, testified: "Finding a place that met our security needs, where the rent was not completely outrageous due to the fact that we were in a war zone, that had required ingress and egress that met what security wanted . . . were all significant issues that had to be overcome."[133]

> [T]he traditional . . . real estate agent just didn't exist . . . there were other channels of information that we would leverage to help us identify what we were looking for. Because that was really the issue, was not a property per se, but a property that we had special considerations for."[134]

These difficulties were further complicated by Stevens' team's inability to find a "landlord that would be willing to cooperate with us and our specific needs. . . ."[135]

As Stevens and his team searched for new property, they temporarily collocated with other U.S. personnel on the ground in Benghazi. Space constraints precluded maintaining this arrangement for the long term.[136] On June 21, 2011, Stevens and his team moved to another interim site, while they narrowed their search for a suitable longer term location.[137] They found a facility that had previously served as a "man camp" for personnel working for the oil industry but had been abandoned at the start of the civil war.[138] The lead Diplomatic Security Agent at the time described the advantages of the camp:

> [I]t had an established perimeter. That perimeter also gave us setback from the road, setback being one of the critical elements that we were looking for given that issues that we had at the Tibesti Hotel with the explosion.
>
> It also was a hardened building. In other words, the mason area was significant enough that it would likely withstand rounds dropping down from the sky or, depending on the

---

[132] Polaschik Testimony at 130.

[133] Testimony of Post Mgmt. Officer for Libya, Bureau of Near Eastern Affairs, U.S. Dep't of State, Tr. at 79 (July 23, 2015) [hereinafter Post Mgmt. Officer for Libya Testimony] (on file with the Committee).

[134] Diplomatic Sec. Agent 7 Testimony at 95.

[135] Id.

[136] See Email from Thomas R. Nides, Deputy Sec'y of State, U.S. Dep't of State, to Special Ass't, Office of Deputy Sec'y, U.S. Dep't of State (June 13, 2011, 1:13 PM) (on file with the Committee, SCB0061059–0061060).

[137] Email from Post Mgmt. Officer for Libya, Bureau of Near Eastern Affairs, U.S. Dep't of State (June 20, 2011, 9:04 AM) (on file with the Committee, C05393024) ("We are treating the interim villa as hotel space—only 30–60 days while we wait for the upgrades to the Villa Compound to come online."); see also Email from Diplomatic Sec. Agent 7 (June 17, 2011, 6:19 AM) (on file with the Committee, C05408710) ("We hope to have the 'interim' villa by next tuesday [sic].").

[138] Testimony of Physical Sec. Specialist, Bureau of Diplomatic Sec., U.S. Dep't of State, Tr. at 9 (Apr. 6, 2016) [hereinafter Physical Sec. Specialist Testimony] (on file with the Committee).

trajectory of a particular round, it provided it afforded us additional protection because of the construction of that particular villa.

It allowed us to control our access onto the compound. That was one of the big problems with the hotel, was we didn't know who was coming and going. It was an active, operating hotel. And so they were there to make money, not to control the access necessarily for the Americans.[139]

Notwithstanding the search for a secure location, traditional security standards did not apply in Benghazi at the time. The physical security specialist in Benghazi testified:

Q: You were advised that OSPB standards did not apply to Benghazi. Is that correct?

A: Yes.

Q: And when they didn't apply to Benghazi, did that mean the city at large or did that mean a specific facility?

A: That meant for our facility.

Q: Okay. But the facility at that point in time was what?

A: The facility that we were going to occupy as the platform was going to be the man camp.[140]

Federal regulation and State Department rules set out the security standards United States facilities located abroad are required to meet to keep Americans safe.[141] Senior State Department officials, nevertheless, made the decision to exclude "temporary facilities," such as Benghazi, from these security rules.[142] Kennedy attempted to justify this exclusion:

When we go into one of these temporary facilities, we take the Overseas Security Policy Board (OSPB) standards—OSPB is how we refer to them—we take the OSPB standards as our goals . . . We treat the temporary facilities as if we were heading towards interim by using the OSPB standards as our goal.[143]

In addition to the OSPB security standards, the Secure Embassy Construction and Counterterrorism Act (SECCA), the applicable federal security law, provides among other things a diplomatic facility ensure: (1) all US Government personnel are located together in the new diplomatic facility; and (2) the diplomatic facility is located "not less than 100 feet from the perimeter of the property on which the

---

[139] Diplomatic Sec. Agent 7 Testimony at 93–94.

[140] Physical Sec. Specialist Testimony at 87–88.

[141] *See* Secure Embassy Construction and Counterterrorism Act of 1999, 22 U.S.C. § 4865 (2012); and *see also,* U.S. DEP'T OF STATE, 12 FAH–6 H–511.1–511.6, OVERSEAS SECURITY POLICY BOARD APPROVED POLICIES AND STANDARDS FOR ALL POSTS; U.S. GOV'T ACCOUNTABILITY OFFICE, GAO–14–655, DIPLOMATIC FACILITY SECURITY: OVERSEAS FACILITIES MAY FACE GREATER RISKS DUE TO GAP IN SECURITY-RELATED ACTIVITIES, STANDARDS, AND POLICIES (2014).

[142] *See* Testimony of Eric Boswell, Ass't Sec'y of State, Bureau of Diplomatic Sec., U.S. Dep't of State, before the H. Comm. On Oversight and Gov't Reform,, Tr. at 65–66 (July 9, 2013) [hereinafter Boswell Testimony] (on file with the Committee).

[143] Testimony of Patrick F. Kennedy, Under Sec'y of State for Mgmt., U.S. Dep't of State, Tr. at 193 (Feb. 5, 2016) [hereinafter Kennedy Testimony] (on file with the Committee).

facility is situated."[144] With regard to Benghazi, however, the State Department Office of the Legal Adviser determined: [T]his facility would not fit within the definition of a 'diplomatic facility' under SECCA, which defines the term as an office that (1) is officially notified to the host government as diplomatic/consular premises or (2) houses USG personnel with an official status recognized by the host government. If the facility will not be notified to the host government then it will not be considered inviolable, and our personnel will not have any official status, then the facility would not meet the definition of a diplomatic facility under the statute.[145]

Without official security standards in place, Stevens and the Diplomatic Security Agents on the ground worked with the landlord of the "man camp" to identify field expedient measures to improve the physical security of the camp. The needed security measures were contracted out to an individual situated in Benghazi.[146] The physical security specialist on site wrote:

> The DS/PSP [physical security programs] funded PSD upgrade contract that was signed . . . was for $75,000 with a specific scope of work to be performed, fabricate two . . . vehicle gates, fabricate concrete jersey type barriers, string barbed wire and fabricate two vehicle drop arm barriers.[147]

Concerns about the owner's title and relationship to the Qadhafi regime forced Stevens and his team to abruptly drop the "man camp" from consideration as a housing facility. With no alternative, Stevens and his team remained at the interim facility, also known as Villa A.[148] Within days of the decision to remain in Villa A, a neighboring property, Villa B, was acquired.[149] The physical security specialist in Benghazi at the time described the sequence of events: "That facility fell through on a Thursday, and on the Friday, Stevens sat down with the Villa A landlord, who brought along the owner of Villa B. Stevens especially liked Villa B and said he wanted A and B together."[150]

The decision made by Washington to exempt the proposed "man camp" site from the official security standards also applied to the

---

[144] See Secure Embassy Construction and Counterterrorism Act of 1999, 22 U.S.C. § 4865 (2012).

[145] Email (June 20, 2011, 11:30 AM) (on file with the Committee, C05396431).

[146] Email from Physical Sec. Specialist, Physical Sec. Programs, Bureau of Diplomatic Sec., U.S. Dep't of State (Aug. 1, 2011, 11:08 AM) (on file with the Committee, C05393020).

[147] Id.

[148] See Email from Physical Sec. Specialist, Physical Sec. Programs, Bureau of Diplomatic Sec., U.S. Dep't of State, to Diplomatic Sec. Agent 25 & James Bacigalupo, Regional Director, Bureau of Diplomatic Sec., U.S. Dep't of State (Feb. 13, 2012) (on file with the Committee, C05411579) ("[T]he decision was made to stay put when Villa B became an option and we stopped looking at the other properties."); see also Email from Diplomatic Sec. Agent (July 04, 2011, 3:59 AM) (on file with the Committee, C05394858) ("We are currently referring to our current residence as Villa A and the neighboring property as Villa B.").

[149] See Email from Physical Sec. Specialist, Physical Sec. Programs, Bureau of Diplomatic Sec., U.S. Dep't, to Diplomatic Sec. Agent 24, et al. (Feb. 13, 2012, 7:52 AM) (on file with the Committee, C05411579).

[150] Summary of group interview with Physical Security Specialist and others (on file with the Committee, SCB0046921–0046923).

Mission compound.[151] The same physical security specialist in Benghazi explained:

> Q: . . . you were told that OSPB standards and SECCA did not apply to the man camp; am I correct?
>
> A: Did not apply.
>
> Q: Did not apply.
>
> So was that analysis then sort of used as it relates to the villa compound?
>
> A: It carried over.
>
> Q: Carried over. So basically and correct me if I'm misstating this but the thought would be that exceptions and waivers to OSPB and SECCA do not apply in Benghazi, generally?
>
> A: When I was there, that's the
>
> Q: Is that a fair characterization?
>
> A: That's the guidance that I was given at that time.[152]

This decision to exclude the Mission compound in Benghazi from official security standards and rules was never formally communicated to the Diplomatic Security Agents who volunteered to serve in Benghazi. One Diplomatic Security Agent told the Committee:

> I was starting to understand then and what I learned later, that if you are a diplomatic facility within the State Department, you have physical security requirements that are in the FAM, the Foreign Affairs Manual. And it is a very detailed, large set of rules that you have to follow to operate a diplomatic facility. It requires you to have physical security standards that are typically going to be expensive and will take time to do.
>
> If you are in a non-diplomatic facility, there are no security standards.
>
> They don't exist.[153]

The Committee also learned "Villas A and B owners were adamant about their residential properties not be[ing] altered by our then short term presence without their explicit approvals being obtained in advance." To assuage the landlords concerns, security improvements to Villas A and B were minimal.[154] According to the physical security specialist:

> [M]inor security improvements were discussed and authorized for B only, open a hole in the perimeter wall between Villa's [sic] A & B wide enough for a roadway, install sev-

---

[151] *See* Physical Sec. Specialist Testimony at 134.

[152] *Id.*

[153] Testimony Diplomatic Sec. Agent, Diplomatic Sec. Serv., U.S. Dep't of State, Tr. at 28 (Apr. 2, 2015) [hereinafter Diplomatic Sec. Agent 10 Testimony] (on file with the Committee).

[154] Email from Physical Sec. Specialist, Physical Sec. Programs, Bureau of Diplomatic Sec., U.S. Dep't, to Diplomatic Sec. Agent 25 and James Bacigalupo, Regional Director, Bureau of Diplomatic Sec., U.S. Dep't of State (Feb. 13, 2012, 7:52 AM) (on file with the Committee, C05411579).

eral window grills on the small Villa B office annex and reposition several large manufacturing machines on the Villa B property to block the vehicle gates because all Mission vehicle activity was to be conducted from Villa A. The owners [sic] representative walked the property with us several times and he agreed to implement these minor security improvements as part of his fiduciary management responsibilities and dismissed other recommendations such as installing razor ribbon on existing perimeter walls were [sic] needed, installing shatter resistant window film and installing vehicle drop arm barriers. Post used available FAV SUV's with maintenance issues (no working A/C) to block the Villa A vehicle gates. There was no PSD/PCB trip report prepared upon return because conditions on the ground were changing on a near daily basis and were discussed on conference calls and/or in email correspondence with concerned offices within WDC as to what Post was proposing and what was being considered an approved for the leased properties.[155]

Villa C, another residence, was acquired shortly after the residences located in Villas A and B. Although no security assessment was conducted on Villa C at the time, one of the Diplomatic Security Agents assessed "[n]o upgrades are needed for Villas A & C."[156]

As Stevens and his team finalized the acquisition of all three Villas in late July 2011, a Diplomatic Security Agent on the ground outlined to Washington D.C. a number of "security-related items," needed to better protect the new compound:[157]

More agents required: Between the three compounds, we're looking at roughly 15 acres of property to secure. This will require additional SAs [special agents] (up to five more) by early to mid-August. For REACT purposes, teams of agents will reside on all three compounds. Once resources permit, RSO [regional security officer] TOC [technical operations center] will be staffed 24/7.

LGF [local guard force]: per the contract already in place with AQM, we'll have 11 unarmed guard positions (all 24/7). This includes a Shift Supervisor and 10 guard posts. Tripoli LGF commander will oversee day-to-day operations. LGF will be in place prior to occupancy. Guard Orders in draft—pending.

Access control policy (drafted and approved by Envoy): Except for select VIPs, visitors will park outside the compound and enter on foot. Visitor/vehicles will be screened by LGF. Visitors/deliveries will be channeled to one access

---

[155] *Id.*

[156] Email from Diplomatic Sec. Agent to Physical Sec. Specialist, Physical Sec. Programs, Bureau of Diplomatic Sec., U.S. Dep't of State, and Post Mgmt. Officer for Libya, Bureau of Near Eastern Affairs, U.S. Dep't of State (Aug. 1, 2011, 6:32 PM) (on file with the Committee, C05393020).

[157] Email from Diplomatic Sec. Agent to DS–IP–NEA (July 21, 2011, 3:22 PM) (on file with the Committee, C05396529).

control point; remaining vehicle gates will be blocked using armored vehicles or similar.

Compound Security/Internal Defense Plan: will incorporate DS [diplomatic security] agents, LGF, and TNC [Transitional National Council] armed guards.

Designation of safe havens within each residential and office structure.

Installation of TSS equipment/arrival of TDY install team—TBD.

Relocation of RSO TOC from Villa A (current location) to Villa B office building.

Request for additional TNC armed guards.[158]

The email introduces several specific elements related to security that later become significant. Already occupying Villa A, Stevens and his team took occupancy of Villas B and C on August 1, 2011.[159] On August 3, 2011, leases for all three villas were executed, forming what would become known as the Benghazi Mission compound.[160]

Diplomatic Security Agents on the ground described their impressions of the compound:

> When I arrived on the compound, it was 13 acres I remember this pretty vividly 13 acres. We occupied three dormitories, I will say. We named them Villa A, B, and C. There was a building that we considered as, you know it was referred to by, you know, us and the other folks there as the tactical operations center, also as the office.

> And then we had another outlying building on the 13 acre compound, which really was three separate, you know, residences, which housed the quick reaction forces I've described before, the 17th February guys, who also lived on compound with us.[161]

> [I]t was not like the other compounds that I had seen. It appeared to be more of a low profile building, lower footprint than your typical embassy or consulate. It didn't have the signs up saying "U.S. Embassy" or "Consulate." It didn't have some of the physical security features you would typically see at an embassy or consulate, such as Delta barriers or chicane. There wasn't the host nation police presence, the military presence that you would find at

---

[158] Email from Diplomatic Sec. Agent to DS–IP–NEA (July 21, 2011, 3:22 PM) (on file with the Committee, C05396529).

[159] *See* Email from Diplomatic Sec. Agent to DS–IP–NEA (July 21, 2011, 3:22 PM) (on file with the Committee, C05396529) (mentioning that "[b]arring any issues, occupancy of villa B&C could be as early as Aug. 1."); *see also* Lease Agreement between [REDACTED] and the United States of America, STS–800–11–L–009 (Aug, 3, 2011) (on file with the Committee, C05394161) (showing term of lease beginning Aug. 1).

[160] *Id.; see also* Letter (July 28, 2011) (on file with the Committee, SCB0047437–42) (authorizing three leases in Benghazi).

[161] Testimony of Diplomatic Sec. Agent, Diplomatic Sec. Serv., U.S. Dep't of State, Tr. at 18 (Apr. 9, 2015) [hereinafter Diplomatic Sec. Agent 12 Testimony] (on file with the Committee).

your typical embassy or consulate. So my impression was, it was a lower or a lower profile mission.[162]

Less than three weeks after leases were signed for the new Mission compound, Tripoli fell to opposition forces.[163] Soon after the fall of Tripoli, elements of the TNC moved from Benghazi to Tripoli.[164] Less than eight weeks after the Mission moved into its new compound, Embassy Tripoli reopened.[165] At that time, Stevens requested his role as representative to the TNC conclude on or about October 6, 2011.[166] He was asked to remain in Benghazi until the TNC's relocation was complete later that fall.[167]

## Uncertain Diplomatic Status

Stevens' Mission in Benghazi fell outside the normal realm, even extending to questions about its diplomatic status.[168] Typically, a Mission and its staff are notified to the host nation under which they receive the full privileges and immunities afforded under international conventions.[169] At the time Stevens and his team went into Benghazi to coordinate with the emerging Transitional National Council,[170] however, the U.S. had not severed formal diplomatic relations with the Qadhafi regime.[171] Gene A. Cretz remained the Ambassador to Libya, and he and a select number of his team were serving "in exile" in Washington D.C.[172] Feltman explained:

---

[162] Diplomatic Sec. Agent 8 Testimony at 41.

[163] See Email from U.S. Embassy Tripoli to Gene A. Cretz, U.S. Ambassador to Libya (Sept. 7, 2011, 12:53 PM) (on file with the Committee, C05390164) (". . . the TNC effectively took control of Tripoli in mid-August and has begun to establish its presence and authority in the city.").

[164] See id. ("Approximately half of the TNC's executive cabinet . . . is currently in Tripoli, joined by 15 of the TNC's 42 council members.").

[165] Id.

[166] Email from William V. Roebuck, Dir. Office of Maghreb Affairs, Bureau of Near Eastern Affairs, U.S. Dep't of State, to Raymond D. Maxwell, Deputy Ass't Sec'y, Bureau of Near Eastern Affairs, U.S. Dep't of State, and Elizabeth L. Dibble, Principal Deputy Ass't Sec'y of State, Bureau of Near Eastern Affairs, U.S. Dep't of State (Sept. 20, 2011, 8:20 AM) (on file with the Committee, C05389443) ("I am forwarding this to socialize Chris' thoughts on the future of the Benghazi Mission, in light of our Embassy in Tripoli. He would like to conclude his service o/ a October 6 and return to Washington.").

[167] Email from Elizabeth L. Dibble, Principal Deputy Ass't Sec'y of State, Bureau of Near Eastern Affairs, U.S. Dep't of Sate, to Raymond D. Maxwell, Deputy Ass't Sec'y, Bureau of Near Eastern Affairs, U.S. Dep't of State, William Roebuck, Dir. Office of Maghreb Affairs, Bureau of Near Eastern Affairs, U.S. Dep't of State, and Lee Lohman, Ex. Dir., Bureau of Near Eastern Affairs, U.S. Dept. of State, et al. (Sept. 20, 2011, 6:38 PM) (on file with the Committee, C05389443) ("I raised with Jeff [Feltman]. He thinks Chris needs to stay in Benghazi until Jalil has relocated more or less permanently to Tripoli. He also thinks we should not rush to shut down the operation there.").

[168] See Email from Senior Desk Officer for Libya, Office of Maghreb Affairs, Bureau of Near Eastern Affairs, U.S. Dep't of State, to J. Christopher Stevens, U.S. Rep. to Transitional Nat'l Council ("stevens chris") (July 27, 2011, 9:22 AM) (on file with the Committee, C05561961) (attaching draft staffing paper discussion of the role of the Mission); see also Email from Senior Desk Office for Libya, Office of Maghreb Affairs, Bureau of Near Eastern Affairs, U.S. Dep't of State, to U.S. Embassy Tripoli, (Sept. 7, 2011, 1:02 PM) (on file with the Committee, C05390164).

[169] See Vienna Convention on Diplomatic Relations, Apr. 18, 1961, 23 U.S.T. 3227, 500 U.N.T.S. 95; Vienna Convention on Consular Relations, Apr. 24, 1963, 21 U.S.T. 77, 596 U.N.T.S. 261.

[170] Email from Special Ass't, Office of Deputy Sec'y, U.S. Dep't of State, to Thomas R. Nides, Deputy Sec'y of State, U.S. Dep't of State (Apr. 5, 2011, 5:38 PM) (on file with the Committee, SCB0061086) ("Chris explained his mission, making it clear that he would like to meet all members of the TNC and as many local council members as possible to understand the extent of the TNC's support.").

[171] See Feltman Testimony at 27.

[172] See Cretz Testimony at 36.

Again, the overall goal was to try to limit the need for a military solution, to focus on a political solution, and convince Qadhafi that his time was over. So you close down the Embassy in Tripoli of course, we closed it down earlier for security reasons but you have no representation in Tripoli, but suddenly you have somebody in Benghazi.

You know, psychologically, did this have an impact on Qadhafi's thinking to realize that the U.K., the U.S., France, Italy, whole lists of countries no longer had representation in Tripoli, but they had representation in Benghazi.

Now, the TNC, as I said, wasn't a government at the time. You know, there's certain attributes that a government has that we didn't think they had achieved those attributes yet. They very much wanted to be recognized as the legitimate government of Libya, and I'm not sure that any country actually recognized them within that period as legitimate government. I don't think they did. But it was important to show who which Libyans did the U.S. think were appropriate interlocutors at the time.[173]

## Keeping Washington Informed

While contending with the civil unrest and seeking a location to house his diplomatic mission, Stevens set out to meet with leaders of the fledgling TNC.[174] He also met with other nations on the ground and leading rebel forces.[175] Throughout his time in Benghazi in 2011 Stevens kept Washington informed of the ongoing developments. For example, on April 10, 2011, he reported to Washington:

> The situation in Ajadbiyah has worsened to the point where Stevens is considering departing Benghazi. The envoy's delegation is currently doing a phased checkout (paying the hotel bills, moving some items to the boat etc.). He will monitor the situation to see if it deteriorates further, but no decision has been made on departure. He will wait 2–3 more hours and then revisit the decision on departure.
>
> \* \* \*
>
> The Brits report Qadhafi's forces are moving from Sirte to Brega, which they interpret as preparation for another assault on Ajadbiyah today.
>
> He plans to discuss the situation further with the Brits, Turks, and the TNC to see if this is an irreversible situation. Departure would send a significant political signal, and would be interpreted as the U.S. losing confidence in the TNC.

---

[173] Feltman Testimony at 27–28.

[174] *See* Email from Special Ass't, Office of Deputy Sec'y, U.S Dep't of State, to Thomas Nides, Deputy Sec'y of State, U.S. Dep't of State (Apr. 5, 2011, 5:38 PM) (on file with the Committee, SCB0061086) ("Chris explained his mission, making it clear that he would like to meet all members of the TNC and as many local council members as possible to understand the extent of the TNC's support.").

[175] *See* Email to SES–O SWO; Tripoli Cooperation, SES–O (Apr. 10, 2011, 6:10 AM) (on file with the Committee, SCB0075057).

Initial message to the TNC would frame the departure as due to security grounds and as a temporary measure only.

Polaschik said she would discuss these developments with Ambassador Cretz.

If the group departs, the contract for the boat stipulates they return to Greece. One scenario could be the group stages elsewhere for a few days.[176]

On April 25, 2011, Stevens reported the following:

*Political/economic developments:*

*The TNC [Transitional National Council]:* This week the Council will focus on strengthening its executive arm, the "Crisis Management Committee," by appointing coordinators (i.e. ministers) for defense, interior, and justice. They will also encourage the head of the Committee Dr. Mahmoud Jabril to remain in Benghazi and focus on managing the affairs of eastern Libya. He has been criticized for spending too much time abroad.

*Libyan Broadcasting:* A number of Libyan contacts told us that Libyan State Television was disrupted in the early morning hours, possibly due to NATO airstrikes. Later in the day, however broadcasting resumed.

*Air bridge?*[sic] The United Nations Humanitarian Air Service (UNHAS) is expected to begin regular passenger service in/out of Benghazi in the next week or so. Details, including its route, are being worked out. The flights would be available on a sign up basis to humanitarian and donor staff (UN, NGOs, and donor Missions).

*New passport and visa procedures:* the TNC issued a press release from Colonel Saad Najm, the head of the immigration office, describing how the historically burdensome passport process will be eased. Colonel Najm said that his office would suspend issuing entry visas until the TNC could better secure the land and sea ports, and said that journalists crossing into Libya over land from Egypt will need to apply for visas at the border town of Msaed and have letters of endorsement from TNC media committee.[177]

In addition, Stevens reported back to the State Department on the security environment in Benghazi.

*Security situation:*

*Benghazi:* TNC member confirmed reports we received yesterday that TNC security forces had uncovered a cell of Libyans sent from Egypt to disrupt life in Benghazi by attacking hotels and even schools (schools have been closed since the mid-March attacks by loyalist forces). [The TNC

---

[176] *Id.*

[177] Email from Staff Ass't, Office of the U.S. Sec'y of State, U.S. Dep't of State, to Jacob J. Sullivan, Dir. Policy Planning, U.S. Dep't of State, *et al.* (Apr. 25, 2011, 4:33 PM) (on file with the Committee, SCB0083338).

Member] said that Qadhafi relative Ahmed Qadhafadam who moved to Cairo after the revolution began was behind the effort. [The TNC Member] said he gave interviews to Egyptian TV channels last night complaining about this problem and calling on Egyptian authorities to stop it. According to press reports, TNC Chairman Abd al-Jalal asked Egyptian authorities to halt Qadhafadam's efforts to raise funds to use against the rebels.[178]

On August 22, 2011, Stevens filed a report on the fall of Tripoli:

TNC caretaker cabinet/members were up until 4am following events in Tripoli and discussing plans for the coming days. Tarhouni said the TNC has been in constant communication with its people in Tripoli, including both fighters and those entrusted with implementing the stabilization plans. Rebels in Tripoli, in coordination with the TNC, have begun to set up checkpoints inside the city and guard public buildings.

TNC chairman Abd al Jalil and PM Jabril made statements to the media last night, urging people to refrain from revenge attacks and destruction of public buildings.

There has so far been 'no bloodbath' or serious looting.

The capture of Saif al-Islam al-Qadhafi and Mohamed at-Qadhafi is significant. The TNC, including Abd al-Jalil himself, intervened with rebels surrounding Mohamed's house to ensure that they didn't harm him. They understood that it would be harmful to the revolution and the TNC if he were killed. These events were captured live by Al Jazeera in interviews with Mohamed. Both brothers are in rebel custody (at this time, it is unclear to us exactly who is holding them, however).

Per Tarhouni, the next steps are: 1) find Muammar Qadhafi; 2) issue a statement announcing the end of the Qadhafi regime and the start of the interim period under the TNC (TNC staff have begun drafting this statement already); 3) insure the delivery of essential services and commodities (esp. addressing the acute shortages of fuel, children's milk, and medication for blood pressure and diabetes); and 4) move the TNC to Tripoli.

Regarding the move to Tripoli, Tarhouni said security arrangements would need to be made before they could send the TNC leadership to the capital. We have heard from another contact that some TNC members are already making plans to fly to Misurata and the Western Mountains, possibly as early as today, and from there drive to Tripoli.[179]

---

[178] *Id.*

[179] Email to Jacob J. Sullivan, Dir. of Policy Planning, U.S. Dep't of State, *et al.* (Aug. 22, 2011, 6:54 AM) (on file with the Committee, SCB0045093).

As Stevens filed his reports, State Department personnel continued to monitor.[180] The Post Management Officer, who handled logistics for Stevens' mission, told the Committee:

> In the initial insertion period, we were speaking to the team on the ground on a regular basis, and we would say we will touch base with you again in X number of hours and have another phone call.
>
> I don't know when we shifted to a regular schedule versus when we were just saying, okay, we've heard from you now. Okay. Let's talk again in 6 hours once things have gone on. We'll give you 8 hours and let you sleep, and then we'll talk to you again, kind of thing.[181]

Polaschik reported:

> I saw my role as his [Stevens] backstop, because having been in a situation where the security environment was very fluid, and having limited resources, knowing that their communications setup was less than ideal as they were getting started, I thought it was very important for him to have a single point of contact that he could reach out to that could then communicate information, requests, et cetera; and also I personally felt very invested in what was happening, and I wanted to be there for him.[182]

Later in her testimony, Polaschik said:

> Quite early on, it looked as if Chris and team had just arrived. There was a moment when it looked like a city called Ajdabiya was about to fall to Qadhafi forces. I remember it was a Saturday, and I was on a conference call, and I remember talking to Chris and saying, are you sure you should stay? Because my perspective is very much with the events in Tripoli when we were evacuating fresh in my mind, things can change on a moment's notice; I would feel much better if he would get out now.
>
> And Chris had, I think, a different tolerance for risk than I did. And he felt that the conditions on the ground were such that it was okay to stay. And, again, these were conference calls that involved a variety of actors in the State Department. I believe Op Center was on it and was probably documenting the call as well. So that was one instance.
>
> But in terms of the overall what is our future, I don't remember the specifics, but I do remember an overall very strong impression from Chris that he felt it was important to stay, and the conditions were such that they should.[183]

---

[180] *See* Post Mgmt. Officer for Libya Testimony at 115.
[181] *Id.* at 108.
[182] Polaschik Testimony at 28.
[183] *Id.* at 30.

## Recognition of the TNC

The discussion in the summer among senior officials in Washington also turned toward supporting the TNC to an even greater degree.[184] The first step in supporting the emerging council was determining when and how to recognize them. Stevens reported to Washington earlier in June "substantial pockets of people in Benghazi and Eastern Libya . . . are questioning the TNC's legitimacy."[185] At the behest of the Secretary, the United States took the unprecedented step of formally recognizing the Transitional National Government on July 15, 2011,[186] terming it the "legitimate representative of the Libya People,"[187] but not the legitimate government of Libya.[188] Fishman explained the difference:

> A: That was how we could recognize the Libyan authorities as the legitimate representative of the Libyan people, which would in essence, derecognize the Qadhafi regime as the Government of Libya.
>
> Q: But did you draw a distinction between recognizing them as the representative of the Libyan people and recognizing them as the legitimate Libyan Government?
>
> A: I believe so, because they didn't have a government at the time.[189]

Notwithstanding the United States' decision to recognize the TNC as the legitimate representative of the Libyan People, the State Department made clear "it did not intend to establish a formal diplomatic Mission in Benghazi."[190] State Department officials were worried:

> [E]stablishment of a formal diplomatic mission in Benghazi would undermine this commitment [to a unified, free Libya with Tripoli as its capital] and send the wrong political message. Establishment of a formal diplomatic mission in Benghazi also would set off a chain of complex legal and administrative requirements that do not make sense for what is intended to be a short-term presence.[191]

While formally recognizing the Benghazi diplomatic mission may have created issues for Washington, especially if the mission were considered "short term," there was a benefit to the TNC: the re-

---

[184] See Fishman Testimony at 22 ("[D]uring the intervention, we were trying, as mandated by the Security Council, to protect the civilian population of the Libyan people, and once their regime was collapsed, we were trying to, as we saw it, help the Libyans stabilize their country and support the interim authorities to do that.").

[185] See Email from Special Ass't, Office of Deputy Sec'y, U.S. Dep't of State, to Thomas R. Nides, Deputy Sec'y of State, U.S. Dep't of State (June 7, 2011, 7:38 PM) (on file with the Committee, SCB0074994) (discussing the TNC's legitimacy).

[186] Hillary R. Clinton, Sec'y of State, U.S. Dep't of State, Remarks on Libya and Syria (July 15, 2011), http://www.state.gov/secretary/20092013clinton/rm/2011/07/168656.htm.

[187] Fishman Testimony at 32.

[188] Id. at 33–34.

[189] Id. at 60.

[190] See Email from Senior Desk Officer to Libya, Office of Maghreb Affairs, Bureau of Near Eastern Affairs, U.S. Dep't of State, to J. Christopher Stevens, U.S. Rep. to Transitional Nat'l Council ("stevens chris") (July 27, 2011, 9:22 AM) (on file with the Committee, C05390164) (attaching draft staffing paper).

[191] Email from William V. Roebuck, Dir. Office of Maghreb Affairs, Bureau of Near Eastern Affairs, U.S. Dep't of State, to Joan A. Polaschik State, Deputy Chief of Mission in Libya, U.S. Dep't of State (July 18, 2011, 8:17 PM) (on file with the Committee, C05579345).

lease of previously frozen funds to them. Fishman told the Committee:

> Well, it led to this complicated process that allowed us to unfreeze some assets because the Central Bank and other financial institutions . . . still had their assets frozen [192]
>
> \* \* \*
>
> [B]y recognizing the NTC [sic], as subsequently other countries did or previously and subsequently other countries did, we [the United States] were able to engage in the process where we were ultimately able to create a temporary funding mechanism where we could release some assets . . . to help defray their cost of running Benghazi.[193]

Private business also stood to gain from the unfreezing of Libyan assets. One such business was Osprey Global Solutions in which Sidney Blumenthal had a financial interest.[194] According to Osprey's Chief Operating Officer, the plan was for the United States to unfreeze the frozen Libyan assets.[195] These assets could then be used by the new Libyan government to fund humanitarian assistance,[196] an idea proposed by the Secretary herself.[197]

According to internal company documents, Osprey identified a 300-foot hospital vessel—including a crematorium.[198] Osprey provided to the Libyans details about this hospital ship, even down to the number of physicians on board (16), nurses (40), custodial and kitchen staff (18). Osprey also provided hard figures on how much it would cost to procure the ship, maintain the ship, and acquire medical equipment.[199]

On July 14, 2011—the day before the United States officially recognized the TNC as the legitimate representative of the Libyan people—Blumenthal emailed the Secretary twice.[200] One email contained the subject "H: IMPORTANT FOR YOUR MEETING. Sid."[201] The other email contained the subject "Re: H: Pls call before you leave for Turkey. Important re your trip. Sid."[202] That email contained the note "read the memo I sent you. Here it is again."[203] The contents of both emails are identical:—Blumenthal

[192] Fishman Testimony at 60.

[193] *Id.* at 33.

[194] Blumenthal Testimony at 44.

[195] *Id.* at 113.

[196] *See* Osprey Global Solutions, Capabilities Brief: Libya Citizens & LSM Initiatives, Osprey Global Solutions, at 71 [hereinafter Osprey Brief] (on file with Committee) ("Citizens Initiative: Phase 2—Frozen Libyan—USA Funds").

[197] Scott Shane & Jo Becker, *A New Libya, With 'Very Little Time Left,'* N.Y. TIMES, (Feb. 27, 2016),

    http://www.nytimes.com/2016/02/28/us/politics/libya-isis-hillary-clinton.html.

[198] Osprey Brief, *supra* note 196, at 31–35 (presenting the "Citizens Initiative: Phase 1—Multi-Purpose Hospital Ship").

[199] *Id.*

[200] Email from Sidney Blumenthal ("sbwhoeop") to Hillary R. Clinton ("H"), Sec'y of State, U.S. Dep't of State (July 14, 2011, 10:38 AM) (on file with the Committee, SCB0078451); Email from Sidney Blumenthal ("sbwhoeop") to Hillary R. Clinton ("H"), Sec'y of State, U.S. Dep't of State (July 14, 2011, 7:03 PM) (on file with the Committee, SCB0078453).

[201] Email from Sidney Blumenthal ("sbwhoeop") to Hillary R. Clinton ("H"), Sec'y of State, U.S. Dep't of State (July 14, 2011, 10:38 AM) (on file with the Committee, SCB0078451).

[202] Email from Sidney Blumenthal ("sbwhoeop") to Hillary R. Clinton ("H"), Sec'y of State, U.S. Dep't of State (July 14, 2011, 7:03 PM) (on file with the Committee, SCB0078453).

[203] *Id.*

described Osprey and the funding issues associated with his venture. The emails read:

> You should be aware that there is a good chance at the contact meeting in Turkey the TNC ambassador to the UAE, a man you have not yet met, whose name is Dr. Neydah, may tell you the TNC has reached an agreement with a US company. The company is a new one, Osprey, headed by former General David Grange, former head of Delta Force. Osprey will provide field medical help, military training, organize supplies, and logistics to the TNC. They are trainers and organizers, not fighters. Grange can train their forces and he has drawn up a plan for taking Tripoli similar to the plan he helped develop that was used by the first wave of Special Forces in the capture of Baghdad.
>
> This is a private contract. It does not involve NATO. It puts Americans in a central role without being direct battle combatants. The TNC wants to demonstrate that they are pro-US. They see this as a significant way to do that. They are enthusiastic about this arrangement. They have held meetings with Grange in Geneva and Dubai this week, Tuesday and Wednesday, that concluded late last night (Wednesday). They have developed a good relationship. This is the group the TNC wants to work with. As I understand it, they are still working out funding, which is related to the overall TNC funding problems.
>
> Grange is very low key, wishes to avoid publicity and work quietly, unlike other publicity hungry firms. Grange is under the radar.
>
> Tyler, Cody and I acted as honest brokers, putting this arrangement together through a series of connections, linking the Libyans to Osprey and keeping it moving. The strategic imperative: Expecting Gaddafi to fall on his own or through a deus ex machina devolves the entire equation to wishful thinking. The TNC has been unable to train and organize its forces. The NATO air campaign cannot take ground. The TNC, whose leaders have been given to flights of fancy that Qaddafi will fall tomorrow or the day after, have come to the conclusion that they must organize their forces and that they must score a military victory of their own over Qaddafi that is not dependent solely on NATO in order to give them legitimacy.[204]

Upon receiving these emails, the Secretary forwarded one to Sullivan and said "Pls read and discuss w me at hotel. Thx."[205] She also responded to Blumenthal. First she wrote: "I just landed and

---

[204] *Id.*

[205] Email from Hillary R. Clinton ("H"), Sec'y of State, U.S. Dep't of State, to Jacob J. Sullivan, Dir. of Policy Planning, U.S. Dep't of State (July 14, 2011, 6:47 PM) (on file with the Committee, SCB0078451).

will call shortly."[206] She followed with: "Got it. Will followup tomorrow. Anything else to convey?"[207]

The following day, the United States formally recognized the TNC as the legitimate representative of the Libyan people, allowing the TNC to access $30 billion in Libyan assets held in the United States.[208]

On August 24, 2011, Osprey and the TNC entered into a Memorandum of Understanding that read, in part:

> Per meetings held 13 July and 20 Aug 2011 in Dubai with Dr. Aref Aly Nayed and in Amman on 23 and 24 August with Mohammad Kikhia, this agreement is entered into this 24th day of August 2011 between the National Transitional Council of Libya (hereinafter referred to as "NTC"), now recognized by the United States Government of America as the legitimate and sole government of the Republic of Libya (ROL), and Osprey Global Solutions, LLC . . . The specific tasks—Scope of Work (SOW) the NTC desires to retain Osprey to perform include but are not limited to . . . Provide ship-to-shore (maritime) logistical support, advanced field hospital services and mobile command and control . . .[209]

The total cost in the Memorandum for the first year of Osprey's services—to include the "multi-purpose 302' ship"—was $114 million.[210]

The head of Osprey, General David L. Grange, also wrote Andrew J. Shapiro, Assistant Secretary for Political-Military Affairs, regarding the hospital ship.[211] In the letter Mr. Grange wrote Osprey was prepared to provide the following services:

> Provide ship-to-shore (maritime) medical and logistical support, advanced field hospital services and mobile command and control; this would include the immediate deployment of a hospital ship equipped with rotary wing assets . . .[212]

Ultimately the National Security Council rejected the hospital ship proposal.[213]

### Senior Official Travel to Libya

Despite the tenuous security environment in the summer of 2011, senior officials from Washington D.C., including Feltman, William Roebuck, Director, Office of Maghreb Affairs, Bureau of

---

[206] Email from Hillary R. Clinton ("H"), Sec'y of State, U.S. Dep't of State, to Sidney Blumenthal ("sbwhoeop") (July 14, 2011, 6:31 PM) (on file with the Committee, SCB0078454).

[207] Email from Hillary R. Clinton ("H"), Sec'y of State, U.S. Dep't of State, to Sidney Blumenthal ("sbwhoeop") (July 14, 2011, 7:37 PM) (on file with the Committee, SCB0078453).

[208] Sebnem Arsu & Steven Erlanger, *Libyan Rebels Get Formal Backing, and $30 Billion*, N.Y. TIMES (July 15, 2011), http://www.nytimes.com/2011/07/16/world/africa/16libya.html?_r=0.

[209] Osprey Global Solutions, Memorandum of Understanding (Aug. 24, 2011) (on file with Committee).

[210] *Id.*

[211] Letter from David L. Grange to Andrew J. Shapiro, Asst. Sec'y for Political-Military Affairs, U.S. Dep't of State (Jan. 4, 2012) (on file with Committee).

[212] *Id.*

[213] Scott Shane & Jo Becker, *A New Libya, With 'Very Little Time Left,'* N.Y. TIMES, (Feb. 27, 2016), http://www.nytimes.com/2016/02/28/us/politics/libya-isis-hillary-clinton.html.

Near Eastern Affairs, State Department, and Fishman, traveled to Benghazi.[214] Feltman wrote to the Secretary during his August 2011 trip to Benghazi:

> I have joined our representative, Chris Stevens, in meetings with a large number of representatives from the TNC, civil society, UN organizations and NGOs, and diplomatic corps. While we had no idea our trip would correspond with the significant military advances in the east and start the coordinated Tripoli uprising dubbed "Operation Mermaid Dawn," the timing gave us the opportunity to note the contrast between the relative bureaucratic quiet here compared to the hyped-up activity in western Libya.[215]

He also described the impact the assassination of General Younis, commander of the rebel forces, had on the security environment in Benghazi.[216] He spoke of the "two realities of Libyan life that TNC officials had previously tried to downplay: tribes and militia . . . On reigning [sic] in the militia we heard no good answers."[217]

It was also during this trip to Benghazi Feltman discussed with Stevens the future of the Benghazi Mission:

> During the August trip, Chris and I talked about, frankly, our shared view that we needed to maintain a longer presence in Benghazi than the fall of Tripoli might otherwise suggest. I was in Benghazi when the battle for Tripoli began, and it was clear that this time, it was inevitable that Qadhafi was leaving Tripoli even though he wasn't, of course, found and killed until later.

> And so Chris and I did talk in that August trip about the fact that both of us believed that we needed to maintain some kind of presence in Benghazi for the foreseeable future. We didn't talk about how long, but given the history of Libya, given the history of the revolution, given the need for Benghazi to remain supportive of whatever government took form in Tripoli, we thought it was politically extremely important that we maintain some kind of presence in Benghazi beyond the fall of Tripoli.[218]

## THE FALL OF QADHAFI

With NATO airstrikes providing cover, by August 2011, the Libyan opposition was finally able to push back against Qadhafi's

---

[214] Email from Huma Abedin, Deputy Chief of Staff to U.S. Sec'y of State, U.S. Dep't of State, to Hillary R. Clinton ("H"), Sec'y of State, U.S. Dep't of State (Aug. 21, 2011, 9:26 AM) (on file with the Committee, SCB0045090–92) (Ms. Abedin forwarding Mr. Feltman's message to Sec'y Clinton).

[215] *Id.*

[216] General Younis, a former Libyan interior minister under Qadhafi, defected to the rebel side when the revolution began and became the commander-in-chief of the rebel forces in Libya.

[217] Email from Huma Abedin, Deputy Chief of Staff to U.S. Sec'y of State, U.S. Dep't of State, to Hillary R. Clinton ("H"), Sec'y of State, U.S. Dep't of State (Aug. 21, 2011, 9:26 AM) (on file with the Committee, SCB0045090–92).

[218] *See* Feltman Testimony at 44–45.

forces.[219] On August 21, 2011, rebels advanced into Tripoli.[220] The next morning, Stevens provided an update to the senior leaders at the State Department on the events in Tripoli and the TNC's urgent request for "essential . . . commodities."[221] Stevens described the events unfolding and made the following request:

> Request for assistance: Tarhouni who also holds US citizenship said items listed above (gas, diesel, baby milk, and medicine) are urgently needed in Tripoli and recommend that USG ship items directly to Zawiya's Port and publicize such assistance as soon as feasible (in coordination with the TNC). He said this would bring the US even more goodwill than it has already earned here.[222]

The Secretary responded to her staff five minutes later asking: "Can we arrange shipments of what's requested?"[223] Sullivan replied seven minutes later saying the NSS and Department of Defense were already pursuing the effort.[224]

The Secretary also told her inner circle she wanted to do a press event as it would be "[g]ood to remind ourselves and the rest of the world that this couldn't have happened [without] us"[225] and "would be a great [opportunity] to describe all we've been doing . . ."[226] She and her staff discussed her traveling to Martha's Vineyard to be seen with the President celebrating their Libyan success.[227] Her top policy director commented: "It will show potus [President of the United States] not on vacation. He's huddling with you. This must be a political boost, right?"[228]

At about the same time, Blumenthal wrote:

> First, brava! This is a historic moment and you will be credited for realizing it.
>
> When Qaddafi himself is finally removed, you should of course make a public statement before the cameras wherever you are, even in the driveway of your vacation house. You must go on camera. You must establish yourself in the historical record at this moment.

---

[219] See John F. Burns, *NATO Bombs Tripoli in Heaviest Strikes Yet*, N.Y. TIMES (May 23, 2011), http://www.nytimes.com/2011/05/24/world/africa/24libya.html.

[220] Kareem Fahim & David D. Kirkpatrick, *Jubilant Rebels Control Much of Tripoli*, N.Y. TIMES (Aug. 21, 2011), http://www.nytimes.com/2011/08/22/world/africa/22libya.html.

[221] Email from Huma Abedin, Deputy Chief of Staff to U.S. Sec'y of State, U.S. Dep't of State, to Hillary R. Clinton ("H"), Sec'y of State, U.S. Dep't of State (Aug. 22, 2011, 7:07 AM) (on file with the Committee, SCB0045093) (forwarding update from Stevens in Benghazi).

[222] *Id.*

[223] Email from Hillary R. Clinton ("H"), Sec'y of State, U.S. Dep't of State, to Huma Abedin, Deputy Chief of Staff to U.S. Sec'y of State, U.S. Dep't of State (Aug. 22, 2011, 7:11 AM) (on file with the Committee, SCB0045095).

[224] Email from Jacob J. Sullivan, Dir. of Policy Planning, U.S. Dep't of State, to Huma Abedin, Deputy Chief of Staff to U.S. Sec'y of State, U.S. Dep't of State & Hillary R. Clinton ("H"), Sec'y of State, U.S. Dep't of State (Aug. 22, 2011, 7:17 AM) (on file with the Committee, SCB0045097).

[225] Email from Hillary R. Clinton ("H"), Sec'y of State, U.S. Dep't of State, to Jacob J. Sullivan, Dir. of Policy Planning, U.S. Dep't of State, Cheryl D. Mills, Chief of Staff and Counselor to U.S. Sec'y of State, U.S. Dep't of State & Huma Abedin, Deputy Chief of Staff to U.S. Sec'y of State, U.S. Dep't of State (Aug. 22, 2011, 7:32 AM) (on file with the Committee, SCB0078489)

[226] Email from Hillary R. Clinton ("H"), Sec'y of State, U.S. Dep't of State, to Jacob J. Sullivan, Cheryl D. Mills & Huma Abedin (Aug. 22, 2011, 7:16 AM) (on file with the Committee, SCB0078489).

[227] Email from Hillary R. Clinton ("H"), Sec'y of State, U.S. Dep't of State, to Jacob J. Sullivan & Huma Abedin (Aug. 22, 2011, 7:09 AM) (on file with the Committee, SCB0078489).

[228] Email from Jacob J. Sullivan to Hillary R. Clinton ("H"), Cheryl D. Mills & Huma Abedin (Aug. 22, 2011, 7:27 AM) (on file with the Committee, SCB0078489).

The most important phrase is 'successful strategy.'[229]

Later in the message, Blumenthal wrote: "Be aware that some may attempt to justify the flamingly stupid 'leading from behind' phrase, junior types on the NSC imagining their cleverness."[230]

The Secretary forwarded this message to Sullivan:

Pls read below. Sid makes a good case for what I should say but it's premised on being said after Q dies which will make it more dramatic. That's my hesitancy since I'm not sure how many chances I'll get.[231]

Sullivan had already developed a detailed timeline of events and actions to demonstrate the Secretary's "leadership/ownership/stewardship of this country's Libya policy from start to finish."[232] He wrote:

HRC has been a critical voice on Libya in administration deliberations, at NATO, and in contact group meetings— as well as the public face of the U.S. effort in Libya. She was instrumental in securing the authorization, building the coalition, and tightening the noose around Qadhafi and his regime.[233]

## Limiting the Future U.S. Role

With the rebels capturing Tripoli in August 2011 and Qadhafi nowhere to be found, the TNC started to shift its leaders and headquarters to Tripoli.[234] As the situation in Libya appeared to stabilize, there was corresponding interest throughout the State Department and the administration to shift the focus back to Tripoli and reopen the U.S. Embassy in Tripoli as soon as possible.[235] Sullivan asked: "[W]hat's it gonna take to get a team on the ground in Tripoli?"[236] His colleague wrote back: "Exception to the BOG [boots on the ground] for Explosive Ordnance Detection and Marine FAST [Fleet Anti-terrorism security team.] An Ambassador to

---

[229] Email from Sidney Blumenthal ("Sid") to Hillary R. Clinton ("H") (Aug. 22, 2011, 11:25 AM) (on file with the Committee, SCB0051597).

[230] *Id.* The phrase "leading from behind" came from a remark by an Obama advisor quoted in a May 2, 2011 article by Ryan Lizza in *The New Yorker*. Ryan Lizza, *Leading from Behind*, NYT (Apr. 26, 2011), http://www.newyorker.com/news/news-desk/leading-from-behind.

[231] Email from Hillary R. Clinton ("H"), Sec'y of State, U.S. Dep't of State, to Jacob J. Sullivan, Dir. of Policy Planning, U.S. Dep't of State (Aug. 22, 2011, 3:46 PM) (on file with the Committee, SCB0051597).

[232] Tick Tock on Libya Email, *supra* note 19 (from Jacob J. Sullivan to Cheryl D. Mills & Victoria Nuland, forwarded to Sec'y Clinton, Aug. 22, 2011, 12:37 PM).

[233] *Id.*

[234] *See* Email from J. Christopher Stevens, U.S. Rep. to Transitional Nat'l Council, to Jeffrey D. Feltman, Ass't Sec'y of State, Bureau of Near Eastern Affairs, U.S. Dep't of State, *et al.* (Aug. 23, 2011, 11:29 AM) (on file with the Committee, SCB00100119) (discussing TNC plans to relocate to Tripoli); *see also* Exec. Secretariat, Operations Ctr., Situation Report No. 14, Libya Task Force TFLY03 (Sept. 4, 2011, 4:00 PM) (on file with the Committee, SCB0074167) ("The TNC's Ministry of Foreign Affairs will move from Benghazi to Tripoli September 4 and will be housed in the Qadhafi-era MFA building.").

[235] *See* Email from Lee Lohman, Ex. Dir., Bureau of Near Eastern Affairs, U.S. Dep't of State, to Patrick Kennedy, Under Sec'y of State for Mgmt., U.S. Dep't of State (Sept. 2, 2011) (on file with the Committee, SCB0096224) ("Jeff send [sic] an email from Paris yesterday expressing frustration that we don't have a presence in Tripoli.").

[236] Email from Jacob J. Sullivan, Dir. of Policy Planning, U.S. Dep't of State (Aug. 30, 2011, 4:47 PM) (on file with the Committee, SCB0060918).

Libya who actually wants to go. Locking Pat Kennedy in a closet for long enough to actually take some real risks."[237]

As events unfolded in Tripoli, senior policy makers within the State Department discussed their goals for Libya, including: 1) bring the Lockerbie bomber to justice; and 2) recover the costs incurred in providing military and humanitarian aid to Libya; 3) recover and improve the position of U.S. Energy firms in Libya.[238] The fourth and final goal was to counter Islamist extremists, noting that there was a need to "avoid allowing the most extreme and certainly violent Islamist groups to use the new Libyan government and civil society as a platform. The American people and the U.S. Congress will be understandably irritated if a revolution that the United States supported ends up spewing hatred or advocating violence against the United States."[239]

These policy goals did not address how the U.S. government would assist Libya in transitioning to a functioning government post-Qadhafi.[240] Nor did they discuss any role the Mission in Benghazi might play in these efforts.[241]

Stevens wanted to maintain a presence in Benghazi for the short term, writing on September 6, 2011: "As the Dept stands up a Mission in Tripoli, the question arises as to how long to keep Mission Benghazi operating. I believe it would be prudent to maintain a small State-run presence here for at least 6 months."[242]

Polaschik also saw the benefits of maintaining a short-term presence in Benghazi. She testified:

> Qadhafi had just fled Tripoli. He was still on the loose, on the lam. We were not yet back in Tripoli. It wasn't clear if or when the leadership of the transitional office or Council would transition from Benghazi to Tripoli, if they all would, what would be there. And given the critical role that Benghazi had played in the start of the revolution and the execution, so to speak, of the revolution and the leadership, of course it made sense to have a presence there for another 6 months."[243]

She elaborated:

> [S]ome officials from the Transitional National Council were beginning to shift to Tripoli. Others were still there,

---

[237] Email to Jacob J. Sullivan, Dir. of Policy Planning, U.S. Dep't of State, (Aug. 30, 2011, 4:50 PM) (on file with the Committee, SCB0060918).

[238] *See* Email to Jacob J. Sullivan, Dir. of Policy Planning, U.S. Dep't of State (Aug. 29 2011, 5:01 PM) (on file with the Committee, SCB0060926–30) (attaching Note for the Secretary re: U.S. Interests in post-Qadhafi Libya).

[239] *Id.*

[240] *Id.* The lack of post-Qadhafi planning is consistent with the President's recent statement that his biggest foreign policy failure was not properly planning for post-Qadhafi Libya. The lack of planning is also in stark contrasts with statements by the Secretary that they did plan for post-Qadhafi Libya but it was "obstruction" by the Libyan people to the United States' efforts that led to the failed state of Libya today. *Barack Obama Says Libya Was 'Worst Mistake of His Presidency,* GUARDIAN (Apr. 11, 2016), http://www.theguardian.com/us-news/2016/apr/12/barack-obama-says-libya-was-worst-mistake-of-his-presidency.

[241] *See* Email to Jacob Sullivan, Dir. of Policy Planning, U.S. Dep't of State (Aug. 29 2011, 5:01 PM) (on file with the Committee, SCB0060926–30) (attaching Note for the Secretary re: U.S. Interests in post-Qadhafi Libya).

[242] Email from J. Christopher Stevens, U.S. Rep. to Transitional Nat'l Council, to Deputy Dir. Office of Maghreb Affairs, Bureau of Near Eastern Affairs, U.S. Dep't of State et al. (Sept. 6, 2011, 9:01 AM) (on file with the Committee, C05389443).

[243] Polaschik Testimony at 160.

so it was clear that there was going to be a period in which the political leadership of a free Libya, . . . the post-Qadhafi government was going to be in a variety of places; so we needed to make sure that we had the ability to touch them in both places, and from my perspective, it made a lot of sense to keep Chris there.[244]

The Post Management Officer for Libya testified closing the Mission was also an option: "In official conversations, as we met to discuss options related to the Benghazi footprint that was always one of the items that was out there as a potential decision point. As we were looking at security and others things, closure was always an option."[245]

Later in September 2011, Sullivan, Feltman, and William B. Taylor, the newly appointed head of the Middle East Transitions office, prepared a note for the Deputy Secretaries advocating U.S. involvement in Libya be significantly scaled back.[246] Outlining the level of priority Libya now had within the State Department, they wrote:

> [P]ost-conflict stabilization in Libya, while clearly a worthy undertaking at the right level of investment, cannot be counted as one of our highest priorities. Strategically for us, Libya does not loom as large as Egypt and Syria.[247]

They cautioned: "We should not allow the momentum of our involvement to date in the Libyan revolution to determine our strategy for longer-term assistance."[248] They emphasized "[t]his means that, for the United States, Libya must not become a state-building exercise."[249] They defined the circumstances under which the U.S. should, or should not, intercede, and argued the U.S. should only assist when 1) the U.S. had a "unique" ability to provide a particular service; 2) the U.S. has a proven track record of success and Congress will provide funds; and 3) Libyans expressly request the U.S. to do so, "[e]ven if we feel the Libyan government or its people are making a mistake in not seeking our help. . . ."[250]

According to these State Department officials, the highest priorities in Libya were to "secure weapons"; ensure an "effective democratic transition"; prevent "violent extremists" from "seizing control"; and "ensuring a level-playing field for U.S. businesses."[251]

Medium priority goals were reconciling former regime elements into Libyan society and "create a judicial system."[252] The lowest priority, according to these policy makers was to support a "broad program of economic reconstruction and diversification" and ensure

---

[244] *Id.* at 39–40.

[245] Post Mgmt. Officer for Libya Testimony at 174.

[246] Note from Jacob J. Sullivan, Dir., of Policy Planning, U.S. Dep't of State, *et al.* to William J. Burns, Deputy Sec'y of State, U.S. Dep't of State, and Thomas R. Nides, Deputy Sec'y of State, U.S. Dep't of State (Sept. 28, 2011) (on file with the Committee, SCB0090954–59), (discussing parameters for U.S. engagement in post-Qadhafi Libya).

[247] *Id.*

[248] *Id.*

[249] *Id.*

[250] *Id.*

[251] *Id.*

[252] *Id.*

the Libyans have the "ability to maintain delivery of basic services."[253]

The sentiment of the memorandum was clear: Once the civil war was over and Qadhafi was removed from power, the United States would move on.[254] The broad policies outlined by the senior State Department officials stood in direct contrast with what the State Department's own experts on the ground in Libya knew was needed to support the country moving forward.

In his interview with the Committee, Cretz described what he saw, knew, and believed needed to be done to stabilize Libya:

Q: . . . what was your sense of what challenges? [sic]

A: Well, number one, you know, Qadhafi ruled for 40 years and didn't allow the emergence of any institution that could rival his power and the influence of he and his small clique over the people and government of Libya, so consequently, after the fall, there really was nothing there. There was no institutions, you know, ministries. They never operated as a real government because Qadhafi ruled the roost.

So my concerns were, number one that we needed to find a way to help them build their infrastructure in terms of developing independent and capable institutions. My second concern was that there had to be a way to end the strife among the militias and that involved getting a strong and capable central government.

We had to deal with, you know, making sure that the oil resource, which was really the only resource that they depended on, was developed in a reasonable way and that the proceeds made their way back to the to the people of Libya. We had to ensure that there was a capable military, a capable counterintelligence, a counterterrorism capability as well.

So these were all kind of concerns that I had mentioned. The borders were porous. There had to be some kind of way to establish a border regime. There was a continuing threat of weapons, which had been collected by the Qadhafi regime and then loose, you know, basically spread throughout the country and began to be making their way through the region in Africa, et cetera, so that had to be a way to get control of that, so there were a lot of problems in the post Qadhafi era.

\*     \*     \*

Q: And with regard to the U.S., United States' engagement, involvement, and to the extent you can recall, would you have recommended that the U.S. become more engaged, less engaged? I know that you've already said that you did not recommend that we leave altogether, but do you have a sense of whether you felt it was important for

---

[253] *Id.*

[254] *See id.* ("The Administration has a primary interest in ensuring that others—the Libyans, the UN, the EU, and NGOs—take overall responsibility for post-conflict stabilization.").

us to increase our engagement as opposed to decrease our engagement?

A: Well, I think it was critical that the United States continue to play a vital role. I mean, given our past history, given what we did on the intervention, and given the fact that there was a real affection for the United States in the country in the aftermath of what we had done along with the French and British and others to overthrow Qadhafi, and I would have liked to have seen a more robust program.

But the truth of the matter was that when you don't have a functioning government, how do you provide resources to that government when there's no absorptive capacity? So this is the main problem that we ran into in the post war situation. You know, I can't say that there was a huge appetite in Washington to put hundreds of millions of dollars into Libya, but I can say there was an interest in ensuring, you know, our role there, ensuring that this evolving nation developed in a democratic tradition. But the truth is that there was no absorptive capacity to receive assistance and to help develop the nation along that way.[255]

## Embassy Tripoli Reopens: Impact on Benghazi Mission

As senior State Department officials were discussing their goals for Libya, nearly seven months after its personnel were evacuated and one month after the fall of Tripoli, the U.S. Embassy in Tripoli raised the American flag and restarted operations.[256] Cretz returned to Tripoli as Ambassador.[257] The precarious security environment in Libya precipitated the need for 16 Security Support Team [SST] members from the Defense Department, eighteen members of the State Department's own highly trained mobile security team, in addition to a temporary duty Diplomatic Security team, to protect the Ambassador and embassy personnel.[258] The Administration's policy of no boots on the ground once again shaped the type of military assistance that would be provided, with the Defense Department and the State Department going to great lengths to ensure the administration's policy was not violated. The Executive Secretariats for both the Defense Department and State Department exchanged communications outlining the diplomatic capacity in which the Defense Department SST security team

---

[255] Cretz Testimony at 145–47.

[256] Polaschik Testimony at 12–15:

> [When "] the Embassy evacuated to Washington, . . . we worked sort of in Embassy in exile . . . In August 2011, our official status as Embassy Tripoli expired because the State Department had run the course of the 180 days of evacuation status for Embassy Tripoli, so we created a new entity that we called the Libya cell. And the purpose of the Libya cell was to either staff the Mission in Benghazi if the situation continued and we needed to have our only representation in country in Benghazi because Qadhafi was still in Tripoli, or the Libya cell would serve as the nucleus of the group that would go back into Tripoli to reopen the Embassy." *Id.*

[257] *U.S. ambassador Gene Cretz returns to Libya*, USA TODAY (Sept. 21, 2011), http://usatoday30.usatoday.com/news/world/story/2011-09-21/us-reopens-libya-embassy/50491638/1.

[258] Cretz Testimony at 89–91.

members would serve, which included wearing civilian clothes so as not to offend the Libyans.[259]

The increased security was important as fighting in Libya continued. Cretz described to the Committee:

> [I]n general, Tripoli was still in the throes—in September of 2011 was still in the throes of civil war. Tripoli had fell—had fallen. But there were still active pockets of resistance throughout the country from Qadhafi loyalists.
>
> The country had also begun to break down in anticipation of a victory over Qadhafi into the militias that, in fact, were fighting Qadhafi. The war against Qadhafi was not by a unified opposition army.
>
> It was made up of a militia. The jihadists had a militia. The people from Zintan had a militia. The people from Misrata had a militia. So in anticipation of the final victory, they were, in effect, fighting it out.
>
> In a sense, a lot of what we see today in Libya, they were fighting it out for a foothold to make sure that they got a piece of the pie—a piece of the power pie once things settled down.
>
> So the situation in Tripoli was very unsettled.[260]

With Embassy Tripoli officially reopened, and Benghazi's future less than certain, Stevens asked the State Department to conclude his Mission on October 6, 2011, but he was asked to remain until Jibril, the interim Prime Minister, completed his relocation from Benghazi to Tripoli.[261] Feltman described his ongoing conversations with Stevens about Benghazi's future:

> The normal response would be once the government's in Tripoli . . . , then you close down Benghazi. That would be sort of a normal response given the budget climate, given all the other complications. And so Chris and I would talk about did we really think this was essential. Why did we think it was essential. And it had to do with, again, the fact that Libya had been essentially a divided country before, where Benghazi had been neglected, oppressed even by Qadhafi, but yet Benghazi was where this uprising had begun. It was where the Libyan revolution had begun, so it was important that Benghazi feel part of

---

[259] *See* Email from Patrick F. Kennedy, Under Sec'y of State for Mgmt., U.S. Dep't of State, to Charlene R. Lamb, Deputy Ass't Sec'y, Bureau of Diplomatic Sec., Int'l Programs, U.S. Dep't of State, (Sept. 6, 2011) (on file with the Committee, SCB0096343); *see also* Email from Patrick F. Kennedy, Under Sec'y of State for Mgmt., U.S. Dep't of State to Denis R. McDonough, Deputy Dir., Nat'l Sec. Council (Sept. 6, 2011, 12:32 PM) (on file with the Committee, SCB0096350) ("I have confirmed . . . [Special Air Services] folks in Tripoli supporting the restart of their Embassy, in civilian clothes. Have also reconfirmed with NEA that civilian clothes [and thus SOF] is the way we have to go.").

[260] Cretz Testimony at 83.

[261] *See* Email from Elizabeth L. Dibble, Principal Deputy Ass't Sec'y of State, Bureau of Near Eastern Affairs, U.S. Dep't of State, to Raymond D. Maxwell, Deputy Ass't Sec'y, Bureau of Near Eastern Affairs, William V. Roebuck, Dir. Office of Maghreb Affairs, Bureau of Near Eastern Affairs, U.S. Dep't of State, Lee Lohman, Ex. Dir., Bureau of Near Eastern Affairs, U.S. Dep't of State *et al.* (Sept. 20, 2011, 6:38 PM) (on file with the Committee, C05389443) (discussing reasons for Special Rep. Stevens to remain in Benghazi).

this process. We felt that having a small diplomatic presence in Benghazi it would not be the Embassy.

Clearly the Embassy would be accredited to the government in Tripoli but that that would keep our presence as well as the presence of others, because we were not the only ones looking at this, as well as the presence of others, would keep Benghazi as part of the political equation. Because if you didn't have Benghazi feeling invested in what was happening in Tripoli, you had the risks of the country splitting again, is what we clearly thought.[262]

Feltman further testified why the State Department did not make the Benghazi Mission official, especially when operations resumed in Tripoli:

So what we were trying to what Chris and I were trying to figure out was, how could we make a compelling enough argument that in the zero sum game that we have in terms of our budget and our resources, that we could find enough resources to keep Benghazi operating through the critical transition period? . . .

[T]he type of budget support out of Congress we would need. This is a time when the U.S. reduces diplomatic presences, doesn't expand them.[263]

Discussions also ensued over how to bring the personnel in Benghazi under the diplomatic umbrella of the Embassy in Tripoli without triggering formal recognition of the Benghazi office.[264]

Polaschik was aware of this issue and wanted to ensure that all personnel in Benghazi had the protections of the privileges and immunities accorded by the Vienna Convention.[265] Listing personnel in Benghazi as a separate office was rejected, however, as "[t]he reference to the establishment of an office in Benghazi may raise congressional notification issues. . . ."[266] Earlier in the year, Kennedy, determined congressional notification was not needed because "the Hill knows we are there."[267]

Ultimately, it was decided to submit "one dip[lomatic] list for Tripoli, but noting on it that certain staff members will be performing their duties on a TDY basis in Benghazi."[268] Thus, with-

---

[262] Feltman Testimony at 58.

[263] *Id.* at 46–47.

[264] *See* Post Mgmt. Officer for Libya Testimony at 131:

At some point in the fall of 2011, we exchanged diplomatic notes with the new Government of Libya in whatever form that happened to be, and with the return of Ambassador Cretz, a Special Representative was not needed at that point, because we had our accredited Ambassador in Tripoli. So at that point, I believe, it when the term 'Special Representative' ceased to be used, but again, I don't have specific recollection of the timeline.

[265] *See* Email from Joan A. Polaschik, Deputy Chief of Mission in Libya, U.S. Dep't of State, to Post Mgmt. Officer for Libya, Bureau of Near Eastern Affairs, U.S. Dep't of State, and Senior Desk Officer for Libya, Bureau of Near Eastern Affairs, U.S. Dep't of State (Oct. 17, 2011, 10:09 AM) (on file with the Committee, C05528533) (discussing listing Benghazi team on diplomatic list).

[266] Email to Post Mgmt. Officer for Libya, Bureau of Near Eastern Affairs, U.S. Dep't of State (Nov. 9, 2011, 5:23 AM) (on file with the Committee, C05528533).

[267] Email (May 18, 2011, 1:13 PM) (on file with the Committee, C05391797).

[268] Email from Deputy Ex. Dir., Bureau of Near Eastern Affairs, U.S. Dep't of State, to Post Mgmt. Officer for Libya, Bureau of Near Eastern Affairs, U.S. Dep't of State, and Joan A.

Continued

out formally notifying the new Libyan government of the Benghazi Mission, the personnel in Benghazi received diplomatic immunity only because the State Department told the Libyan government the personnel in Benghazi were actually assigned to Tripoli.[269]

### Benghazi's Future

Senior officials in Washington discussed several options for Benghazi's future operations. Stevens proposed two options to State Department officials in early September 2011 to continue the Mission:

*Slimmed down compound:* Principal Office (FS–02 level) MGT/IRM and possibly one USAID/OTI officer (if they get requested funding). 4 DS. 1 admin LES [locally employed staff] plus guardforce.

Consolidated to Villa A (combine lodging/offices; beds for 7 plus 2 TDY [temporary duty] in living room; also possible to rent a small 1 bedroom house attached to Villa A belonging to same owner)

Duration: through September 30, 2012 (3 months beyond projected TNC elections)

Purpose: provide platform for POL/ECON [political/economic] reporting; PD and OTI programming;

PM/Conventional Weapons collection effort in east; commercial outreach.

Other Benghazi Missions: UNSMIL [United Nations Special Mission in Libya], EU and UK intend to maintain small branch offices for the next 6 months-one year. Italians and Turks have consulates.

*Virtual presence:* End all 3 compound leases. Zero full-time State Department staff. Use hotels (as Spanish, Greek and foreign NGOs have been doing). Possibly leave FAV in Benghazi **[redacted text]** to support TDY travel in eastern Libya.[270]

Feltman described the discussions to the Committee "[t]hey [sic] were ongoing discussions . . . because we needed to muster our arguments. We needed to muster our rationale. We needed to feel confident ourselves that this was the right thing to do before we would propose something that was going to be, you know, financially difficult."[271]

The Post Management Officer for Libya further explained to the Committee closing the mission was an option. "In official conversations, as we met to discuss options related to the Benghazi footprint that was always one of the items that was out there as a po-

---

Polaschik, Deputy Chief of Mission in Libya, U.S. Dep't of State (Nov. 9, 2011, 7:08 PM) (on file with the Committee, C05528533).

[269] *Id.* ("[C]ertain staff members will be performing their duties on a TDY basis in Benghazi.").

[270] Email from J. Christopher Stevens, U.S. Rep. to Transitional Nat'l Council, to William V. Roebuck, Dir. Office of Maghreb Affairs, Bureau of Near Eastern Affairs, U.S. Dep't of State, Gene A. Cretz, U.S. Ambassador to Libya, and Joan A. Polaschik, Deputy Chief of Mission in Libya, U.S. Dep't of State (Oct. 31, 2011, 3:08 PM) (on file with the Committee, C05394929).

[271] Feltman Testimony at 59.

tential decision point. As we were looking at security and other things, closure was always an option."[272] In September 2011, Cheryl Mills, Chief of Staff and Counselor, State Department, was likely briefed on a plan that would have closed Benghazi in January 2012.[273]

From a security standpoint, Eric Boswell, Assistant Secretary, Diplomatic Security, State Department, explained:

> Benghazi was originally envisaged at [sic] a short term thing. Our expectation in DS was that we were going to support Chris Stevens' effort for 60 days, 90 days, and that once an embassy was reestablished in Tripoli, if that was the outcome of the civil war, once the—well, if the right side one [sic] in Tripoli, once an embassy was to be reestablished, we anticipated that Benghazi would go out of business.
>
> The Embassy was reestablished in September, but the NEA Bureau asked us to keep a little presence in Benghazi, so a little longer a little longer. [sic] It was really quite incremental. A little longer, a little longer.[274]

Benghazi's uncertain future impacted Stevens and his team. The Diplomatic Security Agent in charge in the fall of 2011 testified:

> [W]e were still in this situation where we didn't know how long Benghazi was going to be. Tripoli was kicking off. And so there was a lot of interest in supporting that. So we were trying to figure out—or headquarters was trying to figure out where to prioritize our deficiencies, if you want to call it that. So no one knows.
>
> I mean, we were planning for the worst, phasing people out and trying to figure out how best to support the mission there. If I remember correctly, with the Embassy being opened—it opened towards the latter part of my tenure there. So the Envoy lost his, quote-unquote, status because there was now an Ambassador in country. . . . I think they were going to bring in a political officer, probably my rank. I'm pretty sure he was my rank. He was going to be the foothold there in Benghazi for the short term, but no one knew how long.[275]

While Stevens and his team waited to learn their status, security resources to the Mission decreased.[276] Stevens called an EAC meeting in October 2011 to evaluate the Mission's security posture after

---

[272] Post Mgmt. Officer for Libya Testimony at 174.

[273] See Memorandum to Cheryl D. Mills on Update on Tripoli Operations (Sept. 14, 2011) (on file with the Committee, C05578323) (discussing plans for activities in Benghazi through January 2012).

[274] Testimony of Eric J. Boswell, Ass't Sec'y of State, Bureau of Diplomatic Sec., U.S. Dep't of State, before H. Comm. on Oversight & Gov't Reform, Tr. at 17 (July 9, 2013) [hereinafter Boswell Testimony] (on file with the Select Committee on Benghazi).

[275] Testimony of Diplomatic Sec. Agent, Diplomatic Sec. Serv., U.S. Dep't of State, Tr. at 33–34 (May 21, 2015) [hereinafter Diplomatic Sec. Agent 13 Testimony] (on file with the Committee).

[276] Id. at 33.

the fall of Sirte, Qadhafi's birthplace.[277] Stevens and the Diplomatic Security Agents were concerned about the "recent reduction in DS manpower (the departure of several Agents in past week who ha[d] not . . . been backfilled)."[278] Another EAC was held three days later to discuss "the current situation in Benghazi and to address possible developments . . . that may arise in the next 24 hours."[279] A little more than a week later, a member of the February 17 Martyrs Brigade [February 17] who worked on the Mission compound came under attack on his way home.[280] That incident occurred approximately 500 meters from the compound.[281]

## Qadhafi's Death

With the future of a U.S. diplomatic presence in Benghazi being debated and discussed, the Secretary traveled to Tripoli, Libya on October 18, 2011.[282] During her day trip there, she met with members of the TNC, went to Tripoli University to meet with students, visited the medical center and the U.S. Embassy, and gave several speeches.[283] She did not visit Benghazi even though Stevens was still there. She did "not recall" speaking with Stevens during her trip to Libya.[284] Asked whether she discussed the future of the Mission there, Feltman, who traveled with the Secretary, told the Committee:

> If there were, it was quite light and in passage. She had a very, very busy schedule going to see a variety of Libyan officials, meeting with representatives of Libyan civil society, delivering a speech. It was a jam-packed day and it wasn't the type of quiet time to have sort of policy discussions like that.[285]

Two days later, on October 20, 2011, Qadhafi was captured and killed attempting to escape from his hometown of Sirte. The TNC "declared the liberation of Libya" and the revolutionary war officially ended on October 23, 2011.[286] The NATO-led military action, Operation Unified Protector, formally ended a week later.[287]

---

[277] Email to Diplomatic Sec. Command Ctr. (Oct. 17, 2011, 12:18 PM) (on file with the Committee, C05389778).

[278] Id.

[279] Email from Diplomatic Sec. Agent 13 to NEA–MAG–DL et al. (Oct. 20, 2011, 1:52 PM) (on file with the Committee, C05395038).

[280] Email from [REDACTED] (Benghazi) to 'Spot Reports,' et al. (Nov. 1, 2011, 4:49 AM) (on file with the Committee, C05272056).

[281] Id.

[282] Steven Lee Myers, In Tripoli, Clinton Pledges U.S. to a 'Free Libya,' N.Y. TIMES (Oct. 18, 2011), http://www.nytimes.com/2011/10/19/world/africa/clinton-in-libya-to-meet-leaders-and-offer-aid-package.html.

[283] Id.

[284] Clinton Testimony at 155–56.

[285] Feltman Testimony at 85.

[286] See NTC declares 'Liberation of Libya,' AL JAZEERA (Oct. 24, 2011), http://www.aljazeera.com/news/africa/2011/10/201110235316778897.html; see also Press Release, The White House Office of the Press Secretary, Statement by the President on the Declaration of Liberation in Libya (Oct. 23, 2011), https://www.whitehouse.gov/the-press-office/2011/10/23/statement-president-declaration-liberation-libya ("On behalf of the American people, I congratulate the people of Libya on today's historic declaration of liberation. After four decades of brutal dictatorship and eight months of deadly conflict, the Libyan people can now celebrate their freedom and the beginning of a new era of promise.").

[287] NATO ends Libya mission, CNN (Nov. 3, 2011), http://www.cnn.com/2011/10/31/world/Africa/libya-nato-mission.

When informed of Qadhafi's death, the Secretary said: "We came, we saw, he died."[288]

Approximately a month after Qadhafi's death, Susan Rice, United States Permanent Representative to the United Nations, also traveled to Libya, including Benghazi.[289] Despite "walk[ing] the streets of Benghazi," Rice would not comment to the Committee on whether she visited the Mission compound in Benghazi.[290] Less than a month later, in December 2011, Leon Panetta, the Secretary of Defense, traveled to Libya.[291] Because of security concerns, Panetta's time in Libya was brief and did not include a trip to Benghazi.[292]

## FURTHER EXTENDING THE MISSION

With Embassy Tripoli officially up and running, and the return of Cretz to Libya, Stevens departed Benghazi in late November 2011.[293] Before he left, however, he was asked to return as Ambassador. Cretz was informed of this change as well.[294] According to Polaschik: "[I]t's very inappropriate for someone sitting in country to be working in country. I mean, it's an unusual situation. In order to be nominated and get through the congressional confirmation process, I think it was better for him [Stevens] to be here [in Washington]."[295] Stevens would remain outside of Libya from November 2011 until May 26, 2012.

### Security Remains Unstable

Security continued to be unstable in December 2011. The Security Environment Threat List [SETL] rating for Libya was critical for political violence and high for terrorism and crime.[296] SETL ratings are essential State Department tools in determining the countermeasures a facility must put in place to mitigate a threat.[297] A critical rating is the most serious rating—indicating there is a grave impact to diplomats.[298] A high rating indicates there is a serious impact on American diplomats.[299] In late December 2011, right before holidays, there was open source reporting about a threat to western embassies located in Benghazi during

---

[288] Corbett Daly, *Clinton on Qaddafi: "We came, we saw, he died,"* CBS NEWS (Oct. 20, 2011), http://www.cbsnews.com/news/clinton-on-qaddafi-we-came-we-saw-he-died.

[289] Press Release, U.S. Mission to the U.N., Remarks by Ambassador Susan E. Rice, U.S. Permanent Rep. to the U.N., Following Sec. Council Consultations on Libya (Nov. 28, 2011), http://iipdigital.usembassy.gov/st/english/texttrans/2011/11/20111129113633su0.6971203.html?distid=ucs#axzz48qWq65Vj.

[290] Testimony of Susan E. Rice, U.S. Permanent Rep. to the U.N., Tr. at 134 (Feb. 2, 2016) (on file with the Committee).

[291] *Defense chief Panetta visits Libya,* USA Today (Dec. 17, 2011), http://usatoday30.usatoday.com/news/world/story/2011-12-17/panetta-libya/52019842/1.

[292] *See id.*

[293] *See* Email from J. Christopher Stevens, U.S. Rep. to Transitional Nat'l Council, to Post Mgmt. Officer for Libya, Bureau of Near Eastern Affairs, U.S. Dep't of State (Nov. 10, 2011, 10:39 AM) (on file with the Committee, SCB0079464) ("I'll check in with you all myself when I'm back in [Washington D.C.] the week of Nov 21.").

[294] *See* Email from Gene A. Cretz, U.S. Ambassador to Libya, to Cheryl D. Mills, Chief of Staff and Counselor to the U.S. Sec'y of State, U.S. Dep't of State (Oct. 21, 2011, 4:50 AM) (on file with the Committee, SCB0045106).

[295] Polaschik Testimony at 40.

[296] Email from Diplomatic Sec. Agent 24 to Diplomatic Sec. Agent 10 (Dec. 15, 2011, 9:03 AM) (on file with the Committee, C05388931).

[297] *See* ALEX TIERSKY & SUSAN B. EPSTEIN, CONG. RESEARCH SERV., RL42834, SECURING U.S. DIPLOMATIC FACILITIES AND PERSONNEL ABROAD: BACKGROUND AND POLICY ISSUES 6 (2014).

[298] *Id.*

[299] *Id.*

Christmas and New Year's Eve in 2011.[300] The Mission held an EAC led by the new Principal Officer to discuss its security posture in light of the threat and the overall security environment and to discuss the need for additional security resources.[301]

The incoming Diplomatic Security Agent in charge described the Mission compound when he arrived to the facility in late November 2011.[302] He told the Committee: "While I was in Benghazi . . . the compound was woefully inadequate in terms of physical security. There were a whole number of things that we didn't have, and a lot of things that we did have were completely insufficient."[303]He observed:

> [O]ur perimeter security is nonexistent, we have walls with lattices that somebody can shoot through; we have walls with footholds people can climb over; we have a 4 foot wall back here; we have no lighting. So all these physical security standards, especially around the perimeter of the building were completely insufficient, and we needed large amounts of money and this was going to take time, it was going to be expensive, but we needed this desperately to make this place safe.[304]

With normal security standards not applicable in Benghazi and a decreasing number of Diplomatic Security Agents on the ground, the incoming Diplomatic Security Agents were forced to request the most rudimentary measures to improve security on the compound.[305] The Diplomatic Security Agent on the ground told the Committee: "[O]nce I became RSO, I started a flurry of requests asking for physical security upgrades."[306] He further stated: "I put together a list of, call it a dozen requests in terms of guard platforms, sandbags, sent that out initially in kind of an informal email, because we didn't have any ability to send cables."[307]

For example, on December 21, 2011, the Mission requested funding from Washington for 17 jersey barriers to serve as anti-ram barriers.[308] The barriers were on sale from the British who were closing their compound in Benghazi and moving their operations back to their Embassy in Tripoli.[309] A day later, the agent made another request for "some escape hatches in the iron window bars

---

[300] *See* Email from Diplomatic Sec. Agent 10 to Diplomatic Sec. Agent 25 (Dec. 21, 2011, 8:50 EST) (on file with the Committee, C05396082) (discussing reporting of threat to U.S. compound in Benghazi).

[301] *See* Principal Officer 1, U.S. Dep't of State, to Joan A. Polaschik, Deputy Chief of Mission in Libya, U.S. Dep't of State, *et al.* (Dec. 23, 2011, 7:34 AM) (on file with the Committee, C05392213) (Distributing notes from EAC).).

[302] *See* Diplomatic Sec. Agent 10 Testimony at 19.

[303] *Id.*

[304] *Id.* at 25–26.

[305] *See* Testimony of Diplomatic Sec. Agent, U.S. Dep't of State, Tr. at 26 (Apr. 9, 2015) [hereinafter Diplomatic Sec. Agent 12 Testimony] (on file with the Committee) ("[W]e identified some—you know, identified a contractor to come in and cut those window grilles off and then replace them with a system that was very, very, you know, rudimentary, but it worked.").

[306] Diplomatic Sec. Agent 10 Testimony at 19.

[307] *Id.* at 20.

[308] Email from Diplomatic Sec. Agent 10 to Physical Sec. Specialist, Physical Sec. Programs, Bureau of Diplomatic Sec., U.S. Dep't (Dec. 21, 2011, 12:27 PM) (on file with the Committee, C05396085).

[309] *Id.*

on the villas."[310] That same day, the Diplomatic Security Agent's request was expanded to include:

> [A]dditional security measures that are desperately needed (lighting for areas of the compound that are completely dark, sandbags, platforms that we can place against the perimeter walls so we can see over them—we have significant blind spots in our video camera coverage, a guard shack for outside of the main entrance, etc).[311]

As Benghazi was requesting additional security measures, the Mission was experiencing significant shortages in Diplomatic Security Agents. A Diplomatic Security Agent on the ground at the time described his concern to the Committee:

> It was down to two agents, myself and one other agent. And as I was getting ready to depart, we were going to go to one agent. And if the staffing pattern remained the way it was, with our expected incoming agents, we were going to go down to zero agents. And that would have been around January 4th or 5th or so, we would go down to zero agents.[312]

These requests for security resources and personnel continued into the winter, spring, and summer of 2012.

### The Extension Memorandum

When Stevens left Benghazi for the U.S. in November 2011, Washington still had not made a decision on the Mission's future. A few weeks after he left Libya to return to the United States, Stevens asked the Principal Officer who replaced him in Benghazi about the status of the Mission, writing: "Also, just curious what you guys decided to do re: future of the compound."[313]

Discussions about Benghazi's diplomatic future culminated in the Near Eastern Bureau's decision to request an extension of the Mission for one year.[314] This required the approval of Kennedy, and the Near Eastern Bureau prepared an extension memorandum for his approval.[315] The Post Management Officer for Libya, of the logistics arm of the Near Eastern Affairs Bureau, explained the purpose of the memo:

> [I]ts purpose is to establish the policy priority, that this is what we are going to be doing, and this is what we—we need to make it happen. So this memo says that the pres-

---

[310] Email from Diplomatic Sec. Agent 10 to Physical Sec. Specialist, Physical Sec. Programs, Bureau of Diplomatic Sec., U.S. Dep't (Dec. 22, 2011, 6:09 AM) (on file with the Committee, C05388920).

[311] Email from Diplomatic Sec. Agent 10 to Physical Sec. Specialist, Physical Sec. Programs, Bureau of Diplomatic Sec., U.S. Dep't (Dec. 22, 2011, 7:19 AM) (on file with the Committee, C05388920).

[312] Diplomatic Sec. Agent 10 Testimony at 45–46.

[313] Email from J. Christopher Stevens to Principal Officer 1, U.S. Dep't of State (Dec. 15, 2011, 1:14 PM) (on file with the Committee, SCB0079324).

[314] See Memorandum from Jeffrey D. Feltman, Ass't Sec'y of State, Bureau of Near Eastern Affairs, U.S. Dep't of State to Patrick F. Kennedy, Under Sec'y of State for Mgmt., U.S. Dep't of State (Dec. 27, 2011) [hereinafter Dec. 27, 2011 Action Memo for Under Secretary Kennedy] (on file with the Committee, C05261557) (recommending approval of continued U.S. presence in Benghazi through the end of calendar year 2012).

[315] Id.

ence is approved, and that some of these issues were dealt with to deal with the change in the presence.

Without specific budgets dedicated to these facilities and to this process, there needed to be some sort of mandate to declare this is what we are doing, so that then, the relevant functional bureaus and regional bureau could then say, hey, we have this approval I am waving my document we have this approval, we need to find money to make this happen.[316]

On December 27, 2011, Feltman forwarded the final Action Memorandum to Kennedy requesting approval to extend the Benghazi Mission until the end of 2012.[317] Feltman described the memorandum as reflecting "discussions with my bosses at the State Department about why Chris Stevens and I both thought that we needed to maintain a presence in Benghazi. . . . I was confident that we had done our best to build the consensus that would lead to a yes."[318] When asked whether the Secretary was aware of the discussion about Benghazi's future, Feltman testified he "had ready access to the secretary. I don't think that anything that I would have put in any of these memos would have surprised her just because of the sort of ongoing discussion we had about the Arab Spring."[319]

The Secretary told the Committee:

> There were certainly meetings in which I was advised about the process being undertaken as to determine whether Benghazi should be extended. So, yes, I was aware of the process that was ongoing, and I was kept up to date about it.[320]

In his Action Memorandum, Feltman laid out the policy reasons to remain in Libya:

> A continued presence in Benghazi will emphasize U.S. interest in the eastern part of Libya. Many Libyans have said the U.S. presence in Benghazi has a salutary, calming effect on easterners who are fearful that the new focus on Tripoli could once again lead to their neglect and exclusion from reconstruction and wealth distribution and strongly favor a permanent U.S. presence in the form of a full consulate. They feel the United States will help ensure they are dealt with fairly. TNC officials have said some government agencies may shift their headquarters to Benghazi (such as the National Oil Company). Other government agencies and corporations already have their headquarters in Benghazi and will likely remain there for the foreseeable future. The team will be able to monitor political trends (Islamists, tribes, political parties, militias) and public sentiment regarding the "new Libya," as well as report on the critical period leading up to and through

[316] Post Mgmt. Officer for Libya Testimony at 65–66.
[317] *See* Feltman Testimony at 98.
[318] *Id.* at 100–01.
[319] *Id.* at 101.
[320] Clinton Testimony at 160.

Libya's first post-Qadhafi elections. Programmatic benefits to a continued U.S. presence in Benghazi include building on USAID/OTI's programs to strengthen civil society groups, media training, and capacity building in municipal councils. We should continue to engage with the populace, particularly with the large population of Libyan youth, an important and receptive audience with high expectations for the post-revolution period.[321]

On January 5, 2012, Kennedy approved the memorandum.[322] He explained to the Committee:

This document is essentially in a prime part and a secondary part. The prime part is that I am authorizing us committing to extend the lease on this facility through the end of calendar year 2012. And I am doing that because they have made representations to me that the facility is needed. My conversations with others of my peers indicated that no decision had yet been made about whether to make this operation permanent, continue at interim or close it. . . . And, then secondly, it also sets a ceiling on the number of personnel that will be assigned."[323]

Excluded from the discussions to extend the Benghazi mission for another year were senior officials from the Bureau of Diplomatic Security.

Boswell explained he was not involved, nor consulted, in the extension memorandum:

When the memo came up regarding the—a memo from Assistant Secretary Feltman to Under Secretary Kennedy asking for the extension of the Benghazi mission for another year and asking the Under Secretary to make a couple of decisions about that, one, the overall decision to approve or disapprove, but also a second decision about what kind of property to maintain, I did not see that memo. That memo never got to me. It went up, I gather, on the 23rd of December. It was signed off on by various parts of Diplomatic Security, including—the right parts of Diplomatic Security, including the Countermeasures Directorate. It was cleared by—as I found out in retrospect, it was—after the fact, it was cleared by my Deputy Assistant Secretary for Countermeasures who was acting for Scott Bultrowicz.[324]

Gentry O. Smith, Deputy Assistant Secretary, Diplomatic Security, Countermeasures, confirmed to the Committee he cleared the extension memorandum on behalf of Diplomatic Security. He also confirmed he cleared the memorandum with the comment, "this operation continues to be an unfunded mandate and a drain on per-

[321] Dec. 27, 2011 Action Memo for Under Secretary Kennedy, *supra* note 311.
[322] *See Id.* (signature date stamped); *see also* Post Mgmt. Officer for Libya Transcript at 178 ("['January 5th, 2012'] would indicate that that's the day that action was taken on the memo.").
[323] Kennedy Testimony at 333–334.
[324] Boswell Testimony at 17.

sonnel resources." [325] When asked to explain his comment, Smith testified "it didn't come from Countermeasures, it would not have been solely for physical security. So I would say that it was broader for the operations in Benghazi." [326] He further stated; "The other seniors would have seen the memo as well and had an opportunity to comment based on its accuracy and maybe providing information for the document itself." [327]

Charlene Lamb told the Committee "I did not see it [the memorandum] until after the event in Benghazi." [328]

## Purpose of Mission in 2012: Symbolic Nature of U.S. Presence in Benghazi

With Embassy Tripoli reopened and Stevens back in Washington D.C. awaiting confirmation to become Ambassador to Libya, the Benghazi Mission continued its work through a series of "Principal Officers." [329] The Principal Officers met with leaders of the local council, militia heads, foreign diplomats located in Benghazi, heads of businesses and non-governmental organizations, and regular Libyans. [330] The Principal Officers reported to Washington D.C. their impressions of Benghazi and the state of eastern Libya. [331]

While the Mission continued to operate, it operated much differently than in 2011. As explained by Polaschik:

A: Traditionally [Special Envoys] have been based in Washington, but I know in recent years there has been a special envoy presence in Jerusalem that reports to the Secretary of State. So it's not unprecedented to have special envoy missions.

That said, it is unusual to have a totally separate office in a country in which there is no other consulate or presence. So it was a bit of an odd duck. Let's say it doesn't fit the unusual [sic] State Department pattern, and it's something that as DCM, I struggled with a bit, not in the early days, because it was just a different operation, I think, while Chris was there. Because of his stature, because of his experience, because of his reach back into the State Department, I think he had the ability to get resources and attention in a way that the people who followed him did not.

I was able as DCM to have a good working relationship with Chris and all of his successors just because we made it work. But I did not—you know, in another country, if there's a consulate per se, the principal officer or the consul general reports to the DCM, and the DCM has oversight for operations and hiring and resources and all of those issues. As DCM in Tripoli, I did not have that.

---

[325] Email to Post Mgmt. Officer for Libya, Bureau of Near Eastern Affairs, U.S. Dep't of State (Dec. 23, 2011, 3:27 PM) (on file with the Committee, C05578953).

[326] Smith Testimony at 75.

[327] Id. at 73.

[328] Lamb Testimony at 221.

[329] See Dec. 27, 2011 Action Memo for Under Secretary Kennedy, supra note 311 (discussing staffing of Benghazi Mission).

[330] See id. (discussing programmatic benefits of continued Benghazi Mission).

[331] See id. (discussing the effect of ongoing Benghazi Mission).

Q: Once Chris Stevens left in November of 2011 and was replaced by a series of principal officers, did that change then?

A: The formal relationship?

Q: In that principal officers then became more routine and report to you, and then you reported out to Washington?

A: No. There was never a decision or a procedure put in place to have the Mission in Benghazi report to the Embassy in Tripoli. It was still something that was reporting directly to Washington, staffed by Washington. I had no say in the staffing decisions, resourced by Washington, et cetera.

I played a supporting role. To the extent that I could, I made sure that I coordinated very regularly with the principal officers; and whenever they needed help on anything, I jumped in.[332]

## Security Problems Continue

The security environment also became a factor in the Principal Officer's ability to meet reporting responsibilities. As early as December 2011 and throughout 2012, the Mission was forced to go on lockdown because of the lack of security personnel. This impacted the ability of the Principal Officers to do their jobs. For example, on December 15, 2011, the Principal Officer at the time recommended halting future non-security temporary duty assignments because of the lack of DS Agents on the ground.[333] In January 2012, the Principal Officer reiterated his concerns "the mission will be hard-pressed to support TDY'ers (much less higher-level visitors and out-of-town travel) unless we have better staffing. On that basis, we won't be fulfilling what I understand our mission to be."[334] Later, in February 2012, the incoming Principal Officer expressed similar concerns: "we will be all but restricted to compound for the vital February 12–18 timeframe. This will effectively leave us unable to do any outreach to Libyan nationals during the week and we will be extremely limited in the ability to obtain any useful information for reporting."[335]

On February 11, 2012, the lead Diplomatic Security Agent at Embassy Tripoli, informed Benghazi "substantive reporting" was not the Mission's purpose.[336] In an email to the diplomatic security agent in Benghazi, the Diplomatic Security Agent wrote: "[U]nfortunately, nobody has advised the PO that Benghazi is there

---

[332] Polaschik Testimony at 44–45.

[333] Email from Principal Officer 1, U.S. Dep't of State, to Post Mgmt. Officer for Libya, Bureau of Near Eastern Affairs, U.S. Dep't of State (Dec. 15, 2011, 1:11 PM) (on file with the Committee, SCB0079324–25).

[334] Email from Principal Officer 1, U. S. Dep't of State, to Diplomatic Sec. Agent 25 (Jan. 13, 2012, 2:44 PM) (on file with the Committee, C05393569).

[335] Email from Principal Officer 5, U.S. Dep't of State, to U.S. Embassy Tripoli, *et al.* (Feb 11, 2012, 5:29 PM) (on file with the Committee, C05409829).

[336] Email from Diplomatic Sec. Agent 24 to Diplomatic Sec. Agent 12 (Feb. 11, 2012, 10:41 AM) (on file with the Committee, C05411292).

to support [**redacted text**] operations, not conduct substantive reporting."[337]

These concerns were expressed throughout 2012. Cretz told the Committee:

> The various officers that were there felt that they from time to time didn't that the Mission was not necessarily well staffed enough for them to be able to go out and do their reporting on a regular and aggressive basis.
>
> \*　　\*　　\*
>
> I recall discussions with one or two of them at various times that said that, because of the requirement to protect the facility that it was difficult for them to go out because it required a certain level of accompaniment around the city.[338]

During this time, the Mission evaluated and communicated to Washington D.C. the severity of the security environment. The Mission held more than a dozen EAC meetings to evaluate the security environment; review tripwires and determine if any had been crossed; and to identify any necessary to steps to mitigate the threats.[339] The Mission communicated the outcomes of the EACs to Washington D.C. but senior officials did not respond. The Secretary told the Committee: "There are millions of them, as you point out. They are sorted through and directed to the appropriate personnel. Very few of them ever come to my attention. None of them with respect to security regarding Benghazi did."[340]

Other State Department officers offered similar explanations. Kennedy told the Committee:

> The State Department gets thousands of cables a day. and some of them are brought to my attention, depending upon the nature. An example would be brought up potentially by one of my subordinate units, it might be brought up by a regional functional bureau that has an interest in the subject matter.[341]

Boswell testified:

> I think we followed the Libya situation very closely. Keep in mind, however, that it's a big world out there, and we have 180 posts and some extremely high threat ones, so we spend a lot of time concentrating on the high threat ones. I would say Libya was one of them, but not the only one. There is Iraq, there's Afghanistan, there's Lebanon, there's Yemen, there's Pakistan, and all of those at one time or another were flashing pretty bright.[342]

Lamb told the Committee:

---

[337] *Id.*

[338] Cretz Testimony at 88–89.

[339] *See* Benghazi Spot Report, EAC and Significant Event Timeline (DS/IP/RD) (on file with the Committee, C05394332).

[340] Clinton Testimony at 41.

[341] Kennedy Testimony at 43.

[342] Boswell Testimony at 18–19.

The RSO [Regional Security Officer] and the Ambassador are ultimately responsible for security at post. It is very unfortunate and sad at this point that Ambassador Stevens was a victim, but that is where ultimate responsibility lies. And it's up to headquarters to provide resources when post asks for them, and it's also up to Washington to make sure that we don't have, you know, waste, fraud, and abuse of our resources, because we're covering the entire world as well. So it's you know, when you say who should be accountable, accountable for what?[343]

The U.S.' uncertain and shifting commitment in Libya affected the administration's responses to security threats there. For instance, as detailed in Appendix F, an extensive set of security rules for permanent U.S. diplomatic facilities around the world did not apply to the temporary Benghazi Mission. The lack of security standards made Benghazi an anomaly among U.S. facilities located in Arab Spring countries, such as Tunisia, Yemen, and Egypt. As one Diplomatic Security Agent put it:

[I]f you are a diplomatic facility within the State Department, you have physical security requirements that are in the FAM, the Foreign Affairs Manual. And it is a very detailed, large set of rules that you have to follow to operate a diplomatic facility. It requires you to have physical security standards that are typically going to be expensive and will take time to do.

If you are in a non-diplomatic facility, there are no security standards. They don't exist.

So it's all or nothing.[344]

### Requests for Additional Security Measures

Without security standards in place to guide them, Diplomatic Security Agents were forced to make ad hoc requests for basic security measures. On January 2, 2012, the Benghazi Mission sent an Action Memorandum to Washington D.C. outlining field expedient security measures needed to secure the compound.[345] The request included 17 jersey barriers, 500 sandbags, seven observation platforms, four guard posts, additional lighting, and egress locks on window bars.[346] In addition, the Action Memorandum notified Washington D.C. that additional requests would be forthcoming as well as a request for a physical security specialist to help scope the security needs of the modified compound.[347] The security request was made again on January 5, 2012 and this time included a request for two drop arm barriers and measures to reinforce the pe-

---

[343] Lamb Testimony at 254.

[344] Diplomatic Sec. Agent 10 Testimony at 28.

[345] Email from Diplomatic Sec. Agent 14 to Diplomatic Sec. Agent 25 (Jan. 2, 2012, 5:41 PM) (on file with the Committee, C05579142) (attaching "an Action Memo").

[346] Id.

[347] See id. ("Once a decision has been made on the size and location of Mission Benghazi's compound—perhaps as soon as the coming week—RSO Benghazi will request additional security upgrade requests in support of that shift, and may request a TDY by a facility security expert to help scope them.").

rimeter wall, including concrete and barbed wire.[348] Funding for sandbags, lighting, door upgrades and drop arm barriers was approved on January 26, 2012.[349] On the other hand, the request for observation platforms, guard booths, and escape hatches went unaddressed—as did the request for the help of a physical security specialist.[350]

On February 13, 2012, the Benghazi Mission asked Washington D.C. to reconsider those measures previously requested but not funded.[351] In addition, the Mission made new requests to better secure the compound, including concertina wire, screens to obscure the compound, improvements to the perimeter wall, and . . . film for the compound windows.[352] The Mission also reiterated its request for the help of a temporary duty physical security specialist in Washington D.C. to help scope needed upgrades.[353]

Funding for guard booths was approved on February 23, 2012.[354] A critical request that went unaddressed until early March was a proposal to strengthen the compound's perimeter wall.[355] Modifications to the wall were not completed until May 21, 2012, almost six weeks after the first Improvised Explosive Device [IED] attack on the Benghazi Mission.

### Requests for Additional Diplomatic Security Personnel

In addition to the requests for physical security measures, the Benghazi Mission made constant requests for Diplomatic Security Agents. Concerns about Diplomatic Security Agent staffing shortages in late 2011 and early 2012 precipitated the preparation of an Action Memorandum for Lamb's approval.[356] On January 10, 2012, an Action Memorandum described the Bureau of Diplomatic Security's responsibilities under the December 27, 2011 extension memorandum to provide five Diplomatic Security Agents for Benghazi and recognized the Diplomatic Security's inability to "identify, seek necessary approvals and obtain the required visa ap-

[348] Email from Mgmt. Officer/Information Mgmt. Officer, U.S. Dep't of State, to Post Mgmt. Officer for Libya, Bureau of Near Eastern Affairs, U.S. Dep't of State, Principal Officer 1, U.S. Dep't of State, Libya Mgmt. Issues (Jan. 5, 2012, 1:43 PM) (on file with the Committee, SCB0049988).

[349] See Email from Diplomatic Sec. Agent 25 to Diplomatic Sec. Agent 15 (Jan. 26, 2012, 3:59 PM) (on file with the Committee, C05412127) (notifying that funding for some security measures had been obtained).

[350] See id. (noting that Action Memorandum items 3, 6, 8, and 9 had been funded, but not addressing the funding for other items).

[351] See Email from Diplomatic Sec. Agent 12 to Diplomatic Sec. Agent 25 & James Bacigalupo, Regional Director, Bureau of Diplomatic Sec., U.S. Dep't of State (Feb. 13, 2012) (on file with the Committee, C05394247).

[352] Id.

[353] Id.

[354] See Email to Physical Sec. Specialist, Physical Sec. Programs, Bureau of Diplomatic Sec., U.S. Dep't (Feb. 23, 2012, 8:22 AM) (on file with the Committee, C05394287) ("I just found a clause in our funding matrix that gives us the ability to support his request. There was early on talk about guard towers which we cannot support, however small booths to keep them out of the weather can be supported by our office.").

[355] See Email from Diplomatic Sec. Agent 12 to Physical Sec. Specialist, Physical Sec. Programs, Bureau of Diplomatic Sec., U.S. Dep't, and Diplomatic Sec. Agent 25 (Mar. 1, 2012, 4:59 AM) (on file with the Committee, SCB0049970) ("The current perimeter wall, which was inherited in the leasing agreement, is in poor condition . . ."); Email from Physical Sec. Specialist (Mar. 1, 2012, 9:12 AM) (on file with the Committee, SCB0049971) (recommending funding for a temporary fence).

[356] Email from Diplomatic Sec. Agent 25 to Principal Officer 1, U.S. Dep't of State (Jan. 13, 2012, 10:05 PM) (on file with the Committee, C05411094) ("We have submitted an Action Memorandum that if approved should significantly improve our ability to identify and obtain approvals for staffing Benghazi.").

provals for this many Agents on a continuing basis."[357] The January 10, 2012 Action Memorandum requested Lamb approve efforts to "request assistance from Domestic Operations, so that personnel can be selected and directed from the Field Offices by the DS Command Center as well as authorize funding for five, 45 day ARSO TDYs in Benghazi from Feb.1 through September 30 at a total estimated cost of $283,050."[358] The January 10, 2012 Action Memorandum was never approved by Lamb.[359]

On March 28, 2012, the Embassy in Tripoli made a request on behalf of Benghazi for "five TDY DS agents for 45–60 day rotations in Benghazi."[360]

## Further Erosion of Security in 2012

As the requests for measures and personnel continued, the security environment in Benghazi continued to deteriorate in 2012, with the incidents and attacks increasing in volume and in intensity particularly against westerners.

One event occurred in March 2012:

> Mission personnel were detained at a vehicle checkpoint in the town of Rajma, approximately 15 km southeast of Benghazi International Airport. U.S. Mission Benghazi RSO personnel were there to conduct a site survey near the town of Rajma. Benghazi personnel were detained by 17th February Martyrs Brigade militia members, had their identification temporarily confiscated, and were escorted back to Benghazi to a militia base.[361]

[357] Memorandum from Jim Bacigalupo, Regional Director, Bureau of Diplomatic Sec., U.S. Dep't of State, to DAS Charlene Lamb, Bureau of Diplomatic Sec., U.S. Dep't of State (Jan. 10, 2012) [hereinafter Jan. 10, 2012 Action Memo] (on file with the Committee, C05578986); see also Email from Diplomatic Sec. Agent 25 to Principal Officer 1, U.S. Dep't of State (Jan. 13, 2012, 10:05 PM) (on file with the Committee, C05411094) ("We have submitted an Action Memorandum that if approved should significantly improve our ability to identify and obtain approvals for staffing Benghazi."); Email from J. Christopher Stevens, U.S. Ambassador to Libya, to Diplomatic Sec. Agent 7 (June 5, 2012, 10:55 AM) (on file with the Committee, C05409979) ("We'd feel much safer if we could keep two MSD teams with us through this period to provide QRF for our staff and PD for me and the DCM and any VIP visitors.").

[358] Jan. 10, 2012 Action Memo, supra note 357; see Email from J. Christopher Stevens, U.S. Ambassador to Libya, to Diplomatic Sec. Agent 7 (June 5, 2012, 10:55 AM) (on file with the Committee, C05409979) (Requesting increased security).

[359] See Testimony of James Bacigalupo, Special Agent in Charge/Regional Sec. Officer, Regional Sec. Office before the H. Comm. On Oversight and Gov't Reform, Tr. at 17–18 (Sept. 4, 2012) (on file with the Committee) (Discussing the Jan. 10 Action Memo).

A: I believe it was January, maybe December/January timeframe we had talked about it in the office, and I think I was out on leave because my deputy I had seen a document that my deputy had sent up to Director Lamb, to DAS Lamb requesting we use the system that they use domestically to direct a certain number of agents from the field offices for assignments. We use that on protection. And we sent the memo up suggesting maybe we could use this mechanism for overseas.

Q: Specifically for Libya or

A: It was specifically for Libya.

Q: And do you know what happened to that memo?

A: It was never signed off on.

[360] See U.S. Dep't of State, Cable, Request for DS TDY and FTE Support (Mar. 28, 2012) (on file with the Committee, SCB004625). But see U.S. Dep't of State Cable, Tripoli—Request for DS TDY and FTE Support (Apr. 19, 2012) (on file with the Committee, SCB0046263) (denying request).

[361] Email from Spot Reports to DS Command, et al. (Mar. 15, 2012, 9:24 AM) (on file with the Committee, C05393455).

The situation was eventually resolved and the personnel re-leased.[362]

On April 2, 2012, four days before the first IED attack on the Mission compound, the Mission reported:

> British Diplomatic Mission FAV [fully armored vehicle] was attacked by a mob of demonstrators. The vehicle was damaged but the occupants escaped injury. The demonstrators who numbered between one hundred (100) and two hundred (200) were members of the Traffic Police Force known as "Murur."[363]

On April 6, 2012, the Mission suffered its first IED attack when an IED was thrown over the perimeter wall.[364] According to the spot report: "at approximately 2250 hours (GMT+2), the U.S. Diplomatic Mission Benghazi, Libya Compound came under attack. An IED was thrown over the perimeter walls and exploded within the compound grounds. No one was injured and damage was not visible."[365]

One Diplomatic Security Agent was on the ground at the time of the IED attack.

Four days later, on April 10, 2012, the Mission reported "an IED was thrown at a four (4) vehicle convoy carrying the United Nations Special Representative to Libya, Ian Martin. No one was hurt in the explosion and no one has taken responsibility for the attack."[366]

The March 28, 2012 request for five Diplomatic Security Agents was rejected less than two weeks after the first IED attack on the Mission.[367] In denying the request on April 19, 2012, Washington D.C. responded:

> DS will continue to provide DS agent support in Benghazi. DS/IP recommends that post continues [sic] its efforts to hire LES drivers for Benghazi to enable the DS TDYers to solely perform their protective security function. DS/IP also recommends a joint assessment of the number of DS agents requested for Benghazi to include input from RSO Tripoli, TDY RSO Benghazi, and DS/IP in an effort to develop a way forward.[368]

On May 22, 2012 "a rocket propelled grenade hit the offices of the International Committee of the Red Cross."[369] The International Committee of the Red Cross offices were approximately

---

[362] Id.

[363] Email from Diplomatic Sec. Agent 16 to DS–IP–NEA, Principal Officer 2, U.S. Dep't of State, and Diplomatic Sec. Agent 17 (Apr. 2, 2012, 4:17 PM) (on file with the Committee, SCB0048091).

[364] Email from Diplomatic Sec. Agent 16 to DS–IP–NEA (Apr. 6, 2012, 7:11 PM) (on file with the Committee, SCB0048088).

[365] Id.

[366] Email from Diplomatic Sec. Agent 16 to DS–IP–NEA (Apr. 10, 2012, 1:12 PM) (on file with the Committee, SCB0048085).

[367] See U.S. Dep't of State, Cable, Tripoli—Request for DS TDY and FTE Support (Apr. 19, 2012) (on file with the Committee, SCB0046263).

[368] Id.

[369] Email from OpsNewsTicker to NEWS-Libya (May 22, 2012, 9:06 AM) (on file with the Committee, C05392368).

one kilometer from the Mission compound in Benghazi.[370] Less than a week after the attack on the International Committee for the Red Cross, a Facebook post appeared threatening "to send a message to the Americans."[371]

## Chris Stevens Becomes Ambassador

The U.S. Senate received the President's nomination of J. Christopher Stevens to be Ambassador of Libya on January 24, 2012. The Senate confirmed his nomination by voice vote on March 29, 2012.[372] Stevens was sworn in by the Secretary of State on May 14, 2012.[373]

While in Washington D.C., Stevens met with various individuals including former State Department employee and author Ethan Chorin. Mr. Chorin told the Committee he discussed Benghazi with Stevens in March 2012:

> he [Stevens] said . . . essentially, Benghazi was not only the epicenter of the revolution, but a long-neglected part of the Libyan polity, and that the, essentially—what I got from him was that he was concerned that all of the attention was moving where—all of those factors that you mentioned, militarily, security-wise, medical, to the epicenter activities moving to Tripoli. And I believe what his point was, that he was afraid that the situation in Benghazi could degenerate as a result of that relative shift of the tension.
>
> And we both agreed that Benghazi was particularly important for one, the threat of potential future spread of extremist activity, as well as the fact that, you know, many of Libya's thinkers, intellectuals, you know, people with high levels of education, also came from Benghazi, and that there was a sort of an, essentially, again, without putting words into his mouth, that Benghazi would be critical to future, to Libya's future health as a unified state.
>
> \*   \*   \*
>
> I mean, it was widely known, or believed at the time that either Ansar al-Sharia, or one of its affiliates was responsible for, or had some connection to the death of the assassination of Abdul Fatah Younis. I should actually correct that by saying that it wasn't—it was an Islamist faction that that event was attributed to. But that's the background to our conversation. So there was no explicit mentioning in the Washington conversation about specific names of individuals or groups, but it was clear that that was part of what he was concerned about.

---

[370] Email from Diplomatic Sec. Command Ctr. to DSCC E TIA/PII, DSCC E TIA/ITA & DS–IP–NEA (May 28, 2012, 5:08 AM) (on file with the Committee, C05391864).

[371] Email from Diplomatic Sec. Agent 18 to Diplomatic Sec. Agent 17 *et al.* (May 28, 2012, 5:36 AM) (on file with the Committee, C05392202).

[372] John Christopher Stephens Nomination, PN1233, 112th Congress (Mar. 29, 2012) https://www.congress.gov/nomination/112th-congress/1233 (confirmed on voice vote).

[373] *See* Hillary R. Clinton, Sec'y of State, U.S Dep't of State, *Prepared Remarks at Swearing In Ceremony for Chris Stevens, Ambassador to Libya* (May 14, 2012), http://www.state.gov/secretary/20092013clinton/rm/2012/05/197696.htm.

* * *

He did say that he was very concerned that we were at a turning point, and that things could go badly quickly.[374]

Cretz, whose service concluded on May 15, 2012, communicated his concerns about the negative trends occurring in Benghazi prior to his departure and the need to maintain Department of Defense assets in Libya.[375]

In a classified cable sent on his last day, Cretz warned:

> Nothing threatens the success of the Libyan revolution more than the growing AQIM [al Qaeda in the Islamic Maghreb] links in Libya and the renewed activism of indigenous groups formerly repressed by Qadhafi. AQIM's ability to move senior leaders in and out of Libya and to base them there for months at a time points to the real possibility that parts of Libya-particularly the eastern areas around Derna, which have historically been the source of Libya's homegrown extremist—could turn into a safehaven for terrorists. While we have done some lifting with PM ElKeib to educate the new government of the risks, the Libyans are not fully on board with our concerns. We need to push more vigorously to convince them of the need to actively work with us to build the appropriate intelligence bodies.[376]

Cretz further told the Committee:

> [T]hose events in Benghazi in the spring of 2012 . . . it was a disturbing trend because, in Tripoli, we did not I did not see a piece of intelligence. I did not see any indication that the violence that was taking place was other than the product of the rival militias or whatever fighting it out for their piece of the pie.

> We never had any intelligence report, as I recollect, that specifically targeted U.S. or Western interests in Tripoli. Benghazi began to look like there was something going on there that was disturbing.

* * *

> Well, my view was and I expressed this to General Ham and others, who was the head of AFRICOM at the time was that my belief was that we needed them, especially in Tripoli, because of the ongoing strife and, also, because the elections were going to be held in June.

> And I think our general sense was that this was going to be a time a real problematic time period because it was the first election and for some of the reasons I went over before: first election, a lot at stake.

---

[374] Testimony of Ethan D. Chorin, Tr. at 15–18 (Mar. 11, 2016) [hereinafter Chorin Testimony] (on file with the Committee).

[375] Cretz Testimony at 89–90.

[376] Email from Joan A. Polaschik, Deputy Chief of Mission to Libya, U.S. Dep't of State, to SES–O; SWO-Cables; Dibble, Elizabeth; Maxwell, Raymond; NEA–MAG–DL; Burns, William; Sherman, Wendy; Nides, Thomas; Sullivan, Jacob; Feltman, Jeffrey (May 15, 2012, 10:26 AM) (on file with the Committee, C05395496).

So I felt that, in order again, for us to be able to do the job that we needed to do to get out and to reassure people that we were there to in case we were going to bring in observers or something with the elections, that an SST component would be very, very important for us to maintain up until that time.

\* \* \*

[T]here was a medical component. We had a Navy doctor for a period of time. They brought special skills. For example, we had a bomb that was a 10,000 pound bomb that was in the middle of the Benghazi compound where Qadhafi used to live and kids were playing on it every day.

And I worked with our one of our SST people, and they had a bomb defusing expert. So we were able to work out a plan whereby we defused that bomb. So that kind of skill, the normal kind of skill I think that most DS agents wouldn't possess, counter maybe counterterrorism skills.

I can't describe the level above which our—because our DS agents were very, very capable. But these guys just brought kind of a special force kind of set of skills to the game.[377]

Stevens returned to Tripoli, Libya as Ambassador on May 26, 2012, presenting his credentials to Libyan Foreign Minister Ashour Bin Khyal on May 27, 2012.[378]

## June 2012

Less than ten days after Stevens' return to Libya and a week after the Facebook threat, the Benghazi Mission compound came under attack for the second time in less than two months.[379] On June 6, 2012, the Mission reported back to Washington D.C.:

Approximately, one hour ago (3:30am) an IED exploded next to the front gate. Video camera footage shows a 4-door white pick-up truck in front of the gate, and local guards report seeing a man in 'Islamic' dress placing the IED at what appears to be the base of perimeter wall. The local guards sounded the duck and cover drill after seeing the man and smelling smoke. Approximately 5–6 minutes later the device exploded, creating a large hole in the perimeter wall. No one was injured and all personnel are accounted for.[380]

[377] Cretz Testimony at 86, 90–91.

[378] Email from J. Christopher Stevens, U.S. Ambassador to Libya, to Diplomatic Sec. Agent 7 (June 5, 2012, 10:55 AM) (on file with the Committee, C05409979); see Email to Post Mgmt. Officer for Libya, et al. (May 30, 2012, 11:20 AM) (on file with the Committee, SCB0080338) (regarding the arrival of Ambassador J. Christopher Stevens); Email to SES–O, SWO Cables, NEA–MAG–DL (May 28, 2012, 2:18 PM) (on file with the Committee, SCB0079242) (regarding Tripoli Situation Report).

[379] Id.; Email from Diplomatic Sec. Agent 18 to Diplomatic Sec. Agent 17, et al. (May 28, 2012, 5:36 AM) (on file with the Committee, C05392202).

[380] Email from Principal Officer 2, U.S. Dep't of State, to J. Christopher Stevens, U.S. Ambassador to Libya, Joan A. Polaschik, Deputy Chief of Mission in Libya, William V. Roebuck, Dir.

Continued

A day before the second IED attack on the Mission, Stevens requested the State Department's own highly trained mobile security deployment (MSD) team remain in Tripoli through the end of the summer.[381] More resources in Tripoli meant possibly more available resources to augment security in Benghazi. On the same day Benghazi was attacked for a second time, the Diplomatic Security Agent, who was the head of the MSD division, denied Stevens' request to keep the State Department's highly trained security personnel stating: "Unfortunately, MSD cannot support the request . . . we have two emerging requirements similar to Tripoli that requires the whole of our office essentially." [382]

Five days later, an RPG attack was launched on the United Kingdom Ambassador's motorcade injuring two individuals.[383] According to the Mission, "the UK Ambassador's motorcade was attacked with an RPG and small arms fire in Benghazi, approximately three kilometers away from the US Mission." [384] Concern was expressed the RPG attack was actually directed toward the U.S. Mission. Deputy Assistant Secretary for International Programs suggested to her colleagues and supervisors "it raises the question were they targeting the Brits or us and/or did we just lucky [sic] on this one?" [385] Polaschik told the Committee:

> I personally was very concerned that it might not have been targeted at the British Ambassador, but could have been targeted at us, given the location where it had occurred and given that we had been storing the British embassy's vehicles on our compound. But it was unclear. It was very murky, difficult to determine exactly who was targeted.[386]

The pattern of violence—particularly against westerners raised some concern in Washington. On June 11, 2012, the Near Eastern Affairs regional bureau expressed concern about the security situation in Benghazi to Stevens—suggesting even a pause in staffing.[387] Stevens agreed, indicating it would allow "our RSO team time in Benghazi (perhaps reduced in number) to continue to assess the threat environment and consider ways to mitigate." [388]

On June 12, 2012, Scott Bultrowicz, the Principal Deputy Assistant Secretary, Diplomatic Security, opined after the attack on the

---

Office of Maghreb Affairs, Bureau of Near Eastern Affairs, U.S. Dep't of State (June 6, 2012, 4:49 AM) (on file with the Committee, C05393187).

[381] Email from J. Christopher Stevens, U.S. Ambassador to Libya, to Diplomatic Sec. Agent 7 (June 5, 2012, 10:55 AM) (on file with the Committee, C05409979).

[382] Email from Diplomatic Sec. Agent 7 to J. Christopher Stevens, U.S. Ambassador to Libya (June 6, 2012, 3:00 PM) (on file with the Committee, C05409979).

[383] See Testimony of Gregory N. Hicks, Deputy Chief of Mission at U.S. Embassy Tripoli, U.S. Dep't of State, before H. Comm. on Gov't Oversight & Reform, Tr. 50 (Apr. 11, 2013) [hereinafter Hicks Testimony] (on file with the Committee) (discussing the attack).

[384] Email from Charlene R. Lamb, Deputy Ass't Sec'y, Bureau of Diplomatic Sec., Int'l Programs, U.S. Dep't of State, to Eric J. Boswell, Ass't Sec'y of State, Bureau of Diplomatic Sec., U.S. Dep't of State, et al. (June 11, 2012, 11:09 AM) (on file with the Committee, C05394418).

[385] Id.

[386] Polaschik Testimony at 82–83.

[387] See Email from William V. Roebuck, Dir. Office of Maghreb Affairs, U.S. Dep't of State, to J. Christopher Stevens, U.S. Ambassador to Libya (June 11, 2012, 5:11 PM) (on file with the Committee, C05391335) ("I'm getting quite concerned about the security situation for our folks in Benghazi . . . We are at a(possible) [sic] natural break . . .").

[388] Email from J. Christopher Stevens, U.S. Ambassador to Libya, to William v. Roebuck, Dir. Office of Maghreb Affairs, Bureau of Near Eastern Affairs, U.S. Dep't of State (June 12, 2012, 10:52 AM) (on file with the Committee, C05409960).

UK ambassador's motorcade "this along with last week's incident is troubling."[389] Lamb acknowledged:

> We are not staffed or resourced adequately to protect our people in that type of environment. We are a soft target against resources available to the bad guys there. Not to mention there is no continuity because we do everything there with TDY personnel. The cost to continue to do business there may become more challenging.[390]

On June 14, 2012, the Benghazi Mission held an Emergency Action Committee meeting to discuss the series of attacks and request additional DS staff.[391] The Diplomatic Security Agent in Benghazi wrote to Washington D.C. expressing concern about the intensity and frequency of attacks: "Recent attacks have intensified in frequency with the active targeting of diplomatic personnel (e.g. the IED attack on the U.S. compound, the complex attack on the U.K. motorcade, and a recent rally by heavily armed Islamist militia members)."[392]

That very day the Diplomatic Security Agent in charge in Tripoli underscored the concern raised by Benghazi stating "I fear that we have passed a threshold where we will see more targeting, attacks, and incidents involving western targets."[393] He went on to list five major security incidents in and around Benghazi, including:

> 06/12/2012—0350 hrs—RPG attack on the International Committee of the Red Cross (ICRC) compound in Misrata;

> 06/11/2012—Attack on UK Ambassador's convoy—Benghazi;

> 06/08/2012 2345 hrs—Sabha—Two hand grenades targeted at marked UK vehicles outside of Sabha hotel. One detonated, damaged three tires and an oil pump. The second grenade failed to detonate;

> 06/06/2012—U.S. Mission Benghazi was targeted by an IED which detonated causing damage to the exterior wall of the compound. The Imprisoned Sheikh Omar Abdul Rahman Brigades claimed responsibility for the attack;

> 05/22/2012—International Committee of the Red Cross building attacked by RPG—in Benghazi. The Imprisoned Sheikh Omar Abdul-Rahman Brigades claimed responsibility on 27 May. The brigade accused the ICRC of attempting to convert internally displaced members of the Tawergha ethnic minority to Christianity. It called for the NGO to close its offices; and declared Libya to be an Is-

---

[389] Email from Scott P. Bultrowicz, Principal Deputy Ass't Sec'y of State, Bureau of Diplomatic Sec., to Charlene R. Lamb, Deputy Ass't Sec'y, Bureau of Diplomatic Sec., Int'l Programs, U.S. Dep't of State (June 11, 2012, 1:05 PM) (on file with the Committee, C05388866).

[390] Email from Ms. Lamb to Mr. Bultrowicz (June 11, 2012, 4:16 PM) (on file with the Committee. C05388866).

[391] See Email from Diplomatic Sec. Agent 19 to Diplomatic Sec. Agent 25, James P. Bacigalupo, Regional Director, Bureau of Diplomatic Sec., U.S. Dep't of State, and Diplomatic Sec. Agent (June 14, 2012, 11:40 AM) (on file with the Committee, C05388987) (summarizing staffing needs in light of prevailing security environment).

[392] Id.

[393] Email from Diplomatic Sec. Agent 24 to Diplomatic Sec. Agent 25 (June 14, 2012, 1:56 PM) (on file with the Committee, C05388987).

lamic state. It warned that the Americans would be targeted next.[394]

No additional resources were provided by Washington D.C. to fortify the compound after the first two attacks. No additional personnel were sent to secure the facility despite repeated requests of the security experts on the ground. In fact, the only inquiry from senior State Department officials about the trending violence against westerners was from Victoria Nuland, State Department Spokesperson, asking Stevens how to publicly message the incidents. Nuland wrote:

> I know you have your hands full but we'd like your advice about our public messaging on the spate of violence in Libya over the past ten days.

> Should we now move to something a bit sharper than calling on all sides to work it out? What cd/wd we say about whether the incidents are linked, why they are going after NGO and Western targets now, impact on electoral environment etc. . . .[395]

This exchange is noteworthy. Stevens' expertise was being sought on the messaging of violence in Libya as opposed to his expertise being sought on how best to protect against that violence. Moreover, while the Secretary and others were quick to praise Stevens and his dedication to Libya, they were also quick to note "[h]e [Stevens] definitely understood the risks. Yes."[396]

Saying Stevens "understood" the risks without also acknowledging he repeatedly tried to guard against and defend against those risks is unfortunate. Yes, it is clear Stevens knew the risks associated with his service in Libya from the moment he landed in Benghazi in 2011 on a chartered Greek boat until his final phone call to Gregory Hicks saying "we're under attack." Washington D.C. dismissed Stevens' multiple requests for additional security personnel, while also asking for help in messaging the very violence he was seeking security from.

### Libyan Elections

On July 7, 2012, the first post-revolution democratic elections in Libya occurred, largely without incident.[397] Being in Benghazi during the first national elections was a priority for State Department officials. Feltman told the Committee:

> Libya is a big country. If we only had a diplomatic presence in Tripoli during those elections, I think we would have gotten a very distorted view of [sic] I was already gone from the State Department at this point, but I think it would have been a very distorted view if you are only

---

[394] *Id.*

[395] Email from Victoria Nuland, Spokesperson, U.S. Dep't of State, to J. Christopher Stevens, U.S. Ambassador to Libya (June 13, 2012, 3:42 PM) (on file with the Committee, SCB0079249).

[396] Clinton Testimony at 151.

[397] *See* Jomana Karadsheh, *Liberal coalition makes strides in historic Libyan election,* CNN (July 18, 2012), http://www.cnn.com/2012/07/17/world/africa/libya-election.

reporting what's happening in Tripoli during something as critical as the first elections after Qadhafi's fall.[398]

The Principal Officer in Benghazi at the time described the environment in Benghazi leading up to the elections:

A: Broadly, the elections were the principal focus of attention. There was an international presence there, not just in Benghazi but across the country as these were nationwide elections. It was the object of great public focus. In the immediate run up to the election, there were a number of incidents. On election day itself, I was one of the international observers at polling stations in and around Benghazi.

Q: When you said there were a number of incidents leading up to the election day, can you elaborate further on those?

A: There were reports of attempts to ensure that polling stations did not open, for example. There were reports of attempts to interfere with ballots or ballot boxes, for example.

Q: Were these interferences by one particular organization, or were there multiple organizations involved in these events?

A: There were various allegations as to responsibility for the events. The prevailing theory at that time was that these were the efforts of separatist elements. I did not personally witness any of these events. I want to emphasize that these were largely based on reports in the media or elsewhere, and that in my contacts on election day, I did not see any effort to impede voters or to otherwise interfere in the process.

Q: Okay. And following the election, what was the environment like, within the in the timeframe of a week after the election, what was the environment in Benghazi, Libya, like?

A: There was euphoria, frankly, among most of the Libyans with whom I spoke. They felt that the elections had been successful in terms of their conduct. They thought that this demonstrated Libya's ability to clear a very important hurdle. They felt that the election results themselves represented a consensus for moderate government. And the majority of my Libyan contacts then identified the formulation of a constitution as the next hurdle.[399]

## Making Benghazi a Permanent Presence

As he was awaiting ambassadorial confirmation and re-deployment to Libya, Stevens had lunch with Gregory N. Hicks, who had

---

[398] Feltman Testimony at 64–65.

[399] Testimony of Principal Officer 3, U.S. Dep't of State, Tr. at 14–15 (Mar. 26, 2015) [hereinafter Principal Officer 3 Testimony] (on file with the Committee).

been selected to replace Polaschik as the Deputy Chief of Mission for Embassy Tripoli.[400] They met in Washington D.C. to discuss their upcoming work together in Libya.[401] Part of their discussion centered on the future of operations in Benghazi. Hicks described their conversation as follows:

> I met with Chris, Ambassador Stevens—I may refer to him as Chris, and if I say Chris, that's who I am referring to after his confirmation. And he was, of course, very excited. And we talked about our plans for moving forward, you know, particularly our hope that we could normalize the Mission and bring families back to, you know, to Tripoli in the summer of actually, this coming summer, 2013.

> One of the things he said to me was that, in his exit interview with Secretary Clinton, she expressed the hope that we could make the special Mission in Benghazi a permanent constituent post. And Chris said that one of the first things he intended to do after his arrival was develop a proposal to move forward on that project.[402]

Hicks testified that shortly after he arrived in Libya on July 31, 2012, he asked Stevens about the progress of making Benghazi permanent. He put it as follows:

> Timing was important in this, because we knew that in that particular fiscal year, which was I think 2012, fiscal year 2012, ending September 30th of 2012, we would probably be able to have the resources to do it. We could obligate the money to do that.

> When I arrived on July 31st, I was surprised that the cable had not gone to Washington at that time. And I asked Chris about it, and he said just that things had been much busier than he expected.

> And I basically said, well, we will you know, a friend of mine, a longtime friend of mine, at the time was principal officer in Benghazi. . . . [O]ne of the finest professional officers I know in the Foreign Service. And I told Chris that I would work with [him] to get the project started.[403]

Hicks also described discussions about the Secretary traveling back to Libya, perhaps in October 2012.[404] Emails indicate senior State Department officials, including Mills, Sullivan, and Huma Abedin, Deputy Chief of Staff, were preparing for a trip by the Secretary to Libya in October 2012.[405] Hicks testified he and Stevens

---

[400] Hicks Testimony at 7–8.

[401] Id. at 7.

[402] Id.

[403] Id. at 7–8.

[404] Id. at 15.

[405] Email from Huma Abedin, Deputy Chief of Staff to the U.S. Sec'y of State, U.S. Dep't of State, to Philippe I. Reines, Deputy Ass't Sec'y, Communications, U.S. Dep't of State, Cheryl D. Mills, Chief of Staff and Counselor to the U.S. Sec'y of State, U.S. Dep't of State, Jacob J. Sullivan, Dir. of Policy Planning, U.S. Dep't of State (Sept. 12, 2012, 9:15 AM) (on file with the Committee, SCB0051754) ("Tomorrow is also our first trip meeting for the libya oct trip which we need to discuss."); Email from Huma Abedin, Deputy Chief of Staff to the U.S. Sec'y of State, U.S. Dep't of State, to William Burns, Deputy Sec'y of State, U.S. Dep't of State (Sept. 17, 2012, 1:21 PM) (on file with the Committee, SCB0070473) ("Before our Libya tragedy, we were also

wanted to have a "deliverable" for the Secretary for her trip to Libya, and that "deliverable" would be making the Mission in Benghazi a permanent Consulate.

And I believe I transmitted the policy justification to Washington on August 31st. You know, we are only a month from the end of the fiscal year, so we have to get a [sic] or, we have to help Washington, the executive director's office of the Near Eastern Affairs Bureau to put together a package to get it to Pat Kennedy for a decision by September 30th. Otherwise, we lose the money.[406]

## August 2012

In August 2012—roughly a month before the Benghazi attacks—security on the ground worsened significantly. After a temporary lull around the election, violence escalated. As the security environment deteriorated, security personnel declined. On July 9, 2012, Embassy Tripoli submitted another staffing request on behalf of the Embassy and Benghazi to Washington. Benghazi requested at least one permanently assigned Diplomatic Security Agent from Tripoli be assigned to Benghazi, as well as for Washington to send a minimum of three temporary duty Diplomatic Security agents. The Diplomatic Security Agent in charge in Benghazi at the time explained his reasoning for the Benghazi staffing request:[407]

With all the security situation on the ground going on and putting everything in place, and all the transition taking place in regards to American personnel leaving and coming in, and after discussion with the RSO and chief of Mission, this was a cable suggesting at that time this is what we need to maintain operations in the best safe manner as soon as possible. We wrote this cable on July 9, prior to the Ambassador leaving for Benghazi.

At that time, MSD personnel were, [sic] when we started off with two teams; now there was less teams on the ground. Actually, I don't believe there was any MSD team on the ground. There was just TDYers and two permanent ARSOs on the ground. This is in July. I'm sorry. I'm confused on the dates. Not September. This is July 9. So, at this time, we had another ARSO on the ground that was permanent and myself and the RSO. . . .

\* \* \*

So we wrote this in July because all these elements were leaving. MSD was leaving. The SST team was leaving, or they were going to change their Mission from being in the Embassy to being outside of the Embassy so they could train the Libyan government military. So we came up with this as a suggestion, for example, in line 4, or paragraph

---

considering stops in Libya and Jordan. Given the recent developments, what's your sense about the wisdom of her going to the middle east?").

[406] Hicks Testimony at 16–17.

[407] Testimony of Diplomatic Sec. Agent 21, Diplomatic Sec. Serv., U.S. Dep't of State, Tr. at 78–79 (May 19, 2015) [hereinafter Diplomatic Sec. Agent 21 Testimony] (on file with the Committee).

4, under the current arrangement, and this was the main one, 34 U.S. security personnel, the 16 SSTs, the 11 MSD, the 2 RSOs and 3 TDY RSOs, that was the number that we had there, and it was going to drawn [sic] down to 27. And we said: Wait, we're basically losing people. We need people, specifically because security is not in the best position now.

We requested weapons permits and weapons for the local ambassador bodyguard detail, and funding for security. Yes, and this was the cable that we sent out in concurrence with the Ambassador? [sic] [408]

No response was received. Lamb attempted to explain the lack of response to the Committee.

So when I read this cable in this format, . . . wrote it as a reporting cable in paragraph format, and it's very hard to line everything up by the needs. So I asked the desk officer to have his [sic] . . . at the time was the person working with . . . [sic] for them to get on a conference call and to go through this cable, paragraph by paragraph, line by line, and to switch this into the format that shows how many people do you need for which activities, to support VIP visits, movement security, static security, a quick reaction force. Just tell me exactly what you need and then the numbers will pop out the other side showing what you need.

And they sat down and they did this. And all of that was compiled into the response that unfortunately never went out. But my guidance to them was before that cable went up to Scott Bultrowicz and Eric Boswell, I wanted it to be pre approved at post, because I didn't want to dictate to post their staffing needs, I wanted to support them. But in this format, it was not clear exact because they were coming up on the 1 year transition when everybody was going to leave post and the new team was going to come in, so I wanted it to be laid out, very clear, the current operating support that was being provided for security.[409]

Kennedy explained his involvement in the July 9, 2012 staffing cable and the decision to terminate the Department of Defense's Security Support Team (SST) protective responsibilities in Tripoli. He told the Committee: "I consulted, as I said earlier, with the subject matter experts in this field, and after consulting with them, I responded no, we would not be asking for another extension." [410] This is a much different description of Kennedy's involvement than what Cheryl Mills described to the Committee. She described the Under Secretary as the person "who managed security related issues." [411]

---

[408] Id.
[409] Lamb Testimony at 245–46.
[410] Kennedy Testimony at 46.
[411] Testimony of Cheryl D. Mills. Chief of Staff & Counselor to the U.S. Sec'y of State, U.S. Dep't of State, Tr. at 72 (Sept. 2, 2015) (on file with the Committee).

Beginning in August, the number of security personnel in Embassy Tripoli was 34. Throughout August, security personnel left Embassy Tripoli. By the end of August, the number of security personnel at Embassy Tripoli dropped to six, excluding four members of the Defense Department's SST who were no longer able to serve in an official protective capacity but were on site.[412]

Stevens initially planned to travel to Benghazi in early August. He cancelled the trip "primarily for Ramadan/security reasons."[413] On August 5, 2012, the International Committee for the Red Cross [ICRC] suffered its fifth attack in less than 3 months.[414] As a result, the ICRC suspended its operations in Benghazi and Misrata.[415] On August 8, 2012, the Benghazi Mission reported the changing security environment and the anti-western sentiment back to Washington D.C.[416] In particular, the report described:

> Since the eve of the elections, Benghazi has moved from trepidation to euphoria and back as a series of violent incidents has dominated the political landscape during the Ramadan holiday. These incidents have varied widely in motivation and severity. There have been abductions and assassinations, but there have also been false alarms and outright fabrications.[417]

With the violence continuing to escalate, the Benghazi Mission held an Emergency Action Committee meeting a week later to review the Mission's tripwires, the lack of host nation support, and the overall security environment.[418] Participating in the EAC were the Principal Officer, the Diplomatic Security Agent, and other U.S. government personnel on the ground in Benghazi.[419]

The Diplomatic Security Agent in charge explained to the Committee his concerns with the security environment:

> I had tried to get a contact within the Libyan security apparatus that I could liaise with, which is typical for RSOs wherever they're posted around the world, and I had been unable to do that. I had requested police presence through a diplomatic note, but that had gone unanswered. I was resorting to, you know, flagging police cars down and talking to them to try and get them to stay, and that didn't seem to work.

> There wasn't any sort of information sharing, which is typical, or at least in my experience has been typical, at other embassies or consulates. Where, you know, we provide law enforcement security information to the host nation, they would then, in return, supply us information.

[412] See U.S. Embassy—Tripoli, Libya, Cable (July 9, 2012) (on file with the Committee, SCB0049439–41) (discussing emerging threats in Benghazi) (requesting staffing changes).

[413] Email from J. Christopher Stevens, U.S. Ambassador to Libya, to Principal Officer 3, U.S. Dep't of State (Aug. 2, 2012, 2:45 PM) (on file with the Committee, C05390855).

[414] See Email from OpsNewTicker to NEWS-Mahogany State Department (Aug. 5, 2012, 3:27 PM) (on file with the Committee, C05397147).

[415] See id. ("ICRC suspends work in Misrata, Benghazi after attack (Reuters)").

[416] See U.S. Embassy—Tripoli, Libya, Cable (Aug. 8, 2012) (on file with the Committee, C05262779) (discussing emerging threats in Benghazi).

[417] Id.

[418] See Diplomatic Sec. Agent 8 Testimony at 50.

[419] Id.

And then just the incident the fact [sic] that the prior incident we had with the gelatina or alleged gelatina bomb at the Mission had not been resolved, and it did not appear that local law enforcement was actively pursuing investigation of that, as well as their inability to pursue the possible hostile surveillance incident that was outside our south gate.

All those things I just mentioned led me to believe that they didn't have the ability/desire to prevent/mitigate threats.[420]

He explained the steps the Benghazi Mission took after the EAC "as far as physical security . . . for instance, erect[ed] a, sort of, makeshift chicane outside the north gates or at least the main gate. [redacted text]."[421] One additional outcome of the EAC, the Diplomatic Security Agent described to the Committee, was a response tactic called suspended operations.[422] Under suspended operations, all movements would be curtailed and post would conduct business from inside the compound only.[423] The new status was created because personnel at the Benghazi Mission were already reduced to such levels that authorized and ordered departures were not applicable.[424]

The Benghazi Mission followed the EAC meeting with a cable back to Washington D.C. a day later.[425] The cable described 1) the deteriorating security situation; 2) the departure of organizations such as International Committee on the Red Cross and a U.S. contractor; 3) the increase in hostile militias; 4) the lack of host nation support; and 5) the revisions made to the Mission's tripwires.[426] The cable also put Washington on notice a request for additional security measures would be sent through Embassy Tripoli. The request was made to Embassy Tripoli on August 23, 2012.

A day after the EAC cable was sent to Washington D.C., the Secretary received an update on the security situation in Libya.[427] The Secretary's Information Memorandum described "an upward trend in violence—primarily but not exclusively in the east—since May," and included a list of incidents such as the June 6 attack on the Mission, and the August 6 carjacking of American personnel." [428] It noted "foreign residents of Benghazi have expressed concern about the risks living and working there." [429] Finally, the memo-

---

[420] *Id.* at 59–60.

[421] *Id.* at 60–61.

[422] *Id.* at 89.

[423] *Id.* at 90:

"It wasn't new and novel in that I think it was . . . explained to me they had done something similar to this, I believe when they had the previous gelatina bomb incident at the front gate and they had labeled it as suspended operations, but, no, in my training and experience, I had not seen a suspended operations category before. . . . I had been to places where we had done lockdown, so to speak, for a set period of time, and this seems like a logical outflow of that idea."

[424] Cable, U.S. Embassy—Tripoli, Libya (Aug, 16, 2012) (on file with the Committee, C05261905).

[425] *Id.*

[426] *See id.*

[427] *See* Information Memorandum from Beth Jones, Acting Ass't Sec'y of State, Bureau of Near Eastern Affairs, U.S. Dep't of State to Hillary R. Clinton, Sec'y of State, U.S. State Dep't (Aug. 17, 2012) (on file with the Committee, C05390124) (briefing Sec'y Clinton on the security situation in Libya).

[428] *Id.*

[429] *Id.*

randum noted "there is no coordinated organization behind the incidents."[430] Absent from the Secretary's Information Memorandum was any discussion about the U.S. facilities in Libya and their security posture, or of potential resources and personnel needed in light of the deteriorating security environment.

The same day the Information Memorandum describing the security situation in Libya was sent to the Secretary, an Action Memorandum was also sent seeking her approval to designate Libya as an eligible country to receive funding from the Global Security Contingency Fund.[431] The Secretary approved this designation and the release of $20 million to support Libya's security sector on August 23, 2012.[432] The Global Security Contingency Fund is a joint fund between the State Department and DOD authorized by Congress to help fledgling countries "overcome emergent challenges through security and justice sector assistance to partner countries. State must fund 20 percent of each project. . . . The assistance proposed here [for Libya] is for the security sector. Congressional notification will be required before funds are transferred to GSCF and before initiating any activity."[433]

Less than 2 weeks after the Mission's EAC—on August 27, 2012—the U.S. issued a travel alert for Americans traveling to from and in Libya.[434] Two days later, the Libyan government issued a "'state of maximum alert as from today and until further notice' in the eastern city of Benghazi."[435]

In his handover notes to his successor, the outgoing Principal Officer stated "we are treading water here. . . . We are, for example, on the fourth visit from an Embassy electrician of my brief tenure because we continue to repair rather than replace equipment."[436] Similarly, in handoff notes to the incoming Diplomatic Security Agent, the departing Agent wrote about the dangerous environment in Benghazi, stating:

> there is nothing traditional about this post. Operating in a high threat environment where kidnappings, assassinations and bombings are weekly, if not daily occurrences, post enjoys neither the resources nor the host nation security support one would find at a similarly rated post. DS agents, for all intent purposes, are on their own.[437]

The only inquiry produced to the Committee from the Office of the Secretary to Stevens in August was an August 5, 2012 email

---

[430] Id.

[431] See Memorandum from Thomas R. Nides, Deputy Sec'y of State, U.S. Dep't of State, to Hillary R. Clinton, Sec'y of State, U.S. Dep't of State (Aug. 17, 2012) [hereinafter Aug 17, 2012 Action Memo for the Secretary] (on file with the Committee, SCB0086134–36).

[432] Id.

[433] Id.

[434] Travel Warning—Libya, U.S. STATE DEP'T (Aug. 27, 2012) (on file with the Committee, C05261911).

[435] Email to Gregory N. Hicks, et al. (Aug. 30, 2011, 1:59 AM) (on file with the Committee, C05397292).

[436] Email from Principal Officer 3, U.S. Dep't of State, to Principal Officer 4, U.S. Dep't of State (Aug. 29, 2012, 6:01 AM) (on file with the Committee, C05390852).

[437] Email from Diplomatic Sec. Agent 8 to Diplomatic Sec. Agent 3 (August 27, 2012, 11:49 AM) (on file with the Committee, C05396772–73).

from Sullivan asking: "What is the story here?"[438] regarding another RPG attack on the International Committee of the Red Cross.[439]

## HOST NATION SECURITY:
## FEBRUARY 17 AND LOCAL GUARD FORCE

At the time Stevens entered Libya in April 2011, there was no recognized government to provide security as required by international conventions.[440] The Diplomatic Security Agent in charge of the initial entry into Benghazi described the lack of security resources.

> There wasn't a formalized police I mean, there was probably somebody that called himself a police chief. And then you had the military somewhat of a military presence, you know, that really wasn't focused on anything to do with our security. They had, you know, they were trying to fight the war. Then you had February 17, a militia that assisted us a little bit.[441]

### February 17 Martyrs Brigade

The February 17 Martyrs Brigade [February 17] was one of the largest militias operating in Benghazi and Eastern Libya.[442] February 17 was instrumental in the success of the opposition forces, which eventually overthrew Qadhafi.[443] The emerging TNC recognized February 17 as a quasi- host nation security force—endorsing their efforts to perform basic security functions typically performed by law enforcement.[444] For example, the TNC used February 17 to provide security at the Tibesti Hotel where westerners, non-government organizations, and journalists stayed.[445]

The TNC recommended to Stevens and his team in April 2011 the Mission deal with February 17.[446] Despite being the alleged lead armed presence in Benghazi,[447] Diplomatic Security Agents found February 17 to be undisciplined and unskilled.[448] The Diplomatic Security Agent in charge told the Committee:

> [T]hey were very undisciplined. You know, people over there, a lot of them were not familiar with weapons, you know, because they weren't allowed to have weapons dur-

---

[438] See Email from Jacob J. Sullivan, Dir. of Policy Planning, U.S. Dep't of State, to J. Christopher Stevens, U.S. Ambassador to Libya (Aug. 5, 2012) (on file with the Committee, C05397147).

[439] Id.

[440] Vienna Convention on Diplomatic Relations, 1961, arts. 22, 29, Apr. 18, 1961, 23 U.S.T. 3227.

[441] Diplomatic Sec. Agent 6 Testimony at 33.

[442] See Max Fisher, Libyan Militia's Failed Security at Benghazi, WASH. POST (Nov. 12, 2012), https://www.washingtonpost.com/news/worldviews/wp/2012/11/02/libyan-militias-failed-security-at-benghazi/("[T]he February 17 Brigade 'eastern Libya's most potent armed force,' noting that it 'nominally' reports to the Libyan defense ministry. The command link between Tripoli's senior leaders and on-the-ground militias has proven weak, but the central government still relies heavily on them." (quoting a New York Times report)).

[443] See id. ("[T]he central government still relies heavily on them.").

[444] See id.

[445] See Diplomatic Sec. Agent 7 Testimony at 37 ("The security posture there was they had 17th February Brigade militia personnel that were assigned to the hotel.").

[446] See Diplomatic Sec. Agent 6 Testimony at 34.

[447] See Diplomatic Sec. Agent 7 Testimony at 38–39.

[448] See Diplomatic Sec. Agent 6 Testimony at 35.

ing Qadhafi's rule. So we never could really count on them for much because they just didn't have training. They were undisciplined. We just tried to see if we could get them to post at a couple of locations around the hotel at the entrance and in the parking lot, and to be around at night also in the parking lot.[449]

According to one of the Diplomatic Security Agents in charge, Stevens and his team relied on February 17 at the Tibesti Hotel "only in a case where we specifically needed their help."[450]

When the Mission moved out of the Hotel, February 17 was retained to provide an additional armed security presence to Mission's protective detail.[451] According to the Libya Desk Officer in Washington D.C., February 17 "would assist . . . with our movements as well. So they would be in the vehicles, help . . . get through checkpoints, allow us to get VIP access to certain locations through their very status as 17th of February Martyrs Brigade, which held in high regard in Benghazi, after the fighting."[452] The February 17 members who lived on the Mission compound received an initial stipend of $27/day for their services in addition to housing on the compound.[453] The stipend was increased to $35 in June 2012.[454] In addition to the February 17 members on the Mission compound, a larger contingent of February 17 members lived in "close proximity to the compound" and provided a potential additional response force.[455]

As the number of Diplomatic Security Agents dropped, the need for the February 17 members increased. The Diplomatic Security Agent in charge testified: "we only had three [February 17] at the time. So I was trying to befriend them, trying to get more activity, more interest, additional bodies, because three bodies on 24/7 is [sic] long days, long weeks."[456] Eventually, another guard was added.[457]

February 17 maintained between three and four guards on the compound throughout 2012. They performed drills with the Diplomatic Security Agents and the local guard force and "all plans to defend the compound rely on heavily on both the immediate QRF [quick reaction force] support and the support of their militia col-

[449] *Id.*

[450] Diplomatic Sec. Agent 7 Testimony at 42.

[451] *See* Email from Diplomatic Sec. Agent to DS–IP–NEA (July 21, 2011, 3:22 PM) (on file with the Committee, C05396529) ("[W]e currently have three guards on duty. Ideally, we get two per compound. . . .").

[452] Testimony of Diplomatic Sec. Agent 25, Diplomatic Sec. Serv., U.S. Dep't of State, before the H. Comm. On Oversight and Gov't Reform, Tr. at 88 (Aug. 8, 2013) [hereinafter Diplomatic Sec. Agent 25 Testimony] (on file with the Committee).

[453] Email to Diplomatic Sec. Agent 19 (June 28, 2012, 1:38 PM) (on file with the Committee, C05389864); *see also* Email (Aug. 9, 2011, 12:41 PM) (on file with the Committee, C05396529) (discussing compensation for guards on the compound).

[454] *See* Email (June 28, 2012, 1:38 PM) (on file with the Committee, C05389864) ("FPD approves the increase in stipend payments [from $27 to $35 per day].").

[455] Email from Diplomatic Sec. Agent 25 to Charlene Lamb, Deputy Ass't Sec'y, Bureau of Diplomatic Sec., Int'l Programs, U.S. Dep't of State (June 11, 2012, 1:25 PM) (on file with the Committee, SCB0050094–95).

[456] Diplomatic Sec. Agent 13 Testimony at 44.

[457] *See* Email from Diplomatic Sec. Agent 25 to Charlene Lamb, Deputy Ass't Sec'y, Bureau of Diplomatic Sec., Int'l Programs, U.S. Dep't of State (June 11, 2012, 1:25 PM) (on file with the Committee, SCB0050094–95) ("Currently we have three High Threat Trained TDY DS Agents on the ground and one TDY SST person.").

leagues."[458] February 17 members played critical roles during the first two attacks on the compound. At the time of the first IED attack on April 6, 2012, February 17 members supported the sole Diplomatic Security Agent on the ground. The Diplomatic Security Agent described February 17's role to the Committee:

> I also called our QRF, basically reacted them. We had a plan: On a situation like that, they would take up positions throughout the compound. One of the positions would be outside of our building. As I stepped outside, one of the QRF members was already out there waiting for me. This is possibly, I don't know, 3 minutes after the bombing.
>
> At some point, the guard finally activated the alarm. Our guard force had a push button alarm; in case of any attack, they would activate it. As I step outside, the QRF member is there. We cleared our way to the TOC. Went inside the TOC. I turn off the alarm, and I use our camera system to view or to try to determine if there was any other people, any other attackers in the compound. That took approximately 3, 4 minutes.
>
> I did not see anybody in our camera system. There are some blind spots, but we did have a pretty good system throughout the compound. I thought that with that, I would be able to determine something, something blatant, something that would really stand out.
>
> Afterwards, I stepped outside of the TOC. I had two QRF members with me, and we commenced on clearing the compound.
>
> While we were doing that, I heard two shots. It sounded to me like rifle fire, something bigger than an M4, which is what I had. So I thought initially that it was shooting in the compound. One of the QRF members received, if I am not mistaken, a call that told him that a third QRF member was outside and had detained someone.[459]

At the time of the second IED attack on June 6, 2012, February 17 provided support to the three Diplomatic Security Agents on the ground. One of the Diplomatic Security Agents on the ground during that attack testified:

> [t]he February 17th Martyrs Brigade showed up in a matter of minutes. Then from there we set up a perimeter outside on the street. As we had this large hole in our wall, we wanted to push our security perimeter back even further. We set up the large hole I mean set up the perimeter, sorry; and then from there, once that perimeter was set up, I went with one of our QRF guys **[redacted text]**. And we went there and secured the rest of the compound.

---

[458] Email from Diplomatic Sec. Agent 19 (June 17, 2012, 8:12 AM) (on file with the Committee, C05389864).

[459] Testimony of Diplomatic Sec. Agent, Diplomatic Sec. Serv., U.S. Dep't of State, Tr. at 34–35 (Apr. 13, 2015) (on file with the Committee).

As there was a security incident at the front of our compound, we had lost attention and lost visibility on other aspects of our compound. So, before we decided to let the principal officer out of the safe haven and call the all clear, we went through, me with my M4, him with his AK 47, and we just moved through the compound making sure nobody else had entered and there were no other devices. After that was done, we called the all clear.[460]

Following the June attack, the Diplomatic Security Agents on the ground wanted to increase the number of quick reaction force on the compound. However, February 17 declined expressing "concern with showing active open support for the American's [sic] in Benghazi."[461] Beginning in August, the Diplomatic Security Agent in charge expressed concerns about the trustworthiness of those February 17 on the compound. He told the Committee "I think we, or at least I assumed that he was sharing information with Brigade about what he was doing on the compound and what we were doing."[462] Days later, the Principal Officer at the time expressed concerns about February 17 to Stevens and suggested moving more to a "government-government relationship."[463] Stevens responded "we should be in line with the GOL policy/law on this. What do the local police and SSC leadership recommend."[464]

Two days before the Stevens' trip to Benghazi in September 2012 the Diplomatic Security Agents on the ground were informed February 17 members on the compound would no longer support the Benghazi Mission's off-compound movements—unless the Mission was willing to increase their stipend.[465] In discussing the situation with Embassy Tripoli, one of the Diplomatic Security Agents described the move as "part of a power struggle between the government and brigades over security functions in Benghazi."[466] Nevertheless, the Diplomatic Security Agent expressed concern about the Benghazi Mission's ability to move throughout the city and easily gain access to the VIP areas of the airport.[467] The issue remained unresolved at the time Stevens traveled to Benghazi, with the Diplomatic Security Agents using other U.S. government personnel on the ground in Benghazi to support Stevens' off compound movements.

[460] Testimony Diplomatic Sec. Agent, Diplomatic Sec. Serv., U.S. Dep't of State, Tr. at 50–61 (Mar. 24, 2015) (on file with the Committee).

[461] Email from Diplomatic Sec. Agent 19 (June 17, 2012, 8:12 AM) (on file with the Committee, C05389864).

[462] Diplomatic Sec. Agent 8 Testimony at 26.

[463] Email from Principal Officer 3, U.S. Dep't of State, to J. Christopher Stevens, U.S. Ambassador to Libya, & Gregory Hicks, Deputy Chief of Mission to Libya (Aug. 12, 2012, 5:56 AM) (on file with the Committee, C05411463) (asking if "it is the right signal to send to have a contract with a militia rather than a more usual arrangement with local authorities (the SSC? The Army?) to provide our security? Should we try to readjust to a government-government relationship given the political transition.").

[464] Email from J. Christopher Stevens, U.S. Ambassador to Libya, to Principal Officer 3, U.S. Dep't of State, & Gregory N. Hicks, Deputy Chief of Mission in Libya, U.S. Dep't of State (Aug. 12, 2012, 1:05 PM) (on file with the Committee, C05390836).

[465] See Email from Diplomatic Security Agent 5 to Regional Sec. Officer (Sept. 9, 2012, 11:31 PM) (on file with the Committee, C05396013).

[466] Email from Diplomatic Sec. Agent 5 (Sept. 8, 2012, 9:29 PM) (on file with the Committee, C05396013).

[467] See id.

## Local Guard Force

In addition to the armed presence provided by February 17, Benghazi relied on an unarmed local guard force [LGF] to protect the compound. The local guards were stationed 24/7 around the perimeter of the compound as an "outer ring . . . to give a perception of security."[468] "Local guards provide[d] access control essentially for visitors as well as us moving on and off the compound, and they also serve as the first line of defense in the event of an attack or some other sort of security incident would happened on the premise."[469] In particular,

> they are checking badges, they are checking license plates, that sort of thing. They'll often itemize—the vehicles to make sure there aren't explosives in the vehicles. If something were to happen, for instance, a mob or bomb or some sort of scenario like that, they have the IDNS pendants, which sound our alarm, and then they also have radios so they are instructed to call out a certain thing, DS agents, to alert us what type of attack it is and where they are.[470]

The LGF consisted of 20–25 local guards who rotated in shifts of five to staff unarmed guard posts around the compound.[471] A Guard Force commander oversaw the performance of the guard members who participated in drills and other security operations led by the Diplomatic Security Agents and those February 17 on compound. After the second attack on the compound in June 2012, the Benghazi Mission temporarily increased the number of local guards stationed around the compound at night to eight.[472] On September 11, 2012, there were five local guard force members on duty.[473]

## AN 'INTELLIGENCE FAILURE'

### Intelligence Community Reporting on Deteriorating Environment

As security in Benghazi and Libya deteriorated throughout 2012, the intelligence community's reporting on the burgeoning terrorist environment and the inability of Libyan leaders to curtail the terrorists activities increased in volume and became more alarming and specific in content. As the Office of the Director of National Intelligence told Congress, "[T]he IC [intelligence community] monitored extremist activities . . . and published more than 300 disseminated intelligence reports and finished analytic assessments—for a range of policy makers, the military, and operators—related to Western interests in the region between 1 February and 10 September [2012]."[474] Recipients of these intelligence reports included

---

[468] Diplomatic Sec. Agent 13 Testimony at 51.

[469] Diplomatic Sec. Agent 8 Testimony at 15.

[470] *Id.* at 15–16.

[471] *See* Email from Diplomatic Security Agent 19 to Agent 21 (June 7, 2012, 8:08 AM) (on file with the Committee, C05393670).

[472] *See* Email from Diplomatic Sec. Agent 25 to Charlene Lamb, Deputy Ass't Sec'y, Bureau of Diplomatic Sec., Int'l Programs, U.S. Dep't of State (June 11, 2012) (on file with the Committee, SCB0050094–95).

[473] *See* FN 83, Part I.

[474] *Benghazi Intelligence Review:* Office of the Director of Nat'l Intel., Oct. 22, 2012.

senior government officials such as the Secretary of State, who was briefed daily on the intelligence being collected and reported regarding Benghazi and Libya. The Secretary testified:

> Every morning when I arrived at the State Department, usually between 8:00 and 8:30, I had a personal one on one briefing from the representative of the Central Intelligence Agency, who shared with me the highest level of classified information that I was to be aware of on a daily basis. I then had a meeting with the top officials of the State Department every day that I was in town. That's where a lot of information, including threats and attacks on our facilities, was shared. I also had a weekly meeting every Monday with all of the officials, the Assistant Secretaries and others, so that I could be brought up to date on any issue that they were concerned about. During the day, I received hundreds of pages of memos, many of them classified, some of them so top secret that they were brought to my office in a locked briefcase that I had to read and immediately return to the courier. And I was constantly at the White House in the Situation Room meeting with the National Security Advisor and others.[475]

Kennedy, who was responsible for the security of diplomatic facilities overseas, testified he also received daily intelligence briefings.

> A: I received a notebook every morning.

> Q: And that is a compilation of what?

> A: Compilation of intelligence material from throughout the intelligence community, as well as from the State Department's own Bureau of Intelligence and Research.

> Q: As you sit here today, do you recall receiving anything that week that related to the attacks in Benghazi?

> A: I don't recall anything specific, but I also am sure that there was something in one of the reports from one of the agencies about Libya.[476]

The reports and assessments issued by the intelligence community painted Libya as a country descending into chaos as 2012 wore on. As early as February 2012, "[T]he Community was noting disturbing trends regarding the ability of Islamic extremists to exploit the security situation in Libya."[477]

On February 23, 2012, the Defense Intelligence Agency reported:

**[Redacted text].**[478]

---

[475] Clinton Testimony at 49.
[476] Kennedy Testimony at 121.
[477] *Benghazi Intelligence Review:* Office of the Dir. of Nat'l Intel., Oct. 22, 2012.
[478] *Libya: AQIM's Persistent Efforts,* J. Chiefs of Staff, J. Intel., Feb. 23, 2012.

The same day, the Central Intelligence Agency issued a report titled **[redacted text]** [479] **[redacted text]** [480] **[redacted text]**.[481]

A week later, on February 29, 2012, the Central Intelligence Agency published an assessment titled "Extremist Progress Toward a Safe Haven in Libya." The assessment noted "[t]he progress of two decentralized, al-Qa'ida—aligned groups in Libya and their ability to operate with relative ease throughout many areas of the country suggest Libya is emerging as a terrorist safe haven." [482] The Central Intelligence Agency assessed:

> [T]he decimation of national-level security agencies—which during the Qadhafi regime made Libya a hostile environment for extremists—have allowed al-Qa'ida—associated extremists, including previously Pakistan-based al-Qa'ida members and al-Qa'ida members and al Qa'ida in the Lands of the Islamic Maghreb (AQIM), to procure weapons and develop networks in line with the goals al Qa'ida senior leaders to establish a permanent presence in Libya.[483]
>
> \* \* \*
>
> AQIM's ability to procure a stable supply of newer, more reliable Libyan arms will almost certainly enhance AQIM's ability to counter regional security services and conduct high-profile attacks against local or Western interests.[484]

By mid-March 2012, the Central Intelligence Agency reported **[redacted text]** [485] **[redacted text]**.[486]

On March 21, 2012 the Defense Intelligence Agency published a report titled **[redacted text]**. It stated:

> **[Redacted text]** that these trends and current security situation, if unchecked, will allow al-Qaida and affiliated groups to establish a safehaven within a year.[487]

The Defense Intelligence Agency further stated:

> **[Redacted text]** that militia groups with al-Qaida connections will increasingly adopt an anti-western ideology in the next few months **[redacted text]** that while theses terrorist-aligned militias remain decentralized and possess disparate goals, al-Qaida and AQIM will be unable to unite them and harness their potential in the next few months.[488]

Less than three weeks after the Defense Intelligence Agency's report on the potential for attacks against Western targets, the State Department compound in Benghazi was attacked by an Improvised Explosive Device (IED). An IED was thrown over the compound's

---

[479] **[Redacted text]**.
[480] **[Redacted text]**.
[481] **[Redacted text]**.
[482] *Extremist Progress Toward a Safe Haven in Libya,* Cent. Intel. Agency, Feb. 29, 2012.
[483] *Id.*
[484] *Id.* at 2.
[485] **[Redacted text]**.
[486] **[Redacted text]**.
[487] *Terrorists Using Local Camps and Militias for Future Operations,* Defense Intel. Agency, Mar. 21, 2012.
[488] *Id.*

perimeter wall. At the time, only one State Department Diplomatic Security Agent was at the Mission compound.

Less than a week after the first attack on the State Department compound, the Central Intelligence Agency published an intelligence piece titled "Libya as an emerging destination for foreign fighter training." [489] The same day, the Defense Intelligence Agency issued an intelligence piece reporting "al-Qaeda and al-Qaida in the Lands of the Islamic Maghreb (AQIM) are expanding their contacts with political figures, terrorists, and militia groups in Libya." [490]

AFRICOM issued its own assessment a week later, reporting [redacted text] [491] That same day AFRICOM issued its assessment the U.S. was a target in Libya, the State Department denied Benghazi's request to have five Diplomatic Security Agents deployed in order to better secure the Mission's compound. [492]

The U.S. Army's National Ground Intelligence Center issued an intelligence piece on the 17 February Brigade. [493] At the time, members of February 17 were housed on the State Department's compound in order to augment the State Department's security personnel at the Mission compound, and a larger contingent of February 17 members resided near the State Department compound. In its assessment, the National Ground Intelligence Center reported:

> **[Redacted text].** [494]

Two days later, the CIA assessed "[K]ey militia blocs will most likely remain reluctant to give up their organizational autonomy because of fear of local rivals, distrust of the Transitional National Council, and competition for leadership of newly formed government institutions." [495] The report further noted: "[T]he continued existence of dozens of autonomous militias could undermine Libya's transition by engaging in violence, seizing national infrastructure, subverting election procedures or using coercion to influence the political process." [496]

As the deteriorating security environment accelerated in late spring 2012, AFRICOM reported on the security vacuum created by the Transitional National Council's inability to reign in the competing militias. AFRICOM assessed "Al-Qaida and its affiliates will attempt to capitalize on the turmoil in Libya to garner recruits, mobilize popular Western support, and establish an operational

---

[489] *Libya: Emerging Destination for Foreign Fighter Training,* Cent. Intel. Agency, Apr. 12, 2012.

[490] *Terrorism, Libya: Terrorists Seeking Expanded Influence, Activity,* Defense Intel. Agency, Apr. 12, 2012.

[491] *J2 Intelligence and Knowledge Development, Libya: Al-Qaeda Intent to Target U.S. Aircraft in Libya,* U.S. Africa Command, Apr. 19, 2012.

[492] U.S. Dep't of State, Cable, Tripoli-Request for DS TDY and FTE (Apr. 19, 2012).

[493] *Libya: 17 February Brigade,* U.S. Army Nat'l Ground Intel. Ctr., Apr. 25, 2012.

[494] *Id.*

[495] *Libya: Continued Militia Autonomy Jeopardizing Transition,* Cent. Intel. Agency, Apr. 27, 2012.

[496] *Id.*

presence in Libya to threaten U.S. and Western interests in the Region."[497] AFRICOM further reported **[redacted text]**."[498]

On May 22, 2012, the CIA reported "the eastern city of Darnha, a religiously conservative and historically marginalized areas that was a disproportionate source of Libyan freedom fighters during the Iraq war, is the center of extremist activity in Libya, in part **[redacted text]**."[499] Darnah was located approximately 180 miles from Benghazi. Also on May 22, 2012 the International Committee for the Red Cross (ICRC) was attacked in Benghazi by a rocket propelled grenade (RPG), the first of five attacks that would occur against the ICRC in and around Benghazi during the summer 2012.

On May 30, 2012, in an assessment titled "Terrorism: AQ Bolstering Presence and Influence in Libya," the Defense Intelligence Agency stated **[redacted text]**[500]

On June 6, 2012, less than a week after the Defense Intelligence Agency's reported on al-Qaeda-associated groups planning to launch near term attacks, the State Department compound in Benghazi was attacked again by an IED for the second time in less than two months. According to the Defense Intelligence Agency, **[redacted text]**[501]

On June 11, 2012, the Central Intelligence Agency assessed the "rocket propelled grenade (RPG) and small-arms attack in Benghazi . . . on the British Ambassador's convoy—the third attack on a Western diplomatic target that week—highlights the vulnerability of Western interests posed by the permissive security environment in Libya."[502] Some within the State Department felt the Benghazi Mission compound was the intended target.[503]

The increased number of attacks against Western targets in May and June 2012 led the Defense Intelligence Agency to "assess with high confidence growing ties between al-Qaida regional nodes and Libya-based terrorists will increase the terrorists' capabilities. We expect if the current security vacuum persists, attacks against U.S. and Western interests in Libya (including operations in Tripoli) will increase in number and lethality."[504] On June 12, 2012 a Defense Intelligence Agency assessment titled "Terrorism, Libya: Terrorists Now Targeting U.S. and Western Interests" stated:

> **[Redacted text]**.[505]

A June 18, 2012 Defense Intelligence Agency report titled "Terrorism: Conditions Ripe for More Attacks, Terrorist Safe Haven in Libya" assessed:

---

[497] *J2 Network Analysis of Extremists Operating in Libya*, U.S. Africa Command, May 16, 2012.

[498] *Id.*

[499] *Libya: Weak Security Allowing Al-Qa'ida Associates To Become Entrenched*, Office of Terrorism Analysis, Cent. Intel. Agency, May 22, 2012.

[500] *Terrorism: AQ Bolstering Presence and Influence in Libya*, Defense Intel. Agency, May 30, 2012.

[501] *Brief Notes, Terrorism*, Defense Intel. Agency, June 6, 2012.

[502] *Libya: Attack on British Diplomatic Convoy Underscores Risks to Western Interests*, Office of Terrorism Analysis, Cent. Intel. Agency, June 11, 2012.

[503] Polaschik Testimony at 84–85.

[504] *Terrorism, Libya: Terrorists Now Targeting U.S. and Western Interests*, Defense Intel. Report, June 12, 2012.

[505] *Id.*

**[Redacted text]**.[506]

A June 18, 2012 CIA report issued the same day gave a broader assessment of the variables that would:

> most likely . . . affect the first stage of Libya's transition and the runup to the planned July 2012 National Assembly election. . . . [T]hese variables can be summed into two drivers: the level of effectiveness of the interim government and militias' cooperation with the interim government. Wildcards, including possible attacks by former Libyan leader Muammar al-Qadhafi loyalists or al-Qa'ida-affiliated extremists could also impact events.[507]

The CIA assessment further provided "an attack on interim government officials or infrastructure by loyalists of former Libyan leader Muammar al-Qadhafi and his family or al-Qa'ida-associated extremists could undercut the transition's progress depending on the scope. **[Redacted text]** on the near-term intentions and capabilities of these groups."[508]

On June 26, 2012 the Central Intelligence Agency reported:

> repeated clashes in the past few months underscores the interim government's weak nationwide presence and crisis management capabilities, almost certainly tarnishing public perceptions of its authority and highlighting the many security challenges that will face Libya's post-election government. . . . The government's attempts to stop recurring internal violence often rely on the intervention of local actors whose efforts help stabilize the situation but leave the underlying causes unresolved. The Transitional National Council (TNC) has made little progress toward implementing national reconciliation measures aimed at addressing fissures stemming from last year's conflict and Libyan leader Muammar al-Qadhafi's 42 years in power.[509]

The Central Intelligence Agency's assessment further noted:

> [G]overnment still possesses few cohesive and professional Army and police units because many militias are reluctant to disarm, and its nascent security bodies lack the leadership and organizational capacity to rapidly integrate thousands of poorly disciplined fighters. Many militias that have received official sanction to act as security units almost certainly remain at best loosely controlled by national leaders.[510]

The Defense Intelligence Agency reported the same day:

---

[506] *Terrorism: Conditions Ripe for More Attacks, Terrorist Safe Haven in Libya,* Defense Intel. Agency, June 18, 2012.

[507] *First Stage of Libya's Transition: Key Drivers and Potential Outcomes,* Directorate of Intel., Cent. Intel. Agency, June 18, 2012.

[508] *Id.*

[509] *Libya: Recurring Internal Violence Highlights Security Challenges Facing Successor Government,* Office of Middle East and North Africa Analysis, Cent. Intel. Agency, June 26, 2012.

[510] *Id.*

if the current security vacuum persists, attacks against US and Western interests in Libya will increase in number and lethality. While specific targets of future terrorist attacks are unknown, the DoD presence at US diplomatic facilities and DoD Intelligence, Surveillance, and Reconnaissance assets operating in Libyan airspace may be considered as potential targets. According to AFRICOM's JPERSTAT, as of 21 June 12, . . . [t]he Terrorism Threat Level in Libya is SIGNIFICANT.[511]

In addition to both the Central Intelligence Agency's and the Defense Intelligence Agency's assessment, AFRICOM issued its own assessment of the security environment in Libya, reporting:

**[Redacted text]**.[512]

AFRICOM further assessed:

**[Redacted text]**.

\* \* \*

**[Redacted text]**.[513]

By July 3, 2012, AFRICOM had assessed:

**[Redacted text]**.[514]

AFRICOM further pointed to Libya as a **[redacted text]** [515]

In addition to the threats associated with the formal al-Qaida affiliates, there is a growing threat to Libya-based Western interests from individuals inspired by al-Qaida's ideology with limited or no direction from the organization itself. These individuals or cells are the most likely to conduct attacks, however they are more likely to be unsophisticated or disrupted by local authorities.[516]

AFRICOM emphasized:

[N]o single group likely conducted the series of anti-Western attacks in Libya since 22 May 2012. On 12 June 2012, individuals attacked the International Committee of the Red Cross (ICRC) office in Misrata, wounding the landowner's son and seriously damaging the building. On 11 June 2012, rocket propelled grenades (RPG) fired from an elevated position attack a three-vehicle convoy carrying the British Ambassador to Libya. Two passengers in the lead vehicle were injured. On 6 June, a crude improvised explosive device (IED) detonated adjacent to the main gate of the U.S. Mission Benghazi compound, causing no casualties and minor damage to the compound's wall. The

---

[511] *Id.*

[512] *J–2 Intelligence and Knowledge Development, Theater Analysis Report,* U.S. Africa Command, June 26, 2012.

[513] *Id.*

[514] J–2 Intelligence and Knowledge Development Theater Analysis Report, North Africa: Growing Threat from Al-Qaeda Affiliated Extremists to Western Interests, U.S. Africa Command, July 3, 2012.

[515] *Id.*

[516] *Id.*

'Brigades of Captive Umar Abd-al-Rahman' claimed responsibility for a 22 May rocket-propelled grenade attack on the Benghazi office of the ICRC and the 6 June attack on the U.S. Mission Benghazi.[517]

On July 6, 2012, the Central Intelligence Agency issued its own assessment that al-Qaeda was establishing a sanctuary in Libya. In particular, the report assessed "Eastern Libya, particularly the city of Darnah, provides extremists with the space to plot and train operatives."[518]

The report further pointed out **[redacted text]** [519]

The Defense Intelligence Agency was reporting:

**[Redacted text]** conflict zones or instability provide venues for reengagement **[redacted text]**.[520]

In fact, Abu Sufian bin Qumu, a former Guantanamo Bay detainee who was released back to Libya in 2007, became the "leader of the Ansar Al-Sharia in the city of Darnah."[521] According to the same report, "Qumu trained in 1993 at one of Osama bin Laden's terrorist camps in Afghanistan and later worked for a bin Laden company in Sudan, where the al-Qaeda leader lived for three years."[522]

It was widely reported "[M]ilitiamen under the command of Abu Sufian bin Qumu . . . participated in the attack that killed U.S. Ambassador J. Christopher Stevens and three other Americans."[523]

On July 25, 2012, AFRICOM reported on the spate of attacks on Westerners in eastern Libya. AFRICOM assessed **[redacted text]**."[524]

On August 1, 2012, AFRICOM assessed, "Benghazi's level of violence has escalated following the 7 July 2012 elections; extremists with unknown affiliations are likely targeting foreign and government interests following Islamist groups' poor showing in the elections. Degraded security, which follows recent efforts to establish a regular police force in Benghazi, is also likely a factor."[525]

The same day, the Central Intelligence Agency issued its assessment of an attack on the Libyan military intelligence agency headquartered in Benghazi. The Central Intelligence Agency reported:

[T]he attack yesterday against the Libyan military intelligence headquarters in Benghazi underscores how unidentified assailants are exploiting the permissive security en-

---

[517] *Id.*

[518] *Libya: Al-Qa'ida Establishing Sanctuary,* Cent. Intel. Agency, July 6, 2012.

[519] *Id.*

[520] **[Redacted text]** Defense Intel. Agency, July 19, 2012.

[521] Adam Goldman, *Former Guantanamo detainee implicated in Benghazi attack,* WASH. POST, Jan. 7, 2014.

[522] *Id.*

[523] *Id.*

[524] *J2—Intelligence and Knowledge Development, Theater In-Brief,* U.S. Africa Command, July 25, 2012.

[525] *J2—Intelligence and Knowledge Development, Theater In-Brief,* U.S. Africa Command, Aug. 1, 2012.

vironment to conduct surveillance and attacks. . . . We do not know who was responsible for the strike, and most of the recent attacks do not appear to be linked.[526]

The assessment restated:

**[Redacted text]**.[527]

On August 15, 2012, AFRICOM reported the "threat from extremist groups in Libya remains significant to Western interests."[528]

On August 19, 2012 the Defense Intelligence Agency reported **[redacted text]**."[529] The Defense Intelligence Agency assessed:

**[Redacted text]**.[530]

On August 23, 2012, the Central Intelligence Agency published an assessment finding "Al-Qa'ida-affiliated groups and Libyan militias with extremist ties increasingly are exploiting the permissive security environment in Libya—particularly in the east—to establish training camps, providing these groups with controlled areas in which to improve their operational capabilities."[531] The Central Intelligence Agency's assessment noted again "the proliferation of training camps in eastern Libya is likely to continue unabated absent significant improvements in the technical capabilities, source networks, and infrastructure **[redacted text]**."[532]

On August 27, 2012 the Central Intelligence Agency was reporting:

Al-Qa'ida in the Lands of the Islamic Maghreb (AQIM) is weaving itself into a variety of Libyan extremist circles almost certainly to encourage neighboring extremists to work in concert toward shared goals and increase its influence there. We assess **[redacted text]**, that AQIM seeks a durable presence in Libya because it views itself as the natural jihadist leader for North Africa **[redacted text]**.[533]

On August 29, 2012, the Central Intelligence Agency painted Libya as a country in chaos, reporting:

[A]ttacks by disparate individuals and groups since April against foreign and government targets in Libya underscore Tripoli's inability to prevent and respond to assassinations, bombings, and kidnappings. This violence high-

---

[526] *Libya: Recent Attacks Highlight Persistent Threats in Eastern Libya,* Office of Terrorism Analysis, Cent. Intel. Agency, Aug. 1, 2012.

[527] *Id.*

[528] *J2-Intelligence and Knowledge Development, Theater In-Brief,* U.S. Africa Command, Aug. 15, 2012.

[529] *Libya: Terrorists to Increase Strength During Next Six Months,* Defense Intel. Agency, Aug.19, 2012.

[530] *Id.*

[531] *Libya: Proliferation of Training Camps Aiding Extremist Networks,* Office of Terrorism Analysis, Cent. Intel. Agency, Aug. 23, 2012.

[532] *Id.*

[533] *Terrorism: AQIM Growing Diverse Network in Libya,* Office of Terrorism Analysis, Cent. Intel. Agency, Aug. 27, 2012.

lights the magnitude of reform challenges facing the new government. **[redacted text]**.[534]

On September 5, 2012, AFRICOM reported "Libya-based extremists continue to fuel regional terror groups' operations outside the country through training, recruitment, and facilitation. Libya-based extremists, most notably al-Qa'ida and its adherents, will continue efforts to establish themselves in Libya, taking advantage of the chaotic security environment. Unimpeded these groups may become capable of planning and launching terrorist attacks abroad."[535]

AFRICOM further highlighted a **[redacted text]**[536] "The report stated the best case scenario in Libya was a 'Divided al-Qaida Organization.'"[537] "AFRICOM assessed 'this scenario is likely only if the Western-backed Libyan government is able to effectively disarm extremist militias and exercise control over the majority of Libyan territory.'"[538]

The intelligence community's assessment depicted Libya, eastern Libya, and Benghazi as emerging terrorists' strongholds posing a threat to Western interests. Even with two IED attacks on the State Department's compound, senior government officials believed more intelligence was needed before any step could be taken to strengthen security at the United States facilities in Benghazi.

The Secretary told the Committee although she was fully briefed and aware of the dangers in Libya "there was no actionable intelligence on September 11 or even before that date about any kind of planned attack on our compound in Benghazi."[539]

Kennedy told the Committee "with additional information, we would have known—we would have known more, we would have executed a different security program, because the risks would have been pegged at a higher level."[540]

It is not clear what additional intelligence would have satisfied either Kennedy or the Secretary in understanding the Benghazi Mission compound was at risk—short of an attack. The intelligence on which Kennedy and the Secretary were briefed daily was clear and pointed—Al Qa'ida, al Qa'ida like groups, and other regional extremists took refuge in the security vacuum created by the Libya government and its inability to take command of the security situation.

It is these same groups that were responsible for the spate of attacks against Western interests throughout the spring and summer of 2012. Yet, the risks to the State Department compound in Benghazi were never mitigated. They were only exacerbated by the fact senior officials within the State Department failed to prepare for a worst case scenario in Benghazi. The Benghazi Mission compound not only lacked the resources to ensure the facility physically was secure but failed to ensure enough security personnel were on the ground to carry out the security program.

---

[534] *Libya: Struggling to Create Effective Domestic Security Systems,* Office of Middle East and North Africa Analysis, Cent. Intel. Agency, Aug. 29, 2012.
[535] *J2-Intelligence and Knowledge Development, Libya: Extremism in Libya, Past, Present, and Future,* U.S. Africa Command, Sept. 5, 2012.
[536] *Id.*
[537] *Id.*
[538] *Id.*
[539] Clinton Testimony at 41–42.
[540] Kennedy Testimony at 169–170.

The volume of intelligence regarding extremist activities in eastern Libya in the spring and summer of 2012, in addition to the spate of attacks by these groups against Western interests in Benghazi, was substantial. This intelligence was provided regularly—if not daily—to Kennedy, the Secretary, and others who made decisions with respect to Libya policy and the security of the Benghazi Mission compound and should have manifested substantial risk that could readily have been inferred.

Although this intelligence was available, the analysis was not directed to potential direct threats to U.S. personnel in Libya or Benghazi or the potential consequences of having that many extremists in Libya with respect to U.S. interests.

## PRE-ATTACK WARNING

In his interview with the Committee, Panetta bluntly stated his view "an intelligence failure" occurred with respect to Benghazi.[541] Former CIA Deputy Director Michael J. Morell also acknowledged multiple times an intelligence failure did in fact occur in this respect prior to the Benghazi attacks.[542] This was not necessarily the result of one or two specific instances of inaction, but instead reflected a general lack of planning for a post-Qaddafi environment that began with the U.S. intervention in Libya.

After the fall of Qadhafi, both the NATO Secretary General and the President explained that democracy-building efforts would be up to the Libyans[543]—justified by language in United Nations Security Council Resolution 1973, prohibiting the presence of an "occupying force" in Libya.[544] NATO declared it was concluding the operation "in a considered and controlled manner," yet acknowledged "they [Libyans] still have a lot of work to do—to build a new Libya, based on reconciliation, human rights, and the rule of law."[545] NATO demonstrated a hands-off approach to post-conflict stabilization, leaving Libyans to sort out post-conflict stabilization.[546] At the same time, the President praised the alliance on its successes in Libya, but stated the TNC, the nominally sovereign governing authority of the new Libya, would manage Libya's post-conflict governance and democracy-building effort.[547]

---

[541] Testimony of Leon E. Panetta, Sec'y of Def., U.S. Dep't of Def., Tr. at 111 (Jan. 8, 2016) [hereinafter Panetta Testimony] (on file with the Committee).

[542] Morell Testimony at 82–83; Morell Testimony at 211–212; Morell Testimony at 277.

[543] Although Tom Donilon set up a post-Qadhafi task force to handle issues relating to post-conflict strategy, the group became entrenched with managing the intervention and unable to devote time to extensive stabilization planning. It did produce plans in conjunction with a Libyan reconstruction team, but it was unclear to what extent the plans were used. See CHRISTOPHER S.CHIVVIS, TOPPLING QADDAFI at: LIBYA AND THE LIMITS OF LIBERAL INTERVENTION 143–44. (2014) [hereinafter CHIVVIS, TOPPLING QADDAFI].

[544] Id. at 60; see also Aaron David Miller, Obama's 21st Century War, FOREIGN POLICY (Apr. 5, 2011), http://www.foreignpolicy.com/articles/2011/04/05/obamas_21st_century_war.

[545] Press Release, NATO, NATO Sec'y Gen. Statement on the End of Libya Mission (Oct. 28, 2011), http://www.nato.int/cps/en/natolive/news_80052.htm.

[546] CHIVVIS, TOPPLING QADDAFI, supra note 522, at 164–68.

[547] Lucy Madison, Obama Congratulates Libya on Liberation, CBS NEWS (Oct. 23, 2011), http://www.cbsnews.com/news/obama-congratulates-libya-on-liberation. Despite the fact that the Administration justified the intervention under the doctrine of Responsibility to Protect, advocates for this approach such as Samantha Power, Secretary Clinton, and Susan Rice failed to act on rhetoric from those who helped write the U.N.'s 2001 Responsibility to Protect Report. Authors of the report emphasized that the doctrine embraced the "responsibility to rebuild." See Jayshree Bajoria & Robert McMahon, The Dilemma of Humanitarian Intervention, BACKGROUNDER, COUNCIL ON FOREIGN RELATIONS (June 12, 2013), http://www.cfr.org/humanitarian-intervention/dilemma-humanitarian-intervention/p16524.

The TNC proved unable to exercise meaningful control over the country.[548] After the conflict, Libya faced a growing number of kata'ibas—armed rebel groups not connected with rebels in Benghazi.[549] The rise of these groups distorted efforts to govern from Benghazi, and led to factions within the nation's leadership as a whole.[550] With tens of thousands of Libyans dead and hundreds of thousands displaced,[551] the country needed new a constitution, civil, social, and political institutions, economic management, and management of its oil wealth.[552] As NATO and its partners left Libya, some questioned whether the destruction in Libya would translate into compromising regional security.[553]

The Obama Administration opted to forego the use of military forces to stabilize a post-civil war Libya—an approach described by former Libyan Prime Minister Ali Zeidan as exercising "bad judgment."[554] The State Department exercised its own version of a light footprint, "expeditionary diplomacy," in an attempt to quickly normalize its presence in a country with institutions devastated by more than 40 years of dictatorship, regional strife, and war.[555] The administration also chose to forego post-war planning.[556]

In the aftermath of a multilateral intervention, Libya has erupted into chaos, with both al-Qaeda and the Islamic State of Iraq and the Levant using Libya as a safehaven.[557] While the Secretary of State testified, without specifics, there were a "number of documents" prepared regarding planning for a post-Qadhafi Libya,[558] Morell said otherwise:

---

[548] *See, e.g.,* CHIVVIS, TOPPLING QADDAFI, *supra* note 522, at 183; William Maclean, *If Libyan Rebels Win, Can They Rule?,* REUTERS, (Aug. 21, 2011, *available at*), http://in.reuters.com/article/2011/08/21/idININdia-58891320110821 (last visited Feb. 18, 2016); Jason Pack & Haley Cook, *Beyond Tripoli's Grasp,* MAJALLA, (Oct. 3, 2013, *available at*), http://www.majalla.com/eng/2013/10/article55245761 (last visited Feb. 18, 2016).

[549] CHIVVIS, TOPPLING QADDAFI, *supra* note 522, at 94–95, 183. After the conflict, the State Department was more concerned with Security Council politics in the debate on how to respond to the war than transferring frozen Qaddafi regime funds to the TNC for post-conflict stabilization. *See id.* at 164.

[550] *Id.; e.g., Armed Groups in Libya: Typology & Roles,* SMALL ARMS SURVEY, RESEARCH NOTES (June 2012), *available at*
http://www.smallarmssurvey.org/fileadmin/docs/H-Research_Notes/
SAS-Research-Note-18.pdf (last visited Feb. 18, 2016).

[551] *Biggest Success? NATO Proud of Libya Op Which Killed Thousands,* RT (Oct. 28, 2011), http://rt.com/news/nato-libya-operation-success-999/(last visited Feb. 18, 2016) [hereinafter *NATO Proud of Libya Op*]; Max Boot, *Libya's problems are far from over,* L.A. Times (Aug. 24, 2011), http://articles.latimes.com/2011/aug/24/opinion/la-oe-boot-libya-20110824.

[552] Jayshree Bajoria, *The Perils of Libyan Nation Building,* WORLD POST, (Apr. 7, 2011), http://www.huffingtonpost.com/jayshree-bajoria/the-perils-of-libyan-nati_b_846080.html.

[553] *NATO Proud of Libya Op, supra* note 529.

[554] Mike Krever, *West Should Have Put Boots on the Ground in Libya, Says Former Prime Minister,* CNN (Mar. 25, 2014), http://amanpour.blogs.cnn.com/2014/03/25/west-should-have-put-boots-on-the-ground-in-libya-says-former-prime-minister. *See also* Raphael Cohen & Gabriel Scheinmann, *Lessons from Libya: America Can't Lead From Behind,* TIME (Feb. 15, 2014), http://ideas.time.com/2014/02/15/lessons-from-libya-america-cant-lead-from-behind/; Stanley Kurtz, *Assessing Libya,* NAT'L REVIEW ONLINE (Aug. 22, 2011), http://www.nationalreview.com/corner/275181/assessing-libya-stanley-kurtz.

[555] Fred Burton & Samuel Katz, *40 Minutes in Benghazi,* VANITY FAIR, (Aug. 2013), http://www.vanityfair.com/politics/2013/08/Benghazi-book-fred-burton-samuel-m-katz.

[556] CHIVVIS, TOPPLING QADDAFI, *supra* note 522, at 143–46.

[557] Pamela Engel, *How one major failure allowed ISIS to exploit the chaos in its newest hotspot,* BUSINESS INSIDER (Jan. 27, 2016), http://www.businessinsider.com/isis-libya-rise-2016-1.

[558] The U.S. House Select Committee on Benghazi, *Hearing 4—Part 1: Testimony from Former Secretary of State Hillary Clinton—10/22/2015 (EventID=104082),* YOUTUBE (Oct. 22, 2015), https://www.youtube.com/watch?v=ABFWjZxCAAg; The U.S. House Select Committee on Benghazi, *Hearing 4—Part 2: Testimony from Former Secretary of State Hillary Clinton—10/22/2015 (EventID=104082),* YOUTUBE (Oct. 22, 2015), http://www.youtube.com/watch?v=0hvl1LpZp3Q [collectively hereinafter Benghazi Hearing 4].

One of the problems was not going into it with a very detailed plan for how you were going to maintain stability . . . We never really had a conversation around the table about 'what's going to happen, how's it going to look?' The intelligence community never wrote that paper . . . That conversation was not as rich and rigorous as it should have been.[559]

That view is supported by Anne Marie Slaughter, former Director of Policy Planning, State Department, when she wrote:

It is so much easier to pound our chests and declare that the United States bestrides the world like a colossus and should be able to dictate any outcome it wants. That is no longer true, if it ever were. We found that out the hard way by . . . toppling a government in Libya without any idea of what might come next.[560]

Morell told the Committee Libya was unique among countries involved in the Arab Spring because it was the only place where the United States made a choice to push the Arab Spring forward.[561] As a result, according to Morell, the intelligence community should have furnished the President a plan projecting likely conditions in Libya after the fall of Qadhafi.[562]

Morell attributes the failure to provide predictive intelligence to multiple parties across the spectrum: the intelligence analysts, the leadership of the intelligence community, and even the decision-makers—including the President and the Secretary of State—for not asking those questions and fostering a conversation about what would need to be done to maintain stability in a post-Qadhafi Libya.[563] The Secretary pushed back on this point when she testified: "[W]e can do all the planning we want in Washington, but it's very important to ask the Libyans both what they want and what they expect from us, and so we had an ongoing dialogue that lasted over many months."[564] Her testimony, however, referred to the events after Qadhafi fell, (for example, Nides visited Libya in January 2012, nearly a year after the initial U.S. intervention) and not prior to the U.S. intervention.[565]

In describing this intelligence failure, Morell described to the Committee an additional "intelligence analytic issue."[566] He noted that in authoritarian societies, such as Qadhafi-era Libya, the personality of the leader is "everything," personal relationships with individuals in the rest of the government are "everything," and institutions in that government are all personality-based.[567] The in-

---

[559] Michael Hirsh, 'Here's What I Really Worry About,' POLITICO (May 11, 2015), http://www.pollitico.com/magazine/story/2015/05/Michael-Morell-interview-cia-impending-terror-attack-117821#ixzz4BHB4izvu.

[560] Anne Marie Slaughter, War with Iran is the only alternative to a deal, USA TODAY (Aug. 20, 2015), http://www.usatoday.com/story/opinion/2015/08/20/bombing-iran-only-alternative-deal-column/31940869/ (emphasis added).

[561] Morell Testimony at 82.

[562] Id.

[563] Id. at 83.

[564] Clinton Testimony at 177.

[565] See Request for SST Extension from U.S. Embassy Tripoli, Libya, to Sec'y of State, U.S. Dep't of State (Feb. 12, 2012, 11:58 PM) (on file with the Committee, SCB0049743–48).

[566] Morell Testimony at 277.

[567] Id.

stitutions themselves are empty without the leadership, and when the leader goes away, the institutions simply break down.[568] Morell contended the Intelligence Community did not fully appreciate these factors in the case of Libya.[569] Instead, as he noted, the U.S. instead viewed itself as a "beacon of democracy" without understanding what was next:

> It's ingrained in us, this desire to spread democracy to the rest of the world. I think people's weaknesses flow from their strengths, in organizations and countries. One of our strengths is seeing ourselves as a beacon for democracy. It becomes a weakness when we try to impose it on societies that aren't ready for it. I think of Iraq, Gaza, Afghanistan and Libya. I think it's probably both a failure of intelligence and a failure of policy, in two different administrations.[570]

While the CIA took this dangerous security environment seriously—they sent out a physical security specialist to review its compound in Benghazi and apply immediate upgrades—this analysis all occurred too late to enact meaningful change inside Libya and prevent this threat from emerging and eventually establishing a stranglehold on the country. No predictive analysis occurred within the intelligence community on the front end of the U.S. intervention regarding what might occur if Qadhafi were to lose power. No assessment was made that a power void may be exploited by al Qa'ida and other extremist organizations, and it was this front-end intelligence failure that contributed to the Benghazi attacks.

An additional critical question is why the United States did not have a specific, tactical warning about the attack. Morell addressed this issue when he spoke of what he calls "battlefield intelligence":

> . . . so that you're picking up everything, from a signals perspective and from a humint [human intelligence] perspective. I think the only way to have avoided Benghazi is to have that kind of intelligence footprint over the top of them . . . the real lesson about Benghazi is how do we protect American diplomats, how do we protect American intelligence officers, how do we protect American servicemen and women overseas moving forward, in what is a very, very dangerous world.[571]

Secretary Leon Panetta, himself a former Director of the CIA, also testified about the failure in Benghazi to have the kind of intelligence that would have tipped off U.S. personnel about a specific attack.[572] Panetta labeled this the "most important missing element" regarding Benghazi,[573] and said it should be the first lesson learned about the attacks—improving the intelligence to make

---

[568] *Id.*
[569] *Id.*
[570] *Here's What I really Worry About, supra* note [559] (emphasis added).
[571] *Counterterrorism Efforts,* C-SPAN (May 18, 2015), http://www.c-span.org/video/?326104-1/former-cia-deputy-director-michael-morell-counterterrorism-efforts&start=1060.
[572] *See* Panetta Testimony at 119–20.
[573] *Id.* at 71–72.

sure our personnel are aware there is going to be an imminent attack.[574]

This issue is discussed further in the classified annex to the report, as well as addressing the question of why U.S. government officials did not have what proved to be sufficient, specific, tactical warning about the Benghazi attacks.

The day before the Benghazi attacks, the President convened a phone call with senior administration officials concerning America's preparedness and security posture on the anniversary of the September 11, 2001 attacks.[575] A readout of the meeting notes the "[p]rincipals discussed specific measures we are taking in the Homeland to prevent 9/11 related attacks as well as steps taken to protect U.S. persons and facilities abroad, as well as force protection."[576] Panetta testified there was concern on the call about the anti-Muslim video that was coming out, and there was a specific discussion regarding Tripoli, among other cities in the region.[577] Given the lack of any pre-attack force movement toward North Africa and the Middle East in the wake of the call—especially given the concerns about the video and the forewarning regarding protests in Cairo[578]—there appeared to be no indications an attack in Benghazi, or anywhere else in the region, was anticipated.

Nevertheless, on the morning of September 11, one of the local guards at the TMF witnessed a man, believed to be a police officer, in the second story of a building across the street looking into the State Department facility and taking photographs.[579] Stevens was briefed about the incident,[580] and Sean Smith referenced the incident just hours before the attacks began on an online gaming site.[581]

---

[574] *Id.* at 119–20.

[575] Press Release, The White House Office of the Press Secretary, The White House, Readout of the President's Meeting with Senior Administration Officials on Our Preparedness and Security Posture on the Eleventh Anniversary of September 11th (Sept. 10, 2012), https://www.whitehouse.gov/the-press-office/2012/09/10/readout-president-s-meeting-senior-administration-officials-our-prepared.

[576] *Id.*

[577] Panetta Testimony at 10.

[578] *Id.* at 10–11.

[579] Diplomatic Sec. Agent 5 Testimony at 93.

[580] Email from Assistant Regional Sec. Officer (Sept. 11, 2012, 5:00 pm) (on file with the Committee, C05271656).

[581] The posting by Sean Smith read, "Assuming we don't die tonight. We saw one of our 'police' that guard the compound taking pictures." *See, e.g.,* Lindsay Wise, *Libya attack victim: 'assuming we don't die tonight . . . ,'* SEATTLE TIMES, Sept. 13, 2012.

# PART IV:

# Compliance with Congressional Investigations

*"But now that I am the secretary and I am responsible to you and the Congress, I can promise you that if you're not getting something that you have evidence of or you think you ought to be getting, we'll work with you. And I will appoint somebody to work directly with you starting tomorrow . . . To have a review of anything you don't think you [have] gotten that you're supposed to get. Let's get this done with, folks."*

> Secretary of State John F. Kerry (April 2013—one year before the creation of the Select Committee on complying with congressional questions about the Benghazi attacks.)

*"This is the most transparent administration in history."*

> President Barack Obama (February 2013)

*"Four Americans lost their lives in Benghazi, and this White House has gone to extraordinary lengths to mislead, obstruct, and obscure what actually took place."*

> Speaker John A. Boehner (May 2014—after the White House failed to produce Benjamin J. Rhodes' memo to Congress.)

*"I want the public to see my email."*

> Secretary Hillary R. Clinton (March 2015—after published reports her emails and other public records were returned to the State Department 18 months after she left office.)

## COMPLIANCE WITH CONGRESSIONAL OVERSIGHT

### Introduction

Congress's authority to oversee and investigate the Executive Branch is a necessary component of legislative powers and to maintain the constitutional balance of powers between the branches. As the Supreme Court held in 1927: "[T]he power of inquiry—with process to enforce it—is an essential and appropriate auxiliary to the legislative function."[1] Similarly, the Supreme Court held: "The power of the Congress to conduct investigations is inherent in the legislative process. That power is broad. It encompasses inquiries concerning the administration of existing laws as well as proposed or possibly needed statutes."[2]

When needed information cannot easily be obtained—or if government agencies resist—Congress has legitimate cause to compel responses:

> A legislative body cannot legislate wisely or effectively in the absence of information respecting the conditions which the legislation is intended to affect or change, and where the legislative body does not itself possess the requisite information—which not infrequently is true—recourse must be had to others who do possess it. Experience has taught that mere requests for such information often are unavailing, and also that information which is volunteered is not always accurate or complete, so some means of compulsion are essential to obtain what is needed.[3]

These principles of congressional oversight have been severely tested during the Committee's investigation. The administration's frequently stated pledge to comply with "all legitimate oversight requests" is often a hollow prelude followed by delay or refusal to respond to legitimate inquiries. Other congressional committees have reported similar delay and obstruction.[4] The administration's resistance to this Committee has been especially troubling. The families of the four Americans murdered in Benghazi and the American public deserve to hear the whole truth in a timely fashion. The same government that asked J. Christopher Stevens, Sean P. Smith, Glen A. Doherty and Tyrone S. Woods to serve selflessly and sacrificially delayed and obstructed an investigation into what happened in Benghazi before, during, and after their deaths.

The discussion below details the Select Committee's two-year battle to obtain documents and access to witnesses necessary to understand what happened in Benghazi. The administration's intentional failure to cooperate with this and other congressional investigations warrants changes in congressional rules and amendments to law in order to ensure the Executive Branch cooperates with congressional investigations and the American people know what their government does on their behalf and with their money.

---

[1] McGrain v. Daugherty, 273 U.S. 135, 174 (1927).
[2] Watkins v. United States, 354 U.S. 178, 187 (1957).
[3] *McGrain*, 273 U.S. at 175.
[4] http://www.usatoday.com/story/opinion/2016/02/09/obama-administration-least-transparent-epa-state-doj-clinton-benghazi-column/80050428.

The House of Representatives established the Committee in large part *because* of this administration's delay and obstruction of prior congressional investigations.[5] The House specifically directed the Committee to examine "executive branch activities and efforts to comply with Congressional inquiries" into the Benghazi terrorist attacks and to recommend ways to improve Executive Branch compliance with congressional oversight.[6] The detailed nature of this section is intended to reflect the breadth of the Committee's investigation and the lengths to which the administration went to delay and obstruct the investigation. It also provides a factual record so readers can judge for themselves the responsiveness of Executive Branch agencies and how this lack of responsiveness not only thwarted efforts to find facts but also contributed to the time it took to acquire those facts ultimately uncovered.

## Building the Committee's Record

The discovery and production of all relevant, material documents—and other tangible evidentiary items—is an essential foundation for substantive hearings, public and private, as well as constructive witness interviews. Examining witnesses without knowledge of and access to all relevant information is unproductive, time consuming, and inefficient. The logical chronology of serious investigations is to gather physical evidence and documents prior to questioning witnesses. Not only do the documents serve as a source and foundation for the subsequent interview, they also provide witnesses with the information needed to refresh recollections or put testimony in perspective. Serious investigators understand the logical chronology of access and interview. Regrettably, so too do those seeking to undermine investigations.

### REVIEW OF EXISTING DOCUMENTS

When established in May 2014, the Committee—consistent with the directive in H. Res. 567—sought to obtain all relevant documents from the five House committees previously investigating the terrorist attacks on U.S. facilities in Benghazi.[7]

While previous committees of Congress did investigate certain aspects of Benghazi, no committee investigated all aspects of Benghazi. The House Armed Services Committee focused on Defense Department matters and relied almost exclusively on briefings and public hearings. The Armed Services Committee did not investigate State Department issues, intelligence community issues or White House involvement in the drafting and editing of the public responses after the attacks. The House Permanent Intelligence Committee focused on intelligence issues and did not investigate Defense or State Department issues. Additionally, the Intelligence Committee interviewed some witnesses in groups, which is generally disfavored as an investigatory tool.

---

[5] Eli Lake, *Clinton Can Thank Obama for Her Benghazi Headache,* Bloomberg (Oct. 6, 2015), http://www.bloombergview.com/articles/2015-10-06/clinton-can-thank-obama-for-her-benghazi-headache.

[6] See H. Res. 567, 113th Cong., § 3(a)(6) and (7) (2014).

[7] *See id.* § 5(a) ("Any committee of the House of Representatives having custody of records in any form relating to the matters described in section 3 shall transfer such records to the Select Committee within 14 days of the adoption of this resolution. Such records shall become the records of the Select Committee.").

The Accountability Review Board [ARB] was a State Department investigative entity which did not have jurisdiction over the Defense Department, the Central Intelligence Agency [CIA], or the White House. In addition, there is no transcript from any interview conducted by the ARB, making it impossible to know which questions were asked, of whom, and what the precise responses were. The absence of transcripts requires the reader to simply take the word of those drafting the report.

The failure to honor congressional requests for information and the silo effect of committees being confined to certain jurisdictional lanes is what prompted John A. Boehner, Speaker of the House, and ultimately the House of Representatives, to form a select committee with broad investigatory authority across all jurisdictions and across all facets of what happened in Benghazi before, during and after the deadly attacks.

The Select Committee's broader jurisdiction is reflected in the fact this Committee interviewed 107 witnesses, 81 of whom had not been questioned previously by any committee of Congress. These witnesses came from all parts of government, including the White House, the CIA and Defense and State Departments. It is reflected in the more than 75,000 pages of new documents to which no other committee of Congress had access. In addition, the Committee's investigation discovered emails not previously uncovered from senior government officials including the emails of Stevens and of Hillary R. Clinton, the Secretary of State, and her senior staff.

When the Committee came into existence in May 2014, it accessed approximately 50,000 pages of reports, interview transcripts, depositions, hearing transcripts, memoranda, classified and unclassified documents, and other information not cited or used by the standing committees in their investigations.[8] The Committee reviewed and evaluated the documents page by page.[9] This review took place from July 2014 to October 2014.

Among these materials—many of which were duplicates—were 25,000 pages so heavily redacted as to be useless to investigators.[10] This prompted the Committee to ask the State Department to reproduce the material in less-redacted form.[11] The resulting document productions were delivered in two installments—November 24, 2014, and December 9, 2014.[12]

### INITIAL DOCUMENT REQUESTS TO EXECUTIVE BRANCH AGENCIES

The Committee also sought information through the pending document requests of previous committees. The State Department had yet to comply with two outstanding congressional subpoenas issued

---

[8] Chairman Trey Gowdy, *Interim Progress Update,* H. SELECT COMM. ON BENGHAZI 3 (May 8, 2015), http://benghazi.house.gov/sites/republicans.benghazi.house.gov/files/Interim%20Progress%20Update%2005-08-15.pdf. [hereinafter Interim Progress Update].

[9] *Id.*

[10] *Id.*

[11] *See* Letter from Trey Gowdy, Chairman, H. Select Comm. on Benghazi, to Julia E. Frifield, Assistant Sec'y of State for Legis. Affairs, U.S. Dep't of State, (Sept. 30, 2014) (on file with the Committee).

[12] Letter from Julia E. Frifield, Assistant Sec'y of State for Legis. Affairs, U.S. Dep't of State, to Trey Gowdy, Chairman, H. Select Comm. on Benghazi (Nov. 24, 2014) (on file with the Committee); Letter from Julia E. Frifield, Assistant Sec'y of State for Legis. Affairs, U.S. Dep't of State, to Trey Gowdy, Chairman, H. Select Comm. on Benghazi (Dec. 9, 2014) (on file with the Committee).

in 2013—one subpoena dealt specifically with ARB documents.[13] The other subpoena dealt with documents previously reviewed by congressional investigators but possession of the documents remained with the State Department limiting full and useful access to the information.[14] These subpoenas were and remained legally binding on the State Department and did not need to be reissued at that time.[15] Since those existing subpoenas remained valid, the Committee gave them priority.[16] The State Department produced 15,000 pages of new documents to the Committee on August 11, 2014.[17]

A review of these 15,000 pages of emails and documents, coupled with the 25,000 pages of less-redacted text, revealed significant gaps in the information needed to determine what happened in Libya before, during and after the attacks that led to the murder of four Americans. For instance, this production contained few emails between and among the State Department's senior staff. The email traffic did not reflect roles played in the decision-making process as it related to the U.S.'s intervention into Libya in 2011, the Special Mission to Benghazi in April 2011, the extension of the Benghazi Mission into 2012, the night and early morning hours of September 11–12, 2012, and the post-attack period. Moreover, there were significant gaps in information that could be filled only by interviewing eyewitnesses and other individuals on the ground in Benghazi as well as witnesses who were in Washington DC in the days and months leading up to the attacks on September 11–12, 2012.

On November 18, 2014, the Committee sought specific documents and communications relating to Benghazi and Libya for 11 top State Department officials, including the Secretary and her senior staff.[18] The Committee also requested to interview more than 20 State Department witnesses, all of whom spent time on the ground in Benghazi, including four diplomatic security agents who survived the September 11–12 attacks.[19]

The Committee sent information requests in the fall of 2014 to the CIA, the National Security Agency, the Defense Intelligence

---

[13] Subpoena issued by H. Comm. on Oversight & Gov't Reform to John F. Kerry, Sec'y of State, U.S. Dep't of State (Aug. 1, 2013) [hereinafter OGR Document subpoena] (seeking approximately 25,000 pages of documents referenced in Assistant Sec'y Thomas Gibbons' March 29, 2013 letter).

[14] Subpoena issued by H. Comm. on Oversight & Gov't Reform to John F. Kerry, Sec'y of State, U.S. Dep't of State (Aug. 1, 2013) [hereinafter OGR ARB Subpoena] (seeking documents related to State Dep't's ARB findings regarding the facts and circumstances surrounding the attacks in Benghazi).

[15] Interim Progress Update, *supra* note 8, at 4.

[16] *Id.*

[17] Letter from Julia E. Frifield, Assistant Sec'y of State for Legis. Affairs, U.S. Dep't of State, to Trey Gowdy, Chairman, H. Select Comm. on Benghazi (Aug. 11, 2014) (on file with the Committee).

[18] Letter from Trey Gowdy, Chairman, H. Select Comm. on Benghazi, to John F. Kerry, Sec'y of State, U.S. Dep't of State, (Nov. 18, 2014) (on file with Committee).

[19] *See* Letter from Trey Gowdy, Chairman, H. Select Comm. on Benghazi, to John F. Kerry, Sec'y of State, U.S. Dep't of State (Dec. 4, 2014) (on file with the Committee) (The first of two similarly cited letters requesting interviews of four agents serving in Benghazi the night of the attacks); *see also* Letter from Trey Gowdy, Chairman, H. Select Comm. on Benghazi, to John F. Kerry, Sec'y of State, U.S. Dep't of State (Dec. 4, 2014) (on file with the Committee) (The second of two similarly cited letters requesting interviews of eighteen agents and principal officers who served in Benghazi).

Agency, and the Office of the Director of National Intelligence.[20] In December 2014, the Committee sent information requests to the Federal Bureau of Investigation [FBI] and the White House.[21]

The Committee issued three additional subpoenas to the State Department (detailed below) and made nine individual document requests.[22]

Committee document requests resulted in approximately 75,420 pages of new material:

- The State Department produced approximately 71,640 pages of documents not previously provided to Congress.

- The CIA produced 300 pages of new intelligence analyses.

- The White House produced 1,450 pages of emails.

- Sidney S. Blumenthal produced 179 pages of emails.

- The FBI produced 200 pages of documents.

- The Defense Department produced 900 pages of documents.

- The National Security Agency produced 750 pages of documents.

It is important to rebut a frequent talking point. The number of documents produced is in isolation meaningless without knowing the relevance of the documents actually produced and the number of relevant documents not produced. An agency that compliments itself on the number of pages provided to investigators when it alone knows the number of relevant pages withheld is engaged in propaganda, not transparency.

### MEETINGS, BRIEFINGS, AND PUBLIC HEARINGS

The Committee's first priority was to hear from the families of the four murdered Americans in the Benghazi attacks.[23] These meetings offered the families an opportunity to be heard, to pose questions and concerns to the Committee, and to provide their insights. The Chairman also requested briefings from agencies to discuss survivorship benefits to ensure the families received the benefits to which they were entitled.[24]

The Committee held more than two dozen classified and unclassified briefings with Executive Branch agencies.[25] For example, the Committee met with the State Department to evaluate the events

---

[20] See Letter from Trey Gowdy, Chairman, H. Select Comm. on Benghazi, to John O. Brennan, Dir., Cent. Intel. Agency (Nov. 19, 2014) (on file with the Committee); Letter from Trey Gowdy, Chairman, H. Select Comm. on Benghazi, to Michael S. Rogers, Dir., Nat'l Sec. Agency (Nov. 19, 2014) (on file with the Committee); Letter from Trey Gowdy, Chairman, H. Select Comm. on Benghazi, to David R. Shedd, *acting* Dir., Def. Intel. Agency (Nov. 19, 2014) (on file with the Committee); Letter from Trey Gowdy, Chairman, H. Select Comm. on Benghazi, to James R. Clapper, Dir., Nat'l Intel. (Nov. 19, 2014) (on file with the Committee).

[21] See Letter from Trey Gowdy, Chairman, H. Select Comm. on Benghazi, to James B. Comey, Jr., Dir., Fed. Bureau of Investigation (Dec. 4, 2014) (on file with the Committee); Letter from Trey Gowdy, Chairman, H. Select Comm. on Benghazi, to Denis R. McDonough, White House Chief of Staff (Dec. 29, 2014) (on file with the Committee).

[22] See Letter from Trey Gowdy, Chairman, H. Select Comm. on Benghazi, to John F. Kerry, Sec'y of State, U.S. Dep't of State (July 31, 2015) (on file with Committee).

[23] Interim Progress Update, *supra* note 8, at 3.

[24] Letter from Trey Gowdy, Chairman, H. Select Comm. on Benghazi, and Elijah E. Cummings, Ranking Member, H. Select Comm. on Benghazi to John F. Kerry, Sec'y of State, U.S. Dep't of State and John O. Brennan, Dir., Cent. Intel. Agency (October 8, 2014) (on file with the Committee).

[25] *Id.*

prior to and during the September 11–12, 2012, attacks, including viewing video footage of the attacks.[26] The Committee also met with the Justice Department and the FBI on the capture of Ahmed Abu Khatalla and to view additional footage of the attacks.[27]

The Committee held only four public hearings.[28] The first and second public hearings—on September 17, 2014, and December 1, 2014—examined the State Department's efforts to protect U.S. facilities and personnel currently serving abroad.[29] Immediately following a significant event resulting in serious injury or loss of life, the State Department is required by law to convene an ARB to investigate and make findings and recommendations to protect against similar occurrences in the future.[30] Consequently, the Committee's first hearing focused on the State Department's implementation of the ARB's recommendations as well as those recommendations issued by the Independent Panel on Best Practices. The Independent Panel consisted of independent experts who were asked to evaluate the State Department's security platforms in high-risk, high-threat posts.[31]

The Committee's second public hearing also allowed the Committee to examine the shortcomings identified by the State Department's Office of the Inspector General [OIG] and the Department's efforts to remedy these deficiencies.[32] The OIG's first report, issued in September 2013, contained 20 formal and eight informal recommendations.[33] The OIG conducted a compliance follow-up review from January 15 through March 18, 2015,[34] and in August 2015 reissued one recommendation to the Bureau of Diplomatic Security and the Overseas Buildings Operations.[35] The OIG called on the State Department to "develop minimum security standards that must be met prior to occupying facilities located in designated high risk, high threat locations and include these minimum standards for occupancy in the Foreign Affairs Handbook."[36]

The third public hearing on January 27, 2015, was necessary because of continuing compliance problems with Executive Branch entities.[37] The Committee's authorizing resolution directed it to:

> "[c]onduct a full and complete investigation and study and issue a final report of its findings to the House regarding:
>
> • executive branch activities and efforts to comply with Congressional inquiries into the attacks . . .[38] [and]

---

[26] *Id.*

[27] *Id.*

[28] H. SELECT COMM. ON BENGHAZI, https://benghazi.house.gov/hearings (last visited May 10, 2016).

[29] *Hearing 1 Before the H. Select Comm. on Benghazi,* 113th Congress (2014), *Hearing 2 Before the H. Select Comm. on Benghazi,* 113th Congress (2014).

[30] *See* 22 U.S.C. § 4831 (2005).

[31] INDEPENDENT PANEL ON BEST PRACTICES, DEP'T OF STATE, 1 (Aug. 29, 2013).

[32] *Id.*

[33] *See* Office of Inspector Gen., U.S. Dep't of State, *Special Review of the Accountability Review Board Process: Report No. ISP–I–13–44A,* 39–42 (Sept. 2013), https://oig.state.gov/system/files/214907.pdf.

[34] *See* Office of Inspector Gen., U.S. Dep't of State, *Compliance Followup Review of the Special Review of the Accountability Review Board Process: Report No. ISP–C–15–33,* 39–42 (Aug. 2015), https://oig.state.gov/system/files/isp-c-15-33.pdf.

[35] *Id.*

[36] *Id.*

[37] *See Hearing 3 Before the H. Select Comm. on Benghazi,* 114th Congress, (2015).

[38] H. Res. 567, 113th Cong., § 3(a)(6) (2014).

- recommendations for improving executive branch cooperation and compliance with congressional oversight and investigations . . ."[39]

The administration attempted to the narrow the Committee's investigation and repeatedly asked it to prioritize discovery requests.[40] While the Committee refused to narrow its investigation—the scope of which was mandated by the House of Representatives—the Committee did accommodate the administration's requests to prioritize. This accommodation resulted in the administration disregarding discovery requests that were not prioritized and accusing the Committee of being preoccupied with the witnesses and documents that were prioritized.

The Committee's fourth public hearing was held on October 22, 2015, to receive testimony of the Secretary, a necessary fact witness who oversaw the State Department before, during, and after the Benghazi terrorist attacks.[41] The Secretary had yet to be examined by any investigative panel or congressional committee with access to her emails and other relevant information.[42]

The Committee's preference for private interviews over public hearings has been questioned. Interviews are a more efficient and effective means of discovery. Interviews allow witnesses to be questioned in depth by a highly prepared member or staff person. In a hearing, every member of a committee is recognized—usually for five minutes—a procedure which precludes in-depth focused questioning. Interviews also allow the Committee to safeguard the privacy of witnesses who may fear retaliation for cooperating or whose work requires anonymity, such as intelligence community operatives.

Both witnesses and members of Congress conduct themselves differently in interviews than when in the public glare of a hearing. Neither have an incentive to play to the cameras. Witnesses have no incentive to run out the clock as long-winded evasive answers merely extend the length of the interview. Likewise, Members have no need to interrupt witnesses to try to ask all their questions in five minutes. Perhaps more importantly, political posturing, self-serving speeches, and theatrics serve no purpose in a closed interview and, as a result, the questioning in interviews tends to be far more effective at discovering information than at public hearings. For these reasons, nearly all Executive Branch investigations are conducted in private and without arbitrary time constraints. This is no less true in a Legislative Branch investigation, yet the manner in which the media portrays these investigations is starkly different.

---

[39] *Id.* § 3(a)(7).

[40] Meeting between H. Select Comm. on Benghazi staff and U.S. Dep't of State representatives (February 27, 2015). *See also,* email from Philip G. Kiko, Staff Director and Gen. Counsel, H. Select Comm. on Benghazi, to Julia Frifield, Ass't Sec'y of State, Legislative Affairs, U.S. Dep't of State (March 23, 2015, 6:50 PM) (on file with the Committee).

[41] *Hearing 4 Before the H. Select Comm. on Benghazi,* 114th Congress (2015).

[42] Letter from Trey Gowdy, Chairman, H. Select Comm. on Benghazi, to David E. Kendall, Of Counsel, Williams & Connolly LLP (Mar. 19, 2015) (on file with the Committee). It is important to note that the Committee offered to take Secretary Clinton's testimony in an interview setting. The former Secretary elected to provide her testimony to the Committee in a public setting. *See* Letter from Trey Gowdy, Chairman, H. Select Comm. on Benghazi to David E. Kendall, Of Counsel, Williams & Connolly LLP (Mar. 31, 2015) (on file with the Committee).

No witness interviewed by the Committee complained of poor treatment or a lack of professionalism during these interviews. In fact, witnesses who had no incentive to compliment the Committee did just that, such as Cheryl D. Mills, Chief of Staff and Counselor, State Department, and Huma M. Abedin, Deputy Chief of Staff, State Department.[43]

## The Department of State

Notwithstanding the productions eventually made, the State Department's compliance posture toward the Committee was poor. The Department failed to comply in full with the nine document requests and three subpoenas.[44] Instead, Department officials deflected and delayed their responses, engaged in a pattern of obstruction, and furnished productions and witness interviews slowly—significantly impeding the Committee's investigation and development of a complete record.

RESPONSE TO SUBPOENAS FOR DOCUMENTS RELATING TO THE
ACCOUNTABILITY REVIEW BOARD

As described earlier, two subpoenas issued by Congress to the State Department in 2013 had yet to be satisfied when the Select Committee was formed.[45] One of these subpoenas dealt specifically with documents pertaining to the ARB.[46] Though Congress had been asking for the documents for almost two years, the State Department failed to produce a single document. The Committee emphasized the importance of these documents by reissuing a new subpoena for the 114th Congress. Immediately following the January 27, 2015 compliance hearing, the Committee issued a new subpoena for documents reviewed by the ARB.[47]

The State Department's first production to the Committee consisted of a four-page interview summary for a witness who was scheduled to appear before the Committee the following day.[48] The State Department maintained this posture over the next several weeks with one or two ARB summaries, totaling 38 pages, provided less than a week before the Committee's interviews.[49] It was not until April 15, 2015, the State Department produced approximately 1,700 pages of documents.[50] On April 24, 2015, the Department produced another approximately 2,600 pages of documents.[51]

---

[43] Michael S. Schmidt, *Cheryl Mills, Advisor to Hillary Clinton, Testifies on Benghazi and Email Practices,* NY Times (September 3, 2015), http://www.nytimes.com/2015/09/04/us/hillary-clinton-email-benghazi.html?_r=0.

[44] Letter to John F. Kerry, Sec'y of State, U.S. Dep't of State, to Trey Gowdy, Chmn., H. Select Comm. On Benghazi (July 31, 2015) (on file with the Committee).

[45] Interim Progress Update, *supra* note 8, at 4.

[46] OGR ARB Subpoena, *supra* note 14.

[47] Subpoena issued by H. Select Comm. on Benghazi, to John F. Kerry, Sec'y of State, U.S. Dep't of State (Jan. 29, 2015).

[48] *See* Letter from Julia E. Frifield, Assistant Sec'y of State for Legis. Affairs, U.S. Dep't of State, to Trey Gowdy, Chairman, H. Select Comm. on Benghazi (Feb. 13, 2015) (on file with the Committee).

[49] *See* Comm. Internal Memorandum on State Dep't Records Production.

[50] *See* Letter from Julia E. Frifield, Assistant Sec'y of State for Legis. Affairs, U.S. Dep't of State, to Trey Gowdy, Chairman, H. Select Comm. on Benghazi (Apr. 15, 2015) (on file with the Committee).

[51] *See* Letter from Julia E. Frifield, Assistant Sec'y of State for Legis. Affairs, U.S. Dep't of State, to Trey Gowdy, Chairman, H. Select Comm. on Benghazi (Apr. 24, 2015) (on file with the Committee).

It remains unclear whether production for the January 28, 2015 subpoena is complete. Notwithstanding the more than 4,300 pages produced to the Committee, previous statements made by the State Department to Congress revealed the ARB reviewed "approximately 7,000 State Department documents, numbering thousands of pages."[52] Moreover, the State Department withheld a number of documents from the Committee based on "executive branch confidentiality interests," an administration-constructed privilege not recognized by the Constitution.[53]

## REQUESTS FOR DOCUMENTS OF THE SECRETARY AND OTHER SENIOR STATE DEPARTMENT OFFICIALS

While the State Department produced 15,000 pages of new documents to the Committee on August 11, 2014, there were significant and material omissions. This production contained few emails sent to or received by the State Department's senior staff. In fact, the production included only eight emails sent or received by the Secretary from two email addresses: "HDR22@clintonemail.com" and "H." This was the first time the State Department produced emails from the Secretary. It was also the first time the Committee became aware the Secretary used a private email account to conduct State Department business during her tenure. The Committee was not informed at the time, or at any time until immediately before media reporting, of the extent to which the Secretary relied on private email and a private server to conduct State Department business, or the ongoing discussion between the State Department and the Secretary and her representatives regarding the return of records.

For example, at the time the State Department produced these 15,000 pages of documents, which included these eight emails and pledged a "new relationship with the Committee," it was known within the State Department that the Secretary's email records were not on site.[54] The Chief Records Officer testified:

> Q: One of the things that we wanted to talk with you about was when you first became knowledgeable or aware that all or part of Secretary Clinton's records were not on premises with the State Department. And can you tell us when that was?
>
> A: The end of July 2014.
>
> Q: And how did you become aware that some of her records were not on premises?
>
> A: I was getting ready to enter my new position and one of my colleagues mentioned that in FOIA [Freedom of Information Act] litigation the issue had come up, but I had no idea about the full circumstances.[55]

---

[52] *See* Letter from the Thomas B, Gibbons, *acting* Assistant Sec'y of Legis. Affairs, U.S. Dep't of State, to Darrell E. Issa, Chairman, H. Comm. on Oversight & Gov't Reform (Aug. 23, 2013) (on file with H. Select Comm. on Benghazi).

[53] *See* Letter from Julia E. Frifield, Assistant Sec'y of State for Legis. Affairs, U.S. Dep't of State, to Trey Gowdy, Chairman, H. Select Comm. on Benghazi (Apr. 24, 2015).

[54] Testimony of William Fischer, Chief Records Officer, U.S. Dep't of State, Tr. at 66 (June 30, 2015) [hereinafter Fischer Testimony] (on file with the Committee).

[55] *Id.*

Unknown to the Committee and the public, the State Department and the Secretary were taking remedial action to recover her emails from her private server because of the Committee's investigation.[56] According to the State Department's own Inspector General:

> [i]n May 2014, the Department undertook efforts to recover potential Federal records from Secretary Clinton. Thereafter, in July 2014, senior officials met with former members of Secretary Clinton's immediate staff, who were then acting as Secretary Clinton's representatives. At the meeting, her representative indicated that her practice of using a personal account was based on Secretary Powell's similar use, but Department staff instructed Clinton's representatives to provide the Department with any Federal records transmitted through her personal system. On August 22, 2014, Secretary Clinton's former Chief of Staff and then-representative advised Department leadership that hard copies of Secretary Clinton emails containing responsive information would be provided but that, given the volume of emails, it would take some time to produce.[57]

In July 2014, Mills contacted Platte River Networks, the company contracted to maintain the Secretary's server, to request the Secretary's emails be pulled and sent to her overnight.[58]

The Committee did not publicize the existence of the eight emails identified from the Secretary's private email account, for myriad reasons. The Committee believed these eight emails might represent the beginning of a full production. There also existed the possibility of an explanation other than what was eventually learned. These eight emails could have reflected the Secretary's episodic use of personal email, as other administration officials had done,[59] and a more complete production of state.gov emails could be forthcoming. Of course, while the Committee did not have access to all salient facts in the summer of 2014, the State Department did. The State Department knew then it did not have possession of her public records as these records were not turned over at the end of the Secretary's tenure. The State Department knew then it was in no position to comply with congressional inquiries or FOIA requests related to the Secretary's emails because it did not have custody or access to the full public record. According to a recent report by the State Department's own Inspector General:

---

[56] July 2, 2014 meeting between Comm. Staff Director Philip G. Kiko and State Dep't Chief of Staff David E. Wade.

[57] Office of the Inspector General, "Office of the Sec'y: Evaluation of Email Records Management and Cybersecurity Requirements," at 17–18, footnote 75, (May 26, 2016) (on file with the Committee).

[58] Carol D. Leonning and Rosalind S. Helderman, *State Department's Account of email requirements differs from Clinton's,* Washington Post (September 22, 2015), https://www.washingtonpost.com/politics/state-departments-account-of-e-mail-request-differs-from-clintons/2015/09/22/54cd66bc-5ed9-11e5-8e9e-dce8a2a2a679_story.html ("He [Senator Johnson] cited a July 23, 2014, email in which employees at Platte River Networks, the private company that was then maintaining her server, discussed sending copies of Clinton's emails overnight to Cheryl Mills, a long-time Clinton advisor.").

[59] *See, e.g.,* Letter from Darrell E. Issa, Chairman, H. Comm. on Oversight & Gov't Reform, to Hillary R. Clinton, Sec'y of State, U.S. Dep't of State (Dec. 13, 2012) (on file with the Committee).

In early June 2013, Department staff participating in the review of potential material for production to congressional committees examining the September 2012 Benghazi attack discovered emails sent by the former Policy Planning Director via his Department email account to a personal email address associated with Secretary Clinton. In ensuing weeks, partly as a result of the staff's discovery, Department senior officials discussed the Department's obligations under the Federal Records Act in the context of personal email accounts. As discussed earlier in this report, laws and regulations did not prohibit employees from using their personal email accounts for the conduct of official Department business. However, email messages regarding official business sent to or from a personal email account fell within the scope of the Federal Records Act if their contents met the Act's definition of a record. OIG found that the Department took no action to notify NARA [National Archives and Records Administration] of a potential loss of records at any point in time.[60]

At the time the Committee was formed in May 2014, the State Department was already actively seeking the return of the former Secretary's emails.[61]

The Committee moved forward by issuing its November 18, 2014 document request to the State Department to obtain a clearer understanding of the role the Secretary and her senior staff played prior to, during, and after the terrorist attacks.[62] The Committee made clear the Secretary and her senior staff's documents and emails were necessary to facilitate her testimony before the Committee.[63] The decision to focus on obtaining these documents was the direct result of the Committee Minority's repeated request to move up the Secretary's appearance.

Very senior officials are traditionally interviewed last rather than first so the questions can be informed by as much information as possible. This is standard operating procedure in Executive Branch investigations. The Committee Minority expressly asked that the Secretary's appearance be moved up in the order of witness interviews and pledged in the process to help secure all relevant emails and documents in order to make that a reality. If there is any evidence Minority Committee members attempted to secure access to relevant documents or facilitate the production of documents, the Committee is not aware of it. Instead, the Committee Minority enjoyed the best of all worlds: complain about the Secretary not being interviewed while relying on the State Department to delay, obstruct, and withhold production of the very documents needed to facilitate the interview.

---

[60] "Office of the Sec'y: Evaluation of Email Records Management and Cybersecurity Requirements," *supra* note 69 at 17–18.

[61] Id.

[62] *See* Letter from Trey Gowdy, Chairman, H. Select Comm. on Benghazi, to John F. Kerry, Sec'y of State, U.S. Dep't of State (Nov. 18, 2014) (on file with the Committee). It is also important to note that this letter was accompanied by instructions typically found in subpoenas describing in greater detail the documents and communications sought and the definitions to be applied to the instructions. *See id.*

[63] *See id.*

The State Department did not disclose the fact that it did not have possession of the Secretary's emails, nor that it had been working with the Secretary for the previous seven months to secure their return. The Committee also asked the Secretary for documents and emails. On December 2, 2014, the Committee wrote David E. Kendall, the Secretary's attorney, requesting all of the Secretary's emails related to Benghazi and Libya from her private email account.[64] Knowing the actions already taken by his law firm and Mills to identify and return the former Secretary's emails to the State Department, Kendall did not respond until December 29, at which time he referred the Committee back to the State Department.[65] Kendall stated "[the State Department] is in a position to produce any responsive emails."[66] This "who's on first" routine orchestrated between the Secretary's private counsel and the State Department, which is ostensibly an apolitical governmental diplomatic entity, is shameful. It was not merely Congress and the people it represents who were misled and manipulated, the State Department and the Secretary's email arrangement undoubtedly delayed access to information on what happened to four brave Americans in Benghazi and the government's response before, during and after the attacks. The manner in which the Secretary communicated during her tenure, the manner in which those records were housed during and after her tenure and the manner in which the public record was self-scrutinized and self-selected makes it impossible to ever represent to the families of those killed in Benghazi that the record is whole.

Notwithstanding the Committee's December 2, 2014 request to Kendall, Mills informed the State Department within a matter of days that she was producing 55,000 pages of the Secretary's emails from her personal account.[67] On December 5, 2014, Mills wrote the State Department that the emails were being produced to help the Department "meet its requirements under the Federal Records Act."[68] Mills' letter did not disclose that all of the Secretary's work was conducted on a private email account and server. The letter did not disclose the form in which the 55,000 pages of emails were being produced. It did not disclose how the emails were being delivered to the State Department. The Committee would later learn that, on the same day Mills sent her letter to the State Department, a State Department records official was directed by his supervisor to pick up and transport hard copies of the Secretary's emails from Kendall's law firm, Williams and Connolly in Washington DC, back to the State Department.[69]

Despite receiving the Secretary's emails on December 5, 2014, the State Department failed to produce any document to the Com-

---

[64] Letter from Trey Gowdy, Chairman, H. Select Comm. on Benghazi, to David E. Kendall, Of Counsel, Williams & Connolly LLP (Dec. 2, 2014) (on file with the Committee).

[65] Letter from David E. Kendall, Of Counsel, Williams & Connolly LLP to Trey Gowdy, Chairman, H. Select Comm. on Benghazi (Dec. 29, 2014) (on file with the Committee).

[66] Id.

[67] See Letter from Cheryl D. Mills, Chief of Staff to the Sec'y of State, U.S. Dep't of State, to Patrick F. Kennedy, Under Sec'y of State for Mgmt., U.S. Dep't of State (Dec. 5, 2014) (on file with the Committee).

[68] See Id.

[69] Id.

mittee until February 13, 2015.[70] The Department also resisted scheduling witness interviews in December 2014 and January 2015. The Department's compliance posture resulted in the Committee's third public hearing, held on January 27, 2015. The State Department did not, however, produce a witness of sufficient seniority to make commitments on behalf of the Department.[71]

In fact, the State Department did not respond to the Committee's November 18, 2014 document request until February 13, 2015. At the time, the State Department produced approximately 847 pages of the Secretary's emails in paper copies. The State Department still refused to disclose important, relevant facts such as: the Secretary's emails were not on the State Department's network; the Secretary did not provide electronic copies of her emails; and the Secretary's attorneys—not the State Department—determined which emails would be returned to the Department.

It was not until February 27, 2015, the State Department disclosed to the Committee these facts, days before *The New York Times* would disclose the circumstances.[72] Even then, the State Department failed to disclose the fact that the Secretary used a private server. The Committee learned this fact through subsequent press reports.

Once the Committee learned the State Department had been complicit in the non-production of the Secretary's emails, it issued two preservation letters; one was issued to the Secretary[73] and the other to Web.com,[74] the registrar of the domain name Clinton@clintonemail.com. This was necessary to ensure relevant information in the parties' possession was preserved. The letters requested the Secretary and Web.com:

1. Preserve all email, electronic documents and date ("electronic records") created since January 1, 2009, that can be reasonably anticipated to be the subject to a request for production by the Committee. For the purpose of this request, "preserve" means taking reasonable steps to prevent the partial or full destruction, alteration, testing, deletion, shredding, incineration, wiping, relocation, migration, theft or mutation of electronic records, as well as negligent or intentional handling that would make such records incomplete or inaccessible;

2. Exercise reasonable efforts to identify and notify former employees and contractors who may have access to such electronic records that they are to be preserved; and

3. If it is the routine practice of any employee or contractor to destroy or otherwise alter such electronic records, either: halt such practices or arrange for the preservation of com-

[70] *Id. See also,* Letter from Julia Frifield, Ass't Secretary of State, Legislative Affairs, U.S. Dep't of State, to Trey Gowdy, Chairman, H. Select Comm. on Benghazi, (February 13, 2015) (on file with the Committee).

[71] *See Hearing 3 Before the H. Select Comm. on Benghazi,* 114th Congress (2015).

[72] Michael S. Schmidt, *Hillary Clinton Used Personal Email Account at State Dept., Possibly Breaking Rules,* N.Y. TIMES (Mar. 2, 2015), http://www.nytimes.com/2015/03/03/us/politics/hillary-clintons-use-of-private-email-at-state-department-raises-flags.html?_r=0.

[73] *See* Letter from Trey Gowdy, Chairman, H. Select Comm. on Benghazi, to David E. Kendall, Of Counsel, Williams & Connolly LLP (Mar. 3, 2015) (on file with the Committee).

[74] *See* Letter from Trey Gowdy, Chairman, H. Select Comm. on Benghazi, to Dan Brown, Chairman and Chief Exec. Officer, Web.com (Mar. 3, 2015) (on file with the Committee).

plete and accurate duplicates or copies of such records, suitable for production if requested.[75]

## THE SECRETARY IS SUBPOENAED

On March 4, 2015, a day after the Committee issued two preservation letters, the Committee issued two additional subpoenas. The first compelled production from the Secretary of any documents and communications responsive to the November 18, 2014 letter still in her possession.[76] The Secretary, through her attorney, Kendall, responded to the Committee's subpoena on March 27, 2015. In his letter, Kendall informed the Committee:

> With respect to any emails from Secretary Clinton's 'hdr22@clinontonemail.com' account, I respond by stating that, for the reasons set forth below, the Department of State—which has already produced approximately 300 documents in response to an earlier request seeking documents on essentially the same subject matters—is uniquely positioned to make available any documents responsive to your requests. [77]

Kendall further told the Committee:

> Secretary Clinton is not in a position to produce any of those emails to the Committee in response to the subpoena without approval from the State Department, which could come only following a review process. On March 23, 2015, I received a letter from Under Secretary of State for Management (attached hereto) confirming direction from the National Archives and Records Administration that while Secretary Clinton and her counsel are permitted to retain a copy of her work-related emails, those emails should not be released to any third parties without authorization by the State Department. . . . Thus, while the Secretary has maintained and preserved copies of the emails provided to the State Department, she is not in a position to make any production that may be called for by the subpoena.[78]

The State Department was unmoved by the location of public records during the Secretary's tenure or for nearly two years thereafter until the Committee insisted on their production. The State Department then orchestrated a sophomoric scheme of letters to have these records returned to the State Department. Once this was accomplished, the State Department, previously uninterested in the location, security or fullness of this public record, jealously guarded—indeed prevented—the production of the Secretary's records to Congress.

The State Department made two productions subsequent to February 13, 2015. The Committee received 105 email exchanges from the State Department on June 25, 2015. This production is signifi-

---

[75] See Chairman Gowdy's letters, supra notes 73 and 74.

[76] Subpoena issued by H. Select Comm. on Benghazi, to Hillary R. Clinton, former Sec'y of State, U.S. Dep't of State (Mar. 4, 2015).

[77] Letter from David E. Kendall, Of Counsel, Williams & Connolly LLP to Trey Gowdy, Chairman, H. Select Comm. on Benghazi (Mar. 27, 2015) (on file with the Committee).

[78] Id.

cant because it was made only after a non-government witness provided 179 additional pages of email exchanges with the Secretary on June 12, 2015. 59 of the emails produced by the non-government witness had never been provided by the State Department to the Committee despite the fact these emails were clearly responsive to previous requests and fully within the jurisdiction of the Committee. Moreover, the State Department did not have in its possession, in full or in part, 15 email exchanges produced by the non-government witness—calling into question the completeness of their records from the Secretary.[79] This means that not only was the State Department refusing to produce emails from the Secretary that were unquestionably relevant to this Committee's investigation, it also laid bare the Secretary's assurance that all public records had been returned to the State Department. Neither of those assertions was true.

The State Department made its third production to the Committee—1,899 pages of the Secretary's emails—on September 25, 2015. In its letter accompanying the emails, the State Department noted "it had re-reviewed Secretary Clinton's 2011–2012 emails and today is providing materials in advance of the Secretary's appearance before the Committee on October 22, 2015."[80]

The Committee's interest in the Secretary's emails is limited to their relevance in the investigation of the Benghazi attacks. Her exclusive use of non-official email and a private server for all official communications may raise concerns beyond the scope of this Committee's purview related to Federal records and transparency laws and national security concerns, but jurisdiction for those matters lies either with the Inspector General, the courts, other committees of Congress, or the Federal Bureau of Investigation and the Justice Department.

Simply put, the Committee has an obligation to seek and acquire all relevant information consistent with its jurisdiction. Part of securing that relevant information involved accessing public records, regardless of where and by whom those records were held.

On January 8, 2016, the Department notified the Committee of yet more responsive documents located in the Office of the Secretary.[81] These documents had been "overlooked" by the State Department.[82] On February 26, 2016—20 months after the Committee was formed—the State Department produced approximately 1,650 additional responsive documents.[83]

The odyssey that became the Secretary's email arrangement was fully the result of decisions she made in concert with others at the State Department. Had she used state.gov or employed a method of preserving public records other than simply hiring private legal counsel to store, vet, and disclose these public records, this would

---

[79] Letter from Julia Frifield, Ass't Sec'y of State, Legislative Affairs, U.S. Dep't of State, to Trey Gowdy, Chairman, H. Select Comm. on Benghazi (June 25, 2015) ("In a limited number of circumstances, we did not locate in the tens of thousands of pages of email provided by Secretary Clinton the content of a handful of communications that Mr. Blumenthal produced.")

[80] See Letter from Julia Frifield, Assistant Sec'y of State for Legis. Affairs, U.S. Dep't of State, to Trey Gowdy, Chairman, H. Select Comm. on Benghazi (Sept. 25, 2015) (on record with the Committee).

[81] Email from Eric Schneider, U.S. Dep't of State, to Dana Chipman, Chief Counsel, Sel. Comm. On Benghazi (January 8, 2016,) (on file with the Committee).

[82] Id.

[83] See Letter from Julia Frifield, Assistant Sec'y of State for Legis. Affairs, U.S. Dep't of State, to Trey Gowdy, Chairman, H. Select Comm. on Benghazi (Feb. 26, 2016).

never have become an issue for the Committee. The Committee knew in the summer 2014 the Secretary used private email to conduct at least some official business and never disclosed this fact publicly. The Committee's interest was in accessing the relevant and responsive material needed to accomplish the job it was assigned to do. Moreover, of the more than 100 witnesses the Committee interviewed only one was exclusively connected with her method of producing and preserving emails—Bryan Pagliano, a Special Advisor to the State Department. Pagliano's interview was short when he invoked his Fifth Amendment privilege against self-incrimination. Pagilano was an important witness who could have spoken to the fullness of the Committee's record. The Secretary's server was reportedly down during two key time periods identified during the Committee's investigation—August 2011 and October 2012.

On April 8, 2016, the Committee received another production of approximately 1,150 pages of emails from Sean Smith's email account as well as emails sent to and from senior leaders stored in the Office of the Secretary. On May 5, 2016, the Committee received yet again another production from the State Department of approximately 405 pages of documents from the Office of the Secretary.

Subpoena for 7th Floor Principals' Documents and<br>Communications

The second subpoena issued in the aftermath of the disclosure of the Secretary's email arrangement was issued on March 4, 2015, and sought documents and communications from the remaining ten senior staff officials identified in the Committee's November 18, 2014 letter. More than three months after the Committee first issued its request for these documents, the State Department had yet to produce a single document.[84] A day after issuing this subpoena, the Committee learned the State Department did not start archiving emails of its senior officials until February 2015.[85] The Committee later learned Patrick F. Kennedy, Under Secretary for Management, State Department, wrote to several senior officials identified in the Committee's March 4, 2015 subpoena seeking the return of all work related emails conducted on private accounts.[86] The State Department also kept this second Kennedy letter a secret.[87]

Notwithstanding the specificity and clarity of the documents and communications sought by the March 4, 2015 subpoena, the State Department protested the breadth of the Committee's request.[88] To

---

[84] Subpoena issued by H. Select Comm. on Benghazi to John F. Kerry, Sec'y of State, U.S. Dep't of State (Mar. 4, 2015).

[85] See Lauren French, *Gowdy: Not backing off subpoena of Clinton emails*, POLITICO (Mar. 5, 2015), http://www.politico.com/story/2015/03/house-committee-benghazi-clinton-email-subpoena-115795.

[86] See Letters from Patrick F. Kennedy, Under Sec'y of State for Mgmt., U.S. Dep't of State, to Huma Abedin, William J. Burns, Jeffrey D. Feltman, Cheryl Mills, Thomas Nides, Philippe Reines, Susan E. Rice, Jacob J. Sullivan (March 11, 2015).

[87] Subpoena issued by H. Select Comm. on Benghazi to John F. Kerry, Sec'y of State, U.S. Dep't of State (Aug. 5, 2015).

[88] Email from Philip Kiko, Staff Director, H. Select Comm. on Benghazi, to Julia Frifield, Ass't Sec'y of State for Legislative Affairs, U.S. Dep't of State (March 23, 2015, 6:50 PM) ("let me

Continued

help set priorities, the Committee offered guidance to State Department officials, at their request. For example, on March 23, 2015, the Committee identified four individuals and four discrete timeframes to which the Department could focus its initial efforts.[89]

On April 22, 2015, the Committee again provided guidance outlining a production plan complete with specific individuals and discrete timeframes for the State Department.[90] No documents were produced.

It is worth reiterating that what may appear, at first blush, to be a lack of competence on behalf of the State Department now appears fully intentional and coordinated. Delaying the production of documents sought by letter, informal request, or subpoena has decided political advantages for those opposing the investigation and those in control of the necessary documents and witness access. Asking the Committee for "priorities" or date and time restrictions is calculated to reduce the scope of the investigation—the very thing Committee Minority members asked for in the fall of 2014—and causes the investigation to be drawn out needlessly.

This is an overtly political calculation and has become the typical playbook for an administration that once praised itself for its "transparency."

In an effort to speed the production of documents, the Committee worked to advance the State Department's $2.4 million reprograming request made to the Committees on Appropriations of both the House and the Senate to create a 'document review unit' to help facilitate the production of documents relevant to the Committee's investigation.[91] The Committee was informed 12 full-time employees would be assigned to the 'document review unit,' as well as new technology, to respond to congressional requests. The Committee was told its requests would be the 'document review unit's' highest priority.[92] To the contrary, after the House and Senate Committees on Appropriations approved the Department's reprogramming request, State Department staff did nothing to expedite Committee requests for documents.[93] State Department officials would not disclose how the reprograming request was being implemented, how many employees were assigned to the unit, or whether these individuals were also assigned to respond to FOIA requests. Nor would the officials describe how document requests would be produced with the new technology.[94]

---

reiterate that the subpoena is clear as to what communications and documents the Committee is seeking").

[89] Id.

[90] Email from Philip Kiko, Staff Director, to Julia Frifield, Ass't Sec'y of State for Legislative Affairs (April 22, 2015, 1:03 PM).

[91] James Rosen, *Documents show State Dep't missed target date for special Benghazi unit*, Fox News, May 6, 2016, http://www.foxnews.com/politics/2016/05/06/documents-show-state-department-missed-target-date-for-special-benghazi-unit.html.

[92] Phone call between Philip Kiko, Staff Director, H. Select Comm. on Benghazi, and Julia Frifield, Ass't Sec'y of State, U.S. Dep't of State (May 2015).

[93] Memorandum from Philip G. Kiko, Staff Dir. and Gen. Counsel, H. Select Comm. on Benghazi, to Trey Gowdy, Chairman, H. Select Comm. on Benghazi (June 2, 2014) [hereinafter June 2 Staff Memo] (on file with the Committee) (summarizing the members meeting with State Dep't Chief of Staff Jon Finer).

[94] Id.

## IMPASSE WITH THE STATE DEPARTMENT

On May 22, 2015, more than two months after the March 4, 2015 subpoena, the State Department finally produced approximately 1,200 pages of emails to and from Mills. The documents in this production, however, covered less than a quarter of the timeframes sought and contained less than one-tenth of the contents sought in the subpoena. Furthermore, the State Department withheld documents, telling the Committee "a small number of documents implicate important Executive Branch institutional interests and are therefore not included in this production."[95] The State Department's continued refusal to produce relevant documents delayed the Committee's interview schedule.

Like other investigations, the Committee planned to interview senior level officials within the State Department before interviewing the Secretary. Consequently, delaying document productions for these senior officials in turn delayed the interviews of the same senior officials, which in turn delayed the interview of the Secretary. It is readily apparent this was by design and presented the Committee with a 'Catch-22': either interview senior State Department officials, including the Secretary, without the benefit of the documents needed for a constructive conversation, or postpone those interviews pending document production and be criticized for taking too long.

Recognizing neither public reproach nor the Committee's support for the State Department's reprogramming request would compel the Department to action, the Committee had few alternatives—other than contempt of Congress (dependent on Executive Branch enforcement) or time-consuming litigation. On June 2, 2015, the Committee met with Jonathan Finer, Chief of Staff and Director of Policy Planning, State Department, to discuss the impasse.[96]

With Finer, the Committee made it clear it was necessary to review documents prior to moving forward with interviews.[97] The Committee members personally emphasized to Finer the emails from a number of former senior State Department officials were necessary to have constructive conversations with witnesses.[98] The delays in producing documents thus delayed interviews.[99] While Finer would not agree to a production schedule, he did agree the State Department would make a substantial production within 30 days.[100] The meeting and agreement were memorialized in a subsequent communication sent to Finer.[101] In its letter, the Committee defined "substantial" as "producing," within 30 days, "all documents and emails . . . described in phase one in our April 22, 2015 communication."[102]

---

[95] Letter from Julia Frifield, Assistant Sec'y of State for Leg. Affairs, U.S. Dep't of State, to Trey Gowdy, Chairman, H. Select Comm. on Benghazi (May 22, 2015) (on file with the Committee).

[96] See June 2 Staff Memo, *supra* note 93.

[97] Id.

[98] Id.

[99] Id.

[100] See id.

[101] Letter from Trey Gowdy, Chairman, H. Select Comm. on Benghazi, to Jonathan Finer, Chief of Staff & Dir. of Policy Planning, U.S. Dep't of State (June 4, 2015) (on file with the Committee).

[102] Id.

The "substantial production" of documents never materialized, further delaying the interview schedule. Instead, on June 30, 2015, the State Department produced 3,600 pages of emails, more than 2,000 pages of which were press clippings available chiefly on the internet.[103] The production also focused almost exclusively on two individuals for one month *after* the terrorist attacks, with a scattering of documents from other timeframes.[104] Moreover, the State Department continued its pattern of withholding documents based on what it described as "Executive Branch institutional interests."[105] No other productions arrived for almost another month. On July 29, 2015, the State Department produced approximately 8,000 pages of documents, many of which were press clippings or duplicate emails.

### OTHER DOCUMENT REQUESTS MADE TO THE STATE DEPARTMENT

In addition to seeking enforcement of the March 4, 2015 subpoena, the Committee issued a number of additional requests for information from the State Department. On June 12, 2015, the Committee sought the remaining ARB documents.[106] The Committee requested a list of all documents being withheld and the justification for withholding.[107] The Committee also sought 11 discrete items referenced in the ARB documents.[108] The Committee requested a response by July 8, 2015. Roughly seven months later, on February 25, 2016, the Committee received a four-page document responsive to the June 12, 2015 request.[109]

On July 6, 2015, the Committee wrote the State Department seeking an update on compliance with the March 4, 2015 subpoena. No response was received.

On July 10, 2015, the Committee wrote the Department again expressing concern with the anemic productions made and the Department's lack of candor with regard to the private email use of former senior officials.[110]

The Committee followed this letter with an email highlighting the State Department's inaction in five areas:

1. scheduling of interviews;

2. producing private emails relating to the Committee's jurisdiction sent or received by former senior officials;

---

[103] Letter from Trey Gowdy, Chairman, H. Select Comm. on Benghazi, to John F. Kerry, Sec'y of State, U.S. Dep't of State (July 10, 2015) (on file with the Committee) ("While the meeting may have motivated the Dep't to produce roughly 3,600 pages of documents on June 30, 2015, more than 2,000 of those pages—representing nearly 57 percent were nothing more than basic press clippings. . . .").

[104] Id.

[105] Letter from Julia Frifield, Ass't Sec'y for Leg. Affairs, to Trey Gowdy, Chairman, H. Select Comm. on Benghazi (June 30, 2015) (on file with the Committee) ("In addition, a small number of documents implicate important Executive Branch institutional interests and therefore are not included in this production.").

[106] Letter from Trey Gowdy, Chairman, H. Select Comm. on Benghazi, to John F. Kerry, Sec'y of State, U.S. Dep't of State (June 12, 2015) (on file with the Committee).

[107] Id.

[108] Id.

[109] Interview with [Agent 17], Accountability Review Bd. (Oct. 30, 2012) (on file with the committee State-SCB0098607).

[110] Letter from Trey Gowdy, Chairman, H. Select Comm. on Benghazi, to John F. Kerry, Sec'y of State, U.S. Dep't of State (July 10, 2015) (on file with the Committee) (one of two similarly cited letters).

3. an accounting of the missing documents, including those withheld for executive branch confidentiality interests;

4. producing the remaining aspects of phase one of the March 4, 2015 subpoena; and

5. failing to acknowledge the receipt of the previous letters.[111]

## JULY 31, 2015 DEMAND LETTER

The State Department's untenable posture, coupled with an abject lack of meaningful response to the Committee's outstanding subpoenas and requests, led to a demand letter on July 31, 2015.[112] The letter was a precursor to contempt of Congress action, and reflected the Committee's serious belief the State Department was intentionally impeding the investigation's progress.[113]

The Committee outlined the pattern of concealment and delay employed by the State Department.[114] The Committee noted the State Department's actions with regard to the Committee's questions about production of the Secretary's emails.[115]

The Committee eventually received, in several tranches, document productions subsequent to the July 31, 2015 demand letter. Documents responsive to the March 4 subpoena were produced on August 21 and August 28, 2015; September 18, 2015; October 5, 9, and 15, 2015; November 6 and 24, 2015; December 31, 2015; January 21, 2016; February 26, 2016; April 8, 2016; and May 5, 2016. In addition, the Committee received throughout the fall of 2015 and the early winter of 2016 approximately 9,000 pages of emails from Stevens' email never before produced.[116]

The Committee never received full productions of emails from the accounts of Under Secretary Wendy R. Sherman, Deputy Secretary William J. Burns, or Assistant Secretary Jeffrey D. Feltman—all of whom were listed in the November 18, 2014 document request and the March 4, 2015 subpoena. The State Department never produced all relevant documents reviewed by the Accountability Review Board.[117] Finally, the State Department still has not fully complied with the August 5, 2015 subpoena.

The State Department also withheld documents citing "important Executive Branch institutional interests" or "important Executive Branch confidentiality interests" on four separate occasions.[118] The Committee repeatedly sought additional information on the withheld documents, including the nature and number of documents withheld and the basis in law for withholding them. On June 12,

---

[111] See Email from Philip G. Kiko, Staff Dir. and Gen. Counsel, H. Select Comm. on Benghazi, to Julia Frifield, Catherine Duval, and Austin Evers, (July 14, 2015) (on file with the Committee) (Regarding compliance and requests).

[112] Letter from Trey Gowdy, Chairman, H. Select Comm. on Benghazi, to John F. Kerry, Sec'y of State, U.S. Dep't of State (July 31, 2015) (on file with Committee).

[113] Id.

[114] Id.

[115] Id.

[116] See infra Appendix J for a complete listing of requests and subpoenas for documents as well as productions received pursuant to request or subpoena.

[117] Letter from the Thomas B. Gibbons, acting Assistant Sec'y of Legis. Affairs, U.S. Dep't of State, to Darrell E. Issa, Chairman, H. Comm. on Oversight & Gov't Reform (Aug. 23, 2013) (on file with the Committee) (stating the ARB reviewed approximately 7,000 documents totaling thousands of pages).

[118] See letters from Julia Frifield, Ass't Sec'y of State for Legislative Affairs, U.S. Dep't of State, to Trey Gowdy, Chairman, H. Select Comm. on Benghazi (February 13, 2015, April 24, 2015, May 22, 2015, and June 30, 2015) (on file with the Committee).

2015, July 8, 2015, and July 31, 2015, the Committee wrote the State Department seeking additional information. The Committee also met with State Department representatives to discuss the status of the June 12, 2015, July 8, 2015, and July 31, 2015 requests multiple times, including as late as June 2016. To date, the State Department has yet to account for the withheld documents. The State Department's refusal to provide the Committee with information by which to make reasonable judgements regarding the Department's decisions to withhold documents from Congress and, ultimately, from the American people is yet another example of the Department's pattern of concealment.

## WITNESSES

The Committee interviewed 57 witnesses from the State Department, 50 who had never been interviewed by Congress, including four senior leaders, three Ambassadors, 19 Diplomatic Security agents, four principal officers, and 20 State Department personnel.

On December 4, 2014, the Committee requested the State Department make available for transcribed interviews the eyewitnesses to the attack: the Diplomatic Security agents deployed to Benghazi and the Principal Officers responsible for political reporting. The State Department resisted scheduling interviews for nearly two months. It was not until January 27, 2015 and the threat of subpoenas the State Department began to contact the individuals sought by the Committee.

The Committee sought the testimony of senior State Department officials including those who were not interviewed by the ARB. This included Mills, Jacob J. Sullivan, Deputy Chief of Staff and Director of Policy Planning, and Huma Abedin, Deputy Chief of Staff for Operations. While the Committee sought to schedule these interviews in May 2015, the State Department's failure to produce relevant documents delayed these interviews until early September 2015. The delay in scheduling these interviews in turn necessarily delayed the Secretary's testimony.

The Committee interviewed senior leaders within the Bureau of Diplomatic Security and the regional Bureau of Near Eastern Affairs—the two bureaus with oversight responsibility for security, personnel and policy in Benghazi. The Committee interviewed Kennedy who oversees the Bureau of Diplomatic Security, in addition to the Deputy Assistant Secretaries for Countermeasures and International Programs, Gentry O. Smith and Charlene R. Lamb. The Committee interviewed Jeffrey D. Feltman, Assistant Secretary for Near East Affairs, State Department; Gene A. Cretz, Ambassador to Libya; and Gregory N. Hicks, Deputy Chief of Mission, U.S. Embassy in Tripoli.

Finally, the Committee interviewed those individuals who served as Libya desk officers and were responsible for addressing the day-to-day needs of the Benghazi Mission, including physical security, policy decisions, and logistics relating to Benghazi, Libya.

## The Department of Defense

The Defense Department was initially cooperative but this co-operation dissipated during the course of the Committee's investigation culminating in a factually deficient letter from a political appointee deliberately mischaracterizing efforts to obtain access to witnesses.

The witnesses produced by the Defense Department, both active duty and retired, were cooperative and provided significant new material to the Committee. Identifying those witnesses, locating those witnesses, scheduling their appearances before the Committee and responding to subsequent Committee requests generated by these documents and witness interviews became mired in coordinated partisan responses from a Defense Department political appointee.[119]

## DOCUMENTS

As required by the resolution creating the Select Committee, the House Armed Services Committee provided records in July 2014. Following a review of the information provided by the Armed Services Committee, the Select Committee submitted requests to the Defense Department on April 8, 2015 seeking documents and records not previously provided to the Armed Services Committee.[120] The Select Committee's document request consisted of 12 categories, including a copy of the video of the attack in Benghazi, un-redacted copies of documents provided pursuant to a court order in litigation under FOIA, and copies of the force laydown for U.S. Africa, Europe, and Central combatant commands on September 10, 11, and 12, 2012.[121] The Select Committee also requested assistance in answering 27 questions regarding actions taken by the Defense Department immediately prior to, during, and immediately after the attacks.[122]

On April 27, 2015, the Defense Department responded to the Committee's request providing copies of the force laydown from the respective combatant commands and indicating it would provide "responsive documents not previously provided on a rolling basis" to the Committee.[123] On May 21, 2015, the Defense Department provided 175 pages of classified documents, as well as 551 pages of un-redacted documents provided pursuant to a court order under FOIA litigation.[124] The Defense Department declined to provide 36 pages that "contain[ed] intelligence community or potential target information."[125] It also declined to provide one page "due to con-

[119] Letter from Stephen C. Hedger, Assistant Sec'y of Def. for Legis. Affairs, U.S. Dep't of Def., to Trey Gowdy, Chairman, H. Select Comm. on Benghazi (April 28, 2016) (on file with the Committee).

[120] Letter from Trey Gowdy, Chairman, H. Select Comm. on Benghazi, to Ashton B. Carter, Sec'y of Def., U.S. Dep't of Def. (Apr. 8, 2015) (on file with the Committee) (first of three similarly cited letters); Letter from Trey Gowdy, Chairman, H. Select Comm. on Benghazi, to Ashton B. Carter, Sec'y of Def., U.S. Dep't of Def. (Apr. 8, 2015) (on file with the Committee) (second of three similarly cited letters); Letter from Trey Gowdy, Chairman, H. Select Comm. on Benghazi, to Ashton B. Carter, Sec'y of Def., U.S. Dep't of Def. (Apr. 8, 2015) (on file with the Committee) (third of three similarly cited letters).

[121] Letter from Trey Gowdy, Chairman, H. Select Comm. on Benghazi, to Ashton B. Carter, Sec'y of Def., U.S. Dep't of Def. (Apr. 8, 2015) (on file with the Committee) (one of three similarly cited letters).

[122] Id.

[123] Letter from Michael J. Stella, acting Assistant Sec'y of Def., U.S. Dep't of Def., to Trey Gowdy, Chairman, H. Select Comm. on Benghazi (Apr. 24, 2015) (on file with the Committee).

[124] Letter from Stephen C. Hedger, Assistant Sec'y of Def. for Legis. Affairs, U.S. Dep't of Def., to Trey Gowdy, Chairman, H. Select Comm. on Benghazi (May 21, 2015) (on file with the Committee).

[125] Id.

fidentiality concerns associated with executive branch deliberations."[126] At the time of the Defense Department's letter, Committee staff had received briefings on and reviewed the drone footage on two occasions.[127] The Defense Department did not indicate
whether it would provide a copy of that footage to the Committee.
As to five of the Committee's requests, it indicated its review was
ongoing.

On July 28, 2015, the Committee received the Defense Department's classified response to the Committee's 27 questions.[128] Over
the following months, the Defense Department provided briefings
to the Committee and made witnesses available. It did not, however, furnish any additional documents.

On February 5, 2016, Committee staff met with Defense Department staff regarding the outstanding document requests.[129] During
this meeting the Committee requested an updated list of all air assets situated in the Africa and Europe combatant commands' areas
of responsibility, and whether any assets had not been disclosed
due to special access programs. The Committee also requested documents referring or relating to communications the Defense Department may have had with any foreign militaries concerning coordination or assistance in response to the attacks and any photographs taken by Defense Department personnel during a trip to
Benghazi in October 2012.[130] The Committee also renewed its request for a copy of the video feed from the night of the attack.[131]
The Defense Department failed to respond to the Committee's request.

In total, the Defense Department provided nearly 900 pages of
additional documents not previously provided to Congress.

WITNESSES

The Committee interviewed 24 witnesses from the Defense Department. Of these witnesses, 17 had never been interviewed by
Congress regarding the attacks in Benghazi.

Initially, the Defense Department identified and scheduled witnesses at the Committee's request. For example on July 22, 2015,
the Committee requested the Defense Department make available
the Commander of the Commander's In-Extremis Force [CIF] on
September 11, 2012.[132] The Committee had been unable to identify
this individual and four other individuals by name, but provided
details of their position during the relevant time-frame.[133] The Defense Department identified the five individuals and scheduled
their interviews.

After the initial five witnesses were interviewed and the Committee reviewed the documents provided by Defense Department,

---

[126] Id.

[127] Id.

[128] See Letter from Ashton B. Carter, Sec'y of Def., U.S. Dep't of Def., to Trey Gowdy, Chairman, H. Select Comm. on Benghazi (July 28, 2015) (on file with the Committee).

[129] See Email from Philip G. Kiko, Staff Dir. and Gen. Counsel, H. Select Comm. on Benghazi,
to William Hudson, Dir. of Cong. Investigations, Dep't of Def. (Feb. 5, 2016, 17:19 EST) (on file
with the Committee).

[130] See id.

[131] Id.

[132] Letter from Trey Gowdy, Chairman, H. Select Comm. on Benghazi, to Ashton B. Carter,
Sec'y of Def., U.S. Dep't of Def. (July 22, 2015) (on file with the Committee).

[133] Id.

the Committee requested an additional eight witnesses on February 5, 2016. The Committee also requested an interview with the individual who served as the pilot for the aircraft that transported the CIF.[134] On February 26, 2016, the Committee requested the Defense Department make the individuals who piloted the drone on September 11–12, 2012 that flew over Benghazi and Tripoli available for interviews.[135]

The Committee reiterated both of these requests on March 9, 2016 and March 24, 2016.[136] The Defense Department indicated it was experiencing difficulty in tracking down records which could identify the individuals who piloted the aircraft and had not made progress in meeting the Committee's requests. Consequently, on March 31, 2016, the Committee met with Elizabeth L. George, Deputy General Counsel, Legislation, Defense Legal Services Agency, Defense Department, regarding the outstanding requests. The Defense Department was informed the Committee would issue subpoenas should the Defense Department not provide the names of the pilots immediately.[137]

For the next several weeks, Committee staff sought continued cooperation from the Defense Department. However, on April 28, 2016, Stephen Hedger, the Assistant Secretary of Defense for Legislative Affairs sent an inaccurate and misleading letter to the Chairman regarding the Committee's requests.[138] Not surprisingly, that letter was leaked to the press the following day and was on the Committee Minority's website. Among many of the inaccuracies, the letter stated the Defense Department had expended "significant resources" to locate an individual the Committee had requested to interview who was identified as "John from Iowa" and who had called in to *The Sean Hannity Show* radio program in May 2013. During the call, the individual identified himself as one of the sensor operators of a drone that flew over Benghazi during the attacks. The Committee requested to interview this person during the meeting on March 31. As of the date of Hedger's letter, the Defense Department had failed to provide the names of all the pilots and sensor operators, including "John from Iowa" that had operated the drone on the September 11 and September 12, 2012. Finally, almost a month after Hedger's letter, the Defense Department provided all names of both the pilots and the sensor operators.[139] The Committee benefited from hearing the testimony of the

---

[134] Email from Mac Tolar, Senior Counsel, H. Select Comm. on Benghazi, to William Hudson, Dir. of Cong. Investigations, U.S. Dep't of Def. (Feb. 9, 2016, 1:32 PM) (on file with the Committee).

[135] Email from Mac Tolar, Senior Counsel, H. Select Comm. on Benghazi, to William Hudson, Dir. of Cong. Investigations, U.S. Dep't of Def. (Feb. 26, 2016, 17:00 EST) (on file with the Committee).

[136] *See* Email from Mac. Tolar, Senior Counsel, H. Select Comm. on Benghazi, to William Hudson, Dir. of Cong. Investigations, U.S. Dep't of Def. (Mar. 9, 2016, 12:23 EST) (on file with the Committee) (reiterating interview request); *See also* Email from Mac Tolar, Senior Counsel to Mr. Hudson (Mar. 24, 2016, 16:56) (on file with the Committee) (reiterating interview request).

[137] Email from Philip G. Kiko, Staff Dir. and Gen. Counsel, H. Select Comm. on Benghazi, to Stephen Hedger, Assistant Sec'y of Def. for Legis. Affairs (Mar. 25, 2016, 11:37 AM) (on file with the Committee).

[138] Letter from Stephen C. Hedger, Assistant Sec'y of Def. for Legis. Affairs, U.S. Dep't of Def., to Trey Gowdy, Chairman, H. Select Comm. on Benghazi (April 28, 2016) (on file with the Committee).

[139] See Email from Mac Tolar, Senior Counsel, H. Select Comm. on Benghazi, to Philip G. Kiko, Staff Dir. and Gen. Counsel, H. Select Comm. on Benghazi (May 20, 2016, 11:47 EST) (on file with the Committee) (indicating receipt of all relevant names).

witnesses. These individuals were able to provide the Committee first-hand accounts of their mission that night, the capabilities of the drone, what information was being relayed up the chain of command, and the information they were focused on gathering. The video feed from those drones provided one point of reference for the Committee during its investigation. The witnesses provided another.

Despite Hedger's complaint that the Department had expended "significant resources" to identify "John from Iowa" to "no avail," the Department had actually identified "John from Iowa" within hours of his call in 2013, and had reprimanded him for his actions.[140] Because of Hedger's representation that "significant resources" had been used to find this witness, the Committee issued a subpoena to Hedger to explain what resources had actually been used, and why the Defense Department was unable to respond to a Congressional request in a timely manner.[141]

## The Central Intelligence Agency

The Central Intelligence Agency [CIA] ultimately provided a significant volume of material and witnesses to the Committee, including SameTime messages not previously or generally made available to Congress. Nevertheless, the Committee's work was unnecessarily delayed with respect to documents, witnesses, and other basic requests.

### READ-AND-RETURN DOCUMENTS

When the House of Representatives passed the resolution creating the Committee, it required that "[a]ny committee of the House of Representatives having custody of records in any form relating to [the Benghazi attacks] shall transfer such records to the Select Committee within 14 days of the adoption of this resolution. Such records shall become the records of the Select Committee."[142]

As a result of the resolution, the Chairman of the Intelligence Committee wrote to John O. Brennan, Director, CIA, noting the Intelligence Committee had possession but not custody of records provided by the CIA on a read-and-return basis. Therefore, the Chairman of the Intel. Comm. believed he did not have the authority to transfer these records to the Committee as otherwise required by the resolution. The Chairman, nonetheless, asked the CIA to make these records available to the Select Committee.[143]

> This transmittal is intended to facilitate the CIA's ability to respond to any future requests for these materials from the new Select Committee. I expect you will maintain these materials at CIA Headquarters in a manner such

---

[140] Testimony of Sensor Operator 1, Tr. at 16–17, June 9, 2016 [hereinafter Sensor Operator 1 Transcript] (on file with the Committee). *See also,* Letter from Stephen C. Hedger, Assistant Sec'y of Def. for Legis. Affairs, U.S. Dep't of Def., to Trey Gowdy, Chairman, H. Select Comm. on Benghazi (April 28, 2016) (on file with the Committee).

[141] Subpoena to Stephen C. Hedger, Assistant Sec'y of Def. for Legis. Affairs, U.S. Dep't of Def., H. Select Comm. on Benghazi (June 15, 2016) (on file with the Committee).

[142] H. Res. 567, 113th Cong., § 5(a) (2014).

[143] Letter from Mike Rogers, Chairman, H. Perm. Select Comm. on Intel., to John O. Brennan, Dir., Cent. Intel. Agency (May 8, 2014) (on file with the Committee).

that they could be easily and promptly provided to the Select Committee.[144]

In July of 2014, the Intelligence Committee provided its records to this Committee, including more than 400 pieces of intelligence relating to Benghazi and Libya from 2012, and other reports and correspondence. After acquiring the requisite security clearances and reviewing these documents, on November 19, 2014 the Committee asked that it be able to review the read-and-return records the Intelligence Committee had given back to the CIA.[145] The CIA responded, noting it was "working to try to set up a time next week when we could make the materials available."[146] The CIA did not make the materials available the following week.

On December 8, 2014, the Committee reiterated its request.[147] The CIA responded: "we are in the process of organizing and page numbering the documents so that they are ready for your team to review. I'll check in with the folks who are working on that to see if we can make it all available next week."[148] This hardly squared with what the Intelligence Committee Chairman requested of the CIA.[149]

The Committee made a third request, on December 11, 2014, to review these documents.[150] The CIA's Office of Congressional Affairs responded on December 15, 2014, noting they would "reach out" to the Committee staff that would be reviewing the documents.[151] The CIA never contacted the Committee.

The Committee made a fourth request on January 8, 2015.[152] On January 12, 2015, the CIA responded noting they "have this request as a priority action. We are currently processing the documents. . . . We hope to have them ready for you in a couple of weeks."[153]

It was not until the Committee's January 27, 2015 public compliance hearing with Neil L. Higgins, Director of Congressional Affairs, CIA, that the CIA finally granted the Committee access to these documents.[154] This was nearly three months after the Com-

---

[144] Id.

[145] See Email from Mary K. E. Maples, Office of Cong. Affairs, Cent. Intel. Agency, to Christopher Donesa, Deputy Staff Dir., H. Select Comm. on Benghazi (Nov. 19, 2014, 14:23 EST) (on file with the Committee).

[146] Id.

[147] Email from Christopher Donesa, Deputy Staff Dir., H. Select Comm. on Benghazi, to Mary K. E. Maples, Office of Cong. Affairs, Cent. Intel. Agency (Dec. 8, 2014, 13:57 EST) (on file with the Committee).

[148] Email from Mary K. E. Maples, Office of Cong. Affairs, Cent. Intel. Agency, to Christopher Donesa, Deputy Staff Dir., H. Select Comm. on Benghazi (Dec. 8, 2014, 15:10 EST) (on file with the Committee).

[149] Letter from Mike Rogers, Chairman, H. Perm. Select Comm. on Intel., to John O. Brennan, Dir., Cent. Intel. Agency (May 8, 2014) (on file with the Committee).

[150] Email from Christopher Donesa, Deputy Staff Dir., H. Select Comm. on Benghazi to Mary K. E. Maples, Office of Cong. Affairs, Cent. Intel. Agency (Dec. 11, 2014, 10:47 EST) (on file with the Committee).

[151] Email from Mary K. E. Maples, Office of Cong. Affairs, Cent. Intel. Agency to Christopher Donesa, Deputy Staff Dir., H. Select Comm. on Benghazi (Dec. 15, 2014, 10:33 EST) (on file with the Committee).

[152] Email from Christopher Donesa, Deputy Staff Dir., H. Select Comm. on Benghazi, to Mary K. E. Maples, Office of Cong. Affairs, Cent. Intel. Agency (Jan. 8, 2015, 11:19 EST) (on file with the Committee).

[153] Email from Mary K. E. Maples, Office of Cong. Affairs, Cent. Intel. Agency, to Christopher Donesa, Deputy Staff Dir., H. Select Comm. on Benghazi (Jan. 12, 2015, 15:55 EST) (on file with the Committee).

[154] Interim Progress Update, supra note 8, at 5.

mittee first requested access to these documents—documents the CIA had already produced to the Intelligence Committee and had been set aside specifically for this Committee's access.[155] Having to schedule and conduct public hearings on matters of compliance with requests for clearly relevant documents is a waste of time and resources.

In finally gaining access to these documents, the Committee discovered the records consisted of more than 4,000 pages of emails.[156] The CIA had never indicated they were withholding such a large volume of material from the Committee. Reviewing this material necessitated the redirection of Committee time. The CIA, however, would only allow four Committee staff to review these records during normal business hours at CIA Headquarters in McLean, Virginia. These restrictions unnecessarily limited the Committee's access to the materials and significantly and unnecessarily increased the time needed to review the documents.

In addition, the CIA would not allow Committee staff to retain notes made while reviewing these documents, or even take notes back to Committee offices to discuss with Committee members.[157] The CIA required Committee staff to keep their notes locked in a safe at CIA headquarters.[158] The CIA eventually offered to allow Committee staff to take their notes back to Committee offices—but only if CIA staff first reviewed those notes and applied various redactions to them.[159] This demand raised serious separation of powers concerns and would have compromised the investigation to allow the subject of an investigation to review and redact the notes of its investigator.

The CIA placed none of these onerous and punitive restrictions on the Intelligence Committee's access to these same materials, which the CIA provided to it to keep in its own offices at the Capitol.

### NEW DOCUMENT REQUESTS

After a review of the more than 4,000 pages of 'read and return' documents at the CIA, the Committee issued a new document request to the CIA on April 28, 2015.[160] This request was for 26 specific categories of information to help the Committee better understand the CIA's activities in Benghazi, its response to the attacks, and the analytic processes undertaken in the wake of the attacks.[161] This document request included SameTime messages, emails, operational cables, and intelligence reports.[162]

The CIA resisted this request. In a May 15, 2015 telephone call with the Committee Chairman, David S. Cohen, the Deputy Director of the CIA, expressed concern "with both the breadth and some of the types of documents requested," and claimed "fulfilling the re-

---

[155] *Id.* at 9.

[156] *Id.*

[157] Email from Mary K. E. Maples, Office of Cong. Affairs, Cent. Intel. Agency, to Dana K. Chipman, Chief Counsel, H. Select Comm. on Benghazi et al. (Apr. 17, 2015, 9:16 EST) (on file with the Committee).

[158] *Id.*

[159] *Id.*

[160] Letter from Trey Gowdy, Chairman, H. Select Comm. on Benghazi, to John O. Brennan, Dir., Cent. Intel. Agency (Apr. 28, 2015) (on file with the Committee).

[161] *Id.*

[162] *Id.*

quest could take many months of work." [163] Additional meetings between the Committee and the CIA took place to discuss the request, and it was not until July 8, 2015, two-and-a-half months after the Committee's document request, that the CIA produced additional documents pursuant to this request. [164]

The results of the document production were underwhelming. The CIA delivered only a smattering of material from four general categories. One of the documents was a critical email the CIA had previously withheld from the Committee even though it had been shared with the Intelligence Committee. [165] This document changed the Committee's understanding of what information was shared with Washington from Tripoli in the wake of the attacks—crucial for understanding how the CIA created its post attack analysis. The document production also consisted of cables shared with the Intelligence Committee but not given to this Committee.

Because of this insufficient document production and the withholding of clearly relevant information, on August 7, 2015, the Committee issued a subpoena to the CIA. [166] This subpoena was straightforward and asked for six specific sets of documents. These documents included specific intelligence assessments written by CIA analysts in the wake of the attacks. [167] The subpoena demanded the production of "supporting material" for these assessments. [168] Up to that point the CIA had refused to produce that material, in addition to refusing to produce the assessments with accompanying footnotes. It therefore was impossible for the Committee to understand what material the analysts used to form the basis for their subsequent assessments.

The subpoena also demanded production of additional documents relating to the unclassified talking points requested by the Intelligence Committee on September 14, 2012. [169] Previously, the CIA had refused to produce any additional documents relating to the talking points not already in the public domain, claiming it was the responsibility of the Office of Director for National Intelligence to produce documents, even though the documents in question were all internal to the CIA.

The subpoena also demanded production of SameTime messages from individuals within certain offices in the CIA. [170] Prior witness testimony revealed CIA employees relied heavily on SameTime messages the night of the attacks and in the immediate aftermath, as these were more efficient than typing emails. [171] Simply reviewing the emails previously produced by the CIA, therefore, would

[163] *See* Email from Neal L. Higgins, Dir. of Cong. Affairs, Cent. Intel. Agency, to Dana K. Chipman, Chief Counsel, H. Select Comm. on Benghazi (May 15, 2015, 10:23 EST) (on file with the Committee).

[164] Memorandum from Dir., Office of Cong. Affairs, Cent. Intel. Agency, to Chief Counsel and Deputy Staff Dir., H. Select Comm. on Benghazi, July 8, 2016 (on file with Cent. Intel. Agency, REQUEST 15–001 to REQUEST 15–0004).

[165] Email from employee, Cent. Intel. Agency, to Cent. Intel. Agency (Sept. 14, 2012 4:05 PM) (on file with the Committee, REQUEST 15–0005).

[166] Subpoena issued by H. Select Comm. on Benghazi to John O. Brennan, Dir., Cent. Intel. Agency, (Aug. 7, 2015).

[167] *Id.*

[168] *Id.*

[169] *Id.*

[170] *Id.*

[171] *See, e.g.,* Testimony of employee, Cent. Intel. Agency, Tr. 97–100 (July, 16, 2015) (on file with the Committee).

not tell the full story of what happened the night and early morning hours of the attacks.

On August 28, 2015, the CIA responded to the subpoena.[172] The CIA produced in full the specific intelligence assessments with supporting material.[173] The CIA also produced additional material relating to the Intelligence Committee talking points, but objected to producing SameTime messages, arguing that the CIA "does not produce SameTime messages to Congress because doing so would have serious negative consequences on CIA's work."[174] This is a striking assertion. To suggest the entity that both created and funds the CIA and must provide oversight for myriad reasons cannot have access at some level to the work done by the CIA is staggeringly arrogant. In reality these SameTime messages were both highly relevant and highly probative and fundamentally changed the Committee's understanding of information previously provided to the Committee. This is precisely why Congress must be able to access this information and precisely why the CIA was so resistant to providing it.

A review of the documents ultimately produced by the CIA and subsequent witness interviews necessitated additional document requests to the CIA. The Committee first attempted to request these documents informally. The CIA did not produce them. As a result, on January 13, 2016, the Committee sent a letter to the CIA formally requesting additional documents.[175] This request included two specific operational cables referenced repeatedly during witness interviews, an additional piece of intelligence analysis from after the attacks, and information regarding intelligence given to senior policymakers[176]—the subject of a previous formal request from the Committee to the CIA.[177]

The CIA ignored this request. As a result, the Committee issued a second subpoena on January 20, 2016.[178] This subpoena demanded the production of the two specific operational cables in addition to information regarding intelligence given to senior policymakers.[179]

On February 9, 2016—after months of the Committee applying pressure to produce documents and the possibility John O. Brennan, Director, CIA could be held in contempt of Congress for withholding documents—the CIA finally relented.[180] The CIA agreed to produce SameTime messages to the Committee and came to an agreement on access to the two specific operational cables.[181]

While the CIA claimed the SameTime messages would not change the Committee's understanding of the facts of Benghazi,

---

[172] Letter from Rachel Carlson Lieber, Deputy Gen. Counsel, Cent. Intel. Agency, to Dana K. Chipman, Chief Counsel, H. Select Comm. on Benghazi (Aug. 28, 2015) (on file with the Committee).

[173] Id.

[174] Id.

[175] Letter from Trey Gowdy, Chairman, H. Select Comm. on Benghazi, to John O. Brennan, Dir., Cent. Intel. Agency (Jan. 13, 2016) (on file with Committee).

[176] Id.

[177] Letter from Trey Gowdy, Chairman, H. Select Comm. on Benghazi, to John O. Brennan, Dir., Cent. Intel. Agency (Nov. 4, 2015) (on file with the Committee).

[178] Subpoena issued by H. Select Comm. on Benghazi to John O. Brennan, Dir., Cent. Intel. Agency, (Aug. 7, 2015).

[179] Id.

[180] Letter from John O. Brennan, Dir., Cent. Intel. Agency, to Trey Gowdy, Chairman, H. Select Comm. on Benghazi (Feb. 9, 2016) (on file with the Committee).

[181] Id.

some of the contents of these messages were quite valuable. As a result of the delays—the Agency took more than nine months to fulfill the Committee's request—the Committee lost an opportunity to question some witnesses specifically about these messages. In addition, some of the messages implicated agencies outside the CIA and did in fact change the Committee's understanding of certain facts—something the CIA, with its stove-piped view of the Benghazi landscape, likely would not have known.

## WITNESSES

The Committee interviewed 19 CIA witnesses during the course of its investigation. The Committee understood these witnesses needed flexibility and, in some cases, anonymity. The Committee delayed important interviews to ensure personnel would not take time away from mission-critical duties overseas. On one occasion, the Committee participated in a secure video teleconference with a witness overseas, and on another occasion the Committee waited until a witness was between tours of duty so the interview would not interfere with intelligence activities. The Committee also provided copies of interview transcripts to the CIA so they could have them in their offices rather than reviewing them in the Committee offices.

Although the Committee never issued subpoenas to any CIA witnesses, and all appeared voluntarily, the CIA initially refused to produce some witnesses—including the manager of the analysts. Instead, the CIA produced the former head of the Office of Terrorism Analysis, who was unable to answer granular questions about how the analytic assessments were drafted and what specific intelligence the analysts relied on.[182] Outstanding questions remained after that interview, and it was apparent the Committee needed to speak to the first-line manager of the analysts. The CIA refused to produce this witness, dubbing the individual a "junior analyst" despite a decade of experience at the CIA.[183] Only after the Committee proposed issuing a subpoena for the witness's deposition did the CIA agree to produce the person voluntarily for an interview.[184] This witness proved highly probative, which regrettably, may be why the CIA was reluctant to allow the interview in the first instance.

A similar situation occurred involving a senior employee in Benghazi. The CIA initially refused to produce this individual, who, given his portfolio in Benghazi, was the only person who could speak to a number of different topics and allegations. After the CIA agreed to produce him for an interview, the CIA kept pushing the date of the interview further into the future. Not until the Chairman issued a subpoena and was preparing to serve it did the CIA set a date for this individual's interview. This witness also provided highly probative testimony calling into question previous conclu-

---

[182] See Testimony of employee, Cent. Intel. Agency, Tr. 43, 46 (Nov. 13, 2015)] (on file with the Committee).

[183] Email from Rachel Carlson Lieber, Deputy Gen. Counsel, Cent. Intel. Agency, to H. Select Comm. on Benghazi (Jan. 7, 2016, 10:23 EST) (on file with the Committee).

[184] See Letter from Trey Gowdy, Chairman, H. Select Comm. on Benghazi, to John O. Brennan, Dir., Cent. Intel. Agency (Jan. 13, 2016) (on file with Committee) (on file with the Committee).

sions drawn by other committees of Congress and fundamentally reshaping the Committee's understanding of critical factors.

The Committee is also aware of concerns regarding the accuracy of certain specific witness testimony before the House Intelligence Committee. The Committee carefully reviewed relevant testimony and information and questioned witnesses about this testimony, but was unable to definitively resolve the issue.

## DISPARATE TREATMENT

While the Committee spent months trying to acquire new documents from the CIA, the Committee Minority members had no such difficulty. One day before the Committee's first interview with a CIA witness, the CIA emailed the Committee alerting it that "[i]n response to a request for specific cables from the minority, we have added three documents" to the documents at the CIA available for review.[185] Neither Committee Minority members nor the CIA informed the Committee such a request had been made until the CIA obligingly fulfilled it. In contrast, the CIA refused to produce two specific cables requested by the Committee until a subpoena was issued.[186]

Again on October 17, 2015—just five days before the Committee's hearing with the Secretary—an email was sent on behalf of Committee Minority members to Higgins seeking information regarding a classification issue.[187] The CIA responded 42 minutes later—on a Saturday night.[188]

Two days later Committee Minority members asked the CIA to review seven transcript excerpts from two witness interviews for classification review.[189] The CIA completed these reviews and returned the transcripts in just 40 hours.[190]

When the Committee asked the CIA to conduct a classification review of witness transcripts, however, the CIA refused. As the Chairman noted in a letter to Brennan on January 13, 2016:

> The Agency has indicated it will not conduct a classification review of transcripts of previous Committee interviews but has provided no reason why it is unable to perform this review, which must be performed by the Executive Branch. The refusal to conduct this review threatens to significantly impact both the timelines and constitu-

---

[185] Email from Mary K. E. Maple, Office of Cong. Affairs, Cent. Intel. Agency, to Heather Sawyer, Minority Chief Counsel, H. Select Comm. on Benghazi et al (April 22, 2015, 9:19 EST) (on file with the Committee).

[186] See Letter from Trey Gowdy, Chairman, H. Select Comm. on Benghazi, to John O. Brennan, Dir., Cent. Intel. Agency (Jan. 13, 2016); Email from Rachel Carlson Lieber, Deputy General Counsel, Cent. Intel. Agency, to H. Select Comm. on Benghazi (Jan. 18, 2016), and Subpoena to John O. Brennan, Dir., Cent. Intel. Agency, H. Select Comm. on Benghazi, (Jan. 20, 2016) (on file with the Committee).

[187] Email from Susanne Sachsman Grooms, Minority Staff Dir., H. Select Comm. on Benghazi, to Neal L. Higgins, Dir. of Cong. Affairs, Cent. Intel. Agency (Oct. 17, 2015, 19:02 EST) (on file with the Committee).

[188] Email from Neal L. Higgins, Dir. of Cong. Affairs, Cent. Intel. Agency, to Susanne Sachsman Grooms, Minority Staff Dir., H. Select Comm. on Benghazi (Oct. 17, 2015, 19:44 EST) (on file with the Committee).

[189] Email from Heather Sawyer, Minority Chief Counsel, H. Select Comm. on Benghazi, to Neal L. Higgins, Dir. of Cong. Affairs, Cent. Intel. Agency (Oct. 19, 2015, 20:47 EST) (on file with the Committee).

[190] Email from Neal L. Higgins, Dir. of Cong. Affairs, Cent. Intel. Agency, to Susanne Sachsman Grooms, Minority Staff Dir., H. Select Comm. on Benghazi (Oct. 17, 2015, 19:44 EST) (on file with the Committee).

tional independence of the Committee's final report, as well as the ability of the American people to review transcripts of unclassified interviews. This matter must be resolved promptly to enable the Committee to undertake the process of preparing its final report [191]

The CIA responded to this letter on March 22, 2016—more than two months later—following a meeting on the topic between the Committee and the CIA. In its response, the CIA said a classification review of the transcripts would be "lengthy and laborious." [192] The CIA also reiterated its view the Committee should share its report in advance with the CIA, something the CIA noted was "critically important." [193] This delayed the Committee's final report because the Committee cannot release information without having it cleared for classification purposes and the Executive Branch solely conducts this review.

## The White House

### DOCUMENTS

The Committee sent a document request to the White House on December 29, 2014.[194] While this was not the first time Congress had asked the White House for information regarding Benghazi,[195] it did mark the first time Congress asked the White House for documents. The request consisted of 12 categories, including documents regarding the U.S.'s continued presence in Libya, the response to the attacks, the YouTube video, the Intelligence Committee talking points, and the administration's explanation of the attacks.[196]

On January 23, 2015, the White House objected to some Committee requests, but did commit to "be in a position to begin sharing documents by the end of February." [197]

On February 27, 2015, White House staff met with Committee staff to discuss the requests. At the meeting the White House produced 266 pages of emails to and from White House staff related to Benghazi—the first emails and documents produced to Congress by the White House about Benghazi.[198] These emails, however, were heavily redacted. As a result, the White House and Committee reached an agreement regarding redactions, and on March

---

[191] Letter from Trey Gowdy, Chairman, H. Select Comm. on Benghazi, to John O. Brennan, Dir., Cent. Intel. Agency (Jan. 13, 2016) (on file with Committee).

[192] Email from Neal L. Higgins, Dir. of Cong. Affairs, Cent. Intel. Agency, to Philip G. Kiko, Staff Dir. and Gen. Counsel, H. Select Comm. on Benghazi (Mar. 22, 2016) (on file with the Committee).

[193] *Id.* The CIA acknowledged in a March 4, 2016 meeting that it had simply "assumed" the Committee would do this, without ever once asking with the Committee. This mistaken assumption perhaps contributed to the CIA's hardened posture in refusing to review witness transcripts for classification and sensitivity purposes.

[194] Letter from Trey Gowdy, Chairman, H. Select Comm. on Benghazi, to Denis R. McDonough, White House Chief of Staff (Dec. 29, 2014) (on file with the Committee).

[195] *See, e.g.,* Letter from Buck McKeon, Chairman, H. Armed Servs. Comm., et al., to the President (Oct. 19, 2012) (on file with the Committee); *and* Letter from Darrell Issa, Chairman, H. Comm. on Oversight & Gov't Reform, and Jason Chaffetz, Chairman, H. Subcomm. on Nat'l Sec., to the President (Oct. 19, 2012) (on file with the Committee).

[196] Letter from Trey Gowdy, Chairman, H. Select Comm. on Benghazi, to Denis R. McDonough, White House Chief of Staff (Dec. 29, 2014) (on file with the Committee).

[197] Letter from W. Neil Eggleston, White House Counsel, to Trey Gowdy, Chairman, H. Select Comm. on Benghazi (Jan. 23, 2015) (on file with the Committee).

[198] Letter from Jennifer O'Connor, Deputy White House Counsel, to Trey Gowdy, Chairman, H. Select Comm. on Benghazi (Feb. 27, 2015) (on file with the Committee).

16, 2015, the White House produced these documents with the redactions removed.[199]

On April 23, 2015, the Committee Chairman wrote to the White House again,[200] giving priority to specific categories of documents from the Committee's December 29, 2014 request.[201] As a result, the White House made additional document productions on May 11, 2015;[202] June 19, 2015;[203] and July 17, 2015.[204]

On August 7, 2015, the Chairman wrote a third time to the White House[205] addressing documents responsive to the Committee's December 29, 2014 request which were being withheld by the White House.[206] Subsequently, the White House produced additional documents on August 28, 2015.[207]

On September 9, 2015, White House staff met with Committee staff and made progress on satisfying the Committee's requests for information.[208] The White House briefed the Committee on a specific request, and a path forward was set to identify remaining documents addressing specific categories of information important to the Committee. Additional meetings were held in a classified setting, on October 5, 2015;[209] October 27, 2015;[210] and November 12, 2015.[211] Each meeting was accompanied by a document production from the White House.

In total, the White House made nine productions of documents to the Committee. To be clear the White House did not provide all of the information the Committee requested but the Committee was granted access to information no other congressional committee accessed.

## WITNESSES

The Committee interviewed four witnesses from the White House. On January 21, 2016, three senior White House officials, W. Neil Eggleston, Counsel to the President; Nicholas L. McQuaid, Deputy Counsel to the President; and Donald C. Sisson, Special Assistant to the President; flew to Charlotte, North Carolina, to meet with the Chairman and discuss details regarding these witness

---

[199] Letter from Jennifer O'Connor, Deputy White House Counsel, to Trey Gowdy, Chairman, H. Select Comm. on Benghazi (Mar. 16, 2015) (on file with the Committee).

[200] Letter from Trey Gowdy, Chairman, H. Select Comm. on Benghazi, to W. Neil Eggleston, White House Counsel (Apr. 23, 2015) (on file with the Committee).

[201] Id.

[202] See Letter from Jennifer O'Connor, Deputy White House Counsel, to Trey Gowdy, Chairman, H. Select Comm. on Benghazi (May 11, 2015) (on file with the Committee).

[203] See Letter from Jennifer O'Connor, Deputy White House Counsel, to Trey Gowdy, Chairman, H. Select Comm. on Benghazi (June 19, 2015) (on file with the Committee).

[204] See Letter from Jennifer O'Connor, Deputy White House Counsel, to Trey Gowdy, Chairman, H. Select Comm. on Benghazi (July 17, 2015) (on file with the Committee).

[205] Letter from Trey Gowdy, Chairman, H. Select Comm. on Benghazi, to W. Neil Eggleston, White House Counsel (Aug. 7, 2015) (on file with the Committee).

[206] Id.

[207] See Letter from Jennifer O'Connor, Deputy White House Counsel, to Trey Gowdy, Chairman, H. Select Comm. on Benghazi (Aug. 28, 2015) (on file with the Committee)

[208] See Email from Jennifer O'Connor, Deputy Counsel, White House Office of the Chief Counsel, to Dana K. Chipman, Chief Counsel, H. Select Comm. on Benghazi et al (Sept. 10, 2015, 14:53 EST) (on file with the Committee).

[209] Letter from from Jennifer O'Connor, Deputy White House Counsel, to Trey Gowdy, Chairman, H. Select Comm. on Benghazi (Oct. 5, 2015) (on file with the Committee).

[210] Letter from Jennifer O'Connor, Deputy White House Counsel, to Trey Gowdy, Chairman, H. Select Comm. on Benghazi (Oct. 27, 2015) (on file with the Committee).

[211] Letter from Jennifer O'Connor, Deputy White House Counsel, to Trey Gowdy, Chairman, H. Select Comm. on Benghazi (Nov. 12, 2015) (on file with the Committee).

interviews.[212] The White House and the Committee honored the confidentiality of the meeting and the discussions.

Susan E. Rice, National Security Advisor, and Benjamin J. Rhodes, Deputy National Security Advisor for Strategic Communications, then testified before the Committee.[213]

### ACCESS TO COMPARTMENTED PROGRAMS

Over the course of nearly a dozen interviews with the State Department, the Defense Department, and CIA personnel, witnesses consistently refused to answer questions related to certain allegations with respect to U.S. activities in Libya even though the House specifically gave the Committee access to materials relating to intelligence sources and methods.[214] Most of these questions related in some way to allegations regarding weapons.[215] These refusals meant significant questions raised in public relating to Benghazi could not be answered.

At the meeting between the Chairman and the White House in Charlotte, N.C., in January 2016, the Chairman told Eggleston the Committee would need to review any and all relevant special access programs that might relate to U.S. government activities in Libya. On March 16, 2016, the Committee formalized its request for this access in a letter to Eggleston:

> With this letter, I am also including a classified attachment detailing specific testimony received by the Committee establishing the need to further clarify what specific activities the U.S. government may have conducted, and/or authorized, in Libya in 2011 and 2012. . . . You are in a unique position to help us make sure the record is complete. In order to accomplish this, however, the Committee requires your assistance. I therefore write to formally request access to all special access programs regarding U.S. activities in Libya in 2011–2012.[216]

The letter contained a classified attachment detailing specific testimony from senior and line personnel from the State Department, CIA, and the Defense Department, all of whom did not respond fully to questions from the Committee during their interviews due to access issues. Some of the testimony provided raised substantial further questions in light of the record available to the Committee. The administration ultimately did not provide the requested access.[217]

---

[212] Press Briefing by Press Sec'y Josh Earnest, Office of the Press Sec'y, The White House (Mar. 18, 2016), https://www.whitehouse.gov/the-press-office/2016/03/21/press-briefing-press-secretary-josh-earnest-3182016.

[213] See Testimony of Susan E. Rice, former U.S. Ambassador to the U.N., Tr. (Feb. 2, 2016) (on file with the Committee); Testimony of Benjamin J. Rhodes, Deputy Nat'l Security Advisor for Strategic Communications, Nat'l Security Council, Tr. at 50–51 (Feb. 2, 2016) (on file with the Committee).

[214] H. Res. 567, 113th Cong., § 4(a) (2014).

[215] Letter from Trey Gowdy, Chairman, H. Select Comm. on Benghazi, to W. Neil Eggleston, White House Counsel (Mar. 16, 2016) (on file with the Committee).

[216] Id.

[217] Letter from Neal L. Higgins, Dir. of Cong. Affairs, Cent. Intel. Agency, to Trey Gowdy, Chairman, H. Select Comm. on Benghazi (April 28, 2016) (on file with the Committee).

QUESTIONS TO THE PRESIDENT

In the summer of 2014, the Chairman first discussed sending questions to the President with Eggleston. In the January 2016 meeting, the Chairman again raised with Eggleston the possibility of sending questions to the President. The Chairman offered Eggleston the opportunity to review and comment on the questions in advance as well as to provide the documentary basis behind each question.

Despite this offer by the Chairman, in the three months following that meeting, the White House repeatedly rebuffed offers from the Committee to meet and discuss the questions. On June 7, 2016, the Chairman sent to Eggleston a list of 15 questions for the President regarding the Benghazi attacks.[218] None of these questions had ever been directly addressed by the White House publicly, and for most of the questions the President is the only person able to answer the question. The full text of the letter with the questions is reproduced in Appendix C of this report.

On June 25, 2016, Eggleston responded that he had advised the President not to answer the Chairman's questions. Specifically, Eggleston noted "implications" for the constitutional separation of powers and wrote "if the President were to answer your questions, his response would suggest that Congress has the unilateral power to demand answers from the President about his official acts."[219] Eggleston did not explain how voluntary responses would suggest that Congress could compel answers nor did he mention prior interviews—such as on 60 Minutes on September 12, 2012, and on Univision on September 20, 2012—where the President discussed the Benghazi attacks.

## COMPLIANCE WITH RECORD-KEEPING LAWS AND REGULATIONS

### The Federal Records Act

The Federal Records Act [FRA] "governs the collection, retention, preservation, and possible destruction of federal agency records" by Federal agencies.[220] Federal records include:

[A]ll books, papers, maps, photographs, machine readable materials, or other documentary materials, regardless of physical form or characteristics, made or received by a federal agency under federal law or in connection with the transaction of public business and preserved or appropriate for preservation by that agency or its legitimate successor as evidence of the organization, functions, policies, decisions, proceedings, operations or other activities of the government or because of informational value of the date within them.[221]

---

[218] Letter from Trey Gowdy, Chairman, H. Select Comm. on Benghazi, to W. Neil Eggleston, White House Counsel (June 7, 2016) (Reproduced in Appendix C).

[219] Letter from W. Neil Eggleston, White House Counsel to Trey Gowdy, Chairman, H. Select Comm. on Benghazi (June 25, 2016) (on file with the Committee).

[220] WENDY GINSBERG, CONG. RESEARCH SERV., R43072, COMMON QUESTIONS ABOUT FEDERAL RECORDS AND RELATED AGENCY REQUIREMENTS 2 (2015), https://www.fas.org/sgp/crs/secrecy/R43072.pdf (citing 44 U.S.C., Chapters 21, 29, 31, and 33).

[221] 44 U.S.C. § 3301 (2012). Conversely, non-record materials are broken down into three categories: (1) library and museum material (2) extra copies of documents; and (3) stocks of publications and processed documents—such as catalogs, trade journals, and other publications that are

The FRA requires each agency head to "make and preserve records."[222] Each agency head must "establish and maintain an active, continuing program for the economical and efficient management of the records of the agency" including "effective controls over the creation and over the maintenance and use of records in the conduct of current business."[223] Additionally, each agency head "shall establish safeguards against the removal or loss of records."[224]

The details of implementing an agency's record management program are set out in Federal regulations. Agencies must maintain "adequate documentation of agency business" that "[m]ake possible a proper scrutiny by Congress."[225] The regulations require "[a]gencies that allow employees to send and receive official electronic mail messages using a system not operated by the agency must ensure that federal records sent or received on such systems are preserved in the appropriate agency recordkeeping system."[226]

The State Department's own records management policies reinforce the statutory and regulatory requirements. According to the Foreign Affairs Manual: "[T]he Secretary is required to establish a Records and Information Life Cycle Management Program in accordance with the Federal Records Act."[227] Objectives of the program include fulfilling official requests from Congress,[228] as well as ensuring "[t]he recording of activities of officials of the Department should be complete to the extent necessary to . . . *[m]ake possible a proper scrutiny by Congress and duly authorized agencies of the Government of the manner in which the functions of the Department have been discharged.*"[229]

## The State Department's Record Keeping

The Committee first became aware of the Secretary's use of a non-official email account for at least some official business on August 11, 2014, when the State Department produced to the Committee eight emails to or from the Secretary.[230] These emails indicated the Secretary used a private email account to communicate

---

received from other government agencies, commercial firms, or private institutions. 36 C.F.R. § 1222.14 (2009). The FRA was most recently amended in 2014 to address:

> "[T]he rapid migration over the last several decades toward electronic communication and recordkeeping, federal recordkeeping laws are still focused on the media in which a record is preserved, not the information that constitutes the record itself. To correct this flaw, this legislation will shift the onus of recordkeeping onto the record and not the media it is contained in as a way to better enable NARA, and other agencies, to handle growing amounts of electronic communication."

H. REP. NO. 113–127, at 5 (2013). That amendment was introduced by Ranking Member Cummings (D-MD). H.R. 1233, 113th Cong. (2013).

[222] 44 U.S.C. § 3101 (2012).
[223] 44 U.S.C. § 3102 (2012).
[224] 44 U.S.C. § 3105 (2012).
[225] 36 C.F.R. § 1222.22 (c) (2015).
[226] 36 C.F.R. § 1236.22 (b) (2015).
[227] 5 FAM 414.1 (2015).
[228] 5 FAM 414.3–1(8) (2015).
[229] 5 FAM 422.2(3) (2015) (emphasis added); *see also* 5 FAM 443.1 (establishing principles governing email communications) *and* 5 FAM 754(h) (requiring users to review 5 FAM 443 for responsibilities for handling email correspondence).
[230] *See* August 11, 2014 document production from the State Dep't which included eight emails sent to or received by the Secretary.

about official government business.[231] Well before the State Department made this production of eight emails, it was abundantly clear the State Department knew the complete universe of responsive documents and emails was not housed or situated on State Department servers.[232]

The State Department was aware—as early as June 2013—of the Secretary's use of personal email for official business and the detrimental effect on responses to Congress and obligations under the Federal Records Act, yet the Department said nothing.[233] The State Department was actively retrieving the Secretary's official emails in May 2014—the same time the Committee was formed—still the Department said nothing.

Seventeen days after producing eight of the Secretary's emails, the State Department, through Kennedy, issued a memorandum to State Department principals reiterating the obligation that departing senior staff have to ensure the timely return of records, including email.[234] Specifically, Kennedy's memorandum referenced a "policy in place since 2009 . . . to capture electronically email accounts of the senior officials listed in Tab 1 as they depart their positions."[235] The memorandum attached the relevant Foreign Affairs Manual provisions including those related to email records.[236] During questioning by the Chairman, Kennedy testified about the memorandum:

> Q: On August the 28th, you issued a memo to a whole host of people, subject: "Senior Officials' Records Management Responsibilities." I want to make sure he gets a copy of that so he's looking at the same thing I'm looking at. And we can mark it as committee exhibit 13 here. Does that look familiar? I'm not going to go through the whole thing with you. I just want to. . . .
>
> A: Yes, sir, this is familiar. This is something that we did in response to a NARA program that we call journaling but NARA's official name is Capstone.
>
> Q: And what prompted you to promulgate this memo?
>
> A: NARA's program.
>
> Q: I thought you and I had established that NARA rule had taken place the fall of 2013.
>
> A: The journaling effort, Mr. Chairman, I cannot remember the exact date and how my people had worked this through. But the request to journal these records is some-

---

[231] See id. Some of the emails were identified by the address with domain name "@clintonemail.com." Other emails were designated simply as "H."

[232] See Fischer Testimony at 66, in relevant part:

> Q: Okay. One of the things that we wanted to talk with you about was when you first became knowledgeable or aware that all or part of Secretary Clinton's records were not on premises with the State Dep't. And can you tell us when that was?
>
> A: The end of July 2014.

[233] "Office of the Sec'y: Evaluation of Email Records Management and Cybersecurity Requirements," *supra* note 69 at 17–18.

[234] See Memorandum from "M—Patrick F. Kennedy" to 7th Floor Principals 1 (Aug. 28, 2014) (on file with the Committee).

[235] See id. at 3.

[236] See id.

thing that I'm just reading this now to see if anything else reminds me. Chairman, if I am slow, I am slow. But I have

Q: Having spent the day with you, you will never convince me that you are slow. You will never convince me of that. If you would look at page 3 for me, kind of in the middle, it's a bullet that starts, "As a general matter."

A: Yes.

Q: "As a general matter." I'll let you read the rest of that. You can read it for the record whenever you feel comfortable.

A: Yes, sir, I am ready.

Q: Will you read that for us, for the court reporter?

A: "As a general matter, to ensure a complete record of their activities, senior officials should not use their private email accounts for (e.g., Gmail) for official businesses. If a senior official uses his or her private email account for the conduct of official business, she or he must ensure that records pertaining to official business that are sent from or received on such email account are captured and maintained. The best way to ensure this is to forward incoming e mails received on a private account to the senior official's State account and copy ongoing messages to their State account."[237]

Less than six weeks later, Kennedy sent another State Department announcement restating the obligations of employees to preserve records.[238] Less than 10 days later, on October 28, 2014, Kennedy sent a letter to four former Secretaries of State. That letter sought the return of Federal records, "such as an email sent or received on a personal email account while serving as Secretary."[239] The letter emphasized that "diverse Department records are subject to various disposition schedules with most Secretary of State records retained permanently," a fact that was confirmed in the Committee's interview with William Fischer, Chief Records Officer, State Department.[240] Because of a typographical error, the State Department did not send the letter to Mills until November 12, 2014.[241]

---

[237] Testimony of Patrick F. Kennedy, Under Sec'y of State for Mgmt., U.S. Dep't of State, Tr. at 259–61 (Feb. 3, 2016) [hereinafter Kennedy Testimony] (on file with the Committee).

[238] See Patrick F. Kennedy, Under Sec'y of State for Mgmt., *Dep't Notice 2014_10_115: A Message from Under Sec'y for Management Patrick F. Kennedy regarding State Dep't Records Responsibilities and Policy*, U.S. DEP'T OF STATE (Oct. 17, 2014), https://www.archives.gov/press/press-releases/2015/pdf/attachment2-department-notice.pdf; Patrick F. Kennedy, Under Sec'y of State for Mgmt., *Cable to Field: State Dep't Records Responsibilities and Policy*, U.S. DEP'T OF STATE (Oct. 30, 2014), https://www.archives.gov/press/press-releases/2015/pdf/attachment3-cable-to-the-field.pdf.

[239] See Letter from Patrick F. Kennedy, Under Sec'y of State for Mgmt., U.S. Dep't of State, to former Sec'ys Madeline Albright, Colin Powell, Condoleezza Rice, and Hillary Clinton. (Oct. 28, 2014) (on file with the Committee). It's important to note that because of a drafting error, Cheryl D. Mills letter was sent on November 12, 2014. See Letter from Patrick F. Kennedy, Under Sec'y of State for Mgmt., U.S. Dep't of State, to Cheryl D. Mills. (Nov. 12, 2014) (on file with the Committee).

[240] See Fischer Testimony, *supra* note 54, at 32–33.

[241] See Letter from Patrick F. Kennedy, Under Sec'y of State for Mgmt., U.S Dep't of State to Cheryl D. Mills. (Nov. 12, 2014) (on file with the Committee).

In response to a Committee member, Kennedy told the Committee:

A: Yes, sir. This was in response to a National Archives and Records Administration new policy that they had put out.

Q: Uh-huh. And the letter came from you?

A: The letter came from me, yes, sir.

Q: And

A: It went to the representatives of I believe it was four previous Secretaries of State.

Q: Why did it go to the representatives?

A: That was just a decision that we would write the representatives because it would more likely get the kind of attention, immediate attention, if we sent it to the representatives. And I personally knew all the representatives of Secretary Powell on forward. And so I would write them because I would make sure that they would take it would not get lost, potentially, in the junk mail category.

Q: Okay. And just give me in your words, so I don't have to reread and go through this letter in your words, what were you trying to accomplish exactly with this letter? What were you concerned about?

A: We wanted to make sure that we had in our possession any Federal record that had been created during their tenure that we might not have in our possession.

Q: Uh-huh.

Q: And what prompted you to write the letter when you wrote it?

A: It was basically the NARA, the NARA.

Q: Rule?

A: The NARA rule.

Q: And when was the NARA rule promulgated, do you recall?

A: I believe that it was in late 2013.

Q: If it was late 2013, why did you wait until late 2014 to write the letter?

A: Because this is when I received it, sir.

Q: When you received what?

A: When my staff called this to my attention.

Q: Can you see how the timeline might appear to have been influenced by other factors? Are you at least open to the optics of a congressional committee continuing to ask for her emails, and none are forthcoming, and the State Department says not one word about not having her record?

And I will say again for the record, for the court reporter, because this may be a new court reporter. The person that's currently assigned to aid Congress in collection of records, Mr. Snyder, could not be more professional and easy to work with and fair. And if it's no, it's no, and if it's yes, it's yes, but at least we have an answer. Previous to Mr. Snyder, it was not that way.

So we ask, and we hear crickets. And then we see these letters from you to all the way back to John Jay and Alexander Hamilton saying, can you please produce records. And the rule was promulgated a year before you sent the letter, Ambassador.

A: Mr. Chairman, I absolutely understand your concerns and absolutely agree that your request for records rang some bells in the State Department. Absolutely.

Q: That's what I'm getting at.

A: But, you know, if we wanted to hide something, I would have never sent this letter.

Q: Well, there are two ways to look at that. You sent the letter to more than just the Secretary, which was a very good way to deflect attention onto other Secretaries of State, even though the ones that you [sic] some of the ones you dealt with in the past never sent you an email. Now, the letter does say records and not just emails, I will grant you that.

A: That is correct, sir.

Q: But it is curious why you would wait years and years and years to make sure the public record is complete. Meanwhile, you're getting FOIA requests and congressional inquiries and a host of other things. And yet you wait until our committee is in the throes of asking for her emails for this letter to be sent.

Can you see how that would look suspicious?

A: I can see how it looks suspicious, but, Mr. Chairman, I acted after discussion with my colleagues. You know, you called something to our attention, and we thought, "We could have a problem here." We are now in the email era at the State Department. And the email era of the State Department, access to the Internet, et cetera, et cetera, essentially goes back only to let's see goes back to about late 19——

Q: Whenever Al Gore invented it. All right. I'm going to turn it back over to Jim.

A: So that we went back to the period of time before Secretaries of State who were, in the opinion of myself and others in the State Department, in the Internet email era. And so we went to those four Secretaries of State——

Q: I'm with you.

A: —to make sure that we had your concerns. We also had the NARA concerns. And it seemed to be a rational decision to reach out across the board, because it was only going back

Q: But you would concede you had been getting FOIA requests and you had gotten other congressional inquiries, none of which prompted you to write this letter.

A: This is the first time it had been brought to my attention.

Q: And you've said 'brought to your attention.' Who specifically brought this to your attention?

A: I don't remember. I think it was some combination of our records officers and the Bureau of Legislative Affairs.

Q: All right. You wrote Ms. Mills, among others.

A: Yes.

Q: Did you have any conversations, correspondence, emails, face to face meetings with Ms. Mills prior to sending this letter?

A: Not on this subject.

Q: So, out of the cold blue air, you sent Ms. Mills a letter saying, essentially, 'Send Secretary Clinton's emails back to the State Department,' no warning?

A: I also sent Peggy Sefarino, who was going I wrote who I regarded to be the senior staff officers for four

Q: And you're saying Ms. Mills had no notice that this letter was coming.

A: I did not call her and tell her it was coming, sir. And I am unaware of anyone else who may have called her.

Q: Did you meet with her and tell her it was coming?

A: No, sir, I did not.

Q: The other three designees for the three previous Secretaries of State, did you communicate with them in any fashion prior to them receiving the letter on behalf of the Secretary of State?

A: No, sir, I did not.

Q: And just to be clear, with your question from Chairman Gowdy, you said you did have conversations with Cheryl Mills prior to this letter being sent?

A: Not about this topic, sir. Every once in a while, I would see Cheryl Mills at a social function. I think I even had lunch with her once, discussing old business not related to Secretary I had worked with Cheryl Mills for 4 years.[242]

Less than five weeks after receipt of Kennedy's letter, Mills wrote back to the State Department indicating she was making

---

[242] Kennedy Testimony at 252–57.

55,000 pages of emails sent or received on the Secretary's private email account available to the State Department.[243] The emails were not enclosed with the letter. The Committee would learn later State Department officials were sent to pick up the emails at the law firm of the Secretary's attorney, Williams and Connolly.[244]

In her December 5, 2014 letter to Kennedy, Mills stated:

> Like Secretaries of State before her, Secretary Clinton at times used her own electronic mail account when engaging with other officials. On matters pertaining to the conduct of government business, it was her practice to use the officials' government electronic mail accounts. Accordingly, to the extent the Department retains records of government electronic mail accounts, it already has records of her electronic mail during her tenure preserved within the Department's record keeping systems.[245]

Notably, this was the first time the phrase "it was her practice to use the officials' government electronic emails accounts" was used.[246] Mills further explained in her letter "to the extent the Department retains records of government electronic mail accounts, it already has records of her electronic mail during her tenure preserved within the Department's record keeping systems."[247] Mills letter did not address how emails sent both to and from a personal email account would be captured for federal records purposes.[248] In fact it would be difficult to provide to such an explanation since the Committee's investigation uncovered work-related emails that were sent to and from personal email accounts that were never produced to the State Department.[249]

Collectively, the statements above served as an attempt to shift the burden of the Secretary's recordkeeping responsibilities to other government officials and the State Department.[250] This was apparent in further statements consistently made by the Secretary speculating that "the State Department had between 90–95 percent of all the ones that were work related. They were already on the system."[251] Not only could the State Department not confirm the percentage provided by the Secretary it did not know where the percentage she used originated.[252]

On March 9, 2015, the Secretary revealed her attorneys deleted emails they deemed "personal" before turning over her "work-

---

[243] Letter from Cheryl D. Mills to Patrick F. Kennedy, Under Sec'y of State for Mgmt., U.S. Dep't of State (Dec. 5, 2014) (on file with the Committee).

[244] See Fischer Testimony, supra note 54, at 85.

[245] Letter from Cheryl D. Mills to Patrick F. Kennedy, Under Sec'y of State for Mgmt., U.S. Dep't of State (Dec. 5, 2014) (on file with the Committee).

[246] Id.

[247] Id.

[248] Id.

[249] Letter from Julia Frifield, Ass't Sec'y of State for Leg. Affairs, State Dep't, to Trey Gowdy, Chmn., H. Select Comm. on Benghazi (June 25, 2015) (on file with the Committee) ("In a limited number of circumstances, we did not locate in the tens of thousands of pages of emails provided by Secretary Clinton the content of a handful of communications that Mr. Blumenthal provided. Those communications . . . are documents Bates-numbered in Blumenthal products. . . .").

[250] See id.

[251] Testimony of Hillary R. Clinton, Sec'y of State, U.S. Dep't of State, Tr. at 280 (Oct. 22, 2015) (on file with the Committee).

[252] See id. at 323 where Chairman Gowdy states "when I asked the State Department about ten days ago, what is the source of that figure, they shrugged their shoulders."

related" emails.[253] Neither the State Department nor the Committee could verify no work-related emails were deleted by the Secretary's attorneys or that all of her emails related to Benghazi and Libya were actually produced to the Committee. Concerned about the completeness of the record, the Chairman requested, on March 19, 2015 and again on March 31, 2015, that the Secretary make the email server available to a neutral third party for inspection and review.[254] The requests were rejected.[255] The Committee's concern was confirmed on June 12, 2015 when a non-government witness produced approximately 150 emails and memos sent to or received by the Secretary. [256] Approximately 89 of these emails had never been produced to the Committee. The State Department could not locate 15 of them either in full or part.[257] This is significant for at least two reasons. First, it confirms suspicions the State Department failed to produce relevant, probative information to the Committee until confronted with the reality the Committee had accessed the information through separate channels. In other words, the State Department denied until they were caught. Secondly, this undermines the argument of the Secretary that all of her work-related emails were produced to the State Department. Clearly, these 15 emails are work related and equally clearly they were not produced to the State Department. What remains unknown is whether these emails were lost while housed on the Secretary's private server or whether the Secretary's attorneys screened these emails out when they self-selected which records would be deemed official and which would be deemed personal. Regardless, relevant and probative information the public was entitled to review as public records was withheld.

The fact the Secretary used and maintained a private email account and server for all of her work-related emails prevented the State Department from executing its responsibilities under the FRA and the implementing regulations and policies.

The use of private email for official business was not confined to the Secretary. As noted previously, the Committee also discovered that Mills, Abedin, and Sullivan all made use of private email for official business. Compounding the problem of recovering these records, the State Department did not archive emails sent to or

---

[253] Zeke J. Miller, *Transcript: Everything Hillary Clinton Said on the Email Controversy,* TIME (Mar. 10, 2015), http://time.com/3739541/transcript-hillary-clinton-email-press-conference/.

[254] *See* Letter from Trey Gowdy, Chairman, H. Select Comm. on Benghazi, to David E. Kendall, Of Counsel, Williams & Connolly (Mar. 19, 2015) (on file with the Committee) ("[F]ormally requesting Secretary Clinton make her server available to a neutral, detached and independent third party for immediate inspection and review."); *see also* Letter from Trey Gowdy, Chairman, H. Select Comm. on Benghazi, to David E. Kendall, Of Counsel, Williams & Connolly (Mar. 31, 2015) ("[W]e . . . urge the Secretary to reconsider her position and allow a neutral, detached, and independent arbiter ensure the public record is complete and all materials relevant to the Committee's work have been provided to the Committee.").

[255] *See* Letter from David E. Kendall, Of Counsel, Williams & Connolly, to Trey Gowdy, Chairman, H. Select Comm. on Benghazi (Mar. 27, 2015) (on file with the Committee).

[256] *See* Letter from James M. Cole, Partner, Sidley Austin, to Trey Gowdy, Chairman, H. Select Comm. on Benghazi (June 12, 2015) (enclosing production of documents related to Mr. Cole's client, Sidney S. Blumenthal).

[257] *See* Letter from Julia E. Frifield, Assistant Sec'y of State for Legis. Affairs, U.S. Dep't of State, to Trey Gowdy, Chairman, H. Select Comm. on Benghazi (June 25, 2015) (on file with the Committee).

from senior staff in the Secretary's office during the Secretary's tenure.[258]

Beginning in early March 2015, the Committee sought additional information on the Department's records management activities. The Committee requested briefings on the State Department's record keeping activities as it related to both the Secretary and her senior staff. On March 17, 2015, the Committee met with representatives from the National Archives and Records Administration to better understand their role in the State Department's record keeping practices. On April 10, 2015, the Committee met with Katie Stana, Deputy Director of the Executive Secretariat, State Department, to understand the recordkeeping apparatus in place for the Office of the Secretary.[259] In addition, the Committee interviewed John Bentel, Director of the Office of Information Resource Management for the Executive Secretariat, to understand the technology and systems the Secretary and other senior officials used. When asked about the Secretary's exclusive use of private email and server, the Director testified he became aware when it came out in the papers.[260] He further testified he did not know whether the State Department's general counsel was consulted.[261]

The Committee sought to better understand the State Department's record keeping practices, including additional information on compliance with existing Federal regulations and State Department policy on April 18, 2015.[262] In particular, the Committee requested the State Department respond to 27 questions raised regarding the Secretary's email usage. The Committee emphasized the importance in getting answers to the questions by including them as part of the July 31, 2015 demand letter to Kerry.[263] When asked about the status of a State Department response, the State Department indicated the OIG would respond to the questions.[264] In a January 14, 2016 meeting, the OIG revealed it had not seen the questions until the week of January 5, 2016, contrary to the assertions made by State Department officials. In fact, the OIG suggested at the meeting the Committee would be best served by asking the State Department to respond to the questions.

The questions were subsequently posed to Kennedy on February 3, 2016, who was surprised by the questions. Kennedy testified, when asked about the volume of emails produced to the State Department: "[a]gain, I don't remember when I learned for [sic] it, and that is not, as I said, this is not a subject I prepared for, for this interview."[265]

The Committee's experiences with the State Department's records management and retention practices are consistent with findings by the OIG. It should be noted the position of Inspector

[258] See Lauren French, *Gowdy: Not backing off subpoena of Clinton emails,* POLITICO (Mar. 5, 2015), http://www.politico.com/story/2015/03/house-committee-benghazi-clinton-email-subpoena-115795.

[259] April 10, 2015 meeting between State Dep't officials and Comm. staff.

[260] Testimony of John Bentel, Director, Executive Secretariat, U.S. Dep't of State, Tr. at 37 (June 30, 2015)(on file with the Comm.).

[261] Bentel Testimony at 51.

[262] Email from Philip G. Kiko, Staff Dir. and Gen. Counsel, H. Select Comm. on Benghazi, to Julia Frifield, Assistant Sec'y for Legis. Affairs, U.S. Dep't of State (Apr. 18, 2015, 3:39 PM).

[263] Letter from Trey Gowdy, Chairman, H. Select Comm. on Benghazi, to John F. Kerry, Sec'y of State, U.S. Dep't of State (July 31, 2015) (on file with Comm.).

[264] See conversations between State Dep't personnel and Comm. staff.

[265] Kennedy Testimony at 211.

General [IG] was vacant during the Secretary's entire tenure forcing the OIG to operate without a permanent IG and often without an acting IG.[266] A permanent IG may have had the independence and standing to intervene on these records issues sooner. In September 2012, the OIG found that State Department's Office of Information Program Services, the office responsible for records management practices: "do[es] not meet statutory and regulatory requirements.[267] Although the office develops policy and issues guidance, it does not ensure proper implementation, monitor performance or enforce compliance."[268]

Despite an upgrade in 2009 to spur the preservation of emails as official records, the OIG found in March 2015:

> State Department employees have not received adequate training or guidance on their responsibilities for using the system to preserve 'record emails.' In 2011, employees created 61,156 record emails out of more than a billion emails sent. Employees created 41,749 in 2013. . . . Some employees do not create record emails because they do not want to make the email available in searches. . . .[269]

In its May 2016 report, the OIG found:

> The Federal Records Act requires appropriate management and preservation of Federal Government records, regardless of physical form or characteristics, that document the organization, functions, policies, decisions, procedures, and essential transactions of an agency. For the last two decades, both Department of State (Department) policy and Federal regulations have explicitly stated that emails may qualify as Federal records.

> As is the case throughout the Federal Government, management weaknesses at the Department have contributed to the loss or removal of email records, particularly records created by the Office of the Secretary. These weaknesses include a limited ability to retrieve email records, inaccessibility of electronic files, failure to comply with requirements for departing employees, and a general lack of oversight.

> OIG's ability to evaluate the Office of the Secretary's compliance with policies regarding records preservation and use of non-Departmental communications systems was, at times, hampered by these weaknesses. However, based on its review of records, questionnaires, and interviews, OIG determined that email usage and preservation practices varied across the tenures of the five most recent Secre-

---

[266] Byron Tau & Peter Nicholas, *State Dep't Lacked Top Watchdog During Hillary Clinton Tenure*, WALL ST. J. (Mar. 24, 2015), http://www.wsj.com/articles/state-department-lacked-top-watchdog-during-hillary-clinton-tenure-1427239813.

[267] Office of Inspector Gen., U.S. Dep't of State, *Inspection of Bureau of Administration, Global Information Services, Office of Information Programs and Services: Report No. ISP–I–12–54*, 1 (Sept. 2012), https://oig.state.gov/system/files/199774.pdf.

[268] *Id.*

[269] *See* Office of Inspector Gen., U.S. Dep't of State, *Review of State Messaging and Archive Retrieval Toolset and Record Email: Report No. ISP–I–15–15*, 1 (Mar. 2015), https://oig.state.gov/system/files/isp-i-15-15.pdf.

taries and that, accordingly, compliance with statutory, regulatory, and internal requirements varied as well.

OIG also examined Department cybersecurity regulations and policies that apply to the use of non-Departmental systems to conduct official business. Although there were few such requirements 20 years ago, over time the Department has implemented numerous policies directing the use of authorized systems for day-to-day operations. In assessing these policies, OIG examined the facts and circumstances surrounding three cases where individuals exclusively used non-Departmental systems to conduct official business.[270]

## ANALYSIS AND RECOMMENDATIONS

The necessity and importance of Congress's oversight authority is obvious. Given the administration's lack of responsiveness in most regards and slow and uneven responsiveness in all regards, the Committee makes the recommendations below.

### Restoring the Congressional Contempt Power

#### RECOMMENDATIONS

- House and Senate rules should be amended to provide for mandatory reductions in appropriations to the salaries of federal officials held in contempt of Congress.

- The criminal contempt statute should be amended to require the appointment of a special counsel to handle criminal contempt proceedings upon the certification of a contempt citation against an Executive Branch official by the House or Senate.

- Expedited procedures for the civil enforcement of congressional subpoenas should be enacted to provide timely judicial resolution of disputes.

#### ANALYSIS

As the Chairman noted in the May 8, 2015 Interim Progress Update:

> Compelling compliance with subpoenas requires either the cooperation of the Executive Branch—particularly the United States Attorney—the very entity from which we seek the information and an unlikely ally, or pursuing document production from the Executive Branch via civil contempt, a laborious, slow process and counterproductive to the goal of an expeditious investigation.[271]

This remark concisely describes the dilemma all congressional committees face when demanding information from the Executive Branch. This state of affairs also results, in part, from Congress's failure to adapt the law and its own internal rules to changed circumstances. The recommendations above would restore to Congress

---

[270] "Office of the Sec'y: Evaluation of Email Records Management and Cybersecurity Requirements," *supra* note 69 at Introduction.
[271] Interim Progress Update, *supra* note 8, at iii.

an effective and useful ability to compel compliance from the Executive Branch.

Contempt of Congress has long been recognized as a necessary and inherent component of the legislative power.[272] Without the power to find individuals in contempt, Congress would have no means by which to command compliance with its subpoenas and punish obstruction.[273] For much of our history, Congress wielded the power to enforce a finding of contempt by imprisoning noncompliant individuals—often referred to as the "inherent" contempt power.[274] Congress last used this power in 1935.[275] It has been called "unseemly" and few would advocate a return to the practice in the current hyper-partisan political environment where even the issuing of subpoenas draws howls of protest.[276]

Congress first enacted criminal contempt procedures in 1857 as an alternative to its inherent power to imprison.[277] Under the criminal contempt statute, the House or Senate may cite an individual for contempt of Congress and certify the citation to the U.S. Attorney for the District of Columbia whose "duty" it is to present the contempt citation to a grand jury.[278] Criminal contempt is punishable by a fine of up to $100,000 and up to one year in prison.[279]

The criminal contempt statute was, in practice, the sole enforcement mechanism for Congress after 1935 and was used or threatened with some frequency against senior Executive Branch officials beginning in 1975.[280] Invoking the criminal contempt statute generally resulted in full or substantial compliance with subpoenas.[281]

During recent administrations, the threat of criminal contempt has been insufficient to compel Executive Branch compliance. A recent opinion by the Office of Legal Counsel within the Justice Department likely ended any remaining usefulness the criminal contempt statute had in compelling compliance by Executive Branch officials. In June 2014, the Office of Legal Counsel advised the U.S. Attorney for D.C. that the U.S. Attorney retains prosecutorial discretion not to present a criminal contempt citation to a grand jury despite a statutory "duty" to present.[282] In other words, U.S. Attorneys must substitute their judgment for the judgment of the House or Senate of the United States.[283] While the merits of the Office of Legal Counsel opinion are open to debate, as a practical political matter it is unlikely future administrations would reverse an opinion so obviously favorable to their interests. As a result, an Executive Branch official appointed by the President has discretion whether to hold another Executive Branch official—likely appointed by the same President—accountable for failing to comply

---

[272] E.g., Anderson v. Dunn, 19 U.S. 204, 228–29 (1821) (holding that the House has the inherent power to punish a private citizen for contempt).

[273] Id.

[274] See id.

[275] See Jurney v. MacCracken, 294 U.S. 125 (1935).

[276] See Comm. on the Judiciary v. Miers, 558 F. Supp. 2d 53, 78 (D.D.C. 2008).

[277] 2 U.S.C. §§ 192, 194.

[278] 2 U.S.C. § 194.

[279] 2 U.S.C. § 192, see 18 U.S.C. § 3571 (regarding the maximum fine).

[280] Morton Rosenberg, *When Congress Comes Calling: A Primer on the Principles, Practices, and Pragmatics of Legislative Inquiry,* THE CONST. PROJECT 16 (2009), http://www.constitutionproject.org/wp-content/uploads/2009/07/WhenCongressComesCalling.pdf.

[281] Id.

[282] Letter from Karl R. Thompson, Acting Ass't Attorney Gen., Office of Legal Counsel, Dep't of Justice, to Ronald C. Machen, Jr., U.S. Attorney for D.C. (June 16, 2014).

[283] See id.

with a congressional subpoena.[284] The conflict is obvious and impossible to avoid. Regardless of the merits of a U.S. Attorney's decision not to present a congressional contempt citation to a grand jury, the decision will be colored by that conflict of interest.

Because of the deficiencies of the inherent power and criminal enforcement of contempt, Congress has turned to civil enforcement of its subpoenas with mixed success. While civil enforcement has led to the testimony of officials[285] and the production of a privilege log and substantial numbers of previously withheld documents,[286] Congress must accept very lengthy delays in order to pursue this enforcement option. In its investigation of 'Operation Fast and Furious,' the House Oversight and Government Reform Committee Chairman filed a civil action against the Justice Department in August 2012 to compel the production of documents.[287] Three and a half years later, in January 2016, a Federal district court judge ordered the Justice Department to produce withheld documents,[288] and in April 2016, the Justice Department finally produced the documents to Congress.[289] An enforcement tool requiring three and a half years simply to get a district court order is unacceptable.

While Congress retains its constitutional authority to hold recalcitrant witnesses in contempt of Congress, this authority no longer compels prompt, if any, compliance. All three enforcement mechanisms—inherent powers, criminal charges and civil enforcement— have questionable usefulness today and are largely dependent upon other branches of government agreeing with or pursuing the cause and remedy. The administration's obstruction of congressional oversight is the inevitable and predictable result. The three recommendations above would restore Congress's ability to enforce its subpoenas through its inherent constitutional authority, through criminal law and through civil enforcement.

Restoring Congress's inherent powers to enforce its subpoena must be the first priority. It is the only mechanism solely within Congress's discretion. The inherent power can be restored through simple rules changes in the House. The House should change its rules to allow a point of order against any appropriations measure, including conference reports, and continuing resolutions, that would fund the salary of a Federal official held in contempt of Congress.[290] The House should establish a high bar for waiving the point of order.

---

[284] *See id.*

[285] *See* Comm. on the Judiciary v. Miers, 558 F. Supp. 2d 53, 108 (D.D.C. 2008) (ordering Miers to testify before and produce requested materials to Congress).

[286] *See* Comm. on Oversight and Gov't Reform v. Lynch, No. 12–1332 (ABJ), 2016 WL 225675, at *16 (D.D.C. Jan. 19, 2016) (granting the Comm.'s motion to compel the Justice Dep't to produce documents).

[287] Press Release, H. Comm. on Oversight & Gov't Reform, House Asks Federal Court to Rule Against Attorney General's Stonewalling in Fast and Furious (Aug. 13, 2012), https://oversight.house.gov/release/house-asks-federal-court-to-rule-against-attorney-generals-stonewalling-in-fast-and-furious.

[288] *Lynch*, 2016 WL 225675, at 16.

[289] Press Release, H Comm. on Oversight & Gov't Reform, Chaffetz Statement on Fast and Furious (Apr. 8, 2016), https://oversight.house.gov/release/chaffetz-statement-fast-furious-documents.

[290] For example, House Rules prohibit the inclusion of provisions changing existing law in a general appropriations bill and such provisions may be objected to and ruled out of order. *See* Rules of the H. of Representatives, Rule XXI, cl. 2(b) (114th Cong.). A similar rule could be applied to any provision appropriating funds that would go to the salary of a Federal official held in contempt.

Congress could provide for nearly automatic sanctions against officials held in contempt of Congress, if it included triggering language in an appropriations statute. Under section 713 of the Financial Services and General Government Appropriations Act of 2012, no appropriation in any bill is available to pay the salary of a Federal official who prevents another Federal official from communicating directly with Congress.[291] This rider, which is continued every year, was the subject of a recent ruling by the Government Accountability Office holding that two officials of the Housing and Urban Development Department violated section 713 and that these officials should be required to pay back wages earned while they were in violation.[292]

A rider similar to section 713 could be included in annual appropriations disallowing the use of any appropriation to pay the salary of a Federal official held in contempt of Congress. Such an approach would trigger immediate and automatic sanctions when an official was held in contempt by Congress.

Because the inherent power can be exercised at Congress's sole discretion, the House should establish procedures to ensure the legitimacy of actions pursuant to the power. These procedures should provide for the transparent consideration of timely objections to congressional subpoenas, should require the production of a privilege log, and should require the appearance of the responsible Federal official at a hearing held to consider objections to the subpoena.

As noted above, criminal contempt proceedings against Executive Branch officials are subject to the discretion of the U.S. Attorney for D.C., and raise significant conflict of interest concerns. The Justice Department already has regulations in place for appointing a special counsel in situations presenting a conflict of interest.[293] The criminal contempt statute should be amended to require the appointment of special counsel pursuant to the Justice Department's own regulations whenever the House or Senate presents a criminal contempt citation against an Executive Branch official. This amendment would provide Congress some assurance prosecutorial discretion in contempt matters would be exercised without the appearance of a conflict of interest and should put recalcitrant Federal officials on notice they cannot assume a political ally will ignore a criminal contempt citation.

Finally, the House has increasingly resorted to civil enforcement of its subpoenas. While this mechanism has resulted in substantial compliance, it has also resulted in lengthy delays. This delay is often an unacceptable tradeoff. To increase the usefulness of civil enforcement, the House should consider a bill to require a three-judge panel in civil enforcement actions related to congressional subpoenas with direct appeal to the Supreme Court from the three-judge panel. This would ensure more timely resolution of these actions. An investigation delayed by years of legal deliberations does not allow Congress to make timely legislative decisions.

---

[291] Pub. L. No. 112–74, § 713, 125 Stat. 928, 931 (2012).

[292] Dep't of Housing and Urban Dev.—Application of Section 713 of the Fin. Servs. and Gen. Gov't Appropriations Act, 2012 (Reconsideration), B–325124.2, 2016 WL 1319698 (Comp. Gen. Apr. 5, 2016).

[293] See 28 C.F.R. § 600 (2015) (establishing grounds for appointing a special counsel).

These three recommendations each have limitations and drawbacks, but together they would provide Congress with a far more robust ability to compel cooperation than it has today. It is not acceptable for Congress to simply acquiesce to Executive Branch obstruction. It is Congress' constitutional responsibility to create, fund, and oversee Executive Branch agencies. Congress cannot effectively uphold its responsibilities under the Constitution without the power to ensure compliance with requests for information and witnesses.

## Classification Determinations

### RECOMMENDATION

- Agencies should make express classification determinations with respect to documents and materials provided to congressional oversight committees in accordance with relevant laws and Executive Orders.

### ANALYSIS

The Committee encountered significant practical delays and obstacles to its work arising from the need to quickly develop institutional capabilities to properly handle, work with, and protect classified information. While these difficulties to some degree are inherent in the rapid establishment of a new Committee with jurisdiction for national security matters, the Executive Branch exacerbated these challenges with its repeated efforts to declare certain material should be "treated as classified" even though it had not actually made any administrative determination the material in question met the standards necessary to designate it as classified or followed the process set out and required by Executive Order and relevant regulation to actually designate the material as classified.[294]

The Legislative Branch recognizes the role of the Executive Branch, in accordance with authorities provided under the Constitution and by Congress itself, to determine whether and how national security information should be classified and follows such determinations. Absent an express determination by the Executive Branch or other indication or awareness material is derived from properly classified information, Congress must treat information as unclassified to further the goal of congressional oversight and the responsibilities of the House to the public.[295]

During the course of this investigation, Executive Branch agencies regularly acted in a manner inconsistent with both principles by providing information (both documents and interviews) to the Committee with the request the Committee treat it as classified,[296]

---

[294] See Exec. Order No. 13,526, 75 Fed. Reg. 707 (Dec. 29, 2009).

[295] See, e.g., Letter from Julia Frifield, Assistant Sec'y of State for Legis. Affairs, Dep't of State, to Trey Gowdy, Chairman, H. Select Comm. on Benghazi (Sept. 25, 2015) [hereinafter Frifield Transmittal Letter] (on file with the Comm.). Use of the "Sensitive but Unclassified" designation differs from the broader phenomenon described here—which is not even founded in administrative practice—but strongly illustrates the nature of the problem.

[296] As one example, in a September 25, 2015 letter to the Comm. transmitting emails from the Sec'y, the Dep't stated "these documents should be handled differently from prior productions" even though they had not actually been determined to be classified and review was ongoing. It requested informally for other documents—which had not been properly classified—to be

Continued

even though it had not made any actual determination with respect to the classification of any of the material under the relevant authorities and procedures.[297] Although such requests may be considered in the context of efforts to facilitate Committee access to the material, there is no legal, administrative, or procedural foundation for such a request. National security information should either be properly classified in accordance with clearly stated procedures or treated as unclassified. There is no cognizable middle ground.

Sensitive information can be protected without resort to such arbitrary treatment, as it has been under the Committee's voluntary agreement with the State Department to protect certain types of personal and operational information. The unfounded efforts of the Executive Branch to create new categories of information control posed significant obstacles to the Committee's work—both in handling and using the material and in presenting it to the American people. It is important to note the question here is not alleged "over-classification," but rather failure of the Executive Branch to properly classify the information in question at all. The former is a subjective assessment of whether material should be classified and how. The latter represents attempts by the Executive Branch to control information without following the relevant law or procedure to classify it or, even worse, to control information that doesn't fit within its lawful classification authorities at all. Further, Executive Order 13526 clearly provides material cannot be classified to "conceal violations of law, inefficiency, or administrative error" or "prevent embarrassment to a person, organization, or agency."[298]

## Improving Oversight and Investigations within the House

### RECOMMENDATIONS

- The House should amend its rules to authorize all committees to take depositions.

- The House should amend its rules to require committees to establish oversight subcommittees.

### ANALYSIS

Congressional depositions allow Members and staff, as authorized by a committee, to interview witnesses under oath and, if necessary compel interview testimony by subpoena.[299] The ability to interview witnesses in private allows committees to gather information confidentially and in more depth than is possible under the five-minute rule governing committee hearings.[300] This ability is often critical to conducting an effective and thorough investiga-

---

treated as classified. *Id.* Similarly, the Department asked for certain interviews to be conducted in a classified environment even though the anticipated subject matter had previously been unclassified.

[297] Exec. Order No. 13526, for example, expressly provides: "Information may be originally classified under the terms of this order only if all of the following conditions are met." The stated conditions include specific procedures for identifying and marking classified information "in a manner that is immediately apparent."

[298] Exec. Order No. 13526, 75 Fed. Reg. 707, §§ 1.7(1), (2).

[299] Morton Rosenberg, When Congress Comes Calling: A Primer on the Principles, Practices, and Pragmatics of Legislative Inquiry, THE CONST. PROJECT 11 (2009), http://www.constitutionproject.org/wp-content/uploads/2009/07/WhenCongressComesCalling.pdf.

[300] *Id.*

tion.[301] Committees rely on voluntary interviews to gather information and conduct investigations. If a witness refuses to be interviewed or if the witness's employer—often the Executive Branch—refuses to allow the interview, however, most House committees have no recourse.

At the beginning of the 110th Congress, the Majority, the House, controlled by a Democratic majority, amended its rules to authorize the taking of depositions by members and staff of the Committee on Oversight and Government Reform.[302] Prior to the 110th Congress, depositions had been authorized by the House only for specific investigations.[303] This standing deposition authority applied only to the Committee on Oversight and Government Reform. In the current Congress, the House authorized the taking of depositions by four additional committees.[304] The authority was initially limited to 2015 but was extended to 2016 after its successful implementation in 2015.[305] Lamar S. Smith, Chairman, Committee on Science, Space and Technology, noted:

> During this session there are numerous instances of the Committee obtaining documents and voluntary interviews because of its deposition authority. In fact, as the following examples show, many key interviews and documents would likely not have been obtained without the Committee's ability to compel on-the-record interviews in a private setting.[306]

Jeb Hensarling, Chairman, Committee on Financial Services, similarly noted:

> Deposition authority continues to be critical to the Committee's oversight of an Administration that has been markedly indifferent to the Committee's subpoenas and voluntary information requests.[307]

Given the successful implementation of deposition authority in the 114th Congress to four additional committees, the House should amend its rules to extend the authority to all of its committees.

The small size of committee staffs in comparison to the Federal agencies they oversee necessarily limits the ability of committees to oversee the agencies within their jurisdictions. In addition, committees are already busy wrestling with major reauthorizations and reform plans. As a result, committees sometimes struggle to devote sufficient resources to oversight.

---

[301] *E.g.* This committee conducted 107 interviews in the course of its investigation. Interviews frequently lasted over three hours. This number of witnesses and depth of questioning would be nearly impossible in a hearing setting.

[302] H. Res. 6, 110th Congress § 502 (2007).

[303] Rosenberg, *supra* note 299, at 11, 82. *See, e.g.,* H. Res. 507, 105th Congress (1998) (Providing deposition authority to the Comm. on Education and Workforce for an investigation relating to the International Brotherhood of the Teamsters).

[304] H. Res. 5, 114th Congress § 3 (b) (2015) (The Comms. on Energy and Commerce, Financial Services, Science, Space and Technology, and Ways and Means).

[305] H. Res. 579, 114th Congress (2016).

[306] 162 CONG. REC. H41 (daily ed. Jan. 6, 2016) (letter submitted for the record Rep. Smith).

[307] 162 CONG. REC. H39 (daily ed. Jan. 6, 2016) (letter submitted for the record Rep. Hensarling).

House Rule X, clause 2(b)(2) requires standing authorizing committees with more than 20 members to either establish an oversight subcommittee or to require its subcommittees to conduct oversight.[308] As all House subcommittees have an obligation to conduct oversight within their assigned jurisdictions, this rule is little more than an exhortation to establish an oversight subcommittee. Of the 15 committees to which the rule applies, six did not establish oversight subcommittees in the 114th Congress.[309]

While some committees, such as the Committee on Energy and Commerce, have a decades-long record of active oversight,[310] not every committee in the House has acted accordingly. An oversight subcommittee ensures that at least one subcommittee chair and the staff of that subcommittee will be singularly focused on oversight of the agencies and programs within the full committee's jurisdiction.

## Reforming Record-Keeping Laws

### RECOMMENDATION

- Congress should consider strengthening enforcement authorities and penalties under the Federal Records Act related to the use of non-official email accounts and non-official file-hosting services for official purposes.

### ANALYSIS

The State Department's failure to adhere to Federal law and its own policies governing record management significantly impeded the committee's investigation.[311] Even more important, these failures delayed the flow of information to the families and loved ones of those killed and injured in Libya and delayed that information being made available to the public.

These failures are not indigenous to this Committee and will be familiar to congressional investigators of the Centers for Medicare and Medicaid Services,[312] the Environmental Protection Agency,[313] the Internal Revenue Service[314] and the Energy Department.[315] The destruction of records, use of private email and email aliases, and failure to retain records has impeded multiple congressional investigations over the years. These concerns reach back to prior administrations as well. This is not a political issue; it is a legal,

---

[308] Rules of the H. of Representatives, Rule X, cl. 2(b)(2) (114th Cong.).

[309] H. Comm. on Agric., H. Comm. on Educ. & Workforce, H. Comm. on Foreign Affairs, H. Comm. on Judiciary, H. Comm. on Small Bus., and H. Comm. on Transp. & Infrastructure.

[310] See, e.g., Joel A. Mintz, Agencies, Congress and Regulatory Enforcement: A Review of EPA's Hazardous Waste Enforcement, 18 ENVTL. L. 683, 706 n. 57 (1988).

[311] See supra discussions regarding State Department's record-keeping at 54–66.

[312] Majority Staff of H. Comm. on Oversight & Gov't Reform, Behind the Curtain of the Healthcare.gov Rollout, 113TH CONG. 1, 17 (Sept. 17, 2014), https://oversight.house.gov/wp-content/uploads/2014/09/Healthcare-gov-Report-Final-9-17-14.pdf.

[313] Letter from the members of H. Comm. on Science, Space, and Tech. to Lisa Jackson, Adm'r, Envtl. Prot. Agency (Jan. 23, 2013), https://science.house.gov/news/letters/committee-letter-epa-administrator-jackson-re-alias-emails-january-23-2013.

[314] See Letter from members of H. Comm. on Oversight & Gov't Reform to President Barack Obama (July 27, 2015), https://oversight.house.gov/wp-content/uploads/2015/07/2015-07-27-UPDATED-JC-to-Obama-WH-Koskinen-Resignation.compressed.pdf.

[315] Press Release, H. Comm. on Oversight & Gov't Reform, Oversight Comm. Presses Energy Sec'y on False Denials, Improper Use of Non-official Email Accounts in Solyndra Loan Program (Aug. 15, 2012), https://oversight.house.gov/release/oversight-committee-presses-energy-secretary-on-false-denials-improper-use-of-non-official-email-accounts-in-solyndra-loan-program.

constitutional, and branch equity issue. In 2007, the Secretary—then Senator—denounced "secret White House email accounts" after senior White House officials were found to have conducted some official business over political email accounts.[316] In this Committee's investigation, the Secretary's unusual email arrangement, her senior staff's use of non-official email accounts, and the State Department's own lack of fidelity to the record maintenance rules, all delayed and in some instances prevented the Committee from accessing official records necessary to conduct a thorough investigation.

---

[316] Blake Neff, *VIDEO: In 2007, Hillary Said Secret Emails 'Shredded' the Constitution*, DAILY CALLER (Mar. 4, 2015), http://dailycaller.com/2015/03/04/video-in-2007-hillary-said-secret-emails-shredded-the-constitution.

# PART V:

# Recommendations

## Terrorist Attacks on U.S. Facilities in Benghazi

*Recommendation:* The Executive Branch should provide for a central planning and coordination mechanism (likely within an existing entity) for interagency threat assessment and tracking for "force protection" of U.S. facilities abroad as well as planning, operations, and response to potential attacks.

The coordinating organization should provide for:

- A clear designation of "who is in charge" of managing and following up on response in emergent situations as well as the roles and responsibilities of involved departments and agencies.

- Clear and prompt timeline milestones for resolution of policy issues potentially impacting response to emergent situations.

- Clear and real-time identification of all potential U.S. Government assets potentially positioned to respond to emergent threats.

- A mechanism for prompt consideration of potential waivers to existing policy or other constraints potentially limiting immediate response to an emergent situation.

- Joint training exercises with all agencies present in high threat foreign locations as well as with the host nation's external quick reaction force for emergency and exfiltration plans.

- Interoperability and improved communication during contingencies. As one example, on the ground security personnel need to be able to communicate directly with operational military personnel in a crisis to coordinate surveillance and response.

- Relevant agencies (including the State Department, combatant commands, and the Central Intelligence Agency) need to be involved in each agency's emergency action plans to ensure situational awareness as well as that each agency's facilities, capabilities and response role is known. Where capability on the ground is insufficient and the Defense Department cannot respond immediately, the State Department and other agencies can adjust their respective plans to allow backup local or regional resources to be identified ahead of time.

- Agencies on the ground need to plan for standby military support before a crisis in high threat environments, including where feasible support from U.S. allies. In addition, the coordinating body should provide for a specific mechanism to know and understand assets and capabilities actually available at any given time.

As an example, a Commander's in Extremis Force has now been stood up in Africa, but additional assets available for contingency in high threat environments as well as response times and capabilities should be known to relevant agencies as part of emergency planning. If U.S. resources are not available because of distance, the lack of assets for immediate response should be incorporated in emergency planning with an anticipated timeline for response.

*Recommendation:* Diplomatic Security personnel and or Security Protection Specialists should maintain a state of readiness to counter potential attacks at all times in high threat environments.

- Agents should be armed or have ready access to defensive weapons at all times.

- Additionally, Diplomatic Security Agents and Security Protection Specialists should maintain a 24-hour armed quick reaction force [QRF] capability in all high threat environments manned using internal resources when available.

- When sufficient internal resources are not available, staffing for a QRF should be clearly coordinated in advance with potential responders. Planning should also provide for support and a definitive timeframe for response from other U.S. government resources such as Mobile Security Detachments, Site Security Teams or Fleet Antiterrorism Support Teams [FAST]. When U.S. government assets are not available, planning should consider whether contractors might provide enhanced capability.

*Recommendation:* Operational planners should carefully review whether a heightened posture is warranted on anniversaries of the September 11, 2001 terrorist attacks or other politically significant dates such as Inauguration Day in light of available analysis and threat intelligence.

*Recommendation:* Military planners should review current and future operational planning to prevent recurrence of specific operational issues identified in the response to the Benghazi attacks. These include:

- Ensure that aircraft aligned with response forces maintain the ability to meet specified timelines contained in the relevant concept plans or operations plans.

- Ensure adequate—and actionable—planning and resources for lift and mobility capabilities necessary for response.

- Enhance the capability of Marine FAST to conduct full-scope combat operations.

- Maintain a minimum anticipated timeline to respond to any terrorist attack in the Middle East, North Africa, or Central Asia.

*Recommendation:* The Committee supports funding the State Department's Foreign Affairs Security Training Center as the Department needs a dedicated training facility. The Department also should ensure its personnel satisfactorily complete requisite courses. A security professional should never go to a warzone or high threat environment feeling unprepared to defend themselves and their principal officer.

## Internal and Public Government Communications About the Terrorist Attacks in Benghazi

*Recommendation:* The drafting and editing of talking points and other political communications for policymakers is not an intelligence function. Intelligence agencies and officials should not be drawn into the creating or editing of talking points and other political or policy communications.

- Further, intelligence analysts should generally not produce products other than analytical products adhering to proper analytical tradecraft. Other officials—such as legislative or public affairs, non-analyst management, and White House Staff—should not be involved in the production of any product to be used or represented as the product of analytical tradecraft. Each stream of material must be kept separate and independent.

- Further, when communicating with the public, senior executive branch officials and spokespersons should carefully distinguish analysis of intelligence and other agencies from policy judgments, "spin," opinion and interpretations extrapolated from intelligence analysis by White House staff, political appointees, or senior officials outside the Intelligence Community. Such materials may be derived from properly produced analytical material when distinguished in this manner.

*Recommendation:* An additional step of quality control should be instituted in the review process for analytic products to ensure analytical products accurately reflect the views of analysts consistent with proper analytical tradecraft or are otherwise properly caveated.

- Further, where senior analysts responsible for briefing the President substitute their judgment for the consensus views of line analysts in the President's Daily Brief, the material should be appropriately caveated and accompanied by the consensus view of line analysts.

- Further, a formal mechanism should be put into place to memorialize irregularities arising from significant analytical disagreements or tradecraft deviations, including notification to the Congressional intelligence committees.

*Recommendation:* Claims in analytic products should be supported by substantial evidence, and analysts should clearly understand and place sourcing into context. Open source material should continue to play an appropriate role. However, where analytic products and addressing emergent situations are predominantly based on open source materials, they should be clearly noted as such. As a corollary, while crisis reporting may require flexibility in sourcing and analysis, emergent reporting known to be uncertain or developing should be properly disclosed and caveated.

*Recommendation:* Law governing Accountability Review Boards [ARBs] should be amended to limit the influence of the Secretary of State and offices with potential conflicts of interest in the selection of members and to provide for broader distribution and reporting to Congress with respect to ARB reports or significant findings therein. More specifically:

- Members of ARBs should be appointed in a manner that ensures an independent and objective review of incidents implicating potential accountability.

- The scope of review for ARBs should include all relevant, non-policy conduct of all personnel potentially involved in incidents, including senior officials.

- ARBs should be independent of outside influence up to the point of making recommendations.

- ARB proceedings should be conducted in a manner to ensure appropriate recordkeeping of evidence and support for findings and recommendations.

- If deciding officials disagree with recommendations of ARBs, require them to memorialize reasons in writing.

- All ARB reports or in exceptionally sensitive circumstances significant findings of ARB reports should be provided to Congress.

- ARB reports should presumptively be produced in an unclassified format, and wherever possible a version outlining core findings and issues unrelated to personnel actions should be made public.

- A clear mechanism should be developed to separate personnel accountability from "lessons learned" and general corrective actions following attacks.

- Within the State Department, coordination, oversight and support to an ARB should be provided by a secretariat or other office independent from the secretariats most likely to be reviewed during an ARB proceeding.

*Recommendation:* For an ARB review, the State Department must affirmatively search for all relevant records, including archived records and records of senior leaders.

*Recommendation:* The ARB implementing statute should be amended to allow an assessment of personnel failures not rising to the level of a "breach of duty."

*Recommendation:* Relevant Executive Branch agencies should consider and develop an appropriate long-term framework to provide for appropriate survivor benefits to the families of Americans killed in the line of duty in response to issues identified in the aftermath of the Benghazi attack.

*Recommendation:* Family members of Americans killed in the line of duty should have a central liaison in Departments and agencies where one does not already exist. Such liaisons should be expressly chartered and empowered to act as advocates for family members in—resolving or explaining benefits issues, and providing as much information as possible (including specific information on request) sought by family members. Where classification issues exist, Departments and agencies should consider providing limited security clearances regarding relevant information pertaining to the fate of family members.

## Events Leading to the Terrorist Attacks in Benghazi

*Recommendation:* The Executive Branch should provide Congress with a clear statement of intentions, rationale, plan and strategy (including objectives, contemplated method of execution, and contemplated completion strategy) when entering into major new overseas engagements. Such a statement should also state contemplated results and potential consequences of major initiatives.

*Recommendation:* No facility shall remain in an unofficial status for more than 180 days without the express and direct approval of the Secretary of State.

*Recommendation:* The State Department should comply with the requirements of the Overseas Security Protection Board and the standards provided for in the Secure Embassy Construction and Counterterrorism Act for all premises/facilities occupied for more than 30 days, whether official or unofficial.

*Recommendation:* The State Department should identify a specific funding source for immediate security upgrades for posts in high threat areas.

*Recommendation:* The Intelligence Community and the State Department should specifically recognize and improve collection of intelligence related to civilian "force protection" issues at facilities abroad, particularly with respect to high threat posts.

- This process should include more express recognition and prioritization of collection requirements with respect to threat warning and response within the National Intelligence Priorities Framework.

- This process should include more express coordination and integration with strategic and tactical force protection collection and analysis already conducted by Defense Intelligence Agency and other military intelligence agencies.

## Compliance with Congressional Investigations

*Recommendation:* House and Senate rules should be amended to provide for mandatory reductions in appropriations to the salaries of federal officials held in contempt of Congress.

*Recommendation:* The criminal contempt statute should be amended to require the appointment of a special counsel to handle criminal contempt proceedings upon the certification of a contempt citation against an Executive Branch official by the House or Senate.

*Recommendation:* Expedited procedures for the civil enforcement of congressional subpoenas should be enacted to provide timely judicial resolution of disputes.

*Recommendation:* Agencies seeking to control public dissemination of information provided to Congress should make express classification determinations with respect to documents and materials provided to congressional oversight committees in accordance with relevant laws and Executive Orders.

*Recommendation:* The House should amend its rules to authorize all committees to take depositions.

*Recommendation:* The House should amend its rules to require committees to establish oversight subcommittees.

*Recommendation:* Congress should consider strengthening enforcement authorities and penalties under the Federal Records Act related to the use of non-official email accounts and non-official file-hosting services for official purposes.

# ADDITIONAL VIEWS OF REPRESENTATIVES JIM JORDAN AND MIKE POMPEO

# SUMMARY OF CONCLUSIONS

## I. The First Victim of War is Truth: The administration misled the public about the events in Benghazi

Officials at the State Department, including Secretary Clinton, learned almost in real time that the attack in Benghazi was a terrorist attack. With the presidential election just 56 days away, rather than tell the American people the truth and increase the risk of losing an election, the administration told one story privately and a different story publicly. They publicly blamed the deaths on a video-inspired protest they knew had never occurred.

## II. Last Clear Chance: Security in Benghazi was woefully inadequate and Secretary Clinton failed to lead

The State Department has many posts but Libya and Benghazi were different. After Qhaddafi, the U.S. knew that we could not count on host nation security in a country where militias held significant power. The American people expect that when the government sends our representatives into such dangerous places they receive adequate protection. Secretary Clinton paid special attention to Libya. She sent Ambassador Stevens there. Yet, in August 2012, she missed the last, clear chance to protect her people.

## III. Failure of Will: America did not move heaven and earth to rescue our people

The American people expect their government to make every effort to help those we put in harm's way when they find themselves in trouble. The U.S. military never sent assets to help rescue those fighting in Benghazi and never made it into Libya with personnel during the attack. And, contrary to the administration's claim that it could not have landed in Benghazi in time to help, the administration never directed men or machines into Benghazi.

## IV. Justice Denied: The administration broke its promise to bring the terrorists to justice

After the attacks, President Obama promised "justice will be done." There is no doubt our nation can make good on that commitment. Yet, almost four years later, only one of the terrorists has been captured and brought to the United States to face criminal charges. Even that terrorist will not receive the full measure of justice after the administration chose not to seek the death penalty. The American people are owed an explanation.

## V. Unanswered Questions: The administration did not cooperate with the investigation

Despite its claims, we saw no evidence that the administration held a sincere interest in helping the Committee find the truth about Benghazi. There is a time for politics and a time to set politics aside. A national tragedy is one of those times when as a nation we should join together to find the truth. That did not happen here. So while the investigation uncovered new information, we nonetheless end the Committee's investigation without many of the facts, especially those involving the President and the White House, we were chartered to obtain.

# INTRODUCTION

*Yet tonight, we take comfort in knowing
that the tide of war is receding.*

Barack Obama
President of the United States [1]

The writer F. Scott Fitzgerald once observed, "Show me a hero and I will write you a tragedy." The September 11, 2012 Benghazi attack showed America not one but many heroes—among them Ambassador Christopher Stevens, Tyrone Woods, Sean Smith, and Glen Doherty. The story of Benghazi is their tragic story—which ultimately is the story of four deaths that never should have happened. America owes its people—especially those that work to advance our interests and the interests of freedom around the world—its utmost protection. We failed those Americans in Benghazi.

This is not only the tragic story of two men who died trying to bring freedom to the people of a foreign nation and two others who died trying to save them. It is also the story of a State Department seemingly more concerned with politics and Secretary Clinton's legacy than with protecting its people in Benghazi. It is the story of how the best military in the world never reached Benghazi with men or machines, leaving fellow Americans to fight, and die, alone. And it is the story of an administration so focused on the next election that it lost sight of its duty to tell the American people the truth about what had happened that night.

For the men on the ground in Benghazi, the terrorist attack began at 9:42 p.m. and the threat continued for hours until the planes carrying them and the bodies of the four murdered Americans left Benghazi. For the terrorists the attack was also continuous. It was a plan executed in multiple phases that began at the State facility. It continued when the terrorists ambushed the Americans *en route* to the Annex. The attack continued with multiple assaults on the Annex culminating with deadly mortar fire. According to the Department of Justice, the mission was willful, deliberate, malicious, and premeditated—a coordinated assault aimed at killing or kidnapping America's ambassador.[2]

Those in Washington decided that once the initial attack at the State compound had ended and our men moved to the Annex, the enemy had retreated as well. For those fighting for their lives in Benghazi that night, however, it was one long battle for survival. But the terrorists did not retreat. This view from Washington that the fight had ended is a lapse in judgment that may well haunt our nation for years to come. At the same time Secretary Clinton appears to have concluded that the attack was over, the men on the ground knew better.[3] In the end, two men died from smoke inhala-

[1] President Barack Obama, Remarks by the President on the Way Forward in Afghanistan (June 22, 2011), https://www.whitehouse.gov/the-press-office/2011/06/22/remarks-president-way-forward-afghanistan.

[2] *See United States v. Ahmed Salim Faraj Abu Khatallah,* No. 14–CR–00141 (D.D.C filed Oct. 14, 2014), Indictment at 6, (hereafter "Khatallah Indictment").

[3] During her testimony before the Committee Secretary Clinton testified, *"We knew that the attack was over.* We knew that our diplomatic security team had to evacuate from the compound to the CIA annex, and we were in a frantic search to find Ambassador Stevens." *Hearing*

tion at the State Department's compound during an initial attack involving dozens of extremists. Two more died from mortar fire at the end of a continuous, hours-long siege by approximately a hundred heavily armed and highly trained fighters at the CIA Annex.

Yet, beyond those basic facts other important questions required answers:

- Why were diplomats stationed in Benghazi in the first place and, more importantly, why did they stay as it became more and more dangerous?

- Why did the State Department ignore multiple requests for help from the team in Benghazi, leaving them to fend for themselves in a facility that was no match for a well-organized assault?

- Why did the U.S. military do almost nothing to help and why did it take them so long to arrive in Libya and *never prepare assets* to arrive in Benghazi?

- Why did the administration mislead the American people about the nature and cause of the attack?

- Why, now almost four years later, has only one of the dozens of terrorists who murdered four of our countrymen faced American justice?

Our Democrat committee colleagues suggest all questions about Benghazi have already been asked and answered by earlier congressional investigations and the State Department's Accountability Review Board. While we recognize the contributions some of those other investigations made to our understanding of Benghazi, the questions above and other questions remained, both in our minds and in the minds of many Americans.

We had a duty to seek the entire truth. If we learned nothing new, we would be the first to admit it—and the time and resources devoted would have amounted to a small price to pay to close this chapter once and for all. Yet, our confidence grew that there was more to be learned even as the administration stonewalled at virtually every turn. Our confidence grew even more with each new revelation including the revelation of Secretary Clinton's unprecedented and exclusive use of a private e-mail account and server.

Unfortunately, the administration's efforts to impede the investigation succeeded, at least in part. The White House in particular left large holes in the investigation by denying the Committee access to documents and witnesses—often hiding behind vague notions of "important and longstanding institutional interests of the

---

4 *Before the Select Committee on the Events Surrounding the 2012 Terrorist Attack in Benghazi,* 114th Cong. (2015) (testimony of Hillary Rodham Clinton, Sec'y of State) (emphasis added). Secretary Clinton's certainty about the attack contrasts with the view of those on the ground, where one of our men described the situation after arriving at the Annex, "everybody takes a position to support what we have in store, which we don't know what it is at this point. We are not sure. *We don't know if the fight is over or if it is going to be longer.*" Transcript of Deposition of DS Agent #3 before Comm. on Oversight and Government Reform, 113th Cong. 164 (emphasis added) (on file with the Committee).

Executive Branch."[4] And so the Committee ended its work without having spoken to anyone in the White House Situation Room that night. Nor did we receive all email communication between White House staffers concerning the attack—all off limits to Congress according to White House lawyers. Compounding the problem, the White House refused to identify any of the documents it had withheld. If the administration had a sincere interest in cooperating with the Committee's investigation, as it stated repeatedly, we saw no real evidence of it.

And so we leave the Committee much the same way we joined it—knowing that Congress and the American people did not get every relevant fact from this administration. Nevertheless, we did learn more. Much more.

Most significantly, the administration consistently blamed flawed information from the U.S. Intelligence Community, primarily the Central Intelligence Agency (CIA), for its public misstatements about Benghazi—with the President, Secretary Clinton, Ambassador Rice, and others blaming a video-inspired protest that had never taken place in Benghazi.[5] But flawed intelligence is no excuse for officials who knew better, and we now know that key leaders did. Secretary Clinton in particular learned quickly that Benghazi amounted to an organized terrorist attack, not a spontaneous demonstration turned violent. Yet, Secretary Clinton and the administration told one story privately—that Benghazi was a terrorist attack—and told another story publicly—blaming a video-inspired protest. The misleading public statements led concerned State Department staffers to describe Ambassador Rice as "off the reservation" and another to add the "[White House was] very worried about the politics."[6] A national tragedy, however, is not a time for politics; it is a time to set politics aside and do one's duty.

We also learned that by September 11, 2012 the security situation in Benghazi had deteriorated significantly. Months before the attack one State Department diplomatic security agent viewed the situation as a "suicide mission" where "there was a very good chance that everyone was going to die."[7] Yet, the facility remained open—even as other countries and organizations departed. And yet no one could give a satisfactory explanation for why the State Department remained. While we may never know for certain exactly why the State Department left Benghazi open in the face of such dangerous conditions, the most plausible answer is troubling. Secretary Clinton pushed for the U.S. to intervene in Libya, which at the time represented one of her signature achievements. To leave Benghazi would have been viewed as her failure and prompted unwelcome scrutiny of her choices. But when faced with a dire situation in Libya, Secretary Clinton had an obligation to act. And she

---

[4] Letter from W. Neil Eggleston, White House Counsel, to Rep. Trey Gowdy, Chairman, Select Committee on the Events Surrounding the 2012 Terrorist Attack in Benghazi ("the Committee") (Jan. 23, 2015) (on file with the Committee).

[5] For example, the report issued by the House Permanent Select Committee on Intelligence concluded that "Ambassador Rice's September 16 public statements about the existence of a protest, as well as some of the underlying intelligence reports, proved to be inaccurate." *See* INVESTIGATIVE REPORT ON THE TERRORIST ATTACKS ON U.S. FACILITIES IN BENGHAZI, LIBYA, SEPTEMBER 11–12, 2012 (report by Chm. Rogers and Ranking Member Ruppersberger, Members, H. Perm. Select Comm. on Intel.) (Comm. Print 2014).

[6] E-mail from Senior Advisor for Strategic Communications, State Dep't, Near Eastern Affairs Bureau to various (Sept. 17, 2012) (on file with the Committee, C05580618).

[7] Transcript of Interview of DS Agent #10 at 22 (on file with the Committee).

had a clear chance to do so in August 2012 when presented with the facts in a memo from Assistant Secretary Beth Jones that painted a bleak picture of conditions in Libya. Yet, she failed to lead.

Finally, we learned troubling new details about the government's military response to the attack. Until now the administration has led us to believe the military did not have assets—men or machines—close enough or ready enough to arrive in Benghazi in time to save lives. As one earlier committee put it, "given their location and readiness status it was not possible to dispatch armed aircraft before survivors left Benghazi."[8] The first asset to arrive in Libya—a Marine "FAST" platoon—did not arrive until nearly 24 hours after the attack began. What is troubling is that the administration never set in motion a plan to go to Benghazi in the first place. It is one thing to try and fail; it is yet another not to try at all. In the end, the administration did not move heaven and earth to help our people in Benghazi, as Americans would expect. The contrast between the heroic actions taken in Benghazi and the inaction in Washington—highlights the failure.

In 2011, the President boasted that "[w]ithout putting a single U.S. service member on the ground, we achieved our objectives [in Libya.]"[9] With parts of Libya now terrorist safe havens, it is difficult not to look back on that claim and the claim "the tide of war was receding" as little more than wishful thinking. The same wishful thinking may have also influenced decisions the administration made in Libya and set the background against which four Americans died. Yet, wishes are no match for facts—nor the basis for a sound foreign policy. The facts remain and the tide of war goes in and out. And it was still rising in Libya in September 2012 as Secretary Clinton and the President stood idle.

What follows are the views of two members of this Committee. We choose to add these additional views not to question the Committee's full report. Rather, we write separately to highlight those facts and conclusions uncovered by our investigation that we consider most important to a full understanding of the tragedy that is Benghazi.

---

[8] Staff of H. Armed Services Comm., 113th Cong., Majority Interim Report: Benghazi Investigation Update (Comm. Print 2014) at 19.

[9] See Press Release, Barack Obama, President of the United States, Remarks by the President on the Death of Muammar Qaddafi (Oct. 20, 2011), https://www.whitehouse.gov/the-press-office/2011/10/20/remarks-president-death-muammar-qaddafi.

## I. The First Casualty of War Is Truth: How the administration misled the public about the Benghazi attack

*Was it because of a protest? Or was it because of guys out for a walk one night and decided they would go kill some Americans? What difference at this point does it make?*

Hillary Rodham Clinton
Secretary of State [10]

It began the night of September 11, 2012 and continued for nearly two weeks after. The administration made statements about Benghazi that led the public to believe the attack began spontaneously as a protest over an anti-Islamic video circulating on the Internet. It was, they said, the same video that had sparked demonstrations in Cairo earlier that day. The first statement came from Secretary Clinton. More would follow, from the President, from Ambassador Rice, and from others. Each seemed to blame the murders on a video and a protest.

Yet, in truth, no protest had occurred in Benghazi that night. And even today no clear link between the video and the attack exists. In fact, in the criminal indictment against Ahmed Salim Faraj Abu Khatallah (hereafter "Abu Khatallah")—the only person prosecuted thus far for taking part in the attack—the government does not mention the video or a protest. Rather, it blames the attack on revenge for U.S. intelligence collection efforts in the area—a far different explanation than America received in the immediate aftermath of the attack.[11]

Did the administration mislead the public because it worried a terrorist attack might affect the upcoming election? Or did it simply rely on flawed and changing information from the U.S. Intelligence Community as the administration has maintained? Some critics may say the question alone is evidence of the Committee's alleged partisan agenda. Others may defend the misstatements as little more than election-year "spin"—something for which the public might fault both parties.

For her part, Secretary Clinton simply dismissed the issue—"at this point, what difference does it make?"—in her now famous exchange with Senator Johnson. Yet, the truth is always important. It is especially so during times when we as a nation must face a crisis—and mourn one—together and to learn from it. Instead of sharing that truth, the administration concealed it. And in doing so it misled the American people for political gain. When that happens, whether by Republicans or Democrats, it does, should, and always will make a difference.

---

[10] Benghazi: The Attacks and the Lessons Learned Before the S. Comm. on Foreign Affairs, 113th Cong. at 28 (2013) (testimony of Hillary Rodham Clinton, Sec'y of State), http://www.cnn.com/TRANSCRIPTS/1301/23/se.01.html). Oddly, even well after the fact Secretary Clinton continues the false narrative by leaving out of her answer any reference to it having been a planned terrorist attack.

The statement that begins this section—the first casualty of war is truth—is typically attributed to the late California Senator Hiram Johnson (1866–1945), albeit in a slightly different form.

[11] *See* Khatallah Indictment at 6.

## A. 56 DAYS

The terrorist attack in Benghazi came during a critical time for the President. He faced an increasingly difficult re-election bid as polls showed his lead over Republican presidential nominee Mitt Romney narrowing. The President had few clear successes to highlight from his first term and the economy had yet to recover fully. The political landscape left little room for error—or bad news.

If one bright spot existed in the President's record, nearly four years in office had passed without a significant terrorist incident at home or abroad and killing Osama bin Laden represented an important accomplishment—one the President and his team trumpeted often.[12] As Vice President Biden put it just days before the attack, "Osama bin Laden is dead, and General Motors is alive." It was a powerful political argument, but the tide of war continued to roll in.

September 11, 2012 threatened to take the President's national security argument away. The Romney campaign and others seized on the attack as evidence of a failed policy and criticized the administration's seeming refusal to call the attackers terrorists. To many, Benghazi represented a potential October surprise that could impact the President's re-election bid.[13] As one publication put it, "with the American Presidential election only two months away, the murder of four American diplomats could be a game changer so far as Mr. Obama's re-election prospects are concerned."[14]

The President had a political problem. And his advisors saw it immediately. In fact, the election entered the discussion before the attack even ended. Sometime before 10:35 p.m. on the night of September 11, 2012, Victoria Nuland, the State Department's spokesperson, sent an email to two other high level Clinton aides, Jacob Sullivan and Phillipe Reines:

> ### *This is what Ben [Rhodes] was talking about.*
>
> "I'm outraged by the attacks on American diplomatic missions in Libya and Egypt and by the death of an American consulate worker in Benghazi. It's disgraceful that the Obama Administration's first response was not to condemn

---

[12] For example, just 5 days before the attack, the President in his nationally-televised speech said the following about the war on terror:

> In a world of new threats and new challenges, you can choose leadership that has been tested and proven. Four years ago I promised to end the war in Iraq. We did. I promised to refocus on the terrorists who actually attacked us on 9/11, and we have. We've blunted the Taliban's momentum in Afghanistan, and in 2014, our longest war will be over. A new tower rises above the New York skyline, **al-Qaeda is on the path to defeat, and Osama bin Laden is dead.**

President Barack Obama, Speech to Democratic National Convention (Sept. 6, 2012) (emphasis added), http://www.npr.org/2012/09/06/160713941/transcript-president-obamas-convention-speech).

[13] *See,* e.g., Craig Unger, *GOP's October Surprise? Source reveals "Jimmy Carter Strategy" to make Obama Seem weak on defense in campaign's final month,* Salon (Oct. 1, 2012), http://www.salon.com/2012/10/01/gops_october_surprise/.

[14] Con Coughlin, *The murder of the US ambassador to Libya is a wake-up call for Obama,* THE TELEGRAPH, (Sept. 12, 2012).

attacks on our diplomatic missions, but to sympathize with those who waged the attacks.—Mitt Romney"[15]

The "Ben" in Nuland's email was Benjamin Rhodes, the White House National Security Council's Deputy National Security Adviser for Strategic Communications and one of the President's top aides. The "this" was the accompanying "Tweet" issued from the Romney campaign attacking the administration's handling of the situation. In short, the national security crisis turned into a political problem almost immediately.

And so on this highly charged political stage—just 56 days before the presidential election—events forced the administration to make a choice about what to tell the American people: Tell the truth that heavily armed terrorists had killed one American and possibly kidnapped a second—and increase the risk of losing the election. Say we do not know what happened. Or blame a video-inspired protest by tying Benghazi to what had occurred earlier in the day in Cairo. The administration chose the third, a statement with the least factual support but that would help the most politically.[16]

While the attack loomed largest, and most immediately, for the President and his reelection bid, he was not alone in having a choice to make—or with something to lose. Secretary Clinton would have seen her reputation and legacy—and possibly 2016 election prospects—tied to what had just occurred in Benghazi as well.

Secretary Clinton was the administration's chief proponent of U.S. Libya policy and pushed for the President to join the NATO coalition to topple Qhaddafi. According to then-Secretary of Defense Robert Gates, who opposed intervention, others who pushed to intervene—including Ambassador Rice and Ben Rhodes—are the same people who later worked to mislead the public about the attack.[17]

While that effort succeeded and Qhaddafi is gone, most now agree that the Libya intervention failed, in large part because of inadequate planning for a post-Qhaddafi Libya. As former Secretary of Defense Robert Gates said later, the administration was "playing it by ear" after Qhaddafi's fall.[18] So instead of a burgeoning democracy growing from the Arab Spring, we now have a terrorist safe haven growing in its place.

Secretary Clinton rarely mentions Libya now. Yet, early on her advisors pointed to Qhaddafi's ouster and her role as a historic foreign policy success. In August 2011, Secretary Clinton's Deputy Chief of Staff and Director of Policy Jacob Sullivan described her role as no less than the "leadership/ownership/stewardship of this country's Libya policy from start to finish" and that she was "in-

---

[15] E-mail from Victoria Nuland, State Dep't Spokesperson, to Jacob Sullivan, State Dep't Deputy Chief of Staff and Phillipe Reines, State Dep't Deputy Assistant Secretary for Communications (Sept. 11, 2012) (emphasis added) (on file with the Committee, C05412104).

[16] When asked on the night of the attack whether he knew "of any connection between what had occurred in Cairo and what had occurred in Benghazi," Rhodes testified, "I did not, other than the fact that both events took place in proximity to one another." *See* Transcript of Interview of Benjamin Rhodes, Deputy National Security Advisor for Strategic Communications, White House National Security Council at 13 (Feb. 2, 2016) (on file with the Committee).

[17] ROBERT F. GATES, DUTY 518 (2014).

[18] Nancy A. Youssef, *Hillary's Libya Post-War Plan was "Play It by Ear," Gates Says,* (Oct. 20, 2015, 8:00 p.m.), http://www.thedailybeast.com/articles/2015/10/20/hillary-s-libya-post-war-plan-was-play-it-by-ear-gates-says.html.

strumental in securing the authorization, building the coalition, and tightening the noose around Qadhafi and his regime." [19]

Secretary Clinton's longtime friend and advisor Sidney Blumenthal described the success in even loftier terms:

> First, brava! This is a historic moment and you will be credited for realizing it.
>
> When Qaddafi himself is finally removed, you should of course make a public statement before the cameras wherever you are, even in the driveway of your vacation house. You must go on camera. You must establish yourself in the historical record at this moment.
>
> The most important phrase is: "successful strategy."
>
> \*     \*     \*
>
> Then you can *say whatever on future policy*—but only after asserting the historic success and explaining the reasons why.
>
> This is a very big moment historically and for you. History will tell your part in it. You are vindicated. But don't wait, help *Clio* now. [20]

It is too soon to know how *Clio*—the goddess of history—will ultimately treat Secretary Clinton's push to intervene in Libya. What we do know is that when given a chance to tell the truth to the American people, she did the opposite. It began at 10:08 p.m. in Washington on the night of the murders—before the attack had even ended.

### B. OUT OF THE FOG: TELLING ONE STORY PRIVATELY AND ANOTHER STORY PUBLICLY

Some blame the "fog of war" for the administration's misstatements about Benghazi. While it is true officials in Washington did not have all the facts, the President, Secretary Clinton, and other senior leaders had enough information to conclude almost immediately that Benghazi and Cairo were very different. Benghazi was a terrorist attack and Cairo a large protest that had been publicized in advance on social media and that the State Department prepared for and expected. [21]

The information the President, Secretary Clinton, and other senior leaders had included detailed information about the sophisticated nature of the attack, the weapons used, the complexity of the attack, and the hours-long duration of the siege that spanned two locations. For example, one State Department official was told that night by a witness in Benghazi that the attackers who fired the

---

[19] E-mail from Jacob Sullivan to Cheryl Mills, State Dep't Chief of Staff (Aug. 21, 2011) (on file with the Committee, SCB0075905).

[20] E-mail from Sidney Blumenthal to Hillary Rodham Clinton (Aug. 22, 2011) (emphasis added) (as we now know and as Secretary Gates has pointed, out the day after Qhaddafi fell called for far more planning than "whatever") (on file with the Committee, BLU–094).

[21] *See* Transcript of Press Conference, Statement of Victoria Nuland, State Dep't Spokesperson (Sept. 17, 2012) (on file with the Committee, C05394583).

mortar launcher had significant training and were "not just persons off the street lobbing in mortars."[22]

Significantly, the information known in Washington included reports from a number of eye witnesses on the ground in Benghazi—often in near real time—who remained in almost constant contact with officials in Washington during the attack. None of those eye witnesses mentioned a protest or the video.

One of those witnesses saw the attack begin in real time while watching the Benghazi compound's security monitors inside the facility's tactical operations center. Up to that point, no protests had occurred and all was calm. When asked later about whether a protest had occurred, he said, "No. There was nothing out there up until, well, up until there was. I had been out of the gate at 8:30 that night. We had had personnel leaving the compound, and they drove away from our compound and didn't report anything, and I spoke with them subsequently, there was nothing out there."[23] That same witness updated officials in Washington every 15 to 30 minutes throughout the night—giving the State Department virtually a front row seat to the attack.[24]

The Deputy Chief of Mission in Libya, Gregory Hicks, who was in Tripoli at the time of the attack, spoke to Ambassador Stevens last. As terrorists swarmed the Benghazi compound, Ambassador Stevens managed to call Hicks and said, simply, "Greg, we are under attack."[25] No mention of a protest. No mention of the video. Hicks relayed this same information to Acting Assistant Secretary for Near Eastern Affairs ("NEA") Beth Jones[26] and also spoke to Secretary Clinton and other top State Department officials that night.[27] When asked later whether he would have expected Ambassador Stevens and the security officers in Benghazi to report a protest if it had occurred, Hicks said:

> ***Absolutely,*** I mean, we're talking about both security officers who know their trade, even though they are brand new, and one of the finest political officers in the history of the Foreign Service. You know, ***for there to have been a demonstration on Chris Stevens' front door and him not to have reported it is unbelievable.*** And secondly, if he had reported it, he would have been out the back door within minutes of any demonstration appearing

[22] Transcript of Interview of Charlene Lamb, Assistant Sec'y of State for Diplomatic Security for International Programs at 46–47 (Jan. 7, 2016).

[23] Transcript of Deposition of DS Agent #3 before House Comm. on Oversight and Government Reform at 231 (Oct. 8, 2013) (on file with the Committee).

[24] *Id.* at 165. At approximately 4:38 p.m. the State Dep't Operations Center appears to have set up a direct line to Benghazi. *See* E-mail to Jacob Sullivan, Cheryl Mills, and Secretary Clinton's Executive Assistant (Sept. 11, 2012) (on file with the Committee, C05561866).

[25] Transcript of Interview of Gregory Hicks, Deputy in Charge of Mission in Libya before H. Comm. on Oversight and Government Reform at 18 (Apr. 11, 2013).

[26] Transcript of Interview of Beth Jones, Acting Assistant Secretary for Near Eastern Affairs before House Comm. on Oversight and Government Reform at 38–39 (July 11, 2013) ("He said . . . Greg Hicks has called. Ambassador Stevens is in Benghazi. He called and said, 'We're under attack.'").

[27] *See* Dep't of State, Watch Log, Operations Center (Sept. 11, 2012) (showing call at 7:05 p.m. between Hicks and Secretary Clinton, Deputy Secretary Thomas Nides, Under Secretary Patrick Kennedy, Under Secretary Wendy Sherman, Chief of Staff Cheryl Mills, Deputy Chief of Staff and Director Jacob Sullivan, Spokesperson Victoria Nuland, and Acting Assistant Secretary for Near Eastern Affairs Beth Jones (on file with the Committee, C05872462).

anywhere near that facility. And there was a back gate to the facility, and, you know, it worked.[28]

Days later, one member of the State Department's Diplomatic Security Command Center on duty the night of the attack was asked by a colleague whether a protest had been reported prior to the attack. His response left little doubt: "Zip, nothing nada."[29] That same person in a "Terrorism Event Notification" emailed out the morning of September 12, 2012 described the event just as clearly: "It was a full on attack against our compound in Benghazi."[30] Again, no mention of a protest. No mention of the video.

All of the information coming into the State Department that night and in the days that followed from the witnesses pointed to a terrorist attack. There is no evidence that any of the accounts blamed a video-inspired protest or, in fact, any protest at all. Moreover, this attack did not occur in a vacuum. Rather, it came toward the end—not the beginning—of a long list of terrorist and other violence aimed at the U.S. and other interests in Libya and Benghazi—a history of violence well known to senior State Department officials.

Officials also recognized very quickly the differences between what had occurred in Cairo in response to the video and what occurred in Benghazi. As one official put it the night of the attack, "We can confirm that our office in Benghazi, Libya has been *attacked by a group of militants* [and] [i]n *Cairo,* we can confirm that Egyptian police have now removed the *demonstrators. . . .*"[31] That line between Benghazi and Cairo, however, would soon be blurred and then erased completely.

Notwithstanding clear evidence of a terrorist attack in Benghazi, Secretary Clinton began to connect Cairo and Benghazi in the public's mind almost immediately even as she and others admitted privately the two were unrelated. It began at 10:08 p.m. on the night of the attack—before the attack had even ended—with Secretary Clinton's statement condemning the attack. Other statements would follow as well that week. As shown in the following timeline of administration statements, the administration told two different stories, one publicly that connected the attack to the video and protests in Cairo and another privately that recognized it was a terrorist attack.

### C. PUBLIC VS. PRIVATE TIMELINE

**9/11—Public Statements**

*Secretary Clinton's 10:08 p.m. Statement on the Attack in Benghazi:*

---

[28] Transcript of Interview of Gregory Hicks before H. Comm. on Oversight and Government Reform at 81–82 (emphasis added) (on file with the Committee).

[29] E-mail from DS Agent #30 to DS Agent (Sept. 18, 2012) (on file with the Committee, C05390678).

[30] E-mail from DS Agent #30 to various (Sept. 12, 2012) (on file with the Committee, C05389586)

[31] E-mail from Victoria Nuland, State Dep't Spokesperson to Jacob Sullivan, Patrick Kennedy, Patrick Ventrell, Bernadette Meehan, National Security Council, Assistant Press Secretary (Sept. 11, 2012) (on file with the Committee, SCB000471).

"I condemn in the strongest terms the attack on our mission in Benghazi today. * * * Some have sought to justify this vicious behavior as a response to inflammatory material posted on the Internet." [32]

### 9/11—Private Statements

***Secretary Clinton's Call Sheet for call with President of Libya Mohammed al Magariaf at 6:49 p.m.:***

Under heading Purpose of Call" notes that "Secretary should urge Mr. Magariaf to respond urgently to the attack against the U.S. Mission Benghazi, and security threats against U.S. Embassy Tripoli." No mention of a protest or video. [33]

***Summary of Call between Secretary Clinton and President Magariaf:***

"[O]ur diplomatic mission was attacked[.] . . . [T]here is a gun battle ongoing, which I understand Ansar as-Sharia [sic] is claiming responsibility for." [34] No mention of protest or video.

***Secretary Clinton's E-mail to daughter at 11:23 p.m.:***

"Two of our officers were killed in Benghazi by an Al Queda-like [sic] group[.]" [35]

### 9/12—Public Statements

***Secretary Clinton's Remarks on the Deaths of American Personnel in Benghazi, Libya morning of September 12, 2012:***

"We are working to determine the precise motivations and methods of those who carried out this assault. Some have sought to justify this vicious behavior, along with the protest that took place at our Embassy in Cairo yesterday, as a response to inflammatory material posted on the internet." [36]

### 9/12—Private Statements

***Summary of Discussion between Acting Assistant Secretary Beth Jones and Libyan Ambassador Aujali at 9:45 a.m.:***

"I told him that the group that conducted the attacks—Ansar Al Sharia—is affiliated with Islamic extremists." [37]

***Jacob Sullivan in e-mail to embassy in Kabul, Afghanistan:***

---

[32] Press Statement, Hillary Rodham Clinton, Sec'y of State, Statement on the Attack in Benghazi (Sept. 11, 2012), http://www.state.gov/secretary/20092013clinton/rm/2012/09/197628.htm).

[33] See The Secretary's Call Sheet for Libyan General National Congress President Mohammed al Magariaf (Sept. 11, 2012) (on file with the Committee, C05580497).

[34] Notes of Secretary Clinton's Call with Mohammed al Magariaf (Sept. 11, 2012) (on file with the Committee, C05561906).

[35] E-mail from Hillary Rodham Clinton to "Diane Reynolds" (Sept. 11, 2012) (on file with the Committee, C05794191).

[36] Hillary Rodham Clinton, Sec'y of State, Remarks on the Deaths of American Personnel in Benghazi, Libya (Sept. 12, 2012), http://www.state.gov/secretary/20092013clinton/rm/2012/09/197654.htm).

[37] See E-mail to Victoria Nuland, Deputy Secretary William Burns, Wendy Sherman, Jacob Sullivan, Patrick Kennedy, Cheryl Mills, and others (Sept. 12, 2012) (on file with the Committee, C05391027).

"There was not really violence in Egypt [and] *we are not saying that the violence in Libya erupted 'over inflammatory videos.'"* [38]

### Secretary Clinton's Statements to Egyptian Prime Minister Kandil at 3:04 p.m.:

"*We know* that the attack in Libya had *nothing to do with the film.* It was a planned attack—not a protest. . . . Based on the information we saw today we believe the group that claimed responsibility for this was affiliated with al-Qaeda." [39]

### Under Secretary Patrick Kennedy to congressional staff briefing:

When asked whether "this [was] an attack under the cover of a protest" Kennedy said, "No the attack was a direct breaching attack." More to the point, he was then asked whether "we believe [this was] coordinated with [the] Cairo [protests] to which Kennedy responded, "Attack in Cairo was a demonstration. There were no weapons shown or used. A few cans of spray paint." [40]

## 9/13—Public Statements

### Secretary Clinton's Morocco Remarks:

"I also want to take a moment *to address the video circulating on the Internet that has led to these protests in a number of countries.* * * *

To us, to me personally, this video is disgusting and reprehensible. It appears to have a deeply cynical purpose: to denigrate a great religion and to provoke rage. But as I said yesterday, there is no justification, none at all, for responding to this video with violence.

\*   \*   \*

Violence, we believe, has no place in religion and is no way to honor religion. Islam, like other religions, respects the fundamental dignity of human beings, and it is a violation of that fundamental dignity to wage attacks on innocents. *As long as there are those who are willing to shed blood and take innocent life in the name of God, the world will never know a true and lasting peace. It is especially wrong for violence to be directed against diplomatic missions.* . . .

\*   \*   \*

I wanted to begin with this statement, because, as our Moroccan friends and all of you know, this has been a difficult week at the State Department. I very much appreciate, Minister, the condolences your government expressed to our Embassy in Rabat. *And even though that tragedy happened far away in Benghazi,*

---

[38] E-mail from Jacob Sullivan to Benjamin Rhodes and others (Sept.12, 2012) (emphasis added) (on file with the Committee, SCB0066195).

[39] Notes of Secretary Clinton's Call with Egyptian Prime Minister Hesham Kandil (Sept. 11, 2012) (emphasis added) (on file with the Committee, C05561911).

[40] E-mail from Joy E. Drucker to various (Sept. 13, 2012) (forwarding notes from call between Patrick Kennedy and congressional staff that began at 6:30 p.m. September 12, 2012) (on file with the Committee, C05580110).

*we found a reminder of the deep bounds that connect Morocco to the United States."* [41]

### 9/13—Private Statements

***Summary of call between State Department Deputy Secretary Thomas Nides and Egyptian ambassador to U.S.:***

"Nides said he understood the difference between ***the targeted attack in Libya*** and the way the protest escalated in Egypt." [42]

### 9/14—Public Statements

***White House Spokesman Jay Carney during press conference answering question about Benghazi:***

"We have no information to suggest that it was a preplanned attack. The unrest we've seen around the region has been in reaction to a video that Muslims, many Muslims find offensive. And while the violence is reprehensible and unjustified, it is not a reaction to the 9/11 anniversary that we know of, or to U.S. policy." [43]

***E-mail from White House Advisor Benjamin Rhodes:***

Under heading "Goals" he wrote "To underscore that these protests are rooted in an Internet video, and not a broader failure of policy[.]" [44]

***Return of remains ceremony statement to father of Tyrone Woods recorded in diary:***

"I gave Hillary a hug and shook her hand, and she said we are going to have the filmmaker arrested who was responsible for the death of my son." [45]

***Return of remains ceremony statement to mother of Sean Smith:***

"We were nose-to-nose at the coffin ceremony. She told me it was the fault of the video. I said 'are you sure?' She says 'yes, that's what it was . . . it was the video.'" [46]

### 9/14—Private Statements

***E-mail from State Department press officer in embassy in Tripoli, Libya:***

"Colleagues, I mentioned to Andy this morning, and want to share with all of you, our view at Embassy Tripoli that we must be cautious in our local messaging with regard to the inflammatory film trailer, adapting it to Libyan conditions. . . .

---

[41] Hillary Rodham Clinton, Sec'y of State, *Remarks at Opening Plenary of the United States–Morocco Strategic Dialogue Washington, D.C. Wednesday, September 13, 2012,* http://www.state.gov/secretary/20092013clinton/rm/2012/09/197711.htm.

[42] E-mail from State Dep't Operations Officer to State Dep't Official (Sept. 13, 2012) (on file with the Committee, C05562242).

[43] Transcript of White House Press Conference, Jay Carney, White House Spokesperson (Sept. 14, 2012), https://www.whitehouse.gov/the-press-office/2012/09/14/press-briefing-press-secretary-jay-carney-9142012).

[44] E-mail, Benjamin Rhodes to David Plouffe, White House Political Advisor, Jay Carney, White House Spokesperson, Erin Pelton, aide to Amb. Susan Rice, and others (Sept. 14, 2012 at 8:09 p.m.) (on file with the Committee, C05415285).

[45] *See* Fox News Insider, *Father of Benghazi Victim Reveals Journal Entry Documenting Meeting With Hillary,* YOUTUBE (Jan. 13, 2016), http://www.youtube.com/watch?v=dMx0huMabos.

[46] *See* Fox Business, Benghazi Victim's Mom: Hillary Needs to Tell Me the Truth! (Mar. 10, 2016) (available here http://www.foxbusiness.com/features/2016/03/10/benghazi-victims-mom-hillary-needs-to-tell-me-truth.html).

Relatively few [Facebook comments and tweets] have even mentioned the inflammatory video. So if we post messaging about the video specifically, we may draw unwanted attention to it. ***And it is becoming increasingly clear that the series of events in Benghazi was much more terrorist attack than a protest which escalated into violence. It is our opinion that in our messaging, we want to distinguish, not conflate, the events in other countries with this well-planned attack by militant extremists.*** I have discussed this with Charge Hicks and he shares PAS's view." [47]

### 9/15—Public Statements

*President's Weekly Address titled "Carrying on the Work of Our Fallen Heroes" muddles Benghazi and protests in other countries:*

"This tragic attack takes place at a time of turmoil and protest in many different countries. I have made it clear that the United States has a profound respect for people of all faiths. We stand for religious freedom. And we reject the denigration of any religion—including Islam." [48]

#### 9/15—Private Statements

*Secretary Clinton's call with Prime Minister-Elect of Libya:*

Makes no mention of either a protest or the video. [49]

### 9/16—Public Statements

*Ambassador Rice on Fox News With Chris Wallace*

"But we don't see at this point signs this was a coordinated plan, premeditated attack." [50]

#### 9/16—Private Statements

*Excerpt from Embassy Tripoli Media Report September 16, 2012*

"[T]here is evidence that suggests that the second confrontation at the UM mission's safe house could not have happened without insider knowledge or some degree of organization. This goes against statements that the attacks were not carried out by a single group but by an angry multitude protesting[.]" [51]

### 9/17—Public Statements

*Excerpt from State Department Daily Press Briefing:*

---

[47] E-mail from Public Affairs Officer, U.S. Embassy Libya to Senior Advisor for Strategic Communications, Near Eastern Affairs Bureau, NEA-Libya Desk, Gregory Hicks, Deputy in Charge of Libya Mission, and others (Sept. 14, 2012 at 6:43 p.m.) (on file with the Committee, C05396788).

[48] Barack Obama, President of the United States, Weekly Address: Carrying on the Work of Our Fallen Heroes (Sept. 15, 2012), https://www.whitehouse.gov/the-press-office/2012/09/15/weekly-address-carrying-work-our-fallen-heroes.

[49] E-mail from State Dep't officer to S_CallNotes (Sept. 15, 2012) (notes of call between Secretary Clinton and Libyan Prime Minister-elect Abu Shagur) (on file with the Committee, C05561908).

[50] Transcript of Interview of Amb. Susan Rice on Fox News Sunday with Chris Wallace (Sept. 16, 2012).

[51] E-mail from Public Affairs Officer, U.S. Embassy Libya to Senior Advisor for Strategic Communications, Near Eastern Affairs Bureau, Senior Libyan Desk Officer, Near Eastern Affairs Bureau, and others (Sept. 16, 2012) (attacking Tripoli Media Report for Sept. 16, 2012) (on file with the Committee, C05396830).

"Ambassador Rice, in her comments on every network over the weekend, was very clear, very precise, about what our initial assessment of what happened is. . . . I don't have anything to give you beyond that."[52]

### 9/17—Private Statements

*Excerpt from e-mail discussion between members of NEA press office about what to say about attack:*

**NEA Press Officer Suggested the following language:**

"The *currently available information suggests the demonstrations in Benghazi* were spontaneously inspired by the protests of the US Embassy in Cairo and evolved into a direct assault[.]"

**Senior Libya Desk Officer, Near Eastern Affairs Bureau responding to suggested language:**

"I really hope this was revised. *I don't think we should go on the record on this.*"[53]

### 9/18—Public Statements

*Excerpt from White House Press Briefing by Press Secretary Jay Carney:*

. . . I would point you to what Ambassador Rice said and others have said about what we know thus far about the video and its influence *on the protests that occurred in Cairo, in Benghazi* and elsewhere."

### 9/18—Private Statements

*Deputy Director of CIA Michael Morell in written statement to House Permanent Select Committee on Intelligence:*

"The critically important point is that the analysts considered this a terrorist attack from the very beginning."[54]

*E-mail exchange between State Department security officers commenting on news article titled "White House sees no sign Libya attack premeditated":*

DS Agent #30: "Can you believe this?"

DS Agent: "Was there any rioting in Benghazi reported prior to the attack?"

DS Agent #30: "Zip, nothing nada"[55]

### 9/19—Public Statements

*From "ALDAC"—a worldwide cable—from Secretary Clinton to all U.S. Embassies drafted by Deputy Chief of Staff Jacob Sullivan:*

---

[52] State Dep't of State, Daily Press Briefing—September 17, 2012, Victoria Nuland, State Dep't Spokesperson, http://www.state.gov/r/pa/prs/dpb/2012/09/197821.htm.

[53] *See* E-mail from Senior Advisor for Strategic Communications, NEA to Spokesperson, NEA, Senior Libyan Desk Offier, NEA, Deputy Director, Office of Maghreb Affairs, NEA (Sept 17, 2012) (emphasis added) (on file with the Committee, C05580618).

[54] Michael Morell, Former Acting Director and Deputy Director of the CIA, Written Statement for the Record before the H. Perm. Select Comm. on Intel. (April 2, 2014).

[55] E-mail from DS Agent #30 to DS Agent (Sept. 18, 2012) (on file with the Committee, C05389586).

"Since September 11, 2012, there have been widespread protests and violence against U.S. and some other diplomatic posts across the Muslim world. ***The proximate cause of the violence was the release by individuals in the United States of the video*** trailer for a film that many Muslims find offensive. Diplomatic compounds have been breached in several countries including Libya, Egypt, Tunisia, and Yemen. ***In Benghazi, Libya four U.S. personnel were killed in the violence***[.]"[56]

The administration, including Secretary Clinton, knew that Benghazi was a terrorist attack—from witness accounts, from their understanding of the history of violence in Benghazi, and from the nature of the well-planned, complex attack. Yet, they led the public to believe the video and a protest were to blame in Benghazi.

### 9/20—Public Statements

***Excerpt from interview of the President on Univision Town Hall:***

In response to the question, "We have reports that the White House said today that the attacks in Libya were a terrorist attack. Do you have information indicating that it was Iran, or al-Qaeda was behind organizing the protests?" the President answered, "[W]e're still doing an investigation[.] . . . ***What we do know is that the natural protests that arose because of the outrage over the video*** were used as an excuse by extremists to see if they can also directly harm U.S. interests[.]"[57]

Secretary Clinton has since blamed her statements on changing information received from U.S. intelligence reports. She and others have claimed that the 10:08 p.m. statement was not meant to ascribe a motive to the attack. Yet, Sullivan knew the morning of September 12th—based on the press release from the embassy in Kabul—that people had heard it exactly that way. Moreover, whether or not the intelligence information changed, Secretary Clinton's public and private statements remained consistent—publicly tying Benghazi and Cairo together and privately recognizing the violence in Benghazi was a terrorist attack with nothing to do with a protest or video.

Moreover, to the extent any intelligence analysis incorrectly reported on a protest or a video in connection with Benghazi, Secretary Clinton and other State officials, who knew better, simply ignored them. As just one example, in her conversation September 15, 2012 with the president of Libya, Secretary Clinton made no mention of anything in the CIA talking points that administration officials later claimed were the best assessment available at the time, and those talking points made no mention of a video in connection with Benghazi. In short, Secretary Clinton and the administration knew better than to rely on flawed intelligence reports. Intelligence assessments may have changed. News reports may have changed. But the eye witness accounts remained the same—

---

[56] E-mail from Sullivan Assistant to various (attaching "Immediate ALDAC for transmission" drafted by J Sullivan 9/19/2012 noting approval by "S: The Secretary") (Sept. 2012) (on file with the Committee, SCB0052811) (emphasis added).

[57] Press Release, Remarks by the President at Univision Town Hall with Jorge Ramos and Maria Elena Salinas (Sept. 20, 2012), https://www.whitehouse.gov/the-press-office/2012/09/20/remarks-president-univision-town-hall-jorge-ramos-and-maria-elena-salina (emphasis added).

and not one said a protest had occurred. Yet, once Secretary Clinton and Ben Rhodes set the message, the truth became an afterthought.

### D. AMBASSADOR RICE FACES THE NATION

On September 16, 2012, Ambassador Susan Rice appeared on five Sunday talk shows and blamed Benghazi on the video. She took the brunt of the criticism for doing so when it finally became public that no protest had occurred. It is now clear, however, that connecting the video to Benghazi started far sooner. It began with Secretary Clinton's 10:08 p.m. statement the night of the attack. Rice, however, compounded the deception. And while Secretary Clinton and others blurred the line between Cairo and Benghazi, Ambassador Rice erased it completely.

Ambassador Rice now claims that she did not blame the video for what occurred in Benghazi. The plain wording of what she said, however, refutes her testimony to the Committee. She also claims that she simply relied on the flawed CIA talking points. But even a casual reading of those talking points shows that she went far beyond what the CIA prepared—in a way that helped the President politically.

The original draft of the CIA talking points included key information that would have at a minimum pointed to the possibility of a planned terrorist attack. For example, the initial draft referred to knowing that "Islamic extremists with ties to al-Qa'ida" had taken part in the attack, that "there had been at least five other attacks" previously, and that they could not rule out that "individuals had previously surveilled the U.S. facilities."[58] By the final draft, however, officials had stripped out all of that and other information. It then read simply:

> The currently available information suggests that the demonstrations in Benghazi were spontaneously inspired by the protests at the U.S. Embassy in Cairo and evolved into a direct assault against the U.S. diplomatic post and subsequently its annex. There are indications that extremists participated in the violent demonstrations.

> This assessment may change as additional information is collected and analyzed and currently available information continues to be evaluated.

> The investigation is ongoing, and the U.S. Government is working w/Libyan authorities to help bring to justice those responsible for the deaths of U.S. citizens.[59]

The talking points in their final form make no mention of the video. Nevertheless, and with no discernable basis for doing so, Ambassador Rice drew that inaccurate connection. On Meet the Press she said "putting together the best information we have available to us today our current assessment is that what happened in Benghazi was in fact initially a spontaneous reaction to

---

[58] See *Talking Points Timeline*, ABC NEWS, http://abcnews.go.com/images/Politics/Benghazi%20Talking%20Points%20Timeline.pdf.

[59] *Id.*

what had just transpired hours before in Cairo, almost a copycat of—of the demonstrations against our facility in Cairo, which were prompted, of course, by the video."[60]

The statement Rice made was false. The "best information" available at the time—from the witnesses on the ground—pointed directly to a pre-planned, complex terrorist attack. Many within the State Department came to that conclusion quickly as well. For example, a Senior Advisor for Strategic Communications, Near Eastern Affairs Bureau, "My opinion, that night, was simply that this was a terrorist attack."[61] Likewise, Assistant Secretary of State Beth Jones testified that "there was discussion about was it a demonstration, was it an attack? And I knew very well that the Embassy [in Tripoli] believed it to be an attack. I believed it to be an attack."[62]

No one—and certainly not the CIA or the broader U.S. Intelligence Community—had described Benghazi as a copycat of Cairo. In fact, knowing what they knew at the time it is hard to imagine how the two events could have been more different. On the very night of the attack, Ambassador Rice herself received an e-mail that described the Cairo protests as "2000 protestors in total. 20 got to the top of the wall, 10 got inside the perimeter—they tore down the flag and sprayed graffiti inside the compound. They went after employee cars as well."[63] No one used or showed a weapon in Cairo and no American was hurt. In short, Benghazi was not "almost a copycat" of what occurred in Cairo and Ambassador Rice knew it.

Ambassador Rice's "copycat" claim was particularly troubling in light of the fact that the President said virtually the opposite just days earlier. In an interview with Steve Kroft of 60 Minutes on September 12, 2012 he was asked, "This has been described as a mob action, but there are reports that they were very heavily armed with grenades. That doesn't sound like your normal demonstration."[64] To which the President responded, "As I said, we're still investigating exactly what happened. I don't want to jump the gun on this. *But you're right that this is not a situation that was exactly the same as what happened in Egypt,* and my suspicion is, is that there are folks involved in this who were looking to target Americans from the start."[65] It is troubling that this portion of the President's answer was deleted from the show that aired on September 23, 2012 and was not made public until just days before the election.

Similarly, on CNN's State of the Union Ambassador Rice, almost indignant, insisted "[f]irst of all, let's be clear about what transpired here. What happened this week in Cairo, *in Benghazi,* in many parts of the region . . . was a result—*a direct result* of a

---

[60] Transcript of Interview, Amb. Susan Rice on Meet the Press (Sept. 16, 2012).

[61] Transcript of Interview of Senior Advisor for Strategic Communications, Near Eastern Affairs Bureau at 89 (July 29, 2015) (on file with the Committee).

[62] Transcript of Interview of Acting Assistant Sec'y of State NEA Beth Jones before H. Comm. on Oversight and Government Reform at 138–139 (July 11, 2013) (on file with the Committee).

[63] E-mail from a State Dep't Senior Policy Advisor to Amb. Susan Rice and others (Sept. 11, 2012) (on file with the Committee, C05390691).

[64] Internal Transcript, Interview of the President by Steve Kroft, 60 Minutes at 2 (Sept. 12, 2012) (on file with the Committee, C05527907).

[65] *Id.*

heinous and offensive video that was widely disseminated."[66] Again, nowhere in the talking points did the U.S. Intelligence Community blame the video for what occurred in Benghazi let alone describe it as a "direct result" of the video. When confronted with this, Ambassador Rice seemed to deny the meaning of the very words she used, claiming that she did not "intend[] to include[] Benghazi in that statement[.]"[67]

Nor did Ambassador Rice—or anyone else from the administration—tell the full story. In fact, they only told the half that helped politically. For example, the administration claimed publicly there was no "actionable intelligence" prior to the attack—suggesting the attack was spontaneous.[68] However, it failed to disclose that at the time significant gaps existed in U.S. intelligence collection in Libya that made it virtually impossible to have picked up such warnings in the first place. It also failed to highlight the casing incident that had occurred the morning of the attack just outside the Benghazi compound.[69] The administration also failed to disclose the long history of terrorist violence in Benghazi—information that would have placed the Benghazi attack into its proper context.

Nor did Ambassador Rice show any sincere interest in finding all of the facts—or as she put it—the best information available before going on the Sunday talk shows. In fact, her preparation session the day before, which included Benjamin Rhodes and White House political adviser David Plouffe—appeared to spend very little time on Benghazi at all.[70]

On Monday, September 17, 2012, some State Department officials reacted with shock to Ambassador Rice's claims. Specifically, the Department's NEA Bureau press department—the experts on Libya—reacted with disbelief. The discussion began with NEA's Senior Libyan Desk Officer reacting to draft press guidance that quoted the CIA talking points by saying, "I really hope this was revised. I don't think we should go on the record on this."[71] This led to the Deputy Director, Office of Maghreb Affairs, NEA saying, "Not sure we want to be so definitive[,]"[72] which led to the following e-mail exchange:

***NEA Spokesperson:***

The horse has left the barn on this, don't you think? Rice was on FIVE Sunday Morning shows yesterday saying this. Tough to walk back.

***Senior Advisor for Strategic Communications, NEA:***

[66] Transcript of Interview, Amb. Susan Rice on CNN State of the Union (Sept. 16, 2012).
[67] Transcript of Interview of Amb. Susan Rice at 102 (February 2, 2016), (on file with the Committee).
[68] See US 'had no actionable intelligence' over Benghazi attack, THE TELEGRAPH (Oct. 10, 2012), http://www.telegraph.co.uk/news/worldnews/africa andindianocean/libya/9597738/US-had-no-actionable-intelligence-over-Benghazi-attack.html.
[69] See E-mail from Assistant Regional Security Officer (Sept. 11, 2012) ("We received word from our local guards that this morning they observed a member of the police force assigned to the [Benghazi] Mission at a construction site across the street from our main gate taking pictures of our compound. I briefed the [Ambassador.]) (on file with the Committee, C05271656).
[70] See Transcript of Interview of Amb. Susan Rice at 39 (February 2, 2016) (Rice testified "I don't recall us talking about the CIA talking points" and "we didn't talk about Benghazi, in fact, on the phone call, as I remember") (on file with the Committee).
[71] E-mail from Senior Libyan Desk Offier, NEA to NEA Press Officer (Sept 17, 2012) (on file with the Committee: Doc# C05580617).
[72] Id.

[Nuland] planned on walking it back just a bit, though.

**Senior Libyan Desk Officer, NEA:**

I think Rice was *off the reservation* on this one.

**Senior Advisor for Strategic Communications, NEA:**

Yup. Luckily there's enough in her language *to fudge exactly what she said/meant.*

**NEA Spokesperson:**

Off the reservation on five networks!

**Senior Advisor for Strategic Communications, NEA:**

[White House] very worried about the politics. This was all their doing.[73]

Although these individuals may not have seen the CIA talking points prior to Rice's appearances, they did know what had occurred in Benghazi based on their vantage point that night.[74]

The exchange also highlights another important issue. Toward the end of the exchange the NEA Senior Advisor for Strategic Communications describes it as "luck" that Ambassador Rice had said enough to "fudge" what she meant. A national crisis is no time to fudge the truth; it is a time to find it and to tell it. But what we found here is just the opposite. And for those who appear to have known the truth—such as Secretary Clinton—the American people waited in vain for them to correct Ambassador Rice's misleading public statements.

Possibly most troubling is the evidence suggesting the State Department may have changed its public statements to match Rice's claims. Specifically, on September 17, 2012, a State Department Press Officer in the NEA Bureau circulated a document entitled "NEA Press Guidance Libya: Update on Investigation on Attack in Benghazi,"[75] a document intended as guidance for public comments about the attack. In the original draft it said that "we have not seen any signs that the attack . . . in Benghazi was other than **premeditated or coordinated.**" In a later draft, however, "other than premeditated or coordinated" morphed into "other than spontaneous." The document produced by the State Department to the Committee still contained the insertion (in bold) and deletions (in bold strikethrough) under the heading "Key Points":

> We will continue to wait for the findings of the ongoing FBI investigation before reaching a final conclusion, but at this preliminary stage, ~~time,~~ we have not yet seen any signs that the attack on our consulate in Benghazi was other than **spontaneous.** ~~**premeditated. coordinated.**~~[76]

---

[73] E-mail from Senior Advisor for Strategic Communications, NEA to Spokesperson, NEA, Senior Libyan Desk Offier, NEA, Deputy Director, Office of Maghreb Affairs, NEA (Sept 17, 2012) (emphasis added) (on file with the Committee, C05580618).

[74] *See, e.g.,* Transcript of Interview of Senior Advisor for Strategic Communications, NEA at 89 ("Q: So let me make sure I'm clear. So your opinion on the night of the attack, when you were at the State Department, your opinion was that it was a terrorist attack? A: Correct.") (on file with the Committee).

[75] *See* E-mail from NEA press officer to Bernadette Meehan and others (Sept. 17, 2012) (on file with the Committee, C05578291).

[76] *Id.*

No one asked about it could explain the change. The change—from the truth to a known false statement—is troubling.

Secretary Clinton and others in the State Department clearly knew the truth about Benghazi almost immediately. Yet they only shared that information with others privately, including with Secretary Clinton's daughter. Publicly they told a very different story—one in line with Ben Rhodes's instruction to blame the video and not a failure of the President's policy. In doing so, the President and Secretary Clinton put politics ahead of the truth. The four victims deserved better. And the American people deserved better.

## II. Last Clear Chance

In August 2012 it did not take an expert to see that the State Department facility in Benghazi should have been closed if additional security was not to be provided. The location and the risk demanded Secretary Clinton's attention. The Benghazi facility was wholly unique and there is no evidence that Secretary Clinton asked her experts—let alone Ambassador Stevens who she personally chose for the position—the hard questions. The robust host-nation security forces that the United States takes for granted in other countries did not exist in Libya. Rather, competing militias—some friendly, some not—filled the vacuum left by 40-plus years of Qhaddafi's rule. And escalating violence against the U.S. compound and others in Libya—230 incidents since June 2011 alone—made a terrorist attack all but inevitable. These were the facts known in August 2012. And in August 2012 Secretary Clinton had the last, clear chance to provide adequate protection or, failing that, to close the facility and pull our people out. She did neither.

### A. THE "WILD EAST": POST-QHADDAFI BENGHAZI

*I told him that this was a suicide mission; that there was a very good chance that everybody here was going to die; that there was absolutely no ability here to prevent an attack whatever. \* \* [H]hesaid, "everybody back here in D.C. knows that people are going to die in Benghazi, and nobody cares and nobody is going to care until somebody does die."*

State Diplomatic Security Agent #10 [77]

According to the Diplomatic security agent quoted above, he had this exchange with the State Department's desk officer for diplomatic security in the region that covered Libya, shortly after he arrived in Benghazi on temporary assignment as the regional security officer. The conversation did not occur days before the attack. It did not occur a month before the attack. Rather, he gave the warning nearly nine months before September 11, 2012 shortly after he arrived in Benghazi. Nor was his the only warning.

In June 2012, a second Benghazi security official reported on the "increase in extremist activity" in Benghazi and described his "fear

---

[77] Transcript of Interview of DS Agent #10 at 22–23 (April 2, 2015) (recounting conversation with DS Agent #25 who was the desk officer for diplomatic security in the Near Eastern Affairs Bureau).

that we have passed a threshold where we will see more targeting, attacks, and incidents involving western [sic] targets."[78] The official also listed a series of very recent attacks and noted that a source had warned of a "group attack" on an American facility.[79] He specifically mentioned "[t]argeting [and] attacks by extremist groups particularly in the eastern portion of Libya[.]"[80] These warnings contained troubling information about possible terrorists trying to learn information about U.S. facilities.[81]

The list of incidents in Benghazi that were reported back to Washington was long. And it told a compelling story of a city on the brink. To anyone aware of the conditions, it was not a matter of "if" but rather "when" a terrorist attack on the U.S. compound would occur. The list ran the gamut from minor to major incidents, including a rocket attack on the British ambassador's convoy that prompted withdrawal of British personnel from the city. The incidents included:

- April 10, 2012 explosive device hits U.N. convoy in Benghazi [82]

- May 22, 2012 rocket propelled grenade attack on the International Red Cross facility, which included a warning that "Americans would be targeted next" [83]

- June 6, 2012 attack on U.S. mission in Benghazi [84]

- June 18, 2012 armed attackers storm Tunisian Consulate [85]

- June 11, 2012 rocket attack on the British ambassador [86]

- July 27, 2012 attempted bomb attack on Tibesti Hotel in Benghazi, the hotel used by the State Department during Revolution [87]

- July 31, 2012 seven Iranian-citizen International Committee of the Red Crescent workers abducted [88]

- August 20, 2012 small bomb thrown at Egyptian diplomat's vehicle parked outside of the Egyptian consulate [89]

---

[78] E-mail from DS Agent #24 to DS Agent #25 (June 14, 2012) (on file with the Committee, C05388987).

[79] Id.

[80] Id.

[81] Id. ("LES bodyguard assigned to the Ambassador's Protection Detail informed the RSO that he was asked about specific security questions concerning the embassy by an individual that he believed was an extremist.").

[82] E-mail from Diplomatic Security Agent 16 to DS–IP–NEA (Apr. 10, 2012) (on file with the Committee, SCB0048085).

[83] E-mail from OpsNewsTicker to NEWS-Libya (May 22, 2012, 9:06 AM) (on file with the Committee, C05392368).

[84] E-mail from Principal Officer 2, U.S. Dep't of State, to John C. Stevens, U.S. Ambassador to Libya, Joan A. Polaschik, Deputy Chief of Mission in Libya, William V. Roe-buck, Dir. Office of Maghreb Affairs, Bureau of Near Eastern Affairs, U.S. Dep't of State (June 6, 2012, 4:49 AM) (on file with the Committee, C05393187).

[85] See Mohamed al-Tommy and Hadeel al-Shalchi, *Gunmen Attack Tunisian Consulate in Benghazi*, Reuters (Jun. 18, 2012, 19:03), http://www.reuters.com/article/us-libya-gunmen-tunisia-idUSBRE85H1V620120618

[86] Memo from Regional Director, Near Eastern Affairs Bureau, Diplomatic Security at 44 (June 15, 2012) (on file with the Committee, SCB0048161).

[87] See *Blast and Jailbreak Rock Libya's Benghazi*, AlJazeera (Aug. 1, 2012) (available at http://www.aljazeera.com/news/africa/2012/08/201281818 48269 995.html).

[88] *Iran Red Crescent Team 'Kidnapped' in Libya*, AlJazeera (Jul. 31, 2012), http://www.aljazeera.com/news/africa/2012/07/201273120552473238.html.

[89] See Steven Sotloff, *The Bomb Attacks in Libya: Are Gaddafi Loyalists Behind Them?*, Time (Aug. 24, 2012), http://world.time.com/2012/08/24/the-bomb-attacks-in-libya-are-gaddafi-loyalists-behind-them/.

Without this background one could, in theory, jump to the mistaken conclusion that the terrorist attack in Benghazi and the protests in Cairo were connected in time and in cause. But the State Department and the NEA Bureau in particular knew this history all too well. For those people, it was against this backdrop that they quickly saw Benghazi for what it was: a terrorist attack, not a protest.

Nor did this escalation in violence escape the notice of American policy makers or the U.S. Intelligence Community. Intelligence analysts produced numerous reports on the growing terrorist threat centered in Benghazi—yet the State Department did nothing. Again, why? And so even though the security problems in Benghazi appear to have been well known to State Department officials at the time, no one acted in any meaningful way to protect the Benghazi facility let alone to get the people out. The question remained: Why?

Although the agent's warning quoted at the section heading could not have been clearer, it was ignored even as the situation in Benghazi went from bad to worse. The situation became so grave that it prompted one State Department official to dub Benghazi the "wild east." Sadly, the humor foreshadowed the horror to come as he made this statement in an e-mail sent to Ambassador Stevens just hours before his death.[90]

Some blame the deplorable security conditions in Benghazi on the facility's "made up" State Department designation. To them, the fact the Department labeled the facility "temporary" excused shortcomings in the compound's physical security. A "temporary" designation enabled the facility to skirt a host of written internal security requirements that applied to more permanent locations. We also learned it was an improvised designation not used at any of the State Department's other 275 facilities around the world.[91] The requirements this designation avoided cover everything from setbacks to perimeter wall heights to razor wire placement. Standards that, had the State Department complied with them, would have given the Benghazi staff a fighting chance that night.

In trying to excuse the security conditions in Benghazi, some have argued that it would have been impossible to comply with the State Department's internal requirements in Benghazi. That may be true, but it is also irrelevant. The suggestion that a facility's label should dictate whether men and women have adequate security of course makes no sense.

It makes no sense because it ignores a critical requirement applicable to all facilities regardless of whether it will stand for a day, a year, or a decade. The facility's label did not trump commonsense. Nor did it blind officials to the deadly attack that to trained professionals appears to have been all but inevitable, as the security agent quoted above observed months before. In other words, the State Department cannot hide behind its regulations. It had an

---

[90] E-mail from Public Affairs Officer, U.S. Embassy Libya to Amb. Christopher Stevens (Sept. 11, 2012) (on file with the Committee).

[91] This is the number of facilities identified by Assistant Secretary for Diplomatic Security Gregory Starr in his testimony before the Committee in 2014. Transcript of Hearing 1 H. Sel. Comm. on Benghazi Testimony of Gregory Starr at 97 (Sept. 17, 2014).

obligation to act yet did far too little to secure the facility. The question, again, was why?

The same question came from the former Ambassador to Yemen, who the day after the attack observed:

> People are bound to ask how we can send unarmed civilian diplomats to conduct [U.S. government] business into a region with no local security forces to rely on, only a handful of lightly armed [diplomatic security] agents serving as close protection team, and a couple dozen local militiamen of questionable pedigree with AK–47's providing perimeter security.[92]

It was a question that the ambassador himself could not even answer: "I would suggest that we **begin to think now** of how we explain/justify our presence in these non-permissive environments.[93] To most Americans, the time to think about justifying a presence in Benghazi and other dangerous places should have come before, not after, Americans have died.

So the question remained, what was so important in Benghazi that it meant risking the lives of Americans in what many appeared to view as a suicide mission? It is true that American diplomats cannot hide inside bunkers. That we can never eliminate all risk in diplomacy. That Benghazi was the seat of the revolution and home to important anti-regime leaders. And that the United States was not alone in seeing a good reason to be there, as other Western countries had done the same. Yet, other Western countries left and the U.S. stayed. So while all this may be true, it still begs the essential question: Why Benghazi? The answer that best fits is politics.

### B. PUTTING POLITICS AHEAD OF PEOPLE: FAILING TO CLOSE THE BENGHAZI COMPOUND

It remains unclear why a State Department presence in Benghazi was so important. What is clear, however, is keeping a facility open there was important to Secretary Clinton. In addition, on this matter, many questions remain and much classified information was withheld from the Committee.

In his interview with Secretary Clinton prior to confirmation as ambassador to Libya, Secretary Clinton told Ambassador Stevens that she hoped that Benghazi would become a permanent post. In late July 2012, Ambassador Stevens discussed the issue with his Deputy Chief of Mission Gregory Hicks. According to Mr. Hicks, during their discussion Ambassador Stevens said that Secretary Clinton might travel to Libya again, possibly in October,[94] and that Stevens wanted to have a "deliverable" for her trip. That "deliverable" was to make the mission in Benghazi permanent.

No matter how important a presence in Benghazi was—to Secretary Clinton, to the State Department, to the United States—it

---

[92] E-mail from former ambassador to Yemen to Beth Jones, Acting Assistant Secretary for NEA (Sept. 12, 2012) (on file with the Committee, C05391021).

[93] Id.

[94] Transcript of Testimony of Gregory Hicks, Deputy in Charge of Mission Embassy Libya, before H. Comm. on Government Reform and Oversight at 15 (April 11, 2013).

should have become very clear that the risks of staying without more security outweighed any possible benefit.

On August 17, 2012, Secretary Clinton received a document titled "Information Memo for the Secretary." The memo did not pull punches. Under the somewhat benign heading "Uptick in Violence, Primarily in Eastern Libya" it said, "Since May, there has been a spike in violent incidents, including bombings, abductions, assassinations, and car-jackings."[95] The memo, from Acting Assistant Secretary for Near Eastern Affairs Beth Jones, is quoted at length here:

- "While unpredictable security conditions restrict the movement of U.S. government personnel, they have not limited our assistance work."[96]

- "The attachment lists the major events, which include a June 6 bombing at the U.S. Mission in Benghazi and an August 6 attempted car-jacking of embassy personnel in Tripoli."[97]

- "Recently, foreign residents of Benghazi have expressed concern about the risks of living and working there."[98]

- "In response to five attacks since May, the International Committee of the Red Cross (ICRC) withdrew its personnel from Benghazi and Misrata in early August[.] The ICRC country director believes international organizations in Libya have underestimated the recent rise in violence out of a shared sense of optimism."[99]

- "The variety of the violence points to the overall lack of effective security institutions, particularly in the east."[100]

- "The distance from the already weak central security services, feelings of marginalization from the central government, and a history of Islamist extremism in some eastern towns all seem to contribute to a permissive environment where disparate motivations for violence have found fertile ground in which to germinate. The national Supreme Security Council—a post-revolutionary coalition of militia elements cobbled into a single force and designed to provide interim security in Benghazi—has had limited success as a stabilizing force."[101]

- "The government seems largely unable to gather intelligence in advance of attacks and central security services appear intimidated by the local militias, in some cases tacitly ceding their authority. Some actors see the weak response from the government and feel they can act with increasing impunity. The sense of lawlessness encourages spoilers, predators, and other disruptive players to escalate their actions."[102]

---

[95] Information Memo for the Secretary from Acting Assistant Secretary Beth Jones, NEA (Aug. 17, 2012) (on file with the Committee, C05390124).
[96] *Id.*
[97] *Id.*
[98] *Id.*
[99] *Id.*
[100] *Id.*
[101] *Id.*
[102] *Id.*

- "Benghazi was once palpably safer than Tripoli [but] . . . lawlessness is increasing. . . . Despite the urgency, however, the government's response is likely to continue to be hesitant and tentative[.]" [103]

- "Despite the worrisome aspects of this increase in violence, there is no coordinated organization behind the incidents. . . . Nonetheless, the likelihood of more widespread violence is strong if Libya's political leaders are unable to demobalize [sic] militias and strengthen the government's security institutions." [104]

Despite the colorless bureaucratic language, the Beth Jones memo nevertheless painted a harrowing picture of conditions in the eastern part of Libya where Benghazi is located. Many of the words truly jump at the reader— "urgency," "lawlessness," "unpredictable," "lack of effective security," "limited success," "widespread violence," "act with increasing impunity." The list of specific incidents attached to the memo brought that picture into even starker relief.

When Secretary Clinton was asked about the Beth Jones memo during her Committee interview she deflected, "Well, I think that, again, there was no recommendation based on any of the assessments, not from our State Department experts, not from the intelligence community, that we should abandon either Benghazi or Tripoli." [105]

In the beginning and possibly into the summer of 2012, the situation in Benghazi may have represented one that called out for State Department security experts or the Intelligence Community to speak up. But by August 17, 2012, it had become a situation that now demanded leadership by the Secretary of State herself— leadership that did not sit back and wait for a recommendation.

Just as she had shown—in the words of Jacob Sullivan—"leadership/ownership/stewardship" on the decision to go into Libya, it was now time for her to show that same leadership and upgrade the facility or get our people out—even if it meant criticism from those who opposed the intervention in the first place. She had the last, clear chance to order an immediate closure of the Benghazi facility yet did nothing, and four Americans died.

During her testimony before the Committee, Secretary Clinton almost scolded the Republican members:

> You know, I would imagine I've thought more about what happened than all of you put together. I've lost more sleep than all of you put together. I have been racking my brain about what more could have been done or should have been done. [106]

For one that had spent so much time thinking about what happened, it seems that the answer should have been obvious.

---

[103] *Id.*

[104] *Id.*

[105] Transcript of Hearing 4 before the Select Committee on the Events Surrounding the 2012 Terrorist Attack in Benghazi (hereafter referred to as "the Committee"), 114th Cong. (2015) (testimony of Hillary Rodham Clinton, Sec'y of State).

[106] Transcript of Hearing 4 before the Select Committee on the Events Surrounding the 2012 Terrorist Attack in Benghazi (hereafter referred to as "the Committee"), 114th Cong. (2015) (testimony of Hillary Rodham Clinton, Sec'y of State).

## III. Military Response: Could we have done more?

*I just say, do it. Take the hill. They take the hill.*

Leon Panetta
Secretary of Defense [107]

The U.S. military never reached Benghazi. Not only did it not get to Benghazi, it did not get to Libya during the 7-plus hours of the ongoing attack. The only support unit that did arrive in Tripoli—the Marine "Fleet Anti-Terrorism Support Team" or "FAST" team—was anything but fast, and arrived in Libya nearly 24 hours after the attack had begun and 16-plus hours after the attack ended. In fact, it did not take off until almost 12 hours after the attack ended. Why? Although a Department of Defense drone circled overhead in Benghazi during much of the attack, the military never sent an armed drone that could possibly have changed the course of events during the hours-long siege, especially as terrorists pounded the Annex with mortar fire. An armed drone never came. Why?

Like many Americans, the picture we saw of what happened in Benghazi clashed with our experience and expectations. The brave men and women who serve this country are the greatest fighting force on earth with a capability second to none. We as Americans have grown to expect these men and women to do the near impossible. And time and again they not only meet our expectations, they surpass them. In fact, we saw examples of exactly that heroism on the ground in Benghazi that night.

Our brave soldiers were ready, willing, and able to fight for their fellow countrymen but leaders in Washington held them back. If they had been given the chance they would have, we have no doubt, as Secretary Panetta said, "taken that hill."

In his testimony before the Committee, Secretary of Defense Panetta said that at about 6:00 p.m. on September 11th after meeting with the President, he ordered three assets to deploy: one Marine Fleet Anti-Terrorism Support Team or "FAST" team, one Commanders In Extremis Force or "CIF," and one hostage rescue team based in the United States. He was clear: "My orders were to deploy those forces, period." [108]

After his meeting with the President, which lasted less than 30 minutes, Secretary Panetta had no further contact with the President that night.[109] None. It is hard to accept that the Commander in Chief and the Secretary of Defense had no further contact during the entire unfolding crisis. Possibly just as startling is that Secretary Panetta and Secretary Clinton did not speak at all[110] and Secretary Clinton did not speak to the President until approximately 10:30 p.m., over six hours after the terrorist attack began and approximately five hours after a U.S. ambassador went missing.[111] Secretary Clinton spoke to CIA Director David Petraeus at

---

[107] Transcript of Interview of Leon Panetta, Sec'y of Defense at 57 (Jan. 8, 2016).
[108] Transcript of Interview of Leon Panetta, Sec'y of Defense at 24 (Jan. 8, 2016).
[109] Transcript of Interview of Leon Panetta, Sec'y of Defense at 42 (Jan. 8, 2016).
[110] *Id.* at 48.
[111] *See* Dep't of State, Watch Log, Operations Center (Sept. 11, 2012) (on file with the Committee, C05872462).

approximately 5:38 p.m. but not again that night.[112] The meeting (denoted "M") and calls (denoted "C"), or lack thereof, between the four principals—President Obama, Secretary Clinton, Secretary Panetta, and Director Petraeus—looked like this:[113]

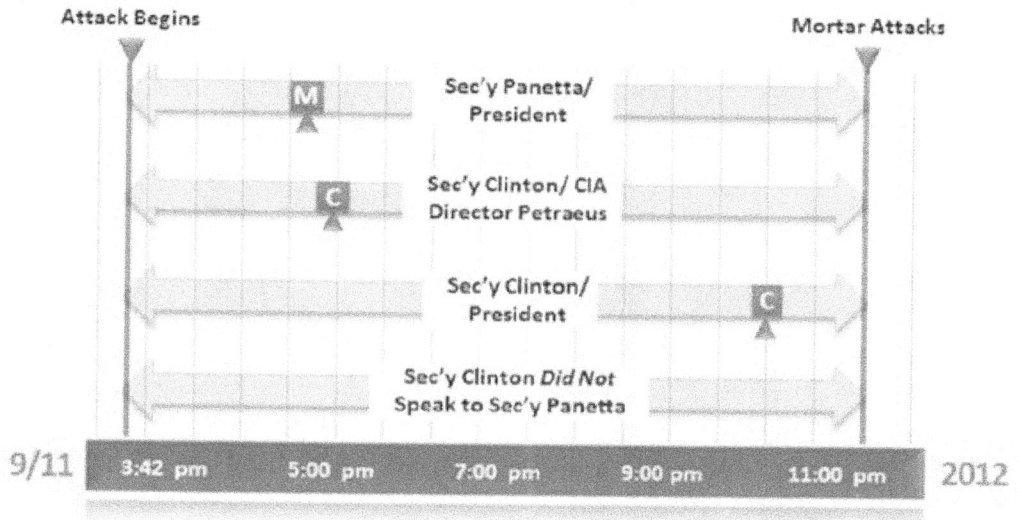

We cannot help but contrast the picture painted by the above with the all hands on deck depicted in the now-famous photo of the President, Secretary Clinton, Defense Secretary Gates, Director of National Intelligence Clapper, and other officials huddled in the Situation Room during the Osama bin Laden raid. Benghazi should have merited the same level of attention and urgency.

Until now, the public has been told that the military could not have reached Benghazi in time to help—either with jet planes, armed drones, or personnel. Had we seen aircraft in the air flying toward Benghazi—flying toward the sound of gunfire as the military often says—only to be recalled mid-flight after hearing that the Americans had left Benghazi safely, we may have been willing to accept that explanation. But the fighter planes and armed drones never left the ground. And, as the chart below shows, the transport planes carrying the FAST, CIF, and hostage rescue team did not leave until hours after the attack was over.

The attack began at 9:42 p.m. in Benghazi, 3:42 p.m. in Washington. It does not appear that Secretary Panetta heard about the attack until sometime after 4:32 p.m. when the National Military Command Center was notified and he did not discuss the matter with the President until approximately 5:00 p.m. From 3:42 p.m. until approximately 10:00 a.m. the next day—nearly 18 hours—no manned U.S. military plane flew on a mission toward Libya. When the first plane did take off with a Marine FAST platoon it did not take off until hours after the attack ended and flew to an intermediate country. The timeline of significant events compared to when the military assets took off and arrived included the following:[114]

---

[112] *Id.*

[113] All times Eastern.

[114] All times shown are Eastern time, which is 6 hours behind local time in Benghazi.

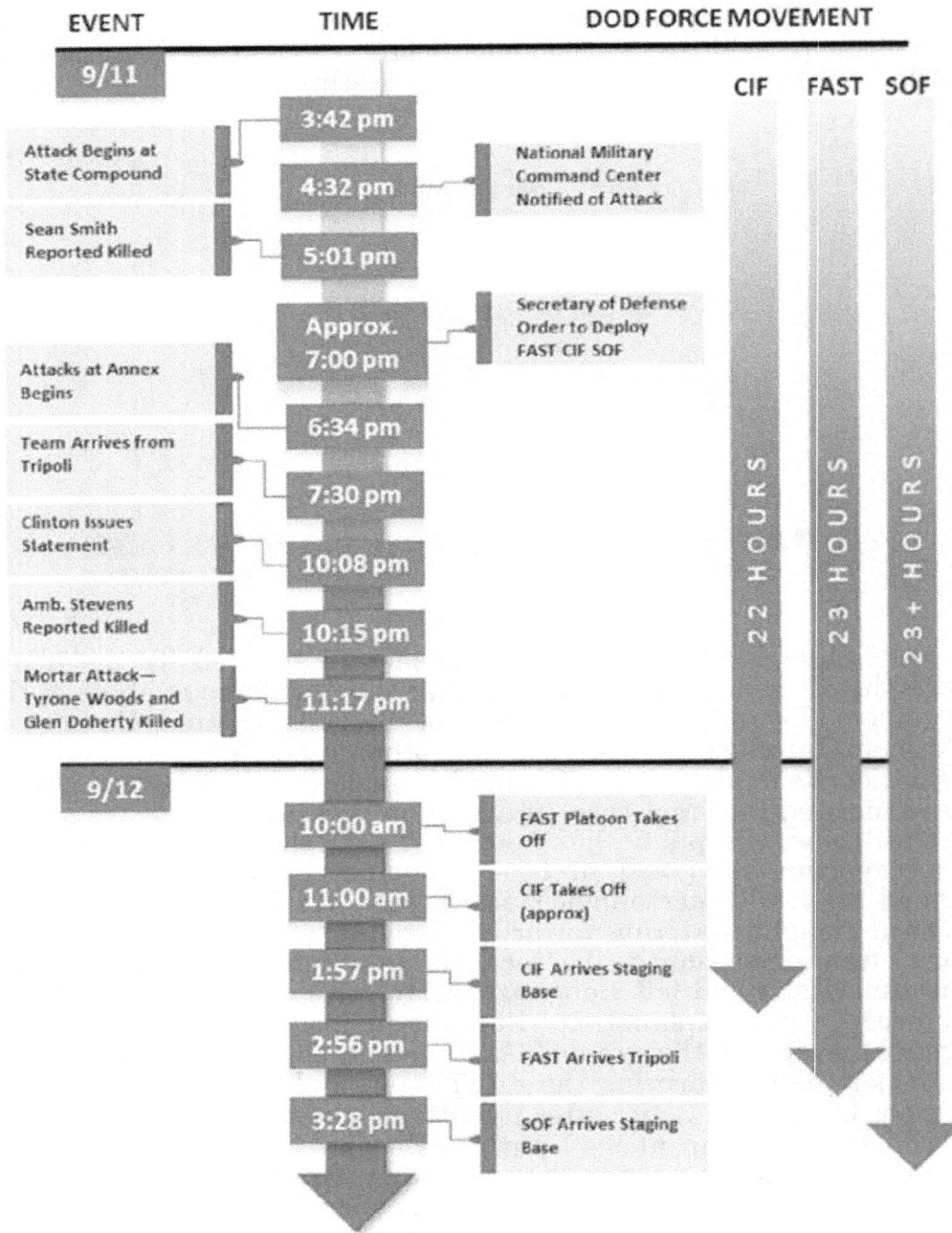

| EVENT | TIME | DOD FORCE MOVEMENT |
|---|---|---|

**9/11**

CIF  FAST  SOF

Attack Begins at State Compound — 3:42 pm

4:32 pm — National Military Command Center Notified of Attack

Sean Smith Reported Killed — 5:01 pm

Approx. 7:00 pm — Secretary of Defense Order to Deploy FAST CIF SOF

Attacks at Annex Begins

Team Arrives from Tripoli — 6:34 pm

7:30 pm

Clinton Issues Statement — 10:08 pm

Amb. Stevens Reported Killed — 10:15 pm

Mortar Attack— Tyrone Woods and Glen Doherty Killed — 11:17 pm

CIF 22 HOURS
FAST 23 HOURS
SOF 23+ HOURS

**9/12**

10:00 am — FAST Platoon Takes Off

11:00 am — CIF Takes Off (approx)

1:57 pm — CIF Arrives Staging Base

2:56 pm — FAST Arrives Tripoli

3:28 pm — SOF Arrives Staging Base

We are now convinced, contrary to the administration's public claim that the military did not have time to get to Benghazi, that the administration never launched men or machines to help directly in the fight. That is very different from what we have been told to date. And the evidence is compelling.

For example, FAST platoons, as of September 2012, were typically used to reinforce embassy security and operated from a fixed location within an embassy. FAST platoons did not deploy with their own vehicles, so they were dependent on other means for ground mobility. In other words, the FAST team was not sent to help in the fight at the CIA Annex. The question then became what was sent. And the answer appears to be nothing. None of the three assets that Secretary Panetta ordered to deploy were intended to join the fight against terrorists at the Annex.

An asset that could have made a difference would have been armed drones. And as the Committee learned, it would have been relatively fast and easy to arm a drone. To date, however, the Committee has not received a detailed inventory of all armed drone assets available that night from the Department of Defense. While we understand that because of time and distance armed drones may not have arrived in time that does not alter the fact that we did not try.

The military has failed to provide a clear, specific inventory of every armed aircraft—whether manned or unmanned—that could have flown to Benghazi during the 7-plus hours from the beginning of the attack to the mortar rounds hitting the CIA Annex. Instead, the military has insisted that the Committee simply accept the word of senior military officers, some without firsthand knowledge of the events, as an adequate substitute for actual eye witnesses.

One of the clearest examples of the Department of Defense's attempt to impede the investigation involved one of its legislative affairs officers, Stephen C. Hedger. Mr. Hedger, appearing to work hand-in-hand with the minority members, wrote a stinging letter to the Committee attacking it on multiple fronts—attacks that quickly found their way into a Democrat press release. The letter even went so far as to imply that the Committee's investigative requests had somehow impaired our national defense.

The most troubling aspect of the letter was the criticism that the Committee had asked for witnesses that "seem unnecessary even for a comprehensive investigation[.]" While it is rare for the subject of an investigation to decide which witnesses are relevant, the Department of Defense felt otherwise. One of the supposedly "unnecessary" witnesses was known to the Committee only as "John from Iowa"—the pseudonym he used when he called into a talk show to discuss the attack. He had operated the video and other sensors on a Predator drone that circled over Benghazi the night of the attack. Given his bird's eye view, the Committee believed he could provide valuable insight into what the Department of Defense knew and therefore could have, and possibly should have, done to help that night.

Mr. Hedger responded to the request with what bordered on sarcasm—describing the Committee's request as one "to interview an individual identified as 'John from Iowa' who described himself as a Remotely Piloted Aircraft (RPA) camera operator on a talk radio show, where he described what he allegedly saw in the video feed from the night of the attack." In short, Mr. Hedger made the request sound like the Committee was chasing crackpots. To drive the point home he then added, "The Department has expended significant resources to locate anyone who might match the description of this person, *to no avail.*"[115]

As it turns out, Mr. Hedger's claim was completely false according to information provided by the witness himself, who the De-

---

[115] Letter from Stephen C. Hedger, Dep't of Defense, Office of Legislative Affairs to the Hon. Trey Gowdy, Chairman, H. Sel. Comm. on the Events Surrounding the 2012 Terrorist Attack in Benghazi (Apr. 28, 2016) (emphasis added) (on file with the Committee).

partment of Defense eventually produced. Mr. Hedger's false and misleading claim, was one of the more troubling examples of the Department of Defense's failure to cooperate fully, although not the only one.

What has also emerged is a picture of the State Department eating up valuable time by insisting that certain elements of the U.S. military respond to Libya in civilian clothes and that it not use vehicles with United States markings. Both restrictions appear to have been concessions to the Libyan government that did not want an identifiable U.S. military presence on the streets of Libya. We will never know exactly how long these conditions delayed the military response but that they were even a part of the discussion is troubling.

And at the same time the State Department appeared to waste time on what our soldiers would wear, it also appeared to waste time and focus on the YouTube video that the administration would later blame, falsely, for the attack. It has emerged that during an emergency call at 7:30 p.m. on the night of the attack involving Secretary Clinton and other high-level officials from the Department of Defense, State Department, and CIA that a full five of the eleven action items from the meeting related to the video.[116]

One such item had Secretary Panetta calling Pastor Terry Jones to ask him to take down the video. At this critical moment, with lives at risk in Benghazi and military assets sitting idle, it is difficult to imagine a worse use of the Defense Secretary's time than to call Pastor Jones about a video having nothing to do with the attack. Rather than diverting the Secretary of Defense's attention, every effort should have been made to marshal assets that could have gone to Benghazi.

We cannot say whether the military could have saved lives in Benghazi. We can say with certainty that our nation's leaders did not move heaven and earth to send military help with the urgency that those Americans deserved. We will never know if a more vigorous, comprehensive, and urgent response could have saved lives.

---

[116] *See* E-mail from State Dep't Operations to various (Sept. 11, 2012) (on file with the Committee, C05562037).

## IV. Justice Denied

*We will not waver in our commitment to see that justice is done for this terrible act. And make no mistake, justice will be done.*

Barack Obama
President of the United States [117]

The President made this promise the day after the attack. Secretary Clinton did much the same. In January 2015, White House Counsel W. Neil Eggleston said something very similar in a letter to the Committee where he claimed "[t]he Administration's focus since the attacks has been . . . an unwavering commitment to bring to justice those responsible for harming Americans[.]" [118] The words of the President and his lawyer were resolute and they were strong. But in the end they were just that, words.

Almost four years have passed since four Americans were killed by radical Islamic terrorists in Benghazi. As of the writing of this report, only one man—Ahmed Abu Khatallah—has been indicted and brought to the United States to face charges. [119] To the Committee's knowledge, no others have been taken into U.S. custody, let alone arrested and prosecuted. Secretary Clinton said, almost two years after the murders, "there's a lot we don't know about what happened in Benghazi." That may be true, but the United States does know the identity of many of the attackers. Yet, the resources devoted to bring them to justice have proven inadequate.

President Obama also claimed that Khattallah "will now face the full weight of the American justice system." To us, that means facing the full measure of punishment for killing four Americans. Yet, the administration has chosen—for reasons it refused to provide Congress—not to seek the death penalty in this case.

And so as we near the fourth anniversary of the attack, the American people, at a minimum, are owed an explanation for the administration's failure to bring more of those responsible to justice.

## V. Notes on the Investigation

For the past two years the Committee pressed for full and complete answers to the important questions left in Benghazi's wake. The American people—and especially the families of the victims and those injured—deserved nothing less.

---

[117] President Barack Obama, Remarks by the President on the Deaths of U.S. Embassy Staff in Libya (Sept. 12, 2012), https://www.whitehouse.gov/the-press-office/2012/09/12/remarks-president-deaths-us-embassy-staff-libya.

[118] Letter from W. Neil Eggleston to Hon. Trey Gowdy, Chairman, H. Sel. Comm. on the Events Surrounding the 2012 Terrorist Attack in Benghazi (Jan. 23, 2015) (on file with the Committee).

[119] It is worth noting that Abu Khatallah's capture demonstrated the capacity of the United States to execute a complex mission in a hostile place to bring a terrorist to justice. It is equally certain that the Obama administration's decision to treat Abu Khatallah and other terrorists as ordinary criminals—affording them the full panoply of legal protections available under U.S. law—has made it harder to capture Abu Khatallah's co-conspirators. That is because the decision denies our Intelligence Community the time and tools necessary to develop facts that might help to apprehend the others responsible. That may, in turn, explain, why dozens and dozens of Abu Khatallah's co-conspirators remain at large.

We approached the investigation believing facts were non-partisan. We knew some hoped the investigation would expose Secretary Clinton and President Obama for serious wrongdoing. Still others hoped, and in fact decided, that the investigation would find nothing—and they did their best to tarnish the Committee's reputation in case something damaging did emerge. But we suspected the vast majority of Americans simply wanted the truth, whatever it may look like, to come out in full.

We had hoped that Democrats on the Committee would join this effort as full partners and that the administration would cooperate with our work. That Republicans and Democrats would feel the weight of history, and the loss of four fellow Americans, and set aside partisan differences in favor of a joint search for the truth. If that had happened, it would not have been without precedent as we saw during the 9/11 Commission investigation. Yet, Minority Leader Pelosi set the tone early, even before the first witness was sworn in, and made clear that a truly bipartisan effort would never happen:

> Our nation deserves better than yet another deeply partisan and political review. It is disappointing that Republicans blocked a proposal offered by Democrats on the House floor today to ensure that this committee is truly bipartisan and fair—a proposal that would have allowed Democrats a real and equal voice on the committee, including on the issuance of subpoenas, the manner in which witnesses would be questioned and deposed, and the specific protocols governing how documents and other information would be obtained, used, and potentially released by the committee.

> It is clear that House Republicans will do anything to divert attention away from their failed leadership and do-nothing record. As they work to feed the most conspiracy-obsessed elements of their base, millions of Americans are languishing thanks to Republicans' refusal to act on the urgent business before our nation: renewing emergency unemployment insurance, raising the minimum wage, and creating jobs.[120]

It bears mentioning that the Democrats on the Committee could have asked for witnesses or documents but in the end asked for one witness and a handful of documents. In other words, we offered them the "real and equal voice on the committee" that Minority Leader Pelosi demanded, but they fell silent when it came time to do the work.

The Democrats on the Committee did not, however, fall completely silent. When they were not attacking the Republicans, they paid lip service to the notion of a bipartisan investigation. Ranking Member Cummings called for just that type of investigation during the first hearing, invoking the same slogan that Minority Leader Pelosi used and, of course, that President Obama had used before

---

[120] Nancy Pelosi, House Democratic Leader, Pelosi Statement on House Vote on Select Committee on Benghazi (May 8, 2014), http://www.democraticleader.gov/newsroom/pelosi-statement-house-vote-select-committee-benghazi/.

her: "Too often over the past two years, the congressional investigation into what happened in Benghazi has devolved into unseemly partisanship. We are better than that." In fact, we are better. But in the end they were just words.

The Democrats on the committee, showed little interest in seeking the truth and routinely turned the investigation into political theater. We had hoped for more from members that included two former criminal prosecutors. Instead, the Democrats and their staff spent the bulk of their time trying to discredit the Republican-led committee and leveling baseless personal attacks. The attacks were often ugly, always without merit, and unfailingly partisan and did nothing to advance the cause of finding the full and complete truth about Benghazi.

## VI. Conclusion

In the end, the administration's efforts to impede the investigation succeeded, but only in part. The minority members' and their staff's efforts to impede the investigation succeeded also, but again only in part. And although we answered many questions, we could not do so completely. What we did find was a tragic failure of leadership—in the run up to the attack and the night of—and an administration that, so blinded by politics and its desire to win an election, disregarded a basic duty of government: ***Tell the people the truth.*** And for those reasons Benghazi is, and always will be, an American tragedy.

MR. JORDAN.
MR. POMPEO.

# APPENDIX A:

## Resolution Establishing the Select Committee on the Events Surrounding the 2012 Terrorist Attack in Benghazi

## H. Res. 567

*In the House of Representatives, U. S.,*

*May 8, 2014.*

*Resolved,*

### SECTION 1. ESTABLISHMENT.

There is hereby established the Select Committee on the Events Surrounding the 2012 Terrorist Attack in Benghazi (hereinafter referred to as the "Select Committee").

### SEC. 2. COMPOSITION.

(a) The Speaker shall appoint 12 Members to the Select Committee, five of whom shall be appointed after consultation with the minority leader.

(b) The Speaker shall designate one Member to serve as chair of the Select Committee.

(c) Any vacancy in the Select Committee shall be filled in the same manner as the original appointment.

2

## SEC. 3. INVESTIGATION AND REPORT ON THE EVENTS SURROUNDING THE 2012 TERRORIST ATTACK IN BENGHAZI.

(a) The Select Committee is authorized and directed to conduct a full and complete investigation and study and issue a final report of its findings to the House regarding—

(1) all policies, decisions, and activities that contributed to the attacks on United States facilities in Benghazi, Libya, on September 11, 2012, as well as those that affected the ability of the United States to prepare for the attacks;

(2) all policies, decisions, and activities to respond to and repel the attacks on United States facilities in Benghazi, Libya, on September 11, 2012, including efforts to rescue United States personnel;

(3) internal and public executive branch communications about the attacks on United States facilities in Benghazi, Libya, on September 11, 2012;

(4) accountability for policies and decisions related to the security of facilities in Benghazi, Libya, and the response to the attacks, including individuals and entities responsible for those policies and decisions;

(5) executive branch authorities' efforts to identify and bring to justice the perpetrators of the attacks on U.S. facilities in Benghazi, Libya, on September 11, 2012;

3

(6) executive branch activities and efforts to comply with Congressional inquiries into the attacks on United States facilities in Benghazi, Libya, on September 11, 2012;

(7) recommendations for improving executive branch cooperation and compliance with congressional oversight and investigations;

(8) information related to lessons learned from the attacks and executive branch activities and efforts to protect United States facilities and personnel abroad; and

(9) any other relevant issues relating to the attacks, the response to the attacks, or the investigation by the House of Representatives into the attacks.

(b) In addition to any final report addressing the matters in subsection (a), the Select Committee may issue such interim reports as it deems necessary.

(c) Any report issued by the Select Committee may contain a classified annex.

**SEC. 4. PROCEDURE.**

(a) Notwithstanding clause 3(m) of rule X of the Rules of the House of Representatives, the Select Committee is authorized to study the sources and methods of entities described in clause 11(b)(1)(A) of rule X insofar as such study is related to the matters described in section 3.

4

(b) Clause 11(b)(4), clause 11(e), and the first sentence of clause 11(f) of rule X of the Rules of the House of Representatives shall apply to the Select Committee.

(c) Rule XI of the Rules of the House of Representatives shall apply to the Select Committee except as follows:

(1) Clause 2(a) of rule XI shall not apply to the Select Committee.

(2) Clause 2(g)(2)(D) of rule XI shall apply to the Select Committee in the same manner as it applies to the Permanent Select Committee on Intelligence.

(3) Pursuant to clause 2(h) of rule XI, two Members of the Select Committee shall constitute a quorum for taking testimony or receiving evidence and one-third of the Members of the Select Committee shall constitute a quorum for taking any action other than one for which the presence of a majority of the Select Committee is required.

(4) The chair of the Select Committee may authorize and issue subpoenas pursuant to clause 2(m) of rule XI in the investigation and study conducted pursuant to section 3 of this resolution, including for the purpose of taking depositions.

(5)(A) The chair of the Select Committee, upon consultation with the ranking minority member, may order the taking of depositions, under oath and pursuant to notice or subpoena, by a Member of the Select Committee or a counsel of the Select Committee.

(B) Depositions taken under the authority prescribed in this paragraph shall be governed by the procedures submitted by the chair of the Committee on Rules for printing in the Congressional Record.

(6) The chair of the Select Committee may, after consultation with the ranking minority member, recognize—

(A) Members of the Select Committee to question a witness for periods longer than five minutes as though pursuant to clause 2(j)(2)(B) of rule XI; and

(B) staff of the Select Committee to question a witness as though pursuant to clause 2(j)(2)(C) of rule XI.

## SEC. 5. RECORDS; STAFF; FUNDING.

(a) Any committee of the House of Representatives having custody of records in any form relating to the matters described in section 3 shall transfer such records to the Select Committee within 14 days of the adoption of this resolution. Such records shall become the records of the Select Committee.

(b)(1)(A) To the greatest extent practicable, the Select Committee shall utilize the services of staff of employing enti-

6

ties of the House. At the request of the chair of the Select Committee in consultation with the ranking minority member, staff of employing entities of the House or a joint committee may be detailed to the Select Committee without reimbursement to carry out this resolution and shall be deemed to be staff of the Select Committee.

(B) Section 202(i) of the Legislative Reorganization Act of 1946 (2 U.S.C. 4301(i)) shall apply with respect to the Select Committee in the same manner as such section applies with respect to a standing committee of the House of Representatives.

(2) The chair of the Select Committee, upon consultation with the ranking minority member, may employ and fix the compensation of such staff as the chair considers necessary to carry out this resolution.

(c) There shall be paid out of the applicable accounts of the House of Representatives such sums as may be necessary for the expenses of the Select Committee. Such payments shall be made on vouchers signed by the chair of the Select Committee and approved in the manner directed by the Committee on House Administration. Amounts made available under this subsection shall be expended in accordance with regulations prescribed by the Committee on House Administration.

7

## SEC. 6. DISSOLUTION AND DISPOSITION OF RECORDS.

(a) The Select Committee shall cease to exist 30 days after filing the final report required under section 3.

(b) Upon dissolution of the Select Committee, the records of the Select Committee shall become the records of such committee or committees designated by the Speaker.

Attest:

*Clerk.*

# APPENDIX B:

# Significant Persons and Organizations

## Persons

Abedin, Huma—Deputy Chief of Staff for Operations for the Secretary of State, Department of State

Bargathi, Abdul Salam—Leader of the Preventative Security Brigade, childhood friend of Abu Khattala

Bash, Jeremy—Chief of Staff to the Secretary of Defense, Department of Defense

Blumenthal, Sidney—Friend and Confidant of Secretary Hillary R. Clinton

Boswell, Eric—Assistant Secretary of State for Diplomatic Security/Director of the Office of Foreign Missions, Department of State

Breedlove, Philip M.—General, United States Air Force; Commander of the U.S. Air Forces Europe/U.S. Air Forces Africa, Department of Defense

Brennan, John Owen—Deputy National Security Advisor for Homeland Security and Counterterrorism, and Assistant to the President, White House

Bukatef, Fawzi—Leader of the February 17 Martyrs Brigade, the group that housed a Quick Reaction Force (QRF) at the Benghazi Mission compound

Bultrowicz, Scott—Director, Diplomatic Security Service and Principal Deputy Secretary of State, Bureau of Diplomatic Security, Department of State

Burns, William—Deputy Secretary of State, Department of State

Carney, Jay—Press Secretary, White House

Chorin, Ethan—Author and Chief Executive Officer, Perim Associates

Clapper, James R.—Lieutenant General, Director, Office of National Intelligence

Clinton, Hillary R.—Secretary of State (January 2009 until February 2013), Department of State

Cretz, Gene Allan—Ambassador to Libya (December 2008 until May 2012), Department of State

Dempsey, Martin E.—General, United States Army; Chairman of the Joint Chiefs of Staff (October 2011 until September 2015), Department of Defense

Dibble, Elizabeth—Principal Deputy Assistant Secretary, Bureau of Near Eastern Affairs, Department of State

DiCarlo, Rosemary—Deputy Permanent Representative (to Susan Rice), then the Permanent Representative to the U.S. Mission to the United Nations, Department of State

Doherty, Glen Anthony—Contractor, Global Response Staff (GRS), Central Intelligence Agency

Donilon, Thomas E.—National Security Advisor to the President, White House

Duval, Catherine—Senior Advisor, Bureau of Legislative Affairs, Department of State

Evers, Austin—Advisor, Bureau of Legislative Affairs, Department of State

Feltman, Jeffrey—Assistant Secretary of State for Near Eastern Affairs (until May 2012), Department of State

Fishman, Benjamin—Member of the National Security Council, White House

Flynn, Michael—Lieutenant General, United States Army; Director, Defense Intelligence Agency (DIA), Department of Defense

Frifield, Julia—Assistant Secretary of State for Legislative Affairs, Department of State

Gharabi, Mohammad—Leader of the Rafallah al-Sahati Brigade

Gibbons, Thomas B.—Acting Assistant Secretary of Legislative Affairs, Department of State

Gordon, Philip—Assistant Secretary for European and Eurasian Affairs Department of State

Ham, Carter—General, United States Army; Commander of U.S. Africa Command, Department of Defense

Hamid, Wissam bin—Commander, Libya Shield Brigade

Hicks, Gregory—Deputy Chief of Mission, Libya, Department of State

Jones, Elizabeth—Acting Assistant Secretary of State, Bureau of Near Eastern Affairs, Department of State

Kelly, John—General, United States Army; Senior Military Assistant to the Secretary of Defense, Department of Defense

Kelly, Thomas—Assistant Secretary for Political-Military Affairs, Department of State

Kennedy, Patrick F.—Under Secretary for Management, Department of State

Kerry, John—Secretary of State (February 2013 to present), Department of State

Khattala, Ahmed Abu—Founded Obeida Ibn al-Jarra Militia, in U.S. custody for his suspected involvement in the Benghazi attacks

Koh, Harold—Legal Advisor, Department of State

Lamb, Charlene—Deputy Assistant Secretary of State for International Programs, Bureau of Diplomatic Security, Department of State

Landolt, Richard B.—Rear Admiral, United States Navy; Director of Operations and Cyber, U.S. Africa Command, Department of Defense

Leidig, Jr., Charles J.—Vice Admiral, United States Navy; Deputy to the Commander for Military Operations, U.S. Africa Command, Department of Defense

Litt, Robert S.—General Counsel, Office of the Director of National Intelligence

Lohman, Lee—Executive Director, Bureau of Near Eastern Affairs/ Bureau of South and Central Asian Affairs, Department of State

Losey, Brian—Rear Admiral, United States Navy; Commander of Special Operations Command (SOC) Africa, Department of Defense

Macmanus, Joseph—Executive Assistant to the Secretary of State, Office of the Secretary, Department of State (from May 2012 until November 2012)

Magariaf, Mohamad Yousef—President, General National Congress of Libya

Maxwell, Raymond—Deputy Assistant Secretary of State for Maghreb Affairs, Bureau of Near Eastern Affairs, Department of State

McDonough, Denis—Deputy National Security Advisor, White House

Meehan, Bernadette—Assistant Press Secretary for the National Security Council, White House

Mills, Cheryl D.—Chief of Staff and Counselor to the Secretary of State, Department of State

Mordente, Patrick—General, United States Air Force; Director of Operations (J3) for the U.S. Transportation Command (TRANSCOM), Department of Defense

Morell, Michael—Deputy Director, Central Intelligence Agency

Mull, Stephen—Executive Secretariat, Office of the Secretary of State, Department of State

Mullen, Michael—Admiral, United States Navy; Chairman of the Joint Chiefs of Staff/Vice Chairman, Benghazi Accountability Review Board

Nides, Thomas—Deputy Secretary of State for Management and Resources, Department of State

Nuland, Victoria J.—Spokesperson, Department of State

Obeidi, Fathi—Lieutenant commander in a branch of Libyan Shield/Commander of Special Operations for Libya Shield

Olsen, Matthew—Director of the National Counterterrorism Center, Office of the Director of National Intelligence

Pagliano, Bryan—Special Advisor, Bureau of Information Resource Management, Department of State

Panetta, Leon—Secretary of Defense (July 2011 until February 2013), Department of Defense

Pelton, Erin—Communications Director and Spokesperson for Ambassador Susan Rice, Department of State

Petraeus, David—Director, Central Intelligence Agency

Pickering, Thomas R.—Chairman, Benghazi Accountability Review Board

Polaschik, Joan—Deputy Chief of Mission for Tripoli, Libya (2009 until June 2012), Department of State

Reines, Philippe—Deputy Assistant Secretary for Public Affairs, Department of State

Repass, Michael S.—Major General, United States Army; Commander, Special Operations Command (SOC) Europe, Department of Defense

Rhodes, Benjamin—Assistant to the President and Deputy National Security Advisor for Strategic Communications and Speechwriting, White House

Rice, Susan E.—U.S. Permanent Representative to the United Nations, Department of State

Roebuck, William—Director, Office of Maghreb Affairs, Bureau of Near Eastern Affairs, Department of State

Ryu, Rexon—Deputy to the U.S. Ambassador to the United Nations, Department of State

Sanderson, Janet—Deputy Assistant Secretary for Near Eastern Affairs, Department of State

Shapiro, Andrew—Assistant Secretary of State for Political-Military Affairs, Department of State

Sherman, Wendy—Under Secretary for Political Affairs, Department of State

Smith, Gentry—Deputy Assistant Secretary of State for Countermeasures, Bureau of Diplomatic Security, Department of State

Smith, Sean—Information Management Officer, Department of State

Starr, Gregory—Assistant Secretary of State for Diplomatic Security (November 2013 to present), Department of State

Steinberg, James—Deputy Secretary of State, Department of State

Stevens, John Christopher—U.S. Representative to the Libyan Transitional National Council/Ambassador to Libya (May 2012 until September 2012), Department of State

Sullivan, Jacob J.—Deputy Chief of Staff and Director of Policy Planning, Department of State

Taylor, William—Special Coordinator for Middle Eastern Transitions, Department of State

Thompson, Mark—Deputy Coordinator, Operations Directorate, Bureau of Counterterrorism, Department of State

Tidd, Kurt—Vice Admiral, United States Navy; Director of Operations (J3) for the Joint Chiefs of Staff, Department of Defense

Ventrell, Patrick—Acting Deputy Spokesperson, Department of State

Winnefeld, Jr., James—Admiral, United States Navy; Vice Chairman of the Joint Chiefs of Staff, Department of Defense

Woods, Tyrone Snowden—Contractor, Global Response Staff (GRS), Central Intelligence Agency

Zeya, Uzra—Chief of Staff to Deputy Secretary Burns, Department of State/ Executive Secretary, Benghazi Accountability Review Board

## Entities

al-Qa'ida in the Arabian Peninsula (AQAP)-al-Qa'ida affiliate

al-Qa'ida in the Islamic Maghreb (AQIM)-al-Qa'ida affiliate

Ansar al-Sharia-Benghazi (AAS-B)—Previously led by the now-deceased Mohammed Ali al-Zahawi, now officially designated as a foreign terror organization

Ansar al-Sharia-Darnah (AAS-D)—Darnah branch of AAS headed by former Guantanamo detainee Abu Sufyan bin Qumo

Blue Mountain Group (BMG)—British company providing unarmed guards used for static security at the Mission

Blue Mountain Libya—Libyan Partner of BMG, signed joint venture with BMG

February 17 Martyrs Brigade—The purported largest militia group in Benghazi, headed by Fawzi Bukatef. The group supplied a four man team of local militiamen to serve as the Quick Reaction Force (QRF) at the Benghazi Mission

Libyan Air Force—The entity that provided the C-130 that evacuated the second set of Americans from Benghazi (this included the uninjured CIA Protective officer, one DS agent, and the remains of the four deceased)

Libya Shield—An umbrella organization of militias to support Libyan Army initiatives throughout the country, the separate Libya Shields were not always cohesive and not all worked in the best interests of the Libyan Army and Libyan government writ-large

Libyan Military Intelligence—The group that helped Americans evacuate from the Annex to the Benghazi airport after the mortar attacks early on September 12th

Mohammad Jamal Network—Group leadership historically affiliated with al-Qa'ida Senior Leader Dr. Ayman al-Zawahiri; other affiliations to AQIM and AQAP

Obeida Ibn al-Jarra Militia—Islamist militia led by Ahmed Abu Khattala, a breakaway faction from Ansar al-Sharia-Benghazi (AAS-B)

Rafallah al-Sahati Brigade—A small militia that also operated under the Libya Shield umbrella; at the time of the attacks, the militia was in possession of kidnapped Iranian hostages

Sheikh Omar Abdel-Rahman Brigades—Islamist militia based in Benghazi, Libya

Supreme Security Council—A quasi-government organization involved in security and policing matters in Benghazi, now defunct

# APPENDIX C:

## Questions for the President

June 7, 2016
W. Neil Eggleston
Counsel to the President
The White House
1600 Pennsylvania Avenue NW
Washington, D.C. 20500

Dear Neil:

Shortly after the formation of the Select Committee on the Events Surrounding the 2012 Terrorist Attack in Benghazi, Libya, you and I spoke on the phone. During that conversation I informed you the Committee would not compel an interview with the President and the Committee was familiar with and would respect the Executive Privilege attached to certain communications with the President. I also told you the Committee would send written questions to the President at the culmination of our investigation. I assured you these questions would not be publicized at the time they were sent and furthermore the questions would be limited to information that could not be obtained from other sources.

At our meeting in Charlotte, N.C. in January of 2016, I further offered to show you the questions in advance and provide the underlying testimony that gave rise to the question. In other words, each of these questions has an evidentiary basis rooted in either documents or other testimony, and I was willing to show you the questions and the foundation for the questions.

While I would have been pleased to meet with you again, the reality is we would have gone over the same ground previously visited. The Executive Branch would, perhaps, argue sending questions to the President is "unprecedented" and would create a "constitutional crisis." The Legislative Branch would argue several prior Committee Chairmen sent an extensive set of questions to the President regarding Benghazi, the President has answered media inquiries about Benghazi without a "constitutional crisis," and the President is uniquely situated to answer these questions. In fact, he is the only person who can answer some of these questions.

As such, below are fifteen questions for the President regarding the Benghazi attacks. Thank you in advance for a reply to these questions no later than June 17, 2016.

Sincerely,
/s/

Trey Gowdy
Chairman


Begin attachment

Questions for the President

1. The White House issued a readout of your meeting with senior administration officials on September 10, 2012, indicating "specific measures" had been taken to "prevent 9/11 related attacks." What were these specific measures, and how did these specific measures differ from specific measures taken on prior anniversaries of September 11?

2. When did you first learn a U.S. facility in Benghazi, Libya, had been attacked? What were you told, and by whom? Were you informed Sean Smith had been killed during the initial attack?

3. What orders or direction, if any, did you give to Secretary of Defense Leon Panetta upon learning of the initial attack? Did you or anyone at your direction ever modify, withdraw, alter, or amplify the initial orders or direction you gave to Secretary Panetta?

4. What were you told about Department of Defense assets in the region that could respond specifically to Benghazi? Did you ask for or receive a list of military or paramilitary assets in the region that could respond to Benghazi during the pendency of the attacks?

5. Were you subsequently kept informed about the initial attack, subsequent attacks, and/or efforts to either send military assistance or evacuate U.S. personnel? By whom?

6. When did you learn Ambassador Christopher Stevens was missing, and who informed you? Were you kept informed on efforts to locate Ambassador Stevens, and if so, by whom? When did you learn Ambassador Stevens was dead, and who informed you?

7. [Classified]

8. Were you aware that prior to any military asset moving to respond to the attacks the State Department expressed concerns to the White House about the number of military assets going into Libya?

9. When did you learn of a mortar attack that killed Tyrone Woods and Glen Doherty? Who informed you?

10. Were you aware of any efforts by White House and Department of Defense officials during the evening of September 11, 2012, and into the early morning hours of September 12, 2012, to reach out to YouTube and Terry Jones regarding an anti-

Muslim video? What specifically connected the attacks in Benghazi to this anti-Muslim [sic] video, and why weren't these efforts made after the protests in Cairo, Egypt?

11. When did you learn individuals associated with terrorist organizations participated in the attack on the U.S. facilities in Benghazi, Libya?

12. Did you receive the President's Daily Brief (PDB) on September 12, 2012 and September 13, 2012? If so, who provided you with the PDB?

13. Have you ever viewed surveillance footage from the cameras (or other sources) located at the U.S. facilities in Benghazi depicting the attacks? Will you declassify this footage so the American people can see for themselves what transpired?

14. Did you authorize a covert action or covert operation to provide lethal assistance to Libyan rebels?

15. [Classified]

# APPENDIX D:

## Significant Events in Libya Prior to the Attacks

**February 22, 2011**—Embassy Tripoli is evacuated because of emerging civil war.

On or around **March 11, 2011**—Decision made to send a representative to Benghazi to liaise with the emerging transitional national council [TNC]. Hillary R. Clinton, Secretary of State, asks J. Christopher Stevens to serve as Representative to the TNC.

**April 5, 2011**—Stevens enters Benghazi and stays at the Tibesti Hotel.

**April 10, 2011**—Stevens and team contemplate leaving Benghazi because of security concerns.

**June 10, 2011**—Stevens and team leave Tibesti Hotel and stay temporarily with other U.S. government personnel in Benghazi.

**June 21, 2011**—Stevens and team relocate to an interim facility later known as Villa A.

**July 15, 2011**—U.S. recognizes the TNC as the "Legitimate Representative of the Libyan People."

**August 3, 2011**—Stevens and team sign leases for Villas A, B, and C.

**August 21, 2011**—Tripoli falls.

**August 22, 2011**—The Secretary takes credit for events in Tripoli.

**August 30, 2011**—The Secretary's staff want team in Tripoli as soon as possible.

**September 22, 2011**—The U.S. Embassy in Tripoli reopens and Gene A.Cretz resumes position as U.S. Ambassador to Libya.

**October 18, 2011**—The Secretary travels to Tripoli but not Benghazi.

**October 20, 2011**—Muammar Qadhafi executed.

**October 23, 2011**—Libya officially liberated.

On or around **November 20, 2011**—Stevens leaves Benghazi.

**November 21, 2011**—First principal officer arrives in Benghazi to replace Stevens.

**December 27, 2011**—Extension Memorandum drafted by the Bureau of Near East Affairs sent to Patrick F. Kennedy, Under Secretary for Management, State Department, outlining continued operations in Benghazi. The memorandum was approved on January 5, 2012.

**December 2011**—Diplomatic Security agent staffing concerns in Benghazi.

**February 2012**—Life Services contract cancelled in Benghazi.

**February 2012**—Local Guard Force service contract awarded to Blue Mountain Group.

**March 28, 2012**—U.S. Embassy in Tripoli requests additional staff including five Diplomatic Security agents for Benghazi Mission compound.

**April 2, 2012**—Attack on United Kingdom [UK] armored vehicle.

**April 6, 2012**—First improvised explosive device [IED] attack on the Benghazi Mission compound.

**April 10, 2012**—IED attack on the motorcade of the United Nations Special Envoy.

**April 19, 2012**—Washington, D.C., denies request for five Diplomatic Security agents to be assigned to Benghazi Mission compound.

**May 14, 2012**—Stevens sworn in as Ambassador to Libya.

**May 22, 2012**—Rocket propelled grenade [RPG] attack on International Committee of the Red Cross

**May 26, 2012**—Stevens returns to Libya.

**May 28, 2012**—Threat to Benghazi Mission compound posted on Facebook.

**June 2012**—Blue Mountain Group issues with Libyan partner.

**June 5, 2012**—Stevens requests State Department mobile security deployment [MSD] team remain in Tripoli.

**June 6, 2012**—Stevens requests MSD team.

**June 6, 2012**—Second IED attack on the Benghazi Mission compound.

**June 11, 2012**—RPG attack on UK Ambassador motorcade

**June 14, 2012**—Emergency Action Committee [EAC] held in Benghazi.

**June 15, 2012**—U.S. Embassy in Tripoli again requests five Diplomatic Security agents for Benghazi Mission compound. Washington, D.C., never responds.

**July 7, 2012**—First national democratic elections held in Libya.

**July 9, 2012**—U.S. Embassy in Tripoli requests to either maintain or replace departing U.S. security personnel with high threat trained Diplomatic Security agents. The Embassy tells Washington, D.C., if you send three agents to the Benghazi Mission compound the Embassy will also send a regional security office. Washington, D.C., never responds to the request.

**August 5, 2012**—International Committee of the Red Cross attacked for fifth time shutting down Red Cross operations in both Benghazi and Misrata, Libya.

**August 15, 2012**—Benghazi holds EAC on deteriorating security situation and requests ability to collocate with other U.S. government personnel.

**August 27, 2012**—U.S. issues travel alert for Libya.

**August 29, 2012**—State of Maximum Alert issued for Benghazi. Alert suspended on September 2.

**August 30, 2012**—Both the Principal Officer and Diplomatic Security agent in charge depart Benghazi. There is a gap in coverage by the Principal Officer until September 15, 2012. Also, no Diplomatic Security agents volunteered to secure the compound during fall 2012. The Benghazi Mission compound was down to two Diplomatic Security agents. An agent is rerouted from the U.S. Embassy in Tripoli to the Benghazi Mission compound bringing the number to 3.

**August 30, 2012**—U.S. Embassy in Tripoli sends one Diplomatic Security agent to ensure three agents are assigned to the Benghazi Mission compound.

On or around **August 30, 2012**—Stevens sends Political/Economic Officer, U.S. Embassy in Tripoli, State Department, to Benghazi Mission compound to cover reporting the first week in September. Stevens himself will cover duties beginning on September 10, 2012.

**September 6, 2012**—Benghazi Mission compound requests presence of Supreme Security Council police from September 10–15.

**September 8, 2012**—February 17 Martyrs Brigade tells Diplomatic Security agents it will no longer support off–compound moves.

**September 8, 2012**—Principal Officer holds meeting with local militia and is told they cannot guarantee the safety of the Benghazi Mission compound.

**September 10, 2011**—Stevens arrives with two Diplomatic Security agents.

**September 11, 2012**—The attacks begin.

# APPENDIX E:

## Security Incidents In Libya

From the outset, the security environment in Benghazi was precarious. Stevens' mission to Benghazi began in the midst of a civil war—with Benghazi serving as the home to the opposition and rebel forces. Notwithstanding the civil war's end in August 2011 with the fall of Tripoli and later Libya's liberation on October 23, 2011, the security environment in Libya, including Benghazi, remained tenuous. At the time the Benghazi mission was extended in December 2011, the State Department's own threat rating system considered Libya to be a grave risk to American diplomats. The security environment only deteriorated from there. The Diplomatic Security agents on the ground tracked the security incidents in Libya between 2011 and 2012. Documents prepared by the agents tracking security incidents are included below.

U.S. EMBASSY – TRIPOLI, LIBYA          REGIONAL SECURITY OFFICE

## SECURITY INCIDENTS SINCE JUNE 2011

### ON 1 JUNE 2011 – BENGHAZI

CAR BOMB EXPLODES OUTSIDE HOTEL: A car bomb exploded outside the Tibesti Hotel in Benghazi. Following this explosion, other devices were discovered and made safe by the local authorities. TNC officials blamed former regime officials for the incident.

### 10 SEPTEMBER 2011 -- LIBYA / TUNISIA / ALGERIAN BORDER

UK CITIZEN KIDNAPPED: According to the UK High Commission, a British national was kidnapped in the Libya/Tunisia/Algeria border area on 10 September 2011 and was subsequently released on 12 September 2011.

### 23 SEPTEMBER 2011 – TRIPOLI

PIPE BOMBS THROWN AT NTC FORCES: At approximately 0042, U.S. Embassy local guard force (LGF) personnel received a report that two crude pipe bombs were thrown at NTC forces manning a nearby checkpoint. The checkpoint was located approximately 500 meters west of the temporary U.S. Embassy residential buildings. According to the NTC personnel at the checkpoint, individuals approached the check point in a 4Dr white, Chevrolet Opra sedan and threw two (2) pipe bombs at the NTC forces. The suspect(s) vehicle was identified as a white Chevrolet Opra (4-door sedan). NTC Forces initiated a search for the suspect(s), and no injuries were reported. U.S. Embassy security officials viewed the site during day time hours and confirmed that a crude device had detonated.

### 26 SEPTEMBER 2011 – TRIPOLI

ALLEGED THREAT FROM PRO-GHADDAFI ELEMENTS AGAINST VARIOUS TARGETS: A letter in Arabic was disseminated to Libyan citizens warning of impending attacks against unspecified targets on/about 27 September. The attacks would allegedly be carried out using explosives and small arms in the Abu Salim and Ghar bin Gashir areas of Tripoli, to include neighborhoods near Tripoli International Airport. The letter called on individuals to support the Ghaddafi regime and warned of potential violence in the streets.

### 27 SEPTEMBER 2011 – BENGHAZI

**Militia Commanders Protest Outside TNC Headquarters** – Fifteen commanders from the Protective Security Brigade, a Ministry of Interior-affiliated militia that protects key infrastructure within the city of Benghazi, protested in front of the headquarters of the TNC. They claimed that Minister of Interior Ahmed Darat was not providing them with equipment and they condemned his ministry's attempts to dissolve their militia. They also complained that members of the old regime, especially in the external and internal intelligence/security organs, were still holding their jobs and should be fired.

**Protests in Downtown Benghazi Over Holdovers from Old Regime** – Hundreds protested in Benghazi's central Freedom Square calling for the removal of "climbers," i.e. those allegedly connected to the regime, from schools and universities, hospitals, the police, Libya's embassies, and private companies. Protesters' chants included "Come on, Benghazi, the revolution still lives!"

U.S. EMBASSY — TRIPOLI, LIBYA                    REGIONAL SECURITY OFFICE                    E-3

## SECURITY INCIDENTS SINCE JUNE 2011

### 28-30 SEPTEMBER 2011 – TRIPOLI

**HOTEL TARGETED BY SMALL ARMS FIRE:**
According to German Embassy officials, the RIXOS hotel received sustained gunfire from an adjacent park during the evenings on 09/28, 09/29, and 09/30 culminating in gunfire which penetrated one of the windows for the German Embassy's security team. The Germans Embassy officials stated that Hotel Security at the RIXOS advised the gunfire was initiated by pro-Ghaddafi forces probing the perimeter security. The German mission left the RIXOS hotel shortly after the incident.

### 03 OCTOBER 2011 – TRIPOLI

**GUNFIGHT NEAR MISSION PROPERTY:** At approximately 2030 hrs, several vehicles and their passengers were engaged in a moving gunfight which passed in front of a temporary U.S. Embassy residential site. One of the chase vehicle struck an Embassy vehicle parked on an adjacent street, although no injuries of US government personnel was reported as a result of the gunfire. Local council officials provided varied accounts of what had caused the gunfire, the most plausible explanation was that local militia members were chasing a former regime supporter who had recently returned from Tunisia.

### 08 OCTOBER 2011 - TRIPOLI

**CELEBRATORY GUNFIRE HITS U.S. MISSION COMPOUND; USG VEHICLE DAMAGED:** On October 8, 2011, at 1715 local time, at least three rounds of celebratory small arms fire (CSAF) impacted on the Embassy residential site in Tripoli. Heavy small arms celebratory occurred in the area surrounding the two Embassy residential sites after the Libyan national soccer team

defeated the Zambian national team. MSD and RSO initiated duck and cover procedures, donning of PPE, and directed all personnel to remain indoors for the duration of the celebratory fire. An MSD agent and POLOFF were returning to one of the residential sites as directed when at least three rounds of fire impacted the three story apartment building. No injuries to Mission personnel resulted from the fire. The all clear was given at approximately 1745 hours and RSO personnel responded to the scene to assess the number of impacted rounds.

On October 9, 2011, at 0845 local time, RSO conducted a subsequent inventory and inspection of Mission vehicles parked in an adjacent lot to the residential site. RSO observed that at least two additional rounds impacted an Embassy soft-skinned vehicle, causing damage to the windshield, and a wall directly in front of the residential compound.

### 12 OCTOBER 2011 - TRIPOLI

**CELEBRATORY GUNFIRE HITS MISSION COMPOUND:** On October 12, 2011, at approximately 2200 local time, heavy celebratory gunfire, including some heavy weapons fire and substantial amounts of tracer fire, erupted throughout Tripoli, Libya to include from properties and personnel adjacent to the Embassy Residential Compound. Local media advised that the gunfire was in response to the reported capture of one of Ghaddafi's sons in fighting in Sirte, Libya. No injuries or significant property damage reported, however, several Mission personnel reported or observed what appeared to be rounds impacting on the residential property. Subsequent review of the residential compound confirmed that two rounds of celebratory small arms fire impacted the Mission Residential Compound.

### 14 OCTOBER 2011 - TRIPOLI

**ARMED ROBBERY OF ORE STAFF:** On the morning of 14 October 2011, a member of the Mission's local official residence (ORE) staff, a citizen of Pakistan, was robbed by three males at knife point of his cellular telephone and approximately 200 LYD while walking to a taxi stand. The incident occurred in daylight hours in the Burg al Fateh area of Tripoli. The victim went immediately to a nearby police station to report the incident and was told by the police that they could do nothing since Libya was "without a government or laws".

**Heavy fighting erupts in Tripoli between TNC militias and alleged pro-Ghaddafi forces:** On October 14, 2011, at approximately 1600 hrs local time, heavy fighting erupted between TNC militias and alleged pro-Ghaddafi forces in the downtown area of Tripoli in the vicinity of the Rixos Hotel. Initial reports claimed units numbering up to 50 individuals were engaged on both sides of the fighting.

U.S. security personnel in downtown Tripoli reported the presence of heavy militia checkpoints in the downtown area, extensive security in the Martyr's Square neighborhood, the deployment of TNC militia heavy weapons 'technical's', and intensive vehicle searches in roads around the Rixos Hotel and Abu Salim neighborhoods; traditional pro-Ghaddafi strongholds.

U.K security personnel advised that an unidentified truck strafed the Radisson Blu hotel with heavy weapons fire and fled the area east bound at approximately 1700 hrs. TNC militia

pursued the vehicle, believed to be affiliated with pro-Ghaddafi forces. The Radisson Blu Hotel is the location for the temporary UK Embassy.

At 1840 hours, U.S. Embassy officials received unconfirmed reports that two hand grenades were thrown at the Al Mahir Hotel, located near the Radisson Blu Hotel.

**QADHAFI SPOKESPERSON DR. MOUSSA IBRAHIM REPORTEDLY CALLS FOR SUPPORTERS TO RISE UP AND ATTACK THE US, FRENCH, AND ITALIAN EMBASSIES IN TRIPOLI.** On October 14, 2011, at approximately 2300 hrs local time, U.S. Embassy security officials received information that Dr. Moussa Ibrahim, Qadhafi's spokesperson, reportedly called upon Qadhafi's "Eagles {supporters}" to rise up and attack the US, French, and Italian Embassies in Libya. The statement reportedly appeared on Allibiya TV (http://www.facebook.com/AllibiyaTV), a pro-Qadhafi news outlet.

The alleged statement is consistent with open source and social media reporting of Qadhafi's calls for a loyalist uprising against the TNC and NATO to start on October 14, 2011. Post received unconfirmed reports that a Facebook campaign, possibly via the AllibiyaTV facebook page, also called on Qadhafi loyalists to target the Radisson hotel which was hit by gunfire earlier in the evening of the 14th.

### 23 OCTOBER 2011 - TRIPOLI

**LGF HIT BY ROCK:** An unidentified individual threw a rock at a member of the U.S. Embassy's local guard force while on patrol near the southern wall of the Embassy's residential compound. The rock appeared to come from a

U.S. EMBASSY – TRIPOLI, LIBYA                    REGIONAL SECURITY OFFICE            E-5

## SECURITY INCIDENTS SINCE JUNE 2011

multi-story apartment building adjacent to the compound.

### 28 OCTOBER 2011 – TRIPOLI

**DIPLOMATIC VEHICLE STOLEN:** Italian Embassy Security Representatives reported the theft of an unarmored, official Embassy vehicle from outside of the temporary Italian Embassy property. The vehicle bore local Libyan license plates and was parked in front of the Italian Embassy property. The Italian Embassy Security Representatives reported that the vehicle was taken during night-time hours.

### 26 OCTOBER 2011 – TRIPOLI

**HAND GRENADE RECOVERED FROM MISSION PROPERTY LAWN - DISARMED AND DISPOSED WITHOUT INJURY:** On 26 October 2011, at approximately 0900 hours, an unused hand-grenade was found on the lawn of a U.S. Embassy annex property located near the airport road. The hand-grenade had not been activated and was uncovered during landscaping in preparation for the visit of a VIP. Embassy security officials responded to the compound and coordinated with the Zintan Military Brigade, who removed and disarmed the grenade. The grenade was a Soviet-era fragmentation grenade, model RDG-5.

The hand grenade had not been activated. Based on its location, Post's assessment is that the grenade was dropped by the prior residents of the compound and uncovered during landscaping and compound rehabilitation activities. A number of TNC militias and local citizens had utilized the property during the Libyan civil war. The property was formally leased to a U.S. company, which evacuated Tripoli at the start of the revolution. No injuries or damage to U.S. personnel or property.

One of the major concerns for post is the uncontrolled and unaccounted for amounts of small arms, explosives, RPGs, and weaponry in circulation within Libya as a result of the civil war. Although the compound had been searched for the presence of UXO prior to occupancy, the lack of landscaping and upkeep of most residential compounds has significantly complicated EOD/UXO recovery and removal efforts.

### 30 OCTOBER 2011 – TRIPOLI

**ATTEMPTED ROBBERY OF WAREHOUSE:** On 30 October 2011, at approximately 0315 hrs, at the Embassy's warehouse located on the eastern side of Tripoli, at least 2 unidentified gunmen in an unidentified vehicle began firing their weapons into the air outside the warehouse gate as part of an apparent robbery attempt. The individuals shouted to the local guards on post to open the gate and the guards refused, asking for the identity of the persons in response. At least one of the unidentified gunmen climbed the front vehicle gate and attempted to view the inside of the warehouse compound. Local guards on post contacted the local guard force commander and the landlord for the warehouse, who resides at a house next to the warehouse. The landlord responded to the warehouse via a secondary gate, and fired two rounds from his personal

AK47 into the air, causing the unidentified gunmen to flee the area. No injuries or damage to USG property were reported.

### 31 OCTOBER 2011 – TRIPOLI

**WAR-WOUNDED PROTESTS:** A group of 25-30 unarmed men apparently protesting the treatment of war-wounded breached the front gate of the TNC Cabinet headquarters today before they were turned away by armed guards at the door after several minutes of heated argument.

### 01 NOVEMBER – TRIPOLI

**MILITIA FIREFIGHT AT HOSPITAL:** A group of Zintan militia affiliated fighters stormed a hospital in Tripoli and demanded the hand-over of a fighter who was wounded earlier in the day. The wounded militiaman had been injured in an earlier clash that also left another militiaman dead. The doctors refused and a Tripoli militia, in charge of hospital security, forced the Zintan affiliated militia out of the hospital. During the altercation, the Zintan affiliated militia reportedly fired rounds at the hospital which escalated the situation. Reinforcements responded to both militias and the fighting escalated to include the use of heavy machine guns and anti-aircraft guns. The gunfight lasted approximately three hours. There were no direct fatalities from the fighting, but three patients at the hospital died due to stress-related causes linked to the clashes. Three Tripoli fighters were wounded. The fighting reportedly ended after calls from a local imam and senior commanders from both groups talked by phone with their men.

### 03 NOVEMBER 2011 - TRIPOLI

**ATTEMPTED CAR-JACKING OF LES:** On 03 November 2011 at 1200 hrs, a US EMBASSY local employed staff member (LES) was targeted for a robbery or car-jacking incident while in the Gargaresh section of Tripoli. According to the LES staff member, he was visiting a local bank on behalf of the Embassy. When the LES pulled into a street near the bank, he noted a vehicle approaching him at a high-rate of speed. The LES staff member reported that the vehicle stopped in front of his car and blocked his path. Two

young males then exited the vehicle, told the LES staff member to wait, and then appeared to reach into their vehicle to retrieve automatic weapons. The LES staff member put his car in reverse and began backing out of the area as he continued to observe the two males in front of him. As he was focused on the persons in front of him, the LES staff member did not check his mirrors and hit a vehicle parked behind him. The two individuals got back in their vehicle and sped away. The owner of the vehicle hit by the LES staff member also observed the incident and was understanding given the circumstances.

**HAND GRENADE RECOVERED FROM MISSION PROPERTY - DISARMED AND DISPOSED WITHOUT INJURY:** On 03 NOVEMBER 2011, at approximately 0900 hours, an unused hand-grenade was found on the lawn of a U.S. Embassy annex property located near the airport road. The hand-grenade had not been activated and was uncovered during landscaping in preparation for the visit of a VIP. Embassy security officials responded to the compound and coordinated with the Zintan Military Brigade, who removed and disarmed the grenade. The grenade was a Soviet-era fragmentation grenade, model RDG-5. The hand grenade had not been activated. Based on its location, Post's assessment is that the grenade was dropped by the prior residents of the compound and uncovered during landscaping and compound rehabilitation activities. A number of TNC militias and local citizens had utilized the property during the Libyan civil war. The property was formally leased to a U.S. company, which evacuated Tripoli at the start of the revolution. No injuries or damage to U.S. personnel or property.

U.S. Embassy — Tripoli, Libya          Regional Security Office          E-7

## SECURITY INCIDENTS SINCE JUNE 2011

One of the major concerns for post is the uncontrolled and unaccounted for amounts of small arms, explosives, RPGs, and weaponry in circulation within Libya as a result of the civil war. Although the compound had been searched for the presence of UXO prior to occupancy, the lack of landscaping and upkeep of most residential compounds has significantly complicated EOD/UXO recovery and removal efforts.

### 14 NOVEMBER 2011 – TRIPOLI

DEMONSTRATION AT RADISSON HOTEL: 200-300 members of the Warshafanna tribe demonstrated at the Radisson Hotel on November 14, protesting TNC Minister of Communications Shammam's statement characterizing the tribe as Qadhafi loyalists. Separately, a senior TNC military official told an Embassy that the clashes were centered on a dispute over control of the former 32$^{nd}$ brigade compound and did not involve any pro-Qadhafi loyalists.

### 08 – NOVEMBER 2011 - NIGER / LIBYAN BORDER

BORDER GUNFIGHT: An allegedly pro-Gaddafi armed convoy attempted crossing the Libyan border into Niger, where they were stopped by elements of the Nigerien army. In the ensuing gun battle, one Nigerian and thirteen (13) Libyan militia members were killed.

### 08 – 13 NOVEMBER 2011 – ZAWIYA / OUTSKIRTS OF TRIPOLI

MILITIA / TRIBAL CLASHES: Large-scale fighting erupted in the outskirts of Tripoli, between Zawiyah and Tripoli, involving a Zawiyah-based militia and a group from the Warshafanna tribe. The Zawiyah group accused the members of the Warshafanna tribe of belonging to Gaddafi loyalist remnants. The Zawiyah group claimed seeing tanks and vehicles with the Gaddafi-era green flag and markings that said "Brigade of the Martyr Muammar Gaddafi". The Warshafanna denied the Zawiya account, adding that the Zawiya militia had been misled by a rumor that pro-Gaddafi fighters were in the area. The fighting was centered around the Imaya military base, with both sides attempting to control the compound. Heavy weapons, to include vehicle mounted weapons and GRAD rocket launchers were used during the clashes. Casualty reports vary, although the Tripoli Medical Center confirmed 27 dead and 25 wounded.

### 14 NOVEMBER 2011 – TRIPOLI

ZAWIYA PROTESTS: 200-300 members of the Warshafanna tribe demonstrated at the Radisson Hotel on November 14, protesting TNC Minister of Communications Shammam's statement characterizing the tribe as Qadhafi loyalists. Separately, a senior TNC military official told Embassy officials that the clashes were centered on a dispute over control of the former 32$^{nd}$ brigade compound and did not involve any pro-Qadhafi loyalists.

### 15 NOVEMBER 2011 – TRIPOLI

OFFICE OF INTERNATIONAL NGO STRAFFED BY SMALL ARMS FIRE: US Embassy security personnel met with the head of the U.S. based NGO regarding an incident wherein at least two unidentified individuals fired AK-47 rounds at the front of the NGO's office and residential property located in the Gargaresh section of northwest Tripoli. The incident occurred at approximately 0330 on Tuesday, 15 November. Embassy security personnel observed approximately 8-10

U.S. EMBASSY — TRIPOLI, LIBYA    REGIONAL SECURITY OFFICE

## SECURITY INCIDENTS SINCE JUNE 2011

impact points on the front of the building, including the front entrance door and an exterior light. The NGO country director added that the round that struck and damaged the exterior light also caused an electrical short and loss of power at the property. He added that the guard on duty reported that two individuals initially parked their vehicle at the adjacent property, which is under construction, at approximately 0300 hours. The unknown individuals then exited their vehicle and fired an entire magazine from an AK-47 into the air, and departed the area. According to the guards, the persons returned to the area after 30 minutes, fired additional rounds, to include several rounds apparently directed at the NGO occupied building.

The NGO country director added that the guards observed an armed robbery occur several days earlier in the vicinity of the Embassy of Oman, located 6-8 residences to the west of the NGO offices. According to the country director, the guard observed 3 individuals armed with AK-47s stealing property, including a television, from the nearby property. NGO staff added that the area near the Embassy of Oman is a source of significant nighttime celebratory gunfire. After speaking with the guards, neighbors, and landlord, the NGO director did not feel that the incident was directed at the NGO but the likely by product of nearby criminal activity. In light of the incident and some physical security deficiencies at the office property, the NGO decided to move from the building.

### 21 NOVEMBER 2011 – TRIPOLI

**INTERMILITIA FIGHTING AT PALM CITY COMPLEX:** U.S. Embassy security officials received confirmed reports from several sources within the local press, business, and diplomatic community that an inter-militia firefight erupted at the front gate area to the Palm City residential area. The Palm City residential area houses the European Union Mission, UN offices, Canadian Ambassador's Residence, German Mission, and several residences of multinational companies. Initial reports indicate that 1-2 militia members, possibly from the Misrata Militia, were killed and 2 more wounded. Reports vary as to the cause of the firefight and whether the Misrata Militia engaged the Zintan Militia, Tripoli Brigade/Tripoli Military Council, or private security at the Palm City complex.

### 23 NOVEMBER 2011 – BANI WALID

**INTER-MILITIA SKIRMISH:** Accounts vary as to the exact cause of the fighting, with one report claiming that fighting began after a militia high-speed chase with a vehicle containing a Ghaddafi loyalist. The loyalist was reportedly killed and the militia attempting to arrest the loyalist was ambushed in an area where residents had blocked roads to create a chokepoint. During the ambush, fifteen (15) militia members were reportedly killed and survivors reported being engaged from adjacent buildings with grenades, RPGs, and small arms fire. One civilian was reported killed during the fighting.

### 26 NOVEMBER 2011 - TRIPOLI

**BELHAJ DETAINED:** Tripoli Military Council leader Abdul Hakim BelHaj was detained for approximately one hour on November 24 while attempting to enter Tripoli following a trip to Qatar. He reportedly was carrying a false passport and a suitcase of cash.

## SECURITY INCIDENTS SINCE JUNE 2011

### 27 NOVEMBER 2011 – TRIPOLI

**CAA CLOSES MITIGA TRAFFIC:** The Civil Aviation Authority (CAA) Director-General halted commercial passenger flights out of Mitiga Airport after a November 26 security breach. The Director-General was reluctant to discuss details, but said an armed group of young men breached airport security and disrupted operations, delaying a Tunis Air flight by six hours. He said no shots were fired and no casualties reported, but that the CAA limited flights out of Mitiga until the security situation is brought under control. Local contacts report the armed group was from a Souq al-Juma' brigade, angered over the inequitable treatment of war-wounded in Tunisian hospitals.

**SKIRMISH IN ZUARA:** A locally employed staff member (LES) of the U.S. Embassy reported a firefight between Zuara forces and a unit out of Ajaali, a nearby town that allegedly was home to pro-Qadhafi fighters during the revolution. According to staff, the sides skirmished over rights to protect a section of the Greenstream project, the Italian natural gas submarine pipeline. No casualties were reported.

**BERBER DISCONTENT:** An Amazigh groups conducted small demonstrations in downtown Tripoli over the weekend to protest the lack of Berber representation in the new TNC cabinet. Amazigh activists advised they want official recognition of their own language and religion and seek ministerial positions in the Ministries of Education, Culture and/or Religious Endowments.

**VANDALISM OF VEHICLE AT US EMBASSY:** On 27 November at approximately 1700 hours, a U.S. Embassy employee discovered that his vehicle had been vandalized in the employee parking area behind the interim Embassy compound. The driver's side window of the vehicle was smashed but nothing was missing from the vehicle.

### 24-27 NOVEMBER 2011 – BENGHAZI

**STUDENT PROTESTS HINDER RESUMPTION OF CLASSES AT THE BENGHAZI UNIVERSITY –** Students at the Benghazi University (formerly known as Gar Yunus University) colleges of engineering, law, and sciences have been holding protests for the past three days that have delayed the resumption of classes. Many students are demanding fairer grading practices, claiming many professors are failing students without cause. Students are also complaining about professors mistreating students and expelling them from classes without cause, and as a result students are demanding changes to the university's rules that offer more protections of students' rights. University professors claim that in fact the students are protesting attempts by faculty to raise academic standards – during the Qadhafi era, universities suffered from grade inflation, as professors and deans would pass students for political reasons.

### 28 NOVEMBER 2011 – TRIPOLI

**VANDALISM OF VEHICLE AT US EMBASSY:** On 28 November at approximately 1430 hours, a U.S. Embassy employee discovered that his vehicle had been vandalized in the employee parking area behind the interim Embassy compound. The passenger side window of the vehicle was smashed but nothing was missing from the vehicle.

**AMCIT REPORTS VEHICLE THEFT:** An AMCIT visited the interim U.S. Embassy and reported to U.S. Embassy security personnel that he was the victim of a carjacking on 31 October 2011 in

U.S. EMBASSY — TRIPOLI, LIBYA

REGIONAL SECURITY OFFICE

## SECURITY INCIDENTS SINCE JUNE 2011

Tripoli. The AMCIT, who is also a Libyan citizen, was abducted by persons known to him who accused him of being a supporter of Ghaddafi. The AMCIT claimed his life was threatened and he was taken to a lawyer, where he was forced to sign over ownership of his vehicle. The AMCIT reported that he was dropped off on a highway by the assailants. The following day, the AMCIT saw his vehicle and the assailants and he notified a local militia. The militia attempted to stop the vehicle and opened fire on the fleeing assailants but was unable to recover the vehicle. The AMCIT added that he had filed a police report but police had not recovered his vehicle.

### 29 NOVEMBER 2011 – TRIPOLI

RAID OF FARM HOUSE; RECOVERY OF 180 ASSAULT RIFLES NEAR MISSION COMPOUND: On 29 November 2011, fifteen members of the Zintan militia converged on and raided a farm house located within 800 meters of the interim Embassy and Residential Compounds. The Zintani militia, supported by three trucks with vehicle mounted heavy weapons recovered 100 FN-FAL and 80 AK series rifles and a computer with weapons information. The home reportedly belonged to a Libyan diplomat who had previously worked at the Libyan embassy in South Korea. Elements of the Zintan militia conducted the raid after reportedly detaining an individual with an unregistered assault rifle, who provided information regarding the weapons cache. The homeowner was not present at the time of the raid, however, the militia remained onsite in an effort to apprehend anyone coming to the property.

### 28 NOVEMBER 2011 – RAS AJDIR, TUNISIAN/LIBYAN BORDER

BORDER VIOLENCE: Tunisian customs officers stopped three cars at the Ras Ajdir border crossing, two of which carried contraband. Relatives of the smuggler retaliated by burning tires in front of the Ben Gardane town hall, requiring national and regional level officials to intervene.

### 28 NOVEMBER 2011 – RAS AJDIR, TUNISIAN/LIBYAN BORDER

BORDER VIOLENCE: On 30 November, a group of Libyans on the Tunisian side of the border crossing assisted several vehicles loaded with contraband cross into Libya. A Tunisian policeman failed an attempt to stop the vehicles and was attacked and threatened with a firearm, an eyewitness reported. Border police went on strike in protest of the lack of security and the Tunisian Armed Forces decided to close the border crossing indefinitely.

### 01 DECEMBER – BENGHAZI

FOUR INJURED IN TEBU-ARAB CLASHES IN KUFRA – Tebu contacts told U.S. Embassy officials that a Tebu border protection militia clashed violently with an Arab militia from the Zuay tribe at the outskirts of Kufra in southeastern Libya. Four Tebu militia fighters were injured and hospitalized. The clashes were the result of a dispute over which militia had jurisdiction – the Tebu and Arab militias set up competing checkpoints, with each side claiming that it had been authorized by the TNC to inspect travelers.

## SECURITY INCIDENTS SINCE JUNE 2011

**DETENTION OF U.S. CITIZEN NGO REPRESENTATIVE:** On December 1, the U.S. citizen chief of party of a U.S. based NGO operating in Libya was detained by members of the Zintan Martyrs Brigade. On Thursday, December 1, 2011 the chief of party was attending an engagement party for a local CDGP colleague at a farm outside of Benghazi. During the event, 50-60 members of the Zintan Martyrs Brigade (a private militia) raided the house, which had been mistaken for another farm, believing the occupants to be "Fifth Column" (pro-Qadhafi) elements. The militia stated they acted under orders from the Prosecutor General's office. Failing to find evidence of "Fifth Column" suspects, the leader of the Zintan Martyrs Brigade ordered his men to round up and detain all 22 men in attendance for listening to loud music and on suspicion of drinking alcohol. There were no women in attendance as this was a traditional Libyan bachelor's dinner.

All 22 men, including the U.S. citizen chief of party, spent the next day and a half in the custody of the Zintan Martyrs Brigade. In the middle of the second day, the Brigade took them to the office of the Prosecutor General of Benghazi, who refused to acknowledge their authority to arrest and investigate possible cases of law breaking. He informed them they should hand the group over to the police, who alone had the authority to arrest and investigate those suspected of breaking Libyan law, or release them.

Later that evening, the men were taken to the local police station, which undertook its own investigation and promptly dismissed the case against all 22 men for lack of evidence. According to the NGO, at no time were the men mistreated, and the Brigade provided a steady supply of water and basic food. The chief of party confirmed that they suffered only material discomfort and general anxiety. They did not face abuse or violence.

### 01 DECEMBER 2011 – JANZOUR (outskirts of Tripoli)

**GUNFIGHT AT MILITIA CHECKPOINT; 1 DEAD –** Accounts of the incident differ, however, Ashraf Abdelsalam Al-Marni Swayha, deputy head of the Janzour military council, was killed at a checkpoint manned by the Zintan militia. According to Janzour militia officials, SWAYHA and his driver stopped at the checkpoint and reportedly informed the Zintan militia of SWAYHA's rank. Allegedly, the Zintan militia told SWAYHA that they didn't care about the Janzour military council and SWAYHA told his driver to depart the checkpoint, at which point the Zintan militia opened fire. SWAYHA was killed and his driver was injured.

### 02 DECEMBER 2011 – TRIPOLI

**EU STAFF MEMBER CARJACKED:** On 02 December, European Union (EU) security reported that a white Hyundai SantaFe was stolen from a local EU staff member during a mid-day carjacking in downtown Tripoli. EU security reported that the vehicle and driver were stopped by what the staff member believed to be militia members at a security checkpoint near Martyrs Square in downtown Tripoli. The militia members reportedly told the EU staff member there was a problem with his vehicle registration and that he needed to follow the militia members to a local police station. The EU staff member was instead led away from downtown Tripoli into a more isolated area, where the militia members forcibly took the Hyundai at gunpoint.

E-12

U.S. EMBASSY — TRIPOLI, LIBYA

REGIONAL SECURITY OFFICE

## SECURITY INCIDENTS SINCE JUNE 2011

### 03 DECEMBER 2011 - TUNISIA/LIBYAN BORDER

**TUNISIA/LIBYAN BORDER CLOSED:** Tunisian authorities closed the border due to continued militia firefights in the vicinity of the Ras Ajdir border post. Specifically, the Tunisians pointed to a series of incidents wherein Libyan militias chased alleged smugglers into Tunisian territory. Libyan militia personnel were asked to withdraw one mile back from the border.

### 04 DECEMBER 2011 — TRIPOLI

**MILITIA FIREFIGHT:** Sustained inter-militia firefights were reported by NGO and diplomatic contacts in the Jam'a Essaga, Al-hani, Zawia Street, Salah eddine and Shara' Edhill, BenAshur, and Noufleen neighborhoods of Tripoli. The gunfight lasted more than 30 minutes with opposing militias utilizing AK series small arms, DSHK 12.7mm and 23mm automatic cannon fire. At least two persons were reported killed in the clash. Sources in the Bashir Sa'dawi's Brigade stated that an intoxicated armed male was arrested in the Ben Ashour neighborhood and held by Al'Asiam Martyrs' brigade in the former Mutassim Ghaddafi residence. Individuals from an unknown militia apparently responded to the area and attempted to forcibly release the detained individual. Elements of security dispatched from the Supreme Security Committee in Tripoli responded to the area and restored calm to the quarter. The former U.S. Embassy compound is located in the neighborhood where the clashes took place. Continued skirmishes in the area also resulted in the closure of Alzawah and Algmehoria streets in Tripoli.

### 05 DECEMBER 2011 – AL-HANI PORTION OF TRIPOLI

**SUFI VERSUS SALAFI CLASHES RESULT IN 4 DEAD:** During a meeting between the Minister of Interior, RSO, and Ambassador, the Minister of Interior confirmed that recent fighting in the Al-Hani area of Tripoli between Salafi and Sufi groups resulted in the death of 4 Salafists. The Minister added that Ministry officials believe that Saadi Ghaddafi, a surviving son of former regime leader Mohammer Ghaddafi, is responsible for inciting violence between the two sects of Islam in an effort to undermine the new government.

### 05 DECEMBER 2011 – UBARI CITY

**CLASHES IN UBARI CITY:** RSO received unconfirmed reports that clashes occurred in Ubari City. No further details available.

### 05-07 DECEMBER 2011 – TRIPOLI

**CITIZEN DEMONSTRATIONS AGAINST MILITIAS:** Local citizens staged peaceful protests in downtown Tripoli, near Nasser and Omar Muktar streets and the new Ministry of Interior building. The protestors called for the departure of militias from the streets of Tripoli. No violence was reported as a result of the demonstrations although the Ministry of Interior and Supreme Security Council established a number of preventative security checkpoints on major roads which affected traffic.

### 10 DECEMBER 2011 – TRIPOLI

**MILITIA FIREFIGHT; CLOSURE OF TRIPOLI INTERNATIONAL AIRPORT:** The TNC closed the airspace at Tripoli International Airport on 10 December due to fighting between two militias on the airport road near the Sidi Saleem fuel

11

487

## SECURITY INCIDENTS SINCE JUNE 2011

depot. The fighting lasted approximately 2.5 hours and occurred within 2 KM of the Embassy Residential Villas (N 32' 47.373' / E 013' 08.747'). U.S. Embassy security personnel activated internal defense and safe haven procedures for all staff as a significant amount of gunfire, to include anti-aircraft rounds, traveled in the direction of the residential villas. None of the U.S. Embassy buildings suffered any damage nor appear to have been directly targeted during the fighting. According to local media reports, two militia members were injured in the fighting. Sources at the UN stated that 4 persons were killed in the clashes, 1 from the Zintan Brigade and 3 from Tripoli based brigades. The firefight involved significant fire from AK series weapons, 14.5 mm machine guns, 23 mm cannons, and RPG fire. Tanks were previously deployed to the area on 08 December and may have been involved in the fighting. A specific clash was reported by local Mission employees at an overpass near the Brega gas terminals, identified by post as waypoint GREY98 ((N 32' 47.373' / E 013' 08.747'). Zintan militia reportedly attacked a national army checkpoint that had been established at the site earlier on 10 Dec. Libyan army spokesman claimed that two gunmen opened fire on a convoy accompanying army chief Maj-Gen Khalifa Haftar earlier in the day.

### 12 DECEMBER 2011 – BENGHAZI

**PROTESTS AND COUNTER-PROTESTS IN THE EAST:** An estimated crowd of about 3,000 mostly youth protesters converged on Benghazi's Shajarah ("Tree") square on the night of December 12 to protest against a range of issues, primarily corruption, the state of the economy, a lack of government transparency and the continued presence of Qadhafi-era figures in government. There were reports of similar,

smaller youth-driven protests in Bayda and Tobruk that same night.

These protests continued during the night of December 13 in Shajarah Square, and were joined by a pro-TNC, pro-Jalil demonstration led by the local "Committee of Wise Men" in Benghazi's Freedom Square. The two protests were estimated to be in the 2,000-3,000 size range each on the night of the 13th. There have been no reports of violence or militia involvement, and the two sites are a considerable distance apart from one another.

### 13 DECEMBER 2011 – TRIPOLI

**LIBYA'S AIR TRAFFIC CONTROLLERS STAGE STRIKE:** Libyan air traffic controllers staged a brief strike on Tuesday that affected flights in the capital and other cities, forcing one passenger plane to be diverted shortly before landing. The air traffic controllers were reportedly unhappy with their pay as well as the appointment of new management. The strike affected airports in the capital Tripoli, the eastern city of Benghazi, and Sabha in the south. Mukhtar Al-Akhdar, commander of the militia unit that controls Tripoli International Airport, said flights resumed after 4:00 p.m. (1400 GMT), and that no civilian aircraft had been allowed to land or depart before then.

According to Abdelrezzaq Zaatout, head of Libya's civil aviation authority, the controllers failed to give airlines the required 72 hour notice regarding the strike, which aggravated its impact. After negotiations with management, the workers agreed to go back to work.

E-14

U.S. EMBASSY — TRIPOLI, LIBYA                    REGIONAL SECURITY OFFICE

## SECURITY INCIDENTS SINCE JUNE 2011

### 15 DECEMBER 2011 – TRIPOLI

GUNFIGHT AT AMAN BANK: The son of Libyan Gen Khalifa Hiftar was injured in a confrontation with members of the Zintan milita at a Tripoli bank. Hiftar's son, Saddam, reportedly triggered the clash by trying to enter the Aman bank armed with a gun and a hand grenade. The Aman bank is guarded by elements of the Zintan militia. A GoL spokesman stated that Saddam was injured in the leg and was taken to a local hospital. Saddam's brother, Belgassim, accused the rebels of abducting Saddam.

REPORT OF MILITIA GUNFIGHT: RSO received an unconfirmed report from an NGO security representative of an inter-militia firefight in Tripoli at MGRS: 33SUS1643833426.

### 16-17 DECEMBER 2011 – BENGHAZI

YOUTH PROTESTS CONTINUE: Youth-led protests in Benghazi and other eastern towns continued on December 16-17, and protesters in Benghazi remained in Shajara square. Protest organizers were not encouraging additional large-scale protests at this time, and local staff in Benghazi confirmed that the numbers of protesters in Benghazi had dropped from crowds in the thousands to perhaps 100 by December 18. According to a protest organizer, this change was implemented because the protests went too far in making their demands — particularly the verbal attacks against NTC Chairman Jalil and calls for the entire NTC to step-down.

### 18 DECEMBER 2011 – TRIPOLI

BREAK-IN AND THEFT FROM LES VEHICLE AT US EMBASSY: At approximately 1645 hours, a U.S. Embassy locally employed staff member reported that unknown individuals broke the driver's side rear window of his vehicle, which was parked in the rear parking lot of the interim Embassy compound. The employee stated that a sound system (portable radio) belonging to the Public Affairs Office was stolen from the rear cargo area of the vehicle. The thief's partial shoe print was noticeable on the rear seat. The employee went to lunch with a 2$^{nd}$ PD section LES at approximately 1200, returning around 1220.

This is the third incident since 11/27 involving vandalism and/or theft of a Mission employee's vehicle at the interim Embassy compound.

### 20 DECEMBER – BENGHAZI – TRIPOLI

PROTECTIVE SECURITY FORCES FOIL AN ATTEMPT DUBBED (PAPA NOEL) OR SANTA CLAUS TARGETING EMBASSIES AND OIL FIELDS IN LIBYA DURING CHRISTMAS AND NEW YEAR EVE HOLIDAYS: Libyan protective security authorities claimed that they foiled plans to attack embassies, consulates and oil fields operating in Libya. According to the GoL, these attacks were allegedly planned for the Christmas and New Years Eve holidays. According to GoL security official Abdessalam Borghathi, a network of Gaddafi loyalists were behind the plot and the GoL arrested the members and dismantled the group. The GoL reported seizure of 150 RPG launchers, and various light weapons and ammunition and undisclosed sums of money. The arrested members of this network reportedly exchanged SMS messages confirming their intent in carrying out this operation as an explosive "Christmas gift" to the Libyan people.

### 20 DECEMBER 2011 – 27 DECEMBER 2011 – TRIPOLI

ONGOING PROTESTS IN ALGERIA SQUARE: Approximately 100-200 protesters participated in

## SECURITY INCIDENTS SINCE JUNE 2011

ongoing protests in Tripoli's central Algeria Square, where they erected a tent and occupied the square. Like protesters in other cities, the Algeria Square protesters' demands included the removal of the symbols of the Qadhafi regime from the government, the suspension of Tripoli's representatives on the TNC, elections for Tripoli local council members, the publication of the minutes of TNC meetings, the sacking of ministers with dual citizenship, and the publication of TNC members' financial holdings and resumes. Social media sites posted videos allegedly showing mistreatment of the protesters: one video shows a person reported to be a bodyguard of Tripoli Local Council president Abd al-Razzag Buhajar threatening protesters with his rifle.

### 21 DECEMBER 2011- TRIPOLI

**POSSIBLE BREAK-IN ATTEMPT:** At approximately 00:50 hours, at a U.S. Embassy annex compound, local guards found a wooden pallet leaning against the interior side of the perimeter wall. Above the wall where the pallet was located, a leather belt was draped over the barbed wire. Security personnel conducted a security sweep of the compound to determine whether an intruder entered the facility or if anything was stolen. No one was found and there were no signs of theft or vandalism.

### 26 DECEMBER 2011 – TRIPOLI

**PEACEFUL DEMONSTRATION:** The Security Attaché for the Embassy of the Netherlands reported a small demonstration, approximately 30 persons, outside of the Prime Minister's office.

**DEMONSTRATION:** The UK Defense Attaché's office reported a planned demonstration at the Radisson Hotel and Martyrs Square by the FIGHTERS UNION regarding lack of pay.

### 27 DECEMBER 2011 – TRIPOLI

**DEMONSTRATION AT TRIPOLI UNIVERSITY:** Students at Tripoli University reportedly protested over the resignation of University president Dr. Faisel Krekshi, who resigned to purpose political aspirations. Krekshi was to be replaced by Dr. Madani Dakhel, formerly the head of the National Committee for Cooperation between Libyan and American Universities. Reportedly, when Dr. Madani attempted to enter the university office, he was attacked by students and kicked out, and the university security personnel were only able to escort him safely out of the university compound. The students then blocked the university entrances and demanded Dr. Krekshi's return.

### 29 DECEMBER 2011 – TRIPOLI

**BURGLARY AT NGO OFFICE:** On 29 December, the office of the National Democratic Institute (NDI), a DoS institutional contractor, was burglarized. NDI attempted to deposit operating funds into their Tripoli bank account on the 28th of December, however, the bank refused to make the deposit without documentation showing how the funds were brought into the country. At the time of the burglary, the offices were empty so no injuries occurred. The perpetrators entered through a ground floor metal office door, gained access to the finance office area, and carried away a 100kg safe. Libyan police investigated the incident and initially detained a guard and driver working on short-term contracts with NDI; they have since been released by the police and their contracts suspended. Police now claim they don't have sufficient evidence or leads to proceed with the investigation.

490

## SECURITY INCIDENTS SINCE JUNE 2011

### In January 2012 – BENGHAZI

**SUFI CEMETARY DESTRUCTION BY SALAFISTS:**
Salafists destroyed the Sufi cemetery of Sidi Ubaid in Benghazi and removed 31 bodies of Sufi saints interred at the site.

### 03 JANUARY – TRIPOLI

**CLASHES IN TRIPOLI:** Clashes between militia elements from Misurata and Tripoli closed down a major area of downtown Tripoli for several hours in the early afternoon on 03 January. The fighting, which lasted for roughly 30 minutes, occurred in an area between the Prime Minister's office and the Ministry of Interior and reportedly involved heavy weapons fire including RPG's. Embassy security officers present in the area witnessed the deployment of several technicals (commercial vehicles with crew served weapons) and at least 20 troops. The media has reported between one and seven casualties but Post was unable to confirm this information. The reasons behind the fighting remain unclear; some reports attributed it to a real estate dispute while others claim that Misurata militia members attempted to free a colleague who had been detained by members of the Tripoli Military Council. According to a GoL official, Misurata militia members attacked Tripoli's Sidi Khalifa militia (part of the Tripoli Military Council). Libyan social media sites focused heavily on these clashes, criticizing the lack of information regarding the events on any of the new Libyan TV channels.

### 01-04 JANUARY 2011 – TRIPOLI

**PORTS STRIKE:** An official from the Ports and Maritime Transport Authority stated on January 4 that a "small" group of port workers have been striking for increased wages. According to press reports, 300 of the 1800 workers have been striking since January 1 demanding better working conditions and government investment to repair war damage and decades of negligence.

**PROTEST AT PM OFFICE:** Voices of Libyan Women (VLW), staged a peaceful protest of approximately 50 women in front of the Prime Minister's office on January to protest a 10% quota for women in office under the newly-released elections law. After several hours, PM Al-Keeb came out and met with the protestors, agreeing to a separate meeting with the leaders on January 5.

### 07 JANUARY 2011 – TRIPOLI

**FRENCH BUSINESSMAN MURDERED:** A French businessman, identified as Hugues de Samie, age 60, a former French serviceman, was killed at his residence in the Zawiet al-Dahmani neighborhood of Tripoli. Sources indicate that Samie may have been targeted by a group of 2-3 individuals, possibly for his former business dealings with the Gaddafi regime. Witnesses stated that nothing of value was taken from the residence, north African domestic workers at the residence were unharmed by the assailants, and Samie was shot at close range with a handgun. Samie, a former member of the French military with a long military career, worked in Libya since 2008 for Construction Mecanique de Normandie (CMN), a French shipyard. He had reportedly been involved in attempts to sell naval patrol boats to Muammar Gaddafi's regime and to win contracts to modernize Libyan frigates bought in the 1970s. Libyan authorities arrested one suspect in the killing, identified as Mohammed al-Kurdi, 28, "The [arrested] criminal is a drug addict and his motive was theft. There are no political motives.

U.S. EMBASSY — TRIPOLI, LIBYA  REGIONAL SECURITY OFFICE

## SECURITY INCIDENTS SINCE JUNE 2011

### 08 JANUARY – TRIPOLI

BANK MANAGER KIDNAPPED:  According to unconfirmed reports from commercial and media contacts, the manager of the Arab Commercial Bank, Mr. Dhawo el Hamdi, was kidnapped today from Tripoli. However, the Libya government had not officially confirmed the incident.

### 09 JANUARY 2011 – TRIPOLI

HOTEL EMPLOYEE ARRESTED:  According to unconfirmed reports from a commercial contact, a man was arrested yesterday at the Rixos Hotel. He was apparently an employee there and attempted to park his car next to the hotel.  The car was searched and a device, described possibly as a grenade, was reportedly found in the car.

### 12 JANUARY 2011 – TRIPOLI

PEACEFUL DEMONSTRATION: RSO noted a small demonstration, approximately 12-15 persons, primarily women, outside of the Prime Minister's office.

### 10 JANUARY 2012 - TRIPOLI

EMBASSY LES VEHICLE BREAK-IN; THEFT:  At approximately 15:30 hours, on 10 January 2012, U.S. Embassy local guard force members reported hearing the sound of glass breaking in the rear parking lot of the interim Embassy compound. Inspection of the parking lot by LGF and LE Staff approximately 5-10 minutes later showed that the front passenger side window of a GSO LES employee's car was smashed. The window had been completely broken and there were traces of blood on some of the glass. Items from the glove box, console and side pockets of Ajaj's car were strewn about the interior of the car.

The LES employee stated that 1,000 Libyan Dinars were missing from the center console storage compartment; he said he had gone to the bank at approximately 08:00 hours. No other items appeared to be missing. The car was parked approximately 15 meters from the wall of the Embassy compound but next to an olive tree blocking any direct view from the back gate.

### 12 JANUARY 2011 -- BENGHAZI

FEMALE POLITICAL ACTIVIST BEATEN IN BENGHAZI: Political activist Azza Ali Orfi was assaulted and beaten by two unknown assailants as she left Al-Fadhel Hotel in Benghazi where she was on business. Azza was present at Maydan Al Shajara in Benghazi on Wednesday where she criticized the TNC for ignoring the demands of "Correcting the Revolution Movement" held in Freedom Square to protest against the current situation.

### 13 JANUARY 2012 – SABHA

4 MEMBERS OF INTERNATIONAL NGO DETAINED:  Four international staff members (Jordanian, Lebanese, US, and German/Somali) of the International Organization of Migration (IOM) were detained at 0030 hrs by several individuals purportedly responsible for security at the Sabha airport. IOM operates a transit assistance center in Sabha and the team planned to travel to the area to discuss future operations with local officials.  The IOM staff members were taken from the airport arrivals area by 3 armed individuals and driven to a compound 10-15 minutes from the airport.  The armed individuals appeared to be militia members involved in security at the airport and claimed they needed to inspect the IOM vehicle and baggage.  Once at the compound, the person in charge, identified as

U.S. EMBASSY – TRIPOLI, LIBYA         REGIONAL SECURITY OFFICE

## SECURITY INCIDENTS SINCE JUNE 2011

Mukhtar Al Heishi, threatened all four staff members, fired his handgun at the feet of the staff members, and struck three of the team members with his hand or handgun. Al HEISHI was identified as the Head of Security at Sabha Airport and the Rebel Commander in charge of Sabha Airport, and a member of the Martyrs of Abdel Jaleel Saif Al-Nasr Regiment. The IOM team was placed into a room that was used as a detention facility and their telephones were confiscated. Also in the room was a Libyan Toureg and a Tunisian citizen, who had also arrived on the same flight into Sabha as the IOM team. According to the IOM team, the Libyan Toureg was taken from the room on at least two occasions and several beaten by Mukhtar and his guards. After approximately 4 hours, militia members from the Saif Al-Nasser brigade came to the compound and transported the IOM team and the Tunisian to a 2nd site, where they were provided water, food, access to a restroom, and usage of their cellphones, although the team was not free to leave. The IOM team and the Tunisian citizen were allowed to depart at approximately 1600 hrs.

### 13 - 15 JANUARY 2012 – GHARYAN

RIVAL MILITIAS CLASH; 3 DEAD, 42 WOUNDED: Clashes between rival Libyan militia have killed three persons and wounded at least 42, the latest in a series of incidents involving armed groups refusing to hand in their weapons. The clashes began late on Friday and continued on Saturday and Sunday. Friday's violence pitted fighters from the town of Gharyan, 50 miles (80 kilometers) south of Tripoli, against a militia from al-Asabia, about 10 miles (16 kilometers) to the southwest. Media reported artillery and rockets were used during the clashes. Ahmed al-Sharif of the Gharyan militia said his fighters had gone to

arrest people suspected of having ties to the former Gadhafi regime. Al-Asabia fighters refused to hand the suspects over, triggering a shootout.

### 15 JANUARY 2012 – GHADAMES

BUS ATTACKED; 1 KIDNAPPED: Members of a Tuareg militia, allegedly aligned with former regime elements, allegedly attached attacked a public bus on its way to Ghadames from Tripoli. The armed attackers stopped the bus and reportedly fired small arms at it, then kidnapped one of its passengers.

### 15 JANUARY 2012 – DERNA

MILITARY COUNCIL ATTACKED: An armed group attached the Military council in Derna, which was defended by the Naser Almadhkour Militia. No reported deaths from the fighting.

### 15 JANUARY 2012 - DERNA

INTERMILITIA CLASHES: In the eastern city of Derna, local militias were engaged in a brief firefight with a group of fighters from outside the city.

### 16 JANUARY 2012 – TRIPOLI

GRENADE FIGHTS: According to diplomatic security contacts, several people were injured, one seriously, when an individual threw a hand grenade in Martys Square. The incident took place between the hours of 2130-2200 hrs. Hospital contacts confirmed that the seriously injured had lost a leg. Tripoli police reportedly sought the support of a police-led militia unit to restore order in the square.

RSO received additional reports of grenades thrown in Souq al Juma at approximately 0200 hrs. No details regarding injuries.

U.S. EMBASSY – TRIPOLI, LIBYA      REGIONAL SECURITY OFFICE

## SECURITY INCIDENTS SINCE JUNE 2011

### 16 - 17 JANUARY 2012 - ALGERIAN/LIBYAN BORDER

**ALGERIAN OFFICIAL KIDNAPPED; FREED IN LIBYA:** Libyan authorities freed Mohamed Laid Khelfi, governor of the southern Algerian province of Illizi, after he was kidnapped by three gunmen and transported across the Algerian/Libyan border. According to the victim, he was kidnapped after returning from official duties in the town of Debdeb when his car was intercepted at 1630 hrs on 16 January by three persons in a Toyota pickup truck. KHELFI stated he was kidnapped in the area of Timeroualine, approximately 80 kilometres from Debdeb. The assailants were described as between 25-30 and carrying AK-47s. The Algerian Interior Ministry added that the kidnappers had been fully identified. Governor Khelfi travelled to the province in response to protests earlier in the week following court judgement against some of the area's residents and family members of an AQIM leader. The governor was released after a Libyan official travelled to Zintan and negotiated with the kidnappers. The Algerian Interior Minister advised that the kidnappers were Algerian and were in Libya, declining to talk about their fate. He also rejected the possibility of submitting an extradition request to Libya.

### 19 JANUARY 2012 – BENGHAZI

**PROTESTORS ROUGH UP NTC VICE PRESIDENT:** A crowd of protesters on 19 January surrounded Transitional National Council (TNC) Vice Chairman Abdul-Hafiz Ghoga and assaulted him before his security guards managed to pull him away. The incident occurred at Gharyounis University in Benghazi, where Ghoga was due to attend a memorial ceremony for those who had been killed during the 2011 uprising and civil war.

During the scuffle, Ghoga's bodyguards reportedly stabbed a student who was demonstrating at the university, though this has yet to be confirmed. The TNC denounced the protest against Ghoga, and claimed that it was an attempt to damage the organisation's reputation. On 22 January, Ghoga resigned from the NTC, saying he did not want the "atmosphere of hatred" to affect the council and its performance.

### 19 JANUARY 2012 – TRIPOLI

**HEAVY GUNFIRE/POSSIBLE FIREFIGHT:** Unconfirmed reports from various commercial contacts regarding a heavy gunfire / possible militia gunfight near the Al Waddan hotel in Tripoli. The gunfire reportedly lasted for approximately 2 hours, beginning at 2100 hrs.

### 20 JANUARY 2012 – TRIPOLI, BENGHAZI, SABHA

**MULTI CITY PROTESTS:** Hundreds of Libyan Islamists demonstrated on Friday, 20 January 2012, to demand that Muslim sharia law form the basis for Libyan legislation. The organizers called the protests a response to the emergence of secular political parties after the fall of the Gaddafi regime. Groups assembled by Islamist political and religious groups demonstrated in squares in Tripoli, Benghazi and in Sabha in the southern desert. In Tripoli's Algeria Square, Islamists burned copies of the "Green Book," Gaddafi's eccentric handbook on politics, economics and everyday life, to underline that the Koran should be the country's main source of legislation.

### 21 JANUARY 2012 – BENGHAZI

**PROTESTS STORM TNC HQ IN BENGHAZI:** Approximately 200 Libyan protesters stormed the TNC's headquarters in Benghazi and demanded a meeting with the country's interim leaders.

U.S. EMBASSY — TRIPOLI, LIBYA

REGIONAL SECURITY OFFICE

## SECURITY INCIDENTS SINCE JUNE 2011

### 23 JANUARY 2012 – TRIPOLI

**MILITIA FIREFIGHT:** On Monday 23 January, at approximately 0115 hrs, local police and security contacts confirmed that a firefight occurred between two militias in the Fashlum area of Tripoli. The fight occurred between a group led by 4 brothers from the Kabuka family and a group from the nearby Abu Salim neighborhood. The firefight lasted 60-90 minutes and involved small arms fire and at least 3 RPG explosions. Two fatalities were confirmed in the fighting (1 Kabuka/1 Abu Salim Brigade), a third individual was listed as deceased (unconfirmed/Kabuka), and at least one seriously wounded, possibly fatally (Kabuka). A subsequent raid of the Kabuka family residence uncovered various small arms, RPGs, an undisclosed amount of funds, and an unknown amount of Ecstasy tablets.

**MILITIA FIREFIGHT:** A second firefight was reported between midnight and 0300 hrs on Monday, 23 January, in the area near the Al Waddan Hotel, along the cornice area of Tripoli. The gunfight started at a check-point a few meters from Al Waddan hotel. The militia in charge in that area insisted on controlling and checking the identification of members of other militias who passed the checkpoint. An argument ensued when the militia in charge of the checkpoint challenged IDs of another militia who were passing the checkpoint. There was sustained gunfire and explosions during the fire fight, although reportedly no wounded or killed in the incident.

However, a source at a local hospital confirmed that a total of 9 individuals died in fighting in Tripoli during the evening and early morning of 22 / 23 January.

**MILITIA FIREFIGHT:** A third firefight was reported at approximately 1640 hours and continued for approximately 45 minutes in the eastern portion of the city, adjacent to the 2nd ring road, in the vicinity of where we maintain a GSO warehouse (MGRS Coordinates: 33SUS31705 39814). There is a former ESO office/operations center in the area and the two militias apparently have been fighting over the control of the site. Roadblocks were placed on several of the primary roads but were removed at the conclusion of fighting. RSO received unconfirmed reports that two persons were killed.

### 23 JANUARY 2012 – BANI WALID

**CLASHES IN BANI WALID:** Multiple Embassy contacts confirmed press reports of renewed fighting in Bani Walid. A TNC official characterized the clashes as between pro-Qadhafi and pro-TNC tribes, and told Embassy officials that the Ministry of Defense dispatched brigades from Misrata to quell the violence. Embassy officials witnessed Zintan brigade members gearing up and heading south. According to the head of Bani Walid's 23 October Brigade (a militia that is reputed to have fought for Qadhafi), the 28 May Brigade (another Bani Walid militia and the hated rival of the 23 October Brigade) started the fighting when it kidnapped a member of the powerful Werfelli tribe. The 23 October brigade leader said that he and various Werfelli tribal leaders are gathering fighters to "deal with the problem" and that everything was "under control" in Bani Walid. He strenuously denied reports that the clashes are between pro- and anti-Qadhafi forces, characterizing the fighting as entirely tribal in nature. Bani Walid has seen several rounds of fighting since Qadhafi's death. The previous incidents included elements of tribal rivalries and

U.S. EMBASSY — TRIPOLI, LIBYA

REGIONAL SECURITY OFFICE

## SECURITY INCIDENTS SINCE JUNE 2011

some anti-TNC sentiment. The October 23 militia leader, for example, stated that he is not pleased by the way that the TNC has treated Bani Walid like an occupied territory.

According to a USG funded mine and ordinance abatement team in Bani Walid at the time of the clashes, a group of armed men, wearing masks and carrying AK-47s and RPGs, set up a barricade around the military council. The members of the military council said that these men were not under the military council and accused them of being "pro-Qadhafi." As the team left the area, the men at the barricade stopped them, but seeing that they were foreigners, let them pass. A member of the same team also reported that the coastal road heading east from Tripoli has been closed off with armed checkpoints. He said that one of their team (a Libyan translator) was heading east to visit his family and was turned around.

### 23 JANUARY 2012 – TRIPOLI

**TRAFFIC POLICE OFFICER KIDNAPPED; KILLED:** A Tripoli Police traffic officer was kidnapped and later killed by unknown assailants while walking home from his duty post south of Grey 4 on the airport road. The officer was wearing his traffic police uniform. The incident occurred at approximately 1400 hrs, and the officer's body was found later along the airport road with hands tied behind his back, and numerous bullet wounds in his back. Ministry of Interior contacts advised that this was the third Tripoli based police officer to be killed since November 2011 in similar circumstances. In at least two of the cases, the officer's vehicle was taken, and the Ministry of Interior is trying to determine the motive for the crimes.

### 27 JANUARY 2012 – TRIPOLI

**ATTEMPTED CARJACKING OF OIL COMPANY VEHICLE:** On 27 January 2011, at 1300 hrs, a vehicle belonging to a Western oil company was enroute to Tripoli International Airport when it was forced to slow down by a group of youths. The vehicle contained one driver and two passengers. The occupants felt that they were being targeted for a robbery or carjacking as the youths attempted to intimidate the occupants and one of the assailants attempted to open one of the vehicle doors. As the vehicle slowly tried to move forward, another youth was 'bumped', but not injured. The group of youth converged on the vehicle and smashed the rear window. The driver took evasive action and departed the scene. The vehicle occupants did not report any injuries. No report of firearms being displayed or used

### 28 JANUARY 2012 – TRIPOLI

**MILITIAS EXCHANGE GUNFIRE:** According to a diplomatic official from a NATO Embassy, there was a sustained gunfight at approximately 1730 hours in the Gargaresh area of Tripoli (N 32° 52.073' E 013°06.383'). The exchange of gunfire occurred at a location previously established as a vehicle checkpoint by one of the militias exercising control over the area.

**FRENCH DIPLOMAT STOPPED AT CHECKPOINT:** In the Gurgi area of Tripoli, a French Diplomat, traveling in a vehicle bearing diplomatic plates, was stopped by militia members manning a checkpoint. Despite the diplomatic plates, the militia members insisted on searching the vehicle. Reports of such incidents have become increasingly common, with untrained and marginally controlled militias failing to abide by

U.S. EMBASSY – TRIPOLI, LIBYA                    REGIONAL SECURITY OFFICE

## SECURITY INCIDENTS SINCE JUNE 2011

or understand international laws governing the protection of diplomats.

PROTEST AT MINISTRY OF DEFENSE: U.S. Embassy security officials observed a group of approximately 75 males, described as between the ages of 18-35, wearing a mix of civilian and military attire, who were protesting and blocking the main gate entrance into the Ministry of Defense. The Embassy's movement security team entered the compound via a secondary entrance. At the conclusion of the 90 minute meeting, Embassy security officials noted the crowd had roughly doubled in size and were interacting with traffic on both the north and west side of the complex. Protesters waved flags, placards and banners allowing vehicles to pass but intermingled in traffic creating disruption. No threatening or malicious action was observed. A rough translation of the protestors placards, criticized acting Minister of Defense Juwali's recent remarks seen as critical of revolutionaries. Juwali reportedly referred to the revolutionaries ('thuwar') as "thieves and pirates".

### 01 FEBRUARY 2012 – TRIPOLI

INTER-MILITIA GUNFIGHT: At approximately, 1500 hrs, a gunfight erupted between elements of the Zintan and Misrata militias when elements of the Zintan brigade used force, including AK47s, heavy weapons and 1-2 RPG's to gain entry to a compound behind the Marriot Hotel, on the seafront. This compound is thought to be occupied by fighters from Misratah (the compound was once owned and used by Saadi Gaddaffi). The Zintan group then freed a fighter that had been arrested by Misratan fighters prior to the gunfight. The main initial engagement lasted 20 – 25 minutes and was limited to the area close to Misratah compound. Fighting was

also reported at Saif al-Islam Gaddafi's beach house that had been occupied by the Zintan militia.

### 05 FEB 2012 - TRIPOLI

PROTESTORS STORM RUSSIAN EMBASSY: From 1400 to 1700 hrs, a demonstration was held outside the Russian Embassy in Tripoli a day after Russia and China blocked a UN resolution on the Syrian crisis. During the demonstration, dozens of pro-Syrian protesters stormed the Russian Embassy, climbed onto the roof of the building, damaged surveillance cameras and hauled down the Russian flag. No injuries resulted from the incident, however, Russian officials complained to the Government of Libya over the lack of response from host nation security officials. The Libyan authorities apologized over the incident and pledged to probe into the circumstances and to ensure security of the Russian diplomatic mission in Tripoli.

### 06 FEBRUARY 2012 – JANZOUR / SUBURB OF TRIPOLI

INTER-MILITIA CLASH: A clash between a Misrata affiliated militia and an unidentified armed group resulted five persons killed and two wounded.

### 06 FEBRUARY 2012 – JANZOUR / SUBURB OF TRIPOLI

REFUGEE CAMP ATTACKED BY MILITIA: On 6 February, seven male black Libyan civilians from Tawergha were killed by militias who raided their makeshift refugee camp at a former naval academy in Janzour, a suburb of Tripoli. The survivors said that they appeared to be from Misrata because of their license plates, though the Misrata militia denied this. The militia

U.S. EMBASSY – TRIPOLI, LIBYA          REGIONAL SECURITY OFFICE

## SECURITY INCIDENTS SINCE JUNE 2011

members who raided the refugee camp claimed to be searching for suspects from an earlier militia clash in Janzour.

### 06 FEBRUARY 2012 – TRIPOLI

**PROTESTORS HURLED ROCKS, EGGS AND TOMATOES AT THE CHINESE EMBASSY:** Syrian and Libyan demonstrators hurled rocks, eggs and tomatoes at the Chinese embassy in Tripoli on Monday, after Russia and China vetoed a U.N. Security Council resolution backing an Arab plan urging Syria's President Bashar al-Assad to give up power.

Armed men, who said they were from the Libyan government's Supreme Security Committee, guarded the embassy from about 50 protesters who waved Syrian opposition flags and had managed to break windows and spray graffiti on the walls. One demonstrator tried to force his way past the guards but was stopped.

Just as protesters had done the day before at the Russian embassy, demonstrators said they wanted to take down the Chinese flag and replace it with the Syrian opposition's flag and the red, black and green flag of Libya's National Transitional Council (NTC).

One of the men guarding the embassy said his colleagues had shot into the air to disperse the crowd when they hurled rocks and tried to push their way through. The crowd later hurled eggs before lining up to pray at prayer hour.

### 10 FEBRUARY 2012 – TRIPOLI

**ALLEGED TERROR CELL ARRESTED IN AIRPORT AREA:** According to the Zintan Military Council, members of a Zintan militia arrested a criminal gang that was operating out of an apartment in Qasr Bin Ghasher area in Tripoli as a base to sell

alcohol, drugs, and weapons. The Zintan Military Council stated that the arrestees carried fake revolutionary ID cards issued by the Ministry of Interior, spoke an Egyptian dialect of Arabic and came from the Eastern Desert (Libyan-Egyptian borders). Zintan officials added that one of the arrestees confessed to planning sabotage and terror attacks in Tripoli to guarantee the instability of the city.

### 12 FEBRUARY 2012 – TRIPOLI

**INDIVIDUAL DETAINED TRYING TO ENTER UN VEHICLE WHILE STOPPED IN TRAFFIC:** A pedestrian attempted to enter a marked UN UNMAS vehicle while it was stopped in traffic on Gurji road, in northwest Tripoli. A militia group driving past the UN vehicle observed the inOne of our drivers witnessed a minor incident on the Gurji road yesterday involving UN vehicle UNMAS 004. Apparently a pedestrian tried to enter the vehicle which was stopped in traffic. A uniformed military group driving by saw the incident, detained the individual, and placed him in the militia vehicle. No further information is available as to what happened to the individual or what he was trying to do.

### 12 FEBRUARY 2012 – AL-KUFRA

**TRIBAL CLASHES:** At least five people were killed in clashes between rival tribes over control of territory in the far southeast of Libya. Violence erupted in the remote south-eastern province of al-Kufra and continued on 13 February. Zwai tribesmen fought with fighters from the Tibu ethnic group. The Zwai claim that the Tibu are bringing in people from Chad and basing them at a nearby oasis, at a camp in the town of Jalu. Both groups were initially utilized light weapons when the fighting initially erupted, but the

U.S. EMBASSY — TRIPOLI, LIBYA　　　　　　　REGIONAL SECURITY OFFICE

## SECURITY INCIDENTS SINCE JUNE 2011

violence escalated, with the two sides firing rocket-propelled grenades and anti-aircraft guns. A TNC spokesperson confirmed the clashes, adding that 20 persons were wounded in the fighting in addition to the five dead.

### 14 FEBRUARY 2012 – TRIPOLI

**EMBASSY SECURITY TEAM MEMBER GRAZED BY CELEBRATORY SMALL ARMS FIRE:** On Tuesday, 14 February at approximately 2345 hours, a member of the U.S. Embassy's security support team (SST) assigned to provide static security support at the U.S. Embassy in Tripoli, Libya, was grazed by one round of celebratory small arms fire (CSAF) while taking out his trash on the Residential Villas Compound. The bullet, believed to be a 7.62mm/AK-47 type round, grazed the SST member's left forearm, leaving an abrasion and 2nd degree burn. The round struck the SST member during its downward trajectory. The SST member was treated by Embassy medical personnel on site at approximately 0015 hours and the injury was treated with a topical anesthetic, burn cream, and placed in a loose dressing.

### 19 FEBRUARY 2012 – BENGHAZI

**US MISSION PERSONNEL DETAINED:** U.S. Mission personnel were detained by militia personnel after they drove through a previously unknown and hastily created checkpoint in Benghazi. The Mission vehicle and personnel were returning from Benghazi's Benina airport at approximately 0100 hours. The Mission vehicle was pursued and stopped by a militia vehicle and additional militia personnel arrived at the site after the Mission vehicle was stopped. The two female Employees in the vehicle identified themselves as U.S. diplomats by referring to their

vehicle license plate, diplomatic placard, and Ministry of Foreign Affairs ID card but they were still prevented from leaving. The one English speaking militia member at the checkpoint demanded to see their passports and demanded to inspect their cargo. Mission personnel refused access to the vehicle and its cargo. The detained employees contacted Mission security personnel and 17 Feb Martyrs Brigade QRF members, who responded to the checkpoint and were able to resolve the situation with the checkpoint commander.

The Mission employees noted that there were 12 checkpoints on the route from the airport. They described the checkpoints as aggressive, with armed personnel who attempted to open the doors of their vehicles.

### 02 MARCH 2012 – DERNA

**DERNA SECURITY COMMITTEE HEAD ASSASSINATED:** The head of the security committee in Derna, Colonel Mohammed Al-Hassi, was shot and killed outside a gas station in Derna. Col. Al-Hassi survived two earlier assassination attempts and was also the head of Derna's anti-drugs unit. He reportedly targeted enforcement efforts directed at local drug smugglers during and before the civil war.

### 03 MARCH 2012 – TRIPOLI

**LOCAL DRIVER THREATENS EMBASSY SECURITY OFFICERS AFTER VEHICLES SCRAPE IN TRAFFIC:** The side mirror of a passing vehicle scraped the side of a U.S. Embassy mobile patrol/quick reaction vehicle while it was operating in downtown Tripoli. The local driver exited his vehicle and made threatening hand gestures toward the Embassy vehicle and its occupants. The local driver pursued the Embassy vehicle

U.S. Embassy — Tripoli, Libya                            Regional Security Office

## SECURITY INCIDENTS SINCE JUNE 2011

multiple times and stopped in front of the Embassy vehicle, causing a block in traffic. The passenger of the car also threatened the Embassy vehicle with a large rock.

### 06 MARCH 2012 – TRIPOLI / BENGHAZI

**SEMI-AUTONOMY DEMONSTRATIONS:** On 6 March, tribal and militia leaders in Benghazi declared semi-autonomy for the eastern region of Cyrenaica. This was met with anger from the NTC government in Tripoli and anti-autonomy demonstrations erupted in Tripoli and Benghazi.

### 08 MARCH 2012 – BENGHAZI

**EXPLOSIONS NEAR US MISSION COMPOUND:** At approximately 2330hrs, several loud explosions occurred near the perimeter of the U.S. Mission compound in Benghazi. Mission security personnel and local 17 Feb Martyrs Brigade personnel secured the compound and investigated the source of the explosions. Additional personnel from the 17 Feb Martyrs Brigade responded to the compound. Security personnel determined that the explosions occurred on a nearby street, within 400 meters of the compound. No injuries or damage were reported from the explosions, believed to be dynamite, 'fish bombs', or 'gelateenas' used in Benghazi for fishing and frequently thrown as part of wedding celebrations.

### 09 MARCH 2012 – ZLITEN

**SALAFISTS ATTEMPT TO DESTROY SUFI SHRINES:** On March 9, over 100 carloads of armed Salafists arrived in Zliten intent on destroying the tomb of one of the most revered Sufis in Libyan history, Sidi Abdul-Salam Al-Asmar al-Fituri. The Salafists, from Benghazi, Tripoli, Misrata, Khoms and other towns and led by Sheikh Salah Al-Kikli from Jebel

Nafusa, were confronted by angry Zliten residents and gun-waving militiamen determined to protect the shrine. These pro-Sufi groups were joined by other militiamen from Misrata. Libya's Grand Mufti, Sadeq Al-Ghariani, subsequently issued a fatwa prohibiting attacks on shrines.

### 08 MARCH 2012 – TRIPOLI

**MILITIA CLASHES:** There were clashes involving militiamen in Tripoli on Thursday night over pay. The clashes occurred in Omar Mukhtar Street, Shara Al-Sarim near Shara Ennasser and in the suburb of Gurgi. The fighting started after militiamen went to area military council offices to collect money promised to them by the government. When many militia members did not find their names on the payroll lists. Making matters were, they claimed that some names on the lists had not played a part in the revolution.

The disgruntled militiamen then started shooting at the local military council offices. The most serious clashes were in Gurgi where heavy weaponry was used.

### 12 MARCH 2012 – KUFRA

**TWO JOURNALISTS DETAINED IN KUFRA:** Two journalists, one U.S. citizen and one Ukrainian citizen, were detained by the Kufra military council for several hours. The journalists had an entry permit for Libya but had been denied permission to travel within Kufra. They were handed over to the local branch of the intelligence service, and then released after several hours, unharmed.

### 16 MARCH 2012 – BENGHAZI

**PRO-AUTONOMY DEMONSTRATORS CLASH:** Pro-federalism demonstrators in Benghazi rallied in support of the establishment of two separate

U.S. EMBASSY — TRIPOLI, LIBYA　　　　　　　　REGIONAL SECURITY OFFICE

## SECURITY INCIDENTS SINCE JUNE 2011

capital cities in Tripoli and Benghazi. The protesters also called for an equal division of seats between the east, west and south in Libya's new constituent assembly, the elections for which are scheduled to take place in June. The demonstrators gathered after Friday prayers and went to Freedom Square, where Ahmed Zubeir Senussi, who was appointed on 6 March as head of the Cyrenaica Transitional Council, made a speech in support of federalism. Pro- and anti-federalism demonstrators clashed in the surrounding streets, using firearms and other improvised weapons. At least one person was killed and five others injured.

### 17 MARCH 2012 – TRIPOLI

**TRASH PROTESTS:** A protest group led by CLEANING UP TRIPOLI, held a demonstration in front of the PM's office in downtown Tripoli to protest the city's escalating waste management crisis, which has resulted in refuse accumulation in many areas of the city.

### 18 MARCH 2012 – TRIPOLI

**MILITIA GUNFIGHT:** On 18 March, a clash erupted between the Zintan militia and residents of Tripoli's Abu Salim district, previously loyal to Gaddafi. One militiaman was killed before a cease-fire was brokered by the district's militia commander. The Zintan militia took control of a school in the neighborhood in August 2011, when Tripoli was overrun by the TNC. The school was turned into a military-style base.

### 18 MARCH 2012 – BENGHAZI

**ARMED ROBBERY OF BRITISH SCHOOL PERSONNEL:** Six unidentified individuals wearing ski masks, dressed in military fatigues, and armed with hand-guns carried out an armed robbery of

teachers and staff of the British School in Benghazi. The assailants threatened the staff and stole handbags, wallets, watches, and vehicles. The incident took place at 0640 hours at the teachers departed a residential compound in route to the school.

### 21 MARCH 2012 - DERNA

**HAND GRENADE ATTACK ON VEHICLE:** Unknown assailants threw a grenade at a car filled with ammunition in Derna, the resulting explosion destroyed the vehicle. No information on fatalities or injuries.

### 22 MARCH 2012 - BENGHAZI

**MILITIA MEMBERS SEARCHING FOR A SUSPECT FIRE WEAPONS NEAR AND ATTEMPT TO ENTER U.S. MISSION COMPOUND:** At 0227 hours seven militia members armed with AK series small arms and traveling in two Toyota Hilux vehicles stopped at the rear gate of the U.S. Mission compound, began kicking the entry gate, and demanded access to the compound. The local guard on duty fled the gate area when the individuals began firing their weapons in the air. As the local guard fled the gate, he activated an internal defense alarm, which caused the Mission security personnel and 17 February Martys Brigade personnel to respond to the area. Mission security officers and the 17 February Martys Brigade determined that the unidentified individuals were part of the Libyan Ministry of Defense, El Awfea Brigade, who were patrolling the area after a recent firefight and noted an unauthorized fire on the US Mission compound. The El Awfea Brigade members apologized to US Mission personnel for their reaction and left the area soon thereafter.

U.S. EMBASSY – TRIPOLI, LIBYA        REGIONAL SECURITY OFFICE

## SECURITY INCIDENTS SINCE JUNE 2011

### 22 MARCH 2012 – TRIPOLI

**CHAIRMAN OF ANTIQUITIES DEPT KIDNAPPED; RELEASED AFTER RANSOM PAID:** Salah Agab, Chairman of the Department of Antiquities, was kidnapped by unidentified militiamen, only to be freed the following day after payment of an undisclosed amount of money.

### 22 MARCH 2012 – TRIPOLI

**PROTESTORS THREATEN PM'S OFFICE:** A group of protestors from Kala'a went to the GoL cabinet offices to demand medical treatment. An official received the group yesterday provided information on the criteria to qualify for GOL-funded care. Apparently dissatisfied by that response, the group came back to the cabinet offices and brandished weapons while making their demands. No one was hurt.

### 23 MARCH 2012 – TRIPOLI

**MILITIA MEMBERS KIDNAP AND BEAT TURKISH HOTEL MANAGER OVER UNPAID BILL:** Armed members the Zintan Militia burst into the Rixos luxury hotel in Tripoli and opened fire after one of their members was told to pay a 6-month lodging bill or vacate. The militia member left returned with dozens of armed men, who smashed through the front door and shot weapons into the air. The Rixos Hotel's general manager, Sukru Kocak, was taken to the militia office in the Fallah area of Tripoli where he said he was beaten, suffering injuries to his knees and a burst ear drum, causing him to lose hearing in his right ear. It's unclear if the damage to his hearing is permanent. Kocak, who is Turkish, said he was released only after the Turkish Embassy and other officials contacted the Libyan government on his behalf. The luxury Rixos is owned by a Turkish company. Before the news of

Kocak's release, Mohammed Madani, a commander of one of the Zintan militias in Tripoli, said the manager was not detained but was taken for questioning and the issue "has been resolved."

### 23 MARCH 2012 – SIRTE

**MILITIA MEMBERS FIRE ON MIN OF INTERIOR VEHICLE; 1 INJURED:** Ministry of Interior vehicles were shot at and threatened by the Al-Jalet Brigade in Jaref, Sirte after they escorted TNC Chairman Abduljalil and PM Al-Keeb's convoy. The attack resulted in the injury of a security officer employed by the Ministry of Interior. Suspects were turned over to the MoI on 27 March 2012.

### 23 MARCH 2012 – LIBYAN / EGYPTIAN BORDER

**ARMED EX-REBELS CLOSE LIBYAN-EGYPTIAN BORDERS:** An ex-rebel group in the border town of Imsa'ed closed the border crossing with Egypt "until further notice". According to sources in Imsa'ed, residents are demanding that the ministries of Interior and Defense take control over the busy border crossing. The ex-rebels say that personnel affiliated with the Ministry of Interior are involved in smuggling operations, and that is why they intervened and closed the borders with Egypt. The border was re-opened on 25 March 2012.

### 23 MARCH 2012 – BENGHAZI

**PROTEST BY POLICEMEN AND SOLIDIERS:** Soldiers and policemen held a protest and march in Benghazi, which ended in Benghazi's Tahir Square. The protestors called for the full reactivation of the army and state security services as the only forces responsible for the country's security.

U.S. EMBASSY — TRIPOLI, LIBYA                    REGIONAL SECURITY OFFICE

## SECURITY INCIDENTS SINCE JUNE 2011

### 23 MARCH 2012 – BENGHAZI

**ARMED MILITIA BLOCKS COASTAL ROAD IN BENGHAZI DEMANDING PAY:** Militia members from the Sidi Khribish area in Benghazi blocked the coastal road at the roundabout near the Mohammed Al-Mgarief School and demanded that the government pay them their promised militia salaries.

### 24 MARCH 2012 – TRIPOLI

**ITALIAN EMBASSY GUARD STRUCK BY CSAF:** An Italian security guard was struck and injured by celebratory small arms fire (CSAF) which landed inside the Italian Embassy compound.

### 26 MARCH 2012 - TRIPOLI

**MILITIA GUNFIGHT NEAR DUTCH EMBASSY:** Two militias engaged in a mid-day (approximately 1200 hrs) gunfight 300 meters west of the Dutch Embassy in downtown Tripoli. Dutch security officers reported extensive small arms and heavy weapons fire but were unable to confirm any injured, dead, or the motive for the fighting.

**GUNFIGHT NEAR POLISH EMBASSY:** At approximately 2100 hours, members of the Polish Embassy security team reported a gunfight lasting approximately 10 minutes within 100 meters of the Embassy. The security officers stated the fight involved unknown individuals, although Libyan Military Police appear to be involved. No information on injured, dead, or a motive for the gunfight.

### 28 MARCH 2012 - DERNA

**HAND GRENADE ATTACK:** An unknown person(s) threw a hand grenade into the courtyard of the Women's Higher Vocational Centre in Derna, in eastern Libya. No details regarding fatalities or injuries.

### 25 - 31 MARCH 2012 – SEBHA

**CLASHES IN SEBHA:** Clashes in Sebha, 660 km south of Tripoli, resulted in more than 160 dead and at least 360 injured. TNC officials stated that the clashes started after a group from the Tebu tribe killed an employee of the General Electricity Co. and stole his vehicle on Sunday; which sparked the clashes between the militias, city residents, and the Tebu tribe. The Libyan Ministry of Transportation confirmed that a Libyan Arab Airlines plane at the Sebha airport was damaged by gunfire and a RPG during the fighting. No passengers were on the plane at the time of the damage. Area hospitals reportedly run out of food and blood and are low on medicine.

**FIGHTING IN UBARI:** Additional fighting was reported between elements of Tuareg tribes and Zintan militia members in the town of Ubari, to the west of Sebha. The area of fighting is located approximately 30 km east of an oil field where a number of operations are ongoing with a significant number of expats. Both Zintan and Misrata militias were reported massing and heading south into the area.

### 29 MARCH 2012 – TRIPOLI

**GUNMEN FIRE ON GHANA AMBASSADOR RESIDENCE:** According to the Embassy of the Republic of Ghana, an unknown number of assailants, operating in three vehicles, fired small arms indiscriminately at the Ambassador's Residence. The incident took place at midnight, and gunfire hit the main gate, front of the residence, and five bullets were fired into the residence bedroom. The Ambassador's spouse

U.S. EMBASSY – TRIPOLI, LIBYA

REGIONAL SECURITY OFFICE

## SECURITY INCIDENTS SINCE JUNE 2011

was injured by window glass shards resulting from the gunfire. The Ambassador was uninjured.

### 01-02 APRIL – GHAT

INTER-MILITIA CLASHES: Media reported approximately twelve persons killed near Ghat, located in southwestern Libya, in fighting between Tuaregs and the Zintan tribe

### 02 APRIL 2012 – BENGHAZI

UK DIPLOMATIC ARMORED VEHICLE ATTACKED BY PROTESTORS: At approximately 1815 hours a U.K Diplomatic Mission armored vehicle was attacked by a mob of demonstrators. The vehicle was damaged but the occupants escaped injury. The demonstrators who numbered between one hundred (100) and two hundred (200) were members of the Traffic Police Force known as "Murur". The Murur Policemen were involved in a clash with local militiamen that escalated into a shooting. The Internal Ministry deployed a third security force the "Al-Nayda" or "Al-Shorta" Police to quell the fighting. A two car UK motorcade, unaware of the protest and related violence, drove near the demonstration site and was attacked by protestors. UK Security officials believe the demonstrators mistook the UK vehicles as local militia units.

### 01 - 05 – APRIL – 2012 – Zuwara, Al-Jumil, and Ragdalin:

INTER-MILITIA FIGHTING/CLASHES: Ongoing clashes between the residents of Zwara, Al-Jumil, and Ragdalin resulted in the death of 26 people and wounded 142 others. Reports on the cause of the fighting vary. Zuwara militiamen claim that they were detained by members of a neighboring town, while Ragdalein fighters stated that they

captured the Zuwara militiamen after months of abuses by Zuwara brigades, including looting of property. The Ministry of Interior added that a Zuwara hunting party shot and killed a person from Al Jumail by mistake and the members of the party were arrested. A TNC spokesperson stated that VP of the TNC and a number of TNC members headed to western Libya to calm the tensions between the clashing neighbors. The TNC spokesperson added forces from the National Army have also been sent there to stabilize the situation. Heavy weapons, including tanks, mortars, anti-aircraft weapons and artillery were used during the fighting.

U.S. EMBASSY – TRIPOLI, LIBYA

REGIONAL SECURITY OFFICE

## SECURITY INCIDENTS SINCE JUNE 2011

### 06 APRIL 2012 – BENGHAZI

CRUDE IED THROWN OVER WALL OF US MISSION; 2 CONTRACT GUARDS ARRESTED AS SUSPECTS: At approximately 2300 hours, one former and one current U.S. Mission contract guards threw a crude IED, referred to as a 'fish bomb' or 'gelateena' over the wall of the U.S. Mission compound in Benghazi. The two suspects were arrested by members of the 17 Feb Martyrs Brigade which provides armed security for the Mission compound. No employees were injured in the incident and limited damage was reported to the interior of the wall. The former guard was dismissed several days earlier for gross misconduct, specifically putting graffiti on USG property.

*Typical home made 'fish bomb' or 'Gelateena'*

### 07-08 APRIL 2012 – RAS JEDIR; LIBYAN-TUNISIA BORDER

TUNISIAN SMUGGLERS DETAINED BY MILITIA: On Saturday, 7 April 2012, five Tunisian smugglers were detained near the Ras Jedir border crossing in the Libyan region of Al-Aql, 50 km from Ras Jedir. The detained smugglers were freed on Sunday, 8 April 2012, after negotiations between the Libyan Military Council of Al-Zawiyah and the Tunisian National Guard, a security source told TAP news agency. The detainees, who had engaged in illegal trading in fuel, were released and were able to retrieve their vehicles, which were full of fuel. Residents from the Tunisian town of Ben Geurdane, where the smugglers originated, blocked the road leading to the border checkpoint to protest against the repeated abduction and detention of Tunisians. The border crossing at Ras Jedir, on primary road leading from Tunisia to Tripoli, has been closed several times over the past year due to clashes or unrest in the border area.

### 10 APRIL 2012 – TRIPOLI

DEMONSTRATIONS AT MOI: Several protests occurred outside the Ministry of Interior (MoI) building in downtown Tripoli. Residents from Zuwara (West of Tripoli) demonstrated about an ongoing conflict between residents of Zuwara and residents of Jmail, and specifically the slow reaction from the MoI to resolve the situation. A number of protestors were demonstrating against the appointment of Salem Al Hassi as the new Intelligence chief. Al Hassi was based in the US and many complain that he is a puppet for the US and should not hold such a critical role. Finally, members of the police, fire brigade and ambulance services demonstrated against the appointment of many of the former regime members into senior positions in the MoI.

### 10 APRIL 2012 – TRIPOLI

DEMONSTRATORS STORM PM OFFICE; 3 EMBASSY EMPLOYEES EVACUATED FROM SITE:

Approximately 125 protestors from a militia based in the Ben Ashour area of Tripoli protested in from of the Prime Minister's office. The protest, which began peacefully around 1100 in the morning, escalated when the protestors

U.S. EMBASSY — TRIPOLI, LIBYA  REGIONAL SECURITY OFFICE

## SECURITY INCIDENTS SINCE JUNE 2011

broke through the outer perimeter fence and stormed the Prime Minister's Office building at approximately 1225 hours. The protestors were able to break through the limited security on-site and entered the first floor of the building. The U.S. Embassy had three employees on-site attending bi-lateral coordination meetings. U.S. Embassy security officers operating in a mobile Quick Reaction Force (QRF) responded to the site and evacuated the employees and a local driver before the demonstration escalated further. Shortly after the U.S. Embassy employees were evacuated, demonstrators beginning firing their weapons at the site.

### 10 APRIL 2012 – BENGHAZI

**CRUDE IED THROWN AT UN CONVOY AND SUPREME SECURITY COUNCIL BUILDING.** At approximately 1430 hours a crude IED, subsequently identified as a 'fish bomb' or 'gelateena' was thrown at a four (4) vehicle convoy carrying the United Nations Special Envoy to Libya. The attack took place in the city of Benghazi just as the motorcade had arrived at the office building of Fawzi Wanis Ghadafi, the head of the Supreme Security Council (SSC). The device exploded approximately 12' from the UN envoy's vehicle. No one was hurt in the explosion, no one has been arrested and no one has taken responsibility for the attack.

### 11 APRIL – 12 APRIL 2012 – BENGHAZI

**MOI FACILITY ATTACKED BY UNKNOWN GUNMEN:** An unknown number of gunmen attempted to steal new vehicles purchased by the former regime and stored at the MoI HQs in Benghazi. The Al Nayda/Al-Shorta Police, subsequently reinforced by elements of the 17 February Martyrs Brigade and Libyan Army

Special Forces from a nearby camp, engaged the assailants in a firefight which lasted from 1800 hrs on 11 April until approximately 0700 hours on 12 April. The MOI Benghazi HQ's is located approximately 4 KM from the US Mission compound in Benghazi. Use of small-arms, anti-aircraft weapons, and RPGs was reported.

### 12 APRIL 2012 – BENGHAZI

**INTER-MILITIA CLASHES:** Unconfirmed reports of armed clashes taking place in the Vinicha area of Benghazi, when one militia allegedly attacked a second militia over 'links to the former regime'. Local militia groups frequently accuse other groups, military, or local leaders of supporting the Ghaddafi and the former regime, often as an attempt to discredit competitors.

### 12 APRIL 2012 – TRIPOLI:

**UK CITIZEN DETAINED BY MILITIA WHILE VISITING FORMER REGIME COMPOUND:** On Thursday, 12 April, a UK expatriate working for an engineering firm and his Libyan driver stopped at the former regime Camp 77 compound, opposite Ghaddafi's former Bab Azzizia compound, in downtown Tripoli. The two entered the compound via a hole in the wall, were immediately stopped by militia personnel, and arrested at approximately 1645 hrs. The two were taken to a military compound near Mitiga Air Base, where they were questioned and allowed to call the engineering firm, who in turn notified the UK Embassy. Questioning and searches of the two, including their personnel effects, laptop computers, and telephones, continued until the UK Embassy arranged for their release around 2100 hrs.

U.S. EMBASSY – TRIPOLI, LIBYA　　　　　REGIONAL SECURITY OFFICE

## SECURITY INCIDENTS SINCE JUNE 2011

### 13 APRIL – 14 APRIL 2012 – TRIPOLI

**EXPATRIATE HOTEL EMPLOYEES DETAINED AT PARTY:** On Friday, 13 April and Saturday, 14 April 2012, a group of expatriates working for a western hotel chain in Tripoli were ejected from their villa by a Janzour Militia. The group was having a party, with loud music and alcoholic beverages. The Militia came to the villa at approximately 0200 hrs on Saturday, 14 April, shut down the party, and gave the party-goers 15 minutes to depart. At least one individual, possibly the villa owner, was arrested. The 'ejected' expatriates departed and obtained rooms at the western hotel chain where they worked.

### 20 APRIL 2012 – KUFRA

**INTER-MILITIA CLASHES:** A ceasefire in the desert town of Kubra ended on April 20 when Arab militias and the Libya Shield brigade began fighting with Tebu militias. The Libya shield brigade is an eastern Libyan militia dispatched by the Ministry of Defense to intervene in earlier tribal conflicts in the area. The head of one of the militias involved in the fighting, the Shield Libya brigade, stated that fighting erupted after Zwai tribesman killed a Tebu man. The leader of the Tebu militias in Kufra reported that six houses in two Tebu residential neighborhoods were destroyed by heavy shelling. According to Tebu militia leaders, sixteen Tebu, both fighters and civilians, were injured and five civilians killed in the fighting.

On April 21, the commander of the Libya Shield brigade signed a ceasefire agreement with Tebu leaders and fighting calmed significantly. Tebu leaders claimed that southern Libya's Arabs are waging a campaign of ethnic cleansing against

them with the tacit support of the Libyan government.

### 23 – APRIL to 09 MAY 2012 - BENGHAZI

**PROTESTS AT OIL COMPANY:** Approximately 50 protesters gathered outside the offices of Libya's largest oil company, Arabian Gulf Oil Company (AGOCO). The protestors demanded more transparency over how the country's new rulers are spending its money, more jobs for youth, and wanted Ghaddafi-era officials removed from government. The protestors blocked the entrances to the company and prevented employees from entering the building. AGOCO has stated that it will have to close the oil operations at midnight on 03 May due to the protests. The oil company complained about the lack of intervention from Libyan security forces to remove the blockade from the facility. The company has cut production by 30,000 barrels per day (bpd) as a result of the ongoing protests.

### 24 APRIL 2012 – TRIPOLI

**GUNFIGHT:** At approximately 1600 hrs, a group of up to a dozen men physically attacked a stationery car on Gorji road in northeast Tripoli. The vehicle began to emit smoke from the damage caused by the assailants. The assailants fled the area when an unknown individual(s) opened fire with small arms and then heavy weapons. A number of persons in civilian clothes were reportedly setting up barriers in the area to stop traffic as a result of the incident. A UK Mission vehicle with security personnel was in the vicinity at the time of the incident. Apparently it was due to an extortion attempt that had gone wrong.

U.S. EMBASSY — TRIPOLI, LIBYA          REGIONAL SECURITY OFFICE

## SECURITY INCIDENTS SINCE JUNE 2011

### 24 APRIL 2012 – KUFRA

**KUFRA RESIDENTS ATTEMPT TO HIT MOD AIRCRAFT WITH GUNFIRE:** Unconfirmed media reports claimed that during his visit to the Kufra area to oversee a recent ceasefire, the Minister of Defense's motorcade and aircraft were fired on in separate incidents. The military council commander in Kufra claimed that local residents fired on the Defense minister's aircraft, possibly with unidentified rocket systems, as it took off. Separate reports claimed that gunfire, including heavy weapons fire, was directed toward the Minister's motorcade during his 5-hour visit to Kufra.

### 17-25 APRIL – ZLITEN and MISRATA

**DEATHS CAUSED BY UXO:** During the past week, two persons were killed in separate incidents related to unexploded ordnance (UXO). In the Zliten incident, the three victims were working on a construction site when they uncovered UXO. The UXO exploded, killing one of the workers and injuring the other two. In Misrata, one man was injured and a second killed when they entered a destroyed ammunition storage area inside the Air Force Academy in search of scrap metal.

### 25 APRIL 2012 – TRIPOLI

**US EMBASSY LOCAL SECURITY OFFICER DETAINED; RADIO SEIZED.** A U.S. Embassy local national security officer was detained at a militia check-point for 2 hours while traveling home after his night-shift. While at the check-point, the security officer was interviewed regarding his employment and a U.S. Embassy radio was seized by the militia. The militia members were unable to explain what type of permission, license, or permit was required for a Libyan national to possess a hand-held radio nor were the militia members able to explain what Libyan law they were enforcing by seizing the radio. The Embassy local security officer was released without further incident. U.S. Embassy security officer is following up with the militia to retrieve the radio.

### 26 APRIL 2012 - BENGHAZI

**FIGHT AT INTERNATIONAL MEDICAL UNIVERSITY; US DIPLOMAT EVACUATED FROM SITE:** A fist-fight escalated to gunfire between the security guards of a Tripoli based trade delegation and militia providing security at the International Medical University. The university is in close proximity to the U.S. Mission in Benghazi and the Principal Officer (PO) from the U.S. Mission was attending the same trade event. As the fight escalated at the front entrance to the university, U.S. Mission security personnel and the 17 Feb Martyrs Brigade QRF personnel supporting the U.S. Mission evacuated the PO while still safe to do so.

### 26 APRIL 2012 – TRIPOLI

**EXPATRIOT NGO EMPLOYEE DETAINED FOR 4 HRS:** At approximately 2100 hrs, an expatriate employee and a contract driver of a U.S. based and funded NGO was stopped by four militia members while traveling north from Tripoli International Airport. The four militia members traveling in two unmarked sedans approached the NGO vehicle from behind at high-speed and directed the vehicle to pull over to the side of the road. Two unidentified individuals, believed to be members of a militia based on statements they made to the driver, asked for the documents of the NGO employees. The expat NGO employee, a Palestinian citizen, was directed into one of the militia vehicles and the NGO driver was directed to follow the two militia vehicles into the city.

U.S. EMBASSY – TRIPOLI, LIBYA     REGIONAL SECURITY OFFICE

## SECURITY INCIDENTS SINCE JUNE 2011

The Palestinian employee of the NGO was placed in the back of the vehicle with two of the militia members in the front seat. The militia members would not allow the Palestinian NGO employee to take his cell phone but he was able to retrieve his backpack and laptop from the NGO vehicle. While in the militia vehicle, the Palestinian NGO employed noted he was left alone in the back of the vehicle, with access to a militia members' AK-47 on the rear seat beside him. He was not searched. Once in downtown Tripoli, the militia members met with another individual, identified as a 'sheik', who also questioned the NGO's Libyan driver and Palestinian officer. The NGO's Libyan driver was advised he was free to go after the militia reviewed his documents, although the NGO's Palestinian employee was transported to a 'military police' compound in southeastern Tripoli, where he underwent additional questioning by three additional militia members and military police. The military police advised that the facility was used to process, investigate, screen persons believed to be illegally present in Libya. Upon verification of the NGO's Palestinian's work and travel documents, he was transported back to the NGO's downtown office at approximately 0100 hrs and released.

### 26 APRIL 2012 – TRIPOLI

PROTEST AT NTC HQ: A number of lawyers protested in front of the NTC headquarters in Tripoli over plans to integrate them into the justice ministry. The lawyers are from the Public Defense Lawyers Group ("Muhama Shaabia"), from which lawyers are appointed by the state to defend Libyans in court at government expense.

### 27 APRIL 2012 – BENGHAZI

FAILED PRISON BREAK: In the early morning hours a Benghazi prison was the site of an attempted prison break in which prisoners and prison guards exchanged gunfire. Officials claimed that the fighting killed three prisoners and three guards.

### 27 APRIL 2012 – BENGHAZI

COURTHOUSE BOMBED: At approximately 0500 hours, the Benghazi courthouse was targeted by three crude IEDs, believed to have been contained within packages at the site. Initial reports claimed that four security guards were injured and both the courthouse and an adjacent building were damaged. A Benghazi security official later claimed that the explosives were thrown out of a passing car. No group or motive claimed credit for the attack.

### 27 APRIL 2012 – BENGHAZI

EXPATRIOT DEMINING/ WEAPONS ABATEMENT STAFF DETAINED, QUESTIONED, and RELEASED: Two South African nationals, in Libya as part of a U.S. funded weapons abatement, UXO removal, and demining project, were detained at gunpoint while walking in an residential area. At approximately 0630 hrs, a Ford sedan passed the two men while they were walking, turned around

U.S. EMBASSY — TRIPOLI, LIBYA                                           REGIONAL SECURITY OFFICE

## SECURITY INCIDENTS SINCE JUNE 2011

and returned to where the men were, and a soldier with an AK series assault rifle exited the vehicle. The soldier directed them to get in the vehicle. The soldier took one of the South African's company ID, read the Arabic version on the back of the ID card, and examined the passport and visa. The two South Africans were driven to a house at high speed, where the soldier crashed the gate open with his vehicle. A second militia member wearing a hood and armed with an AK47, entered the vehicle, and questioned the two expatriates regarding their nationality, employer, and purpose for being in Libya. The vehicle departed the residential building at high-speed but stopped in order for the militia members to blindfold the two South Africans. The South Africans were then driven to a second property where a third, unidentified person joined the first two militia members. The militia members reviewed the passports, employer ID cards, and appeared to be discussing next steps. The militia members returned the South Africans' documents and cards and then drove them back to the initial point where they were directed into the vehicle. The South Africans' remained blindfolded until they were brought to the initial pick-up point. The militia members told the South Africans' that they were detained for "their own safety", shook hands with the South Africans' and allowed them to return to their residence. The incident lasted for approximately 2 hours.

### 27 APRIL 2012 – TRIPOLI

GUNFIGHT: At about 2030 hours, an argument between 2 youths in the Alheshan area (Souk Al Juma) escalated to gunfire, killing one bystander and injuring two others. The motive behind the fight was suspected to be part of an ongoing drug

war. Reason behind it not clear but suspected to be part of an ongoing drug war.

### 28 APRIL 2012 – TRIPOLI

DRIVE-BY REVENGE KILLING: Two individuals were shot and killed late on Saturday night in what appears to be a drive-by revenge attack for a shooting incident which took place on 27 April in Alheshan/Souk Al Juma area of Tripoli. Gunfire went on until the early hours. The police emergency number (1515) was called and the answer reportedly given was: "We're aware of the problem but there's nothing we can do."

### 28 APRIL 2012 – BENGHAZI

AIRPORT CLOSED DUE TO PROTESTS: Multiple sources confirmed that Benghazi's Benina airport was closed yesterday due to a protest by the 'Qatar' Battalion of the Barqa Militia. The Barqa Militia has not been paid their salaries in some time. The intent of the Barqa Militia in halting the flights was to prevent PM Al-Keib from flying to Tripoli. Al-Keib and other government ministers were in Benghazi to inaugurate the new government headquarters in the city. The Prime Minister met with representatives of the protestors at the airport; however, the meeting was unable to resolve the protestors' demands. As a result of the closure, the Prime Minister flew back to Tripoli from Abraq airport.

### 01 MAY 2012 – KUFRA

THREAT OF MORE VIOLENCE AFTER INDIVIDUAL KILLED: Media sources reported that an unidentified member of the Al-Majabra tribe was shot and killed around 8pm in the town's Ashoura district while walking home from a market. The Ashoura district is considered to be a largely Tebu area and the killing could re-ignite new clashes in the area.

### 01 MAY 2012 – TRIPOLI

**PROTESTS AT TNC OFFICES IN TRIPOLI:** Several hundred armed revolutionaries from the Union of Revolutionary Battalions surrounded the TNC's offices in Tripoli as part of protests over benefits for former fighters. Between 300 - 400 fully armed ex-rebels surrounded the NTC's offices with gun-mounted trucks. The NTC's offices are located opposite the luxury Rixos Hotel. The demonstrators claimed to represent 200 militia brigades and met with NTC Chairman Jalil. The protestors presented a list of demands to the NTC, including having a direct voice in governing the country, seats assigned to them in the new National Assembly, and amnesty for any crimes committed during the revolution. The protestors also demanded an extension to the voter registration period from 2 weeks to 30 days and for candidates from 7 to 25 days. The group also demanded proper care for all injured ex-rebels and proper distribution of monetary grants being paid to the ex-rebels.

### 01 MAY 2012 – TRIPOLI

**CLASHES IN TRIPOLI:** On May 1, militias from the Souq al-Jumaa and Tajoura neighborhoods joined with the Tripoli branch of the Supreme Security Council to successfully oust what they characterized as "criminal gangs" that had occupied the former headquarters of the Libyan External Security Organization and the Jedayda prison. The gangs had allegedly used the ESO building and the prison as bases to conduct rent-seeking activities such as operating illegal checkpoints and stealing residents' cars. One Tajoura militia member was killed in the clashes

and at least three others were injured. In a public statement issued in reaction to the fighting, the SSC called on militias to comply with orders issued by the GOL to hand over occupied government facilities.

The clashes continued on into the evening, with an increase in militia patrols throughout Tripoli as well as the closure of portions of the Tripoli Ring Road in the eastern side of the city.

Supreme Security Committee (SSC) contacts stated that a group of criminals posing as militia members had indiscriminately fired at residential buildings and the Ministry of Interior building at the intersection of December 24th Street and Al-Naser Street in downtown Tripoli. Two individuals were arrested with no confirmed casualties.

In Suq Al-Jouma, SSC sources reported members of a militia brigade attacked a building belonging to the Foreign Ministry. A number had been arrested with no further details as to casualties or the motive behind the attack.

In the Hadba Al-Khadra neighborhood, the SSC confirmed clashes between members of the Tripoli Revolutionary Brigade and the Shara Ajdabiya Revolutionary Brigade over a government building. Forces from the SSC were directed to the area to resolve the fighting. No further details as to casualties or the motive behind the attack.

### 01 MAY 2012 – TRIPOLI

DEPUTY LGF COMMANDER DETAINED, ASSAULTED, AND US EMBASSY LGF VEHICLE STOLEN BY ARMED INDIVIDUALS AT AN IMPROMPTU CHECK-POINT NEAR POST'S GSO WAREHOUSE. On 05/01/2012, at approximately

U.S. EMBASSY — TRIPOLI, LIBYA                REGIONAL SECURITY OFFICE

## SECURITY INCIDENTS SINCE JUNE 2011

1040 hours, the U.S. Embassy's Deputy LGF Commander was detained, assaulted, and the US Embassy LGF vehicle he was operating stolen by armed individuals at an impromptu check-point near Post's GSO Warehouse. The armed youth detained the LGF deputy along with several other Libyan citizens at a former Ghaddafi regime compound in Tripoli, Libya for more than 3 hours. The LGF deputy, assisted by a Libyan National Transitional Government (NTC) guard in the group of detainees, scaled a wall, escaped the compound, and fled to the U.S. Embassy's GSO warehouse. RSO coordinated recovery of the vehicle with NTC security officials, who directed two militia (Tajoura & Souk Al-Juma) brigades and national army units to the area. On the evening of 5/1/2012, NTC officials recovered the Embassy vehicle although heavy fighting in the area where the incident occurred, to include clashes with the armed group responsible for the vehicle theft, prevented RSO and Embassy officials from retrieving the vehicle until the following day. Libyan security forces, including national army units and militia falling under the control of the Supreme Security Council, recovered 4 vehicles, including two vehicles stolen from other militias, a UN vehicle, and the US Embassy vehicle, and released thirty detainees. During the fighting, security elements killed 2 members of the group, arrested approximately 12 individuals, gained control of the former ESO compound, and continue to search for 5 additional suspects.

### 02 MAY – 10 MAY 2012 – BENGHAZI

WORKERS STRIKE AT LIBYAN CEMENT COMPANY: Approximately 65 workers of the Libyan Cement Company, a joint venture between the Economic and Social Development Fund/Ministry of Industry and an Austrian company, ASAMERR, have been on strike since 02 May outside the Benghazi plant. While the production facility remains open despite the striking workers, the managing director of the company has evacuated 33 expatriate employees of the company as a preventative measure in the event of further unrest and violence.

### 03 MAY 2012 – TRIPOLI

POLICE AND SECURITY FORCES CLASH WITH ARMED DRUG GANG: At approximately 1630hrs, police and security forces engaged an armed drug gang in the Qadasiya area of Tripoli. Police attempted to arrest the members of the gang when the drug dealers opened fire with automatic weapons. The gunfight was sustained for approximately 15 minutes, with witnesses describing persons firing in several directions. Casualties were unknown.

### 06 MAY 2012 – BENGHAZI TO TOBRUK

THREE KILLED AND TWO INJURED IN AN ARMED ROBBERY OF BANK VEHICLE; 2 MILLION LYD TAKEN; THIEVES PART OF BRIGADE HIRED TO PROTECT LIBYAN CENTRAL BANK IN BENGHAZI: According to the Tobruk based Ali Hassan Al-Jaber Brigade, an unidentified group of 3 armed individuals carjacked a bank truck carrying 2 million Libyan Dinars while it was in route to a bank in the eastern Libyan city of Tobruk. The Brigade's commander stated that three of the guards accompanying the bank truck were killed and one injured by the armed assailants and the driver of the truck is still missing. The bodies of the guards were left by the roadside when the attackers fled with the vehicle and cash. Two of the murdered guards were shot and the third had his throat slit. Investigators believe that the assailants wanted the attack to be carried out by Islamist extremists. The vehicle attack took place

U.S. EMBASSY – TRIPOLI, LIBYA

REGIONAL SECURITY OFFICE

## SECURITY INCIDENTS SINCE JUNE 2011

while the guards were transporting money from the Central Bank of Libya in Benghazi to the Bank of North Africa in Tobruk.

Hospital officials in Al-Marj confirmed that three bodies were transported to Al-Marj's main hospital along with the injured guard. Brigade members claimed they arrested the assailants and recovered the stolen money. Subsequent investigation revealed that the assailants were from the brigade hired to protect the Benghazi premises of the Libyan Central Bank. Investigators determined that the gang planned to murder all the guards to avoid being recognized as security from the Central Bank. The wounded guard was able to identify the attackers to investigators.

### 05 MAY 2012 – SEBHA

RENEWED FIGHTING: Clashes broke out in the Al-Jadid area in Sebha between Libyan 'Special Forces' and purported Qadhafi loyalists. Officials within the Libyan special forces claimed that heavy weapons were used during the fighting, with two Libyan special forcers members wounded and two 'loyalists' injured and arrested.

### 08 MAY 2012 – TRIPOLI

PROTEST AT PM's OFFICE: Individuals who were prisoners under the Qadhafi regime protested at the PM office in Tripoli. This protest was unrelated to a subsequent protest by militia members from Yefren and Kikla, which escalated into a violent confrontation between the militia members and trhe MOI/SSC.

### 08 MAY 2012 – TRIPOLI

CLASHES AT PM OFFICE; 4 INJURED AND 1 KILLED: Approximately 200 militia members from the western Nafusa Mountains (Yefren and Kikla)

clashed with Ministry of Interior and Supreme Security Council members outside of the Prime Minister's Office in down town Tripoli. A security officer from the MoI/SSC assigned to the PM's office was killed and three others wounded. One of the militia members was injured. SSC officials claimed to have seized sixteen militia vehicles and arrested fourteen militia members. The incident began with militia members protesting at the PM's office for wages when it escalated into exchanges of gunfire, to include use of heavy weapons.

### 08 MAY 2012 – ZAWYIA

ATTACK ON OIL REFINERY: Senior GOL officials reported an attack on an oil refinery in Zawyia, although the officials could not provide additional details as to who had carried out the attack or what the motive was. No information on damage, injuries, or fatalities.

### 11 MAY 2012 – TRIPOLI

TRIPOLI RESIDENTS PROTEST AND CALL FOR REMOVAL OF WEAPONS AND MILITIAS: Thousands of Tripoli residents demonstrated in Martyrs' Square demanding the removal of arms and the departure of unofficial and unsanctioned militias. Protestors also called for the establishment of a National Army and the absorption of the militia groups under its control.

The demonstrators called for the activation of the legal system, the National Army and the collection of arms in order to achieve safety, security and stability.

### 12 - 13 MAY 2012 – BANI WALID

CLASHES IN BANI WALID: Clashes broke out this evening on the outskirts of Bani Walid between

U.S. EMBASSY — TRIPOLI, LIBYA      REGIONAL SECURITY OFFICE

## SECURITY INCIDENTS SINCE JUNE 2011

government troops and local fighters opposed to the TNC and the revolution.

Ministry of Interior officials confirmed the deployment of additional government forces, including militia under the Libya Shield Brigades, were deployed to the southern area of Tripoli, near Tarhuna, and also to Bani Walid. Reinforcements from Misrata were reportedly blocked from entering Bani Walid by sympathizers in Tarhouna.

### 9-14 MAY 2012 – TRIPOLI

PROTESTS AT TRIPOLI INTERNATIONAL AIRPORT: For the past several days, a small number of airport employees have been striking at Tripoli International Airport, demanding higher wages, among other requests. On May 13, U.S. Embassy observed that the employees have positioned themselves at the entry point for outbound passengers to pass through customs, significantly slowing down customs' ability to process passengers. As a result of the disruption, recent flights to Rome, Frankfurt, and Vienna on international carriers have reportedly taken off from three to five hours late. Air Malta and Alitalia each cancelled at least one flight to Tripoli because of the strike. Airport officials reported that while all flights are eventually taking off, the protesters have slowed down the process to allow just one flight per hour. According to airport officials, the issue was resolved on 14 May 2012.

### 13 MAY 2012 – LIBYAN/EGYPTIAN BORDER

TWO DIE IN MINE BLAST CROSSING FROM EGYPT TO LIBYA: Two men were killed and 29 other people were injured after their convoy that was illegally crossing from Egypt into Libya entered a minefield. Mahmoud Zahran, a Health Ministry official in the northern Egyptian city of Marsa Matrouh, confirmed that an Egyptian and a Sudanese man died when their vehicle, which was travelling in a convoy with two others, hit landmines inside Libya. The injured were transported to a hospital in Salloum, an Egyptian town near the border. The north coast of Egypt and Libya is littered with landmines laid during World War II. It is unknown if the landmine dated from the 1940s or was more recently planted.

### 14 MAY 2012 - MURZUQ

CANDIDATE ASSASSINATED IN SOUTHERN LIBYA: A local candidate from Murzuk, located in southwestern Libya, was assassinated shortly after registering to stand in the June elections as a candidate for the National Congress.

Khaled Bukhatwa Abu Salah, a prominent political activist and physician from the oasis town of Murzuq, was attacked and killed by an armed gang some 30 kilometers from Awbari. Supreme Security Council (SSC) officials stated that an armed gang traveling in five cars followed him after he registered with the electoral commission. They surrounded his vehicle and killed him. Two colleagues travelling with Abu Salah managed to escape the attack.

Bukhatwa Abu Salah was a member of the Fazazna, an ethnic group of dark-skinned former African slaves who identify culturally and politically with Libya's Arabs. One prevailing theory among Murzuq residents is that Bukhatwa was killed by a Tebu militia for his frequent statements in the Libyan media criticizing human rights violations committed by the Tebu, such as torturing prisoners. A Supreme Security Council spokesman told Al Jazeera that the killing remains

U.S. EMBASSY — TRIPOLI, LIBYA          REGIONAL SECURITY OFFICE

### SECURITY INCIDENTS SINCE JUNE 2011

under investigation and its perpetrators and motivation are not yet clear.

### 14 MAY 2012 - MURZUQ

**CLASHES IN GHADAMES; TUAREQ LEADER AND 9 OTHERS KILLED:** A Tuareg leader and eight others were killed in clashes that lasted for more than seven hours. One man from the Ghadames brigade was also killed and more than 20 people injured. Local officials added that Tuareg militia had also attacked a National Army checkpoint located at 50 km outside the city on 11 May. Ghadames brigade members reportedly called on the National Army, Army Chief of Staff, and Special Forces from Benghazi, but no reinforcements arrived. The clashes lasted for more than seven hours and included mortar fire and 106mm anti-tank rockets. A hospital, the airport, and several residential houses were reportedly damaged during the fighting. The Libyan Army Chief of Staff subsequently attributed responsibility for the attacks on a irregular militia called the "Western Region Military Junta".

### 14 MAY 2012 – RAS JEDIR; LIBYAN-TUNISIA BORDER

**BORDER CLASHES BETWEEN SMUGGLERS AND AUTHORITIES:** Thirty trucks loaded with bananas, apples, and a variety of electrical and household equipment were stopped at the border crossing in the southeastern town of Ben Guerdane, triggering clashes between authorities and locals.

During the confrontation, an angry crowd of locals from Ben Guerdane joined the fight, clashing with police and army officials. As tensions rose, protests spread into downtown Ben Guerdane, forcing roads and shops to close

throughout the city. Tunisian armed forces succeeded in restoring order until the following morning. The director of Ben Guerdane Hospital confirmed to Tunisia Live that the hospital admitted two men following the clashes, one of whom was badly burnt.

### 15 MAY 2012 - SORMAN

**TWO KILLED IN CLASHES IN BEACH RESORT AREA:** At least two persons were killed and a third wounded in clashes in the northwestern resort town of Sorman. The clash occurred at the Electricity institute, which is located in the resort area of the town, which is located approximately 45 km west of Tripoli on the road to Sabratha. The clashes reportedly occurred following a dispute between a man from Sorman and another from the Mutrud area. After the fight, a weapons store in Sorman was destroyed by Mutrud residents as retribution for the attack.

### 15 May 2012 - BENGHAZI

**MILITARY POLICE HEADQUARTERS IN BENGHAZI TARGET OF GRENADE ATTACK :** An unknown attacker threw a hand grenade at the Military Police (MP) headquarters in Benghazi. Currently, the MP headquarters is being used as a makeshift prison where a number of Qadhafi loyalists are detained. No injuries were reported and no inmates were able to escape.

### 15 MAY 2012 - BENGHAZI

**DIRECTOR OF BENGHAZI'S MEDICAL CENTER INJURED IN SHOOTING :** Director of Benghazi's Medical Center Dr. Fathi Al-Jhani was wounded in the chest after he was shot on Wednesday afternoon when leaving work. Dr. Al-Jhani was taken to a Benghazi hospital for treatment and doctors there said he is in a stable situation.

U.S. EMBASSY – TRIPOLI, LIBYA

REGIONAL SECURITY OFFICE

## SECURITY INCIDENTS SINCE JUNE 2011

Armed men followed Dr. Al-Jhani as he headed to his vehicle in the center's parking lot and fired at him, injuring him in the chest. Security officials reportedly captured the assailants as they attempted to flee the scene. Subsequent reports indicated that the shooting was related to

### 16 MAY - NATIONWIDE

BANK EMPLOYEES STAGED DEMONSTRATIONS FOLLOWING MURDER OF COLLEAGUES IN ARMED ROBBERY: Employees of the Bank of North Africa staged a nationwide protest following the murder of four of their colleagues in an armed robbery. The robbery took place on a convoy transporting LD 2 million from the Central Bank of Libya in Benghazi to the Bank of North Africa in Tobruk on 6 May. Demonstrations were witnessed at Bank of North Africa branches in several Libyan cities, with the demonstrators demanding swift action to bring the perpetrators to justice. The money has subsequently been recovered and the robbers arrested.

### 16 MAY 2012 - SIRTE

VEHICLE BOMB ASSASSINATION ATTEMPT: Embassy commercial contacts provided details on a 16 May assassination attempt against a Libyan national in Sirte. The Libyan national was the target of a bomb placed underneath his vehicle while it was parked at his residence in Sirte. The bomb detonated, destroyed the car but missed the intended target as he was opening his residential vehicle gate at the time of the explosion. The commercial contact traveled to the scene and spoke with EOD personnel who described the attempt as 'professional' and likely triggered by a timer. No group claimed responsibility for the attack. No further specifics

as to the background of the individual or who might have targeted him were available.

### 17 MAY 2012 – BENGHAZI

TNC MEMBERS ATTACKED AT BENGHAZI AIRPORT: An armed group allegedly attempted to shoot NTC members, Khaled Saleh and Fathi Al Baaja at Benghazi Airport on the evening of 17 May 2012. According to Saleh, he had been trying to speak to the group regarding militia payments when the group became agitated and began shooting at the TNC officials. The group reportedly was linked the Cyrenaica military council.

### 18 MAY 2012 – BENGHAZI

PEACEFUL DEMONSTRATION AT UNHCR: A peaceful demonstration was held at the UNHCR office located in the Hawary area of Benghazi. Approximately, 200 pro-federalists gathered in front of the UN building to express their dissatisfaction with the current distribution of parliamentary seats for the Barqa area. The protestors arrived in approximately 60 vehicles and were accompanied by press from Al-Jazeera and Al-Arabiya. The participants delivered a petition to the UN and remained on site for approximately 2.5 hours.

### 21 MAY 2012 – TRIPOLI

FIGHTING IN JANZOUR AREA: Libyan National Army units reportedly gave notice to the militia currently occupying the Regatta area to leave the site. The Army units reportedly returned in the afternoon to evict them by force. Additionally, diplomatic contacts reported a 2nd, possibly related incident, approximately 500 meters south of Palm City near the 'Little Janzour' roundabout. Diplomatic vehicles were in the vicinity when a

U.S. EMBASSY — TRIPOLI, LIBYA                    REGIONAL SECURITY OFFICE

## SECURITY INCIDENTS SINCE JUNE 2011

gunfight took place at the roundabout, followed by the dispatch of heavy militia, police, and SSC/MOI response. SSC officials confirmed that two SSC officers died during the clashes in Janzour.

### 21 MAY 2012 – TRIPOLI

CZECH DIPLOMATIC VEHICLE STOPPED/SEARCHED BY MILITIA: A Czech Embassy vehicle, bearing red diplomatic license plates, was stopped and searched by approximately 20 members of the Suq Al Juma militia. Reportedly, the diplomatic passengers were told to exit the vehicle and taken to a nearby location by the militia while the search was being conducted. Czech Embassy officials were able to arrange for intervention by SSC officials via a dual-national (Czech/Libyan) contact within the SSC.

### 22 MAY 2012 – BENGHAZI

ICRC BUILDING AND BANK STRUCK BY RPGs: The International Committee for the Red Cross/Red Crescent (ICRC) building was hit by two RPG rounds, one at approximately 0330 hours and a second at 0530. The first RPG struck the front of the building, damaging a shipping container. The second was an 'airburst' with no damage. No casualties were reported given the time of the incident. There were also reports of a third RPG explosion approx 1 km away at 0540 hours, which struck the Sahara Bank's Fuwaihat branch. The ICRC compound is located near the al-Nasser Athletic Sports Club on Shari Al-Andalus near the intersection of Third Ring Road, approximately 1km from Benghazi Mission. The Imprisoned Sheikh Omar Abdul-Rahman Brigades claimed responsibility on 27 May for the attack of the International Committee of the Red Cross

(ICRC). The brigade accused the ICRC of attempting to convert internally displaced members of the Tawergha ethnic minority to Christianity. It called for the NGO to close its offices, and declared Libya to be an Islamic state.

### 22 MAY 2012 – TRIPOLI

ANGRY VISA APPLICANT FIRES WEAPON AT GERMANY EMBASSY: At approximately 1200 hrs, a Libyan militia veteran applied for a Schengan visa at the German Embassy. The Libyan militia veteran, identified as Hassam BELHAJ, DOB: 15-Sept-1987, was planning to travel to German for follow-up treatment but his visa application was rejected as being incomplete. Enraged, he began firing his AK-47 into the air, causing further confusion on the street outside the German Embassy. During the shooting, German Embassy officials were instructed to remain in the building, away from the windows. German personnel off-site were directed to remain off-site.

### 23 MAY 2012 – LIBYAN/TUNISIA BORDER

RAS JEDIR BORDER CROSSING CLOSED BY LIBYAN GOVT: Media sources reported that the Libyan side of the Ras Jedir border crossing was closed, possibly in protest over news that Tunisia would not extradite former Libyan PM Baghdadi. The border was re-opened later on the 23rd.

### 23 MAY 2012 – TRIPOLI

SHOOTING AT TRIPOLI AIRPORT AFTER ARREST OF LIBYAN DEFENSE MINISTER'S RELATIVE: Members of the Al-Zintan Brigade at Tripoli International Airport arrested a relative of Libyan Defense Minister Usamah al-Juwayli. According to sources at the airport, after the arrest, members of the Al-Zintan Brigade started shooting near one of the African Airways planes.

## SECURITY INCIDENTS SINCE JUNE 2011

Reportedly, the minister's relative was arrested after "verbal exchanges" between the minister's relative and security officials the airport. Security officials reportedly asked the relative for a license for the car he was driving, which he was unable to produce. After the relative's arrest by security officials, members of the Al-Zintan Brigade attempted to intervene in the situation.

### 23 MAY 2012 – TRIPOLI

DETENTION AND SEARCH OF DIPLOMATIC CARGO BY LOCAL MILITIA: Shipments of diplomatic supplies, including a 20' container of security equipment, cameras, and electrical supplies, were seized and searched by members of the SSC outside of Tripoli port. The cargo, including goods destined for the German Embassy, were diverted to a TNC Customs side near the WICS/MOD site, and then to Mitiga Airport. Although clearly marked and manifested as diplomatic cargo, the SSC failed to acknowledge TNC customs guidance that the shipments were exempt from search and seizure. The U.S. Embassy goods were released after approximately 6 hours due to intervention by Embassy officials. However, a number of items were removed from the shipment during the searches.

### 23 MAY 2012 – TRIPOLI

KIDNAPPING/DETENTION OF MITIGA CUSTOMS CHIEF BY ARMED GROUP: The head of the customs department at Mitiga airport, Col Ibrahim Umar Qasudah, was kidnapped by an armed group on Wednesday, 23 May, while on his way to his office at the airport. It is unknown if his detention was related to the seizure of diplomatic cargo on the same day.

### 24 MAY 2012 – TRIPOLI

TRIPOLI CUSTOMS STAFF PROTEST CHIEF'S KIDNAP, LIBYAN BRIGADE DENIES INVOLVEMENT: On 24 May, customs officers staged a protest outside the Council of Ministers in Tripoli to demand the transitional government's intervention to free Col Ibrahim Umar Qasudah, the head of customs at Mitiga airport in Tripoli who was kidnapped/detained by armed men on 23 May. The protestors demanded the GoL provide protection to all customs staff at all border crossings and the swift punishment of kidnappers and criminal groups targeting customs staff and offices. The protestors threatened to stop work at all Libyan land, sea and air customs ports. The commander of the Badr Misratah Brigade denied that his forces "are linked in absolutely any way" with the kidnap of a customs officer at Tripoli's Mitiga International Airport.

### 25 MAY 2012 – TRIPOLI

DRUG RAIDS BY SSC: Supreme Security Committee (SSC) forces, brigades under Interior Ministry control and members of the NTC-affiliated Abu Salim Military Council conducted a series of night time raids of drug dens in the Abu Salim and Al-Huadba districts of Tripoli. According to NTC spokesman Mohammed Harizi, the raids began at 02:00hrs and continued for several hours. Sustained exchanges of fire took place, with unconfirmed reports of six fatalities, including two SSC officers, and approximately fifteen persons wounded. The wounded men have been taken to Abu Salim hospital for treatment. Large quantities of drugs and alcohol were reportedly seized during the raids, which were subsequently disposed of at the Abu Salim Military Council HQ.

U.S. EMBASSY – TRIPOLI, LIBYA                REGIONAL SECURITY OFFICE

## SECURITY INCIDENTS SINCE JUNE 2011

### 26 MAY 2012 – TRIPOLI

**SENEGALESE AMBASSADOR CARJACKED:** On 5/26/2012, the Senegalese Ambassador had his vehicle carjacked while waiting to enter his residential compound. A militia vehicle with a crew served weapon followed the Ambassador's vehicle to his residence where the Ambassador was forced out of his vehicle and his vehicle taken by the individuals in the militia vehicle. The Ambassador was driving in a diplomatic plated vehicle although did not have a security escort or team. The Ambassador believed that the vehicle was providing his diplomatic vehicle with an armed escort.

### 26 MAY 2012

**FAILED ATTACK ON HEAD OF WESTERN MILITARY COUNCIL:** According to various media reports, the head of the military council for the western region, Mukhtar Fernana, was the target of an attack by gunmen. Fernana's vehicle was reportedly attacked by assailants traveling in five vehicles. No further details regarding the identity of the assailants nor was any information available on casualties.

### 26 MAY 2012 – WADI AL-AHMAR

**OIL WORKER PROTESTS:** Protesters in Wadi Al-Ahmar threatened to suspend oil production on 28 May 2012, unless the government agrees to federalist demands for eastern Libya, particularly Barqa. The protests also sought more equitable sharing of oil revenue between the three historical regions of Libya.

### 28 MAY 2012 – SIRTE

**EXPLOSION KILLS 7, INCLUDING MOI CONTROLLED MILITIA MEMBERS:** An explosion took place inside the base of the Sirte Revolutionary Brigade last night, killing seven people. An unknown number of people were also injured. According to the MoI, three members of the brigade, who are under Interior Ministry control, were killed, along with two men from the Al-Fergan tribe and two from Derna. Conflicting reports identified the source of the explosion as a fire in a weapons/ammunition storeroom or an RPG attack, possibly by former regime elements (FRE).

### 28 MAY 2012 – ZLINTEN

**BODY OF ZLINTEN MAN TORTURED TO DEATH DUMPED IN LOCAL HOSPITAL:** The body of a man has been found dumped at Zliten hospital. Investigations have revealed that the dead man, named as Hussein Omar Attir and in his forties, was tortured to death. His body was covered in bruises and his hands had been tied. According to the Libyan Human Rights Observatory, it has sent a report to the Attorney General which is to said to claim that Attir was tortured and murdered by five named members of a local brigade after being held for six days during at one of the brigade's command centers in the town.

### 04 JUNE 2012-TRIPOLI

**AL-AWFEA BRIGADE SEIZES AIRPORT:** On June 4, 2012, A gun battle took place at Tripoli International Airport between members of a Tarhouna based militia and government forces, after the Tarhouna militia men stormed the airport demanding the release of a rebel leader. Libyan authorities allegedly deployed 5,000 security forces to the airport, regained control of the facility, and arrested 30 militia members. The

## SECURITY INCIDENTS SINCE JUNE 2011

attack on the airport was carried out by members of the al-Awfea brigade, a volunteer militia from the town of Tarhouna about 80 km (50 miles) south-east of Tripoli. Flights were diverted to Mitiga airport while black smoke could be seen rising from fires set in the runway area. Sporadic gunfire could be heard for several hours.

### 06 JUNE 2012-BENGHAZI

**US MISSION TARGET OF IED:** On June 6th 2012, at approximately 0325 hrs the U.S. Mission in Benghazi was the target of an IED attack. The Mission's local guard force reported a suspicious male individual wearing "Islamic" dress exit a passing vehicle and approach the front gate of the Mission. The guards observed stated they saw the subject place a device at what appeared to be the ledge of the perimeter wall, approximately 3 feet from the ground. The local guard force initiated the Mission's emergency, imminent danger alarm Approximately 6 minutes after the IDNS alarm was initiated, an IED exploded next to the front gate. No one was injured and all personnel are accounted for. Video camera footage shows a 4-door white pick-up truck departing the area in front of the main gate. The guards confirmed that the subject was driving the vehicle. The local guards then stated that they smelled and saw smoke coming from the area of the wall where the subject had approached. Approximately 6 minutes after initiating the IDNS, the device exploded, creating a large hole in the perimeter wall. US Mission Benghazi QRF, and their support unit from Local Militia (17th February Martyrs Brigade) responded quickly to the incident. The Imprisoned Sheikh Omar Abdul-Rahman Brigades reportedly claimed credit for the attack.

### 08 JUNE 2012-SABHA

**GRENADE ATTACK ON UK VEHICLES:** At approximately 2345 hours, two hand grenades were used by unknown persons to target marked UK diplomatic vehicle while they were parked outside of a Sabha hotel. One grenade detonated, causing damage to three tires and an oil pump. The second grenade failed to detonate and was removed by local security forces. No injuries resulted from the incident.

### 10 JUNE 2012 – KUFRA

**CLASHES IN KUFRA:** On 10 June, fighting flared up again in Kufra. Tobu tribesmen were engaged in clashes with former rebels who had become members of the new Libyan National Army. A Kufra official said the Tobu had launched an attack on the city with tanks and other heavy weapons. A Tobu representative said it was the tribe that had come under attack. The Tobu rep stated that the fighting started after the former militiamen, known as the Libya Shield Battalion, shelled the tribe's district. A third official claimed that an attack on a security checkpoint in the town triggered the violence. The fighting continued into the 14th of June with at least 38 people were killed and as many as 150 wounded.

### 10 JUNE 2012 – TRIPOLI

**ATTEMPTED BREAK IN / ARMED ROBBERY OF SUV OF EXPAT:** At approximately 2250 hours, ten (10) unidentified men carrying AK-47s and traveling in 3 vehicles, attempted to scale the wall of the expat's villa after the security guard at the villa refused to grant them entry. ' Military police providing security to a nearby refugee camp, alerted by the efforts of the thieves, responded to the villa and the armed gang fled before any gunfire was exchanged. The vehicles used by the armed gang were described as two

U.S. EMBASSY — TRIPOLI, LIBYA          REGIONAL SECURITY OFFICE

## SECURITY INCIDENTS SINCE JUNE 2011

unmarked Toyota Land Cruisers with tinted windows, and one Chevrolet (or similar) sedan car. There were no insignia or number plates evident.

### 10 JUNE 2012 – TRIPOLI

**ZINTAN MILITIAMEN SEIZE GOVERNMENT CARS IN TRIPOLI:** A group from one of the Zintan militias, Brigade 14, which was assigned to protect the Algerian-Libyan borders, seized a number of government vehicles in Tripoli on Monday. The vehicles seized by the militia included cars belonging to the protocol department as well as police vehicles. Brigade 14 militia members stated that they seized the government vehicles due to the government's failure to provide financial "entitlements" to the brigade. The Ministry of Interior confirmed that at least 33 government vehicles were taken by the brigade, adding that negotiations between the government and the brigade were ongoing. The vehicle in which the Maltese Central Bank Governor Josef Bonnici was traveling was among those seized. Bonnici, in town for official meetings with the Central Bank of Libya, was told to exit the protocol vehicle he was traveling in when the motorcade was stopped at a Zintan checkpoint. Protocol and police vehicles, including those in Bonnici's motorcade, were taken to the brigades' Tripoli headquarters, near the airport road.

### 11 JUNE 2012 – BENGHAZI

**RPG ATTACK ON UK AMBASSADOR'S CONVOY; 2 SECURITY OFFICERS INJURED:** At approximately 1530 hours, a 3-car motorcade carrying the UK Ambassador was targeted by an RPG attack. The security personnel in the motorcade indicated that they were initially engaged by an RPG and then possible AK-47 fire within 500 meters of the rear entrance of their compound. The attack occurred as the convoy was en route to the British office compound, which is located approximately two kilometers from U.S. Mission Benghazi. One RPG round struck the rear of the lead armored vehicle, injuring two of the security personnel in the vehicle. The motorcade was not flying the British flags. Security and medical personnel from the U.S. Mission in Benghazi responded and provided initial trauma medical care until the Supreme Security Council (SSC) could respond. No suspects have been identified and no group has claimed responsibility for the attack. Both injured security officers were medevaced out of Libya for further treatment.

### 12 JUNE 2012 – MISRATA

**IED/EXPLOSION AT THE ICRC COMPOUND IN MISRATA; 1 PERSON INJURED.** The ICRC confirmed that an explosion occurred in our Misrata office at 3.50am on 12 June. A crude, time-delayed IED was the cause of the explosion, which wounded one person. informed and were on site early at five in the morning."

### 13 JUNE 2012 – SEBHA

**CLASHES IN SEBHA:** Two persons were killed and eleven wounded in fighting between the National Army and 'wanted individuals' in Sebha. According to the Supreme Security Committee in Sebha, the two men killed were part of the SSC and described the wounded as soldiers and SSC members. According to the Sebha SSC, the 'wanted individuals' were from Ghaddafi's tribe.

### 13 JUNE 2012 – BENGHAZI

**INDIVIDUAL KILLED IN CAR BOMB ASSASINATION:** One individual was killed at the Zamzam market area of Benghazi when a bomb

## SECURITY INCIDENTS SINCE JUNE 2011

placed inside his vehicle detonated. The victim was identified as Ibrahim al-'Arabi by the Benghazi Security Directorate's spokesman Majdi al-'Arfi. The bomb went off as the man was leaving the market in route to his residence. The victim was reportedly the aid to a former internal security service officer.

### 21 JUNE 2012 – BENGHAZI

BENGHAZI JUDGE LINKED TO YOUNIS'S DEATH ASSASSINATED: On the evening of June 21, the former military prosecutor who reportedly ordered the arrest of General Abdul Fatah Younis was shot and killed in Benghazi. Judge Jumah Hasan al Jawzi had survived two earlier attempts on his life in January and March. The judge was blamed for Younis's death, when Younis was killed after being summoned by the TNC last July for questioning. No one has yet to be charged with killing Younis. It is unclear who was behind al Jawzi's assassination.

### 23 JUNE 2012 – BENGHAZI

ARMED ROBBERY OF UK CITIZEN BY LOCAL TAXI DRIVER: On 23 June, a UK citizen was robbed at gunpoint by the driver of a local taxi. Shortly after the UK citizen entered the local taxi, a black and white Hyundai sedan with no local license plates, the driver pulled a 9mm pistol on the passenger and demanded money. The passenger gave the taxi driver a small amount of funds and was able to exit the vehicle. No injuries reported.

### 24 JUNE -- 02 JULY 2012 – KUFRA

RENEWED FIGHTING: Clashes in Al-Kufra between Tebu, Zwai, and elements of the Libya Shield Brigade, which falls under the Libyan ministry of Defense, left numerous dead and wounded. Sources in the Supreme Security Council and the Ministry Defense confirmed that both sides utilized armored vehicles, including tanks, during the fighting and that residential neighborhoods and the local hospital were struck during the fighting. During the three weeks' of fighting, Tebu spokesmen claimed that at least 56 of their people have been killed, most recently two on Saturday, 6/30 during shelling of the town's Tebu districts of Qaderfi and Qarah Tebu.

### 24 JUNE 2012 – TRIPOLI

POLICE RAIDS AGAINST ARMED GANG: According to the Tripoli police and Supreme Security Committee (SSC), the two organizations carried out a raid against an armed gang involved in drug smuggling and kidnappings. The raid took place on Sunday on a property formally owned by the Ghaddafi regime located on the outskirts of Tripoli. No further details were provided on the number of persons arrested or the exact location of the raid. No casualties were reported. The raid is part of a series of recent raids in May and June 2012 carried out by authorities in Tripoli to improve law and order in the city.

### 24 JUNE 2012 – TRIPOLI

HEAD OF ROADS AND BRIDGES AUTHORITY KIDNAPPED: According to officials at the Roads and Bridges Authority, the Director of office, Dr. Naas Mohamed was kidnapped by eight. The

## SECURITY INCIDENTS SINCE JUNE 2011

Director was reportedly taken by the armed group from his office in Got Alshaal area on Sunday morning. Authorities were informed of the incident and continue to investigate.

### 26 JUNE 2012 – TRIPOLI

**TUNISIAN CONSULATE TARGETED BY CRUDE IED:** According to the Tunisian Embassy, shortly after 1500 hrs, two to four men in a Mitsubishi Lander drove up to the front of the Tunisian Embassy located in the Nouflein area of Tripoli. The individuals threw a small explosive device at the outside of the building. There were no reported injuries as a result of the explosion, however, the consulate's rear gate was charred, two nearby cars were damaged, and a large hole was created in the ground. Many believe the incident is connected with the extradition of Al-Mahmoudi from Tunisia to Libya, which occurred on 24 June.

### 01 JULY 2012 – BENGHAZI

**HNEC OFFICES STORMED; ELECTION MATERIALS AND BALLOTS BURNED:** Between 100-200 demonstrators ransacked the office of the High National Electoral Commission (HNEC) in Benghazi, burning election materials and chanting pro-federalist slogans.

### 01 JULY 2012 – TOBRUK

**HNEC OFFICES STORMED; DEPUTY CHAIRMAN BEATEN:** The HNEC office in Tobruk was stormed by protestors, who who also assaulted its deputy chairman, Mufta Othman.

### 02 JULY 2012 – MAREJ

**POLITICAL PARTY OFFICE FIREBOMBED:** According to unconfirmed media reports, the campaign office of the Justice and Construction Party in Marej was the target of a firebombing.

The office was reportedly destroyed. No suspects were identified. A Molotov bomb was thrown at an electoral office that belongs to Justice and Construction Party in Marej city and burned it down.

### 03 JULY 2012 – MUSAID (LIBYAN-EGYPTIAN BORDER)

**SECURITY FORCES ABANDON POST IN PROTEST OVER DANGEROUS CONDITIONS:** Security forces on the Libyan-Egyptian border crossing at Musaid abandoned their posts in protest at what they said are the dangerous conditions they have been exposed to, which included being regularly shot at by smugglers involved in human trafficking.

### 04 JULY 2012 – BENGHAZI

**BORDER SECURITY OFFICER ASSASSINATED IN BENGHAZI :** A border control department officer, identified as Colonel Sulaiman Hasan Bortima, was assassinated on Wednesday. Colonel Bortima, who was assigned to the Gharyonis district, was struck by three bullets fired by a group of unidentified assailants driving in a Mitsubishi Lancer. Neither a motive nor the assailants have been identified.

### 03 JULY 2012 – KUFRA

**ZWAY TRIBESMAN STOP OIL PRODUCTION AT THREE SITES TO PROTEST VIOLENCE AND GOVT RESPONSE IN KUFRA:** Zway tribesmen surrounded and stopped production at three oil fields in the Kufra region after their prior warning four days prior went unheeded by the government. The Zway leaders in Kufra demanded that the NTC take decisive action to put an end to the violence in the town within 72 hours or they would stop oil flowing. The three fields include Wintershall's Nafura C96

## SECURITY INCIDENTS SINCE JUNE 2011

concession at Jakhira and the nearby concession in the Amal field held by Harouge (formerly Veba) Oil. Oil production at the two locations was estimated to be approximately 75,000 barrels per day. The Zway are the primary security guards at the Nafura fields, which aided their ability to cause a work stoppage. The Zway are also threatening to stop water following in the Man-made River in their attempts to force the government to take decisive action in Kufra.

### 05 JULY 2012 - AJDABIYA

**ARSON SUSPECTED IN LIBYAN POLL OFFICE FIRE:** The main storage center for election materials in Ajdabiya caught fire in a suspected arson attack. The fire destroyed ballot papers and other election equipment. Security sources confirmed that the fire was being investigated as a possible arson attack. National election commission officials planned to replace the materials before the elections on Saturday. The storage center is located on the outskirts of Ajdabiya, but the main election commission headquarters in the center of town were not affected, according to witnesses.

### 06 JULY 2012 – BENGHAZI

**LIBYAN AIRFORCE HELICOPTER STRUCK BY GUNFIRE; ONE HNEC EMPLOYEE KILLED:** A Libyan air force helicopter transporting polling material was struck by gunfire, suspected of being from a 14.5 millimeter anti-aircraft weapon, and was forced to land at Benghazi's Benina Airport. The aircraft was flying to Al Abyar Benghazi Sub Constituency. One HNEC staff member was killed during the attack and another was wounded.

### 07 JULY 12 – QAMINIS / OUTSKIRTS OF BENGHAZI

**ARMED INDIVIDUALS STORM THREE POLLING STATIONS:** A group of Pro-Federalist gunmen reportedly stormed three polling stations in the Qaminis area, located approximately 47 km west of Benghazi city. The group took ballots, voting material, and burned the material in the street. No reports of casualties.

### 07 JULY 2012 – AJDABIYAH

**POLLING STATIONS CLOSED DUE TO THEFTS OF ELECTION MATERIAL:** According to election officials and media sources, voting was suspended in some polling stations in Ajdabiyah following the theft of election material. The election material was reportedly stolen just before dawn on Saturday, 7 July.

### 07 JULY 2012 – AJDABIYAH

**GUNMAN OPENS FIRE NEAR POLLING STATION:** One person was killed and another was wounded when unknown gunmen opened fire near a polling station in the city of Ajdabiya.

### 08 JULY 2012 – SABHA

**CONTINUED CLASHES:** Additional clashes were reported in the Al-Jadid district between members of the national army and the Maqarihah tribe. No casualties were reported

U.S. EMBASSY — TRIPOLI, LIBYA                    REGIONAL SECURITY OFFICE

## SECURITY INCIDENTS SINCE JUNE 2011

from the clashes, which lasted approximately 30 minutes. The incident reportedly occurred after the national army surrounded a district which houses members of the Maqarihah tribes.

### 09 JULY 2012 – DERNA

**MOSQUE TARGETED BY IED:** The Sahaba Mosque in Derna was targeted by an IED at approximately 7 am on Monday morning. The blast damaged the tomb of Zuhayr Ibn Qais Al-Balawi at the Sahaba Mosque in Derna causing what could be irreparable damage to the monument to the seventh century commander who helped bring Islam to the region. No casualties have been reported. The bomb destroyed the building over Balawi's grave but the actual grave is reported not to have been damaged. No group claimed responsibility for the explosion, but local residents blame a small group of Salafists active in the area. Reportedly, the Salafist group refused to pray in the mosque because of Zuhayr Ibn Qais Al-Balawi tomb. Conservative Salafist Muslims have been blamed for the attack, which follows similar incidents at other shrines around the country in recent months.

### 08 -15 JUL 2012 – BANI WALID / MISRATA

**LIBYAN JOURNALISTS DETAINED/KIDNAPPED:** Gunmen kidnapped two journalists, Youssef Badi and Abdelqader Fessouk, who work for Misratah-based Tobacts TV station. The journalists were abducted near the town of Bani Walid while on their way back from Mizdah where they were covering the elections. The Misratan journalists were released on 15 July 2012, reportedly in exchange for an unspecified number of detainees from Bani Walid being held in Misrata. The release of the journalists came after a week of heightened tensions between Misrata and Bani

Walid, which included a second abduction incident in Bani Walid.

### 12 JULY 2012 – BANI WALID / MISRATA

**JOURNALIST AND SECURITY MEMBER ATTACKED AND ABDUCTED IN BANI WALID:** Three more Misratans were abducted in Bani Walid after a shooting incident. The three individuals, two members of the Libya Shield brigade and an independent journalist, came under attack after passing through the Bir Dufan checkpoint 20 kilometres northeast of the town. The two shield members, Omran Shaban and Mohammed Al-Ouyb, were taken to a hospital in Bani Walid where they are now receiving treatment. Shaban was reportedly wounded in the neck by a bullet. The journalist identified as Abdul Aziz Harous is not believed to have been wounded and is being held separately. The release of all three is said to be still under negotiation.

### 15 – 22 JULY 2012 – TRIPOLI

**LIBYA'S OLYMPIC CHIEF KIDNAPPED IN TRIPOLI:** Libya's Olympic committee president was taken from his car by gunmen in Tripoli on Sunday and his whereabouts are unknown. Nabil Elalem was in his car with a colleague when two vehicles carrying men in military-style clothing blocked them in. The gunmen, estimated to be approximately eight in number, reportedly claimed to be from the national army and asked for Elalem to come with them. Elalem was not allowed to take a phone or laptop with him. The other passenger in Elalem's vehicle was not harmed or abducted. Elalem was released unharmed on 21 July 2012. It is believed that Elalem was held by a criminal group, although the exact circumstances of his abduction remain unclear.

U.S. EMBASSY — TRIPOLI, LIBYA       REGIONAL SECURITY OFFICE    E-51

## SECURITY INCIDENTS SINCE JUNE 2011

### 17 JUL 2012 – DERNA

**UN VEHICLES TARGETED BY SMALL ARMS FIRE NEAR DERNA:** UN officials confirmed that three of their vehicles were fired upon while passing under an overpass in Derna while returning to Benghazi from Tobruk on July 17. The UN staff had been observing local elections in Tobruk. Bullets struck one of the vehicles but the incident resulted in no casualties.

### 17 JULY 2012 – TRIPOLI

**ARMED CLASHES:** Following an accidental killing between two friends, four brothers of the deceased decided to seek revenge on the family of the boy who killed their family member. At approximately 1745hrs a small group of four men attacked a house and shop in the Gargarsh area close to the police station belonging to the family of a brother involved in the incident earlier in the day, which led to the fatality at the beach. The group fired 2 RPG rounds and threw petrol bombs at the house followed by small arms fire. During this period a further 3 RPG rounds were fired at the house and further small arms fire. The group then attacked the shop and vehicle belonging to the family with petrol bombs resulting in the shop and the vehicle being destroyed. The incident lasted for approximately two hours after which the local security committee intervened and put an end to street confrontations between the two families. No further incidents were reported.

### 19 JUL 2012 – BENGHAZI

**BENGHAZI PLANNING OFFICE CLOSED BY PROTESTORS OVER SALARY DISPUTE:** The Planning Office in Benghazi was stormed Protesters reportedly stormed the Planning Officer in Benghazi, causing a work stoppage when they blockaded the offices over unpaid salaries and living expenses. The protesters are reportedly owed past salary payments totaling 15 million LYD, which has been paid by the city of Benghazi on behalf of the Ministry of Social Affairs (MSA). Despite promises from the MSA that this loan would be refunded, nothing had yet been received.

### 19 JULY 2012 - TRIPOLI

**ARMED ROBBERY OF RESTAURANT:** At approximately 1800 hours, unidentified gunmen robbed all of the patrons of a Chinese Restaurant located on Gargaresh Road in western Tripoli. No casualties were reported.

**CLASHES NEAR AIRPORT:** Heavy weapon fire was reported northeast of the Tripoli International Airport at approximately 15h00. Air traffic was not disrupted in any way. Reports indicate that two rival militia groups were clashing in the vicinity of Kaser Ben Gasher (Qaser Bin Gasher) area located near the Airport facilities. No further reports.

### 21 JULY 2012 - TRIPOLI

**INTER-MILITIA CLASHES:** At approximately 2130 hours, inter-militia clashes involving small arms and hand-grenades reported in the vicinity of the Tripoli Towers near Alrasheed and Omar Mukhtar Streets.

U.S. EMBASSY — TRIPOLI, LIBYA        REGIONAL SECURITY OFFICE

## SECURITY INCIDENTS SINCE JUNE 2011

GENERAL ASSESSMENT ON THE SECURITY ENVIRONMENT:

Crime levels in Tripoli have significantly increased with the fall of the Ghaddafi regime as local militias are demobilized in the absence of a reconstituted security/police infrastructure. Tripoli residents reported being subjected to looting and robbery by gunmen. Carjackings, robberies, burglaries, and thefts have noticeably increased in Tripoli, particularly given that the majority of the 16,000 criminals released by Ghaddafi during the revolution have yet to be re-apprehended. While the Ministry of Interior is in the process of absorbing a large percentage of the demobilized militia, many of its records and infrastructure was destroyed during the revolution. The MoI estimates that only 60% of police have returned to their pre-revolution posts. Widespread small arms distribution coupled with lack of employment for former regime supporters, and demobilized or current militia members, has added to the increased crime rate. The government estimates that between 200,000 and 250,000 people in Libya are armed. It has attempted a number of schemes, including offering people jobs in exchange for handing over their weapons or offering to buy their weapons, in order to disarm the militias. So far the offers have shown few results.

RSO has received regular reporting about clashes between rival militias, and some reports of vigilante revenge killings. The government struggles to establish its legitimacy with weapons freely available and various armed brigades having unclear lines of command and control. While authorities had so far successfully contained any outbreaks of violence, they could escalate and widen in scope, he warned.

The lack of oversight by the central government over militias creates an environment conducive to torture and ill treatment of those suspects arrested or detained by the various militias, often on limited evidence. Diplomatic personnel and expatriates are increasingly being detained by poorly trained militia groups, often for arbitrary or unclear reasons. The government has acknowledged the problem of the Militias in torture and detentions, but it admits that the police and Justice Ministry are not up to the task of stopping them. On Tuesday, it sent out a text message on cell phones, pleading for the militias to stop.

The risk of U.S. Mission personnel, private U.S. citizens, and businesspersons encountering an isolating event as a result of militia or political violence is HIGH. The Government of Libya does not yet have the ability to effectively respond to and manage the rising criminal and militia related violence, which could result in an isolating event.

Officials have described the Ghaddafi legacy on the ability of the interim government to govern as "weak, at times absent, state institutions, coupled with the long absence of political parties and civil society organizations, which render the country's transition more difficult". Local officials remain concerned with the chaos and radicalization that could result from protracted civil conflict in Libya. Neighboring countries fear extremist groups who could take advantage of the political violence and chaos should Libya become a failed state.

**From:**
**Sent:** Tuesday, August 21, 2012 4:06 AM
**To:**
**Cc:**
**Subject:** Updated Benghazi incident chart
**Attachments:** Incident Chart Updated 8-21.xlsx

An updated incident list for you. We are also adding them into the website to track as well. We will likely meet with 17 February today about the detained American. Last night the 17 February commander confirmed that they did have him in custody and further more they were going to publicize it on their webpage today, with some sort of propaganda aim. I'll keep you posted.

*Libya Herald 20 August 2012*
A small bomb hit the vehicle of an Egyptian diplomat in Benghazi today, Monday, in the latest sign of unrest in the eastern city. The diplomat, First Secretary Abdelhamid Rifai, was reported to have been at home at the time. Nobody was hurt in the blast. Maged Al-Urfi, a Benghazi internal security spokesman, said the device contained only a small quantity of explosives, not enough to injure passangers. "This is meant to send a message, not hurt", he said, refusing to give further details. The vehicle was parked outside of the Egyptian consulate in Fwyhat, one of Benghazi's wealthier districts, home to a number of foreign diplomats. In recent months Benghazi has been hit by a number of attacks on foreign diplomats, including attacks on the Tunisian consulate, the American consulate and a vehicle carrying the British Ambassador. The city has also been plagued by a spate of assassinations directed at high-profile former Qaddafi officers, with 14 having been killed so far this year. It is not known who is behind the latest incident or what their motivations were.

### Benghazi Non-Revolutionary Incident Chart Since June 2011 to Present

| | Location | Victim | Date/ time | Type |
|---|---|---|---|---|
| | Tibesti Hotel | | 6/1/2011 | Car Bomb |
| | US Mission | US Mission | 4/6/2011 @ 2300 | Gernade (gelateena) |
| | SSC building | UN motorcade | 04/10/2012 @ 1430 | Gernade (gelateena) |
| | Courthouse | Parliment | 04/27/2012 @ 0500 | 3 IEDs |
| | Benghazi Police Headquaters | Benghazi Police | 5/15/2012 | Gernade (gelateena) |
| 6 | Benghazi Hospital | Hospital Director | 5/15/2012 | Shooting |
| 7 | ICRC | ICRC Staff | 5/22/2012 @ 0330 & 0530 | RPG |
| | Sahara Bank Fuwaihat | Staff | 5/22/2012 @ 0540 | RPG |
| | UK  Compound Access Road | UK CG Motorcade | 6/11/2012 @ 1530 | RPG |
| | US Mission | Mission Staff | 6/6/2012 @ 0325 | IED |
| | Zamtam Market | Fmr. Qadhafi Security Ofc. | 6/13/2012 | Car Bomb |
| | High National Electoral Commissio | HNEC Ballot office stormed | 7/01/12 @ 0100 | Vandalism |
| | Unknown | Assassination Gaddafi Officials | 7/26/2012 | Car bomb |
| | Benghazi Appeals Court | N/A | 7/27/2012  @ 0600 | Gernade (gelateena) |
| 14 | Kwaifiya Correctional Facility | Prison Break attempt | 7/27/2012 | RPG |
| | Military Police Station | IED (suspicious package) | 7/27/2012 | Bomb |
| | Military Police Station | IED (suspicious package) | 7/27/2012 | Bomb |
| | Universtiy of Benghazi | IED (suspicious package) | 7/28/2012 | Bomb |
| | Tibesti Hotel | IED (suspicious package) | 7/29/2012 | Bomb |
| | D1 Pizza | Sudanese CG | 7/30/2012 @ 1400 | Car Jacking |
| | Tibesti Hotel | ICRC | 7/31/2012 @ 0100 | Kidnapping |
| | Military Intellegence Bldg | Bombing | 8/1/2012 @ 0400 | Bomb |
| | Islamic Center | (American) | 8/9/2012 @ 1300-1530 | Kidnapping |
| 23 | Fwayhat Benghazi Mosque | Col. | 8/10/2012 @ 1300 | Shooting |
| 24 | Benghazi Power Station | N/A | 8/10/2012 | RPG |
| | Unknown | Col. | 8/11/2012 | Kidnapping |
| | Benghazi Ocean Road | Police Ofc. | 8/13/2012 @ 0530 | Gernade (gelateena) |
| | Home of Col. | Col. | 8/14/2012 @ 1800 | Bomb |
| 28 | Unknown | Former MI officer | 8/3/2012 | Shooting |
| | Central Benghazi | Police Station | 8/13/2012 | Armed Attack |

| 30 | Unknown | Gen. | | 8/10/2012 | Shooting |
|---|---|---|---|---|---|
| | Da'wah al Islamiya Building | Unknown | | 8/16/2012 | Failed bombing |
| | Al Bilad newspaper offices | Unknown | | 8/17/2012 | Armed Attack |
| | Benghazi University | C | (American) | 8/20/2012 | Kidnapping/Detention |
| | Dubai Street Home | Egyptian CG first secretary | | 8/20/12 @ 1600 | Bomb |

# APPENDIX F:

## Deterioration of Mission Compound Security

### Overview

The decision by State Department senior officials to leave the Benghazi Mission in an undefined status left it without typical security measures and a dedicated funding stream that would otherwise apply to official overseas posts. Benghazi's security posture was further eroded by other factors such as constant equipment failures and insufficient quantities of personal protection equipment. Furthermore, notwithstanding the insufficient number of Diplomatic Security Agents sent to Benghazi, intervening factors such as problems with the Libyan visa system further limited the number of Diplomatic Security Agents deployed to Benghazi.

### Funding Issues

The Benghazi Mission's requests for even the most basic security measures were impacted by the lack of dedicated funding made available by the State Department. Senior officials within the State Department were well aware of the funding implications associated with continuing the Benghazi Mission into 2012. Jeffrey D. Feltman, Assistant Secretary of State, Bureau of Near Eastern Affairs, testified:

> What we were trying to . . . figure out was, how could we make a compelling enough argument that in the zero sum game that we have in terms of our budget and our resources, that we could find enough resources to keep Benghazi operating through the critical transition period? [sic] [1]

Patrick F. Kennedy, the Under Secretary of State for Management, testified: "OBO has the funding authority . . . for our permanent facilities. . . . It [funding authority for temporary facilities] ranges between the regional bureau in which the facility is located or the Bureau of Diplomatic Security." [2] To that end, there was awareness at the senior level that the Benghazi Mission's limited duration prevented it from receiving any type of dedicated

---

[1] Testimony of Jeffrey D. Feltman, Ass't Sec'y of State, Bureau of Near Eastern Affairs, U.S. Dep't of State, Tr. at 47 (Aug. 8, 2015) [hereinafter Feltman Testimony] (on file with the Committee).

[2] Testimony of Patrick F. Kennedy, Under Sec'y for Management, U.S. Dep't of State, Tr. at 18 (Feb. 3, 2016) [hereinafter Kennedy Testimony] (on file with the Committee).

funding for its physical security needs from the State Department's Overseas Building Office [OBO], the office responsible for funding security measures.[3]

The December 27, 2011 Action Memorandum, approved by Kennedy, outlining the future operations of the Benghazi Mission for another year would have been an appropriate place to address the funding limitations within the OBO; and to designate a funding source to ensure the Benghazi Mission's security needs were met in 2012.[4] The Action Memorandum's failure to address the issue forced nontraditional funding sources to be identified, with quick turnaround, in order to respond to Benghazi Mission's basic security needs.[5]

Gentry O. Smith, the Deputy Assistant Secretary of State for Countermeasures, Bureau of Diplomatic Security, testified funding was never an issue for physical security.[6] Nevertheless, on January 12, 2012, the physical security desk officer was informed "OBO/SM . . . advised . . . they cannot provide the funding" for the security requests.[7] As a result, the State Department's physical security specialist was forced to locate other offices within the Department to find the funds the Benghazi Mission needed.[8] On February 15, 2012, the physical security desk officer explained to the Benghazi Mission "how the funding process normally works . . . with short term leases in place at Benghazi, OBO/SM cannot get involved due to OBO policy . . . funding security upgrades would have to be identified from other sources (DS)."[9]

The Diplomatic Security Agents on the ground described the impact the lack of funding had on the Mission.

> I was told that the only way that we can get you security upgrades is if they basically don't cost anything and we

---

[3] Summary of group interview with Physical Security Specialist and others (on file with the Committee, SCB0046921) ("OBO is precluded from funding upgrades to short term leases, so it did not fund upgrades in Benghazi.").

[4] Memorandum from Jeffrey D. Feltman, Ass't Sec'y of State, Bureau of Near Eastern Affairs, U.S. Dep't of State, to Patrick F. Kennedy, Under Sec'y for Management, U.S. Dep't of State (Dec. 27, 2011) (on file with the Committee, C05261557).

[5] Summary of group interview with Physical Security Specialist and others (on file with the Committee, SCB0046922) ("nontraditional DS funding was identified for Benghazi."). *See also* Testimony of Diplomatic Security Agent, Diplomatic Security Service, U.S. Dep't of State, Tr. at 80 (April 2, 2015) [hereinafter Diplomatic Security Agent 10 Testimony] (on file with the Committee) ("In terms of funding issues for programmatic stuff and security upgrades, . . . you're not going to get the money because Pat Kennedy hasn't given you guys any money. So there's no money at all that exists for the security budget for Benghazi. Every single penny you get we have to take from some other operational budget from some other office somewhere.").

[6] Testimony of Gentry O. Smith, Deputy Ass't Sec'y of State, Bureau of Diplomatic Security, Countermeasures, U.S. Dep't of State, Tr. at 76 (Feb. 25, 2016) [hereinafter Smith Testimony] (on file with the Committee);

> Q: Let me ask you this. As the DAS for Countermeasures, were you concerned about the ability to fund sufficiently the physical security measures needed to secure the facility?

> A: It had not become an issue for me yet at that time, based on, as we spoke of in the first hour, the sources that were providing funds for the operation, particularly from the physical security side. You had Physical Security Programs, you had International Programs, you had OBO, and then you had the regional bureau as well.

> Q: You said it had not been a concern at that time. Did it ever, did funding for physical security upgrades ever become an issue for you or a concern of yours?

> A: No.

[7] Email from Physical Security Specialist, Physical Security Programs, Bureau of Diplomatic Security, U.S. Dep't of State (Jan. 12, 2012 6:29 AM) (on file with the Committee, C05397166).

[8] *Id.*

[9] Email from Physical Security Specialist, Physical Security Programs, Bureau of Diplomatic Security, U.S. Dep't of State, to Diplomatic Security Agent 24, U.S. Dep't of State, *et al.* (Feb. 15, 2012 2:39 PM) (on file with the Committee, SCB0048394).

can, sort of, you know, steal a couple bucks here and there from other pots of money, that there is no budget for Benghazi.[10]

If we had the money at post and if I had the money at post, you know, if I was able to spend the money you know, I'm an official for the U.S. Government. I'm entrusted with a lot as a DS agent. You know, I wanted the ability to go ahead and perform work, pay for that work, and then on the back end be able to tell people, 'This is what I spent it for,' and be able to you know, justify it that way, because it just made sense in my mind. Not necessarily I don't know if that's the appropriate way to do it, but for me, that was some of my frustration.[11]

Further complicating the funding issue was the fact that Benghazi was a cash economy. Diplomatic Security Agents on the ground told the Committee "it was a cash economy at the time, so that money had to get to us before we could identify contractors and work to be under way."[12] Yet, even getting the money to Libya was a problem. State Department officials indicated: "[s]ince it [Benghazi] was not a post, it had no formal designation in Department systems, and no electronic way to get the fund transfers."[13]

## Technical Equipment

The security challenges at the Mission compound were not limited to the rudimentary security measures that were being requested by the Diplomatic Security Agents or the challenges with funding the requests. The Benghazi Mission was constantly requesting assistance with routine items such as door locks, monitors, batteries, radios, and cameras.[14] More often than not the Benghazi Mission sought help fixing constant equipment malfunctions.

The challenges with finding, installing, and fixing the equipment were exacerbated by the fact it could not be done locally.[15] The Benghazi Mission was dependent on "the Cairo engineering center . . . [which had] responsibility for US Missions in Libya."[16] When the U.S. Embassy in Cairo was not available, other embassies, such as Frankfurt, "augment[ed] the Cairo team."[17] Thus, notwithstanding the logistics of getting into Benghazi, the Benghazi Mission was subject to the U.S. Embassy in Cairo's schedule as well

---

[10] Diplomatic Security Agent 10 Testimony at 27.

[11] Testimony of Diplomatic Security Agent, Diplomatic Security Service, U.S. Dep't of State, Tr. at 24 (Apr. 9, 2015) [hereinafter Diplomatic Security Agent 12 Testimony] (on file with the Committee).

[12] Id. at 21.

[13] Summary of group interview with Physical Security Specialist and others (on file with the Committee, SCB0046921).

[14] Email from Principal Officer 3, U.S. Dep't of State, to Principal Officer 4, U.S. Dep't of State (Aug. 29, 2012, 6:01 AM) (on file with the Committee, C05390852).

[15] Testimony of Diplomatic Security Agent, Diplomatic Security Service, U.S. Dep't of State, Tr. at 46 (Mar. 12, 2015) [Hereinafter Diplomatic Security Agent 15 Testimony] (on file with the Committee) ("I was asking for things that were not just readily available in Benghazi. And it wasn't I could go to the drop arm store. There wasn't one. So they would have to be locally procured and then put together.").

[16] Email from Regional Dir. for Security Engineering, Cairo, Egypt, U.S. Dep't of State, to Travel Specialist, Cairo, Egypt, U.S. Dep't of State, and Security Engineering Officer, U.S. Dep't of State (Jun. 11, 2012 12:00 PM) (on file with the Committee, C05392482).

[17] Id.

as that of other embassies. For example, in early January 2012, Benghazi Mission personnel requested the assistance of the Electrical Security Officer [ESO] in Cairo to, among other things, help decommission Villa A and install equipment in Villas B and C.[18] The ESO could not travel to Benghazi until February 26, 2012 to assist with the requests.[19]

Compounding the equipment challenges was the Benghazi Mission's constant need for technical assistance throughout 2012. For example, in early February 2012, the Benghazi Mission sought help from the Radio Program Branch in Cairo for new radio equipment because "DS [Diplomatic Security] Washington has requested that the majority of radio equipment initially brought into Benghazi now must be returned."[20] This was preceded by a request for, among other things, replacing the radio antenna and repeater.[21] This was followed by a request in late February 2012 to help again with radio repeaters. The Benghazi Mission wrote:

> [T]he government authority in Libya responsible for allocating/assigning radio frequencies has declined our current frequencies in use and has provided us with an "acceptable" frequency range for use. As a result, we need to replace the current radio repeaters at site (Benghazi and Tripoli) with repeaters that will accommodate the frequencies that the Libyan government has agreed to let us use.[22]

In late April 2012, after the first improvised explosive device [IED] attack on the perimeter wall at the Mission compound, Benghazi had problems with much of its security equipment, including: the loud speaker, the itemizer, walk-through metal detector, and camera 1.[23] In addition to fixing the malfunctioning equipment, the Mission sought help procuring additional equipment to strengthen the security on the compound such as a camera to screen the C-gate; monitors in [quick reaction force] QRF bungalow, and locks for doors. Finally, the Benghazi Mission needed help relocating its lighting around the perimeter.[24]

In June 2012, the second IED attack on the Mission compound damaged not only the perimeter wall but also cameras and the secondary metal detector. The Benghazi Mission sought help from the U.S. Embassy in Cairo to fix the damage but also sought help with the installation of additional cameras to strengthen security.[25] Three weeks later, power surges in Benghazi damaged the "voltage regulator and 220–110V transformer," shutting all of the Benghazi Mission's technical equipment down and necessitating the need for

---

[18] Email from Information Management Officer, U.S. Dep't of State, to Diplomatic Security Agent 15 (Jan. 11, 2012, 10:28 AM) (on file with the Committee, C05392732).

[19] Email from Diplomatic Security Agent 15 to Diplomatic Security Agent 24 (Jan. 31, 2012 7:32AM) (on file with the Committee, C05410045).

[20] Email from Information Management Officer, U.S. Dep't of State (Feb. 1, 2012 4:08 AM) (on file with the Committee, C05395451).

[21] See id.

[22] Email to Deputy Ex. Dir., Bureau of Near Eastern Affairs, U.S. Dep't of State (Feb. 21, 2012 2:09 PM) (on file with the Committee, C05393043).

[23] Email from Diplomatic Security Agent 17 to Diplomatic Security Agent 24 (Apr. 21, 2012 10:20 AM) (on file with the Committee, C05409948).

[24] Id.

[25] Email from Diplomatic Security Agent 19 to Security Engineering Officer, U.S. Dep't of State (Jun. 6, 2012, 5:07 PM) (on file with the Committee, C05392482).

technical help from Cairo again.[26] Because the U.S Embassy in Cairo couldn't make the trip, the post in Frankfurt Germany sent personnel and equipment to make the necessary repairs.[27]

Later, in August 2012, the Benghazi Mission sought the assistance of Cairo to fix additional malfunctioning equipment, including: seeking a new Immediate Distress Notification System [IDNS], old pendants for the current IDNS system, camera and monitors for its technical operations center and Villa Safe Haven, additional cameras with visibility outside the compound walls, upgraded critical cameras for night vision, louder IDNS system and a hardened [technical operations center] TOC door.[28]

The constant malfunctions frustrated personnel on the ground.[29] In his turnover notes, the departing principal officer in Benghazi told his replacement: "[t]he tendency has been to conduct triage in the interim. We are, for example, on the fourth visit from an Embassy electrician of my brief tenure because we continue to repair rather than replace equipment."[30]

On August 23, 2012, the Benghazi Mission requested additional technical equipment to help secure the compound. The request included an expert to analyze the loss of exterior lighting, new IDNS panel and pendants, weapons cabinet, better personal tracking device software, disintegrator if post increases its footprint, belt-fed crew-served weapon with bi-pod, CS gas canisters, badging machine, computer program to make access requests and computer at the guard house to view the approved access requests, an additional itemizer and an alarm system for the office villa.[31]

### Protective Equipment

The Benghazi Mission was constantly securing adequate supplies of protective equipment for personnel in 2012. For example, on January 24, 2012, the lead Diplomatic Security Agent on the ground requested additional helmets, vests and [e]scape hoods after an insufficient number were sent to the Benghazi Mission.[32] The U.S. Embassy in Tripoli acknowledged it mixed up the Benghazi Mission's request for the equipment.[33] In sending the protective equipment to Benghazi, the U.S. Embassy in Tripoli stated: "It's not exactly what you asked for but is what we could get together to get up to you."[34]

In early February 2012, the Benghazi Mission requested ballistic vests, ballistic plates, complete personal medical kit, radio wires

---

[26] Id.

[27] Email from Information Management Officer, U.S. Dep't of State, to Security Engineering Officer, U.S. Dep't of State (Jun. 25, 2012, 9:23 AM) (on file with the Committee, C05392482).

[28] Email from Diplomatic Security Agent 26 to Security Engineering Officer, U.S. Dep't of State (Aug. 6, 2012 2:58 PM) (on file with the Committee, C05390265).

[29] See email from Principal Officer 3, U.S. Dep't of State, to Principal Officer 4, U.S. Dep't of State (Aug. 29, 2012 6:01 AM) (on file with the Committee, C05390852).

[30] Id.

[31] Email from Diplomatic Security Agent 8 to Diplomatic Security Agent 23 (Aug. 23, 2012 2:44 PM) (on file with the Committee, C05390126–C05390127).

[32] Email from Diplomatic Security Agent 15 to Diplomatic Security Agent 25 (Jan. 24, 2012 9:38PM) (on file with the Committee, C05393735).

[33] Email to Diplomatic Security Agent 15 (Jan. 29, 2012 1:56 PM) (on file with the Committee, C05412863).

[34] Id. ("It is not exactly what you asked for but is what we could get together to get up to you. We believe the original order that was made is mixed in with the commo [sic] equipment that needs to get up to you. We'll have to open the crates to see if your original order is included.").

with pig tail, low profile holster, magazine pouches, low profile chest vest, individual GPS, flashlight, strobe, multi-tool, camel pak hydration system, and go bags.[35] With one Diplomatic Security Agent arriving without luggage and protective equipment in Benghazi, the Mission was concerned future Diplomatic Security Agents would also arrive without their personal protective gear. Further prompting the request was an incident that occurred on the compound while the Diplomatic Security Agent was without [his] equipment.[36] To ensure this didn't happen again, the Benghazi Mission sought to have additional equipment at the ready.[37] The equipment was not sent until March 2012.[38]

Additional requests for personal protection equipment were made on June 24, 2012, three weeks after the second attack on the facility. The request first went to Washington D.C. and then to the U.S. Embassy in Tripoli for a response.[39] The Embassy in Tripoli responded it had some items but that the others "will have to be post procured."[40]

## Security Staffing and the Mission

In addition to physical security, the Benghazi Mission's security deficiencies extended to State Department's unwillingness to commit the number of personnel needed to adequately secure the compound and personnel. The December 27, 2011 Action Memorandum authorized five Diplomatic Security Agents to serve at the Benghazi Mission compound.[41] It was the expectation of those personnel on the ground that five Diplomatic Security Agents would be deployed to secure the compound.

Yet Benghazi "achieved a level of five DS Agents (not counting Defense Department provided temporary duty [TDY] Site Security Team personnel sent by the U.S. Embassy in Tripoli) for only 23 days between January 1 and September 9, 2012."[42] Efforts to secure five Diplomatic Security Agents were either ignored or dismissed. As a result, the Benghazi Mission did not have five Diplomatic Security Agents on the Mission compound during the first IED attack on April 6, 2012. The Benghazi Mission did not have five Diplomatic Security Agents on the compound during the second IED attack. The Benghazi Mission did not have five Diplomatic

---

[35] Email from Diplomatic Security Agent 12 to Diplomatic Security Agent 25 (Feb. 5, 2012 6:42 AM) (on file with the Committee, C05394222).

[36] Email from Diplomatic Security Agent 25 (Feb. 14, 2012, 8:54 AM) (on file with the Committee, C05393444).

[37] See Id.

[38] Email to Diplomatic Security Agent 25 (Mar. 5, 2012 11:27 AM) (on file with the Committee, C05393444).

[39] Email from Diplomatic Security Agent 19 to Diplomatic Security Agent 24 (Jun. 24, 2012 11:28 AM) (on file with the Committee, C05411697).

[40] Email from Diplomatic Security Agent 24 to Diplomatic Security Agent 19, (Jun. 24, 2012) (on file with the Committee, C05411697).

[41] Testimony of Diplomatic Security Agent, Libya Desk Officer, U.S. Dep't of State, Tr. at 17 (Aug. 8, 2013) [hereinafter Diplomatic Security Agent 25 Testimony] (on file with the Committee) ("[A]t the time it was Acting Regional Director . . . to come to that number. I don't know specifically what was his thinking on the matter, but I know in the summer of 2011 they were down to five agents for several months, so that was the in Benghazi that was the lowest number that was on the ground in Benghazi that I'm aware of at that time timeframe prior to December of 2012.").

[42] See Department of State, Accountability Review Board for Benghazi Attack of September 2012, December 19, 2012, at 31.

Security Agents at the time Ambassador Stevens arrived at the Mission compound on September 10, 2012.

## PROTECTIVE DETAIL—OFFICE OF DIGNITARY PROTECTION

Because of the Defense Department's "no boots on the ground" policy, military security assets were only available in emergency circumstances.[43] Hence, only State Department Diplomatic Security Agents traveled with J. Christopher Stevens, U.S. Representative to the Transitional National Council [TNC] and his team into Benghazi. The Diplomatic Security Agents accompanying Stevens and his team needed certain skills for the Benghazi Mission in order to conduct "protective security functions."[44] The Diplomatic Security Agent in charge of Stevens' protective detail described the qualifications of his team.

> A: I think it was pretty much people were selected because of their skill sets. You know, they spent, they spent time to make sure they had the right team makeup. And, for example, my shift leader . . . , he had, I would estimate he had been on Diplomatic Security for eight years. He had some advanced training on a mobile training team where they it's a tactical team that the State Department has. He was on that team, and they trained for like nine months.
>
> Q: Is that known as the MSD [mobile security deployment]?
>
> A: MSD.
>
> Q: Okay.
>
> A: And anybody else on the team either had prior military experience, which I think all but two had prior military experience, and they had all gone through the State Department's high threat training.
>
> Q: Okay.
>
> A: As I recall.
>
> Q: Okay. And you had too?
>
> A: Yes.
>
> Q: To your knowledge, was that a requirement that everyone have this high threat tactical course prior to going?
>
> A: I think that was a requirement as far as the boss' thought when they were trying to put the team together, you know, that they wanted people to have that experience.[45]

---

[43] Benghazi Party Ops Plan (March 30, 2011)(on file with the Committee, SCB0095930)("DOD provide QRF for security and medical extraction").

[44] See Action Memorandum For DSS Director Jeffrey W. Culver (June 30, 2011)(on file with the Committee, C05579256).

[45] Testimony of Diplomatic Security Agent, Diplomatic Security Service, U.S. Dep't of State, Tr. at 20 (Feb. 10, 2015) [hereinafter Diplomatic Security Agent 6 Testimony] (on file with the Committee).

Two additional Diplomatic Security Agents traveled to Benghazi in late April 2011 to augment the Stevens' protective detail. The two additional Diplomatic Security Agents brought the total number of Agents to ten.[46] The Diplomatic Security Agents assigned to the Stevens' protective detail served in temporary capacities contingent on the Mission's duration.[47] When senior State Department officials made the decision to extend Stevens' Mission in Benghazi beyond the initial 30-day mark, the next Diplomatic Security Agent team rotated in for another 30–45 days.[48] The incoming Diplomatic Security Agent in charge described the process: "The first team that went in, the Dignitary Protection team that went in, it was a 30-day Mission, and they were in need of an agent in charge to go in and take over from that agent in charge and to continue on the Mission."[49]

The number of Diplomatic Security Agents dropped from ten to five when Stevens and his team were forced to leave the Tibesti Hotel and find other accommodations. When Stevens and his team relocated to Villas A, B, and C in early August 2011, additional Diplomatic Security Agents were needed again to secure the 13 acre compound. The Diplomatic Security Agent in charge informed Washington D.C.:

> [m]ore agents required: Between the three compounds, we're looking at roughly 15 acres of property to secure. This will require additional SAs (up to five more) by early to mid-August. For REACT purposes, teams of agents will reside on all three compounds. Once resources permit, RSO TOC will be staffed 24/7.[50]

By mid-September, the Mission had increased back to "10 bodies [DS agents] on compound."[51]

### SHIFT IN SECURITY POSTURE FROM A PROTECTIVE DETAIL TO A QUASI-RSO PROGRAM

By mid-September 2011, efforts were also under way to restart operations at the U.S. Embassy in Tripoli. Predictably, resources and personnel shifted away from the Mission in Benghazi back to the U.S. Embassy in Tripoli.[52] This precipitated a number of con-

---

[46] See Memorandum from Exec. Dir., NEA–SCA/EX, to Patrick F. Kennedy, Under Sec'y of State for Mgmt., U.S. Dep't of State (Apr. 15, 2011) (on file with the Committee, C05390734); see also email from SMART Core (Apr. 19, 2011, 12:17 PM) (on file with the Committee, C05390733).

[47] See Diplomatic Security Agent 6 Testimony at 14 ("I was on a 60 day TDY, but I think I spent less than 45 days in Benghazi because I know I did. I spent 30 some days in Benghazi because it took time for us to get there."). See also, Testimony of Diplomatic Security Agent, Diplomatic Security Service, U.S. Dep't of State, Tr. at 25 (Feb. 26, 2015) [hereinafter Diplomatic Security Agent 7 Testimony] (on file with the Committee) ("[T]he first team that went in, the Dignitary Protection team that went in, it was a thirty day Mission.").

[48] Diplomatic Security Agent 7 Testimony at 26 ("I would say that when they recognized that the Mission was viable and that they were going to continue it, they started to look for a replacement knowing that the agreement was that the agent in charge was going to do 30 days. So then they thought, okay, now we need to find somebody to continue on.").

[49] Id. at 25.

[50] Email Diplomatic Security Agent to DS–IP–NEA (Jul. 21, 2011, 3:22 PM) (on file with the Committee, C05396529).

[51] Testimony of Diplomatic Security Agent, Diplomatic Security Service, U.S. Dep't of State, Tr. at 24 (May 21, 2015) [hereinafter Diplomatic Security Agent 13 Testimony] (on file with the Committee).

[52] See email from Joan A. Polaschik, Deputy Chief of Mission in Libya, U.S. Dep't of State, to John C. Stevens, U.S. Representative to Transitional National Council, William V. Roebuck, Dir. Office of Maghreb Affairs, Bureau of Near Eastern Affairs, U.S. Dep't of State, Post Man-

versations about the Benghazi Mission's future. At the time the
U.S. Embassy in Tripoli restarted operations, the Benghazi Mission's security posture changed from that of a protective detail to
a regional security officer [RSO] program, a program similar to
those implemented in embassies and official posts located abroad.[53]
Unlike the protective detail that focused primarily on the security
of Stevens and his team using U.S. security assets, the new security posture would be overseen by a rotation of volunteer Diplomatic Security Agents. In addition, the Benghazi Mission focused
more on employing host nation support for security, including
using the February 17 Martyrs Brigade as a QRF team and employing an unarmed local guard force [LGF]. The Diplomatic Security Agent in charge in September described his response when
learning about the change in security:

> When I got solicited to go out, I was supposed to be the
> agent in charge of this detail. So I assumed as you know,
> you don't want to do that too often that the 10 would be
> part of my bodyguard staff and that's all I would have to
> deal with.

> So when I got close to the drop date or the day I arrived,
> they basically said, "We don't know how long we're going
> to be here. So we're going to make you the RSO, and we're
> going to make your number two the AIC," at which time
> I tried to get back on the airplane.

> But, nonetheless, it was myself and my number two. Rank
> wise, he was senior. He did more of the movement portion
> with Ambassador Stevens, but I did the overall security
> aspects of the job, access control and all the policy crap.[54]

When asked to describe the caliber of host nation support available, he told the Committee:

> [W]e were a quasi RSO office at best, so meaning Benghazi
> was unique in the fact that Benghazi really didn't know
> who they were either. . . . They were still jockeying to fig
> ure out who was going to be in power and who wasn't.

> So, normally speaking, you would have already known that
> when you go into an environment. If you were going to es
> tablish yourself or an embassy, you'd already know who
> your minister of security is or who your DOD counterparts
> would be.

> There it was a little different because you had different I'll
> say tribal, for lack of a better term. But you had different
> groups there and sects that you were trying to figure out
> who were friendly and who weren't.

> And, I mean, for all intents and purposes, we thought ev
> erybody was friendly at that time. But, from my perspec
> tive, we didn't want to befriend one group versus somebody

---

agement Officer for Libya, Bureau of Near Eastern Affairs (Sept. 18, 2011, 11:54 AM)(on file
with the Committee, C05395962)(stating "and when can we get . . . here").
[53] Diplomatic Security Agent 25 Testimony at 18.
[54] Diplomatic Security Agent 13 Testimony at 28–29.

else without you know, we didn't want to cause an international incident.

At the time, 17 Feb. had already stepped up and said that they were going to be the point people for diplomatic interests or security purposes under this function.

So my interest while I was there was trying to plus that contingent up because knowing they only had a local guard force contingent of 10 people or 12 or whatever it was, unarmed and poorly equipped and poorly trained, I wanted at least some firepower. At least I could put them to at least have a presence.

But we only had three at the time. So I was trying to befriend them, trying to get more activity, more interest, additional bodies, because three bodies on 24/7 is long days, long weeks.[55]

The change in security posture together with the reopening of the U.S. Embassy in Tripoli left the Diplomatic Security Agents on the ground uncertain about their future in Benghazi and their ability to do their jobs. The Diplomatic Security Agent in charge in September testified:

As we downsized to a lesser number, it's more difficult to run, keep up with the off tempo. That's where the 10 bodies kind of helped because, with additional bodies there, I could farm them out to support USAID interests or the MANPAD guy or . . . and what have you. But as you start reducing those resources, then you have to prioritize your Missions.[56]

\* \* \*

[W]e were still in this situation where we didn't know how long Benghazi was going to be. Tripoli was kicking off. And so there was a lot of interest in supporting that. So we were trying to figure out or headquarters was trying to figure out where to prioritize our deficiencies, if you want to call it that. So no one knows.

I mean, we were planning for the worst, phasing people out and trying to figure out how best to support the Mission there. If I remember correctly, with the Embassy being opened it opened towards the latter part of my tenure there. So the Envoy lost his, quote unquote, status because there was now an Ambassador in country. . . . I think they were going to bring in a political officer, probably my rank. I'm pretty sure he was my rank. He was going to be the foothold there in Benghazi for the short term, but no one knew how long.[57]

As Stevens closed out his time in Benghazi, the number of Diplomatic Security Agents assigned to secure the Benghazi Mission

---

[55] *Id.* at 43–44.
[56] *Id.* at 32.
[57] *Id.* at 33–34.

continued to decrease. By the end of October 2011 the number of Diplomatic Security Agents assigned to secure the Benghazi Mission decreased to six.[58] By the end of November 2011, as Stevens' was departing, the number of Diplomatic Security Agents assigned to the Benghazi Mission was expected to drop to three.[59]

Diplomatic Security personnel responsible for staffing overseas posts including Benghazi recognized early on the problems associated with finding Diplomatic Security Agents available to serve in Benghazi. With a protective detail, the Diplomatic Security Command Center could direct Diplomatic Security Agents to serve on a temporary basis. Under a RSO program, temporary duty positions were filled by volunteers.[60] The desk officer in charge of staffing in Benghazi testified:

> The Mission in . . . September, October, the Mission in Benghazi changed essentially from a protection Mission, which was run by our dignitary protection unit here in Washington, to a more traditional RSO program management position, which pushed it back into DS/IP's, my office's realm.

> So at that time the mechanism to get agents changed, they have a task oriented system, we have a it's hard to describe, but it's a system where basically we get volunteers to go. It's usually the high threat posts. And our system is, generally we cover traditionally we cover one RSO position like over a summer transition or during a break. It was very difficult for us to get the type of numbers on kind of a continuous basis through the volunteer system.[61]

> \* \* \*

> Typically we just cover the gaps, but we did do occasionally we would do particularly in the beginning of Arab spring, it was very busy, and we had to find TDY support. But generally it wasn't near that number. It was never near that number. And it was for a much shorter timeframe, usually only one or two 60 to 30 day deployments for agents.[62]

To address the emerging issue, the desk officer drafted an Action Memorandum for the approval of Charlene Lamb, the Deputy Assistant Secretary of State for International Programs in the Bureau of Diplomatic Security.[63] The October 24, 2011 Action Memorandum described the emerging problems associated with identifying enough volunteer Diplomatic Security Agents to serve 30–45 day rotations in Benghazi on a consistent basis and identified solu-

---

[58] See id. at 72. See also Memorandum from Regional Director, Bureau of Diplomatic Security, U.S. Dep't of State, to Charlene Lamb, Deputy Ass't Sec'y of State, Bureau of Diplomatic Security, Int'l Programs, U.S. Dep't of State (Oct. 24, 2011) (on file with the Committee, C05391928).

[59] Memorandum from Regional Director, Bureau of Diplomatic Security, U.S. Dep't of State to Charlene Lamb, Deputy Ass't Sec'y of State, Bureau of Diplomatic Security, Int'l Programs, U.S. Dep't of State (Oct. 24, 2011) (on file with the Committee, C05391928).

[60] Id.

[61] Diplomatic Security Agent 25 Testimony at 18–19.

[62] Id.

[63] Memorandum from Regional Dir., Bureau of Diplomatic Security, U.S. Dep't of State, to Charlene Lamb, Deputy Ass't Sec'y of State, Bureau of Diplomatic Security, Int'l Programs, U.S. Dep't of State (Oct. 24, 2011) (on file with the Committee, C05391928).

tions including deploying Diplomatic Security Agents through the Diplomatic Security Command Center as had been done previously.[64] When asked by the Committee whether the October 24, 2011 Action Memorandum was approved, Lamb testified:

> I had actually requested that they draft this memo because it's very easy for people to take for granted when there's a need for TDY people, they don't take the budget into consideration. And when we don't have full time positions authorized, this TDY money is coming out of the international program's budget. And at $9,000 per agent for 45 days on a continual basis for a year, this money adds up very, very quickly and depletes the budget that I have for worldwide TDY assignments. So I wanted this to be documented and I wanted to be able to forward this forward and to go to the DS budget people to make sure that we had appropriate funding, and that they knew we were going to need additional funding, should this TDY status continue for a long period of time.[65]
>
> \*　　\*　　\*
>
> I'll be honest, there were so many operational things going on, my intent with this memo was to get this into the hands of the budget people and to have the budget people work together to come up with a solution to get the money that was needed.[66]
>
> \*　　\*　　\*
>
> We never ran we never ran out of money to the point where we said, okay, we can't send anybody else, there's no more money. We never went anti deficient with funding. So the Department, collectively, between DS, financial personnel, and the Department, we were always funded for these types of posts.[67]

When asked by the Committee directly whether funding was approved for five, 45-day assistant regional security officer [ARSO] TDYs in Benghazi, Lamb testified: "yes."[68] However, the October 24, 2011 Action Memorandum, which outlined proposed solutions including funding for five Diplomatic Security Agents, was never signed.[69] The desk officer testified:

> A: I identified the problem immediately because you can see the staffing chart as was coming down. So when I took

---

[64] Id.

[65] Testimony of Charlene Lamb, Deputy Ass't Sec'y, Bureau of Diplomatic Security, Int'l Programs, U.S. Dep't of State, Tr. at 77–78 (Jan. 7, 2016) [hereinafter Lamb Testimony] (on file with the Committee).

[66] Id. at 92.

[67] Id. at 92–93.

[68] Id at 93.

> Q: But, specifically, this request for $47,000, do you recall whether that was approved?
>
> A: Yes.
>
> Q: That was approved?
>
> A: It would yes.

[69] Memorandum from Regional Dir., Bureau of Diplomatic Security, U. S. Dep't of State, to Charlene Lamb, Deputy Ass't Sec'y, Bureau of Diplomatic Security, Int'l Programs, U.S. Dep't of State (Oct. 24, 2011) (on file with the Committee, C05391928).

over the program in October, I immediately had conversations with my direct supervisors, and we generated an action memorandum with numerous recommendations on how we thought or I thought we could alleviate this problem.

Q: And was this just specifically focused on Benghazi or

A: I believe it was Libya centric——

Q: Libya.

A: But I can't remember if it was Benghazi specific.

Q: And do you recall the timeframe that that actual memorandum circulated?

A: The date was mid to late October of 2011.

Q: And was that ever signed?

A: It was approved by my immediate supervisors.

Q: Did that help alleviate the concerns?

A: It was not approved through their superiors, so it never

Q: So where did it stop?

A: It stopped, as far as I know, at the I don't know where it went. I know it went up to the Deputy Director/DAS level. Which one of them looked at it or which one didn't, I don't know.

Q: Did you ever understand why it didn't get approved at that level?

A: No, I did not.[70]

Lamb informed the Committee that Kennedy was aware of the funding issues associated with staffing the Mission in Benghazi.

Q: So is it fair to say that Pat Kennedy was aware of the funding issues that were associated with the TDYs in Benghazi?

A: It would he, during his regular staff meetings when we discussed all of the Tripoli and Benghazi issues, he was aware, and he had financial people there from his staff that reported to him directly.

Q: So he was shifting resources as it relates to . . .

A: If it was necessary, he would not hesitate to do that.[71]

STAFFING SHORTAGES—DECEMBER 27 ACTION MEMORANDUM:
FUTURE OF BENGHAZI OPERATIONS

By December 2011, Diplomatic Security Agent staffing in Benghazi was a problem. Two Diplomatic Security Agents secured the 13 acre compound in mid-December. Without reinforcements from Washington D.C. there was every expectation it would drop

---

[70] Diplomatic Security Agent 25 Testimony at 20.
[71] Lamb Testimony at 89.

to one and then to zero in January.[72] One of the Diplomatic Security Agents on the ground expressed his concerns:

> It was down to two agents, myself and one other agent. And as I was getting ready to depart, we were going to go to one agent. And if the staffing pattern remained the way it was, with our expected incoming agents, we were going to go down to zero agents. And that would have been around January 4th or 5th or so, we would go down to zero agents.[73]

The principal officer who replaced Stevens also alerted Washington D.C. about the impact of the shortages in Diplomatic Security Agents in December 2011. He wrote:

> [o]n a much more serious matter, something I flagged for Bill [Roebuck] yesterday on the phone, but pledged to send the details. We're going to be short on the RSO end of things from December 19 through the end of the year. During that period, we will be down to just 2 A/RSOs or the practical equivalent thereof. . . .

> What this all means is that all non-DS TDYs to Benghazi should be discouraged through the end of the year for sure (and we're still pretty limited the first week of January as the new folks get spun up), as even the basic movements are going to overextend us. . . .

> We are a little too close to being down to a single agent here if arrival dates (or visa issuance?) slips to the right . . . and if we're going to need to extend anyone here (one of whom has already done so), we need to get that sorted out sooner rather than later. Also, it's a little curious to hear about DS intensions to staff Benghazi with a RSO and 4 A/RSOs, while at this rate, we won't hit that target during my first two months here.[74]

At the time Benghazi Mission was experiencing shortages in Diplomatic Security Agents, the December 27, 2011 Action Memorandum was being circulated for approval. The Action Memorandum acknowledged "Diplomatic Security's current presence consists of two Special Agents, with an additional three slots currently unfilled" and attributed the unfilled slots "to budget constraints and the reduced footprint."[75] The Action Memorandum authorized a "full complement of five Special Agents."[76] Kennedy provided a different interpretation to the Committee:

---

[72] Diplomatic Security Agent 10 Testimony at 41–42.
[73] Id.
[74] Email from Principal Officer 1, U.S. Dep't of State, to Post Management Officer for Libya, Bureau of Near Eastern Affairs, U.S. Dep't of State (Dec. 15, 2011, 1:11 PM) (on file with the Committee, C05391603).
[75] Action Memorandum from Jeffrey Feltman, Ass't Sec'y of State, Bureau of Near Eastern Affairs, U.S. Dep't of State, to Patrick F. Kennedy, Under Sec'y for Mgmt., U.S. Dep't of State (Dec. 27, 2011) (on file with the Committee, C05261557).
[76] See id. See also Diplomatic Security Agent 25 Testimony at 17 ("at the time it was Action Regional Director to come to that number. I don't know specifically what his thinking on the matter, but I know in the summer of 2011 they were down to five agents for several months, so that was the—in Benghazi—that was the lowest number that was on the ground that I'm aware of at that time timeframe prior to December of 2012 [sic].").

It says eight U.S. direct hire employees and two slots for political military and USAID. So that's 8, plus 2 is 10, of which 5 are substantive or management and 5 are Diplomatic Security. So you have five to protect five.[77]

\* \* \*

How many people the Near East Bureau, looking at what was going on, how many people the Near East Bureau ultimately decided to deploy, kind of a cost benefit analysis. How much activity are they going to do? How much reporting do they want to do? That's a call made by the Near East Bureau. My point is that you judge the number of Diplomatic Security on two factors. It's the facility and the number of sorties that you need to make out into the city.[78]

Lamb described Diplomatic Security's responsibilities to provide five Diplomatic Security Agents in Benghazi as "kind of the cap of what the bureau was asking . . . Kennedy to approve. What they're saying is, at the most, we're not going to exceed this staffing level in Benghazi."[79] Others such as the Diplomatic Security Agents on the ground and the principal officers they were protecting saw Diplomatic Security's staffing obligations as five Diplomatic Security Agents for Benghazi.[80]

Though the effect of budget constraints on Diplomatic Security Agents assigned to the Benghazi Mission was known well before the decision to extend the Benghazi Mission, the December 27, 2011 Action Memorandum was silent on a funding solution.[81] The Bureau of Diplomatic Security cleared the December 27, 2011 Action Memorandum with the "comment that this operation continues to be an unfunded mandate and a drain on personnel resources."[82] Neither Gentry O. Smith, Deputy Ass't Sec'y, Bureau of Diplomatic Sec., Countermeasures, U.S. Dep't of State, whose office was responsible for ensuring security standards and adequate physical security measures were in place at the Benghazi Mission and who cleared the Action Memorandum for Diplomatic Security, nor Lamb whose office was responsible for staffing, had any recollection of why the comment was made.[83]

### REQUESTS FOR ADDITIONAL DIPLOMATIC SECURITY AGENTS

Concerns about Diplomatic Security Agent staffing shortages going into 2012 precipitated another Action Memorandum for

---

[77] Kennedy Testimony at 301.

[78] *Id.* at 302.

[79] Lamb Testimony at 224.

[80] Email from Diplomatic Security Agent 15 to Diplomatic Security Agent 12 (Jan. 27, 2012, 11:10 AM) (on file with the Committee, C05411094). ("U/S Kennedy stated there should be 5 agents here and I agree.").

[81] Action Memorandum from Jeffrey Feltman, Ass't Sec'y of State, Bureau of Near Eastern Affairs, U.S. Dep't of State, to Patrick F. Kennedy, Under Sec'y for Mgmt., U.S. Dep't of State (Dec. 27, 2011) (on file with the Committee, C05261557).

[82] Email from Special Ass't to the Ass't Sec'y for Diplomatic Security, Bureau of Diplomatic Security, U.S. Dep't of State, to Post Management Officer, Bureau of Near Eastern Affairs, U.S. Dep't of State (Dec. 23, 2011, 3:27 PM) (on file with the Committee, C05578953).

[83] Lamb Transcript at 221 ("I did not see [the Action Memorandum] until after the event in Benghazi."). *See also* Gentry O. Smith at 75 (Feb. 25, 2016) [hereinafter Smith Testimony] (on file with the Committee) ("[I]t didn't come from Countermeasures, it would not have been solely for physical security.").

Lamb's approval.[84] The January 10, 2012 Action Memorandum highlighted Diplomatic Security's responsibilities under the December 27, 2011 Action Memorandum to provide five Diplomatic Security Agents for Benghazi and recognized the Offices' inability to "identify, seek necessary approvals and obtain the required visa approvals for this many agents on a continuing basis."[85] The January 10, 2012 Action Memorandum requested Lamb approve efforts to:

> request assistance from Domestic Operations, so that personnel can be selected and directed from the Field Offices by the DS Command Center as well as authorize funding for five, 45 day ARSO [assistant regional security officer] TDYs [temporary duty] in Benghazi from Feb.1 through September 30 at a total estimated cost of $283,050.[86]

The January 10, 2012 Action Memorandum was never approved.[87]

Without a mechanism to identify a constant pool of Diplomatic Security Agents to serve in Benghazi, the Mission continued to experience shortages. The principal officers on the ground expressed concern back to Washington D.C. about the impact the Diplomatic Security Agent staffing shortages was having on the security of the compound, in addition to their reporting obligations.[88] Moreover, the principal officers were concerned about the vulnerabilities created by the shortages in relation to the overall security environment in Benghazi. For example, the principal officer was concerned only two Diplomatic Security Agents were scheduled to be at the compound during the upcoming February 17th anniversary.[89] With no option available within Diplomatic Security, members of the Defense Department's SST who were currently deployed to the U.S. Embassy in Tripoli offered to travel to Benghazi to address the Diplomatic Security Agent shortage.[90] SST agents deployed to the

---

[84] Email from Diplomatic Security Agent 25 to Principal Officer 1, U.S. Dep't of State (Jan. 13, 2012, 10:05 PM) (on file with the Committee, C05411094) ("We have submitted an Action Memorandum that if approved should significantly improve our ability to identify and obtain approvals for staffing Benghazi."); Action Memorandum for DAS Charlene Lamb (January 10, 2012) (on file with the Committee, C05578986).

[85] *Id.*

[86] *Id.*

[87] *See* Testimony of James Bacigalupo, Regional Dir., Bureau of Diplomatic Security, U.S. Dep't of State, Tr. at 17–18 (Sept. 4, 2013) (on file with the Committee).

> A: I believe it was January, maybe December/January timeframe we had talked about it in the office, and I think I was out on leave because my deputy had seen a document that my deputy had sent up to Director Lamb, to DAS Lamb requesting we use the system that they use domestically to direct a certain number of agents from the field offices for assignments. We use that on protection. And we sent the memo up suggesting maybe we could use this mechanism for overseas.
>
> Q: Specifically for Libya or——
>
> A: It was specifically for Libya.
>
> Q: And do you know what happened to that memo?
>
> A: It was never signed off on.

[88] *See* email from Principal Officer 5, U.S. Dep't of State, to U.S. Embassy in Tripoli, *et al.* (Feb. 11, 2012, 5:29 PM) (on file with the Committee, C05409829). *See also* email from Principal Officer 1 to Diplomatic Security Agent 25 (Jan. 17, 2012, 8:38 AM) (on file with the Committee, C05411094).

[89] *See id.*

[90] Email from Diplomatic Security Agent 24 to Joan Polaschik, Deputy Chief of Mission in Libya, U.S. Dep't of State (Feb. 6, 2012, 11:05 AM) (on file with the Committee, C05411434) ("From DS HQ (DAS Lamb and MSD Director) has indicated, they are not in favor of pulling MSD out of Tripoli to support from Benghazi and from what I understand they are keeping the staffing in Benghazi at 3–4 agents. DS HQ continues to complain about Benghazi being an unfunded mandate and there are no agents or funds to support it, so I doubt anything is going

Benghazi Mission compound on three more occasions: March 27–30, 2012, April 12–27, 2012, after the first attack, and June 9–23, 2012, after the second attack.[91]

On February 16, 2012, Joan Polaschik, the Deputy Chief of Mission in Libya, met with Lamb to discuss among other things the staffing issues in Benghazi. According to personnel in the meeting:

> Joan essentially briefed Charlene on the situation in Tripoli, primarily because that's where Joan was currently serving. They then discuss Benghazi some. And Joan was primarily seeking to get clarity from Charlene on DS' plan moving forward for security in both Tripoli and Benghazi.

> During the meeting, there was what appeared to be a different policy set forward by Charlene about our security posture in Benghazi that advocated for local hire drivers and only one armed DS officer per vehicle with some reference to maybe in the future, once people had the foreign affairs counter threat training, some individuals could potentially self-drive. That seemed very different from what the previous stated policy of having two DS in any vehicle leaving the compound in Benghazi. It seemed a significant difference in policy, which raised alarm bells.[92]

The policy change made by Lamb to cap the number of Diplomatic Security Agents assigned to the Benghazi Mission at three was confirmed by the desk officer responsible for staffing in Benghazi.

> A: In mid-February, in conversations with DAS Lamb, it became quite she made it quite apparent that she wanted three agents on the ground in Benghazi. From that time on, I was attempting to get three agents into Benghazi at all times.

> Q: How did you I mean, you said she made it clear. How did that become clear to you that was her position?

> A: I don't specifically remember. I believe the on or about February 16th we were preparing for DCM from Tripoli to come in for a meeting on security related issues, and at that time I specifically recall the conversation about the number of agents in Benghazi. So that's the last thing I can recall specifically?

> Q: Can you elaborate on that conversation?

> A: Certainly. While discussing RSO staffing in Libya, the topic came up in Benghazi, and DAS Lamb became aware of the fact that two of the agents were essentially excuse me their primary duty was driving the movement team vehicle. And traditionally overseas posts, the vast majority of

---

to change unless the status of Benghazi is formalized. SST has indicated that they would be willing to support.").

[91] See Benghazi DS and SST TDY staffing for Jan. 2012-September 11 (on file with the Committee, C0539433).

[92] Testimony of Post Management Officer for Libya, Bureau of Near Eastern Affairs, U.S. Dep't of State, Tr. at 165–166 (Jul. 23, 2015) [hereinafter Post Management Officer Testimony] (on file with the Committee).

them, their drivers are provided by the post. They're locally engaged staff drivers. So she wanted to alleviate that program or that duty, so to speak, in her mind. That was one of the factors. There could have been more. That was the factors that she made known to me and my superiors.[93]

The policy change was not communicated to the Diplomatic Security Agents on the ground or other State Department personnel who nonetheless believed five Diplomatic Security Agents were needed to adequately secure the Benghazi Mission. For example, the lead Diplomatic Security Agent in Benghazi at the time wrote:

I've enjoyed four agents for six days now and it's been a treat to allow agents to properly turnover programs with one another. We'll be back down to three tomorrow and then 2 on March 21 . . . Having been here for six weeks now, I've had to deal with two Principal Officers who expect five DS agents to accommodate their travel, maintain the security integrity (and programs) on the compound.[94]

Further to same, on March 28, 2012, Embassy Tripoli made a request on behalf of Benghazi for "five TDY Diplomatic Security agents for 45–60 day rotations in Benghazi." Advocating for the Benghazi Mission, Gene A. Cretz, U.S. Ambassador to Libya, wrote in his cable to Washington D.C:[95]

This number is required to ensure that we have an appropriate USDH [direct hire] presence to protect our COMSEC; support the two long term USDH TDYers, and support an increasing number of program/assistance TDY's from both Tripoli and Washington. The number of TDY'ers in Benghazi is expected to increase in the run up to the elections. Embassy Tripoli is in the process of recruiting four LES drivers and an RSO LES SPSS, which will support operations in Benghazi. Post also plans to deploy a TDY RSO from Tripoli once expanded permanent staffing is established and stabilized. Once these positions are filled; Post anticipates requiring fewer TDY DS agents to support Benghazi. Although an LGF contractor has begun operations in Benghazi, initial discussions regarding contractor-provided armed close protection/movement support does not appear viable based on complications regarding GOL firearms permits. Currently, the LGF contractor is able to obtain only short term (48–72 hr) firearms permits for specific VIP visits.[96]

---

[93] Diplomatic Security Agent 25 Testimony at 23–24.

[94] Email from Diplomatic Security Agent 12 to Diplomatic Security Agent 25 (March 14, 2012, 11:02 PM)(on file with the Committee, C05411904).

[95] U.S. Dep't of State, Cable, Request for DS TDY and FTE Support (March 28, 2012) (on file with the Committee, SCB004625–27).

[96] Id.

VISAS

At the time the March 28, 2012 staffing request was sent to Washington D.C., the number of Diplomatic Security Agents at the compound dropped to two.[97]

Notwithstanding Lamb's decision to limit the number of Diplomatic Security Agents serving at the Benghazi Mission to three, those Diplomatic Security Agents who were available to deploy were prevented from traveling because they could not get visas from the Libyan Government.[98] Thus, the pool of Diplomatic Security Agents available to serve was further limited. The desk officer in charge of staffing in Benghazi described the problem with the Libyan visa system:

> When they first initiated it, it was a surprise to us, we weren't aware it was going to happen. So basically you went from airport visas where you just kind of show up and was having to see if you had the right passport and you get stamped. And then you go to a visa process where they weren't quite ready yet, this end in at the Embassy to issue visas. So it was very confusing. They didn't have their process down. The bureaucracy wasn't working too well in their Ministry of Foreign Affairs, we call it the MFA, and back here in Washington. And that was in the December 2011 timeframe.

> That kind of got sorted out in the early January 2012 timeframe and it did that way the process at least, it would take 2 or 3 weeks, but as long as we know the process, we can usually work around it.

> And then it collapsed again in that end of March/April timeframe, and that one was pretty significant. That one was much longer, and it was difficult, and they were essentially, to my knowledge, they were changing from a they were using stamps before. This is probably too much detail for you guys, but and then they went to foils, and they didn't have the foils, so they had to get the foils, no one had the foils. I mean, it was convoluted. . . .

> It actually got longer after the foil issue was resolved. So it was probably it usually took me about 6 weeks to get from identified to out there, and 4 weeks of that would be about for the visa process. I tried to get the visas in 1 month before the departure date, and that was standard until basically 9/11.[99]

---

[97] *See* Email from Diplomatic Security Agent 12 to Diplomatic Security Agent 25 (Mar. 21, 2012, 8:03 AM) (on file with the Committee, SCB0049976) ("[W]e are down to 2 agents in Benghazi which stifles movements and puts [us] in bad shape on compound.").

[98] *See* Email from Diplomatic Security Agent 25 to Post Management Officer for Libya, Bureau of Near Eastern Affairs, U.S. Dep't of State, *et al.* (Mar. 20, 2012, 9:09 PM) (on file with the Committee, SCB0049977) ("I just went to the Libyan Embassy and was told that their 'system' was down. They could not check the status of currently approved visas nor do anything having to do with visas. When asked when the system may be back up, the clerk told me that there was no way of telling when (or if) it will be up at any point in the future. 'It is being worked on' is what I was told.").

[99] Diplomatic Security Agent 25 Testimony at 34–35.

The visa delays prevented two Diplomatic Security Agents from traveling to the Benghazi Mission in late March and early April.[100] As a result, only one Diplomatic Security Agent was on the compound at the time of the first IED attack.[101] On April 6, 2012, an "IED was thrown over the perimeter wall at 1650 EDT/2250 Benghazi."[102] The single Diplomatic Security Agent described the sequence of events to the Committee:

> Shortly after I went inside, I know the principal officer and the IMO had already retired. I was sitting there, and I just turned on the TV, and I heard a very loud explosion. And, as I told you before, you heard explosions throughout, but you would know by the force of this explosion, not only the noise but also the way it rocked the building, I knew that it was inside the compound.
>
> At that point, I was sitting in the living room. I had my weapons with me. I did not have my vest. I ran into my bedroom, grabbed my vest. I spoke to the IMO and to the principal officer. I instructed them to allow me out, lock themselves lock the door and lock themselves in the safe haven. I had an extra pistol and an extra shotgun. I left it there for them. I left two radios. One that is communication for them and me and communications for them and the Annex building. I told them that I would be [in] constant contact with them on the radio or on the phone; if they did not hear from me, then to contact the Annex building for assistance.
>
> I also called our QRF [quick reaction force], basically reacted them. We had a plan: On a situation like that, they would take up positions throughout the compound. One of the positions would be outside of our building. As I stepped outside, one of the QRF members was already out there waiting for me. This is possibly, I don't know, 3 minutes after the bombing.
>
> At some point, the guard finally activated the alarm. Our guard force had a push button alarm; in case of any attack, they would activate it. As I step outside, the QRF member is there. We cleared our way to the TOC. Went inside the TOC [technical operations center]. I turn off the alarm, and I use our camera system to view or to try to determine if there was any other people, any other attackers in the compound. That took approximately 3, 4 minutes.
>
> I did not see anybody in our camera system. There are some blind spots, but we did have a pretty good system throughout the compound. I thought that with that, I would be able to determine something, something blatant, something that would really stand out.

---

[100] See Email from Diplomatic Security Agent 25 (Apr. 7, 2012, 2:56 PM) (on file with the Committee, C05392858).

[101] See Email from Diplomatic Security Agent 24 to Principal Officer 2, U.S. Dep't of State, and Deputy Dir. Office of Maghreb Affairs, Bureau of Near Eastern Affairs, U.S. Dep't of State (Apr. 7, 2012, 9:10 AM) (on file with the Committee, C05409502).

[102] Email (Apr. 6, 2012, 8:28 PM) (on file with the Committee, C05409502).

Afterwards, I stepped outside of the TOC. I had two QRF members with me, and we commenced on clearing the compound.

While we were doing that, I heard two shots. It sounded to me like rifle fire, something bigger than an M4, which is what I had. So I thought initially that it was shooting in the compound. One of the QRF members received, if I am not mistaken, a call that told him that a third QRF member was outside and had detained someone.

\* \* \*

There was a third QRF member, **[redacted text]**, who was outside of the compound and had detained two Libyan nationals. Eventually I found out that he's the one who fired the two shots. It is common; it is standard operating procedure for Libyans to shoot warning shots, and that is what he did.

So we were clearing the compound when I learned that he was outside and he was possibly engaged with the attackers. I kept one of the QRF members guarding the entry to our house. I communicated with the principal officer that everything was still okay; we are still clearing. I went outside, and **[redacted text]** had two people on the ground.

Shortly afterwards, reinforcements from the 17th February Militia arrived. They took them away. I requested from the militia to provide a security ring outside of the compound. I made contact with the Annex building. And I asked them to hold off on sending reinforcements to prevent a blue on blue situation the Militia did not know who they were; they did not know who the Militia were but to be on stand-by in case we needed additional assistance.

At that time, all QRF members and myself cleared the whole compound. It took us several hours to do so. We did not find evidence of any other intruders, attackers, enemy on the grounds. I went back inside, and I briefed the principal officer as to what had taken place. She and I then commenced our notifications to D.C. and our report writing.[103]

The principal officer in Benghazi expressed concern to the lead Diplomatic Security Agent in Tripoli "had the attack been even slightly less amateur, I don't know what we would have done."[104]

Less than two weeks after the first IED attack on the Benghazi Mission compound occurred, Washington D.C. rejected the March

---

[103] Testimony of Diplomatic Security Agent, Diplomatic Security Service, U.S. Dep't of State, Tr.at 30–32 (April 13, 2015) [hereinafter Diplomatic Security Agent 16 Testimony] (on file with the Committee).

[104] See Email from Principal Officer 2, U.S. Dep't of State, to Diplomatic Security Agent 24 and Deputy Dir. Office of Maghreb Affairs, Bureau of Near Eastern Affairs, U.S. Dep't of State (April 7, 2012, 3:25 AM) (on file with the Committee, C05409502).

28, 2012 request to deploy five Diplomatic Security Agents to Benghazi.[105] In denying the request, Washington D.C. stated:

> DS will continue to provide DS agent support in Benghazi. DS/IP recommends that post continues its efforts to hire LES drivers for Benghazi to enable the DS TDYers to solely perform their protective security function. DS/IP also recommends a joint assessment of the number of DS agents requested for Benghazi to include input from RSO Tripoli, TDY RSO Benghazi, and DS/IP in an effort to develop a way forward.[106]

Throughout the remainder of spring 2012, the number of Diplomatic Security Agents deployed to the compound never exceeded three.[107] Half the time, there were only two Diplomatic Security Agents.[108] During this time, the security environment in Benghazi started to deteriorate. Less than one week before Stevens returned to Tripoli as the Ambassador in May 2012, a rocket propelled grenade [RPG] attack occurred on the International Committee of the Red Cross.[109] The International Committee of the Red Cross was located approximately one kilometer from the Benghazi Mission. A "vague Facebook post claiming responsibility for the RPG attack" also indicated it was "preparing to send a message to the Americans."[110]

On June 6, 2012, a week after the threat to the Mission compound, the Benghazi Mission was attacked for a second time. An IED along the Benghazi Mission's perimeter wall—blowing a hole "6 feet by 4 feet," large enough for an individual to walk through.[111] At the time of the second IED attack, three Diplomatic Security Agents were on the ground. A Diplomatic Security Agent on the ground at the time described the attack to the Committee:

> Around 3:00 in the morning, give or take 20, 30 minutes, the imminent danger and notification system alarm went off, affectionately called the duck and cover alarm. That woke all of us up. I got up. I put on my armor, grabbed my weapon, got dressed of course, and then went outside to find out what was going on. I go outside, and I see a bunch of our I see our local Guard Force members around the front of the gate making, gesturing with their hands, you know, towards their nose. I did not speak Arabic. At the time they did not speak English, so, that's how we communicated. I believe at the time during that shift there was one person that didn't speak English. So, you know, I started smelling; then I had this distinct smell, not like something burning, but some kind of chemical burn, what-

---

[105] U.S. Dep't of State, Cable—Tripoli, Request for DS TDY and FTE Support (April 19, 2012)(on file with the Committee, SCB0046263).

[106] See id.

[107] See Benghazi DS and SST TDY staffing for Jan. 2012-September 11 (on file with the Committee, C0539433).

[108] See id.

[109] Email from Diplomatic Security Agent 24 to Diplomatic Security Agent 25 (June 14, 2012, 1:56 PM)(on file with the Committee, C05391830).

[110] Email from Diplomatic Security Agent 18 to Diplomatic Security Agent 17 (May 28, 2012, 5:36 AM) (on file with the Committee, C05392202).

[111] Testimony of Principal Officer 2, U.S. Dep't of State, Tr. at 109 (Mar. 13, 2015) [hereinafter Principal Officer 2 Testimony] (on file with the Committee).

ever. Come to find out, you know, 5 minutes later that it's a fuse.

But at that point so I asked everyone to start backing away from the wall. Then as I back away, that's when the bomb detonates.

From there it knocked me down. Ears were ringing. I get up with the local guards. We run back. There are some sandbags right there at the corner. Get behind those sandbags, point my M4 at the hole in the wall and wait for any follow up attack that may occur. And that was the

And no follow up attack did occur, so after that the February 17th Martyrs Brigade showed up in a matter of minutes. Then from there we set up a perimeter outside on the street. As we had this large hole in our wall, we wanted to push our security perimeter back even further. We set up the large hole I mean set up the perimeter, sorry; and then from there, once that perimeter was set up, I went with one of our QRF guys **[redacted text]** And we went there and secured the rest of the compound.

As there was a security incident at the front of our compound, we had lost attention and lost visibility on other aspects of our compound. So, before we decided to let the principal officer out of the safe haven and call the all clear, we went through, me with my M4, him with his AK–47, and we just moved through the compound making sure nobody else had entered and there were no other devices. After that was done, we called the all clear.[112]

Two days after the second attack on the compound the number of Diplomatic Security Agents dropped to two.[113] Five days later, on June 11, 2012, an RPG attack was launched on the UK Ambassador's motorcade. Some speculated the RPG was directed toward the Mission given the proximity of the attack to the Mission Compound. Polaschik testified:

A: There were two main reasons. One was the physical location of the attack. It occurred, I believe, on Venezia Street, which is right by our compound. And it was actually, as I understood it, not having been there at the time of the attack, close by our rear exit from our compound. And, also, given the fact that we had been storing British armored vehicles on our compound, again, if someone had been watching, you know, did they know for sure whether that was British or American.

Also, around the same time, a figure named Abu Yahya is it Abu Yahya al Libi? a senior Al Qaeda operative, had been killed, I believe, in either Pakistan or Afghanistan. So I was——

---

[112] Diplomatic Security Agent, Diplomatic Security Service, U.S. Dep't of State, at 59–61 (Mar. 24, 2015) [hereinafter Diplomatic Security Agent 22 Testimony] (on file with the Committee).
[113] Email from Diplomatic Security Agent 25 to Diplomatic Security Agent 21 (Jun. 7, 2012, 3:03 PM) (on file with the Committee, C05391125).

Q: By the U.S. Government?

A: Correct.

Q: In a drone strike or something like that?

A: Correct. In some U.S. operations. So, given that he was a Libyan, I was concerned whether or not there could have been some retaliatory action taken by Al Qaeda, you know, for that act. So it was murky. There were a lot of things that were unclear, but I was concerned that there could have been links to the U.S. Government.

Q: At that time, in June of 2012, the Brits were storing their vehicles and their weapons on the U.S. compound, the Benghazi compound; is that correct?

A: Correct.[114]

In fact, between the first attack on the Benghazi Mission on April 6 and June 2012, there were more than 21 separate incidents in Benghazi.[115] While a member of the Defense Department's SST was temporarily diverted to bolster security after the series of attacks against the Mission compound and U.K. Ambassador's motorcade, Diplomatic Security Agent staffing never increased to five.[116] The sequence of attacks raised enough concern in Washington D.C., for Lamb to acknowledge to her supervisors there were not enough resources diverted to Benghazi.

We are not staffed or resourced adequately to protect our people in that type of environment. We are a soft target against resources available to the bad guys there. Not to mention there is no continuity because we do everything there with TDY personnel. The cost to continue to do business there may become more challenging.[117]

Washington D.C. did nothing to provide additional resources or personnel. For example, a day before the second IED attack on the Mission compound, Stevens requested the support of the State Department's highly trained mobile security deployment team to remain in Tripoli through the end of the summer.[118] More resources in Tripoli meant possibly more available resources at the Benghazi Mission. However, on the day of the second IED attack against the Benghazi Mission on June 6, 2012 the request was denied.[119]

On June 14, 2012, eight days after the second IED attack on the compound, the Diplomatic Security Agent in charge sent a staffing

---

[114] Testimony of Joan Polaschik, Deputy Chief of Mission in Libya, U.S. Dep't of State, Tr. at 95–96 (Aug. 12, 2015) [hereinafter Polaschik Transcript] (on file with the Committee).

[115] Security Incidents in Benghazi, Libya, from June 1, 2011- Aug. 20, 2012 (on file with the Committee); see also Benghazi Spot Report, EAC and Significant Event Timeline (DS/IP/RD) (on file with the Committee, C05394332).

[116] See Benghazi DS and SST TDY staffing for Jan. 2012-September 11 (on file with the Committee, C0539433).

[117] Email from Charlene Lamb, Deputy Ass't Sec'y, Bureau of Diplomatic Security, Int'l Programs, U.S. Dep't of State, to Scott Bultrowicz, Principal Deputy Sec'y of State, Bureau of Diplomatic Security, U.S. Dep't of State (Jun. 11, 2012, 4:16 PM) (on file with the Committee, C05388866).

[118] Email from John C. Stevens, U.S. Ambassador to Libya, to Diplomatic Security Agent 7 (Jun. 5, 2012, 10:55 AM) (on file with the Committee, C05409979).

[119] Email from Diplomatic Security Agent 7 to John C. Stevens, U.S. Ambassador to Libya (Jun. 6, 2012, 3:00PM) (on file with the Committee, C05409979).

request to Diplomatic Security requesting "five DS agents be deployed to secure the facility, with a MSD team on standby."[120] One day later, on June 15, 2012, an Action Memorandum requesting five additional staff for Benghazi was directed to Lamb for approval.[121] The Action Memorandum described "the uncertainty of the security situation in Benghazi and the fact that their appears to be an active terrorist cell in Benghazi, Libya planning and implementing attack operations against western interests including the U.S. Mission in Benghazi."[122] No response was ever received.[123] The desk officer responsible for staffing in Benghazi described his role in developing the Action Memorandum.[124]

> A: The RSO in Benghazi also requested and received additional local guard support, which was the Blue Mountain Group. So they had additional guards on at night. And then the RSO in Benghazi, they requested me for additional staffing, RSO staffing, agents staffing.
>
> Q: How did that request come in?
>
> A: I believe we definitely talked on the phone and then he sent an email to follow up with that. But first we spoke on the phone and then we sent an email.
>
> Q: And what was the number requested or——
>
> A: Sure.
>
> Q: How did that proceed when that after that request came in?
>
> A: Certainly. The number he requested at the time was I think he said five agents, and he specified a timeframe through the election period, which was going to be probably in a month, so on or about I think it was earlier scheduled it was early July, so roughly about a month, and then he recommended having four agents remain at the compound.
>
> Q: Based on your experience, just from a personal perspective, did you support that number or support that assessment?
>
> A: Yes. Not only did I support it, I sent it to the RSO for clearance as well, which he supported fully, and I drafted an action memorandum stating the RSO's request.
>
> Q: And what happened to that action memorandum?
>
> A: It was approved by my direct supervisors, and then it was upstairs for a while. And we didn't hear anything. We felt it urgent enough, my supervisor scheduled a meeting with DAS Lamb, and in the meeting with DAS Lamb, es-

---

[120] Email from Diplomatic Security Agent 19 to Diplomatic Security Agent 25, James Bacigalupo, Regional Dir., Bureau of Diplomatic Security, U.S. Dep't of State (Jun. 14, 2012, 11:40 AM) (on file with the Committee, C05393692).

[121] Memorandum from James Bacigalupo, Regional Dir., Bureau of Diplomatic Security, U.S. Dep't of State, to Charlene Lamb, Deputy Ass't Sec'y, Bureau of Diplomatic Security, Int'l Programs, U.S. Dep't of State, (Jun. 15, 2012) (on file with the Committee, C05578316).

[122] Id.

[123] Diplomatic Security Agent 25 Testimony at 42–43.

[124] Id.

sentially the long and short of it, the memo was denied for additional resources, personnel wise.

Q: Can you walk us through that in a little more detail? How long was it upstairs? So your immediate supervisor, that would be Mr. Bacigalupo?

A: At that time it was James Bacigalupo, correct.

Q: So he approved this action memorandum, and then it would go to Charlene Lamb. Is that correct?

A: It went to I know it was in I don't know where it went in between. Probably to her staff assistants or the deputy prior to her. But it definitely made it to her because that's who we had the meeting with.

Q: And how long was it up there before the meeting?

A: I think the memo actually didn't get sent up until after the incident with the UK protective detail, so it was probably mid-June, June 15th, I believe, the date on the memo. So I think it was late that week. Maybe June 18th. I can't recall it specifically.[125]

Concerned about the impending loss of security personnel and the deteriorating security environment in Tripoli and in Benghazi, the U.S. Embassy in Tripoli sent a staffing request to Washington D.C.[126] The July 9, 2012 staffing request included a request for a minimum of four additional Diplomatic Security Agents for the Benghazi Mission—which would be comprised of at least one permanently assigned Diplomatic Security Agent from the U.S. Embassy in Tripoli, as well as a minimum of three temporary duty Diplomatic Security Agents identified by Washington D.C. The Diplomatic Security Agent in charge in Benghazi in July explained his reasoning for the request.[127]

With all the security situation on the ground going on and putting everything in place, and all the transition taking place in regards to American personnel leaving and coming in, and after discussion with the RSO and chief of Mission, this was a cable suggesting at that time this is what we need to maintain operations in the best safe manner as soon as possible. We wrote this cable on July 9, prior to the Ambassador leaving for Benghazi.

At that time, MSD personnel were, when we started off with two teams; now there was less teams on the ground. Actually, I don't believe there was any MSD team on the ground. There was just TDYers and two permanent ARSOs on the ground. This is in July. I'm sorry. I'm confused on the dates. Not September. This is July 9. So, at this time, we had another ARSO on the ground that was permanent and myself and the RSO.

---

[125] Id.

[126] U.S. Dep't of State, Cable, Request for Extension of TDY Security Personnel (July 9, 2012) (on file with the Committee, SCB0049439).

[127] Testimony Diplomatic Security Agent, Diplomatic Security Service, U.S. Dep't of State, at 78–79 (May 19, 2015) (on file with the Committee).

* * *

So we wrote this in July because all these elements were leaving. MSD was leaving. The SST team was leaving, or they were going to change their Mission from being in the Embassy to being outside of the Embassy so they could train the Libyan government military. So we came up with this as a suggestion, for example, in line 4, or paragraph 4, under the current arrangement, and this was the main one, 34 U.S. security personnel, the 16 SSTs, the 11 MSD, the 2 RSOs and 3 TDY RSOs, that was the number that we had there, and it was going to drawn down to 27. And we said: Wait, we're basically losing people. We need people, specifically because security is not in the best position now.

We requested weapons permits and weapons for the local ambassador bodyguard detail, and funding for security. Yes, and this was the cable that we sent out in concurrence with the Ambassador? [128]

Again, going based on the numbers of agents that were going to Benghazi while we were averaging one, two, or three, and we never actually had five, we're suggesting: Hey, international programs, how about you making sure that we always have three, and we're going to put a permanent RSO on the ground, and that would give us at least four if you cannot provide us with enough TDYers to do the job. That's basically why we went with that number. It was an average of the amount of agents that we had at any time at that post. [129]

No response was received. Lamb explained the lack of response to the Committee:

So when I read this cable in this format, **[redacted text]** wrote it as a reporting cable in paragraph format, and it's very hard to line everything up by the needs. So I asked the desk officer to have his . . . at the time was the person working with **[redacted text]** for them to get on a conference call and to go through this cable, paragraph by paragraph, line by line, and to switch this into the format that shows how many people do you need for which activities, to support VIP visits, movement security, static security, a quick reaction force. Just tell me exactly what you need and then the numbers will pop out the other side showing what you need.

And they sat down and they did this. And all of that was compiled into the response that unfortunately never went out. But my guidance to them was before that cable went up to Scott Bultrowicz and Eric Boswell, I wanted it to be pre approved at post, because I didn't want to dictate to post their staffing needs, I wanted to support them. But in this format, it was not clear exact because they were com-

---

[128] *Id.* at 79.
[129] *Id.* at 80.

ing up on the 1 year transition when everybody was going to leave post and the new team was going to come in, so I wanted it to be laid out, very clear, the current operating support that was being provided for security.[130]

She further explained: "And just because it didn't get sent out with a cable number on it, I am testifying to you that everything in that cable was followed through and carried out." [131]

Kennedy explained his involvement in the July 9, 2012 staffing cable and the decision to terminate the Defense Department's SST protective responsibilities at the U.S. Embassy in Tripoli. He testified to the Committee: "I consulted, as I said earlier, with the subject matter experts in this field, and after consulting with them, I responded no, we would not be asking for another extension." [132] This is a much different description of Kennedy's involvement than what Cheryl D. Mills, Chief of Staff and Counselor to the Secretary of State, described to the Committee. She described the Under Secretary as the person "who managed security related issues." [133]

Additional resources were never sent to Tripoli or Benghazi, despite the requests of the security professionals on the ground. Beginning in August, the number of security personnel at the U.S. Embassy in Tripoli was 34. By the end of August, the number of security personnel at Embassy Tripoli dropped to six Diplomatic Security Agents.[134] In Benghazi, the number of Diplomatic Security Agents continued to fluctuate. By August, the desk officer responsible for staffing in Benghazi conveyed to the Regional Bureau "DS has had no volunteers for Benghazi for the upcoming few months . . . DS's plan is to maintain 3 DS staff in Benghazi at all times by drawing on Tripoli's resources." [135]

On September 1, 2012, a Diplomatic Security Agent, who was originally scheduled to serve at the U.S. Embassy in Tripoli, arrived at the Benghazi Mission to serve as the Diplomatic Security Agent in charge. With the addition from Tripoli in early September 2012, three Diplomatic Security Agents secured the Benghazi compound, including on the morning of September 10, 2012 prior to Stevens' arrival.

---

[130] Lamb Testimony at 245–246.

[131] *Id.* at 248.

[132] Kennedy Testimony at 46.

[133] Testimony of Cheryl Mills, Chief of Staff and Counselor to the U.S. Sec'y of State, U.S. Dep't of State, Tr. at 72 (Sept. 2, 2015) (on file with the Committee).

[134] Testimony of Gregory Hicks, Deputy Chief of Mission at U.S. Embassy Tripoli, U.S. Dep't of State, Tr. at 13–14 (Apr. 11, 2013, U.S. House Committee on Oversight and Gov't Reform) (on file with the Committee); *see also* Cable from Embassy Tripoli to U.S. Dep't of State (Jul. 9, 2012) (on file with the Committee, SCB0049439).

[135] Email from Deputy Dir. Office of Maghreb Affairs, U.S. Dep't of State (Aug. 27, 2012, 4:47PM) (on file with the Committee, C05394203).

# APPENDIX G:

## Timeline of Significant Events During the Attacks

**Tuesday, September 11, 2012** [1]

EDT/EET

3:42 pm/9:42 pm—First attack on the Benghazi Mission compound begins.

4:21 pm/10:21 pm—The White House Situation Room convenes a meeting.

4:32 pm/10:32 pm—The National Military Command Center [NMCC] at the Pentagon is notified of the attacks.

5:00 pm/11:00 pm—Secretary of Defense, Leon E. Panetta, and Chairman of the Joint Chiefs of Staff, Martin E. Dempsey, meet with the President at the White House.

5:10 pm/11:10 pm—The first Drone arrives in Benghazi.

5:23 pm/11:23 pm—All State Department personnel evacuate to the Benghazi CIA Annex. Ambassador Christopher Stevens is unaccounted for.

5:38 pm/11:38 pm—The Secretary of State calls David H. Petraeus, Director, Central Intelligence Agency.

6:00 pm/12:00 am—The Secretary of Defense convenes a meeting at the Pentagon.

6:49 pm/12:49 am—The Secretary of State calls the Libyan President.

6:58 pm/12:58 am—Gregory Hicks, Deputy Chief of Mission, Tripoli, reports another mob gathering at Annex.

7:05 pm/1:05 am—The Secretary of State holds a conference call with Cheryl Mills, Chief of Staff, State Department, Patrick F. Kennedy, Under Secretary for Management, State Department, Gregory Hicks, Deputy Chief of Mission, Libya, Stephen Mull, Executive Secretariat, State Department, Thomas Nides, Deputy Secretary for Management and Resources, Jacob Sullivan, Deputy Chief of Staff for Policy and Director, Office of Policy Planning.

---

[1] Eastern Daylight Time (Washington, DC) and Eastern European Time (Benghazi) are used.

7:19 pm/1:19 am—Jeremy Bash, Chief of Staff, Department of Defense emails potential response forces to Jacob Sullivan, Cheryl Mills, and others.

7:30 pm/1:30 am—Team Tripoli arrives at the airport in Benghazi.

7:30 pm/1:30 am—The White House convenes a meeting via secured teleconference video with representatives from the State Department, the Defense Department, and the intelligence community on the U.S. response to the attacks in Benghazi.

7:40 pm/1:40 am—The Embassy in Tripoli receives a call from a missing Diplomatic Security Agent phone about an American at the hospital.

8:30 pm/2:30 am—NMCC holds a conference call with AFRICOM, EUCOM, CENTCOM, TRANSCOM and the four services about the military response to Benghazi.

8:39 pm/2:39 am—The NMCC conveys authorization to the FAST to prepare to deploy and the CIF to move to an intermediate staging base.

8:53pm/2:53 am—The NMCC conveys formal authorization to deploy the U.S. Based Special Operations Force to an intermediate staging base.

9:57 pm/3:57 am—Bash emails Sullivan and asks, "Any word from the hospital?"

10:27 pm/4:27 am—The President calls the Secretary of State.

10:34 pm/4:34 am—The Diplomatic Security Command Center at the State Department issues an update that Libyans have confirmed Stevens is in a hospital and has been killed.

10:39 pm/4:39 am—Kennedy sends a photo of Stevens from Twitter to Mills.

11:00 pm/5:00 am—The established N-hour.

11:05 pm/5:05 am—Team Tripoli arrives at the Annex in Benghazi.

11:17 pm/5:17 am—The first mortar hits the Annex in Benghazi.

11:38 pm/5:38 am—The Secretary of State emails: "Cheryl told me the Libyans confirmed his death."

11:41 pm/5:41 am—Diplomatic Security Command Center reports mortar fire at the annex and new injuries to the American personnel.

11:45 pm/5:45 am—A McDonough email notes the Secretary of Defense called Pastor Jones.

## Wednesday, September 12, 2012

12:05 am/6:05 am—AFRICOM orders a C–17 aircraft to prepare to deploy to Libya.

12:12 am/6:12 am—Mills informs McDonough "we're pulling everyone out of Benghazi."

1:00 am/7:00 am—The CIF is ready to deploy

1:19 am/7:19 am—Admiral James Winnefeld, Vice Chairman of the Joint Chiefs of Staff, emails we "now have dip clearance for FAST platoon to Tripoli . . ."

1:31 am/7:31 am—The first plane leaves from the Benghazi airport with the survivors *en route* to Tripoli.

1:40 am/7:40 am—Winnefeld sends another email: "first airplane departs Ramstein at 0600z [2:00 am/8:00 am]"

2:25 am/8:25 am—Steven's death is confirmed when the security officers from CIA and the State Department receives his body.

~ 4:00 am/10:00 am—The second plane provided by the Libyan Air Force departs with all remaining U.S. personnel in Benghazi for Tripoli.

~ 6:00 am/12:00 pm—A C–130 aircraft arrives at Rota Spain to transport the FAST to Tripoli.

~ 7:00 am/1:00 pm—The FAST completes loading the C–130 aircraft and is ready to depart.

8:15 am/2:15 pm—The C–17 aircraft departs Germany to Tripoli to evacuate Americans.

~ 10:00 am/4:00 pm—The FAST departs Rota Spain *en route* to Tripoli.

~ 10:00 am/4:00 pm—The CIF's C–130 aircrafts arrive at the airport.

~ 11:00 am/5:00 pm—The CIF departs *en route* to the intermediate staging base.

~ 2:00 pm/8:00 pm—CIF arrives at an intermediate staging base.

2:56 pm/8:56 pm—FAST platoon arrives in Tripoli.

3:28 pm/9:28 pm—The Special Operations Force deployed from the U.S. arrives at the intermediate staging base.

4:19 pm/10:19 pm—The C–17 aircraft with Americans evacuated from Tripoli arrives in Germany.

The following timeline, the "Comprehensive Timeline of Events—Benghazi," provides further detail about the events that occurred during the attack. This is a timeline of events compiled by the State Department using information obtained from the DVR footage of the Benghazi Mission compound and the Annex, as well as interviews, and logs maintained at the Tactical Operations Center at the Embassy in Tripoli and at the Diplomatic Security Command Center.

The Committee makes this timeline available to the public with the following corrections:

- Time stamp 0503.00: The "unidentified LN Motorcade" was not February 17 Martyrs Brigade. It was the Libya Shield.

- Time stamp 0614.00: The motorcade that arrived was the Libyan Military Intelligence.

Last Edit: 20121101          <u>Comprehensive Timeline of Events - Benghazi</u>

<u>Source Material</u>

This timeline is constructed from DVR footage of the U.S. Special Mission Compound (USSMC)
and U.S. Special Mission Compound Annex (Annex) from the Federal Bureau of
Investigation (FBI) as well as FBI interviews conducted with relevant parties in the days immediately
following the events, logs of events maintained by the Tactical Operations Center at U.S. Embassy
Tripoli and at the Diplomatic Security Command Center (DSCC), and the DSCC phone logs. No further
information has been utilized. All information sources for events are listed in the far right column.
**This document is a draft working product unless expressly indicated otherwise.**
**This document is Law Enforcement Sensitive (LES) and should not be utilized for follow-on analysis**
**unless expressly indicated. All labels, identities, and assumptions are subject to change.**

<u>Time References</u>

Analysis of both DVR systems indicates that the Annex DVR system's timestamp is 02 minutes and
04 seconds behind the timestamp for the USSMC. For accuracy, the time adjusted to the USSMC
system has been provided in the "Synched to USSMC" column. In addition, a comparison of observed
sunrise with recorded sunrise by the U.S. Naval Observatory, while imprecise, does provide
assurance that times provided by both DVR systems are accurate to within a few minutes of real time.
(Recorded Sunrise: 0622  Observed through treeline by Annex Camera 5: 0628 on Sep 12, 2012)

September 11-12, 2012

| DVR Time (Local) | Synched to USSMC | Location | Event | Source |
|---|---|---|---|---|
| 1939.26 | | USSMC | 2 individuals (presumed to be Ambassador Stevens and Turkish dignitary) walk through garden north of Villa C to Gate C1. | USSMC 12 |
| 1940.08 | | USSMC | Vehicle departs to East (presumed to be Turkish dignitary). | USSMC 8 |
| 1941.34 | | USSMC | Individual (presumed to be Ambassador Stevens) returns from Gate C1 through garden to Villa C vicinity. | USSMC 12 |
| 2010.09 | | USSMC | Motorcade x3 enters compound from Gate C1 (presumed to be British security team). | USSMC 12 |
| 2027.26 | | USSMC | Four individuals depart USSMC (presumed British security team). | USSMC 12 |
| 2102.50 | | USSMC | Supreme Security Council truck arrives at C1 | USSMC 8 |
| 2142.14 | | USSMC | Supreme Security Council truck departs C1 Gate. Occupant(s) never exit vehicle. | USSMC 8 |
| 2142.20 | | USSMC | 2 Local National Guards (Blue Mountain Libya) seen fleeing south from Gate C1. | USSMC 4 |

| Time | | Source | Description | Ref |
|---|---|---|---|---|
| 2142 - 2202 Approx | | USSMC | ___ moves to Villa C. Places Ambassador STEVENS and IPO Sean SMITH into safe haven | |
| 2142.43 | | USSMC | 2 LNG run to Villa B followed by ___ ___ and ___ run to Office. ___ runs to Villa B. | USSMC 6, 1 |
| 2142.53 | | USSMC | 1st Explosion near C1 Gate | USSMC 12 |
| 2143.20 | | USSMC | 20-30 armed intruders seen moving right to left on road outside compound near C1 Gate | USSMC 4 |
| 2143.50 | | USSMC | Armed intruders seen on compound | USSMC 12 |
| 2144.00 | | USSMC | 2nd Explosion near C1 Gate | USSMC 8 |
| 2144.58 | | USSMC | ___ and ___ attempt to move to Villa C but see multiple armed intruders blocking Alley. They return to Villa B and barricade inside. | USSMC 6, |
| 2145-2232 Approx | | USSMC | ___ and ___ remain inside Villa B | |
| 2144.58 | | USSMC | Armed intruders seen in Alley between Villa B and Villa C | USSMC 5 |
| 2145 | | Tripoli | RSO Tripoli notified of attack | Tripoli TOC Log |
| 2145.38 | | USSMC | Embassy Vehicle Stolen and C3 Gate left Open | USSMC 10 |
| 2146.33 | 2148.37 | Annex | Annex Personnel begin donning body armor | Annex 8 |
| 2147.13 | | Tripoli | ARSO ___ Tripoli) calls DSCC for 1 min, 3 sec | DSCC Call Record |
| 2148.36 | | USSMC | 2 Attackers dragging 1 LNG - probable wound to leg. | USSMC 9 |
| 2150.27 | | USSMC | 2 armed intruders find 1 LNG hiding behind TOC | USSMC 2 |
| 2154.13 | | USSMC | 1 armed intruder makes first unsuccessful attempt to breach TOC. | USSMC 1 |
| 2157.13 | | USSMC | 1st Fireball at QRF / Guest House | USSMC 4 |
| 2201.23 | | USSMC | 2nd Fireball at QRF / Guest House | USSMC 12 |
| 2202.07 | | USSMC | Heavy smoke at location of Villa C suddenly visible from Alley. | USSMC 5 |
| 2202.25 | | USSMC | Heavy smoke suddenly visible from Camera 9 mounted on Villa C. | USSMC 9 |

| | | | | |
|---|---|---|---|---|
| 2202-2235 Approx | | USSMC | becomes separated from STEVENS and SMITH in Villa C due to smoke. _____ receives SAF upon exiting via window. _____ searches Villa C multiple times and ultimately retreats to Villa C rooftop. | |
| 2202.42 | | USSMC | Multiple armed intruders breach Villa B. | USSMC 1 |
| 2203.20 | 2205.24 | Annex | 2 Vehicle motorcade (armored) departs Annex. Mercedes G-Series Wagon and Mercedes Sedan. Presumed departure of Annex QRF Team | Annex 6, 8, 13, 14 |
| 2203.53 | | USSMC | Multiple armed intruders make second unsuccessful attempt to breach TOC. (Note: TOC is not breached during the attack) | USSMC 1, 6 |
| 2208.11 | | USSMC | Presumed tracer rounds seen streaking by. _____ reports receiving tracer fire from beltfed machine gun. | USSMC 6, |
| 2205.00 -2209.10 | | USSMC | The majority of armed intruders on compound appear to exit out of Gate C1. | USSMC 9, 12, 6, 1 |
| 2214.00 | | USSMC | Last armed intruder seen by camera on compound moving past Villa C toward Gate C1 | USSMC 9 |
| 2215 | | Benghazi Unknown | Annex QRF en route and taking fire | Tripoli TOC Log |
| 2217.29 | | USSMC | _____ moves from TOC to Villa B | USSMC 1, 6 |
| 2232.59 | | USSMC | _____ and _____ move Villa B to TOC to get FAV. | USSMC 1, 6 |
| 2235.25 | | USSMC | _____ and _____ drive FAV from TOC to Villa C. | USSMC 6, 5 |
| 2236.35 - 2237.05 | | USSMC | _____ and _____ attempt entry to Villa C | USSMC 12 |
| 2238 | | USSMC | 17 February Martyrs' Brigade arrives at compound | Tripoli TOC Log |
| 2239.26 | | USSMC | DS Agents interact at Villa C w/ Unknown male - possible 17 February QRF Member | USSMC 9 |
| 2240.00 | | USSMC | Multiple armed LN arrive at Villa C. Likely members of 17 February Martyrs' Brigade. | USSMC 9 |
| 2241.50 | | USSMC | FAV moves back to TOC (to retrieve gas masks). | USSMC 6, 5, 9 |
| 2243.22 | | USSMC | FAV returns from TOC to Villa C (presumably with gas masks). | USSMC 6, 5, 9 |

| | | | | |
|---|---|---|---|---|
| 2247.22 | | USSMC | Dark Colored Vehicle parks at C1 exterior. Presumed to be 1st of 2 Annex QRF elements. Footage after indicates personnel (likely militia) holding north side perimeter | USSMC 4 |
| 2248.30 | | USSMC | 2nd of 2 Annex QRF elements enters compound on foot through C3 Gate. Footage after shows personnel (likely militia) holding south side perimeter. | USSMC 10 |
| 2249.32 - 2307.15 | | USSMC | DS Agents, Annex QRF, and 17 February Martyrs' Brigade members attempt search and rescue of Villa C. | USSMC 12 |
| 2256.34 | | USSMC | Annex QRF element and 17 February Martyrs' Brigade members enter TOC after _____ opens door. | USSMC 1, |
| 2258.17 | | USSMC | _____ departs TOC w/ 2 USG laptops. | USSMC 6 |
| 2301 | | USSMC | Sean SMITH reported KIA | Tripoli TOC Log |
| 2304.07 | | USSMC | Annex QRF members x2 depart TOC with unknown equipment (possible encryption device for ClassNet laptops) | USSMC 6 |
| 2305.25 | | USSMC | USSMC Exterior Lighting goes offline | USSMC 12 |
| 2307.45 | | USSMC | Dark Colored SUV moves onto compound through C1 Gate - likely Annex QRF SUV - FAV Mercedes G-Series Wagon staging for evacuation. | USSMC 4 |
| 2310.00 | | USSMC | Unknown explosive detonates several meters interior to C3 Gate. | USSMC 10 |
| 2312 | | USSMC | Annex QRF reported inside compound | Tripoli TOC Log |
| 2316.24 | | USSMC | Dark Colored SUV (presumed to be FAV Toyota Land Cruiser containing 5x DS Agents + body of Sean SMITH) departs C1 Gate heading east. | USSMC 4 |
| 2316.39 | | USSMC | Dark Colored SUV (presumed to be FAV Toyota Land Cruiser containing 5x DS Agents + body of Sean SMITH) crosses camera POV heading west. | USSMC 4 |
| 2317 | | Benghazi Unknown | All DS Personnel w/ SMITH depart compound en route to Annex. FAV receives SAF | Tripoli TOC Log |
| 2318.42 | | USSMC | Multiple SAF and small explosions in vicinity of C3 Gate | USSMC 10 |

| | | | | |
|---|---|---|---|---|
| 2319.07 | | USSMC | Large dark colored SUV (presumed to be FAV Mercedes G Series Wagon containing Annex QRF Team) departs C1 Gate heading east. Multiple individuals (presumed to be February 17 Martyrs' Brigade Militia members) depart C1 Gate on foot. | USSMC 4 |
| 2319.44 | | USSMC | RPG launched through open C3 Gate. Multiple SAF continues. | USSMC 10 |
| 2319.52 | | USSMC | Unknown explosive detonates directly interior to C3 Gate. | USSMC 10 |
| 2320.37 | | USSMC | RPG launched through open C3 Gate. Multiple SAF continues. | USSMC 10 |
| 2320.50 | | USSMC | Unknown explosion - exterior to C3 Gate | USSMC 10 |
| 2320.51 | | USSMC | Unknown explosion - exterior to C1 Gate | USSMC 4 |
| 2321.47 | 2323.51 | Annex | Dark Colored Toyota Land Cruiser arrives at Annex. Presumed to be 5x DSS Agents from USSMC | Annex 6, 8, 13, 14 |
| 2323.44 | | USSMC | Camera 10 for the C3 Gate goes offline | USSMC 10 |
| 2324.22 | | USSMC | Unknown explosive round (possible mortar?) recorded passing overhead of Gate C1 and impacting in vicinity of north road near Villa A. | USSMC 4, 7 |
| 2330 | | Annex | _____ reports arrival at Annex | Tripoli TOC Log |
| 2330-0530 | | Annex | Annex receives sporadic SAF and RPGs | |
| 2336.24 | 2338.28 | Annex | Mercedes G Series Wagon returns to Annex | Annex 6, 8, 13, 14 |
| 2340.52 | 2342.56 | Annex | Possible flare or tracer round passes overhead to North | Annex 10 |
| 2342.56 | | USSMC | Possible flare or tracer round x2 passes overhead - moving west to east. | USSMC 6 |
| 2345.46 | 2347.50 | Annex | Mercedes G Series Wagon moved to physically block primary entrance into Annex. | Annex 8 |
| 2345.53 | | USSMC | Unknown armed intruders (presumed rioters/looters) walk north from C3 Gate. | USSMC 9 |

| 2346.54 | | USSMC | Armed Intruders approach TOC, loot FAVs | USSMC 6 |
|---|---|---|---|---|
| 2348.40 | | USSMC | Camera 6 for USSMC TOC goes offline | USSMC 6 |
| 2349.09 | | USSMC | A mix of armed and unarmed intruders enter TOC | USSMC 1 |
| 2351.42 onward | | USSMC | Armed and Unarmed Intruders begin removing gear and papers from TOC. | USSMC 1 |
| 2354.40 | | USSMC | QRF / Guest House shows new or renewed fire. | USSMC 4 |
| 2355.40 | | USSMC | Camera 9 covering the C3 Drive goes offline | USSMC 9 |

## 12 September 2012

| 0001.24 | | USSMC | FAV Toyota Land Cruiser stolen from vicinity of TOC | USSMC 1 |
|---|---|---|---|---|
| 0003.17 - 0031.33 | | USSMC | Cameras 1, 4 go offline for approx 28 min | USSMC 1, 4 |
| 0032.49 | 0034.53 | Annex | Individuals moving in far east field | Annex 3 |
| 0032.53 | 0034.57 | Annex | SAF originating (probable) NE | Annex 3 |
| 0033.15 | 0035.19 | Annex | SAF destroys flood light near NE corner | Annex 3 |
| 0034.27 | 0036.31 | Annex | Individual approach perimeter wall from east field. | Annex 2 |
| 0034.35 | 0036.39 | Annex | Possible IED or RPG near NE perimeter corner | Annex 3, 4, 10, 2, 5 |
| 0034.38 | 0036.42 | Annex | Armed Unknown Individual approaches perimeter wall from east field. | Annex 3 |
| 0035.08 | 0037.12 | Annex | Armed Unknown Individual departs perimeter wall from east field. | Annex 3 |
| 0035.51 | | USSMC | Flash of Light visible - east side of TOC. Likely beginning of vehicle fire. | USSMC 1 |
| 0037.02 | | USSMC | Unknown event occurs inside TOC (likely beginning of fire) which causes large crowd of intruders to attempt to flee the building. | USSMC 1 |
| 0037.07 | | USSMC | 1st of 3 explosions from within Villa C | USSMC 12 |
| 0037.25 | | USSMC | 2nd of 3 explosions from within Villa C | USSMC 12 |
| 0037.45 | | USSMC | 3rd of 3 explosions from within Villa C | USSMC 12 |
| 0037.45 | | USSMC | Smoke visible eminating from TOC | USSMC 1 |
| 0038.16 | | USSMC | Camera 12 for C1 Drive goes offline | USSMC 12 |
| 0038.16 - 0039.48 | | USSMC | Camera 1 goes offline for 1 min, 32 sec. | USSMC 1 |
| 0038.22 | 0040.26 | Annex | Flashlight by white sedan in east field and SAF near NE corner of perimeter wall | Annex 3, 10 |
| 0039.33 | 0041.37 | Annex | Sustained SAF and unknown explosive shot impacts on east side of perimeter wall. Again at 0039.57 | Annex 3 |
| 0043.59 | | USSMC | Large explosion in vicinity of Villa B | USSMC 1 |

| | | | | |
|---|---|---|---|---|
| 0045.07 | | USSMC | Large explosion in vicinity of Villa B | USSMC 1 |
| 0048.18 | | USSMC | Intruder disables Camera 5 | USSMC 5 |
| 0052.38 | | USSMC | White Crewcab Pickup (probable Toyota Helix) heading to SW - towing black SUV (possibly Mercedes G5) | USSMC 1 |
| 0057.47 | 0059.51 | Annex | Flashlight visible on tree line in east field. | Annex 3 |
| 0059.50 | | USSMC | Small white subcompact car turns around between TOC and Villa B | USSMC 1 |
| 0108.38 | 0110.42 | Annex | Likely RPG fired from east field. Likely strikes Bldg B. | Annex 3, 2 |
| 0110.31 | 0112.35 | Annex | SAF impacts on east side of perimeter wall | Annex 3 |
| 0111.03 | 0113.07 | Annex | SAF near NE corner of perimeter wall | Annex 3 |
| 0111.15 | 0113.19 | Annex | Annex Cameras 11 and 13 go offline | Annex 11, 13 |
| 0111.30 | 0113.34 | Annex | Likely Wire-Guided Munition hits compound from east field. | Annex 3 |
| 0111.50 | 0113.54 | Annex | Possible richocet or returned fire from Annex personnel - Impacts near white sedan in east field. | Annex 3, 2 |
| 0112.11 | 0114.15 | Annex | Sustained SAF | Annex 3, 2 |
| 0146.50 | 0148.54 | Annex | Dark, small SUV/Hatchback staged due east of Annex on south road; vehicle drives by at 0148.30, U-turns, and drives by again before departing camera view. | Annex 6 |
| 0149.19 | 0151.23 | Annex | Unknown Individual - White T-shirt, Blue running pants, emerges from villa | Annex 1, 6, 12 |
| 0150.42 | 0152.46 | Annex | Unknown individual from villa meets unknown male - white capris, white tanktop, carrying cell phone. This 2nd individual walks down to Annex and back at 0153.35 | Annex 1, 6, 12 |
| 0156.24 | 0158.28 | Annex | Multiple individuals seen moving through sheep herd due north of Annex. Probable surveillance. No weapons visible. Cellphones in use. | Annex 10 |
| 0203 | | Benghazi Unknown | U.S. Embassy receives call from unknown individual stating that individual matching Ambassador's description is currently in hospital. | Tripoli TOC Log |
| 0203-0415 Approx | | Annex | ⬚ tasks ⬚ to obtain info on possible location of STEVENS at hospital | ⬚ |
| 0238.18 | 0240.22 | Annex | Annex personnel drop glow stick in front of main entrance. | Annex 14 |
| 0415 | | Benghazi Unknown | ⬚ notifies ⬚ that STEVENS is KIA | ⬚ |

| 0503.00 | 0505.04 | Annex | Unidentified LN Motorcade (Likely Feb 17 Martyrs' Brigade) arrives and parks in front of annex, 10-12 vehicles, some with markings and police lights. Approx. 6 AmCits - armed and w/ body armor. Presumably the QRF-Medical Team from Tripoli. | Annex 6, 14 |
|---|---|---|---|---|
| 0515.31 | 0517.35 | Annex | Motorcade car alarms appear to go off. Drivers remove vehicles from the scene with great haste (likely due to sound of mortar launching or arriving.) | Annex 1, 6, 12 |
| 0515.36 | 0517.40 | Annex | Likely first mortar impacts against exterior of north perimeter wall. | Annex 4, 5, 7, 9 |
| 0515.56 | 0518.00 | Annex | Cameras 1, 3, 4, 2, and 10 go off line | Annex 1, 3, 4, 2, 10 |
| 0515.57 | 0518.01 | Annex | Likely second mortar impacts against or just inside of north perimeter wall. | Annex 5 |
| 0516.04 | 0518.08 | Annex | Multiple tracer rounds pass east to west along north perimeter wall. | Annex 5 |
| 0516.17 | 0518.21 | Annex | Likely third mortar impacts interior of compound; likely impacts on/near Bldg C. | Annex 5, 7 |
| 0516.28 | 0518.32 | Annex | Likely fourth mortar impacts interior of compound. | Annex 5, 7, 8 |
| 0516.36 | 0518.40 | Annex | Likely fifth mortar impacts against exterior of north perimeter wall. | Annex 5, 7, 9 |
| 0516.48 | 0518.52 | Annex | Camera 8 goes off line | Annex 8 |
| 0516.49 | 0518.53 | Annex | Likely sixth mortar impacts interior of compound. Camera 7 catches path of either a component or tracer round. | Annex 5, 7, 9 |
| 0554.58 | 0557.02 | Annex | Partial damage visible to Bldg. C | Annex 9 |
| 0614.00 | 0616.04 | Annex | Probable Feb 17 Martyrs' Brigade Militia motorcade arrives and stages in front of Annex. Approx. 30-60 vehicles, including technicals w/ mounted weapons. | Annex 6, 14 |
| 0632.33 | 0634.37 | Annex | Annex personnel evacuate in Annex vehicles w/ LN motorcade support. 8 vehicles including a flatbed and pick up truck with KIA and WIA. | Annex 6, 14 |
| 0635.40 | 0637.44 | Annex | Heavy smoke suddenly visible from vicinity of Bldg. C | Annex 7 |
| 0635.50 | 0637.54 | Annex | Annex Vehicle (Toyota Helix Pickup) departs Annex alone w/ 2 black gear bags. | Annex 14 |

571

| | | | | |
|---|---|---|---|---|
| | | | | DSCC Chronological Log |
| 0731 | | Benghazi Airport | 1st Aircraft departs Benghazi with [ ] [ ] and [ ] | |
| 0825 | | Benghazi Airport | [ ] receives body of STEVENS at Benghazi Airport | |
| 0838 | | Tripoli | 1st Aircraft arrives Tripoli | DSCC Chronological Log |
| 0954 | | Benghazi Airport | 2nd Aircraft departs Benghazi with [ ] and bodies of SMITH and STEVENS | DSCC Chronological Log |
| 1133 | | Tripoli | 2nd Aircraft arrives Tripoli | DSCC Chronological Log |

This timeline gives preference to time/date stamps over interview recollections where they conflict.

The following timeline, the "Timeline of Department of Defense Actions September 11–12, 2012," provides further detail about the Defense Department actions that occurred during the attack. This is a timeline of events compiled by the Defense Department. The timeline does not disclose when the forces were ready to deploy or when those forces actually moved.

Timeline of Department of Defense Actions on September 11-12, 2012
All times are Eastern Daylight Time (EDT, Washington, DC)
and Eastern European Time (EET, Benghazi)

Tuesday, September 11, 2012
EDT // EET

~3:42 pm // 9:42 pm    The incident starts at the facility in Benghazi.

3:59 pm // 9:59 pm    An unarmed, unmanned, surveillance aircraft is directed to reposition overhead the Benghazi facility.

4:32 pm // 10:32pm    The National Military Command Center at the Pentagon, after receiving initial reports of the incident from the State Department, notifies the Office of the Secretary of Defense and the Joint Staff. The information is quickly passed to Secretary Panetta and General Dempsey.

5:00 pm // 11:00pm    Secretary Panetta and General Dempsey attend a previously scheduled meeting with the President at the White House. The leaders discuss potential responses to the emerging situation.

5:10 pm // 11:10 pm    The diverted surveillance aircraft arrives on station over the Benghazi facility.

~5:30 pm // 11:30 pm    All surviving American personnel have departed the facility.

6:00-8:00 pm //
12:00-2:00 am    Secretary Panetta convenes a series of meetings in the Pentagon with senior officials including General Dempsey and General Ham. They discuss additional response options for Benghazi and for the potential outbreak of further violence throughout the region, particularly in Tunis, Tripoli, Cairo, and Sana'a.
During these meetings, Secretary Panetta directs (provides verbal authorization) the following actions:

1) A Fleet Antiterrorism Security Team (FAST) platoon, stationed in Rota, Spain, to prepare to deploy to Benghazi, and a second FAST platoon, also stationed in Rota, Spain, to prepare to deploy to the Embassy in Tripoli.
2) A EUCOM special operations force, which is training in Central Europe, to prepare to deploy to an intermediate staging base in southern Europe.
3) A special operations force based in the United States to prepare to deploy to an intermediate staging base in southern Europe.

During this period, actions are verbally conveyed from the Pentagon to the affected Combatant Commands in order to expedite movement of forces upon receipt of formal authorization.

~6:30 pm // 12:30 am    A six-man security team from U.S. Embassy Tripoli, including two DoD personnel, departs for Benghazi.

~7:30 pm // 1:30 am    The American security team from Tripoli lands in Benghazi.

~8:30pm // 2:30 am    The National Military Command Center conducts a Benghazi Conference Call with representatives from AFRICOM, EUCOM, CENTCOM, TRANSCOM, SOCOM, and the four services.

8:39pm // 2:39 am    As ordered by Secretary Panetta, the National Military Command Center transmits formal authorization for the two FAST platoons, and associated equipment, to prepare to deploy and for the EUCOM special operations force, and associated equipment, to move to an intermediate staging base in southern Europe.

8:53pm // 2:53 am    As ordered by Secretary Panetta, the National Military Command Center transmits formal authorization to deploy a special operations force, and associated equipment, from the United States to an intermediate staging base in southern Europe.

~11:00 pm // 5:00 am    A second, unmanned, unarmed surveillance aircraft is directed to relieve the initial asset still over Benghazi.

~11:15 pm // 5:15 am    The second facility in Benghazi comes under mortar and rocket propelled grenade fire.

Wednesday, September 12, 2012

12:05 am // 6:05am    AFRICOM orders a C-17 aircraft in Germany to prepare to deploy to Libya to evacuate Americans.

~1:40 am // 7:40 am    The first wave of American personnel depart Benghazi for Tripoli via airplane.

~4:00 am // 10:00 am    The second wave of Americans, including the fallen, depart Benghazi for Tripoli via airplane.

8:15 am // 2:15 pm    The C-17 departs Germany en route Tripoli to evacuate Americans.

1:17 pm // 7:17 pm    The C-17 departs Tripoli en route Ramstein, Germany with the American personnel and the remains of Ambassador Stevens, Sean Smith, Tyrone Woods, and Glen Doherty.

1:57 pm // 7:57 pm    The EUCOM special operations force, and associated equipment, arrives at an intermediate staging base in southern Europe.

2:56 pm // 8:56 pm    The FAST platoon, and associated equipment, arrives in Tripoli.

3:28 pm // 9:28 pm    The special operations force deployed from the United States, and associated equipment, arrives at an intermediate staging base in southern Europe.

4:19 pm // 10:19 pm    The C-17 arrives in Ramstein, Germany.

# APPENDIX H:

## The September 12 Situation Report and the President's Daily Brief

The very first written piece produced by CIA analysts regarding the Benghazi attacks was an overnight Situation Report written very early in the morning on September 12, 2012. This piece included the line "the presence of armed assailants from the outset suggests this was an intentional assault and not the escalation of a peaceful protest." While that line was correct—the attacks were an intentional assault and not the escalation of a peaceful protest—Michael Morell, Deputy Director, Central Intelligence Agency, noted it was a "crucial error that [came] back to haunt [the CIA]."[1] This was an error, according to Morell, because that line was not written by analysts but rather a "senior editor" who "believed there needed to be some sort of bottom line" in the piece.[2] Morell labeled it a "bureaucratic screw-up" and claims that since similar language did not appear in the CIA assessment the following day, September 13, it was evidence to critics that "the intelligence community was politicizing the analysis."[3]

Though Morell learned this information second-hand[4] and put it in his book, the Select Committee spoke directly to individuals with first-hand accounting of the events. In reality, the "senior editor" was the Executive Coordinator of the Presidential Daily Brief; she included the language about the intentional assault and not the escalation of a peaceful protest; and this "bureaucratic screw-up" resulted in this individual taking the piece to the White House, presenting it to Jacob Lew, Chief of Staff to the President, and delivering it to an usher to give to the President.

### Insertion of the Language

The Executive Coordinator described to the Committee when she first saw the September 12 update:

> A: So the analysts came in to brief me—I don't remember what time that was, but my guess is probably somewhere between 3 and 4. And the piece that he gave to me was much longer than this.

---

[1] MICHAEL MORELL, THE GREAT WAR OF OUR TIME: THE CIA'S FIGHT AGAINST TERRORISM—FROM AL-QA'IDA TO ISIS 217 (2015) [hereinafter MORELL].

[2] Testimony of Michael Morell, Deputy Dir., Central Intelligence Agency, Tr. at 25 (Sept. 28, 2015) [hereinafter Morell Testimony] (on file with the Committee).

[3] MORELL, *supra* note 1, at 218.

[4] Morell Testimony at 28.

And we had a difference of opinion on one piece of the intelligence. He believed that this was a spontaneous event and was not open to the idea that it wasn't a spontaneous event. And I disagreed because, you know, I had 20 years of Army experience. You know, this is the military person in me. And I said, I just can't buy that something that's, you know, this coordinated, this organized, and this sophisticated was something that they just, you know, did on, you know, the spur of the moment. I said, we have to consider the fact that that might not be the case.

He had a lot of good arguments. You know, it was the anniversary of 9/11, there was the video in Cairo, there were a number of other things happening that, you know, would seem to suggest that it was spontaneous. But just being military and seeing, you know, what we were seeing in the traffic, I was like, I don't think that this is—I don't think we can discount the possibility that this was a, you know, coordinated, organized, preplanned attack.

Q: When you say when you were seeing what you were seeing in the traffic, what does that mean?

A: So the things they were talking about, how organized that it was, in the press reporting. There was a lot of press that was coming back and talking about, you know, like, how they were breaching and, you know, like, how it was sort of phased, right? It was coming across to me, reading, you know, the open press at the time, that this was a phased attack. And I would be very surprised if a phased attack was something that was just, all of a sudden, you know, "Hey, guess what? Let's go have an attack today because these other things are happening." I don't think that—that just didn't make sense to me.[5]

While the analyst believed it was a spontaneous event, given her experience the Executive Coordinator believed the piece needed to leave open the possibility that something else occurred other than a spontaneous event. She testified:

Q: You said there was a disagreement between you and the analyst. A piece came in; it was lengthy. You wanted to cut it down because that's what you normally do. Can you describe a little bit more about the disagreement that you had?

A: Well, that was really it. Like, he was pretty convinced that this was a spontaneous attack, that it was, you know, as a result of this confluence of events—the 9/11 anniversary, the video being released, the protest in Cairo. [**redacted text**].

And, to me, that wasn't enough. I was like—like I said, just my gut feeling. I said, we need to leave the door open

---

[5] Testimony of the President's Daily Briefer, Office of Dir. of Nat'l Intelligence, Tr. at 24–26 (Apr. 29, 2016) [hereinafter PDB Testimony] (on file with the Committee).

for the possibility that it might not have been spontaneous.[6]

The manager of the analysts testified that her analysts did not
agree with this approach and that the disagreement with the Executive Coordinator became hostile:

> The POTUS coordinator, according to my two analysts,
> who I trust and continue to trust, was that they got into
> an argument, which is highly unusual, with the POTUS
> coordinator, that was actually quite hostile. And she in-
> sisted that based on her personal experience of 15 or how-
> ever many years as a captain in the Air National Guard,
> that there was no way that was true.[7]

According to the manager of the analysts, none of her analysts
believed the sentence regarding an intentional assault should have
been included. The manager testified:

> A: And so the POTUS coordinator inserted this sentence
> because she felt strongly that it was an intentional assault
> against our consulate.
>
> Q: And——
>
> A: But there was no—nothing to base that on, no report-
> ing.
>
> Q: And that view is the view of that single editor. Is that
> right?
>
> A: Yes.
>
> Q: Was there anyone—any of the analysts on your team
> that thought that sentence should have been included?
>
> A: No.
>
> Q: And the reason your team and your analysts felt so
> strongly was because there was no reporting to support
> that. Is that correct?
>
> A: Correct. We just—you can't make a call without an evi-
> dentiary base to support it.[8]

However, without solid evidence pointing in either direction—
spontaneous or not—the Executive Coordinator was sure to be
careful with her language. She merely wanted to leave open the
possibility that it was an intentional assault and the language she
chose reflected that possibility—not a conclusion. She told the Committee:

> Q: —your choice of the word "suggests," is that to couch
> it——
>
> A: Yes.

---

[6] *Id.* at 28.
[7] Testimony of **[redacted text]** Team Chief, Office of Terrorism Analysis, Central Intelligence
Agency, Tr. at 32 (Feb. 10, 2016) [hereinafter **[redacted text]** Team Chief Testimony].
[8] *Id.* at 100–101.

Q: —to say that this may have happened, as opposed to it definitively happened?

A: Correct.

Q: Okay. And was that a deliberate ——

A: It was leaving the door open that this is what it suggests, but that doesn't mean this is what it is.[9]

The analysts and the Executive Coordinator were not able to reach a consensus on the language in the piece. The analysts, who went up to the 7th Floor of the CIA headquarters to brief the Executive Coordinator on the piece, returned to their desks. The Executive Coordinator testified:

Q: Okay. And was there a resolution between you and him——

A: Not really.

Q: —on how to proceed?

A: No.

Q: No. Okay. So how did your conversation or interactions with him end?

A: I told him I would think about, you know, what he had said. And I said, you know, I will to talk to somebody.[10]

The Executive Coordinator, however, did not make the decision to include the language of an intentional assault on her own, and she did not do it in a vacuum based solely on her experience. Members of her staff, which numbered roughly 15, talked with individuals outside CIA headquarters about what was going on. She told the Committee:

Q: In terms of picking up the phone and calling anybody outside of the building, is that something you did to acquire information?

A: We did. Yes.[11]

She also discussed the matter with another analyst who had expertise in regional issues. The Executive Coordinator testified:

We had—I was very lucky because we had another—we had a MENA analyst that was a PDB briefer. She was the, I want to say, the SecDef briefer. And so I went over and I talked to her and I said, "Hey, this is what the analyst says. Here's my opinion. You know, what are your thoughts, having covered this area, you know, pretty extensively in your career?" And she agreed with me.

We discussed it, we had a conversation about it and—you know. And so I made the decision to change the wording

[9] PDB Testimony at 37.
[10] Id. at 29.
[11] Id. at 26.

to make sure that we at least addressed the possibility that this was a planned attack.[12]

She also testified:

A: There was a lot of discourse about this at the PDB. I mean, the other PDB briefers and I, that's the only resource I have at the time. And I never would make an assessment all on my own and just be like, this is it. I mean, we would do——

Q: I understand.

A: We talk about it, we're sounding boards for each other. So there was a lot of discussion. And, yes, I'm sure that the supervisor of the young man who wrote this, we had that conversation. Like, are you sure that this is what you want to say. And yes, when I wrote this, I didn't feel like I was saying you're wrong and I'm right. All I was trying to do was say, look, we need to leave the door open in case this is not a spontaneous attack. We want to be able to wait until there's more information, and so that's why I use the word "suggests." I didn't say this is an intentional assault. It suggests that it is.

The manager of the analysts who disagreed with the Executive Coordinator, however, concedes that the Executive Coordinator was right with her analysis. She testified:

Q: And she was right?

A: In the event, yes, she was right.[13]

Similarly, Michael Morell concedes the sentence was accurate. He testified:

Q: So the sentence ended up being accurate?

A: Yeah. Absolutely.[14]

### The President's Daily Brief

When the Executive Coordinator finished inserting the accurate sentence regarding the "intentional assault and not the escalation of a peaceful protest" into the September 12 piece, she put it into the "book" she prepared each day for the President and his Chief of Staff.[15] This "book" is otherwise known as the President's Daily Brief, or the PDB.

Normally, upon completion of the PDB, the Executive Coordinator would travel to the White House, brief the Chief of Staff, and if the President required a briefing, she would brief the President. She testified:

So during the weeks that I produced the PDB, I would produce it, and then they would drive me to the White

---

[12] *Id.* at 29.
[13] Testimony of Dir. of the Office of Terrorism Analysis, Central Intelligence Agency, Tr. at 23 (Nov. 13, 2015) [hereinafter OTA Director Testimony] (on file with the Committee).
[14] Morell Testimony at 25.
[15] PDB Testimony at 41.

House, and I would produce—or I would brief Jack Lew first, who was the Chief of Staff. And if the President required a brief during that day or chose to take a brief, then I would give him a brief, and if not, then his briefer— then the DNI would brief him.

When we were on travel, I always briefed the President. That was my responsibility whenever we would fly.[16]

On September 12, 2012, the morning after the Benghazi attacks, the Executive Coordinator—the individual presenting the President with his Presidential Daily Brief—traveled to the White House. That day, however, she did not present the PDB to the President.[17] Instead, she gave it to an usher. She testified she presented the PDB—with the accurate sentence regarding the "intentional assault and not the escalation of a peaceful protest"—to Lew:

A: So it depends. If we're traveling, then I present it to the President personally. And if he has questions—usually the only questions he usually asks——

Lawyer. We're not going to talk about what the President said or your conversations with him.

A: Okay. So if we're in town and we're not traveling then I bring it to the White House, and I personally brief Jack Lew. And I hand the President's book to the usher, and the usher presents it to the President.

Q: So normally in Washington, when you're here in town, you're not sitting across from the President, him looking at the book, and he may be asking you questions?

A: No.

Q: How did it happen on the 12th that day?

A: I was here. So we were not traveling yet. We were in D.C. So I would have—I had a driver, and the driver drives me to the White House. I drop off the book first with the usher and then I go down and I brief Jack Lew.

Q: Okay. And what time was that on the 12th?

A: So we always arrive by 7:00, and so it would've been around 7:00. I mean, I'm assuming around 7:00.

Q: So that day at 7:00, the booklet that has been put together, you take it to the White House, you visit with Jack Lew and then someone walked it into——

A: No. First we give the brief to the usher. So my driver drops me off at the front gate. I go through——

Q: You actually physically hand the document—or the material.

A: Yeah, I physically hand the material to the usher and then I walk back down with my briefcase and go see Jack Lew and wait for him and then I brief him.

[16] *Id.* at 6.
[17] *Id.* at 41.

Q: Okay. And with Mr. Lew, did you talk about this SITREP?

Lawyer: We're not going to discuss what specific information was provided to any White House staff in any PDB.

Q: But you did talk with Mr. Lew that day?

A: I did.[18]

### Fallout

Morell labeled the insertion of the language by the Executive Coordinator a "bureaucratic screw-up." This language made it into a piece that was put in the President's Daily Brief, which was briefed to Lew, and possibly shared with the President. Such a "bureaucratic screw-up," therefore, has far reaching implications if it occurs with any regularity.

Michael Morell told the Committee that what occurred was a "big no-no." He testified:

> She was, I'm told, a long-time military analyst with some expertise in military matters, no expertise in North Africa and no expertise in this particular incident. She added that, right? That's a no-no, that's a no-no in the review process business.[19]

The manager of the analysts who disagreed with the Executive Coordinator called what occurred an analytic "cardinal sin." She testified:

> What she did was, frankly, in the analytic world, kind of a cardinal sin. I mean, the job of the POTUS coordinator—so we had the two analysts stay overnight. Their job is to copy edit these things and make sure that if there is some analysis in there, that the evidentiary techs sort of hang together; that it actually makes sense because it does go to the—it's a big deal. I mean, it goes to very senior policymakers. So——[20]

The OTA Director also said that what occurred was a problem:

> Q: Okay. Is that a problem that the senior DNI editor had the final sign-off on this as opposed to the analysts, and that person is inserting something in there that the analysts adamantly disagree with?
>
> A: In my personal view, yes.[21]

Despite this "bureaucratic screw-up"—which occurred in relation to the Benghazi attacks, one of the few, if only, times in history outside scrutiny has ever been applied to the PDB process—Morell and others at the CIA told the Committee this occurs infrequently. Morell testified:

> Q: So from my perspective, I'm very new to this arena, it seems like it's a problem that you have these rigorous processes in place, and on this particular occasion a piece

---

[18] *Id.* at 66–67.
[19] Morell Testimony at 25.
[20] **[Redacted text]** Team Chief Testimony at 30–31.
[21] OTA Director Testimony at 43.

is going before the President and somebody inserts a sentence that substantively changes the meaning of a bullet point without any additional review by the analysts who wrote the piece.

A: Yes. You're absolutely right.

Q: That's a problem in your eyes as well?

A: Yes.

Q: And how often does something like that occur?

A: Not very. You know, in my experience, once or twice a year.[22]

The manager of the analysts who disagreed with the Executive Coordinator testified:

Q: Is that something that in your 8 years prior you had ever seen or heard of happening?

A: No.[23]

She also testified:

A: Oh, I'm sure I did, yeah. I mean, it was unheard of and it hasn't happened since.

Q: Okay.

A: It's a big deal.[24]

Morell, himself once the head of the PDB staff, told the Committee how he would have responded if a senior editor had made such a substantive edit over the objections of the analysts:

A: And this—you know, I ran—I've ran the PDB staff, right, as part of the jobs I had. I would have reprimanded, orally reprimanded, not in a formal sense, right——

Q: Sure.

A: —called this person in my office and said, you know, what happened? And if it turned out to be exactly what I just explained to you, I would have said, don't ever do that again.[25]

Morell also suggested how to ensure such a "bureaucratic screwup" doesn't happen in the future. He told the Committee:

Q: Is there any way to prevent these types of insertions by senior reviewers in the future?

A: Well, I said, it doesn't happen very often, right.

Q: But it happened in this case, though.

A: So it's not a huge problem, right, it doesn't happen very often. The way you prevent it is twofold, right? You make it very clear when somebody shows up to the PDB staff

---

[22] Morell Testimony at 25–26.
[23] **[Redacted text]** Team Chief Testimony at 30–31.
[24] **[Redacted text]** Team Chief Testimony at 35–36.
[25] Morell Testimony at 26.

what their responsibilities are and what their responsibilities are not, you're not the analyst. And, two, when something—when something does happen, even something very minor, right, you make it very clear then that they overstepped their bounds. That's how you prevent it.[26]

The Executive Coordinator, however, has a different point of view than Morell, the OTA Director, and the manager of the analysts. She did not view this as a "bureaucratic screw-up" at all, but rather exactly the job she was supposed to be doing. She acknowledged the disagreement with the analysts the night of the Benghazi attacks, testifying:

> Q: Okay. And I know we talked about it, but how unusual, I guess, was this disagreement, this type of disagreement?

> A: It was pretty unusual. Most of the time, we were able to, you know, just sort of agree on language, and they'll gave you a face like, "Okay," they'll roll their eyes, they'll be like, "All right, you know, that's not as strong of language as I would like." But, you know, a lot of times, you know, we soften the language because we just don't know for sure. So, you know, we'll change from, you know, "believe with high confidence" to—I'm like, do you really believe with high confidence, or do you really think that's maybe medium confidence?

> And I sort of saw my role as, you know, like, a mentor because I'd been in intelligence for 20 years. So a lot of times, you know, I would tell the analysts, you know, this is good tradecraft, but it will be better analysis if you take into consideration these things which you may or may not have considered.[27]

However, the fact that she inserted language into the piece was not a "no-no" or a "cardinal sin," but rather something that was ultimately her decision, not the analysts'. This directly contradicts what Morell said about the Executive Coordinator overstepping her bounds. She testified:

> But I do know that, you know, when I talked to [senior CIA official], you know, in the interview process and also, you know, subsequent to that, he basically said that you're the PDB briefer, you are the last, you know, line of defense and, you know, it's your call. So if there's something in there that, you know, bothers you, you know, coordinate it out, and then if you can't come to an agreement, it's your, you know, responsibility. So I did not take that lightly.[28]

Since it was a responsibility she did not take lightly, she only modified such language when there was ample evidence to support it. She told the Committee:

---

[26] *Id.* at 27.
[27] PDB Testimony at 38.
[28] *Id.* at 31.

But yes. I mean, we don't—I rarely ever—in fact, I can't remember any time that I've ever made, you know, a call just based on press reporting, so I'm sure there was other intelligence.[29]

Perhaps as a result of the direction she was given during her interview, the Executive Coordinator experienced no fallout or reprimand as a result of her actions the night of the Benghazi attacks. She testified:

Q: Okay. Were you told by anybody never to do that again?

A: No.

Q: Okay. Were you told by anybody that what you did was a big no-no?

A: No.[30]

As a matter of fact, she and her PDB colleagues agreed that her actions—inserting the language about the intentional assault and not the escalation of a peaceful protest—were the right call. She testified:

Q: Okay. So you said you have a roundtable. I mean, who is comprised, just roughly, of that roundtable?

A: So it's all the PDB briefers. Some weren't there because a lot of times their principals, like, keep them there or, you know, they don't get back in time. But also it's whoever—it'll be either [CIA individual] or [State Department individual] or [DIA individual] that's leading it.

Q: So I just want to make sure I understand your testimony correctly. You were told by someone at the roundtable that the analysts were upset, but you say that's too harsh a word——

A: Yeah.

Q: —for lack of a better word.

A: I can't think of a better—it was somewhere in between, like, upset and——

Q: Sure. Sure.

A: Yeah.

Q: There was discussion. It seemed to be—the consensus was that it was the right call.

A: Yes.

Q: Okay. The consensus by those at the roundtable.

A: At the roundtable, yes.[31]

One of the briefers at the roundtable was an analyst who came from the Middle East and North African desk at the CIA, and was

---

[29] Id. at 26.

[30] Id. at 44.

[31] Id. at 43–44.

a colleague of the analysts who disagreed with the Executive Coordinator the night of the attack.[32]

The testimony received by the Committee on this topic presents a dichotomy between two parties. On the one hand, CIA personnel present a picture that what occurred was a major error and breach of protocol. On the other hand, the Executive Coordinator, who works for ODNI, testified she was told when she took the job that she had the final call on language in analytic pieces, though changing substantive language was something exercised judiciously. Since the Benghazi attacks, the analysts have been instructed to stay with the PDB editors until the final piece is with the ODNI official.[33] Given how the situation unfolded early in the morning of September 12, 2012, it is unclear how this new guidance would have altered that particular outcome.

Two of the first pieces produced by the CIA analysts in the wake of the Benghazi attacks contained errors either in process or substance. Both of these pieces became part of the President's Daily Brief. While the Committee only examined intelligence pieces regarding the Benghazi attacks, discovering errors in two pieces—on successive days, on one single topic—that became part of the President's Daily Brief is extremely problematic for what should be an airtight process. Whether these errors are simply a coincidence or part of a larger systemic issue is unknown. The September 12 piece, along with the egregious editing and sourcing errors surrounding the September 13 WIRe, discussed in detail above, raise major analytic tradecraft issues that require serious examination but are beyond the purview of this Committee.

---

[32] *Id.* at 42.
[33] OTA Director Testimony at 43.

# APPENDIX I:

# Witnesses Interviewed by the Committee

## State Department Officials

### DIPLOMATIC SECURITY AGENTS

Of the more than 50 agents who served temporary assignments of approximately 30–45 days in Benghazi, 19 were interviewed.[1] Of this 19, four were agents who survived the attacks on September 11, 2012, and who had not been previously interviewed by any committee of Congress. The fifth survivor had been interviewed previously by the House Committee on Oversight and Government Reform.

The five agents from Diplomatic Security who were in Benghazi on the night of the attacks deserve the enduring gratitude of all Americans for their heroic efforts on the night of the attacks. The Committee commends their dedication to their country, the selflessness shown to their colleagues, and the bravery and astuteness they demonstrated during the attacks.

Fifteen other agents interviewed by the Select Committee served in Benghazi between April 2011 and September 2012. Each agent served at different times and therefore was able to provide the Committee with insight on the continuing spectrum of security challenges faced in Benghazi during the 18 months the United States maintained a presence. The Committee notes that these agents, as well as those not interviewed, served in Benghazi under difficult circumstances. Their ability to protect U.S. government personnel under such circumstances is a testament to the commitment each has to this country and to their colleagues. They all deserve our thanks.

Apart from those who served in Benghazi, the Committee interviewed other agents and employees of the Diplomatic Security Service. One agent was in the Diplomatic Security Command Center on the day of the attacks. Another agent coordinated staffing assignments for Benghazi, among other things. The Committee interviewed the former Deputy Assistant Secretary for International Programs who was involved in staffing the Benghazi Mission. The Committee also interviewed two persons who dealt with the physical security of the facilities, one was a physical security

---

[1] Out of security and privacy concerns, the Committee has not used the names of certain executive employees, and has, instead, used the person's title or some other descriptor to identify the person. For example, given security concerns facing Diplomatic Security agents who serve around the world—often in dangerous places—the Committee assigned numbers to these agents. Throughout the report, and in this appendix, the Committee listed the person's title or position held during the relevant time period.

specialist and the other was the Deputy Assistant Secretary for Countermeasures in 2011–2012.

*Attack Survivors*

**Diplomatic Security Agent #3**—Interviewed by the House Committee on Oversight and Government Reform on October 8, 2013: The fifth agent present in Benghazi on September 11, 2012. This Special Agent joined Diplomatic Security in 2009 and his first permanent or long-term overseas assignment was as an Assistant Regional Security Officer to Embassy Tripoli. He arrived in Tripoli in June 2012 and on August 30, 2012, was sent to Benghazi to be the head agent, or Acting Regional Security Officer.

**Diplomatic Security Agent #1**—March 6, 2015: Joined Diplomatic Security as a Special Agent in 2011 after eight years in the U.S. military, where he specialized in explosives disposal. Arrived in Tripoli in mid-August 2012 for a 60 day assignment. Traveled with Stevens and another agent to Benghazi on September 10, 2012.

**Diplomatic Security Agent #4**—March 16, 2015: Joined Diplomatic Security as a Special Agent in 2010 after serving approximately five years in the Army. He arrived in Benghazi in early to mid-August for a temporary assignment. He was on the roof at the Annex as the attacks continued and was severely injured by mortar fire.

**Diplomatic Security Agent #2**—March 19, 2015: Joined Diplomatic Security as a Special Agent in 2011 following seven-and-a-half years in the Army. Arrived in Tripoli in early August for a temporary assignment. Traveled with the Ambassador and another agent to Benghazi on September 10, 2012.

**Diplomatic Security Agent #5**—April 1, 2015: Joined Diplomatic Security as a Special Agent in 2011 following five years with the Navy, where he specialized in search and rescue operations. Arrived in Benghazi in early August for a temporary assignment. Secured the Ambassador and Sean Smith in the makeshift safe haven when the attacks began.

*Other Agents Assigned in Benghazi*

**Diplomatic Security Agent #6**—February 10, 2015: Headed the protective detail for Stevens when Stevens first went into Benghazi in April 2011. The agent met up with Stevens in Europe in mid-March and then traveled to Benghazi in early April and remained there until early May 2011.

**Diplomatic Security Agent #9**—February 12, 2015: Along with another agent, was sent to join the initial protective detail approximately two weeks after Stevens and his team arrived in Benghazi, bringing the number of agents in Stevens's protective detail up to 10.

**Diplomatic Security Agent #27**—February 19, 2015: Was the second agent sent to join the initial protective detail approximately two weeks after Stevens team arrived in Benghazi, bringing the number of agents in Steven's protective detail up to 10.

**Diplomatic Security Agent #18**—February 24, 2015: Joined Diplomatic Security in 1999 following ten years of prior military service. This agent was sent to Benghazi in late October 2011 for approximately 55 days to be the lead security agent.

**Diplomatic Security Agent #7**—February 26, 2015: A Special Agent since 1986, and in 2011 was the Director of the State Department's specialized tactical unit in Diplomatic Security, known as Mobile Security Deployment. This agent went to Benghazi in early May 2011 to take over as head of Stevens' protective detail, replacing the initial agent-in-charge. He was in Benghazi when the initial search for a State Department diplomatic and housing compound began.

**Diplomatic Security Agent #15**—March 12, 2015: Joined Diplomatic Security in 2001 and went to Benghazi in early January 2012 until mid-February. This agent was in Benghazi for the first anniversary of the revolution.

**Diplomatic Security Agent #22**—March 24, 2015: A Special Agent since 2012, he was in Benghazi from late May through the end of July 2012. He was present for the second attack against the compound wall, the attack against the British Ambassador, and the Libyan elections.

**Diplomatic Security Agent #10**—April 2, 2015: A Special Agent since 2009, this agent went to Benghazi for six weeks from late November 2011 through the end of the year. Before he left, there was a real concern that no agents would be in Benghazi in early January.

**Diplomatic Security Agent #12**—April 9, 2015: A Special Agent since 2006 following service in the Marine Corps. This agent was temporarily assigned in Benghazi from early February through March 2012.

**Diplomatic Security Agent #16**—April 13, 2015: Joined the Diplomatic Security Service in 2011 following both service in the Marine Corp and as a Special Agent with other federal law enforcement agencies. This agent was temporarily assigned to Benghazi from early March through mid-April 2012.

**Diplomatic Security Agent #8**—April 15, 2015: Special Agent with the Diplomatic Security who was in Benghazi from the end of July 2012 to the end of August 2012 as the Acting Regional Security Officer or lead agent.

**Diplomatic Security Agent #21**—May 19, 2015: A Special Agent with Diplomatic Security since 2003, was permanently assigned to Tripoli in summer 2012. In August 2012, he covered Benghazi for a short period of time and was back in Tripoli on the night of the attack.

**Diplomatic Security Agent #13**—May 21, 2015: A Special Agent since 1999 with former Marine Security Guard experience, was temporarily assigned to Benghazi from mid-September 2011 to late October. Initially he had 10 agents in his detail to protect Stevens and his staff.

**Diplomatic Security Agent #17**—August 21, 2015: A Special Agent since 1997, she was assigned to Benghazi as the lead agent from early April to the end of May 2012.

**Diplomatic Security Agent #29**—April 28, 2016: This agent was part of the initial eight-member protective detail for Stevens, arriving in Benghazi on April 5, 2011.

*Headquarter Special Agents*

**Lamb, Charlene**—January 7, 2016: Deputy Assistant Secretary for International Programs, Diplomatic Security. The International Programs section manages programs and policies that protect the Department of State's missions and personnel overseas.

**Smith, Gentry**—February 25, 2016: Deputy Assistant Secretary for Countermeasures, Diplomatic Security. The Countermeasures section is responsible for all the physical and technical security requirements for all U.S. diplomatic missions, both domestic and overseas, as well as manages the diplomatic courier operations for the State Department.

**Physical Security Specialist**—April 6, 2016: A Special Agent with Diplomatic Security until retirement in 2001, he returned to Diplomatic Security as a contractor working as a physical security specialist with agents assigned overseas, including Libya, on implementing physical security projects.

**Diplomatic Security Agent #30**—August 19, 2015: A Special Agent with Diplomatic Security since 2001, was assigned to the Diplomatic Security Command Center [DSCC] from 2011 through 2013 as the senior watch officer. The DSCC operates around the clock to monitor and report threat information concerning all U.S. diplomatic facilities worldwide.

PRINCIPAL OFFICERS WHO SERVED IN BENGHAZI

Following the departure of Stevens from Benghazi in late November 2011, the State Department sent a series of Foreign Service officers to Benghazi to conduct outreach with the rebel leaders and report on the political, economic and security situation in the eastern portion of Libya. The Committee interviewed four of the six individuals who served as the "Principal Officer" in Benghazi. Three who served the longest periods of time, ranging from 60–100 days, were interviewed. The fourth interviewed was in Benghazi for 13 days in early September 2012, and returned to Tripoli before the attacks.

**Principal Officer #1**—March 3, 2015: A Foreign Service officer since 1998, who was temporarily assigned to Benghazi from November 2011 to February 2012. Principal Officer #1 was the first principal officer assigned following the departure of Stevens from Benghazi.

**Principal Officer #2**—March 13, 2015: A Foreign Service officer since 2003 who was temporarily assigned to Benghazi from early March to mid-June 2012. This officer was present when an explosive was detonated at the compound wall and when there was an assassination attempt made against the British Ambassador. At times, the officer was protected by a single Diplomatic Security agent.

**Principal Officer #3**—March 26, 2015: A Foreign Service officer since 1991, he temporarily served as the Principal Officer in Benghazi from July through August 2012. He was present for the Libyan elections and then witnessed and reported on the declining security environment in Benghazi that followed.

**Principal Officer #4**—May 8, 2015: A Foreign Service officer since 2002, he went to Tripoli in June 2012 on a permanent assignment to be the political reporting officer. He served as the Principal Officer in Benghazi from September 1 through September 10, 2012, departing Benghazi on the morning of September 11. He returned to Tripoli and was present in the operations center during the attacks and following the attacks, met with the surviving agents.

### EMBASSY TRIPOLI

**Cretz, Gene**—July 31, 2015: Ambassador to Libya from December 2008 through May 2012. Returned to Washington, D.C., in December 2010 due to personal security concerns and returned to Libya in September 2011.

**Polaschik, Joan**—August 12, 2015: Deputy Chief of Mission for Libya from 2009 through mid-June 2012. With the departure of Ambassador Cretz in December 2010, she was the highest ranking Foreign Service officer in Libya, known as the Chargé d'Affaires or Chargé.

**Hicks, Gregory**—April 14, 2016: Deputy Chief of Mission for Libya, arriving in Libya on July 31, 2012.

### "MAIN STATE" OFFICIALS

*Bureau of Near Eastern Affairs*

**Feltman, Jeffrey**—December 8, 2015: Assistant Secretary of State for Near Eastern Affairs from August 2009 until his retirement in May 2012. In February 2008, he was appointed the Principal Deputy Assistant Secretary in the Bureau of Near Eastern Affairs and as of December 2008, served concurrently as Acting Assistant Secretary of State for the Bureau.

**Maxwell, Raymond**—March 8, 2016: Deputy Assistant Secretary of State for Near Eastern Affairs, Office of the Maghreb Affairs. The Maghreb Affairs Office, known as NEA/MAG, covers foreign policy issues for the North Africa countries of Morocco, Algeria, Tunisia, and Libya.

**Deputy Director, Office of Maghreb Affairs, Near Eastern Affairs Bureau**—December 17, 2015: A Foreign Service officer since 1999, served as the Deputy Director for the Office of Maghreb Affairs within the Near Eastern Affairs Bureau, known as NEA/MAG, from 2011 to 2013. NEA/MAG was responsible for oversight and coordination of diplomatic activities of the U.S. Government within the countries in the region.

**Senior Libyan Desk Officer, Office of Maghreb Affairs, Near Eastern Affairs Bureau**—November 18, 2015: A career Foreign

Service officer, served as the Senior Libya Desk officer in the Office of the Maghreb Affairs within the Near Eastern Affairs Bureau, known as NEA/MAG, from 2011 to 2014. NEA/MAG was responsible for diplomatic policy issues arising in the North Africa countries of Morocco, Algeria, Tunisia, and Libya.

**Spokesperson, Near Eastern Affairs Bureau**—October 9, 2015: A career Foreign Service officer who served as the spokesperson for the Near Eastern Affairs Bureau from 2011 to 2013.

**Senior Advisor for Strategic Communications, Near Eastern Affairs Bureau**—July 29, 2015: A career Foreign Service officer who, in 2012, served as deputy spokesperson for the Near Eastern Affairs Bureau and then transitioned in the Bureau to be the Senior Advisor for Strategic Communications.

**Post Management Officer for Libya**—July 23, 2015: From 2010 through June 2012, was the Post Management Officer or logistical officer for Libya within the Executive Office in the Near Eastern Affairs Bureau, known as NEA/SCA/EX. From 2011 through June 2012, this officer focused nearly exclusively on Libya matters. The Post Management Officer reports to the Executive Director or "EX" who is charged with overseeing all administrative and management activities for the bureau and for Foreign Service posts in the region and develops and executes programs for the bureau in support of substantive policy decisions.

## U.S. Mission to the United Nations

**DiCarlo, Rosemary**—August 11, 2015: From 2008 until retirement in September 2014, held various positions for the State Department at the U.S. Mission to the United Nations. The U.S. Mission to the United Nations [USUN] serves as the United States' delegation to the United Nations. At the time of the Benghazi attack, was the Deputy Permanent Representative (to Susan Rice), then the Permanent Representative to the USUN.

**Ryu, Rexon**—August 25, 2015: Deputy to the U.S. Ambassador to the United Nations, Susan Rice, and directed the Ambassador's Washington office at the State Department.

**Pelton, Erin**—February 11, 2016: At the time of the Benghazi attacks, was the communications director and spokesperson for the U.S. Permanent Representative to the United Nations, where she had been in that position less than two months. Immediately prior to this position, was director of communications and assistant press secretary for the National Security Council at the White House.

## Speechwriters

**Dan Schwerin**—October 9, 2015: Speechwriter for the Secretary of State between 2009 and early 2013.

**Megan Rooney**—October 9, 2015: Speechwriter for the Secretary of State between 2009 and early 2013.

*Records Management*

**Agency Records Officer**—June 30, 2015: At the time of the interview was the Division Chief of the Records and Archives Management Division and was the designated agency records officer for the Department of State.

**Director, Information Resource Management, Executive Secretariat, Office of the Secretary**—June 30, 2015: Until his retirement in November 2012, was the Director of the Office of Information Resource Management within the Office of the Secretary's Executive Secretariat, where he oversaw the information technology division exclusively used by the Office of the Secretary and senior leaders within the State Department.

**Pagliano, Bryan**—September 5, 2015: From May 2009 to February 2013, was a special advisor within the information technology section known as the Information Resource Management Bureau for bureaus and offices other than the Office of the Secretary. He continued to work as a contractor for the State Department until March 2016.

## CONTRACTORS

**Sterling Contractor #1**—February 26, 2016: Worked for Sterling International (now Sterling Global Operations) in Libya on a weapons removal and abatement program for the State Department. Was in Benghazi on the night of the attacks.

**Sterling Contractor #2**—March 31, 2016: Worked for Sterling International (now Sterling Global Operations) in Libya on a weapons removal and abatement program for the State Department. Was in Benghazi on the night of the attacks.

**Locally Employed Staff**—March 22, 2016: Was a contract employee in Benghazi, Libya for the State Department.

## OTHER

**Contracting Official**—August 27, 2015: A procurement and contracting specialist at the State Department, who in May 2012 began supporting Diplomatic Services and local guard programs. This official was involved in management of the contract with Blue Mountain Group for local guard service in Benghazi.

**Managing Director, Office of Management Policy, Rightsizing and Innovation**—March 4, 2016: Since 1997, has been with the Office of Management, Policy, Rightsizing and Innovation, an office that works directly for the Under Secretary for Management. Since 1999, has been assigned the duty of managing the Accountability Review Board [ARB] process. This official has worked on 11 ARBs, including the Benghazi ARB.

## SENIOR LEADERS

**Mills, Cheryl**—September 3, 2015: Chief of Staff and Counselor to the Secretary of State from May 2009 until February 2013.

**Sullivan, Jacob**—September 4, 2015: Served as Deputy Chief of Staff for Policy for the Secretary of State beginning in January

2009 and also served as the Director of Policy Planning beginning in February 2011. He left the State Department and both positions in February 2013.

**Abedin, Huma**—October 16, 2015: Served as Deputy Chief of Staff for Operations for the Secretary of State from January 2009 through February 2013.

**Nides, Thomas**—December 16, 2015: Joined the State Department in January 2011 to serve as the Deputy Secretary for Management and Resources, a position he held until February 2013. Similar to a chief operating officer, the Deputy Secretary for Management and Resources has overall responsibility for resource allocation and management activities at the State Department.

**Rice, Susan**—February 2, 2016: From January 2009 until July 2013, served as the U.S. Permanent Representative to the United Nations and a member of the President's Cabinet. The U.S. Mission to the United Nations serves as the United States' delegation to the United Nations.

**Kennedy, Patrick**—February 3, 2016: Has been the Under Secretary for Management since 2007 and has been a career Foreign Service officer since 1973. The Under Secretary for Management is responsible for finances, budgets and contracting, resources (both personnel and facilities), logistics, and security for Department of State overseas and domestic operations.

## OTHER COMMITTEES' ACTIVITIES

The Select Committee also had available transcripts of hearings, briefings, and interviews from other committees, including interview transcripts from:

Bacigalupo, James—Regional Director, Bureau of Near Eastern Affairs, Bureau of Diplomatic Security

Boswell, Eric—Assistant Secretary of State for Diplomatic Security

Bultrowicz, Scott—Director, Diplomatic Security Service and Principal Deputy Secretary of State for the Bureau of Diplomatic Security

Dibble, Elizabeth—Principal Deputy Assistant Secretary, Bureau of Near Eastern Affairs

Diplomatic Security Agent #3—Special Agent, Bureau of Diplomatic Security and Regional Security Officer in Benghazi, Libya

Diplomatic Security Agent #19—Special Agent, Bureau of Diplomatic Security who served temporarily in Benghazi

Diplomatic Security Agent #23—Special Agent, Bureau of Diplomatic Security and Regional Security Officer in Tripoli, Libya on the night of the attacks

Diplomatic Security Agent #24—Special Agent, Bureau of Diplomatic Security and former Regional Security Officer in Tripoli, Libya

Diplomatic Security Agent #25—Special Agent, Bureau of Diplomatic Security and Libya Desk Officer, International Programs, Bureau of Diplomatic Security

Hicks, Gregory—former Deputy Chief of Mission, Libya

Jones, Elizabeth—Acting Assistant Secretary, Bureau of Near Eastern Affairs

Lamb, Charlene—Deputy Assistant Secretary of State for International Programs, Bureau of Diplomatic Security

Lohman, Lee—Executive Director, Bureau of Near Eastern Affairs

Maxwell, Raymond—Deputy Assistant Secretary for Maghreb Affairs, Bureau of Near Eastern Affairs

Mullen, Michael (Adm.)—Vice Chairman, Benghazi Accountability Review Board

Nuland, Victoria—Spokesperson, Department of State

Pickering, Thomas—Chairman, Benghazi Accountability Review Board

Roebuck, William—Director, Office of Maghreb Affairs, Bureau of Near Eastern Affairs

Special Assistant to Under Secretary Patrick Kennedy

Sullivan, Jacob—Deputy Chief of Staff for Policy and Director, Office of Policy Planning

## Intelligence Community Officials

**CENTRAL INTELLIGENCE AGENCY—to be inserted following classification review**

*Headquarters*

**Petraeus, David**—January 6, 2016, and March 19, 2016: Director of the Central Intelligence Agency from September 2011 to November 2012. At the time of the attacks, the CIA had personnel in Benghazi and Tripoli. The CIA's Annex facility in Benghazi was attacked on September 11–12, 2012, following the attack on the State Department facility.

**Morell, Michael**—September 28, 2015: Joined the Central Intelligence Agency in 1980 and was its Deputy Director from May 2010 to August 2013. At the time of the attacks, the CIA had personnel in Benghazi and Tripoli. The CIA's Annex facility in Benghazi was attacked on September 11–12, 2012, following the attack on the State Department facility. Deputy Director Morell edited the highly criticized talking points that were developed after the attacks.

**Director, Office of Terrorism Analysis**—November 13, 2015: The Office of Terrorism Analysis, part of the CIA's Counterterrorism Center, develops and disseminates analytical pieces regarding known and suspected terrorist acts and actors. OTA developed and disseminated analytical reports immediately after the Benghazi attacks.

**Chief of Operations, Near East Division**—December 10, 2015: Head of the CIA's headquarter coordination and support office for operations in the Middle East and Africa, which included Libya.

**Team Chief, Office of Terrorism Analysis**—February 10, 2016: Leader of the team that produced analytical pieces. Was involved in the Benghazi post-attack analytical reporting.

*Benghazi*

**GRS #1**—May 22, 2015: A member of the Global Response Staff [GRS] who responded to the State Department facility when it was attacked and was present when the Annex facility was attacked.

**GRS #2**—May 27, 2015: A member of the GRS who was present when the Annex facility was attacked.

**GRS #3**—May 29, 2015: A member of the GRS who responded to the State Department facility when it was attacked and was present when the Annex facility was attacked.

**GRS #4**—March 1, 2016: A member of the GRS who responded to the State Department facility when it was attacked and was present when the Annex facility was attacked.

**GRS #5**—May 24, 2016: A member of the GRS who responded to the State Department facility when it was attacked and was present when the Annex facility was attacked.

**GRS-Team Lead**—April 19, 2016: The leader of the Benghazi Global Response Staff [GRS] who responded to the State Department facility when it was attacked and was present when the Annex facility was attacked.

**Chief of Base**—November 19, 2015: The head of the U.S.-based intelligence group at Benghazi Base who was present for the attacks on September 11–12, 2012.

**Deputy Chief of Base**—June 4, 2015: The second-in-command of the U.S.-based intelligence group at Benghazi Base and was present for the attacks on September 11–12, 2012.

**Officer A**—March 2, 2016: Part of the U.S.-based intelligence group at Benghazi Base and was present for the attacks on September 11–12, 2012.

**Officer B**—April 23, 2015: Part of the U.S.-based intelligence group at Benghazi Base but who had traveled from Benghazi on the morning of September 11, 2012.

**Officer C**—June 19, 2015: Part of the U.S.-based intelligence group at Benghazi Base and was present for the attacks on September 11–12, 2012.

*Tripoli*

**GRS Tripoli**—June 23, 2015: A member of the Tripoli-based Global Response Staff (GRS) who became part of Team Tripoli and responded to Benghazi when the State Department facility attacked and was present when the Annex Base in Benghazi was attacked.

**Chief of Station**—July 16, 2015: A Chief of Station is the lead CIA official stationed in a foreign country and is responsible for the U.S.-based intelligence group.

*Other*

**CIA Official**—June 2, 2015: In September 2012, this official was serving in Europe on the night of the attacks and played a role in responding to the attacks.

The Select Committee also had available to review information from the House Permanent Select Committee on Intelligence including transcripts of hearings, briefings, and interviews of agency heads, senior officials and other individuals from the Office of the Director of National Intelligence, Central Intelligence Agency, National Counterterrorism Center, Department of State, Department of Defense, National Security Agency, and Federal Bureau of Investigation.

### OFFICE OF THE DIRECTOR OF NATIONAL INTELLIGENCE

**Olsen, Matthew**—February 16, 2016: Director of the National Counterterrorism Center (NCTC) from August 2011 through July 2014. A part of the Office of the Director of National Intelligence, NCTC oversees analysts from other federal agencies, including the CIA, the FBI, and the Department of Defense to collect, analyze and disseminate counterterrorism threat information and intelligence.

**ODNI Analyst**—April 29, 2016: Was involved in the production of the first analytical piece generated in the wake of the Benghazi attacks.

### DEFENSE INTELLIGENCE AGENCY

**Flynn, Michael (Lt. Gen)**—September 29, 2015: Served as the Director of the Defense Intelligence Agency at the time of the attack. Provided information on the intelligence picture before and after the attack.

**Tripoli Analyst**—November 10, 2015: An analyst with the Defense Intelligence Agency who was assigned in Tripoli and present in Tripoli during the attacks and was involved in intelligence collection and reporting in Libya.

## Department of Defense

**Panetta, Leon**—January 8, 2016: Served as the Secretary of Defense at the time of the attacks. He provided information on the President's direction to him, which forces he ordered to deploy, and when he gave the order to deploy those forces.

**Bash, Jeremy**—January 13, 2016: Served as Chief of Staff to the Secretary of Defense and was a liaison between the Defense Department and the State Department. He provided information about which forces were identified to be deployed on the night of the attack. He also participated in a meeting with the White House and the State Department on the evening of September 11.

**Breedlove, Philip M. (Gen.)**—April 7, 2016: Served as the Commander of the United States Air Forces in Europe at the time of the attacks. He provided information regarding the available transport aircraft on the night of the attack, when those aircraft were ordered to deploy, and when those aircraft deployed.

**Ham, Carter (Gen.)**—June 8, 2016: Served as Commander for Military Operations United States Africa Command [AFRICOM] at the time of the attacks. He provided insight into the decisions made at the Pentagon and AFRICOM regarding the attacks.

**Kelly, John (Gen.)**—March 23, 2016: At the time of the attacks, served as the Senior Military Assistant to the Secretary of Defense. Provided information regarding meetings and decisions made at the Pentagon in response to the attack.

**Landolt, Richard B. (Rear Adm.)**—May 5, 2016: Served as Director of Operations and Cyber, United States Africa Command (AFRICOM) at the time of the attacks. He provided information regarding meetings and decisions made at AFRICOM.

**Leidig, Jr., Charles J. (Vice Adm.)**—April 22, 2016: At the time of the attacks, served as Deputy Commander for Military Operations United States Africa Command [AFRICOM]. He provided information regarding meetings and decisions made at AFRICOM.

**Losey, Brian (Rear Adm.)**—June 16, 2016: Served as Commander, Special Operations Command-Africa in September 2012. He provided information regarding meetings and decisions made at SOC-AF.

**Miller, James (Ph.D.)**—May 10, 2016: At the time of the attacks, served as Under Secretary of Defense for Policy, a principal advisor to the Secretary of Defense on matters of national security and defense policy.

**Mordente, Patrick (Gen.)**—April 28, 2016: Served as Deputy Director of Operations and Plans at TRANSCOM in September 2012. He provided information regarding the C-17 aircraft that evacuated the wounded and deceased from Tripoli.

**Repass, Michael S. (Maj. Gen.)**—April 15, 2016: Served as the Commander of Special Operations Command Europe at the time of the attack. He provided information regarding when the Commander's in-Extremis Force [CIF] was ordered to deploy, when it deployed, and any delays in deploying the CIF.

**Tidd, Kurt (Adm.)**—April 4, 2016: Served as the Director of Operations (J3) for the Joint Chiefs of Staff. Provided information regarding when the forces were ordered to deploy, who set the N-hour for those forces, and any issues he was made aware of regarding those forces deploying. N-hour specifies a time that commences formal notification to a rapid response unit and requires deployment within a specified time.

**Winnefeld, Jr., James (Adm.)**—March 3, 2016: Served as the Vice Chairman of the Joint Chiefs of Staff at the time of the attack. He provided information regarding the Pentagon's response to the attack.

**CIF Commander**—August 26, 2015: The Commander's in-Extremis Force [CIF] is at a Combatant Commander's disposal for rapid deployment. The CIF Commander provided information about when his team received their orders, when they were ready to deploy, and when they left Croatia for Libya.

**C-17 Pilot**—March 16, 2016: Piloted the C-17 aircraft that was deployed from Ramstein Airbase to Tripoli, Libya to evacuate US personnel. He provided information regarding when he received his orders, and when he deployed.

**Defense Attaché**—June 17, 2016: Served as Defense Attaché, U.S. Embassy Tripoli, Libya, in September 2012.

**Drone Pilot #1**—May 25, 2016: This remotely piloted aircraft pilot operated a remotely piloted aircraft, commonly known as a drone, over Benghazi during the attacks.

**Drone Pilot #2**—May 25, 2016: This remotely piloted aircraft pilot operated a remotely piloted aircraft, commonly known as a drone, over Benghazi during the attacks.

**FAST Commander**—September 2, 2015: The Marine Corps' Fleet Antiterrorism Security Team [FAST] is a special operations team on standby to respond to US government interests and to temporarily augment existing security. The FAST Commander was in charge of the FAST Team ordered to deploy to Tripoli. He provided information about when his team received their orders, when they were ready to deploy, and when they actually deployed.

**Sensor Operator #1**—June 9, 2016: Operated the sensor controls on a remotely piloted aircraft, commonly known as a drone, flown over Benghazi during the attacks.

**Sensor Operator #2**—June 9, 2016: Operated the sensor controls on a remotely piloted aircraft, commonly known as a drone, flown over Benghazi during the attacks.

**DOD Special Operator**—September 22, 2015: One of two Special Forces operators who responded as part of Team Tripoli to Benghazi as the attacks occurred and were present at the Benghazi Base when the mortar attacks occurred.

The Select Committee also had available to it transcripts of hearings, briefings, and interviews from other committees, including interview transcripts from:

Ham, Carter (Gen.)—Commander for Military Operations, United States Africa Command [AFRICOM]

Landolt, Richard B. (Rear Adm.)—Director of Operations and Cyber, AFRICOM

Leidig, Jr, Charles J. (Vice Adm.)—former Deputy to the Commander for Military Operations, AFRICOM

Losey, Brian (Rear Adm.)—former Commander, Special Operations Command—Africa [SOCAFRICA]

Tidd, Kurt (Vice Adm.)—Assistant to the Chairman, Joint Chiefs of Staff

Zobrist, Scott (Brig. Gen.)—Wing Commander, 31st Fighter Wing, Aviano Air Base, Italy

## White House

**Fishman, Benjamin**—January 12, 2016: A staff member of the National Security Council who, beginning in April 2011, handled Libya matters and who continuously coordinated with the State Department, including Envoy/Ambassador Stevens, and other executive branch agencies regarding Libya.

**Meehan, Bernadette**—December 18, 2015: Deputy Spokesperson for the National Security Council (NSC) at the White House at the time of the attack. A Foreign Service Officer with the State Department since 2004, was detailed, meaning on loan to, the National Security Council (NSC) as of July 2012.

**Rhodes, Benjamin**—February 2, 2016: Assistant to the President and Deputy National Security Advisor for Strategic Communications and Speechwriting.

## Other

**Blumenthal, Sidney**—June 16, 2015: Longtime friend and confidant of Hillary R. Clinton. Blumenthal sent her numerous "intelligence reports" and other advice on Libya.

**Chorin, Ethan**—March 10, 2016: Co-director of a non-profit organization that envisioned building relationships between U.S. medical centers and Benghazi medical centers who was in Benghazi at the time of the attack. He was to meet with Ambassador Stevens on September 12, 2012. He is also a former State Department Foreign Service Officer who had been assigned to Libya in 2004–2006 and is an author on books and articles on Libya.

# APPENDIX J:

# Requests and Subpoenas for Documents

## State Department

**September 20, 2012**—Letter from the House Committee on Oversight and Government Reform [OGR] to Hillary R. Clinton, Secretary of State, requesting seven categories of documents pertaining to the Benghazi attacks: 1) Benghazi security situation; 2) threat assessment for US personnel; 3) preliminary attack site exploitation; 4) pre-attack warnings; 5) evidence supporting or contradicting Rice statement blaming video; 6) evidence supporting or contradicting Magariaf's statement that attacks were premeditated; 7) attack information.

The State Department provided OGR eight batches of documents totaling 25,000 pages on a "read and return" basis. OGR was allowed to review the documents, but custody and control of the documents, which were returned to the Department at the end of each day, was retained by the Department.

---

**December 13, 2012**—Letter from OGR to the Secretary requesting information on, among other things, whether the Secretary used personal email for official business.

The State Department's written response on March 27, 2013, did respond to the question regarding the Secretary's use of personal email for official business.

---

**August 1, 2013**—Subpoena from OGR to State Department for records previously produced on a 'read and return" basis. The subpoena required copies of these documents previously provided on a "read and return" basis.

---

The State Department produced 25,000 pages of heavily redacted documents to OGR, with the last installment being produced on April 17, 2014.

---

**August 11, 2014**—Letter from the State Department to the Committee accompanying the production of approximately 15,000 pages of documents never before produced to Congress. This production included eight emails sent to or from "H" or HDR22@ clintonemail.com. This production also excluded documents involving purported "institutional interests."

According to the State Department, this production fulfilled compliance with OGR's September 20, 2012, request and OGR's August 1, 2013, subpoena for "reading room" records. However, as the Committee later determined, responsive records of senior leaders were not included in any production, revealing notable gaps in the records of the Secretary of State and other senior leaders.

---

**September 30, 2014**—Letter to the State Department formalizing prior informal requests for lesser redacted versions of documents provided to OGR only on a "read and return" basis. The letter also requests production of any Administrative Review Board [ARB] documents requested by Congress.

---

**November 18, 2014**—Letter to the State Department requiring production of the records of the Secretary and ten senior leaders. The specific request was for "any and all documents and communications referring or relating to policies, decisions, or activities regarding: (1) security of the United States facility in Benghazi that was attacked on 9.11.2012 (the "Special Mission"); (2) the State Department's decision to open or maintain the Special Mission; (3) the attacks on the Special Mission on 9.11.2012; or (4) weapons located or found in, imported or brought into, and/or exported or removed from Libya, authored by, sent to, or received by [one of the named individuals]."

The State Department produced only 847 pages of the former Secretary of State's emails and other documents before subpoenas were issued on March 4, 2015, commanding production of these records. Following the issuance of the subpoena, additional records were produced. In all, the Committee received just over 42,000 pages of documents to and from the Secretary of State and senior leaders. However, not all records were produced.

---

**November 24, 2014**—Letter from the State Department accompanying the production of the first set of less-redacted "reading room" documents.

---

**December 2, 2014**—Letter to David Kendall, attorney for the Secretary, requesting production of official documents in her custody.

In response, on December 29, 2014, Kendall informed the Committee that the Secretary returned records to the State Department and the State Department would be providing any relevant records to the Committee. The Secretary produced no records to the Committee.

---

**December 4, 2014**—Letter to the State Department requesting interviews of four agents who survived the attacks in Benghazi and who have not been previously interviewed by a congressional committee.

It took the State Department until March-April 2015 to schedule interviews for these agents.

---

**December 4, 2014**—Letter to the State Department requesting interviews of 18 agents and four principal officers who served in Benghazi before the attacks.

The State Department did not begin to schedule interviews until February 2015.

---

**December 9, 2014**—Letter from the State Department accompanying production of the second and final set of less-redacted "reading room" documents previously reviewed by the OGR.

The total of the two productions was approximately 25,000 pages of documents.

---

**December 17, 2014**—Letter from the State Department acknowledging receipt of document and interview requests and requesting that the Committee prioritize its requests.

---

**December 29, 2014**—Letter from the Secretary (via attorney) stating the State Department, not the Secretary, will comply with Committee's December 2, 2014, request for any official records personally retained by the Secretary.

---

**January 28, 2015**—Subpoena for ARB documents with cover letter. Note: The Committee subpoena was identical to an OGR subpoena previously issued on August 1, 2013.

The request was fulfilled according to the State Department by production of documents on April 15 and 24, 2015, of approximately 4,300 pages. However, the Committee sent a letter to the State Department on June 12, 2015, regarding various missing documents. A missing four-page interview report was subsequently delivered on February 25, 2016. The State Department previously claimed the ARB had reviewed over 7000 documents totaling thousands of pages.

---

**February 13, 2015**—Letter from the State Department accompanying the production of 895 pages of emails and documents, including approximately 847 pages of emails to and from the former Secretary of State; approximately four pages relating to the January 28, 2015, subpoena, and approximately 43 pages of documents omitted from previous productions.

---

**March 3, 2015**—Letters sent from the Committee to registrar of domain name and internet service provider used by the Secretary ordering the preservation of relevant records.

---

**March 4, 2015**—Subpoena from the Committee to the State Department for records of ten senior officials for documents referring or relating to: (1) Libya; (2) Libyan weapons programs; (3) Benghazi attacks; (4) post-attack statements for years 2011–2012.

The State Department produced records of senior leaders, however, the production did not include records for all ten senior leaders named in the subpoena and the prior request. Moreover, the productions covered only discrete time frames, not the two-year time period called for by the requests. Additionally, the State Department affirmatively stated it was withholding relevant documents that pertained to "executive interests."

Approximately 39,875 documents were produced on these dates:

| | |
|---|---|
| May 22, 2015 | 1,199 pages |
| June 30, 2015 | 3,636 pages |
| July 28, 2015 | 8,254 pages |
| Aug. 21, 2015 | 7,452 pages |
| Aug. 28, 2015 | 4,703 pages |
| Sept. 3, 2015 | 110 pages |
| Sept. 18 2015 | 1,090 pages |
| Oct. 5, 2015 | 193 pages |
| Oct. 9, 2015 | 3,456 pages |
| Oct. 15 2015 | 122 pages |
| Nov. 6, 2015 | 812 pages |
| Nov. 24, 2015 | 2,789 pages |
| Dec. 31, 2015 | 2,448 pages |
| Jan. 21, 2016 | 886 pages |
| Feb. 26, 2016 | 1,650 pages |
| April 8, 2016 | 1,075 pages |

**March 4, 2015**—Subpoena from the Committee to the Secretary (via her personal attorney) for documents referring or relating to: (1) Libya; (2) Libyan weapons programs; (3) Benghazi attacks; (4) post-attack statements for years 2011–2012.

Notwithstanding the State Department's claim that it had produced all relevant records and "erred on side of inclusion" when it produced 847 pages of records on February 13, 2015, additional productions of official records of the former Secretary of State were produced by the State Department:

| | |
|---|---|
| June 10, 2015 | 1 page |
| June 25, 2015 | 105 pages |
| Sept. 25, 2015 | 1,899 pages |

**March 26, 2015**—Letter to the State Department reiterating demand for ARB documents; reiterating demand for records of senior leaders; and outlining State Department's hindrance of Committee's efforts to obtain additional information and answers to basic questions on records management. A briefing on records management is requested within two weeks.

**March 27, 2015**—Letter from the Secretary's attorney regarding purported inability to comply with subpoena. Enclosed was a letter from Under Secretary for Management Patrick Kennedy sent on March 23, 2015, to the Secretary affirming any official records belong to the State Department. Letter also contains a disclosure that all information during the requested time period on the Secretary's server had been deleted.

**April 15, 2015**—Letter from the State Department accompanying the first production of ARB records consisting of approximately 1758 pages of documents.

This production was in response to January 28, 2015, subpoena from the Committee and its predecessor subpoena issued by the House Oversight and Government Reform Committee on August 1, 2013.

---

**April 24, 2015**—Letter from the State Department accompanying production of a second set of ARB records consisting of approximately 2,523 pages. The letter explains that, in the view of the State Department, this completes compliance with ARB subpoena(s).

The two productions of documents totaling just over 4,300 pages conflicts with a letter from the State Department to the House Oversight and Government Reform Committee stating that the ARB reviewed over 7000 documents totaling thousands of pages. Upon review of the documents provided to the Committee, a letter was sent June 12, 2015, outlining missing documents and requesting additional productions. However, only one missing interview summary consisting of four pages was produced ten months later on February 25, 2016.

---

**May 11, 2015**—Letter from the Committee to the State Department requesting interviews with head of information technology for the Executive Secretariat during 2011–2012 and with the Agency Records Officer within next ten days.

These two interviews were ultimately conducted on June 30, 2015, more than a month later.

---

**May 14, 2015**—Letter to the State Department that the Department's lack of production of relevant documents is the reason the Committee will be unable to interview the Secretary in a timely manner.

---

**May 15, 2015**—Letter from the State Department in response to the Committee's May 14, 2015, letter, detailing compliance to date and incorrectly asserts that the Committee narrowed the subpoena's demand.

---

**May 19, 2015**—Letter to Sidney Blumenthal requesting records regarding Libya and the State Department from September 11–30, 2012.

Superseded by the Committee request on May 29, 2015, for a larger time frame.

---

**May 19, 2015**—Letters to Cheryl Mills, Jacob Sullivan, Philippe Reines, Susan Rice, Huma Abedin (via her attorney) & Caitlin Klevorick for records related to Libya and the State Department from September 11–30, 2012.

Superseded by the Committee request on May 29, 2015, for larger time frame.

For the initial limited time frame, on July 2, 2015, Cheryl Mills produced 30 pages and Jacob Sullivan produced 38 pages to the State Department for review by the State Department before production to the Committee.

---

**May 22, 2015**—Letter from the State Department accompanying production of approximately 1,199 pages of Cheryl Mills emails and documents.

---

**May 29, 2015**—Supplemental letter to Sidney Blumenthal via his attorney for records sent to the executive branch from 2011 to 2012.

On June 12, 2015, 179 pages of documents were produced to the Committee.

---

**June 1, 2015**—Supplemental letter to Huma Abedin via attorney for records from 2011 to 2012.

On July 9, 2015, Huma Abedin via her attorney notifies the Committee that 338 pages were sent by Abedin to the State Department for further review and for compliance with the requests of the Committee.

---

**June 2, 2015**—Committee Member meeting with Jon Finer, Chief of Staff, State Department to discuss lack of document production by the State Department. Additional request made of the State Department for all emails/records of Ambassador Stevens for 2011–2012 as well as for emails of Sean Smith.

Ambassador Stevens records were produced on the dates listed below in the approximate number of pages listed below:

| | |
|---|---|
| Oct. 5, 2015 | 1,370 pages |
| Oct. 9, 2015 | 1,828 pages |
| Oct. 16, 2015 | 2,587 pages |
| Oct. 20, 2015 | 1,296 pages |
| Oct. 21, 2015 | 866 pages |
| Nov. 6, 2015 | 344 pages |
| Nov. 24, 2015 | 647 pages |
| Total pages: | 8,939 |

By agreement, a select portion of Sean Smith records were reviewed and approximately 175 pages were produced on April 8, 2016.

---

**June 4, 2015**—Letter to the State Department confirming an agreement reached that the State Department would substantially comply with outstanding requests. Substantial compliance defined as completion of the first phase of production of senior leader records within 30 days.

---

**June 9, 2015**—Supplemental letters sent to Cheryl Mills, Jacob Sullivan, Philippe Reines via attorneys to produce records related to Libya from 2011 and 2012.

---

**June 10, 2015**—Letter from the State Department accompanying production of one email, initially discovered in the production of Cheryl Mills records but was not in the production of Secretary Clinton's records. The State Department acknowledged the email was previously produced by the Secretary to the State Department but omitted from prior production to the Committee.

---

**June 12, 2015**—Sidney Blumenthal via his attorney produces approximately 179 pages of email exchanges with the Secretary regarding Libya.

Of the 81 email exchanges produced, 59 were email exchanges not contained in prior production of Secretary Clinton's emails by the State Department in February 2015.

---

**June 12, 2015**—Letter from the Committee to the State Department detailing documents missing from the ARB productions. The letter provides list of additional discrete documents needed. The letter further requests a privilege or Vaughn index detailing documents withheld and precise reasons for not producing relevant records.

The only additional record produced was a four (4) page interview summary. The privilege log was never produced.

---

**June 19, 2015**—Email from the Committee to the State Department requesting explanation and production of documents provided by Sidney Blumenthal that were not among documents in the State Department's production on February 13, 2015, of Secretary Clinton's records.

State Department produced an additional 105 pages of records in response to this inquiry but acknowledged it was unable to locate 15 email exchanges between the former Secretary and Mr. Blumenthal that Mr. Blumenthal produced to the Committee.

---

**June 25, 2015**—Letter from the State Department accompanying production of approximately 105 additional Secretary Clinton email exchanges with Sidney Blumenthal regarding Libya. The letter further discloses, however, the State Department was unable to locate nine entire exchanges between Secretary Clinton and Sidney Blumenthal and was unable to locate an additional six email exchanges where significant portions were omitted.

---

**June 30, 2015**—Letter from the State Department accompanying the production of approximately 3,636 pages of emails to and from Jacob Sullivan, Cheryl Mills, and Susan Rice.

More than half of production consisted of press clippings. The remaining substantive emails were primarily for one month time frame, September 11, 2012, to October 12, 2012.

---

**July 2, 2015**—Letters from the personal attorney for Mills and Jacob regarding production of documents to the State Department for limited time period of September 11–30, 2012, recounting that 30 pages for Mills and 38 pages for Sullivan were returned to the State Department. Acknowledges that a further production to be done by July 27, 2015, for larger time frame in the second request from the Committee.

---

**July 6, 2015**—Email exchange between the Committee and the State Department outlining several issues: 1) request for production of letters sent by Kennedy to senior officials seeking return of official records retained in personal email accounts; and 2) inquiry as to an expected production of the first phase of documents of senior leaders.

Response from the State Department received the next day, July 7, 2015, summarily stating the State Department is working on all requests.

No response to the request for the letters from Kennedy to senior leaders until a subpoena was issued on August 5, 2015, for these records. The records were produced on August 6, 2015.

---

**July 8, 2015**—Letter from the Committee to the State Department regarding documents intentionally withheld from the Committee. The letter requests a privilege log or "Vaughn Index" outlining details of "Executive Branch confidentiality interest" for withheld documents from productions made on April 24, 2015, May 22, 2015, and June 30, 2015.

Despite repeated assurances that summary was being prepared detailing the documents withheld and the precise reason for withholding, no summary was ever received.

---

**July 9, 2015**—Letter from attorney for Huma Abedin regarding 338 pages of documents pertaining to Libya produced by her to the State Department for further review by the State Department for production to the Committee.

---

**July 10, 2015**—Letter from the Committee to the State Department seeking information regarding allegations of retaliation against a whistleblower.
Letter received on October 9, 2015, in response.

---

**July 27, 2015**—Letter from the State Department regarding a scheduled July 29, 2015, hearing on State Department document production and promising "meaningful production of several thousand pages to the Committee.

---

**July 28, 2015**—Letter from the State Department accompanying production of approximately 8,254 pages of documents of senior leaders.

---

**August 5, 2015**—Subpoena issued to the State Department seeking the March 11, 2015, letter from Kennedy to the ten senior officials identified in the Committee's March 4, 2015, subpoena and the emails submitted to the State Department as a result of the March 11, 2015, letter from the State Department to the senior officials.

These items were previously requested by letter on July 6, 2015, but request was ignored. Production of the letter from Kennedy subsequently occurred on August 7, 2015, following issuance of the subpoena. Official records found in the personal email accounts of Sullivan and Mills subsequently produced to the Committee.

---

**August 7, 2015**—Production of correspondence between Kennedy and former senior leaders requesting return of official records maintained on personal email accounts.

---

**August 21, 2015**—Letter from the State Department accompanying production of approximately 7,452 pages of documents of senior leaders.

---

**August 28, 2015**—Letter from the State Department accompanying production of approximately 4,703 pages of senior leaders records including a classified portion.

---

**September 3, 2015**—Letter from the State Department accompanying production of approximately 110 pages of emails from Sullivan from his personal email account.

---

**September 18, 2015**—Letter from the State Department accompanying production of approximately 1,090 pages of emails from senior leaders.

---

**September 22, 2015**—Email to the State Department outlining documents needed prior to October 22, 2015, hearing.

---

**September 25, 2015**—Letter from the State Department accompanying production of approximately 1,899 pages of emails from the Secretary.

---

**October 5, 2015**—Letter from the State Department accompanying production of approximately 1,563 pages of documents, including approximately 1,370 pages of Stevens emails and approximately 193 pages of documents from senior leaders.

---

**October 9, 2015**—Letter from the State Department accompanying production of approximately 3,456 pages, including emails from the personal email accounts of Mills, Sullivan, and Abedin regarding Libya and additionally approximately 1,828 pages of Stevens emails.

---

**October 15, 2015**—Letter from the State Department accompanying production of approximately 122 pages of Abedin emails.

---

**October 16, 2015**—Letter from the State Department accompanying production of approximately 2,587 pages of Stevens emails.

---

**October 20, 2015**—Letter from the State Department accompanying production of approximately 1296 pages of Stevens emails.

---

**October 21, 2015**—Letter from the State Department accompanying production of approximately 866 pages of Stevens emails.

---

**November 6, 2015**—Letter from the State Department accompanying production of approximately 344 pages of Stevens emails and approximately 812 pages of Kennedy emails.

---

**November 24, 2015**—Letter from the State Department accompanying production of approximately 647 pages of Ambassador Stevens emails and approximately 2789 pages of Under Secretary Kennedy emails.

---

**December 31, 2015**—Letter from the State Department accompanying production of approximately 2448 pages of Under Secretary Kennedy emails/documents.

---

**January 21, 2016**—Letter from the State Department accompanying production of approximately 866 pages of Under Secretary Kennedy emails.

---

**February 25, 2016**—Letter from the State Department accompanying production of approximately 4 pages consisting of one missing ARB interview summary.

---

**February 26, 2016**—Letter from the State Department accompanying production of approximately 1,640 pages of documents of former Secretary Clinton and emails from senior leaders, recently discovered from the Office of the Secretary.

---

**February 26, 2016**—Letter from the State Department accompanying production of approximately ten pages of emails of Cheryl Mills previously withheld from the Committee.

---

**April 8, 2016**—Letter from the State Department accompanying production of approximately 1,146 pages of documents of former

Secretary Clinton and emails from senior leaders, recently discovered from the Office of the Secretary.

**May 5, 2016**—Letter from the State Department accompanying production of approximately 405 pages of documents recently discovered from the Office of the Secretary.

## Department of Defense

**April 8, 2015**—Letter to the Defense Department requesting briefings on Operation Jukebox Lotus, Operation Oaken Lotus, Defense Department personnel's 1208 mission in Libya, EUCOM/AFRICOM's Commander's in-Extremis Force [CIF], and others.

**April 8, 2015**—Letter requesting answers to 20 questions (57 subparts) pertaining to 1) heightened alert/deployment status for various U.S. military forces or assets; 2) commands or orders, given, rescinded, or status and manner of compliance.

**April 8, 2015**—Letter to the Defense Department requesting production of: 1) Defense Department documents/communications relating to the Benghazi attack; 2) After-action reports on the attack; 3) documents sent to Defense Department (excluding DIA) relating to the attack; 4) documents relating to orders or commands given to defend against the attacks or rescue Americans in Benghazi; 5) documents relating to the preparation to respond to such orders or commands; 6) documents relating to the recission or cancellation of such orders or commands; 7) copy of the Predator video on the night of the attack; 8) documents relating to the Annex attack; 9) unredacted versions of the 486 pages of AFRICOM-related documents produced to Judicial Watch; 10) AFRICOM AOR Force Laydown slides; 11) EUCOM AOR Force Laydown slides; 12) CENTCOM AOR Force Laydown slides.

**April 27, 2015**—Letter from the Defense Department in response to the three April 8, 2015, letters stating the Defense Department will schedule briefings requested; will answer questions posed; and will provide documents requested. Defense Department included one slide in response to items 10, 11, 12 of document request.

**May 21, 2015**—Letter from the Defense Department on status of document request and production of 726 pages of documents, including: 1) Defense Department documents/communications relating to the Benghazi attack are pending production; 2) 175 pages produced on the after-action reports on the attack; 3) documents sent to the Defense Department (excluding DIA) relating to the attack has been referred to DIA for production; 4) documents relating to orders or commands given to defend against the attacks or rescue Americans in Benghazi is pending production; 5) documents relating to the preparation to respond to such orders or commands is pending production; 6) documents relating to the rescission or cancellation of such orders or commands is pending production; 7) a copy of the Predator video on the night of the attack was made available for staff review; 8) documents relating to the Annex attack is pending production; 9) 551 pages (which includes some withheld pages) but includes unredacted versions of the 486 pages of AFRICOM-related documents produced to Judicial Watch; 10) AFRICOM AOR Force Laydown slides have been previously provided; 11) EUCOM AOR Force Laydown slides have been previously provided; 12) CENTCOM AOR Force Laydown slides have been previously provided.

---

**July 28, 2015**—Written answers received to questions in letter sent January 7, 2016, pertaining to 1) heightened alert/deployment status for various U.S. military forces or assets; and 2) commands or orders, given, rescinded, or status and manner of compliance.

---

**January 7, 2016**—Letter from Defense Department accompanying the production of 61 pages in response to the Committee's April 24, 2015, request. Letter notes that another 54 pages of relevant documents have been withheld based on an assertion of "longstanding Executive Branch interests."

## NATIONAL SECURITY AGENCY

**November 19, 2014**—Letter to NSA Director requesting production of all finished intelligence analysis products regarding Libya.

---

**April 28, 2015**—Letter to NSA Director requesting specific documents, including: certain NSA reports, Critical Intelligence Communications (CRITIC) messages, attack-related documents, NSA collection requirements for Libya, NSA activities related to the NIPF.

---

**May 11, 2015**—Letter from NSA acknowledging receipt of April 28, 2015, letter.

## DEFENSE INTELLIGENCE AGENCY

**November 19, 2014**—Letter to DIA Director requesting production of all finished intelligence analysis products regarding Libya.

---

**April 23, 2015**—Letter to DIA Director requesting production of: 1) "DCTC's Benghazi Binder" containing timeline of terrorist events and acts against western interests; 2) DCTC's DIA intelligence reports on the attacks; 3) photos/videos of Benghazi mission/annex and related document; 4) analysis of social media covering Benghazi; 5) documents relating to video-conferences in September 2012 pertaining to Libya; 6) documents/communications regarding responsibility for the Benghazi attack; 7) documents and communications regarding the Benghazi attacks sent to or from the White House Situation Room, the National Military Command Center, or the Defense Intelligence Operations Coordination Center.

---

**May 8, 2015**—Letter from DIA accompanying production of a binder of materials in response to the April 23, 2015, request. The letter notes that some documents still in clearance process.

## Central Intelligence Agency

**November 19, 2014**—Letter from the Committee requesting "all finished intelligence analysis products regarding Libya" issued between 9/11/2012 and 12/31/2012.

———

**April 28, 2015**—Letter from the Committee requesting production of the following documents or communications, including reports, cables, emails, and instant messages, relating to the Benghazi attacks: 1) to or from Tripoli Station; 2) between Tripoli Station and the State Department; 3) to or from Benghazi Base; 4) to or from Director Petraeus or his immediate staff; 5) to or from Deputy Director Morell or his immediate staff; 6) to or from CIA Operations Center.

The letter also requested production of documents or communications relating to: 7) development of a 9/13/2012 WIRe article; 8) development of a 9/15/2012 WIRe article; 9) CIA's strategic priorities in Libya; 10) security situation in Benghazi; 11) vulnerability assessments of Benghazi Base; 12) CIA personnel and AFRICOM; 13) eyewitness accounts of the attack; 14) final report produced and referenced in 1–001405; 15) Team A/Team B analysis of the attacks; 16–19) specific document requests; 20) February 17 Martyrs Brigade; 21) unclassified HPSCI talking points; 22) cables regarding the Benghazi attacks; 23) Tripoli Station SIGINT strategy; 24) Ambassador Stevens Benghazi trip; 25) FBI trips to Benghazi following the attacks; and 26) cables requested by Secretary Clinton or Chief of Staff Cheryl Mills.

———

**August 7, 2015**—Subpoena to CIA for document production of: 1) Same Time (instant) messages relating to the Benghazi attacks sent to or from a) Director, b) Deputy Director, c) OTA, d) Ops/NE division, d) MENA, e) Tripoli Station; 2) unclassified HPSCI talking points; 3) development of a 9/13/2012 WIRe article; 4) development of a 9/15/2012 WIRe article; 5) development of a 9/12/2012 MENA Situation Report; 6) development of a 9/12/2012 Libya Spot Commentary.

———

**November 4, 2015**—Letter from the Committee requesting production of a "list of all intelligence products from the BIR [Benghazi Intelligence Review] that were included in the PDB [President's Daily Brief] between February 2012 and November 2012."

———

**January 13, 2016**—Letter from the Committee outlining areas of noncompliance: 1) Same Time Chats (instant messaging) requested in the August 7, 2015, subpoena; 2) outstanding document requests from the August 7, 2015, subpoena, including, a) initial analysis of the attacks, b) critical cable written in the aftermath of the attacks, c) intelligence regarding the deteriorating security situation in

Benghazi, d) specific cable reflecting calls made on the night of the attack and related records; 3) refusal to certify compliance with talking points request; 4) outstanding witness interview requests (4 referenced); 5) access to information about certain CIA activities; and 6) classification review of interview transcripts.

## White House

**December 29, 2014**—Letter from the Committee to White House Chief of Staff requesting 12 categories of documents pertaining to Libya and the Benghazi attacks, specifically documents pertaining to: 1) Libya policy; 2) attack response; 3) the President's actions and communications; 4) identities and content of communications of others with President about attacks; 5) identities and content of communications of White House staff about attacks; 6) persons present in White House Situation Room on September 11–12, 2012; 7) movement logs, photographs, etc. of President on evening of September 11, 2012; 8) drafts, notes, revisions to President's Rose Garden remarks made on 9/12/2012; 9) documents pertaining to public response/messaging about the attacks; 10) documents pertaining to protests at U.S. overseas facilities; 11) documents pertaining to the video, Innocence of Muslims; 12) documents related to the President's meeting on September 10, 2012, with Senior Administration Officials in preparation for the 9/11 anniversary.

---

**January 23, 2015**—Letter from White House stating that other Executive Branch agencies are in best position to respond to document requests. The letter further complains that request is broader than the Committee's mandate. The letter outlines how the requests intrude "on longstanding Executive Branch confidentiality and other institutional interests." The letter asserts the White House will begin producing documents by February and welcomes further discussion on how to narrow the requests made.

---

**February 27, 2015**—Letter from the White House accompanying the production of approximately 266 pages of documents responsive to the December 29, 2014, request.

---

**March 17, 2015**—Letter from the White House accompanying the re-production of approximately 266 pages of documents with lesser redactions.

---

**April 23, 2015**—Letter in response to White House position on scope of mandate of the Committee and the Committee requests, including that the White House cannot rely on productions by other agencies to fulfill its obligation to respond to a congressional request; disagrees with the narrow interpretation of scope of the Committee's mandate; and requests that future productions give priority to certain areas (Items 1, 2, 8, 9, 10, 11 from December 29, 2014, letter) and further give priority to certain specific time frames.

---

**May 11, 2015**—Letter from the White House accompanying the re-production of approximately 203 pages of documents.

---

**May 19, 2015**—Letter from the Committee requesting production of any email communications to or from a personal address regarding Libya from National Security Advisor Susan Rice.

---

**June 19, 2015**—Letter from the White House accompanying the re-production of approximately 266 pages of documents responsive to requests.

---

**July 17, 2015**—Letter from the White House accompanying the re-production of approximately 340 pages of documents responsive to requests.

---

**August 7, 2015**—Letter to White House resetting priorities: compliance has not been achieved notwithstanding lapse of 7 months; many documents produced have been publically available press clippings; and the White House needs to identify what documents will be produced and what documents it will refuse to produce and the precise legal basis for non-production.

---

**August 28, 2015**—Letter from the White House accompanying the re-production of approximately 247 pages of documents responsive to requests.

---

**October 5, 2015**—Letter from the White House accompanying the re-production of approximately 34 pages of documents responsive to requests.
Meeting/briefing between the Committee staff and White House counsel staff regarding production of documents.

---

**October 27, 2015**—Letter from the White House accompanying the re-production of approximately 47 pages of documents responsive to requests.

---

**November 12, 2015**—Letter from the White House accompanying the re-production of approximately 48 pages of documents responsive to requests.

---

**March 16, 2016**—Letter formally requesting "access to all special access programs regarding U.S. activities in Libya" specifically in reference to "weapons trafficking, weapons diversion, and the monitoring of weapons transfers."

White House forwarded the letter to the Central Intelligence Agency for response. Response received on April 28, 2016.

# APPENDIX K:

## Analysis of Accountability Review Board, House Armed Services Committee and House Permanent Select Intelligence Committee Reports

### Was the Accountability Review Board Independent and Comprehensive?

#### INTRODUCTION

On October 3, 2012, the Secretary of State announced the formation of a panel known as the Benghazi Accountability Review Board [ARB].[1] The five member ARB was charged with examining "the circumstances surrounding the deaths of personnel assigned in support of the U.S. Government Mission to Libya in Benghazi, Libya, on September 11, 2012."[2] Federal law and State Department procedures outline the process for convening and conducting an ARB investigation—a process typically overseen by career personnel.[3] Notwithstanding the processes already in place, the Secretary's senior staff oversaw the Benghazi ARB process from start to finish. The senior staff's participation ranged from selecting the ARB members to shaping the ARB's outcome by editing the draft final report. The decisions to deviate from longstanding processes raise questions about the ARB's independence, thoroughness, and therefore the fullness of their findings of accountability.

#### BACKGROUND

Accountability Review Boards are designed to play a critical role in ensuring the State Department learns from past incidents so as to ensure future security and safety related incidents can be prevented. According to the State Department, the "ARB process is a mechanism to foster more effective security of U.S. missions and personnel abroad by ensuring a thorough and independent review of security-related incidents."[4] Through its investigations and recommendations, the Board seeks to determine accountability and promote and encourage improved security."[5]

---

[1] Convening of an Accountability Review Board, 77 Fed. Reg. 60741 (Oct. 4, 2012), Pub. Notice 8052.
[2] Id.
[3] 22 U.S.C. § 4831 et seq. and 12 FAM 030.
[4] Id.
[5] 12 FAM 013. Objective.

By law, Accountability Review Boards are charged with examining five aspects of an incident, including:

1. The extent to which the incident or incidents with respect to which the Board was convened was security related;

2. Whether the security systems and security procedures at that mission were adequate;

3. Whether the security systems and security procedures were properly implemented;

4. The impact of intelligence and information availability; and

5. Such other facts and circumstances, which may be relevant to the appropriate security management of United States missions abroad.[6]

Prior to 1986, no formal mechanisms were in place to examine, review, and make recommendations after significant incidents involving State Department facilities of personnel. Following several attacks against U.S. missions in the 1980s, the State Department created an independent review panel to examine the incidents. The Advisory Panel on Overseas Security, chaired by Admiral Bobby Inman, issued its report in 1985. Concerned that the State Department did not consistently examine serious and significant incidents as did other federal agencies, the Panel recommended the "Secretary of State [be required] to convene a Board of Inquiry with powers of establishing accountability in all cases involving terrorism or security related attacks that result in significant damage and/or casualties to United States personnel or property."[7] The Advisory Panel's recommendation to establish the Accountability Review Board was adopted by the State Department and later incorporated in the Omnibus Diplomatic Security and Antiterrorism Act of 1986.[8]

Since 1986, nineteen (19) ARBs have been convened to review the most significant attacks against U.S. diplomatic personnel or facilities.[9] The findings and recommendations of each ARB investigation are in effect cumulative. Cheryl Mills, Chief of Staff and Counselor to the Secretary of State, explained to the Committee, "ARBs . . . have an enduring life, meaning that the learnings that came from those ARBs should be acted on and implemented."[10] Two significant ARBs convened subsequent to 1986 were those formed in the aftermath of the August 7, 1998, dual terrorist attacks in the east African cities of Dar es Salaam, Tanzania, and Nairobi, Kenya.

Speaking on behalf of both East African ARB panels, ARB Chairman William Crowe wrote former Secretary of State Madeline

---

[6] 22 U.S.C. § 4834(a).

[7] Report of the Secretary of State's Advisory Panel on Overseas Security, Accountability and Acceptance of Risk, 1 (1985) http://www.fas.org/irp/threat/inman [hereinafter Inman Report].

[8] 22 U.S.C. § 4831 through 4835.

[9] OIG Special Review of the Accountability Review Process, ISP-I-13-44A, 10 (September 2013) ("Within the 14-year period covered by this review [1998-2012], a significant number of security-related incidents, more than 222 in all, were not subject to [ARB] consideration."), found at https://oig.state.gov/system/files/214907.pdf.

[10] Testimony of Cheryl D. Mills, Chief of Staff, U.S. Dep't of State, Tr. at 269 (Sep. 3, 2015) [hereinafter Mills Testimony] (on file with the Committee) ("It was my impression that ARBs are supposed to have an enduring life, meaning that the learnings that came from those ARBs should be acted on and implemented").

Albright expressing concern about the Department's commitment to security:[11]

> [H]ow similar the lessons were to those drawn by the Inman Commission over 14 years ago. What is most troubling is the failure of the U.S. government to take the necessary steps to prevent such tragedies through an unwillingness to give sustained priority and funding to security improvements.

> We are advancing a number of recommendations that deal with the handling of terrorist threats and attacks, the review and revision of standards and procedures to improve security readiness and crisis management, the size and composition of our missions, and the need to have adequate and sustained funding for safe buildings and security programs in the future. We recognize that the Department of State and other U.S. government agencies are already making adjustments and taking measures to enhance the protection of our personnel and facilities abroad. It is clear, however, that much more needs to be done.[12]

Two recommendations identified by the East African ARBs were directed specifically to the Secretary of State:

> Recommendation #4: The Secretary of State should personally review the security situation of embassy chanceries and other official premises, closing those which are highly vulnerable and threatened but for which adequate security enhancements cannot be provided, and seek new secure premises for permanent use, or temporary occupancy, pending construction of new buildings.[13]

> Recommendation #13: First and foremost, the Secretary of State should take a personal and active role in carrying out the responsibility of ensuring the security of U.S. diplomatic personnel abroad. It is essential to convey to the entire Department that security is one of the highest priorities. In the process, the Secretary should reexamine the present organizational structure with the objective of clarifying responsibilities, encouraging better coordination, and assuring that a single high-ranking officer is accountable for all security matters and has the authority necessary to coordinate on the Secretary's behalf such activities within the Department of State and with all foreign affairs USG agencies.[14]

---

[11] Letter from Admiral William J. Crowe, to Madeline Albright, Sec'y of State, U.S. Dep't of State (Jan. 8, 1999) (on file with the Committee).

[12] *Id.*

[13] Report to the Congress on Actions Taken by the Department of State In Response to the Program Recommendations of the Accountability Review Boards on the Embassy Bombings in Nairobi and Dar es Salaam, 14 (April 1999), http://fas.org/irp/threat/arb/accountability_report.html.

[14] *Id.* at 29–30.

*Decision to Convene an Accountability Review Board Panel*

The Secretary convened the Benghazi ARB on the recommendation of the State Department's permanent coordinating committee [PCC], a seven member committee with convening authority.[15] State Department procedures provide "the ARB/PCC will, as quickly as possible after an incident occurs, review the available facts and recommend to the Secretary to convene or not convene a board."[16] The Managing Director for the State Department's Office of Management Policy, Rightsizing and Innovation [M/PRI] and the Chair of the ARB/PCC, explained:

> [W]e put together . . . some facts as we know it, about the incident. We tell our director. He contacts the legal adviser, who is not a voting member but is there to provide advice to the PCC, and Diplomatic Security and the regional bureau. And we say hey, this looks to us like it meets the criteria, I'm going to call the PCC together. And it's the chairman's right to assemble this group.[17]

After the attacks on the U.S. diplomatic facility on September 11, 2012, the ARB/PCC did not meet in person but discussed the situation by email.[18] The Managing Director of M/PRI explained:

> A virtual meeting, we do that on incidents that we think do not need the PCC to meet. That is our standard operating procedure. But since this was well known by everyone in the Department, we felt comfortable in doing it electronically.[19]

The PCC agreed an ARB should be convened and made the recommendation to the Secretary on September 19, 2012.[20] In making the recommendation, the PCC noted:

> Should you agree to this recommendation, we will prepare the appropriate appointment letters for the Chair and proposed members of the ARB, the letters to the Congress and notifications to the public via the Federal Register announcing your decision.[21]

---

[15] 12 FAM 032.

[16] 12 FAM 032.1.

[17] Testimony of the Managing Director, Office of Management Policy, Rightsizing and Innovation, U.S. Dep't of State, Tr. at 20 (Mar. 4, 2016) [hereinafter M/PRI Managing Director Testimony] (on file with the Committee).

[18] Email from the M/PRI Managing Director, U.S. Dep't of State to Eric Boswell, Ass't Sec'y of State, Bureau of Diplomatic Security, U.S. Dep't of State, Beth Jones, Acting Ass't Sec'y of State, U.S. Dep't of State, *et. al* (Sept. 19, 2012) (on file with the Committee, SCB0049611) ("The Under Secretary from Management asked M/PRI to get the ARB/PCC together today to provide a recommendation to the Secretary as to whether to convene an ARB in response to the September 11, 2012 attack in Benghazi, Libya. Due to conflicting schedules we are conducting the vote via email.").

[19] M/PRI Managing Director Testimony at 24.

[20] Memorandum from M/PRI Managing Director, U.S. Dep't of State, to the Sec'y of State, (Sept.19, 2012) (on file with the Committee, C05456350) ("The Permanent Coordinating Committee (PCC) on Accountability Review Boards (ARB) was asked on September 19, 2012 to examine the recent incident, and has recommended that you convene an ARB to examine this incident.").

[21] *Id.*

The Secretary approved the PCC's recommendation to convene the ARB the same day.[22]

*Selection of the ARB Panel*

"The law requires four nominees [to be selected] by the Secretary of State and one nominee by now the Director of National Intelligence."[23] State Department procedures outline the process for selecting State Department representatives to the Board once a decision to convene an ARB has been made. The procedures specify "[i]f the ARB PCC recommends that the Secretary convene a board, it will forward a list of potential board members to the Secretary for approval." However, the Benghazi ARB/PCC did not prepare a list of prospective board members, nor did it share a list of candidates with the Secretary as required by State Department procedures.[24] The Managing Director who also served as the ARB/PCC Chair, explained to the Committee:

> Q: Did you put together a list of names to recommend to be members of the ARB?
>
> A: I don't believe I did.
>
> Q: Okay. Why not?
>
> A: Well, because they went for option two and did more of the celebrity approach as I would say. As I mentioned earlier, they got Ambassador Pickering, who I consider to be in that category as Ambassador Crowe, for when he was chosen for Nairobi Dar.[25]

The PCC did not prepare or send a list of prospective members to the Secretary because the senior staff were already in the process of identifying panelists to serve.

As Mills told the Committee, "I worked with Under Secretary Kennedy and Deputy Secretary William Burns in identifying who might be talent that could actually serve in this role."[26] Talent would later be defined as individuals who would understand the Secretary's narrative of expiditionary diplomacy. On September 15, 2012, William Burns, Deputy Secretary of State, recommended Ambassador Pickering to the ARB.

In an email to Mills, Burns wrote:

> On arb, I'd suggest Pickering in addition to Armitage. They're both very experienced and fair minded and understand entirely demands of expeditionary diplomacy.[27]

On September 18, 2012, Burns informed Mills and Patrick Kennedy, Under Secretary of State for Management, that "Tom Pickering is willing to chair. . . . He liked very much the idea of in-

---

[22] *Id.*

[23] Testimony of Patrick F. Kennedy, Under Sec'y for Management, U.S. Dep't of State, Tr. at 278 (Feb. 3, 2016) [hereinafter Kennedy Testimony] (on file with the Committee).

[24] M/PRI Managing Director Testimony at 29 (A list of potential board members was not forwarded to the Secretary for approval).

[25] *Id.* at 27.

[26] Mills Testimony at 137.

[27] Email from William Burns, Deputy Sec'y of State, U.S. Dep't of State, to Cheryl D. Mills, Chief of Staff, U.S. Dep't of State (Sep. 15, 2012, 1:09 PM) (on file with the Committee, SCB0057846).

cluding Mike Mullen." [28] Admiral Michael Mullen retired as Chairman of the Joint Chiefs of Staff on November 1, 2011.[29] At the time they served on the Benghazi ARB, both Mullen and Pickering were also members of the Secretary's Foreign Affairs Policy Advisory Board.

> The Foreign Affairs Policy Board was launched in December 2011 to provide the Secretary of State, the Deputy Secretaries of State, and the Director of Policy Planning with independent, informed advice and opinion concerning matters of U.S. foreign policy. The Board serves in a solely advisory capacity, with an agenda shaped by the questions and concerns of the Secretary. Its discussions focus on assessing global threats and opportunities; identifying trends that implicate core national security interests; providing recommendations with respect to tools and capacities of the civilian foreign affairs agencies; defining priorities and strategic frameworks for U.S. foreign policy; and performing any other research and analysis of topics raised by the Secretary of State, the Deputy Secretaries, and the Director of Policy Planning.[30]

The Foreign Affairs Policy Advisory Board's formation occurred contemporaneously with the decision to extend the operations in Benghazi as well as the restart of operations in Tripoli.

Mills explained her communications with ARB panelists Mullen and Catherine Bertini:

> I reached out to, I believe Admiral Mullen myself. . . . And, I reached out to, I believe, Cathy Bertini, who had been recommended to us by the Under Secretary of Management.[31]

Kennedy described his role in the selection of the ARB panel members to the Committee:

> I had met Catherine Bertini when I was one of the alternate representatives to the United Nations and she was at the United Nations as the she was I think at that point the senior American serving in the United Nations Headquarters Secretariat. So I worked with her on a professional basis because I was representing the United States and she was a senior official within the United Nations. I did not recommend her for the position.

> I provided one name, Richard Shinnick. That was the only name that I was solicited and asked to provide a suggestion for, in effect, a type of expertise.[32]

---

[28] Email from Jacob J. Sullivan, Deputy Chief of Staff and Dir. of Policy Planning, U.S. Dep't of State, to William Burns, Deputy Sec'y of State, U.S. Dep't of State (Sept. 18, 2012, 9:35 AM) (on file with the Committee, SCB0057775).

[29] *Biography of Admiral Mike Mullen,* U.S. Navy (Jul. 12, 2013), http://www.navy.mil/navydata/bios/navybio.asp?bioID=11.

[30] *Foreign Affairs Policy Board,* U.S. Dep't of State, http://www.state.gov/s/p/fapb/.

[31] Mills Testimony at 138.

[32] Kennedy Testimony at 265.

Kennedy explained further:

A: As I said earlier, I was asked only to make one recommendation name somebody who was not in the State Department but knew a lot about Secretary of excuse me Department of State construction activities. So I made one recommendation and I made no recommendations for any of the other four.

I was advised, because I also head the unit that publishes the names in the Federal Register, I was advised that the selections were Pickering, Mullen, Turner, I think it was, Bertini and Shinnick.

Q: And so did Cheryl Mills ask you for that, or did Jake Sullivan? Or who asked you for——

A: Cheryl Mills asked me for the name of someone who knew about State Department facilities management and construction.

Q: And did she share with you who the other members who she was thinking about

A: No.

Q: appointing?

A: No. I was informed who the selections were.[33]

On September 28, 2012, Mills shared with Kennedy, Stephen Mull, the Executive Secretariat, Uzra Zeya, the ARB executive secretary, and Burns about Catherine Bertini agreement to participate as an ARB member.[34] Within hours of Bertini's acceptance, Kennedy shared with Mills and Mull the additional news: "Dick Shinnick has accepted as the fifth member of the panel."[35]

The Intelligence Community recommended Hugh Turner, a former CIA deputy director, to serve as the intelligence Community's representative.[36] Burns spoke early on with Michel Morrell, Deputy Director of the CIA, and Robert Cardillo, Deputy Director of ODNI about their choice of representatives on the ARB panel—reporting back to the Mills and Kennedy "they will coordinate on a nominee."[37]

As panelists confirmed their participation on the ARB, Mills shared the information with the Secretary. For example, within minutes after sharing the news about Catherine Bertini with the

---

[33] Id. at 278.

[34] Email from Cheryl Mills, Chief of Staff and Counselor, U.S. Dep't of State, to Stephen Mull, Executive Secretary, Office of the Secretariat, U.S. Dep't of State (Sept. 28, 2012, 2:37 PM) (on file with the Committee, SCB0057607) ("Catherine Bertini agreed to serve on the ARB panel today"). See also Email from Cheryl Mills, Chief of Staff and Counselor, U.S. Dep't of State, to Catherine Bertini, Accountability Review Board Member (Sept. 28, 2012, 2:28AM) (on file with the Committee, SCB0054582) ("[I]f you could tomorrow, I would welcome connecting with you." From Bertini "Thank you for reaching out to me. I am pleased to say Yes to your request and I very much look forward to contributing to the work of the panel on this critically important issue").

[35] Id. ("Dick Shinnick has accepted as the fifth member of the Panel").

[36] Mills Testimony at 138.

[37] Email from Jacob J. Sullivan, Deputy Chief of Staff and Dir. of Policy Planning, U.S. Dep't of State, to William Burns, Deputy Sec'y of State, U.S. Dep't of State (Sept. 18, 2012, 9:35 AM) (on file with the Committee, SCB0057775) (containing exchange from William Burns to Cheryl Mills and Patrick Kennedy).

senior staff, Mills also relayed the news to the Secretary.[38] Mills explained to the Committee:

We certainly apprised her that it looked like we had a team of five that represented a balance of those who understood diplomacy, who understand national security, who understood what it meant to operate in environments that were insecure, and that we thought the balance of who we had identified met that criteria.[39]

### ARB Executive Secretary

The senior staff's involvement in the ARB process also extended to selecting the Executive Secretary to the ARB. According to the State Department's regulations, the Executive Secretary to the ARB is considered to be part of the ARB staff and "serves to coordinate and facilitate the work of that Board."[40] On September 25, 2012, the Managing Director wrote Mull and his Deputy:

I would appreciate knowing how this ARB is going to work since it is not going in the normal way. Can we talk this morning or tomorrow morning about the roles and responsibilities?[41]

The Managing Director explained to the Committee: "I was a little bit concerned about being behind the tide."[42] "I was hungry for information myself."[43] She described her normal responsibilities with regard to selecting the Executive Secretary to the ARB:

A: [W]hat I normally do is go to our H.R. Bureau and see who is available at the senior ranks to take on a function such as this.

Q: And what does the Executive Secretary to the ARB do?

A: They arrange the meetings. They make sure that the board has access to the Department for interviews and, you know, because usually these people are removed from the Department, you know, they're retirees, they're unfamiliar with the Department's ways. So in sitting in on the interviews, the exec sec would know who they should contact next, who this leads them to in a bureau. So they act, as I call it, the bridge from the ARB to the building.

Q: And in the 10 prior ARBs that you had been involved in, as the ARB officer, had you made the selection of the executive secretary?

A: I wouldn't say made the selection. I nominated people in the past, sure.

Q: And had they been selected then?

---

[38] Email from Cheryl Mills, Chief of Staff and Counselor, U.S. Dep't of State, to H (Sept. 28, 2012, 2:46 PM) (Subject: FYI) (on filed with the Committee, SCB0045509).

[39] Mills Testimony at 141.

[40] 12 FAM 032.3b.

[41] Email from Managing Director, Office of Management Policy, Rightsizing and Innovation to Stephen Mull, Exec. Sec'y, Office of the Secretariat, U.S. Dep't of State (Sept. 25, 2012, 7:58 AM) (on file with the Committee, SCB0093148).

[42] M/PRI Managing Director Testimony at 32.

[43] Id. at 33.

A: Yes, normally.[44]

On September 21, 2012, Mull informed Burns about Mills' decision to select Burns' Chief of Staff for the position of Executive Secretary to the ARB. He wrote to Burns:

Hi Bill, Cheryl [Mills] asked me to talk to Uzra about the possibility of her serving as Exec Sec for the ARB through the end of November. She seemed very reluctant, but Cheryl agreed that Uzra had all the right qualities. Uzra asked to hold off giving a decision until she talked to you, so she'll be seeking you out on this today.

Steve Mills recounted a different version of events to the Committee: [45]

She [Uzra] was recommended by Deputy Secretary Burns. She had been his chief of staff. She also, I thought was a good recommendation in the sense that Deputy Secretary Burns is well-respected and well-regarded in the building. He's the most senior foreign service officer. And she, in being his chief of staff, when she reached out to people, when she did that, people responded.[46]

On September 22, 2012, Burns conveyed Uzra Zeya's decision to serve as Executive Secretary to Mills stating:

Hi,

Uzra has agreed to serve as Exec Secretary of ARB. She'll call Steve to let him know.

We talked at length about this, and she is comfortable with decision, for all the right reasons. She'll do a great job.[47]

## Documents Reviewed By the ARB

The ARB panel's primary sources of information were documents and witness interviews.[48] Documents were collected from State Department personnel with "information relevant to the Board's examination of these incidents."[49] Even before the ARB was convened, the Bureau of Legislative Affairs, with oversight from Mills, put in place a system to transmit, store, and review documents relevant to the myriad requests for information, including Congress,

---

[44] Id.

[45] Email from Stephen Mull, Exec. Sec'y, Office of the Secretariat, U.S. Dep't of State, to William Burns, Deputy Sec'y, U.S. Dep't of State (Sept. 21, 2012, 8:45 AM) (Subject: re: Uzra/ARB) (on file with the Committee, SCB0057773).

[46] Mills Testimony at 194.

[47] Email from William Burns, Deputy Sec'y, U.S. Dep't of State, to Cheryl D. Mills, Chief of Staff and Counselor, U.S. Dep't of State (Sept. 22, 2012, 1:37 PM) (on file with the Committee, SCB0057772).

[48] Testimony of Ambassador Thomas Pickering, Chairman, Benghazi Accountability Review Board, before the H. Comm. on Oversight and Gov't Reform, Tr. at 52 (Sept. 19, 2013) [hereinafter Pickering Testimony] (on file with the Committee).

[49] Patrick F. Kennedy, Under Sec'y of State for Mgmt., *Department Notice, Convening of Accountability Review Board to Examine the Circumstances Surrounding the Deaths in Benghazi, Libya on September 11, 2012.* U.S. Dep't of State (on file with the Committee, SCB0050689).

Freedom of Information [FOIA], and the ARB.[50] The Deputy Director, Office of Maghreb Affairs, Bureau of Near Eastern Affairs, described the process for submitting documents:

> A: There was a request to produce documents . . . I think that we were given, you know, kind of the general search terms to look for and scan in our computer and files.
>
> Q: So you eventually, did you produce a PST file, or did you produce hard copies in response to that request?
>
> A: We produced hardcopies in response to that request.
>
> Q: So you physically would have identified the documents that were responsive, printed them out from your computer, and then handed that stack over to somebody?
>
> A: That's what I recall.[51]

The Deputy Director further elaborated on her role and the role of other individuals within the State Department in reviewing and identifying relevant documents:

> A: I received a call from our Principal Deputy Assistant Secretary [Elizabeth Dibble] in NEA. It was Columbus Day weekend. I recall it because I changed my plans for the weekend very quickly as a result of her request. And she noted that I believe it was a group in H, was the Legislative Affairs Bureau, was reviewing all of the—was preparing documents to be provided for, I thought it was the ARB, and then whatever subsequent use, presumably congressional review or whatever the case may be. But I wasn't sure. They were going through the documents for release, and she said could I join the group the following day and look at, you know, kind of looking whether we needed to redact any sensitive information. That was my role to help in the release of those documents, and she indicated that night, you know, depending on how big of a task it is, could you help me setting up a work flow like other officers from NEA who could be involved in, you know, going through and looking for sensitive information that we might recommend for redaction.
>
> Q: And you said, you recall that it was Columbus Day weekend?
>
> A: Or close to Columbus Day weekend, because I had plans to see my brother that I cancelled.
>
> \* \* \*
>
> It had started before that weekend, but DAS Dibble learned of it, or she realized there wasn't an NEA participant on that Saturday, so she called me and I went in the following morning, yeah.

---

[50] Testimony of the Deputy Director, Office of Maghreb Affairs, Bureau of Near Eastern Affairs, U.S. Dep't of State, Tr. at 112 (Dec. 17, 2015) [hereinafter NEA Deputy Director Testimony] (on file with the Committee). *See also* Mills Testimony at 150 ("I had been managing, as you know, our response effort and collaborating with our leadership team on Benghazi in particular.").

[51] NEA Deputy Director Testimony at 105.

Q: And did you go any other days other than that Saturday morning? Were you also there on Sunday? Did you continue on Monday?

A: I went in on Sunday and Monday and then through that first week, and then I helped develop a rotation schedule for other colleagues from NEA to kind of make sure we had an NEA colleague. There were colleagues from DS and IRM. You know, other subject matter experts were in the room as well, kind of looking and looking at documents for I can't recall how long that lasted, but I helped develop the work schedule.

\*     \*     \*

I was primarily focused myself on redacting names and titles of individuals who were private citizens, either Libyan, American, U.N. staff, other internationals who were in Libya doing work, because they were talking to American diplomats. That's a sensitive thing that could endanger people if that's generally known in some circumstances. So that's primarily what I was recommending redacting. And then I also recommended redacting the names of junior people who were drafting emails or cables as well.[52]

Mills' involvement in the process was described by Charlene Lamb, Deputy Assistant Secretary, Bureau of Diplomatic Security. Lamb testified:

She [Mills]—it was my understanding, she was responsible for getting all of the documents that were being requested in—and compiled in, you know, organizing the documents so they made sense, and making sure nothing got left out.

Because Mills is not a security expert, she had a lot of questions about security policies, procedures, you know, what was routine, what was done under exigent circumstances. So there were several DS [Diplomatic Security] people there, not just myself, that were working to help bring all these documents together and to answer questions that she had.[53]

Mills told the Committee certain documents were set aside for her specific review. As she told the Committee:

The documents I would see were documents where the team had looked through them and thought that there was a subset that I should see. Those typically meant that they were sharing new information, new facts, or other information that they thought was important for the senior leadership to know.[54]

---

[52] Id. at 101.

[53] Testimony of Charlene Lamb, Deputy Ass't Sec'y of State for Diplomatic Security, Int'l Programs, Tr. at 108 (Jan. 7, 2016) [hereinafter Lamb Testimony] (on file with the Committee).

[54] Mills Testimony at 182.

\*     \*     \*

I acknowledge I was pushing pretty hard for them to get them out the door because our goal was to try to do that.

Mills explained the ARB's access to these documents:

They [ARB] were looking at records already being assembled in response to a request that had already been posed to our department by Members of Congress, as well as they had their own individual interviews that they were conducting where they might ask for records or materials that they felt would be relevant that they came to have knowledge of.

\*     \*     \*

Separate and apart from that, the ARB could both reach to the Administration Bureau to be able to access any of those records that were being collected, which would have been records regarding anything related to the night of September 11 and 12. And, they could also initiate their own requests for documents.
They [the Administration or "A" Bureau] were the actual repository and kept copies of everything and they would only make copies to allow other individuals to review them as opposed to disturb their copy set.

\*     \*     \*

Their [ARB] mechanisms were threefold, if I really think about it. One, obviously, they could reach out to the A Bureau and say, we want to look at all of them or we want to look at documents of this nature. Two, they could make requests. Three, they would ask, as our reviews were going on of records, were there any records that were relevant that they should be either looking at or that they would be at least apprised of. And so that was another mechanism that they had. And so those could be collected to them if that's what they reached to ask for. They might have asked for that on a particular subject matter; has anybody seen anything on this topic or that topic?
But those were the three ways that they could get it, with each of those being avenues for them to be able to ascertain whatever information they believed they needed, because people didn't have visibility into how they were making those judgments.[55]

According to the State Department, the ARB reviewed more than 7,000 documents numbering thousands of pages as part of its investigation.[56] Excluded from the ARB panel's review were documents and emails sent to or by the Secretary or her senior staff. As the Secretary told the Committee:

---

[55] Mills Testimony at 142–147.
[56] Letter from Thomas B. Gibbons, Acting Ass't Sec'y, Bureau of Leg. Affairs, U.S. Dep't of State, to Hon. Darrell E. Issa, Chairman, H. Comm. on Oversight & Gov't Reform (Aug. 23, 2013) (on file with the Committee).

I don't know what they [the ARB] had access to. I know that, during the time I was at the State Department, there was certainly a great effort to respond to your predecessor, Congressman Issa's inquiries. And many thousands of pages of information was conveyed to the Congress.[57]

The ARBs access to information from the Secretary and her senior staff was extremely limited. The nearly 3,000 pages of emails from the Secretary were made available only to the Committee with productions occurring on February 13, 2015, June 25, 2015, and September 25, 2015—well after the conclusion of the Benghazi ARB. Furthermore, it is unclear whether the ARB had access to the more than 60,000 pages of senior leader records produced separately to the Committee during its investigation.[58] This was further corroborated by Jacob Sullivan, Deputy Chief of Staff and Director of Policy Planning, who told the Committee:

Q: Did you provide any documents to the ARB?

A: I don't think they asked me for any documents, so I don't think I provided any.[59]

The State Department informed the Committee, Department records for senior officials are stored separately.[60] This includes a separate email system, which until February 2015 did not have archiving capability.[61] Unless separate searches were conducted by State Department personnel on these systems and personnel saved their emails, senior leader emails and records would not have been accessible by the ARB panel.[62]

*Subpoena for ARB documents*

Like previous Congresses, the Committee sought access to the underlying documents reviewed by the ARB to better understand the ARB panel's review and findings. The documents sought are required by law to be physically separated and stored by the State Department and should be easily accessible by the State Department.[63] Congress issued its first subpoena for documents reviewed by the ARB on August 1, 2013.[64] No documents were produced. On January 28, 2015, the Committee reissued the subpoena for ARB documents.[65]

---

[57] Testimony of Hillary R. Clinton, Sec'y of State, U.S. Dep't of State, Tr. at 321–322 (Oct. 22, 2015) [hereinafter Clinton Testimony] (on file with the Committee).

[58] This number excludes the approximately 4,300 pages of documents produced to the Committee.

[59] Sullivan Testimony at 82.

[60] April 10, 2015 meeting with the Director of the Office of Executive Secretariat.

[61] *Id.*

[62] *Id.*

[63] 22 U.S.C. 4833(c) (the statute contemplates that ARB records will become publically available following the conclusion of its work).

[64] August 1, 2013 subpoena to John F. Kerry, Secretary of State seeking all documents provided by the Department of State to the Accountability Review Board convened to examine the facts and circumstances surrounding the September 11–12, 2012 attacks on U.S. facilities in Benghazi, Libya and all documents and communications referring or relating to ARB interviews or meetings, including but not limited to notes or summaries prepared during and after any ARB interview or meeting.

[65] *See* January 28, 2015 subpoena issued to John F. Kerry seeking:

Continued

Almost two and a half years after Congress issued its first subpoena in 2013, the State Department for the first time produced an ARB record—a four page interview summary for a witness who was scheduled to appear before the Committee the following day.[66] The State Department maintained this posture over the next several weeks with the production of one or two ARB interview summaries, totaling 38 pages, each provided less than a week before the Committee's interviews.[67] It was not until April 15, 2015, the State Department produced a larger trove of ARB documents consisting of 1,758 pages. On April 24, 2015, the State Department produced another 2,523 pages of documents. Accompanying the April 24, 2015, production was a letter stating:

> [t]his production, together with our production on April 15, 2015, constitutes our delivery of ARB documents that were physically set aside following the ARB's completion and archived. In addition to these materials, the Department searched for and included in this production, as responsive to your subpoena's second a request, a small number of interview summaries that had not been stored within these physically set aside files.[68]

Although the State Department produced 4,319 pages to the Committee, previous statements by the State Department that the ARB reviewed "7,000 State Department documents numbering thousands of pages" suggest the Committee does not have all the documents reviewed by the ARB.[69] Moreover, the State Department by its own admission withheld a number of documents from the Committee. On April 24, 2015, the State Department informed the Committee "a small number of documents" were being withheld because of "executive branch confidentiality interests."[70] The State Department's basis for withholding the documents was a concocted administrative privilege—one made up entirely by the Administration and not recognized by the Constitution.[71] The State Department has yet to explain the discrepancy.

*Witness Interviews*

The ARB interviewed more than 100 people.[72] However, neither the Secretary, nor her inner circle, were interviewed by the ARB. Mullen offered this explanation:

---

1. "all documents and communications produced by the Department of State to the Accountability Review Board ("ARB" or the ARB) convened to examine the facts and circumstances surrounding the September 11–12, 2012 attacks on U.S. facilities in Benghazi Libya.

2. All documents and communications referring or relating to the ARB interviews or meetings, including but not limited to, notes or summaries prepared during and after any ARB interview or meeting."

[66] Letter to Trey Gowdy, Chairman, H. Select Comm. on Benghazi, from Julia E. Frifield, Ass't Sec'y of State for Leg. Affairs, U.S. Dep't of State (Feb.13, 2015) (on file with the Committee).
[67] H. Select Comm. on Benghazi Internal Working Document (on file with the Committee).
[68] Letter to Trey Gowdy, Chairman, H. Select Comm. on Benghazi, from Julia E. Frifield, Ass't Sec'y of State for Leg. Affairs, U.S. Dep't of State, (Apr. 24, 2015) (on file with the Committee).
[69] Letter from Thomas B. Gibbons, Acting Ass't Sec'y, Leg. Affairs, U.S. Dep't of State, to Darrell E. Issa, Chairman, H. Comm. on Oversight & Gov't Reform (Aug. 23, 2013).
[70] Id.
[71] Letter to Trey Gowdy, Chairman, H. Select Comm. on Benghazi, from Julia E. Frifield, Ass't Sec'y of State for Leg. Affairs, U.S. Dep't of State, Apr. 24, 2015 (on file with the Committee).
[72] Press Release, U.S. Dep't of State, Briefing on the Accountability Review Board Report (Dec. 19, 2012), http://www.state.gov/r/pa/prs/ps/2012/12/202282.htm ("We interviewed more than a hundred people, reviewed thousands of documents, and watched hours of video. We spoke with

Q: And, there was no interview of Deputy Secretary Nides or Secretary Clinton?

A: There was not.

Q: And was there any discussion as to at what level the interviews would not take place at? For example, was there a common—excuse me, I'll start over. Was there a decision by the board not to interview Mr. Nides?

A: There was early on a discussion, and certainly I had a discussion, private discussion with Ambassador Pickering about at least my expectation, and I would say this was in the first couple weeks, that this certainly could present the requirement that we would have to interview everybody up the chain of command, including the Secretary, and he agreed with that. So the two of us had sort of set that premise in terms of obviously depending on what we learned over time, and our requirement to both affix both responsibility and accountability per se were, again, based on the facts as we understood them. So there was a consensus, and it was a universal consensus over time that we did the interviews we needed to do and that we didn't do the interviews we didn't do, which would have included the ones obviously that we didn't do, which were Nides and Burns and Secretary.

*　　*　　*

Q: So it's fair to say the board decided it didn't need to interview Cheryl Mills or the Secretary about events that night?

A: No. And I think to your point about Ms. Mills and the Secretary, it was really through the, both the discussions with so many people that we interviewed and the affirmation and the validation of what happened that evening, including the conversation the Secretary had with Mr. Hicks, that we just didn't, we didn't see any need to clarify that, we knew that had happened. We were comfortable in the case of Mr. Hicks that he was walking us through what had happened. So there just wasn't any further need to go anywhere else.[73]

### Senior Staff Communications with the ARB Members

In addition to selecting members of the ARB and its staff, identifying and reviewing documents, Mills played a peculiar role during the ARB's investigation. Within days of the ARB's start, Mullen reached out to Mills to express concerns about Lamb's testimony

---

people who were on the scene in Benghazi that night, who were in Tripoli, who were in Washington. We talked to military and intelligence officials, including to many State Department personnel, and to experts who do not work for the United States Government.").

[73] Testimony of Admiral Michael Mullen, Vice Chairman, Accountability Review Board, before the House Oversight and Government Reform Committee, Tr. at 26–28 (Jun. 19, 2013) [hereinafter Mullen Testimony] (on file with the Committee).

before Congress.[74] Mullen explained his reasons for contacting Mills:

> Shortly after we interviewed Ms. Lamb, I initiated a call to Ms. Mills to give her—what I wanted to give her was a head's up because at this point she was on the list to come over here to testify, and I was—so from a department representation standpoint and as someone that led a department, I always focused on certainly trying to make sure the best witnesses were going to appear before the department, and my reaction at that point in time with Ms. Lamb at the interview was—and it was a pretty unstable time. It was the beginning, there was a lot of unknowns. To the best of my knowledge, she hadn't appeared either ever or many times certainly. So essentially I gave Ms. Mills a head's up that I thought that her appearance could be a very difficult appearance for the State Department, and that was—about that was the extent of the conversation.[75]

Mills did not recall the conversation about Lamb, telling the Committee:

> A: I don't recall it [the conversation with Admiral Mullen], but I would have no reason to believe that he wouldn't be accurate about that.
>
> Q: Okay. He related that he told you that Charlene Lamb was not going to be a good witness for the State Department. Does that ring a bell with you?
>
> A: No, because if I was aware of that, I might have been thoughtful about that in all the ways of which—how we could best communicate information. But I don't dispute that. I'm sure that if that's his memory that he would be accurately reflecting what he recalls.[76]

Weeks later, Mullen reached out again to Mills and the Secretary to discuss the ARB's work to date. Mullen explained:

> So shortly after we met, first couple weeks there were some there were some things that we could see early that we thought it was important that the Secretary of State know about, not so much in terms of what had happened, but steps that we thought she might want to take initially as opposed to wait weeks or months to see the results of the board. So we put together a list of—and I honestly can't remember the number, but somewhere between 10 and 20 recommendations for her to take a look at immediately. So, for example, one of them clearly, because there was a fire issue, was consider getting breathing apparatuses out to high threat posts immediately. So there were things like that, and we sent that list up, and to the best of my knowledge, that's something that Ambassador

---

[74] Mills Testimony at 184.
[75] Id. at 23–24.
[76] Id. at 173.

Pickering either handed, transmitted to Ms. Mills and the Secretary.

At the end of the ARB we met with Secretary Clinton for about 2 hours to give her a briefing on what we had come across, and at least at that point, and we hadn't finished or signed it out, but at least the major recommendations that we had concluded up to that point. The only other State Department employee that was in the room with Secretary Clinton then was Ms. Mills.[77]

Mills confirmed the meeting with Pickering and Mullen:

In the course of their investigation, we had one briefing where they stepped through where they were in their process—and, by that, the other person who was briefed was the Secretary—that they stepped through where they were in their process and that they anticipated being on time and what their own assessments were, but that they had not come to conclusions yet about accountability. So this was basically a briefing before they had stepped through their accountability elements.[78]

*Editing the Report*

Mills also described Pickering and Mullen's outreach as they were drafting their final report:

A: And then, as they were preparing their report, they reached out to say, "We have a draft of the report." They shared that draft with me. I shared back my observations of instances where there were issues or facts that I thought were relevant for their consideration. They took them, or they didn't. Ultimately, they had to make that judgement.

Q: So you reviewed the draft before it went public, before it was released?

A: Well, the draft before it went to—ultimately, it goes to the Secretary——

Q: Right.

A: —and then it actually gets—we made a determination to release it. ARBs are not always released publicly, but the Secretary had said she wanted to release this one publicly.

Q: And can you tell me the extent of edits that you and/ or the Secretary made to the report?

A: The Secretary didn't. And the Secretary did not, at least to my knowledge, review a draft.

Q: So Secretary Clinton didn't review it; you just reviewed it.

A: I reviewed the draft. That's correct.

---

[77] Mullen Testimony at 25.
[78] Mills Testimony at 187–188.

Q: All right. And were there—you said there was some suggestions. So what were the edits, what were the changes that you asked the ARB to make?

A: I can't tell you that were the different issues now, because that's obviously too long away. But basically what I stepped through was, if there was information that we had that didn't seem to be reflected there, I would flag that. If there were other reactions or observations I had, I would share that. And that's what I would have done.

Q: So I just want to be clear. First, you reviewed it. Second, you said there are changes that need to be made, and you gave those changes to the ARB. Is that right?

A: No.

Q: Okay. Well, then tell me what's right.

A: Okay. I reviewed it, and I identified areas where I either saw that there was, from my perspective, based on where I was sitting, information that wasn't present, information that might be different, or other factors that I thought were relevant for their consideration in deciding what went in the document. And they then made their own judgement.

Q: Well, that sounds like changes.

A: I certainly——

Q: So you suggested changes?

A: I certainly made recommendations for places where I thought there were inaccuracies or misstatements or other information that might not be fully reflective of what the information was that was there. I certainly made those, yes.

A: You reviewed it, and you recommended changes. It was up to them whether they implemented the changes or included them in the——

A: Yes. Recommend changes or flagged areas where I thought there might be inaccuracies.

Q: Change this, delete that, that kind of—that kind of——

A: No.

Q: I just want to be clear.

A: Oh. Thank you.

Q: All right?

A: I appreciate that.

Q: You recommended changes. Then what happened? Did they do it or not?

A: So some they took probably, and some they didn't. My impression is that——

Q: Why is there a "probably" there? I mean, the final report—you didn't look at the final report? The Secretary looked at it.

A: I did look at the final report, but what I didn't have is an errata sheet and say, "Oh, that's not there. Oh, this is there." I didn't do that, so that's why I don't have a frame of reference.[79]

Mills' peculiar role in the ARB investigation extended beyond the selection of members to approving senior State Department officials meeting with the ARB. On November 3, 2012, Thomas Nides, Deputy Secretary of State, sought approval from Mills for the ARB's request to meet with him. On November 3, 2012, Nides wrote Mills "I assume this is a y."[80] Mills responded "Y".[81]

*Accountability of State Department Personnel*

Among the 29 recommendations made to the State Department, the ARB found:

Systematic failures and leadership and management deficiencies at senior levels within two bureaus of the State Department ("the Department") resulted in a Special Mission security posture that was inadequate for Benghazi and grossly inadequate to deal with the attack that took place.[82]

The ARB identified one official from the Bureau of Near Eastern Affairs and three officials from the Bureau of Diplomatic Security at fault for Benghazi security failures. Notwithstanding their finding of inferior performance in these two bureaus, the ARB "did not find reasonable cause to determine that any individual U.S. government employee breached his or her duty,"[83] the performance standard set out in law. A breach of duty must rise to "willful misconduct or knowingly ignor[ing] his or her responsibilities."[84] The Board noted that poor performance does not ordinarily constitute a breach of duty that would serve as a basis for disciplinary action but is instead addressed through the performance management system.[85]

Mills shared with the Committee her reaction upon learning of the ARB's findings on personnel:

---

[79] *Id.* at 187–191.

[80] Email from Thomas Nides, Deputy Sec'y of State for Management and Resources, U.S. Dep't of State, to Cheryl D. Mills, Chief of Staff, U.S. Dep't of State (Nov. 3, 2012 12:26 PM) (on file with the Committee, SCB0058538).

[81] Email from Cheryl D. Mills, Chief of Staff, U.S. Dep't of State, to Thomas Nides, Deputy Sec'y of State for Management and Resources, U.S. Dep't of State (Nov. 3, 2012 1:10 PM) (on file with the Committee, SCB0058537).

[82] Unclassified Benghazi Accountability Review Board, U.S. Dep't of State [hereinafter Unclassified ARB].

[83] *See* Finding # 5, *id.,* at 7; *see also* Classified Accountability Review Board, U.S. Dep't of State, at 10 [hereinafter Classified ARB].

[84] *See* Statement of Admiral Mullen, U.S. Dep't of State, Briefing on the Accountability Review Board Report (Dec. 19, 2012), http://www.state.gov/r/pa/prs/ps/2012/12/202282.htm; *see also* Statement of Ambassador Thomas Pickering, U.S. Dep't of State, Briefing on the Accountability Review Board Report (Dec. 19, 2012), http://www.state.gov/r/pa/prs/ps/2012/12/202282.htm.

[85] *Id.*

What I do recall is that they had made determinations around personnel, and I recall one of them being surprising to me, and I told her [the Secretary] that I was surprised that they had made a conclusion about one particular individual.[86]

Emails between Burns and Mills suggest others were surprised by the ARB's finding with regard to personnel. On December 18, 2012, Burns wrote to Mills:

Hi,

Went down to talk to Eric this evening but missed him. Sent him note, and will follow up tomorrow. Also had long talk with Pat. He's coping, but as you well know its not easy.[87]

Emails between Kennedy and Mills indicate discussions were underway to reassign staff as an eventual, or perhaps even preventative, response to the ARB's finding. On December 13, 2012, five days before the ARB report was released, Kennedy proposed to Mills a staffing change dealing with three of the four individuals ultimately named in the ARB, all of whom were under Kennedy's supervision. His plan called for placing two individuals identified by the ARB with the Office of Foreign Missions. The third individual under Kennedy's supervision would have been responsible for security at non-high threat posts. Unsure of the plan, Kennedy wrote:

Cheryl

As we discussed, I'm sending along my first-cut on staffing

Still playing with it

But think its worth a gut check

Regards

Pat[88]

Notwithstanding Kennedy's proposal, all four individuals were placed on administrative leave and eventually reinstated within the State Department. Lamb described her experience to the Committee:

A: We were put on four State Department employees were put on administrative leave for a short period of time.

Q: Right. With pay or without pay?

A: With pay.

Q: And was there any due process for you to go through to what was the due process measures? They come to you State Department comes to you and says, you're going to

[86] Mills Testimony at 192.

[87] Email from William Burns, Deputy Sec'y of State, U.S. Dep't of State, to Cheryl D. Mills, Chief of Staff and Counselor, U.S. Dep't of State (Dec. 18, 2012, 7:26 PM) (Subject: Fw: DS) (on file with the Committee, SCB0045827).

[88] Email from Patrick F. Kennedy, Under Sec'y for Management, U.S. Dep't of State, to Cheryl D. Mills, Chief of Staff and Counselor, U.S. Dep't of State (Dec. 13, 2012, 10:12 AM) (on file with the Committee, SCB100920).

be suspended on administrative leave not suspended on administrative leave for 4 weeks. Was there some kind of due process rights that you had when that was first given to you?

A: I was not given any guidance.

Q: They didn't tell you had any way to appeal that or anything?

A: No.

Q: Okay. And who told you that? Who told you that you were going to be suspended? Or you were going you were going to be on a 4 week administrative leave?

A: Eric Boswell.

Q: All right. And when he told you that, he didn't say there's tell me how he gave it to you, he told you that information.

A: He called me and Scott Bultrowicz in, and he said that we were to be out of the building by the end of the business day, and that we were on administrative leave.

Q: And did you ask him what was your response? I think I would say, really? Can I talk to anyone? Can I give my side of the story or

A: No, I Scott and I have been around DS a long time. And, I mean, we've seen this process, and we knew that there were administrative things that people were looking into, and we just said, yes, and did as we were told.

Q: And then how were you notified that you were you were when you could come back? Did you know right ahead that today you are going to leave and you can come back to a date in the future? What did they tell you?

A: We were sent a letter telling us when to report back to duty.

Q: Okay.[89]

While the ARB's findings of accountability extended to three individuals within the Bureau of Diplomatic Security, the findings were limited. The ARB correctly assessed the State Department's inadequate security posture at the Benghazi Mission both in terms of its physical security as well as the lack of security staffing. However, the ARB failed to distinguish between responsibility for security staffing and responsibility for physical security. This confusion is reflected in the Chairman of the ARB's testimony:

Q: So the decisions about additional physical security, who were those made by?

A: The Bureau of Diplomatic Security.

\* \* \*

Q: How high up did they go?

---

[89] Lamb Testimony at 106–107.

A: To Assistant Secretary Boswell principally, but to [Deputy Assistant Secretary] Charlene Lamb in fact.[90]

Contrary to the Chairman of the ARB's understanding, responsibility for the physical security of the Benghazi Mission did not fall within the Office of International Programs but within the Office of Countermeasures and the relevant offices under its purview.

Moreover, the decisions to exclude the Benghazi Mission from the physical security rules were generally made at the Assistant Secretary for Near Eastern Affairs and Under Secretary for Management levels. The Benghazi ARB described "the flawed process by which Special Mission Benghazi's extension until the end of December 2012 was approved," determining it was "a decision that did not take security considerations adequately into account."[91] Yet, the ARB failed to ascribe responsibility to those who drafted and approved the Benghazi Mission's 12 month extension.

The Benghazi ARB's failure to recognize deficiencies at the highest levels of the State Department's leadership is curious. As stated above, the State Department has been told repeatedly by past ARBs that change is needed both in its culture and with respect to security. Following two of the most significant terrorist attacks in State Department history, the Nairobi and Dar es Salaam embassy bombings in 1998, the ARB described steps the State Department should take to bolster the security of facilities abroad; chief among them, the application of the security rules at U.S. diplomatic facilities abroad. The State Department rejected these past ARB recommendations and excluded the Benghazi Mission from the security rules.

Furthermore, it is ironic that in the summer of 2009 the State Department conducted a Quadrennial Diplomacy and Development Review, which was intended to be a "sweeping review of diplomacy and development, the core missions of the State Department and USAID."[92] The report came out in December 2010 and was lauded as a "sweeping assessment of how the Department of State" could "become more efficient, accountable, and effective in a world in which rising powers, growing instability, and technological transformation create new threats, but also new opportunities."[93] The report cautioned that the State Department must change in order to:

> [I]nstitute procedures to integrate security and risk management into every stage of policy and operational planning in Washington and the field. Including security considerations in the design and development of policy and programs from the outset will make it easier to find effective ways to mitigate risk. We will also ensure Diplomatic Security Regional Directors are more actively and regularly involved in regional bureaus' policy development so there is a shared understanding between those responsible

---

[90] Ambassador Thomas Pickering Testimony at 153.
[91] Unclassified ARB, *supra* note 81, at 30.
[92] *See* U.S. Dep't of State, Quadrennial Diplomacy and Development Review Fact Sheet, http://www.state.gov/documents/organization/153109.pdf.
[93] *Leading Through Civilian Power*, Quadrennial Diplomacy and Development Review, U.S. Dep't of State, at 72 (2010).

for ensuring security and those responsible for developing and implementing policy.[94]

Yet the State Department maintained the status quo and rejected the findings of this report. In fact, every ARB review has concluded that the State Department needs a significant change in its culture and organizational structure to improve security. Lasting and significant change must be directed from the top.

### House Armed Services Committee Majority Interim Report: Benghazi Investigation Update

Between September 2012 and April 2014, the House Armed Services Committee conducted its own review of the events surrounding the September 11–12, 2012, terrorist attacks, including the days leading up to and following the attacks. Specifically, the Armed Services Committee looked at the military's role: "the response of the Department of Defense", "what preparations the U.S. military had made for the possibility of an attack", and "what arrangements have subsequently been put in place to minimize the possibility of a similar occurrence."[95] In February 2014, the Armed Services Committee issued a "Majority Interim Report: Benghazi Investigation Update" outlining its findings to date. At the time of its interim report, the Armed Services Committee had conducted seven classified briefings, two public hearings and one transcribed witness interview. Based on the information obtained, it issued six findings in its February 2014 report:

1. In assessing military posture in anticipation of the September 11, 2012 anniversary, White House officials failed to comprehend or ignored the dramatically deteriorating security situation in Libya and the growing threat to U.S. interests in the region. Official public statements seem to have exaggerated the extent and rigor of the security assessment conducted at the time.

2. U.S. personnel in Benghazi were woefully vulnerable in September 2012 because a.) the administration did not direct a change in military force posture, b.) there was no intelligence of a specific "imminent" threat in Libya, and c.) the Department of State, which has primary responsibility for diplomatic security, favored a reduction of Department of Defense security personnel in Libya before the attack.

3. Defense Department officials believed nearly from the outset of violence in Benghazi that it was a terrorist attack rather than a protest gone awry, and the President subsequently permitted the military to respond with minimal direction.

4. The U.S. military's response to the Benghazi attack was severely degraded because of the location and readiness posture of U.S. forces, and because of lack of clarity about how the terrorist action was unfolding. However, given the uncertainty about the prospective length and scope of the attack, military

---

[94] Id.
[95] House Armed Services Committee, Majority Interim Report: Benghazi Investigation Update, at 3 (Feb. 2014) (on file with the Committee).

commanders did not take all possible steps to prepare for a more extended operation.

5. There was no "stand down" order issued to U.S. military personnel in Tripoli who sought to join the fight in Benghazi. However, because official reviews after the attack were not sufficiently comprehensive, there was confusion about the roles and responsibilities of these individuals.

6. The Department of Defense is working to correct many weaknesses revealed by the Benghazi attack, but the global security situation is still deteriorating and military resources continue to decline.[96]

## SCOPE LIMITATIONS: MAJORITY INTERIM REPORT

Notwithstanding its findings, the Armed Services Committee acknowledged at the outset the limitations of its report stating "This report should be considered one component of continuing comprehensive Benghazi related oversight underway in the House of Representatives."[97] Moreover, the Armed Services Committee recognized the scope of its review of the terrorist attacks was limited, stating, "[i]n keeping with the committee's jurisdiction, however, this document addresses only the activities and actions of personnel in DOD."[98] Finally, the report acknowledged "the committee's inquiry continues", "staff . . . [will] interview additional witnesses in coming weeks, including individuals who were involved in responding to the Benghazi events and other officials. Some individuals who have already provided information will appear for further questioning and clarification."[99] The Armed Services Committee conducted eight transcribed interviews after releasing the interim report.[100] The last transcribed interview occurred in April 2014, one month prior to the Select Committee's formation.

## CONTENT LIMITATIONS: MAJORITY INTERIM REPORT

The value of information obtained was necessarily limited. Public hearings and briefings typically do not lend themselves to uncovering new facts or witnesses. The Defense Department was positioned to influence the content of information presented in these settings. As a result, the Armed Services Committee was limited in its understanding of the policies and procedures that contributed to the military's posture prior to and its response during the September 11–12, 2012, attacks.

For example, the Armed Services Committee had not conducted transcribed interviews of the top military officials prior to its 2014 report to understand the discrepancies in the discussions that took place during the September 10, 2012, meeting with the White House regarding the nation's preparedness and security posture on September 11, 2012.[101] It did not interview Secretary Panetta to discuss his December 2011 trip to Libya, his understanding of the

---

[96] *Id.* at 2.
[97] *Id.* at 1.
[98] *Id.*
[99] *Id.* at 4.
[100] Committee on Armed Services: Benghazi Materials, p. 5.
[101] *Id.* at 7.

Benghazi Mission compound, and his role in the military's response—specially why only one asset made it to Libya more than 24 hours after his verbal order to deploy the Commander's in Extremis Force, special operations forces located in the United States, and two Fleet Antiterrorism Security Teams including one to Benghazi and one to Tripoli.[102] Further, it did not interview many military personnel on the ground at the installations and intermediate staging bases in Europe to understand the orders given and status of assets on September 11–12, 2012. Finally, the Armed Services Committee did not have access to other agency documents referencing military discussions that could shed light on issues relating to military planning and operations prior to and during the attacks.

Broadly speaking, the Armed Services Committee predominantly confined its inquiry to whether the military had assets close enough to have "made a difference" in Benghazi. Further, it did not have access to new information with respect to assets potentially available outside of then-established military planning for such contingencies. Nowhere does the Armed Service Committee's report consider: Was Benghazi ever part of the military's response? Why did it take the military so long to get to Tripoli? What assets received orders to deploy? Why did it take so long to put U.S. forces into motion? And, most basically, whether it is accurate to state no assets could have arrived in time for the second fatal attack on the annex?

## SELECT COMMITTEE'S INVESTIGATION

The Select Committee sought to answer these and other important questions based on all the evidence presented not just the facts as presented by Defense Department. At the Select Committee's insistence, it conducted 24 interviews, 16 of whom had never been interviewed. The Select Committee also received approximately 900 pages of documents never before produced to Congress. The Select Committee's insistence on additional information was met with opposition from the Defense Department, a department seemingly more used to dictating the terms of congressional oversight. From the perspective of the Defense Department, the Select Committee should have been satisfied with the witnesses and documents it provided. For example, the Defense Department chided the Committee for wanting to speak to a low-level service member that may have evidence contradicting the Department's version of events. In the Department's view, however, "locating these types of individuals are [sic] not necessary since such claims are easily dismissed by any one of the multiple high-level military officers already interviewed." The Select Committee, however, was not in the business of accepting the word of anyone single person, "high-level military officers" or otherwise. The Select Committee was interested in finding and confirming facts wherever those facts emerged to understanding the truth about the military's role on the night of September 11–12, 2012.

---

[102] *Id.* at 16.

## The Permanent Select Committee on Intelligence
## Chairman's Report

The House Permanent Select Committee on Intelligence released its report to the public on November 21, 2014. The report was limited in scope, its focus narrowly aimed at reviewing the performance of the Intelligence Community related to the deaths of four Americans in Benghazi on September 11, 2012. The Select Committee, having the benefit of time, breadth of inquiry and resources has identified facts that contradict a key, overly broad conclusion contained in the Chairman's report. Namely, the Chairman's report asserted that there was "no evidence of an intelligence failure."

The Select Committee received testimony from two senior Obama Administration officials who stated that in their view an "intelligence failure" had taken place with respect to Benghazi.

Further, the Select Committee received testimony with respect to not one, but two, important analytical tradecraft irregularities that career line analysts uniformly described as significant and gave rise to important concerns. Both directly impacted significant analysis with respect to Benghazi, including an assessment given to the President of the United States. This too was a significant intelligence failure.

The Intelligence Committee interviewed less than one-third of the CIA personnel on the ground that night in Benghazi—two-thirds of whom held the exact same position. It did not interview key witnesses who would have helped it better understand the overall CIA mission in Benghazi and its response to the attacks, including analytical issues in the wake of the attacks. The Intelligence Committee did not interview any of the CIA analysts at headquarters. The Select Committee's interviews with these analysts allowed it to draw conclusions about the errors of the products produced by the analysts involved in drafting.

Finally, the Chairman's report draws several conclusions about the analytical assessments done by the CIA. As described previously in this report, the Select Committee received testimony with respect to two separate serious analytical tradecraft incidents with respect to Benghazi: sloppy analytical work gave rise to key fallacies of the Administration's talking points with respect to the attack, and another incident where the President's briefer substituted her own personal assessment for the properly coordinated and vetted work of line analysts in the President's Daily Brief.

In short, the Select Committee has had access to and received evidence from numerous witnesses and documents that the Intelligence Committee never obtained. It has had the time and resources to inquire into the intelligence efforts before, during and after the attacks in Benghazi. This Committee believes this report provides a truly thorough review of the intelligence community's performance related to the attacks.

# APPENDIX L:

# Biographies of Glen A. Doherty, Sean P. Smith, J. Christopher Stevens, and Tyrone S. Woods

## Glen A. Doherty

Glen Doherty (born 1970) was a personal security specialist serving in Libya. He was raised in Massachusetts and joined the Navy SEALS in 1995 and became a paramedic and sniper specializing in the Middle East. He responded to the attack on the USS Cole in 2000 and served two tours in Iraq. After a decorated Navy career, Mr. Doherty worked as a private security contractor in a number of countries, including Afghanistan, Pakistan, and Yemen.

## Sean P. Smith

Sean Patrick Smith (born 1978) was an Information Management Officer with the United States Foreign Service. He lived in The Hague, Netherlands and was on temporary duty to Benghazi in September 2012.

Smith previously served in the Air Force, where he spent six years as a ground radio maintenance specialist, including a deployment to Oman. Smith was awarded the Air Force Commendation Medal.

Smith was an only child and grew up in San Diego. As a Foreign Service employee, he lived in The Hague, Netherlands, with his wife and two children.

He was posthumously awarded the Thomas Jefferson Star for Foreign Service on May 3, 2013.

## J. Christopher Stevens

Ambassador J. Christopher Stevens (born 1960) served as U.S. Ambassador to Libya from May 2012 to September 2012. He had previously served in Libya as the Deputy Chief of Mission from 2007 to 2009 and as the Special Representative to the Libyan Transitional National Council from March 2011 to November 2011. Stevens also served overseas in Jerusalem, Cairo, and Riyadh.

While in Washington, Stevens served as Director of the Office of Multilateral Nuclear and Security Affairs; Pearson Fellow with the Senate Foreign Relations Committee; special assistant to the Under Secretary for Political Affairs; Iran desk officer; and staff assistant in the Bureau of Near Eastern Affairs.

Prior to joining the Foreign Service in 1991, Ambassador Stevens was an international trade lawyer in Washington, DC. From 1983 to 1985 he taught English as a Peace Corps volunteer in Morocco.

He was born and raised in northern California. He earned his undergraduate degree at the University of California at Berkeley in 1982, a J.D. from the University of California's Hastings College of Law in 1989, and an M.S. from the National War College in 2010. He spoke Arabic and French.

## Tyrone S. Woods

Tyrone Woods (born 1971) was a personal security specialist in Libya. He was a highly decorated Navy SEAL for almost twenty years, serving in various locations, including Iraq. After his retirement in 2010, he protected U.S. facilities around the world.

Woods was raised in Portland, Oregon, and was an avid runner, surfer, and car enthusiast in addition to being a registered nurse and certified paramedic. He is survived by his wife and three sons.